I0815222

ALL THE WORLD ON A PAGE

All the World on a Page

A CRITICAL ANTHOLOGY OF MODERN RUSSIAN POETRY

SELECTED AND WITH ESSAYS
BY ANDREW KAHN AND
MARK LIPOVETSKY

PRINCETON UNIVERSITY PRESS
PRINCETON & OXFORD

Published by Princeton University Press
41 William Street, Princeton, New Jersey 08540
99 Banbury Road, Oxford OX2 6JX

press.princeton.edu

Library of Congress Cataloging-in-Publication Data

Names: Kahn, Andrew, editor. | Lipovet͡skiĭ, M. N. (Mark Naumovich), editor.
Title: All the world on a page : a critical anthology of modern Russian poetry / selected and with essays by Andrew Kahn and Mark Lipovetsky.
Description: Princeton : Princeton University Press, 2025. | Includes bibliographical references and index.
Identifiers: LCCN 2024035105 (print) | LCCN 2024035106 (ebook) | ISBN 9780691207162 (hardback) | ISBN 9780691269399 (epub)
Subjects: LCSH: Russian poetry—20th century. | Russian poetry—20th century—Translations into English. | Russian poetry—21st century. | Russian poetry—21st century—Translations into English. | Russian poetry—20th century—History and criticism. | Russian poetry—21st century—History and criticism. | BISAC: POETRY / Anthologies (multiple authors) | LITERARY CRITICISM / Modern / 20th Century | LCGFT: Poetry. | Literary criticism. | Essays.
Classification: LCC PG3237.E5 A45 2025 (print) | LCC PG3237.E5 (ebook) | DDC 891.71/408—dc23/eng/20240920
LC record available at https://lccn.loc.gov/2024035105
LC ebook record available at https://lccn.loc.gov/2024035106

British Library Cataloging-in-Publication Data is available

Editorial: Ben Tate and Josh Drake
Production Editorial: Kathleen Cioffi
Jacket Design: Haley Chung
Production: Danielle Amatucci
Publicity: Alyssa Sanford and Carmen Jimenez
Copyeditor: Leah Caldwell

This book has been composed in Arno

Printed in the United States of America

10 9 8 7 6 5 4 3 2 1

CONTENTS

NOTE ON THE TEXT

THE FOLLOWING transliteration conventions have been adopted in our book: we use a modified Library of Congress system of transliteration in the text, adopting *-y* in names to match the ending *-ii*. We use the standard spelling of first and last names adopted in the West: Alexander Pushkin, Vladimir Mayakovsky, Osip Mandelstam. The soft sign is indicated with a curly apostrophe. When citing Russian sources in the notes and references, we use the Library of Congress system without diacritics.

For poetry quoted in the body of the chapter, we generally provide original Russian block quotations in Cyrillic. Otherwise, when we quote a phrase, English translation comes first followed by transliteration in parentheses except in instances where the chapter focuses on elements of style and language, in which case close attention to the Russian takes precedence.

Introduction

ENDURING MODERNISM

POETRY OF the twentieth and early twenty-first centuries possesses enormous cultural capital for Russophone readerships globally. The thirty-four poems that form the anthology in this book are, we believe, outstanding works of the lyric art, to be enjoyed as individual texts alongside their translations and illuminated through the chapter-length essays that accompany each one. Out of each text there emerges a personal view of the world, as the book's title, drawn from an early poem by Pasternak, suggests; yet the hope is that this volume will also suggest the richness, relevance, and pleasure of a tradition that is national and international, playful and existential, historical and contemporary. Many of the poets included here found themselves on the right side of history but on the wrong side of their country's politics. One traditional role of the poet has been to voice the principle of the independence of the imagination in moral judgment. This tradition of poetic authority, established in the nineteenth century by giants such as Pushkin and Lermontov, continues to reverberate and provide opposition. It would strike a jarring note to claim for the Russian context what Auden said of the Anglo-American world, namely, that poetry makes "nothing happen." The history of the art form in Russia is littered with many examples of governments, Imperial and Soviet, as well as readers being energized to act by works of poetry they take to heart. As the essays about a number of works in this book may show, Russian poetry offers a context, a way of happening—when we begin to see that the social function of the poem, if it has one at all, is to provoke reflection and sometimes reaction.

The present selection contains works that explore the familiar terrain of lyric poetry, including love (Mayakovsky, Tsvetaeva), desire and sexuality (Nabokov, Brodsky, Rymbu), friendship and betrayal (Akhmadulina), the human condition existentially (Blok, Losev, Vysotsky, Stepanova), cultural memory (Mandelstam,

Shvarts, Barskova), religious and metaphysical insights (Kuzmin, Khlebnikov, Vvedensky, Kharms, Goralik), terror and war (Satunovsky, Oleinikov, Zabolotsky, Gor, Galich, Fanailova), the mundane (Kholin, Prigov, Rubinshtein), and, not least, the subject of poetry itself (Gumilev, Guro, Khodasevich, Pasternak, Mandelstam, Akhmatova, Sedakova, Nikonova).

The reader will not find here examples of so-called Soviet poetry, or, more specifically, poetry that became part of the state-sponsored literary institution named socialist realism.[1] As a literary institution, socialist realism determined a spectrum of permissible lyrical roles and personae by imposing on writers a perpetual negotiation between individual and state-mandated poetic styles in order to satisfy the expectation that poets adhere to prescribed functions and limit their own creative activity. Many talented poets contributed to the advance and expansion of this system. It did not completely deprive poets of the opportunity to express themselves (examples of Soviet poets such as Andrei Voznesensky or Yevgeny Yevtushenko come to mind in this regard). But the ideological, political, and even aesthetic limits of self-expression were always clearly marked for both authors and readers.

Although they are distinctive individually, the poets collected here form a tradition based on their relation to modernism, whether as original participants in the Silver Age, a convenient term for the period from 1900 to 1918, or as its heirs. This introduction will set out how we see some of the larger contexts informing these works, give an explanation of how the volume is conceived and organized, and touch on the critical methods we have adopted in relation to the history of Russian lyric. While the last is a separate story, the politicization of Russian culture shaped how poets wrote as well as how they were read.

The Constants of Russian Poetry

Endurance and invention are hallmarks of the Russian lyric tradition. Claims made for a literary tradition on the basis of some notional moral stature—here an element of endurance—can be compelling, but on their own they look insufficient and even suspect. It is necessary both to acknowledge that cultural, historical, and psychological pressures shape works of art of great individuality and variety—and to acknowledge they can be entirely withstood when poets withdraw into their own world. For that reason, the essays in this book, while attentive to form and language, regularly aim to situate writers and poems in their context or, to use a more current term, "literary field," which in the modern period often included conditions of state control such as censorship, dislocation, and sometimes persecution. Through the series of revolutions, crises, catastrophes, and repressions that twentieth-century Russian history presents, poetry never failed to find ways to talk about the interior life and explore individual consciousness. Even when poets were silenced, whether singled out as victims of terror for bearing witness or in times of strife, their voices were eventually recovered and heard. From the time of Pushkin, if not earlier, Russian lyric poets claimed a mandate they never lost to combine the perspectives of the personal and national, the historic and timeless, condensed into memorable, expressive language and form.

The tradition is so crammed with experience of life and art that it has become a source of strength for poets and readers alike. In his Nobel lecture of 1987, Joseph Brodsky argues that lyric poetry, more than any other verbal forms, teaches the "privateness of the human condition." He then moves on to a larger claim about the types of freedom of individual consciousness that poetry can instill:

> Lots of things can be shared: a bed, a piece of bread, convictions, a mistress, but not a poem by, say, Rainer Maria Rilke. A work of art, of literature especially, and a poem in particular, addresses a person tête-à-tête, entering with them into direct—free of any go-betweens—relations. It is for this reason that art in general, literature especially, and poetry in particular, is not exactly favored by the champions of the common good, masters of the masses, heralds of historical necessity. For there, where art has stepped, where a poem has been read, they discover, in place of the anticipated consent and unanimity, indifference and polyphony; in place of the resolve to act, inattention and fastidiousness.

Despite its focus on the private self, however—or, perhaps, thanks to it—the Russian cultural tradition, according to Brodsky, treats poetry as the supreme artistic form and has for centuries regarded poets as secular prophets whose introspections have tremendously wide resonance.[2] How Russian poetry achieved the prestige it enjoys—dubbed by G. S. Smith "a surrogate religion"[3] in its native culture—is a story that has been told elsewhere by scholars, commentators, and writers themselves. The story is of course complex, and this is not the place for an account that also takes stock of the sociological and institutional factors that contributed to the myths of the poet that developed at home and abroad.[4] Still, the reader can turn to literature itself to see how the myth of the poet as a charismatic figure grew cumulatively, starting in the early nineteenth century when the glamorous lives and tragic fates of Pushkin and Lermontov tapped into the romantic cult of celebrity.

A foundational text in this regard was Pushkin's "The Prophet" (1826). Its opening lines describe a spiritually depleted subject cast into "the desert" or spiritual despondency. The poem's turning point comes unexpectedly with the sudden appearance of an angel.[5] Once touched by the wings of this seraph, the speaker's eyes and ears acquire visionary powers. Through the physical transformation of his senses, the speaker can penetrate the mysteries of nature; and through a moral transformation he can bring a message of rebirth to mankind. But Pushkin's message to the poet is about the cost of inspiration. It comes in the form of the mutilation the angel performs by replacing the speaker's tongue with that of the wise serpent, and ripping out his old heart and substituting a burning piece of coal: poetry redolent of the prophet Isaiah looks back to the moment in the Old Testament when, by placing a cinder on Moses's tongue, an angel curbed his speech and saved his life to do future good. In the final lines of "The Prophet," the voice of God enjoins the poet to take up a moral mission to enlighten the people. These are the lines that have encapsulated for so many later Russian poets a sense of responsibility to their art and society:

Arise, prophet, and see and hear,
Be filled with my will
And, setting forth over land and seas,
Ignite the hearts of men with your Word.

In one of his last poems, written a decade after "The Prophet," Pushkin boasted that posterity would remember him for writing in the vernacular of the people and for his daring to supplicate from rulers "mercy for the fallen." It would be some time before his view that art could be both creatively free and socially significant came to shape attitudes toward literature. After Pushkin's death in a duel in 1837, with his works much distorted by censorship and political interference, his standing faltered for some decades. In the 1860s, the increasingly ideological Radical critics gave short shrift to Pushkin's political history and battle for creative freedom. They associated him with an art-for-art's-sake aestheticism detached from their own dogmatic utilitarianism about the social mission of literature. Dostoevsky's famous "Pushkin Speech" in 1880 was an important step in reestablishing Pushkin as a moral authority, a view that gained traction in the 1920s and 1930s as he became the most popular Soviet poet. His fate as a victim of court and society politics was taken to corroborate the general view that speaking truth to power could only be exercised perilously. Here it is hard not to recall the famous remark, attributed by Nadezhda Mandelstam to her husband Osip Mandelstam, that "poetry is respected only in this country—people are killed for it. There's no place where more people are killed for it."[6] Poets, whether or not their own style had anything in common with Pushkin's, continued to take to heart the vision of art as uplifting, and the art form has been unstintingly responsive and illuminatingly vital for a broad social spectrum, even at the darkest historical times.

At least in the Soviet period, the impulse to turn experience into verse was a wide, popular reflex, even (and affectingly) in dire circumstances. One proof comes in an anthology of Gulag poetry containing thousands of texts written by a vast range of the prison population (not just the intelligentsia).[7] Few if any of the writers of these poems were literary professionals; yet however linguistically modest and derivative their achievements, it was to verse, set out in traditional stanzaic forms, rather than prose that many prisoners authors turned in order to record ephemeral sensations of beauty and hope as much as despair. More dramatic evidence of poetry's staying power can be found in the heroic efforts of samizdat (the practice of underground publication) and tamizdat (the practice of clandestine publication abroad) works to preserve legacies menaced by the Soviet state have been carefully documented, as has the remarkable survival of works by Mandelstam, Kharms, Vvedensky, Oleinikov, and others through the efforts of devoted and brave readers who strove where possible to preserve poetic speech from oblivion, often making of poetry a life-and-death matter. Following the tradition of civic poetry, the more un-Pushkinian Nikolai Nekrasov, a contemporary of Tolstoy and Dostoevsky, used his novelistic gift for speaking in many voices to capture the experience of the marginal and neglected. Anna Akhmatova, an avowed Pushkinian, whose original fame derived from her exquisite small-scale lyrics about love, revealed another dimension of gravity in *Requiem*, a piece written clandestinely "for the drawer." Akhmatova assumed what she regarded as an ethical obligation to record and articulate the suffering of the victims of the Great Purges. A similar generational sense of artistry and conscience is a feature one might also identify as a particular quality of the poetry of Maria Stepanova, whose book of poems *The War of Beasts and Animals* treats Russia's war against Ukraine polyphonically.

The idea of the poet's societal mission is not the only legacy of Pushkin's "The Prophet." The poems included here that draw on this masterwork shift emphasis away from the didactic content onto the idea of poetry as a form of spiritual inspiration. Vladimir Nabokov and Vladislav Khodasevich made noteworthy contributions to the perpetuation of the Pushkin cult in émigré circles. More accessibly, we can note that literature itself in the twentieth century made the fate of the poet a rich topic. Nabokov's *Gift*, his final and greatest Russian-language novel, created a hero devoted to Pushkinian artistic values explicitly juxtaposed with the tradition of utilitarian criticism associated with the literary and revolutionary radicals who, for Nabokov, epitomized the vulgarity later embodied by the Bolsheviks. As Irina Shevelenko points out, the theme seems to culminate in novels such as *The Works and Days of Svistonov* (1929) by Konstantin Vaginov and *Pushkin House* (1978) by Andrei

Bitov, important postmodernist fictions that anticipate Victor Pelevin's sarcastic treatment of the fate of the poet in post-Soviet Russia, as depicted in *Homo Zapiens* (1999).[8] For Khodasevich and Zabolotsky, among others, what matters is the access to exaltation and renewal that poetry brings them, even in trying personal circumstances. These poems look to Pushkin not for didacticism but rather to recover moments of unworldliness, the "inattention and fastidiousness" of which Brodsky speaks.

Some of the poets included here doubled down on the integrity of art detached from politics. Others enjoyed a negotiated freedom with the authorities. Recognizing that poetry can begin in unlikely contexts, whether in a prison line or on the brink of dying, other writers subverted completely the idea that poets had an exalted status. Even when ideological roadblocks diverted writers and thwarted them into self-censorship, the spirit of modernist invention persisted. The poems included here written between the death of Stalin and before Perestroika testify to that capacity for end-running stagnation and accessing a tradition that was never entirely sealed off.

Life stories and feeling, while the stuff of art, are of course not art. Lyric poets have at their call the linguistic and formal resources that make it possible to universalize experience and move outward from a seemingly personal moment to some greater connectedness to the world and the human condition. Ironic, comical, visionary, poignant, incandescent with convictions, mini-dramas of horror and terror or of transcendence and love, Russian lyric poems have no limit on range, treatment of feelings and states of being, and no limit either to their capacity for artistic innovation. Seeing how the style of individual poets has been conditioned by a national tradition adds a further dimension to the experience of reading poems.

How poems transform the personal into the national-cum-historical constitutes one pattern to be discerned in poems across the span of the chapters. Poems that take their departure from a single moment can also compact an entire historical period. For instance, poems that situate the poet in a historically charged moment or location tend to bring together the micro and the macro. In talking about the tension that poems set up between the individual and the social, Brodsky, some of whose greatest poems are about empire and tyranny, has in mind the view that the political is the personal, a maxim that would hold true for history as well given how famously (not to say notoriously) tragic the past century has been in Russian history. Numerous poems in this book—and the most striking may be Mandelstam's "The Horseshoe Finder" (1922), Kuzmin's "Not a governor's lady with an officer" (1924), Gor's "I lie together with my wife, the two of us in the apartment . . ." (1942–44), Galich's "The Night Watch" (1963), Barskova's "Children's Literature" (2019),

Stepanova's "A little like this: instead of coming out of the closet" (2021)—find a language and form for the effects of historic and political cataclysm on national experience.

In "The Horseshoe Finder," the reader encounters Mandelstam opening up his poetic sights in an explosive picture of time and history, his poem about found classical objects cast in the visionary mode of Rimbaud. In a poem that tracks the interior thoughts of Gulag prisoners following a plough (and in a literal sense making verse with their feet), Nikolai Zabolotsky renews Romanticism in perceiving the relation of Man, History, and Nature—what he calls "the magical mystery of the universe." Behind Barskova's work about individual fates lies the tragedy of the Great Terror. Many poems will offer diverse perspectives, subverting official attitudes. Akhmadulina's response to contemporary literary politics blurs the boundary between the categories of Soviet and dissident, showing the need to take an ethical stance and critique the *sauve qui peut* hypocrisy writers exhibited under pressure from the authorities. Fanailova engages with the brutality of the invasion of Afghanistan, the Soviet Union's ill-fated colonial project, taking aim at post-Soviet neocolonialism as well. A generation later, as freedom of speech was withdrawn and state-sanctioned pieties were mandated in Putin's Russia, Stepanova and Rymbu find a language in which to defend the autonomy of the self and the right of art to speak out. The latter's "My Vagina" is a poem in which her sexual organs rebel, reproaching the male gaze and patriotic culture and eroticizing her reading; while the former makes a timely political allegory out of Covid at a moment when political repression was putting an entire culture back in the closet.

In their cosmic view of the contemporary and the larger workings of history, these poems all omit to name outright the historical crisis they reflect. That degree of obliquity allows each poet to foreground some other vital aspect, creating a particular aesthetic to render revolutionary dynamism, historical despair, the insidiousness of political oppression, the brutality of war. A sense of dynamism and colossal destruction attends Mandelstam's poem, which wonders in which direction the new Soviet state, an argonaut, will head and what it will leave behind of earlier civilization and its own. Kuzmin renders the same historical period with the care of an icon painter for whom the tragedy of apostasy and sacrilege is appropriate. Whether readers bring a little or much knowledge about Stalinism to Galich's poem is secondary to the poem's nightmarish, Gothic evocations of power and authoritarian idolatry. In the post-Soviet cultural space, the discovery of lost voices—the writer suppressed, censored, erased by the state machine—has led to a recuperation of lost biographies, works, and entire chapters of literary history. For Barskova, the lives behind the lines and the agonies suffered elicit a poetry of dry-eyed sympathy. The poet who could not bear witness at the time can remind and lay down a marker for the future in only twenty-five or so lines that reconnect and project, memorializing and extending: "They stand for poetry and weave their thread."

The Legacy of Modernism

When the cast of poets and choice of lyrics feel truly like a representative selection—a mini literary history of trends and movements as well as a great reading offering to poetry lovers—then the best anthologies may seem like more than the sum of their parts and a step toward a literary history. The poems and poets included here can also be seen in the light of their affiliation with literary movements: symbolism (which emerged in the 1890s); acmeism (often seen as close to Anglo-American Imagism); futurism of the 1910s–20s; absurdism (OBERIU) of the 1920s–30s, pioneers of nontraditional poetics known for linguistic experimentation; and concretism and conceptualism of the late-Soviet period.[9] Despite disruptions and interventions of the state and political circumstance, the vitality of the modernist legacy, connecting poets to one another within the Russian canon, across traditions and borders, remained a touchstone throughout the Soviet and post-Soviet eras.

Modernism as a term is notoriously hard to pin down. It is seen as supranational, international, and local, a single movement as well as a plurality of modernisms. That very breadth and internationalism make it preferable in the present context to an alternative term, "Silver Age."[10] Many versions of modernism share common preoccupations with explorations of many kinds, whether linguistic, technological, eschatological, or psychological. All of these can be attested in Russia's modernist poets and beyond.[11] Viewed from a distance, the term stands for numerous literary groups and subgroups that splintered over personalities and sometimes aesthetic manifestos, many of them aware at the time of their own mission to articulate a new aesthetic.[12] It has been seen as allied to symbolism with its theurgic thrust and radical departure from realism; futurism with an emphasis on invention, fragmentation, and disruption; or versions of reinvention to be seen in the cultural collage and preservations of the classical in acmeism.[13]

In contending here that modernism is a common factor in the poems selected for the present book, the aim is not to insist that all relate, in the same way, to a single movement and in the same way. Insofar as chapters historicize and contextualize individual careers and aesthetic profiles, the chapters themselves address in passing the specific way in which the writer is modernist by drawing attention to their development and affiliations. We start with Alexander Blok in 1908 representing the early phase of modernism that absorbed into poetry numerous other trends in literary study (such as aesthetic techniques like defamiliarization, as pioneered by Formalism), visual art (such as the World of Art, cubo-futurism, suprematism, and later constructivism), and cinema. In the Soviet period, modernism continues to develop not only as a nostalgic reference to the past but as an independent phenomenon that, however, remains "officially" unacknowledged. Later poets, perhaps expectedly, expand the modernist into the postmodernist with their ironic and self-ironic discourses.[14]

Modernism, in our understanding, also embraces the avant-garde as its extreme manifestation, and defines itself through permanent crossing of borders and limits—social, political, linguistic, aesthetic, metaphysical, historical. Presenting a subject as the center of the cosmos with its own mythology, history, ethics, and sometimes religion, modernist poets included facts and phenomena of "real life" in these individualized universes, invariably subjugating them to the subject's perspective and thus, inevitably, transgressing societal norms and constraints. The absolutist subjectivity underpinning modernist poetry determines the logic of the development of an artistic language that constantly and radically renews itself, breaking with the dominant traditions, striving for a continuous "defamiliarization" and expressing a highly individualized view of the world. The paradox of modernist self-mythologizing is defined by the knowledge of the relativity of a myth that stands in a problematic relationship with other mythologies and belief systems—from religious to political.

Until the 1920s, Russian modernism was fully alive to international currents in the arts and flourished by contact. Mandelstam's Pindaric fragment "The Horseshoe Finder" owes its propulsion to Rimbaud's "Bateau ivre," while Blok's "Free Thoughts" is a vehicle for his reinvention of Baudelaire's flâneur in the mold of a Nietzschean philosophical hero who makes out of his urban world an existential journey. The continuance of Silver Age culture into the First Wave of emigration that saw millions of Russians settle in Berlin and Paris in the 1920s had a looking-glass effect: convinced that their own values were incompatible with Soviet aesthetics, writers pondered the question of whether a spiritual home could be created outside Russia. Both Nabokov and Khodasevich carried into the emigration their worship of Pushkin as the supreme genius of Russian poetry. Physical dislocation also telescoped the development of literary trends. Viewed against a timeline of European art, the erotic sophistication of Nabokov's "Lilith," a poem inspired by Mallarmé, may look like a holdover from fin de siècle decadence; yet, in the context of the conservative aesthetics fostered by émigré critics, the poem was daring.

Proof of Russia's poetic vitality and capacity to hear old and new voices through the Iron Curtain can be found in quiet acts of internationalism such as Olga

Sedakova's rewriting of Keats, absorbing his voice into her own poetry and idiom, already enriched by her mastery of allusion. Imitation can be read in one way as a reflection on poetry's survival tactics in the coldest possible climate, both literally and metaphorically. Engagement with a broad mixture of cultures was typical of Russian modernism and remained an important aspect of Russian lyric poetry (including a distinguished tradition of verse translation) even when it went underground or abroad in avoidance of the state's demand for socialist realism. A similar internationalism during the Perestroika period from the 1980s informed postmodernist poetry of the 1980s–90s.

Modernism continued to develop from the 1920s to the 1990s, producing new branches and new poetic languages among émigré poets and also in the USSR.[15] This evolution was partially visible in publications of the 1920s, before socialist realism established its monopoly.[16] Later on, modernist quests relocated into the realm of "nonofficial" literature, either appearing in the samizdat or, more frequently, manifested in the milieu of underground circles and groups, where poetry existed in the form of recitations and performances. These alternative forms of existence proved part of the culture of transgression and experimentation (sometimes bohemian, sometimes more risky) favored by modernism.[17]

The Silver Age gave birth to three major lineages of Russian modernist poetry: symbolism, acmeism, and futurism. Russian symbolism had reimagined poetry as "theurgic art" (as named and practiced by a seminal practitioner, Viacheslav Ivanov) whose purpose was to create new myths and reveal hidden links between the real and metaphysical. Essentially, the symbolists treated each word as a potential symbol, emphasizing its musical aspects through poetic rhythm and rhyme, thus transforming a poetic text into an act of magic. For them, a symbol became the nexus of the phenomenal and spiritual, of the visible and invisible, the real and ideal. In Andrei Belyi's words, "The symbol awakens the music of the soul. [. . .] Music is the window from which the enchanting streams of Eternity pour into us and splash magic."[18] Blok's "Free Thoughts. On Death" (1908) is a vivid example of such transformations: first, the lyrical subject recognizes in mundane events symbols of the ubiquitous presence of death beneath a thin film of life, but the musicality of the verse itself, resonances between the subject's internal state and the world, paradoxically lead to the poem's optimistic finale and its call "to sing songs! And listen to the wind!" The music generated by poetry visibly overcomes the tragedy of existence.

One can detect the echo of symbolism in much later poems, such as Elena Shvarts's "A Rubbish Heap" (1983), which sculpts and ironizes a new sense of the sacred from the abject. The poem also reads as a demonstration of a poetic magic—the musicality of the verse, the stream of metaphors and similes, in front of our eyes—that transforms an ugly rubbish heap into a symbol of world culture, metamorphizing apparent death, rot, and destruction into sources for the new art. Similarly, Maria Stepanova's poem "A little like this: instead of coming out of the closet" transforms pandemic isolation into a series of self-generating symbols signifying the indistinguishability of life and death, the emergence of some "lifedeath" as a metaphysical status quo of contemporary civilization.

Acmeism appeared as a reaction to symbolism, supplanting metaphysics and the occult with the worship of art and architecture, texts and beautiful objects, and showing greater attention to the human body and psychologically concrete emotions. In the words of Mandelstam's manifesto "The Morning of Acmeism" (1912):

> The Acmeists share their love of the organism and organization with the physiological genius of the Middle Ages. In the pursuit of sophistication, the nineteenth century lost the secret of true complexity. [. . .] We do not want to entertain ourselves with a walk in the "forest of symbols," because we have a more pristine, more slumbering forest—the divine physiology, the infinite complexity of our dark organism.[19]

The tradition of acmeism established by Gumilev, Mandelstam, and Akhmatova also left an indelible mark on the modernist poetry of the Soviet era. The legacy is still visible in Akhmatova's and Mandelstam's lyrics of the 1920s and 1930s (and for Akhmatova also of the 1940s to 1960s). Over several generations, and sporadically, acmeism was adopted and enriched by such highly individual poets as Kuzmin, Khodasevich, and Nabokov. Brodsky and Losev gave this aesthetic new life in the 1960s and 1970s by infusing it with caustic (self-)irony and various forms of philosophic and emotional detachment. All these and other poets explore the dramatic relationship between world culture, Russian history, and the author's personal memory. What is also distinctively acmeist is the orientation of verse toward a permanent, more or less explicit, intertextual dialogue with poetic classics. In this they found the means to renew traditions without breaking with them. The (neo)acmeist lyric is marked by "an unusually developed sense of historicism" and an awareness of the "experience of history in oneself and oneself in history . . ." Meditation on memory and recollection serves as "a profoundly moral ground that stands against forgetfulness, oblivion, and chaos, as the foundation of creativity, faith, and loyalty."[20]

The acmeist matrix continues to evolve in post-Soviet poetry as well. Polina Barskova uses the acmeist method of conversing with objects of culture treated as accumulators of historical memory when she creates a virtual palimpsest in her "Children's Literature." In this poem, images and rhythms from Soviet children's books hide images of their creators as well as reflections of torture they underwent during the Great Terror, and all this is inscribed above Bosch's *Garden of Earthly Delights*. Mandelstam's "infinite complexity of our dark organism" resonates with Elena Fanailova's "reading" of her protagonists' bodies as the text consisting of scars left by traumatic history (". . . Again they're off for their Afghanistan," 2003) and "My Vagina" by Galina Rymbu (2018), which became an aesthetic manifesto for an entire generation of feminist poets.

The avant-garde offers a radicalized version of modernism. According to the Russian scholar Maxim Shapir, "In avant-garde art, pragmatics comes to the fore. The main thing is the potency of the art—it's meant to shock, to stir up, to provoke an active reaction in a person from the outside."[21] Avant-garde work always implies crossing the boundary that separates the artistic world from the nonaesthetic, a direct and frequently outrageous invasion of the reader/viewer's unconscious. The proverbial "slap in the face of public opinion" can be manifested in a variety of ways: in shocking subjects of poetry, in formal radicalism, in poetic performances by the author—in any case, the resort to shock value remains a constant of the avant-garde.Modernism does not break with existing cultural languages, whereas the avant-garde seeks to smash them and create new languages instead—including transrational ones (*zaum'*). These new languages are supposed to transform the reader/viewer's perception and, through it, to revolutionize society. Russian futurism was the epitome of the avant-garde in Russian poetry, and after 1917 it fueled such diverse cultural phenomena as LEF (Left Front of the Arts—a literary group and journal), constructivism in art and architecture, Formalism and the Moscow Linguistic Circle in theory, and "literature of the fact" in literature.

Khlebnikov, Mayakovsky, and Guro represent classical futurism in this volume. The first two poets are famed for their extravagant metaphors, linguistic innovations, and performative Nietzscheanism. By those linguistic criteria, Elena Guro's traditional-sounding lyric does not fit the avant-gardist model. Yet, when considered from the perspective of her use of biographic self-fashioning (a key element in modernist aesthetics), "Gone to sleep, gone quiet now, so kind" looks startling and even has shock value. The poets of OBERIU (Union of the Real Art), an unofficial group that combined playfulness with an absurd, dark, and tragic vision of the world, are direct heirs to futurism. Daniil Kharms, Nikolai Oleinikov, Alexander Vvedensky, and Nikolai Zabolotsky emphasize different aspects of the futurist legacy (although late Zabolotsky almost entirely departs from it), but all of them remain radical in their rethinking of metaphysics, irreverent inversions of the aesthetic canons, and attempts to break through conventional logic, exercising bracing forms of estrangement and mockery directed at canonized and dogmatized perspectives on history and culture.

Shocking subjects were a staple of futurist art. The nightmarish poems of Gennady Gor about the Leningrad siege escalate the aesthetic by combining elements of ugly and deadly everyday routine with the absurdist language inspired by the OBERIU poets. Working in the same vein were the underground concretists, represented here by Ian Satunovsky and Igor Kholin, both members of the circle of artists and poets active in the 1950s and 1960s. Their poems train their lens on an offensively close view of everyday Soviet life, and they achieve their shocks by conveying the horror of the mundane. Among underground poets of the next generation, Ry Nikonova carried into her work a futurist energy of rebellion against stale language. In her lyrics of the 1970s and 1980s, she resurrected the search for a transrational language (*zaum'*) and positioned her philosophy of poetry in an intense dialogue with avant-gardist poets of the 1910s and 1920s. A distant yet recognizable echo of futurism comes to life in the works of the Moscow conceptualists Dmitri Prigov and Lev Rubinshtein, who in their nonconformist poetry either deconstructed the Soviet self (Prigov) or reconceptualized the work of language to piece together the real from fragments of discourses and figments of imagination (Rubinshtein). These poets' experimental forms fully correspond to Jean-François Lyotard's famous definition of postmodernism as "incredulity toward metanarratives" because they explode traditional concepts of lyrical form and lyrical mind. Although thoroughly postmodernist, the conceptualists were true to the legacy of futurism by targeting cultural conventions and pieties.

However, the description of Russian modernist poetry of the twentieth and, arguably, twenty-first centuries would forfeit numerous masterpieces and poetic personae if we were to limit its genealogy to the direct heirs of symbolism, acmeism, and futurism. Another lineage can be captured with the term "neoromantic," to denote poets who, despite other differences, developed shared strategies for expressing their nonconformism, even within Soviet poetry. It is on the basis of these poetic principles that poets as dissimilar as Nikolai Gumilev (also a founding father of acmeism), Alexander Galich, Vladimir Vysotsky, Marina Tsvetaeva, Bella Akhmadulina, and Linor Goralik can be grouped loosely as neoromantic. The first common practice is the reconsideration of the romantic quest for transcendence: stylization and irony replace the ideal, blurring the boundary between fiction and reality and, above all, creating a sense of estrangement. In this attempt to materialize fantasy and expose the instability of even an imagined reality, the neoromantic poets typically employ oxymoron as a favored trope.

A second common practice among neoromantic authors affects the configuration of the poetic subject. The neoromantic poet is comfortable creating a contradictory self, one that straddles the literal and fictional and can fragment into multiple personalities, sometimes inhabiting multiple spheres. Gumilev's "Sixth Sense" distills a sentiment prevalent among neoromantic writers, namely, that poetry can be counted on to manifest the highest and most enduring acts of transcending and transgressing limits. The neoromantic speaker frequently breaks the boundaries of his or her selfhood through theatrical transformations of the subject. Galich and Vysotsky are particularly famous for their socially diverse lyric speakers. In Galich's ballads, the perspective of an ordinary Soviet slob conveys the grotesque transformations of a living person into an automaton, and the parade of Stalin monuments in "The Night Watch" demonstrates the driving force of this process. Vysotsky's poetry comprises verse monologues delivered by pirates, thugs, alcoholics, space travelers, psychiatric patients, prisoners, as well as a jet plane and a wolf. Given that all of these characters represent manifestations of the lyrical self, it is not surprising that some critics have argued that Vysotsky's encyclopedia of voices represents a new, polyphonic poetic subjectivity.

Yet, if Vysotsky is exceptional in degree and inventiveness, he is not alone. Other neoromantic poets also gravitate to extreme life-and-death situations as moments of consummate freedom from social and cultural conventions, when everything superficial vanishes and something "solid" and "reliable" comes to the fore. Marina Tsvetaeva makes every emotional gesture transgressive, and love in her poems is an unstoppable force that is able to curtail the horizon. This may explain the popularity of both the ballad genre and war poetry among neoromantics, including Gumilev, Galich, and Vysotsky. The extreme conditions treated in neoromantic poetry place multiple subjectivities in relation to one another: they reinforce the striving for moral clarity and a more unified personality, invoking the timeless oppositions between good and evil, heroism and treason. However, when Linor Goralik conflates an extreme scenario by imagining the Magi walking toward a star in a stylized version of a children's tale about a hare and a baby wolf ("wolfie"), the result of this fusion appears to be radically transgressive. In crossing lines, breaking rules, and subverting expectations, neoromantic poetry triumphantly embodies a form of emancipation.

Lyric Subjectivity

Another way to think about the history of poetry in Russia, and a story arc the reader can trace in this book, concerns the changing treatment of subjectivity in lyric poetry. How the subject has been reinvented and conditioned by history, and what the formative values have been in the development of poetry, is a question that consciously and unconsciously informs many of the works we discuss. The beginnings of modern Russian poetry date to the eighteenth century. Literary conventions and proof of competent command of neoclassical taste were the priorities for writers. Only a few exceptional writers such as Gavriil Derzhavin became canonical beyond their time. Recognized by contemporaries for his genius (using the word in the period sense to mean "rare gift of inspiration"), Derzhavin was precocious because his poetry was a vehicle for setting out an internal conception of his own identity, the workings of heart and intellect, and for trying to see himself in relation to a world he understood as complexly layered socially, politically, and metaphysically as a matter of some partly fathomable design. Most other contemporary poets made use of stock figures, stereotyped emotions, clichéd gestures, all the depersonalizing elements of a genre system widely applied.

The great poets of the Golden Age, the name for the Pushkin period, had a richer view of interiority, freedom, and personal autonomy, acquiring a keen sense of how their creativity affected their own identity and the outside world. Understanding of the self in any art form may stand in relation to conceptions developed by contemporary philosophy and science. In the Pushkin period, the engagement with German Idealism, which was important to the history of Russian thought in the 1830s, brought a new conceptual vocabulary that was not firmly grounded in scientific or philosophical and pedagogical research practiced in Russia. Some echoes of Schelling and Schiller, even fewer of Coleridge, the sources on theories of the creative imagination described famously by M. H. Abrams, achieve limited penetration in the thought and work of Russian poets of that nineteenth-century generation, and, while poetry now finds its material in lived experience, few earlier poems genuinely sought to know the human person individually. For all the increase in meditative postures and attention to the interpersonal, the presentation of the self remains highly rhetorical and external to true psychological portraiture. Pushkin's vaunted classical style almost always universalizes emotions at first contact, Baratynsky's famous use of irony by definition treats the personal with detachment, and Tiutchev sublimates deep feeling, even when achingly felt, into symbolic language. Subjectivity tends to be configured impersonally. The use of language is performative, but interiority is sparsely psychologized. Style of expression, marked by self-possession and rhetorical poise, follows how far understanding of the imagination, empathy, and the passions had developed in the period, and even memory, which might be thought to be the most personal perspective intuitively open to every poet, objectifies the self as detached from experience. Poems are more memorable for restraint, irony, and dignity than for personality, and the overall character of Russian poetry seems consistent with Louis Menand's view of the nineteenth century as committed to a "doctrine of impersonality."[22]

By the first decade of the twentieth century, when the earliest poem in this book was written, the human sciences had altered received attitudes to the social sphere, newly understood as man-made and subject to human agency. Attitudes to human nature also changed greatly with what the historian Daniel Beer calls the reception of "biopsychological theories of human nature."[23] The status of the perceiving and feeling subject developed in the twentieth century within the matrix of scientific, psychological, and artistic changes that contributed to and constituted modernism. The self became a fractionalized entity to be understood in instants of time phenomenologically, seen as divided between unconscious and conscious states, as socially conditioned and also biologically determined. As Leonid Livak, the most recent historian of Russian modernism, puts it, the movement was a carrier of a "new consciousness" and new sensibility that drew on a "cognitive system that gave meaning to events in artistic, social, and private life."[24] Relativity and cultural relativism, fostered by anthropology, linguistics, biology, and science, fundamentally altered the perspective on the past, making the remote past more immediate and the personal past mobile, layered, uncertain.[25]

These are vast generalizations, intended only to frame the basic observation that, from the Silver Age, Russian poets exploit these new attitudes and perspectives on the representation of self-definition as an open process of discovery. Yet that is how one of the greatest poets, and most eloquent essayists, understood the shift in the way lyric poetry conceptualized the self. For Brodsky, all of the many states of mind and terms of identity predicated on reading poetry concern the production of conscience in the individual. In this he is following in the footsteps of Marina Tsvetaeva, a predecessor he particularly admired, whose essay "Art in the Light of Consciousness" also explored connections between reading and readers as an unfathomable and unpredictable relationship. She puts the matter pithily in a section on Goethe when she writes, "One person reads Werther and shoots himself; another reads Werther and, because Werther shoots himself, decides to live."[26] The point is about the fluidity of experience that goes into poems as well as the fluidity of each reader's own experience of the poem.

While the poems chosen for this anthology were not intended to exemplify the theme of subjectivity, which we view as a distinctive feature of Russian (as distinct from Soviet) poetry, it is no coincidence that many of the poems treat aspects of subjectivity and carry forward the practices and legacy of modernism.[27] Not least among factors was literature itself. Nabokov's prurient "Lilith" depicts an erotic reverie as it takes place in the mind of the subject gripped by a dream that is itself informed by borrowings from Mallarmé. The poem looks back to decadence, artfully pastiching it while sharing the fascination with the psychology of uncontrolled desire at work in novels like *Despair* and *Laughter in the Dark*. The young Pasternak, immersed in the vortex of his love for philosophy and art, repeatedly in his earlier poetry captures the moment when language and perception fuse, nowhere better demonstrated than in "Poetry," in which consciousness attempts to transcribe on the page poetic consciousness. Into its phenomenological project, this short lyric seems to distill a view of consciousness that would mark modernist novels of the period, both in Russia and abroad.

The account of inspiration endorsed by Pushkin and then Mikhail Lermontov continued to make its presence felt well into modernism. Vladislav Khodasevich, while capable of great self-irony, nevertheless felt most true to his Russianness when portraying inspiration as a sudden flash, and he looked not into his own psyche but to other poets for the idea of poetic birth. Many poets of the Silver Age, in keeping with broader trends in modernism, brought a new psychologism to their understanding of memory and imagination. The self-conscious awareness of the poem in the process of its own creation has been a feature of modernist and then modern poetry, internationally, whether one looks at Rilke or Mallarmé or Mandelstam. Pasternak's "Poetry" enacts its own process of discovery. Born out of his philosophical studies and phenomenological alertness, influenced by his superb musical and painterly senses, Pasternak's poem verges on a definition of poetry as a harmony of mood and language that comes alive in the subject in the moment in which it is lived or even experienced on the page.

Other factors conditioning subjectivity were cultural (emigration or internal immigration into the literary underground) as well as historical and political. For all the Pushkinian qualities Vladislav Khodasevich absorbed into his lyric poetry, his portrayal of the poetic self pays close attention to the cultural moment. In his "Ballad" (1922), written on the eve of permanent emigration, the question of poetic inspiration is not a purely internal mechanism. His threadbare situation, the sense of the self and poetic vision as fugitive and reduced, impinges sharply on the subject's capacity to step outside his actual life and recover the power of poetry that is individual and also Pushkin-conditioned, whereas, in Kharms's "Werld," the text so radically and defensively detaches individual consciousness from the contingencies of the body and the world that the uncertainty about using even basic words challenges the identity of "I." The loss of fixed referents, whether an entire literary tradition or belief in the logic of the world, finds the self grappling to reestablish habitual associations or confront their loss, factors that remain active decades later as we see in Lev Losev's "One Day in the Life of Lev Vladimirovich." No literary work with such a title can escape the shadow of Solzhenitsyn's hero, lightly ironized here since Losev's alter ego is serving his sentence of "exile" in a liberal arts college. Here the problems of how to identify oneself pile up, and the poet makes of this long poem an experience-filled form that cannot stave off a final, new moment of nonrecognition. The only two love poems in the book, by Tsvetaeva and Mayakovsky, share a more than hyperbolic style of amatory declaration. Both are poems of voice and self-inquiry, and the two aspects are fused together because each searches for its own space to be filled by the beloved, projecting the self onto the other in Tsvetaeva's mountain-wide embrace and Mayakovsky's star-filled sky.

How This Book Works

The poems in *All the World on a Page* are drawn from a long century that witnessed the incalculable political, historical, and cultural changes of late Imperial Russian, Soviet, and post-Soviet history. The reader will find here a mixture of classic names as well as great poems by some lesser-known poets. World-class names include Blok, Akhmatova, Mandelstam, Pasternak, Mayakovsky, Tsvetaeva, Khlebnikov, and Brodsky, as well as poets regarded in Russia as near-equals but who have been relatively neglected abroad such as Kuzmin, Khodasevich, Zabolotsky, Guro, Vvedensky, and Kharms. At the same time, readers persuaded by a choice of author may wonder about the choice of a particular poem. For instance, there has always been a debate about Nabokov's standing as a poet. "Lilith" does not typify Nabokov's usual lyric nostalgia for Russia and other quests for lost time, his more familiar great theme. It does, however, intersect captivatingly with the modernist and decadent materials he explored in his fiction at the time. Similarly, the choice of Brodsky's "Homage to Chekhov" might also look offbeat when compared to the more classicizing works, elegies to empire, and metaphysical meditations that are his great themes. Yet this work's humor and its intrinsic statement on the hierarchy of art and the authority of poetry over other literary genres are also the quintessence of Brodsky and perhaps worth emphasizing.

Each chapter contains the original Russian poem and an English translation. Many of the latter are new commissions and reflect the dynamic state of Russian poetic translation at the present time. One inherent challenge for all interested in working on poetry across languages is the famous *traduttore–traditore* slogan often invoked to bemoan the gaps and awkward fits in idiom, structure, and voice that translators negotiate. Circumstances of receptivity to languages and traditions can and do change. In the early twenty-first century, the art of literary translation is now more widely practiced and extensively studied, and that has been to the benefit of the Russian tradition, among others. A century ago, Roman Jakobson's landmark essay "On the Generation That Squandered Its Poets" delivered a moving elegy to the final expiration of the Silver Age culture represented by the suicide of Mayakovsky, an admired innovator and great friend. While Jakobson felt that "what distinguished Russia is not so much the fact that her great poets have ceased to be, but rather that not long ago she had so many of them," he concluded that it was likely to go unappreciated by the larger world because Russia's poetry "has never really been an export item" and was "unlikely to survive the misfortunes of translation."[28]

A century ago, Jakobson could not have anticipated the skill and ingenuity successive generations have brought to their task. Between 1960 and 1990s, the translation of Russian poetry had its own moral valor, particularly if it also recovered the work of poets banned in the USSR or expressed the sense that literary affinities could circumvent the Iron Curtain. Advocates of a certain narrative of poetic heroism unique to Russia could be found among the ranks of contemporary poets in exile—not only Joseph Brodsky, though he was first and foremost—as well as among Western poets of authority such as Seamus Heaney, who, always appreciative of the artistry of poems even when read secondhand in English, understood the weight credited to the words of Eastern European and Russian poets. English-speaking audiences have increasingly gained access to the work of Russian poets and groups through translations, biographies, memoirs, and anthologies. In "The Poet's Essay," Randall Jarrell, writing about the American poetry scene in 1959, mused that the "ideal public would just read the poet; read him [*sic*] with a certain willingness and interest; read him imaginatively and perceptively."[29] The aim of this book is to help readers, with or without knowledge of Russian, to have that sort of experience in their encounter with the Russian tradition. Since the 1980s, there has been a notable step change in quantity and quality of translations, both of classics and of new poetry, making newly available household names such as Akhmatova, introducing writers who are canonical Russian voices but unfamiliar to the Anglophone reader such as Khodasevich, and capturing in real time cutting-edge new poets such as Barskova, Goralik, Fanailova, Stepanova, and Rymbu, all represented here.

The principles of selection set out in this introduction suggest that the role of subjectivity and the modernist dimension constituted powerful generative principles across the entire time period. Readers will be in a position to look at many other poems and consider how closely they conform to and depart from criteria that we believe are valid for our selection. While this book is not an attempt at canon formation, the set of poems illustrates an underlying coherence to the history of lyric in a period marked by much historical discontinuity and dispersal. In chronological order, the chapters afford the reader a chance to experience the richness of Russian poetry through poems and poets rather than through movements (although the essays situate each poet in relation to their artistic context). We have focused on poems as much as poets in showcasing the art of the Russian lyric, and, while some of the choices may represent a familiar aspect of the poet's work, some also represent lesser-known elements of their art. Even so, the inevitable sins of omission in any anthology can perhaps be somewhat extenuated by frankly admitting that we considered many other poets. In some cases the choice between representatives of different aesthetic schools such as Prigov and Parshchikov meant that the choice fell between one rather than the other. We regret that there was no space to include, for example, works by Boris Slutsky, who, even as he paid his dues to official literature, kept his best poems "for the drawer" and exemplified a type of voluntary dislocation from the Soviet mainstream; the neo-modernist lyric of Viktor Krivulin, a member of the same Leningrad underground circle to which Elena Shvarts belonged; and the richly experimental work of Arkady Dragomoshchenko, akin to American Language Poetry and expert in forms of philosophical monologue—all remarkable and very different writers whose range of lyric techniques and linguistic variety would have been important additions. The subjective element of taste will inevitably play a part in what Vladimir Markov, a distinguished literary scholar and anthologist, called the "torture of choice." It is to be hoped that the final selection of poems, made after sifting through countless alternatives, will provide readers, whether new to Russian poetry or inveterate readers and scholars, with rich encounters of voices, personalities, forms, and themes.

The chapter-length essays in the book stand on their own; the larger story they tell about Russian poetry as an art, and the state of the art to the present, emerges through their connected stories. Readers may choose to read selectively or sequentially, and they might also observe that there are considerable affinities between poems, some brought out in the chapter essays. Readers may see for themselves poems clustered according to overarching themes, left implicit, relating to self, history, God, society, and poetry. Works belonging to these categories share a theme but remain irreducibly different as poetic performance. What we see as distinctive about Russian poetry over this span (and beyond the end of the Soviet period) is its gravitation toward certain themes that regularly embody the national/historical in the personal. even in periods when fractured cultural politics cut across modernist trends (felt acutely in the diaspora of several generations); the perpetual, even chronic, attentiveness of poems to the individual subject and the nature of subjectivity; and its sometimes playful, sometimes elevated interest in how poetry comes to the poet.[30]

In poetry studies generally, the method of close reading retains its position as an important mode of analysis that has also over time acquired more compendious expectations than the internal focus favored by New Critical techniques. Poems will be read here for their perceptual nuances, surface novelties, language, sensations, and structuring of lyrical details, but our understanding also expands when they are not read in isolation, and users of this critical anthology will also benefit from the broader picture it presents. Metrically, musically, thematically, poets have stamped their personalities on the lyric, whether in the short confines of the quatrain or in the expansiveness of semi-narrative of a cycle such as Akhmatova's *Secrets of the Craft*. In the Russian tradition, examples of the lyric sequence go back to the eighteenth century and include the pioneering book of elegies published by Alexander Sumarokov. While notable examples in the nineteenth century include Alexander Pushkin's "Songs of the Western Slavs" ("Pesni zapadnykh slavian," 1835) and Nikolai Nekrasov's *Who Lives Well in Russia* (*Komu na Rusi zhit' khorosho*, 1874), the use of poetic cycles united through thematic coherence or narrative sequence entered its full flourishing mainly in the Silver Age. The older and younger symbolists Innokenty Annensky in his *Cypress Chest* (*Kiparisovyi larets*) and Alexander Blok in his *Snow Mask* (*Snezhnaia maska*) innovated by making the lyric sequence an organizing principle of a book of poems, a practice that poets of the next generation such as Anna Akhmatova, Marina Tsvetaeva, and Mikhail Kuzmin developed. Kuzmin and Akhmatova, in their respective *The Trout Breaks the Ice* (*Forel' razbivaet led*, 1925–28) and *Poem Without a Hero* (*Poema bez geroia*, 1935–61), composed single books comprising an entire cycle of poems. Akhmatova remained a keen practitioner both of the cycle embedded in a larger book of poems, such as the "Northern Elegies" (*Severnye elegii*, 1921–64), and the separate freestanding sequence such as *Requiem* and the "Secrets of the Craft." The history of the use of the lyric sequence and its patterns in Russian poetry has yet to be written. It is clear, however, that as in modern British and American poetry, in Russian the dynamic structuring of a relational ordering of poems has taken different approaches. The traditional, and still helpful, New Critical approach to the poetic cycle has seen it primarily as a twentieth-century device used by poets to bring together often disparate and sometimes clashing voices. By subordinating the individual lyric to the sequence, the lyric series establishes an organic relation of part and whole and achieves unity through associative relations between the lyric units. More recent studies have moved away from the tonal equilibrium and unity postulated of the cycle to many more examples in which fragmentation, erasure, contradiction and nonnarrative can dominate. In this vein, Joseph Conte draws a distinction between serial poems and procedural forms. The serial poem is not a sequence because the reader can start reading anywhere. Priority of information and plot line do not determine content, and the reader does not need a specific order or arrangement of information to understand. This is very much in keeping with Elena Shvarts's observation in the prose introduction to her "miniature epic" *Homo Musaget* (*Khomo Musaget*, 1996) that the series "departs from the narrative poem by virtue of its extremely discontinuous development of plot. The plot of the typical narrative poem flows like a river, the plot of the series hides underground, now suddenly darting from the heights, now touching base with its source."[31] Serial poems may generally resist closure. And, while an open series can be extended ad infinitum, even a finite series can end on an open note. The procedural form, in Conte's definition, imposes a set form that serves as a fixed vehicle, and these "arbitrary constraints are relied on to generate the context and direction of the poem during composition."[32] While he argues that his categories apply only to postmodernist poetry, reviewers of his book have disputed that narrowness and seen the utility of these categories as much broader, a point that looks helpful in relation to single poems discussed in this book that either originate in a cycle or constitute a separate sequence. The lyric sequence that made its mark on modernist poetry (and best attested here by the example of Akhmatova) has remained one of the more productive structures in Russian poetry of the past quarter century, practiced inventively by the likes of Olga Sedakova, Joseph Brodsky, Elena Shvarts, and Maria Stepanova.

Finally, a word is in order about the term "critical" and what the book's title promises. A critical anthology is not a literary history of poetry in disguise. The essays we have written, the methods and techniques they apply, reflect the interpretative traditions that have evolved and shaped the discipline of Russian poetry studies over a long period. Much like Anglo-American criticism, though with its own emphases, Russian literary criticism in the domain of poetry has undoubtedly gone through its own battles. In the 1900s, where this book begins, formalist approaches akin to the pragmatics of New Criticism from the 1950s refocused attention away from biography and history onto verbal structures and genre, acknowledging but downplaying message. A second generation of younger formalists, anticipating the New Historicism of the 1980s, explored fascinatingly literary texts as historical artifacts bearing the traces of cultural codes. The influence of these schools, while interrupted during the heyday of structuralism, was never completely extinguished, and lines can be drawn between them and later fashions in critical reading, semiotics, and a renewal of philological interest in poetry. Structuralist poetics as an outgrowth of larger trends also had its roots in the early apprehension by theorists and poets in the 1910s and 1920s that poetic language could be understood as a special instance of language seen in Saussurean terms as the relationship of *langue* and *parole*. Between the 1970s and 1990s, numerous studies of Russian poetry and poets saw the business of interpretation largely based on the analysis of intrinsic formal and logical patterns to be found in poems, a method perhaps most famously exemplified in the classic grammatical, lexical, and syntactic parsing that Claude Lévi-Strauss and Roman Jakobson applied in their close reading of Baudelaire's "Les Chats."[33] Compatible with deconstruction as well as some types of New Criticism, the method at its apogee put clear water between a tradition of biographical reading of poetry still dominant in Soviet literary studies and the study of the verbal artifact for its language and form. While this school of criticism lasted longer in the Slavic discipline than in other fields, the fashion was not entirely parochial. Its preferred methods of subtextual and intertextual analysis coincided at the time with comparable interest in citational practices in English literary studies (even if Harold Bloom's psychoanalytical spin-off into anxiety of influence was a second chapter that largely passed Russian poetry criticism by).

Over the postwar period until at least the 1990s, critical methods had a doctrinaire cast. It was a rare work like Yuri Lotman's *Structure of the Literary Text*, something of a textbook of close reading, that treated the ahistorical aesthetic value of the artwork and literary contexts, like the biographical, historical, and sociological, as equally relevant. Whether methods privileged subtextual, structuralist, or biographical elements or genre and form, they tended to anchor the understanding of the text in one set of descriptors detached from other factors that condition horizons of expectation. The reasons behind the fossilization of these schools lie beyond the present discussion. It suffices to note with some confidence that the present state of poetry scholarly criticism in Russian studies has outgrown ideologies, retaining the lessons of each of these methods yet aiming to provide more layered descriptions of poems sensitive to the works of texts as well as the creative imagination of individual poets. Here you will find a variety of spaces, including metaphysical landscapes, bare rooms, the sun, a lightbulb, a battlefield, a garbage heap, an archaeological dig, a dacha, ancient Rome, English and Siberian summers, a racecourse and racehorses, a talking angel, and a militant vagina. And you will hear remarkable voices.

1

Alexander Blok, "Free Thoughts. On Death" (1908)

IN BAUDELAIRE'S SHADOW

Вольные мысли. О смерти

Всё чаще я по городу брожу.
Всё чаще вижу смерть - и улыбаюсь
Улыбкой рассудительной. Ну, что же?
Так я хочу. Так свойственно мне знать,
Что и ко мне придет она в свой час.

Я проходил вдоль скачек по шоссе.
День золотой дремал на грудах щебня,
А за глухим забором - ипподром
Под солнцем зеленел. Там стебли злаков
И одуванчики, раздутые весной,
В ласкающих лучах дремали. А вдали
Трибуна придавила плоской крышей
Толпу зевак и модниц. Маленькие флаги
Пестрели там и здесь. А на заборе
Прохожие сидели и глазели.

Я шел и слышал быстрый гон коней
По грунту легкому. И быстрый топот
Копыт. Потом - внезапный крик:
"Упал! Упал!" - кричали на заборе,
И я, вскочив на маленький пенёк,
Увидел всё зараз: вдали летели
Жокеи в пестром - к тонкому столбу.
Чуть-чуть отстав от них, скакала лошадь
Без седока, взметая стремена.

А за листвой кудрявеньких березок,
Так близко от меня - лежал жокей,
Весь в желтом, в зеленя х весенних злаков,
Упавший навзничь, обратив лицо
В глубокое ласкающее небо.
Как будто век лежал, раскинув руки
И ногу подогнув. Так хорошо лежал.
К нему уже бежали люди. Издали\',
Поблескивая медленными спицами, ландо
Катилось мягко. Люди подбежали
И подняли его . . .

    И вот повисла
Беспомощная желтая нога
В обтянутой рейтузе. Завалилась
Им на плечи куда-то голова . . .
Ландо подъехало. К его подушкам
Так бережно и нежно приложили
Цыплячью желтизну жокея. Человек
Вскочил неловко на подножку, замер,
Поддерживая голову и ногу,
И важный кучер повернул назад.
И так же медленно вертелись спицы,
Поблсскивали козла, оси, крылья . . .

Так хорошо и вольно умереть.
Всю жизнь скакал - с одной упорной мыслью,
Чтоб первым доскакать. И на скаку
Запнулась запыхавшаяся лошадь,
Уж силой ног не удержать седла,
И утлые взмахнулись стремена,
И полетел, отброшенный толчком . . .
Ударился затылком о родную,
Весеннюю, приветливую землю,
И в этот миг - в мозгу прошли все мысли,
Единственные нужные. Прошли -
И умерли. И умерли глаза.
И труп мечтательно глядит наверх.
Так хорошо и вольно.

Однажды брел по набережной я.
Рабочие возили с барок в тачках
Дрова, кирпич и уголь. И река
Была еще синей от белой пены.
В отстегнутые вороты рубах
Глядели загорелые тела,
И светлые глаза привольной Руси
Блестели строго с почерневших лиц.
И тут же дети голыми ногами
Месили груды желтого песку,
Таскали - то кирпичик, то полено,
То бревнышко. И прятались. А там
Уже сверкали грязные их пятки,
И матери - с отвислыми грудями
Под грязным платьем - ждали их, ругались
И, надавав затрещин, отбирали
Дрова, кирпичики, бревёшки. И тащили,
Согнувшись под тяжелой ношей, вдаль.
И снова, воротясь гурьбой веселой,
Ребятки начинали воровать:
Тот бревнышко, другой - кирпичик . . .

И вдруг раздался всплеск воды и крик:
“Упал! Упал!” - опять кричали с барки.
Рабочий, ручку тачки отпустив,
Показывал рукой куда-то в воду,
И пестрая толпа рубах неслась
Туда, где на траве, в камнях булыжных,
На самом берегу - лежала сотка.
Один тащил багор.

А между свай,
Забитых возле набережной в воду,
Легко покачивался человек
В рубахе и в разорванных портках.
Один схватил его. Другой помог,
И длиннос растяпутое тело,
С которого ручьем лилась вода,
Втащили на берег и положили.

Городовой, гремя о камни шашкой,
Зачем-то щеку приложил к груди
Намокшей, и прилежно слушал,
Должно быть, сердце. Собрался народ,
И каждый вновь пришедший задавал
Одни и те же глупые вопросы:
Когда упал, да сколько пролежал
В воде, да сколько выпил?
Потом все стали тихо отходить,
И я пошел своим путем, и слушал,
Как истовый, но выпивший рабочий
Авторитетно говорил другим,
Что губит каждый день людей вино.

Пойду еще бродить. Покуда солнце,
Покуда жар, покуда голова
Тупа, и мысли вялы . . .

Сердце!
Ты будь вожатаем моим. И смерть
С улыбкой наблюдай. Само устанешь,
Не вынесешь такой веселой жизни,
Какую я веду. Такой любви
И ненависти люди не выносят,
Какую я в себе ношу.

Хочу,
Всегда хочу смотреть в глаза людские,
И пить вино, и женщин целовать,
И яростью желаний полнить вечер,
Когда жара мешает днем мечтать
И песни петь! И слушать в мире ветер![1]

Free Thoughts. On Death

More and more often I wander through the city.
More and more often I meet death—and smile
a philosophical smile. But what of that?
It's how I am. I like to know
that death will come for me in his good time.

I was walking on the road beside the racetrack.
A golden light dreamed on the piles of gravel,
beyond a thick-set hedge the hippodrome
gleamed greenly in the sun. The stalks of corn
and dandelions, swollen by the spring,
dreamed in its warm caresses. In the distance
the flat roof of the stand was bearing down
on gawpers and flappers. Little colored flags
were scattered over the scene. And on the railings
sat people who had stopped to gawp.

I walked along and listened to the horses
galloping over the soft earth—the rapid
beat of the hooves. Then . . . a shout: "He's fallen!
He's fallen!" the watchers on the railings shouting.
I jumped up on a little stump and all at once
I saw it all—jockeys in their bright shirts
flashing toward the distant finishing post,
and close to them a horse without a rider
racing along, the stirrups flying wildly.
And just behind the tender, curling foliage
of birch trees, close beside me, lay a jockey,
all yellow in the green of the spring corn;
he lay there on his back, turning his face
to the sky's deep caressing blue
as if he'd been lying there a hundred years
at ease, his arms stretched wide, his legs bent up.
People were already running to where he lay.
Far off, sedately, with a flash of spokes,
a carriage moved. The people rushed to him
and lifted him.

And I could see a leg
helplessly yellow hanging there
in its tight breeches. On his shoulders
somehow his head was lolling down. The carriage
drove up to where he was. On the cushions
all tenderly and carefully they laid

the chicken-yellow jockey, and a man
scrambled up to the running board and froze there,
giving support to head and legs,
and the staid coachman turned the horses' heads.
And once again the spokes were slowly turning,
the box, the axles and the wings all shining . . .

To have so good, so free a death . . .
All his life he had raced, with just one thought,
to be first past the post. And, as they galloped,
his panting horse had lost its footing, he
had tried in vain to keep the saddle steady,
the useless stirrups gave beneath his feet,
and he went flying, jolted from its back . . .
His head struck backwards on the friendly earth
so full of spring, so much his native place,
and in that moment thoughts flashed through his brain,
only the thoughts he needed. They flashed through
and died. And then his eyes died too.
And dreamily his corpse stared heavenward.

So good, so free a death . . .

One day I was wandering on the river bank.
Workers were wheeling barrows from the barges
with logs and bricks and coal. The river
was bluer still against the foaming whiteness.
The shirts were flung wide open on the brown
of sunburned bodies, and the men's clear eyes,
bright with the soul of free and open Russia,
shone sternly from their blackened faces.
And round about them barefoot kids were playing,
mixing and stirring piles of yellow sand,
and making off with bricks or blocks of wood
or logs and planks. Then they would hide, and you
could see the light reflected off their dirty heels,
and mothers—sagging breasts concealed beneath
their grubby dresses—waited for them, cursing,

and boxed their ears and took away from them
the logs, the bricks, the planks. And dragged it off
into the distance, bent beneath the load.
And back the children came, a merry gang,
and once again they started on their games,
one stealing bricks, another logs . . .

And suddenly I heard a splash, a shout:
"He's fallen! He's fallen!" they shouted from the barge.
A workman, letting go his barrow handle,
was pointing with his hand toward the water,
a crowd of bright shirts rushing to the place
where in the grass, among the cobblestones
right on the river bank, a bottle lay.
One man carried a boat-hook.

Between the piles
fixed in the water close by the embankment
a man was rocking gently in the river,
wearing just a shirt and ragged gaiters.
Somebody grabbed him, another lent a hand.
Together they dragged him up and laid him there,
a long-limbed body stretched out on the bank,
with river water pouring off him.
Clashing his sword against the stones, a policeman
bent down and laid his ear against the man's
damp chest, and listened carefully, no doubt
to catch the heartbeat. People gathered round,
and every new arrival thought to ask
the same inevitable stupid questions:
when had he fallen, how long was he floating
there in the river, how much had he drunk?
Then everybody quietly moved off
and I went on my way, but listened
while one impassioned worker, who'd been drinking,
authoritatively held forth to his mates,
informing them that liquor is a killer.

I'll keep on walking, while the sun stays out,
and while my head is thick with the fierce heat
and my thoughts flounder helplessly.

O heart!
it's you who must be my guide, and with a smile
consider death. You also will grow tired,
too tired to bear the kind of merry life
that I am leading. People are not able
to bear the kind of love and hate
that fill my heart.

What I want, constantly,
is to look deep into the eyes of people
and to drink wine, and to kiss women's lips
and fill the evenings with the rage of passion,
when days are stifling and you cannot dream.
And to sing songs! And listen to the wind!

(TRANSLATED BY PETER FRANCE)

By the early 1900s symbolism was the dominant literary movement in Russia, and Alexander Blok was the towering poet of its younger, or second, generation. Fundamental to the aesthetic of symbolism, and evident most especially in the works of Blok and Andrei Belyi, was a type of postromantic idealism. Its premise was the existence of a noumenal realm beyond its imperfect manifestation on earth, captured in the famous slogan *ab realibus ad realiora,* and its goal for art was to capture this unearthly vision.[2] In the poetry of Blok's early maturity, most famously the poems published as *The Verses on the Beautiful Lady* (*Stikhi o prekrasnoi dame,* 1901–2) and in his second collection *The Snow Mask* (*Snezhnaia maska,* 1907), the self had been tragically divided in the symbolist manner between earthly existence and metaphysical longing. His dominant symbols were the lady of the night or Beautiful Woman, wine and absinthe, the rose, and the window as a portal into a higher realm. Much of Blok's lyric poetry falls within and illustrates this symbolist purview and sense of metaphysical yearning. His longer poems and theatrical works, such as *The Fair-Ground Booth* (*Balganchik,* 1906) and *King on a Square* (*Korol' na ploshchadi,* 1906), more conspicuously inscribe themselves within Russian modernism's complex cultural moment. Their openness to popular cultural, urban life, and the influence of cinema partake of (and contributed to) the ferment that made the period between the 1905 and 1917 revolutions especially dynamic. The most spectacular example would be the narrative poem *The Twelve* (*Dvenadtsat'*, 1918), which, written in polyphonic style, makes use of diverse voices to capture the chaos, violence, and dynamism of the revolution in relation to immediate contexts of social disintegration and the millenarian vision for revolutionary utopia.

The poem discussed in this chapter comes from a short cycle named for its most significant work. The iambic pentameter of "Free Thoughts" is in complete contrast to the mixed meters of *The Snow Mask*, the collection that preceded it, and Avril Pyman sees a sharp contrast between the former's Dionysian storms and the Apollonian clarity of "Free Thoughts."[3] The only point of continuity, she notes, is the theme of death, given great prominence in the new poem's subtitle. When he wrote "Free Thoughts," the "validity of symbolism as a transcendental idea" had come into doubt, giving way to feelings of disenchantment displayed in "The Stranger" ("Neznakomka," 1906), one of Blok's most anthologized lyrics.[4] He was also the same age as Pushkin when the latter wrote, also in blank verse, one of his most moving philosophical poems on time, aging, and death, "Once again I revisit" ("Vnov' ia posetil'," 1835).

One of Blok's longest lyric poems, and an important contribution to the line of city poems pioneered a generation earlier by the nineteenth-century radical poet Nikolai Nekrasov, "Free Thoughts" integrates into his urban settings the Baudelairean figure of the flâneur. Blok's attention has moved to the disconnected wanderer from the symbolist dreamer.[5] Possessed of a fatalistic streak, Blok gravitated to lyric personae (including Hamlet and Don José in adaptations of Prosper Mérimée's *Carmen*) that overlapped with the persona he cultivated in his private life—or at least in the private life he and his intimate circle projected to the public and posterity. Life-creation or *zhiznetvorchestvo* was an important aesthetic trend in the period, extending from Romanticism a tendency to read the real through the ideal.[6] The deliberate blurring of boundaries between the literary and the real, and the prosaicization of romantic situations, influenced readers and writers in the period and well beyond.[7] Given this deliberate interplay of life and work, it is not for nothing that, in the years following his death in 1921, Blok himself would come to be seen as a martyr to his own literary biography.[8]

In 1909, Andrei Belyi, a key figure in Blok's personal and creative life as well as a seminal force in symbolism, proclaimed Baudelaire together with Nietzsche "the patriarch of symbolism."[9] His influence had already been felt in European and American city poems in which "small deaths" become "a routine mechanical business."[10] Aware of these trends, and an admirer of Baudelaire, Blok renewed the city poem in Russia.[11] He crafted his alter ego with an understanding of the cityscape in which the flâneur figure seeks to settle an inner need.[12] In its portrayal of a flâneur, "Free Thoughts" combines a primacy of sensation familiar from Baudelaire and elegiac sentiments drawn from Pushkin and develops a new type of viewer of modern urban life.

"Free Thoughts" creates situations that pit a psychologically realized character against a particular conundrum: How can the speaker reconcile the experience of living with the recognition of one's own mortality? This is the origin of its philosophical content. Throughout his urban journey, the speaker is unable to shake off his morbid wish to find proof that he will die, which he regards as a right (*svoistvenno mne znat'*, line 4), seeking also to ascertain when his death will occur.[13] To that end, led by his gaze toward the lurid, the flâneur acts as a spectator of other lives until he takes stock of his own situation at the end. In the nineteenth century, Romantic heroes, perennially alienated from society, fled abroad, usually to the exotic Orient. Modernist heroes, alienated both from society and from themselves, had no need to travel very far once decadent writers and symbolists had established affinities with Baudelaire.[14]

The poem's paragraphing follows its narrative segments until two final short sections that take the speaker from experience to an emotional crisis. The opening section is in the present tense, framing a story in which the speaker relates in the past tense sudden deaths he witnessed. The melancholy tone struck in lines 1–5 remains prevalent throughout. The two main narrative sections contain accounts of two deaths the speaker witnessed. Such reportage, while increasingly associated with literature about the city, is not a common feature of Blok's poetry.[15] This is of a piece with the hybrid nature of "Free Thoughts" as a lyric poem containing plot elements. The long narrative or epic poem (*poema*) is his usual vehicle for storytelling and subplots, and Baudelaire, whose figure of the flâneur came to inhabit European modernism, may as a prose writer be the model for a work that threads the main elegiac theme through subordinate stories.[16] The effect of this type of sensational report on the spectator is twofold, beginning with a moment of surprise and then generating a recapitulation and a way of seeing death. In Blok's other city poems, the alienated urban figure may be a decadent hero whose ennui can be assuaged by drink or a dalliance with a prostitute, experiences that sometimes unlock an otherworldly transport.[17] On this occasion, however, redemption through epiphany and transfiguration is not part of the deal.

He decides at the beginning to apply to experience a jaundiced eye or to smile. The smile itself is literally translated a "rationalist smile," and Peter France perfectly captures its nuance with his choice of "philosophical." The aim of the speaker's itinerary is to harden his responsiveness to death as a fact, to make him confront directly that instantaneous transformation the individual undergoes from animate to inanimate, what it looks like, what it means. The drama of the poem is about the battle between the will to live and capitulation to morbidity. Unexpected tragedies catch the attention of the speaker, who is on a mission to prepare himself for death by observing the deaths from a vantage point just outside the crowd.[18] His walk is therefore an act in persuading himself of his own mortality and its inescapability based on the two deaths he witnesses: first that of a jockey at a racecourse (lines 20–35) and, second, that of a barge hauler.[19] These shocking moments lead to an emotional reckoning. Z. G. Mints, the foremost Russian scholar of Blok, identified the period from 1906 as a third phase in his development, marked by a "turning to reality and daily life" ("obrashchennost' k deistvitel'nosti, k bytu").[20] While realism necessarily concerns everyday detail, as Mints rightly observed, for Blok the new style jettisoned both the symbolist language of mystery and the occult in favor of a spiritual loftiness. That loftiness of tone, evident especially in the poem's final lines with its exaltation of freedom, contributes to the creation of an individual psychology. It sits alongside descriptive features of the poem—graphic violence, the crowd, workers, questions of justice—associated with Naturalism in the period.

Yet, for all the realistic detail, a basic unanswered question may contribute to the poem's character as a universal statement. Do we know where the speaker is, can we say which city? The answer is negative, and the absence of other geographical information to pinpoint location amounts to a deliberate vagueness. Blok situates his hero in cityscapes that for the reader look real, and for the hero are relentless when read at a symbolic level. Focalization through the first-person narration contributes to the sense of a double narrative, analyzing the hero's experiences as he wanders. That blurred perspective also gives Blok the opportunity to create a poem that maintains a highly rational tone until its emotionally charged conclusion. For a self-absorbed speaker, consumed by his own thoughts, even the reliving of the two episodes requires a retinal vividness in reviewing what he saw. While Blok dispenses with all the nonessential details of city, country, even language, he pays close attention to spatial relations and makes frequent use of adverbs. In the first tableau at the horse race, the speaker locates himself "on the road beside the racetrack" (line 6), things that happen start behind a barrier ("beyond a thick-set hedge," line 8) and "in the distance" (*vdali,* line 11), with other marks creating a division between foreground and background ("scattered over the scene" is the translation for "here and there," line 14), and when the first accident occurs he is nearby (*blizko ot menia*, line 26). In the second tableau, set among the dockers, the effects are repeated, putting the speaker at a distance as he wanders along the river bank (*po naberezhnoi*, line 62), watches workers closer to him and then "into the distance" (*vdal'*, line 79), observing minutely their process and with such attentiveness to the way the children chop wood that the reader might reasonably expect the accident to take place there rather than, as it does, on the river when for a second time there is a victim from a fall.[21] Other parts of speech also accentuate the impression of perfect recall, especially the use of temporal markers to coordinate action and indicate repetition: once (*odnazhdy*, line 62), suddenly (*vdrug, tut*, lines 83, 70), already (*uzhe*, line 74), once again (*snova, vnov'*, 80, 103), frequently (*chashche*, lines 1, 2), then (*potom*, lines 18, 107), every time (*kazhdyi den'*, lines 103, 111). The senses are taut, sight and sound alert to every change—and these changes are, invariably, unexpected because the psychological anxiety of the poem is to steel oneself for unexpected death. The reaction of the crowd to the jockey's fall is "sudden"; not only is it repeated, but it attracts the speaker who "jumped up on a little stump" (line 20) to get a better view. When the docker falls and drowns, once again there is a jarring noise and "shout" (line 83).

In these two episodes, a pattern is established. Correspondingly, the repetition of words and phrases suggests overlaps between the two episodes that reflect a consistency to the way the speaker processes experience. The cry "He's fallen!" (*Upal! Upal!*, line 19) occurs with the first death, again as a pair to mark the second death (*Upal! Upal!*, line 84). Interior thoughts mute the outside world for a speaker who is visually oriented (and the crowd he watches at the races also "gawp" without making noise). Quoted speech stands out on the page. When speech occurs again, it is indirect reported speech within the monologue and its reflection on the second death (lines 105–6). This had already happened a first time at line 28, where *upavshii* (lit. "having fallen") repeats the word in a different verbal form. Alongside the telling literalism to the moment, there is a symbolic nuance. The motif of the fallen angel, a Lucifer figure, once an important motif in Russian Romanticism, was also a key figure in decadence (the movement's name itself etymologically deriving from "to fall" [*cadere*]). For Russian symbolist poets and painters, the fallen-angel figure was the legacy of Mikhail Lermontov, connecting romanticism and decadence. In the world of "Free Thoughts," death is a literal reality whose transcendence no longer figures. After the jockey falls, the speaker fixates on the body parts rather than the body as a whole, focusing on his "helplessly yellow" leg (line 37), the relaxed posture, the "chicken-yellow" figure (line 42), and twice the narrator says that the body literally "lies well" (lines 31, 61). The description, suggesting the body's strange contortion, deliberately reminds one of Baudelaire's "Carcass" ("Une charogne") from *Les Fleurs du mal*, transferring to the jockey the grotesque beauty of the horse:

> Rappelez-vous l'objet que nous vîmes, mon âme,
> Ce beau matin d'été si doux:
> Au détour d'un sentier une charogne infâme
> Sur un lit semé de cailloux,
>
> Les jambes en l'air, comme une femme lubrique,
> Brûlante et suant les poisons,
> Ouvrait d'une façon nonchalante et cynique
> Son ventre plein d'exhalaisons.[22]

The twofold nature of each death scene constructs a scene of surprise, arresting the gaze theatrically, and then a static point of assimilation in which the speaker tests his own poise and refuses to forfeit his illusion of beauty in the face of the real. The reader's immediate reflex might be to conclude that the first death is meaningful because it culminates a life dedicated to racing in which the reward for risk was a sense of freedom in the present; and that, by contrast, the death of the docker is meaningless because it is a random accident. Yet in the first case the poem shows that routine, indifferent to life, continues. Why should the wheels on the carriages or landaus not revolve and shine? It is while he observes them that, at the end of the section (lines 59–60), the reference shifts from "jockey" to "corpse." The drowning occasions a similar set of conditions, starting with the crowd, a shout, a close shot of the victim being laid out, and then a replay (from line 91) of the entire scene as if in slow motion. In both instances the effect is to create a sense of déjà vu: first, internal to the actual scene as the speaker takes in the death from a distance and then up close; second, the pattern the speaker's language imposes on the two scenes also creates a strange effect of sameness.

If the redoubling of tragic vignettes creates an effect of déjà vu, psychologically the juxtaposition of these two scenes, one about sport and risk, the other about work and routine, exposes the morbidity of the speaker who seems fatally drawn to tragic accidents that drive home the conclusion that death affects the extraordinary and the ordinary alike. Despite the parallel structures and overlapping phrases, the episodes contain subtle differences. The account of the jockey is shot through with irony. The horserace has an element of spectacle and implicit risk, which adds to the thrill. The speaker's language in the first part tends to extremes. The descriptions of nature are archly poetical, even vulgar: the word used for "grass" (*zlak*) is high style, the description of dandelions "swollen by the spring" (*oduvanchiki razdutye vesnoi*) that doze in the sun's "warm caresses" (lines 10–11) is mannered, effects that are repeated lower down (lines 25–30) and even later in the description of the jockey's fall onto "the friendly earth / so full of spring" (lines 55–56). Correspondingly, the speaker heroicizes the jockey in tones of great pathos. When he speaks of single-mindedness, he does not seem to be paying tribute to the dedication of the professional athlete. Life in the phrase in which he uses the word (*zhizn'*, line 49) seems to be a metaphorical race that is conducted only by a hero determined to be a victor and gripped by an *idée fixe* (of which the phrase *upornaia mysl'* is a translation into Russian). And, despite the grotesque description of the sightless eyes voided of all thought, the speaker ennobles the death, asserting that to lie this way, and to die this way, is "good" and "free." Philosophically, the speaker convinces himself that the scene illustrates the definition of a good death, one that is consistent with the shape of an entire life dedicated to defying risk. Descriptively or emotionally, the language strikes many false notes and pleads harder than the speaker can consciously acknowledge. Can the values lauded here survive class division and also apply to the proletariat? That hardly seems to be the case, since the examples function in counterpoint, juxtaposing the jockey's costume and the worker's "shirt and ragged gaiters" (line 94); the dead body of the former is graceful in repose, unlike the "long-limbed body" (line 97) stretched out on the bank, and the motley crowd are castigated for asking the same "stupid questions" (line 104). The narrator refrains from comment, showing neither pity nor disdain and relaying the moralizing conclusion of fellow workers that drink is to blame. The inclusion of figures from daily life is consistent with the trend to represent ordinary Russians, which "reverberated through Russian society at almost every level [. . .] from the semi-literature public for the new cheap popular fiction to the elite readership of modernist prose and poetry."[23]

Blok's vision of the modern city follows a Baudelairean pattern of beauty and estrangement, amalgamating the loneliness the city wanderer feels with a self-induced mood of despair brought upon by a sense of the human condition. The poem builds an experiential base to help the narrator reach his own ethical position on death, and while he initially regards the horserace as an example of a "good death" (line 48), disillusion sets in: the description of a "corpse" (*trup*) and lifeless eyes is unheroic. The overall effect is to underscore his sense of predicament, and it leaves unresolved, at least initially, the impression that the bewildered speaker has condemned himself to continuing his existence as a solitary individual facing the endless examples of the same phenomenon that urban reality can throw up. The speaker's thoughts follow his language. If he employs similar phrases in both episodes it is because ultimately these deaths look remarkably the same. Can one understand what death means by observing the deaths of others? The dogged profession to carry on searching belies the poem's title. The speaker's thoughts, "stale" and "dulled," turn out to be anything but free. The way out of this impasse of mood and thought may lie through a poetic rather than perceptual jolt.

"Free Thoughts" is not the first poem in Russian to explore a fascination with death. In fact, its wording, use of urban space, and psychological posture put it in dialogue with Pushkin's "Whether I wander along the noisy streets" (1835). Blok signals the connection immediately at the opening by replaying the beginning of Pushkin's lyric:

Брожу ли я вдоль улиц шумных,
Вхожу ль во многолюдный храм,
Сижу ль меж юношей безумных,
Я предаюсь моим мечтам.[24]

Whether I wander along noisy streets,
Or enter a thronged church,
Or whether I sit among madcap youths
I surrender to my daydreams.

Blok's poem constructs a spectator who lives through comparable existential anguish. But, whereas Pushkin's speaker rapidly reviews a series of fantasies that are remote and indirect, Blok's flâneur encounters reality in the streets. The shock of experience, the sensation of viewing death up close, is the perceptual reckoning the speaker seeks, turning away from the focus on a Platonic realm that was habitual in the symbolist mode. For Blok, an affinity with Pushkin was obvious on the level of personal taste and sympathy. Looking to him as a spiritual source and artistic model was, however, in his immediate context not obvious, and Blok acknowledged in his diaries how unfashionable Pushkin was, asking, "But what if [. . .] they learned to love Pushkin again in a new way—not Briusov, Shchegolev, Morozov, etc., but the futurists. They abuse [*braniat*] him in a new way, and he grows closer in a new way."[25]

Both Pushkin's and Blok's poems situate their hero in an unnamed city, Blok's hero consumed with the same foreboding about death that causes the Pushkinian hero to wander. Each speaker makes the poem into a drama about the impossibility of predicting when their own demise will occur, and only such knowledge, they feel, will stabilize their state of mind. The posture of the Pushkinian speaker is solipsistic, already detached from the hustle and bustle of daily life as he encounters it on his strolls because morbid fantasies grip him. In "Whether I wander along the noisy streets," stanzas rapidly conjure potential moments of death. The speaker's every step confronts him with reminders of the inescapability of death. Scenes flash past the speaker's eyes, each distilling the finiteness of his own life. Awareness of aging provokes the anxiety of mortal terror. He longs to know when and how his death will come, aware that none of the questions can find an answer. It is a sign of the depth of his despair that he turns every sign of life into a negative sign of death. Ultimately the resolution of this aporia is to be found in the very cause of despair. The only way to come to terms with the realization that life means his decay and physical disintegration into dust—in the biblical sense of "ashes to ashes"—is to contemplate what that means. The speaker originally sought consolation in knowledge of what his death would look like—fruitless speculation—and his later attitude quietly relinquishes that as an impossibility.

Until this moment, and with adjustments for its modernist aesthetic, Blok's meditation extends Pushkin's script. Blok reduces the multiple scenarios or "fancies" that the Pushkinian speaker entertains, focusing only on the two situations discussed above. He also chooses not to follow the conclusion of Pushkin's poem in which the speaker embraces the "indifference" of Nature, setting up a counterpoint rather than confirmation. Having gone so far, he follows a shift in the mood of his speaker and takes the poem toward a resolution of its own. Closure in Pushkin's elegy occurs when a rational premise stops the catalog of morbid fantasies, whereas Blok's ending replaces resignation with ambivalence. At line 115, the invocation of the heart is an appeal to feeling and also a moment of reckoning that cannot to be assuaged. At this point, he finds relief to an "unbearable" burden in the possibility of cynicism and irony. An ending to the poem that recapitulated only the instruction to face death with "a smile" had been conceivable. It is part of the cynic's logic to project himself as death-obsessed when in fact he is just as obsessed with living.

This change in tone raises the key question as to what motivates the exalted optimism of the last two sections. The banal fact of death in itself is not the poem's discovery. Behind the human dramas of Pushkin's poem, one sees the fateful work of inescapable destiny. In Blok's work, the sight of death stimulates an act of volition, given imagistic and emotional weight by attention to the "heart" (*serdtse*) and the declaration "I want" (*Khochu*). The key to his reaction is not in the experience of death, which strikes him as meaningless. It lies in his perspective. Seized, like the Pushkinian speaker, with a need to know, he remains until the final expostulation gripped by the intensity of that focus on his destiny. His aim of comparing experiences has revealed uneven reactions.

Martha Kelly has argued that Blok's earlier poetry, imbued with a vision for changing Russia and emblematic in its use of the body, is consistent with his "vision of a more integrated, less atomized cultural and sense of self."[26] "Free Thoughts" opens a great distance between that vision and its spectator's solipsistic state. Encoded in the vignettes is a distinctively pessimistic thought: that the actuality of the city erases these characters and reduces them into anonymity and lost humanity. The aesthete in him admires the jockey, the aloof bourgeois turns away from the worker class, and the overall impression is that, while death defines the human condition, it also isolates individuals. Alongside the reckoning with mortality is a comfortless attitude to society that goes with the alienated modern hero. By assuming the position of the flâneur, Blok seems to adopt the modern position of immunity to death that Baudelaire described in the subchapter "The Artist, Man of the World, Man of the Crowd, and Child" in *The Painter of Modern Life*:

> Do you remember a picture (it really is a picture!) painted—or rather written—by the most powerful pen of this age and entitled "The Man of the Crowd"? In the window of a coffee-house there sits a convalescent, pleasurably absorbed in gazing at the crowd, and mingling, through the medium of thought, in the turmoil of thought that surrounds him. But lately returned from the valley of the shadow of death, he is rapturously breathing in all the odours and essences of life; as he has been on the brink of total oblivion, he remembers, and freely desires to remember, everything. Finally he hurls himself headlong into the midst of the throng, in pursuit of an unknown, half-glimpsed countenance that has, on an instant, bewitched him. Curiosity has become a fatal, irresistible passion! Imagine an artist who was always, spiritually, in the condition of that convalescent, and you will have the key to the nature of Monsieur G.[27]

In his earlier collections, and especially in the way he theatricalized the bohemian if not fully decadent nature of his private life, Blok directed his criticism at stagnant bourgeois society. His earlier persona is full of the yearning for liberty, often symbolized by the image of the window through which a better realm is to be glimpsed. In those years, salvation came to the poet, often as he was in a drunk state, in a vision of female figures, representing extremes of female sexuality such as the streetwalker, who is twinned with Carmen (as a symbol of destiny), and Ophelia, who is twinned with his own wife Lyubov'. "Free Thoughts" ends with a declaration of the will to live. The affirmation, underscored by the image of the heart as the source of volition, comes from within rather than from a surrogate Muse. Blok's lines once again hark back to a Pushkinian moment, this time from his celebrated "Elegy" (1830). The ending of that poem can be heard in Blok's more affirmative stance. Both poems repudiate a morbid fascination with the past and explicitly reject death:

I do not wish to die, friends
I wish to live so as to think and suffer.[28]

And here is Blok's elaboration:

What I want, constantly,
is to look deep into the eyes of people
and to drink wine, and to kiss women's lips
and fill the evenings with the rage of passion
when days are stifling and you cannot dream.
And to sing songs! And listen to the wind!

Pushkin's poem is the monodrama of a figure divorced from reality, submerged in his own thoughts and oblivious to the world. In these lines, as is also true of Pushkin, after a quick return to morbidness on the subject of a good death, Blok ponders the matter of a good life, one that is hedonistic, destructive, with no restraints. "Free Thoughts" has moved from despondency to detached curiosity to despair to life affirmation, at once depleted and gloomily defiant. In a poem written in free verse (*vol'nyi stikh*), free thoughts are about the exercise of free will (*volia svobody*) and willpower itself (*sila voli*).

Yet Blok's poem also departs from Pushkin. To be as free as the wind is to reprise an image not from Pushkin but from Ibsen's play *Brand* (1867). Blok was an avid reader of Ibsen, who enjoyed huge popularity in Russia.[29] That drama's eponymous hero, a lonely figure in a state of revolt and committed to doing the right thing, believes in the will of man. The realist quality of the "Free Thoughts," reminiscent of Nekrasov and Dostoevsky for their attention to poverty and the commotion of the crowd, is not only significant as an element of style. While "Free Thoughts" has no overt social program to propose, as a work of realism it carries a burden of social relevance, and this is expressed through the plight of the hero dreamer who is, finally, frustrated. The double combination of urban oppressiveness and mortal intimations energize the speaker eventually to an assertion powerfully expressed in the concluding section. Yet at the same time, with an irony characteristic of Blok, the speaker shows awareness that his dramatic utterance is formulaic. At this point in "Free Thoughts," the hero could have committed to social action in the manner of an Ibsen hero—and does not.

Blok's protagonist could be said to fall into the famous novelistic tradition of the nineteenth century, perpetuating the superfluous man as a type. And he may have learned another lesson from Ibsen's dramas, namely, that "truth is something individual and subjective."[30] If there is a further element of Ibsen here in the language of volition and fate, this is not entirely a poem about the individual in opposition to society, the classic theme of Ibsen's plays. And that is the point: cut adrift in urban space at a time when Russia was convulsed with the aftermath of the 1905 Revolution, this speaker has not yet found a purpose or understood what individual freedom in life, an ideal of Ibsen's characters, means. An existential hero, and the most fully realized of Blok's Baudelairean creations, he ends with a resolution worthy of a Nietzschean superman and yet remains earthbound, a transitional figure trapped by mundanity and mortality.

2

Elena Guro, "Gone to sleep, gone quiet now, so kind" (1912)

PERFORMING SINCERITY

* * *

Памяти моего незабвенного
единственного сына В. В. Нотенберг.

Вот и лег утихший, хороший—
Это ничего—
Нежный, смешной, верный, преданный—
Это ничего.

Сосны, сосны над тихой дюной
Чистые, гордые, как его мечта.
Облака да сосны, мечта, облако . . .

Он немного говорил. Войдет, прислонится.
Не умел сказать, как любил.

Дитя мое, дитя хорошее,
Неумелое, верное дитя!
Я жизни так не любила,
Как любила тебя.

И за ним жизнь, жизнь уходит—
Это ничего.

Он лежит такой хороший—
Это ничего.

Он о чем-то далеком измаялся . . .
Сосны, сосны!

Сосны над тихой и кроткой дюной
Ждут его.

Не ждите, не надо: он лежит спокойно—
Это ничего.[1]

* * *

In memory of my only unforgettable son,
V. V. Notenberg

Gone to sleep, gone quiet now, so kind—
Nothing to be done—
Tender, clumsy, loyal, devoted—
Nothing to be done—

The pines, pines above the quiet dunes,
Pure and proud as his hopes and dreams.
Clouds and pines for miles, a dream, a cloud . . .

Spoke little, rarely. Leaned on a wall if he'd come in.
He loved, but couldn't say it, how he loved.

My child, my own good-natured child,
My bumbling, loyal child!
Life I loved far less
Than how I loved you.

And life follows him, life leaves me—
Nothing to be done.

There he sleeps, so good, so kind—
Nothing to be done.

He wore himself down over some far away thing . . .
Pine trees, pine trees!
Pines above the meek and quiet dune
Await him.

No need to wait: he sleeps serenely—
Nothing to be done.

(TRANSLATED BY MATVEI YANKELEVICH)

The poet and artist Elena Guro (1877–1913) contributed to all the early collections and manifestos of the Russian futurists. Yet her poems bear little resemblance to the radical verses of Velimir Khlebnikov and Vladimir Mayakovsky with their grotesque hyperboles, bold neologisms, broken rhythms, and *zaum'*, i.e., phonetic and/or trans-sense poetry consisting of neologisms whose meaning can be opaque. Nor do her minimalist, fragmentary, melancholic, and impressionistic works flaunt the anti-aestheticism and rebelliousness against cultural authorities indelibly associated with the avant-garde. And, while scholars have traced the influences of symbolism and impressionism on Guro's oeuvre, her participation in futurist circles was no accident.[2] It speaks to her own version of a radicalism expressed in the way she creates the poetic persona rather than through the techniques of verse form.

Guro led a tragic life, and her biography is full of gaps. She died at the age of thirty-five from leukemia, having published three collections of poetry, prose, and drama, and she was already ill by the time her second book, *Autumn Dream*,[3] appeared in 1912. The title page of this book features a dedication: "I give this book to those who understand and who do not chase away. E. Guro + Eleonora f. Notenberg." Next to this dedication, we see Guro's portrait of a young man who appears to be her deceased son Willy Notenberg. He is the dedicatee of the book's opening poem and the subject of the poem analyzed in the present chapter: "In memory of my only unforgettable son, V. V. Notenberg." The collection closes with the notes of a violin suite written by Mikhail Matyushin, composer, artist, and Guro's husband. The caption to the musical phrase reads: "From my violin suite *Autumn Dream*, dedicated to my friend Willy Notenberg."

Guro's contemporaries read *Autumn Dream* as an epitaph to her dead son. Moreover, many subsequent dictionaries and encyclopedias have claimed that "Elena Guro" was merely her pseudonym and that her real name was Eleonora von Notenberg. This supposition proved false. The manipulation of names has been shown to be a successful literary mystification: "There was no son, as there was no original Germanic name masked by the pseudonym Guro. But the real question is why the fantasy of a son who died was proffered in the first place."[4] A third collection, *The Poor Knight*, left unfinished at her death and published posthumously, sheds light on this hoax. Guro borrowed the expression "poor knight" (*bednyi rytsar'*), from Pushkin's poem "Once there lived a poor knight" (1832). Even before Guro used the phrase to title her final collection, it had already been linked the motif of motherly love in the *Autumn Dream* collection in the poem that follows "Gone to sleep":

Но в утро осеннее, час покорно-бледный,
Пусть узнают, жизнь кому,

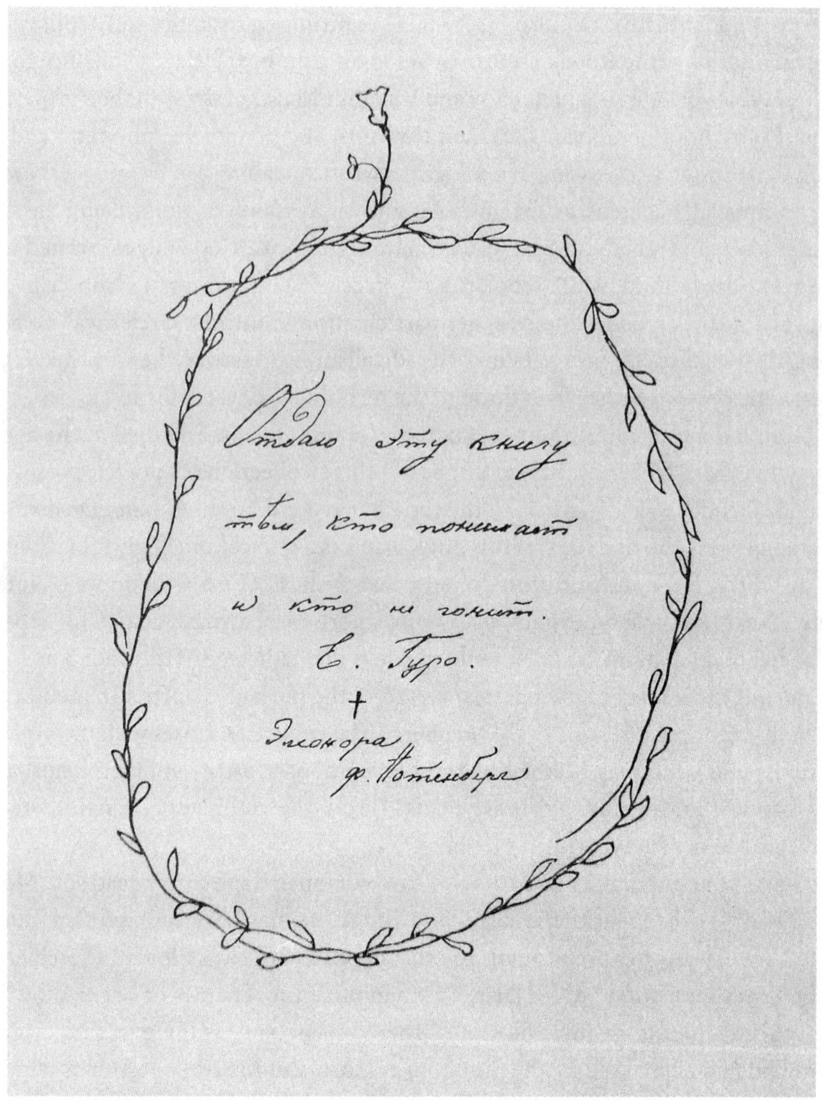

FIGURE 2.1. Elena Guro. *The Autumn Dream* (1912). A dedication: "I give this book to those who understand and who do not chase away. E. Guro + Eleonora f. Notenberg." Open source: https://traumlibrary.ru/book/guro-osenniy-son/guro-osenniy-son.html.

FIGURE 2.2. Elena Guro. *The Autumn Dream* (1912). Guro's portrait of a young man who appears to be Willy Notenberg, who is presented as her dead son. Open source: https://traumlibrary.ru/book/guro-osenniy-son/guro-osenniy-son.html.

Как жил на свете рыцарь бедный
И ясным утром отошел ко сну.
Убаюкался в час осенний,
Спит с хорошим, чистым лбом,
Немного смешной, теперь стройный—
И не надо жалеть о нем.

But in the autumn, at an early hour,
let it be told to those who want to learn
of the poor knight who lived his life and suffered,
who went to sleep forever one clear morn.
Was lulled to sleep one hour in autumn,
his forehead smooth, and clean, and white.
A funny man, now cold and slender.
Please do not pity the poor knight.[5]

In the last collection, her protagonist, a certain "Madame Elsa," sees a ghost-like young man whom she believes to be her son and also takes for a Christ-like knight. "I am but a tiny spark of God. I am only mercy and compassion. I have no other qualities,"[6] he says. The heroine finds herself full of "longing and yearning, for motherly love has been awakened in her and cannot be quenched . . ."[7]

Vladimir Toporov has identified the motif of a dead son as a key theme running through Guro's entire oeuvre, and he concludes that the archetype of the mother of all living things is a constant in her work. He sees in Guro's adaptation a polemic with what he calls a central myth of early futurism. In his words, this "'basic' myth, or arguably a natural force that carries and crystallizes this myth [. . .], contains extreme, paradoxical meanings, including hate for one's father, infanticide, suicide."[8] According to Toporov, Guro subverted this myth: "She could never permit herself—neither in life nor in her creative work—to be a witness (let alone a perpetrator) of the destruction of young life; and to be present at the extinction of young life, even without violence, was unspeakably hard for her, painful to the point of self-destruction."[9] This is the context in which her invention of a phantom son takes on the "'reality' of motherly consciousness," embodying its "potency, hope, pity, its joyful expectation, and its bitter farewell."[10]

Of course, it was only after her death that readers began to see through the pretense of the dead son as a legend. Her hoax was one of the most audacious in a period full of notorious mystifications. For example, the poet Elizaveta Dmitrieva, a friend of Guro's, had a long and successful career as Cherubina de Gabriak, a mysterious Catholic countess whose romantic poems were published in the celebrated modernist magazine *Apollon*. To this end, Guro consciously used her fake "real name" and the dedication as a platform on which to stage a performance of maternal grief, exploiting an emotion surrounded by a halo of sacredness in European and Russian culture. For a noteworthy example of the hallowed status of maternal grief, we have only to look ahead to Akhmatova's *Requiem* (1935–61), in which the mother's tragedy essentially overshadows that of her son, a victim of the Great Purges. The *blasphemous* essence of Guro's performance has much in common with the performances of other futurists, who sought to offend public taste by making scandalous gestures.[11] Unlike her fellow futurists, however, Guro does not indulge a mother's grief blatantly; on the contrary, the works dedicated to her imaginary son are marked by their understated pathos. Even Korney Chukovsky, author of scathing articles about the futurists and an astute connoisseur of literary jokes, was taken in: "Her poems on the death of her only son, so simple and terrible, cannot be read without empathy." He illustrated this thesis with the very poem we are presently discussing.[12]

Guro's mystification has a larger cultural resonance. It provides a striking example of the modernist phenomenon of life creation or *zhiznetvorchestvo*. While the aestheticization of how a writer lives and behaves has been traced back to the romantic period, in Russian modernist culture it acquired particularly striking, eccentric forms and even generated an original theory of performativity (Nikolai Evreinov's "theater for oneself"). In her study of *zhiznetvorchestvo* strategies in Russian modernism, Schamma Schahadat distinguishes two basic types—theatrical and ritual:

> Artists focused on the theatrical model build the story of their life according to the laws of a play and, demonstratively exposing themselves, cultivate distance between their own *self* and the chosen role. [. . .] As for the theurgic *zhiznetvorchestvo* [. . .]it is oriented toward ritual. Here, the ritual is meant to bring the artist closer to God and to restore the original harmony of being.[13]

Guro's case clearly falls under the second type of *zhiznetvorchestvo*. Her grief for an imaginary departed son is a private, individual *ritual of mourning*, closed to outsiders, imbued with a longing for God and harmony with the world. At the same time, however, it is also a mystification: "The peculiarity of a mystification is the introduction of an additional level into the space between the text and the author, a space for the self-assertion of another author—the 'other' of the author. Thus, the fictitious merges with the real, and the boundary separating them becomes blurred."[14] Insofar as no greater moment of sincerity can be imagined than mourning a child, the creation of a successful alter ego and the convincing performance of grief are inextricably linked. Striking the right tone of melancholy and mourning were essential, and the poem's prosody is crafted entirely with these effects in mind. The rhythm of her *vers libre* is created primarily by verbal and syntactic repetition. We find it in the refrain *eto nichego*—literally "this [is] nothing," translatable as "there, there" or even "it's okay"; "nothing to be done" in the present translation. Repetitions with slight variations appear in many other lines, such as "The pines, pines above the quiet dunes" (line 5), "Pines above the meek and quiet dune" (line 20). Words are repeated in the same or adjacent lines: "*Pines, pines* [. . .] proud as his *dream*," "*clouds* and *pines, dream, cloud* . . ." (lit. lines 5–6, 7); "Life *I loved* far less / Than how *I loved* you" (lines 12–13); "My *child*, my good *child* / my bumbling, loyal *child* . . ." (lit. lines 10–11); "*Life, life* is leaving . . ." (lit. line 14); "*Pines, pines*! / *Pines* above a meek and quiet dune . . ." (lit. lines 19–20); "*Waiting for* him. / Do not *wait* . . ." (lines 12–13). The characteristics of the dead son ("good," "loyal") are also repeated; *utikhshii* ("gone quiet") in line 1 is echoed by the description of the "quiet dunes" in line 5 as well as by the "meek and quiet dune" in line 20. At the same time, the rhythm is quite loose, with one to four stressed syllables per line. There are no rhymes, unless we count repetitions. The alternation of longer and shorter lines (1–4, 14–17, 18–21) arguably has a rhythmic function, albeit not a strong one.

As for the son himself, he appears only as a ghostly image, intermittent and flickering. His features are projected onto a sparse landscape that appears to be surrounding his grave: the dunes ("meek and quiet") and the pines (lit. "pure and proud, like his dream"). The refrain *eto nichego* adds to the impressionistic effect of pathetic fallacy by expressing both the mother's reconciliation with grief and the final dissolution of the young man's features into the bareness of the Baltic landscape. Furthermore, the refrain "Nothing to be done" adds only a minimal musicality, giving a near primitive quality to this monodrama. Stark and devoid of melody, this poetry is arguably the antithesis of a performance. The verse has a palpably unsteady quality, the result of the rhythmic irregularity of three consecutive stresses in line 14: *I za nim zhizn', zhizn' ukhodit* ("And life follows him, life leaves me"). The halting cadence anticipates the elegiac tones of the subsequent refrain in which the speaker, consumed by an emptiness about to engulf her, mourns not only the young man but life itself. Beginning with a statement of death ("Gone to sleep, gone quiet now," line 1), the poem ends by abandoning all hope for resurrection. This note sounds even more pronounced in the translation: while *eto nichego* literally means "it's nothing," it also conveys a sense of resignation caught in the English "nothing to be done": "No need to wait: he sleeps serenely—/ Nothing to be done." The positioning of this poem in the collection next to a poem overtly inspired by Pushkin's

"Once there lived a poor knight" may add a further irony. Pushkin's chivalric knight is a crusader who has just returned from the Holy Land, and he marks his return by praying to the Virgin. The poem has had a controversial reception since some versions contained a blasphemous suggestion that the knight's prayer leads him to sexual climax.

What does Guro's poem actually tell the reader about the dead son? The words describing him are deliberately devoid of specific content and border on tautology: he is said to be faithful, loyal, and, as is obsessively repeated, good—*khoroshii*[15]—the most vague description imaginable. Even his age is unclear. "Spoke little, rarely. Leaned on a wall if he'd come in. / He loved, but couldn't say it, how he loved" (lines 8–9). Does this describe a toddler with a limited vocabulary or a teenager hesitating to express his feelings? "He wore himself down over some far away thing" (line 18) is another vague characteristic that can be interpreted both as a longing for the transcendent and as a desire to travel, to escape the restrictions of home. Even the very phrase expressing the mother's tragedy is merely a variation on a banal idiom: after all, "Life I loved far less / Than how I loved you" (lines 12–13) is only another way of saying "I loved you more than life."

However, this reading proceeds from the belief in the reality of the son and his death. Once we reread the poem in the awareness of the mystification, we must revise our attitude to this elegy because the same phrases and verbal formulas take on new meaning. For example, in this context, the significance of the refrain *eto nichego* ("it's nothing") changes radically. It is as if Guro wishes to hint to us that her son, his death, and her grief are not real; in other words, "it's nothing" because all this is a fiction, a nothing. But, paradoxically, the love and pain evoked by this fiction turn out to be strong, deep, and nothing if not "sincere." The poem exposes the very essence of the creative process: out of nothing, out of a game of imagination, something real is born, or at least something real enough to affect the inner world of the poetic persona and of the reader, too. Moreover, grief for a son who never lived animates the "other" authorial persona, nourishing her life-creation. The repeated *eto nichego* thus creates a tension within the text: a constant reminder of fictionality, it keeps destroying the hypnotic emotional illusions created by the poem. Again and again, they are shattered—only to be recreated in the next line.

This reading implies a new and rather radical rethinking of what constitutes poetry and the poetic persona. Instead of following the romantic tradition and regarding poetry as the ultimate expression of the author's individuality, Guro with her minimalist style suggests viewing verses as a set of *hollow* forms. What, then, is the function of these forms? Clearly not to express the author's unique experience since the text does not contain any. If one reads it without the dedication to her "unforgettable only son" and not through the optic of the legend the poet created, this elegy turns into a set of highly generalized expressions devoid of personal meaning. It takes no more than a set of familiarly poignant triggers to provoke the reader's emotions, sentiments that ring hollow depending on biographical circumstance. Poetry thus only *imitates* the unique worldview of the poetic persona or the author.

Such a reading undermines a crucial assumption, central to the romantic tradition, that positions poetry as an expression of the author's unique inner universe. The exceptionality of individual experience was taken to be a prerequisite of great poetry. In the case of Guro, the fictive persona who speaks in the poem emanates from her grasp of *zhiznetvorchestvo*. Once the veil of the refrain ("It's nothing") is torn away, feeling turns out to be as hollow a form as all the other elements of the poetic process. So does the poetic persona. It resembles a photo stand-in from some quaint beach, one of those with a hole for a face: readers are left to fill the void left by the author/speaker with their own emotions. Only then is the world miraculously and poetically transformed when a new reality is born out of nothing. Only then do the boundaries between the fictitious and the real become blurred.

Implicit in Guro's "Gone to sleep" is a conceptualization of poetry that attacks the fundamental notions of the romantic tradition and also questions the essential tenets of the emerging modernist paradigm with its emphasis on the uniqueness and authenticity of the poet's personality. In this sense, Guro anticipates a postmodernist or conceptualist understanding of poetry and the poetic persona. This makes her after a fashion a predecessor to a fierce experimentalist like Dmitri Prigov (1940–2007). In 1980, in the preface to his samizdat collection *Sincerity on Contractual Terms, or Tears of a Heraldic Soul* (*Iskrennost' na dogovornykh nachalakh, ili Slezy geral'dicheskoi dushi*), Prigov wrote:

> The poet, too, is human. This is to say, nothing human is alien to the poet.
>
> So I, too, was moved to say something direct, sincere, even sentimental. [. . .] And just as I felt so moved, lines started floating from the darkest and sweetest strata of my memory: "The weary sun sunk meekly in the sea . . ."; "There was a maple by the church, who loved so tenderly a birch . . ."; "Comrade, oh comrade, my wounds are aching so . . ." And I cried.
>
> And I realized that there is nothing more ornamental than a sincere and suffering poet [. . .] But I also realized that there are certain callsigns that evoke from the heart of the author and the reader deeply personal tears, which, spilling over, sincerely shine on all the fractures of this almost canonical ornament, this sign of the "Lyrical," which does not sneak a peek at life but tells life what it should be.[16]

As though prefiguring this conceptualist manifesto, Guro's poem is an example of "sincerity on contractual terms," with the paratext and the authorial "legend" serving as the contract. The poem's minimalist devices really do function as Prigov's "callsigns that evoke from the heart of the author and the reader deeply personal tears." The paradox exposed by Guro resonates with Prigov, given his ironic awareness of how easily hollow forms arising from "nothing" (*nichego*) still manage to generate a powerful emotional response. Her poem does precisely what Prigov would describe so much later: it "does not sneak a peek at life but tells life what it should be." Perhaps it is in this sense that Guro's poetry is truly a futuristic (rather than futurist) work: it anticipates the future of literature.

3

Vladimir Mayakovsky, "Listen!" (1914)

LOVE AND THE EGOTISTICAL SUBLIME

Послушайте!

Ведь, если звезды зажигают —
значит—это кому-нибудь нужно?
Значит—кто-то хочет, чтобы они были?
Значит—кто-то называет эти плевочки
жемчужиной?
И, надрываясь
в метелях полуденной пыли,
врывается к богу,
боится, что опоздал,
плачет,
целует ему жилистую руку,
просит—
чтоб обязательно была звезда! —
клянется—
не перенесет эту беззвездную муку!
А после
ходит тревожный,
но спокойный наружно.
Говорит кому-то:
"Ведь теперь тебе ничего?
Не страшно?
Да?!"
Послушайте!
Ведь, если звезды

зажигают—
значит—это кому-нибудь нужно?
Значит—это необходимо,
чтобы каждый вечер
над крышами
загоралась хоть одна звезда?![1]

Listen!

So if the stars are kindled,
doesn't it happen in answer to someone's pleas?
Doesn't it mean someone wants them very much to exist?
Doesn't it mean someone calls these droplets of spittle pearls?
And, breaking down,
in the blizzard of noontime dust,
bursts in on god,
hurried, worried, astir,
crying,
kissing his sinewy hand,
begging:
"Let there please be a star!"
swearing:
"This starless torture he cannot stand!"
And after,
walks about anxious,
pretending to be at ease,
asking the one:
"You not afraid anymore?
Are you better?
You are?"
Listen!
If the stars are kindled,
doesn't it happen in answer to someone's pleas?
Doesn't it mean someone needs to see
every single night
above the rooftops
at least one star?

(TRANSLATED BY ALEXANDRA BERLINA)

Mayakovsky is the most dramatic first-person writer of Russian and Soviet modernism: "we" (*my*) and "I" (*ia*) are his two standard viewpoints, and the first-person singular pronoun usually takes the lead. The title of his first collection was the single word *I!* (*Ia!*), and the first-person dominates that entire, handwritten book (printed lithographically in three hundred copies), from the crayon portraits of the poet done by the artists V. Chekrygin and Lev Zhegin and then in each of the short poems ending with fourth and final "Several Words about Myself." The book constitutes an ego-document, and even Mayakovsky's occasional use of a third-person subject to distance himself seems only to intensify that self-referential effect.[2] His orbit radiates out from his person, as in "Several Words about Myself," extends to individuals, as in "Several Words about My Wife" and "Several Words about My Mother," before expanding to the stars, the key image in this chapter's poem.

Do the stars revolve around him? In "Several Words about My Wife," a cluster of stars, variegated and shouty, adhere to his "equipage." His conceit, and the poetic conceit, reach astronomic proportions when the speaker apostrophizes "Sun" and exclaims "My father!". Having already compared his soul to a "cloud that has been torn apart" he then apostrophizes time self-pityingly and at the very end manages to make the final word not "I" but "person" (*chelovek*) although he is referring to himself as the lyric subject:

Я одинок, как последний глаз
у идущего к слепым человека!

I am alone like the last eye
Of a person going to visit the blind!

Mayakovsky republished these poems in his substantial second collection *Simple As Bellowing* (*Prostoe kak mychanie*, 1916). It consists of thirty-five lyrics, the poem-cum-drama *Vladimir Mayakovsky: A Tragedy*, and *A Cloud in Trousers* (*Oblako v shtanakh*) divided into six parts reflecting the life of prerevolutionary man, things, and the city.[3] Part One consists of a verse dedication to Lilya Brik, whom he met in 1915. Here she has already become the lifelong love and source of emotional upheaval and the essential "you" with whom the lyric "I" is in dialogue.[4] "Listen!" was originally published separately in a newspaper, but it appears as the first poem in Part Three. That part bears the title "I Shout to the Brick" ("Krichu kirpichu"). Part Four, bearing the title "Magnificent Absurdities" ("Velikolepnye neleposti"), includes a poem of that title, two poems about war, and a fourth lyric titled "Me and Napoleon" ("Ia i Napoleon"). Parts four and five contain, respectively, the long work *Vladimir Mayakovsky: A Tragedy* and the poetic drama *A Cloud in Trousers*, the last a work written in 1914 about a then-unrequited love for Maria Denisova (and not Lilya Brik).

The whole collection showcases his growing versatility, establishing Mayakovsky as an energetic practitioner of artistic life-creation (*zhiznetvorchestvo*), self-centered but not solipsistic. The figure of Mayakovsky who emerges from these pages is perhaps more multifaceted than the critical literature has sometimes appreciated, given the emphasis usually placed on his myth-creation vision in the context of the new world. The Mayakovsky of this poetic book straddles old and new, the small and the grand, the urban and cosmic, and is mainly unpolitical until the burst of revolutionary energy brought about by an existential crisis and manifested in *A Cloud with Trousers*, about failure in love. For the most part, however, he has his feet on the ground in Petrograd, an eye on history—he promises to lead the urban crowds and defend Russia against pretenders like Napoleon—and sometimes his head in the clouds, either out of rapture or because he is also, as a futurist, a utopian visionary of cosmic change. The modernist poet sometimes operates like the eye of the camera ("Still Petrograd," "Theatres," "Port," "Night"), and vignettes ("A Word About the Conductor") and these shorter poems, written in traditional meters, look outward to urban settings, taking in restaurants, automobiles, hairdressers, the prosaic world that Blok's generation had by precedent made fit for use in poetry. The collection as a whole is a rich example of the avant-garde book. Evidence of speed, noise, and violence abound in the collection's cityscapes. The speaker is often to be found out and about in the city stomping on the pavement. His verbal and visual technique work together. Partial views and montage-like comparisons (such as "there is the moon / my wife")[5] feature, and choppy phrases and word dislocations go together with the incursion of free-verse forms and irregular rhyme.

To judge by contemporary reactions, the collection typifies why Mayakovsky polarized readers. P. E. Shchegolev, an important scholar of Pushkin, a political activist, and a historian of anti-tsarist underground movements, who might well have been an admirer, in fact dismissed this collection as pure bombast, making it clear it was time for Mayakovsky to dial down the volume:

> This is not the first year in which Mayakovsky is making noise on the literary scene. His period of youthfulness and first youth has passed, and the youthful resonance of his voice has been replaced by a brashness that is slightly fattened up. Brashness is the fundamental element of his verse technique; it is on brashness that his noisy fame rests.[6]

The strong motif of anti-philistinism may have struck Shchegolev as antidemocratic. Even when a collection like *Simple As Bellowing* gestures to the masses, the poet's attitude is fickle, hesitating between a camaraderie and contempt. This may say more or as much about a tension in Mayakovsky's development between lyric and public postures than it does about class loyalties. In the poem "Here you are!" ("Nate!"), about halfway through this part of the book, he exclaims, "You are all piling up, filthy in your galoshes and even without galoshes on the butterfly of the poetical [*poetinogo*] heart." Grotesque and satirical scenes do not undermine his boast of "having opened for you so many boxes of verse," and he goes on to show solidarity by claiming, fancifully in the poem "We," that together they will be the "feathers of a boa" that "girdles the comets circling the sky."

In *Simple As Bellowing* the claims of love are no less fraught than the drama of establishing revolutionary culture. While most of the twenty-six poems in this part of the book are about the poet and the city, the self and the masses, the theme of love is positioned in the first and final, twenty-sixth poem, "The Violin and a little nervously, too." In "I shout to the brick" he comes back down to earth: the Russian word *kirpich* puns on its English of "brick," a homonym for Lilya's married surname Brik.[7]

His preference for the empyrean remains unchecked, for Mayakovsky consistently uses stars and constellations metaphorically and visually, often guided by a visual rather than symbolic logic. Generally, in the first decade of his work until 1923, there is a division of purpose in Mayakovsky's astronomic language between stars and constellations. In the vision imagined in "We," millions will inhabit the sky and galaxies, whereas in "Listen!" there is a lone star to whom the poet speaks. In a "Hymn to Lunch" he promises those who eat themselves to death that in the afterlife they can make preserves from stars; he describes streetlamps as both "gaslight signs" and "constellations" ("Morning"), ornamental when he compares to the moon a woman he calls his wife (presumably Denisova, the addressee of *A Cloud in Trousers*) and her entourage to "constellations"; and stars will also serve as political imagery whether as military decorations on uniforms, a pattern on a flag ("Red Flag"), the five-pointed red star on the Kremlin. Stars can also represent a utopian vision of renewal, as in the 1917 poem "Revolution. A Poetic Chronicle," in which Russia is its own cosmos and its "stars are lances"; or similarly in 1916 when he enjoins Russia ("To Her") to grab the sky and move it higher and think up new stars and create a new land in which the souls of artists, ecstatically scratching the roofs, climb up to the sky. Evocations of a single star or constellations feature in poems about national destiny, and when it comes to personal fate he seems to deliberately smash such familiar usage, calling himself in *Vladimir Mayakovsky: A Tragedy* the "king of lamps" ("Ia—tsar' lamp!") who ascends to his throne "through the holes in the sky." In the militantly revolutionary narrative poem *150,000,000*, the poet, in a rhetorical extravagance worthy of the eighteenth-century ode Mayakovsky admired, apotheosizes the gods and asks them to vacate the old constellations where they hand out and create a new world, a world in which people are "tender, like love that ascends toward a star by the light."

In Pushkin, Lermontov, Mandelstam, and Zabolotsky the metaphoricity of the star has some stability in relation to hope, change, and fate. Mayakovsky's stars are more theatrical, almost like stage props, and while stars do not represent symbolic forces the image signals an acute consciousness of longing and exaltation, of aspiration and unfading emotion.[8] A single star marks out a vivid perception and a desire for future fulfillment; and the success of a future reality, which may be difficult to grasp, can be embodied by the image of an exalted experience that turns brick/Brik into light. The plurality of stars is his default mode in much of his writing, and that makes the lone star of exceptional value. As Mayakovsky confided to his diary when analyzing the passion he felt from 1915 until his death for Lilya Brik: "Love is life, this is the main thing. From love unfold poems and actions and everything else. Love is the heart of everything."[9] The pair first began to meet in the summer of 1914, and the rapturous despair of a destabilized self conveyed in this poem captures that moment of coup de foudre.[10]

"Listen!" is a poem written in sublimely plain language—about rejection, belonging, worship, and love. Its three protagonists are the speaker, the beloved, and God, a third character who is mute but present. Mayakovsky's free verse is a form purpose-built for transcribing spontaneous feeling, and its flexible lineation, a hallmark of his poetic style, is ideal for following the intonational imperatives of the voice. Yet his is also the avant-garde aesthetic of the futurist, committed to texture (*faktura*) often built out of slight deformations, preferring the off-rhyme or pseudo-rhyme to exact rhyme, reveling in rhythmic variation, scattering echoes of key sounds across a text.[11] The opening imperative plunges us into his emotional storm. The declaration of love is both a persuasive as well as performative utterance. Elsewhere, especially in his epic *150,000,000*, Mayakovsky aims to exercise the magic power of the poetic word, in keeping with the futurist ethos, to animate things. Here his aspiration is less Promethean to create anew and more immediately human: to close the gap between the earthly and heavenly and through love to reveal the recognition of something bigger and higher.

While the repeated direct address (lines 1, 23) involves the reader, it is aimed at himself. It is typical of this kind of monologue to capture the poet at a moment in which the poet talks about himself by talking about an object—the stars—and in which he talks about an object in talking about himself.[12] This is an intimate lyric about identity made precarious by love to such an extent that the busy world present in the rest of this book of poems has been sidelined in an intense moment of questioning because the fixation on *you* has brought the rest of the world into doubt, and that even includes the existence of god. The main trope of the poem is interrogative: questions are asked eight times, twice with an exclamation to convey even greater emphasis. What kinds of questions? Are they genuinely speculative? Are they mainly rhetorical? Works with a high number of nonverbal devices like exclamation and question marks throw onto the reader doubts about the speaker's emotional state, psychology, and attitude to the addressee (and the identity of the recipient is also a consideration in thinking about the communicative act).[13] Another repeated element of the poem is the word *znachit* (lit. "that means"), which can be read as declarative and a factual statement of equation ("x means y") but can also convey doubt, as in a hint or leading question asked to invite the speaker to agree and by way of that confirmation reassure.

In Mayakovsky's case, inwardness coexists with highly rhetorical and even oratorial qualities. The poem opens with a call to attention, Mayakovsky commanding an addressee or all those listening to heed his story. The first word following this call to attention introduces hesitation and justification. *Ved'* (lit. "after all") offers imprecise extenuation justifying the bold opening and is intended to imply defensiveness ("You might not have expected that, but this is the reason why . . ."), reticence ("Sorry to draw attention to myself, but I have something to tell you that you will want to hear"), or urgency ("The thing I have to tell you is really quite important, never mind the abruptness"). The purpose of the opening salvo of questions, voiced extravagantly not to say hyperbolically, is to set up an interior drama expressed between lines 6 and 22. Even though he has no doubt that the cloudy sky will clear and that the stars will appear, he elevates the sadness of his lover into a problem of global dimensions and in doing so subordinates God to the addressee. Hyperbole, a patent way to flatter, is an awkward trope: if naive and totally heartfelt, its use risks ridicule as too casual; if ironical, the poet risks losing control of the feelings they wish to elicit; and if sincere and not hackneyed, then the need is to manage excess with some sophistication mixing self-irony and sincerity. In this instance, one thing the comparison achieves is to show that both lover and beloved enjoy a proximity to one another that distances them from their context and the political and historical inklings that seep into many other poems in the book. Metaphors even in a single text are not static; they are "context sensitive, relating to specific (fictional or real) frames of reference and dependent on interpretations."[14] The star represents an article of faith, and the relation of supplicant to divinity is transactional: fear of a void rather than religiosity compels this act of beseeching.

Here are all the elements of a narrative—lover, beloved, turmoil, the universe—that will eventually culminate in the long poem *About That* (*Pro eto*, 1923). In this short lyric, he pursues the different struggle of coming to terms with the jolt of love to the ego. It is in looking at the stars that Mayakovsky ponders causation in three questions about utility (who needs this?), design (who has willed this?), and aesthetics (why are stars like pearls rather than like spittle?). Mayakovsky's speaker finds no need to situate himself in relation to nature or even to bother about a setting of any kind. Mayakovsky's voice is all the stage that is required for his dialogue with the reader (or dialogue with himself, to be overheard by the reader). The insistence that the appearance of the stars has meaning, an existential statement, is voiced from a conspicuously emotional point of view, staged as a struggle against the void that will open up if love is disappointed, and perhaps an example of a larger battle Mayakovsky wages against an instinct for nihilism that makes him a romantic fallen angel or tragic Prometheus.[15] Wherever we peg his status, Mayakovsky sees himself as mediator between his lover and God.

In his great love sequence *At the Top of My Voice* (*Vo ves' golos*), written a year before his suicide, Mayakovsky contemplated the power of his voice to outlast time and to survive (at least as received among the "planets of the proletariats") as a living force, unlike the dead light of the stars:

Мой стих дойдет,
　　но он дойдет не так,—
не как стрела в амурно-лировой охоте,
не как доходит
　　к нумизмату стершийся пятак
и не как свет умерших звезд доходит.[16]

My verse will arrive,
　　But it will not arrive that way—
Not like an arrow in an amorous-lyre-like hunt
It will not arrive
　　Like a worn-out fivepence to a numismatist
And will arrive not like the light of stars that have died.

What is never in doubt is Mayakovsky's use of lyric to give voice unembarrassedly to his state of mind. Yuri Tynianov also identified the tragicomic as a key feature in Mayakovsky's prerevolutionary work and regretted its loss from the writings of his final years.[17] Bathos of a tragicomic kind comes out of the juxtaposition of "droplets of spittle" and "pearls." Thinking of the religious language in which the poet has couched his emotional doubts, the reader may also wonder whether the metaphor of the pearl also alludes to the Gospel injunction "not to cast idols to dogs and not to throw pearls before swine." It would not be beyond Mayakovsky to question the entire universe because his own star—or the star he feels has been kindled for him—is in doubt, or perhaps to intimate that, if he is rebuffed, then it is because God (or the lover symbolized by the star) may not be worthy of him. The early tendency to project his suffering on a grand scale will acquire a cosmic and Christological dimension in *About That*.

In the emotional predicament that escalates, the speaker places himself as a supplicant. Pronominal contortions perform a double set of alienations from the self. The unnamed "I," alienated from himself, is also a "someone," who speaks to himself as "you." Action is the key to identity rather than vice versa. The verb is the most frequently used part of speech in the poem, front-loading lines 9–14. The verb "to be overwrought" is cognate with the idea of speech containing an emotional "rip" or "tear" that is expressed as the speaker depicts the abject state in which he tears himself apart (lit. "in storms of dust") as he reaches for God. Doubt has given voice to insistence, the question mark displaced by the exclamation mark. The entire predicament is encapsulated in the rhyming (lines 11, 15) of "sinewy hand" and "starless torture": to kiss the first is also to worship the second. The image takes the poem one step closer to divulging an emotional truth. Rather than stay focused on the stars, by metonymy an image for God, the quest is for a single star—and that is a different matter entirely because it shifts the discourse from the language of metaphor to the language of the symbol.

The emotional and rhetorical logic operates according to a double axis of two contrasting pairs: the hidden rhyme of *trevozhyni/spokoinyi* stacked on top of one another (lines 17–18) and a hidden pseudo-rhyme in *byla zvezda* and *bezzvezdnuiu* (lines 13, 15). Line 16 provides a good example of how layout can add a semantic boost. While words belie the idea that "after" will transform his emotional state, the placement of the words and the space that leaves the phrase hanging at the end of the line provide a pause vocally, and a break visually. Do we wonder what comes next? Will the poem further intensify its tortured expression? The answer to such a large question is surprisingly understated and subsumed into the verse flow. The tone is deceptive because these lines contain the poem's central moment of the poem, its dramatic peripety (lines 19–22):

Говорит кому-то:
"Ведь теперь тебе ничего?
Не страшно?
Да?!"

"You not afraid anymore?
Are you better?
You are?
Listen!

Perhaps the double punctuation marks of question and exclamation are intended to suggest that hope can do no better than mitigate doubt. If the assertion of "Yes" that follows is less than emphatic then perhaps it is because terror of the void cannot be dispelled. But, in the effort to overcome it completely and to make himself whole, the speaker repeats the process of internal debate. These lines clarify for the reader that everything "he" is doing—running, asking, kissing a hand, suffering anxiety—is done not for the lyric hero's sake but for the "you," whose anxiety and disquiet are his main concerns.

The enormous ego that drives the "I" to speak directly to God scales the heights to verify that love exists: the universe exists because of love rather than the converse. Mayakovsky is not a visionary poet as exemplified by other poets discussed in this book (such as Zabolotsky and Sedakova); yet he is a poet of strong emotion whose relation of the personal and beautiful to the universal and divine strive toward an immensity of space. As Thomas Weiskel noted long ago in his classic study *The Romantic Sublime*, "It is a commonplace that twentieth-century literary consciousness is a late variant of Romanticism."[18] The unironic upward thrusting, the vertiginous fantasy, the spatial immensity, and the use of the imaginary faculty to feel the divine presence and sense nature's grander aspect, in this case love as a star and a star as love, approach the hallmarks of a sublime moment. Insofar as Mayakovsky believes that the universe will be provident and that the stars will shine, attesting the presence of love, the vision is not of the traumatized, stranded ego of what Weiskel calls the "negative sublime." In this projection of love into the phenomenal field, called the "egotistical sublime," the speaker overcomes a feeling of being under threat: "Nature does not betray the heart that loves her; objects are overflowing with a presence that flows into the mind; perception is the acceptance of plenitude."[19] It is a measure of the poem's gestalt as a cathartic act that now, from a position of greater calm, as the dilemma has been overcome, and in a gesture of closure, line 25 reiterates line 2. The experience of that original splitting of perspective into his subjective and objective points of view becomes part of the poem itself, making us aware of "both perceiver and perceived, the observer and the object."[20] For a poet of the Romantic sublime, the self can be the entire universe, collapsing time and space into that interior world and then projecting subjectivity back again onto nature as an objective fact.

Mayakovsky flourished in the public sphere and he vocally chastised writers who made their own "private, personal business" the material of the socialist poet.[21] In the immediate aftermath of the Russian Revolution, he championed the "poet-worker" (*poet-rabochii*), propagandized class warfare and global communism, and invited poets and drummers onto the streets nowhere more hyperbolically than in the communist epic *150,000,000* (1920). After the end of the civil war, the new aesthetic line determined by LEF, the Left Front of the Arts that was influential from 1923 to 1925, espoused mass culture, producing manufactured art (*proizvodstvennoe iskusstvo*) that was utilitarian and socialist in message but conceived with avant-garde filmic and theatrical techniques in mind.[22] Mayakovsky the revolutionary poet of the 1920s set himself the task of writing "poetry for all" that required the minimal possible education and was "free of any type of culture." He was already in his lifetime seen as a new classic in the canon of Russian poetry and largely accepted on his own terms as a great figure.[23] Boris Pasternak, himself briefly a futurist, was enthralled by both the personality and the verse technique, identifying Mayakovsky's signature device of the verse ladder and his extravagant use of metaphor as the hallmarks of an "artist."[24] Yet the contradiction between the private and public remained impossible to resolve even by making the personal into the cosmic. Although Mayakovsky tried to separate his political poetry after the revolution from his intimate lyric written earlier, his sense of his own identity remained unchanged. Despite his efforts to subjugate himself to the Party's requirements for art, he found it impossible. His very last poems return to the idea of cosmic intimacy (most strikingly in the poem "It is already two a.m."). For the post-Stalin generations to come, *Simple As Bellowing* was the first volume with Mayakovsky's early lyric that was read and memorized, poetry that was not in the eyes of that readership spoiled by Mayakovsky's role as a public tribune for revolution and communism. Even so, the poetry of his final decade could not suppress the torments of his own private life, and if there is an element of contradiction between his position and practice, the solution he found that originates in "Listen!" was to make the universal, and even cosmic, a vehicle for the personal, and the present text is a memorable example of that lyric audacity.

4

Nikolai Gumilev, “The Sixth Sense” (1920)

POETIC DARWINISM

Шестое чувство

Прекрасно в нас влюбленное вино
И добрый хлеб, что в печь для нас садится,
И женщина, которою дано,
Сперва измучившись, нам насладиться.

Но что нам делать с розовой зарей
Над холодеющими небесами,
Где тишина и неземной покой,
Что делать нам с бессмертными стихами?

Ни съесть, ни выпить, ни поцеловать.
Мгновение бежит неудержимо,
И мы ломаем руки, но опять
Осуждены идти всё мимо, мимо.
Как мальчик, игры позабыв свои,
Следит порой за девичьим купаньем
И, ничего не зная о любви,
Все ж мучится таинственным желаньем;

Как некогда в разросшихся хвощах
Ревела от сознания бессилья
Тварь скользкая, почуя на плечах
Еще не появившиеся крылья;

Так век за веком—скоро ли, Господь?—
Под скальпелем природы и искусства

Кричит наш дух, изнемогает плоть,
Рождая орган для шестого чувства.[1]

The Sixth Sense

Splendid the wine that loves us, the good bread
that slides into the oven just for us,
splendid the woman in whose welcoming bed
we go from anguish to sweet happiness.

But what shall we do with rosy-fingered dawn
high in the cold expanses of the sky,
the place of quietness and unearthly calm,
what shall we do with deathless poetry?

We cannot eat or drink or kiss these; still
the moment flashes by unstoppably,
and once again, lament it as we will,
we are condemned to passing, passing by.

And as some boy may turn away from sports
to watch a girl go swimming in the pond,
and though still ignorant of love, his thoughts
he does not understand;

As once in marshlands where mare's tail grew thick
a slimy creature roared the misery
of impotence, feeling upon its back
the place where wings would spread themselves one day;

Just so, from age to age—how long, O Lord?—
under the knife that art and nature wield,
our soul cries out, and our poor flesh grows tired,
bringing to birth the sixth sense that we need.

(TRANSLATED BY PETER FRANCE)

"The Sixth Sense" is one of Nikolai Gumilev's (1886–1921) most famous works. Written a year before his tragic death, when he was shot by the Bolsheviks on charges of counterrevolutionary conspiracy, it may look retrospectively like an artistic testament and philosophical manifesto addressed to the future. The critical tradition has generated an enormous range of possible interpretations.[2] Some critics see this poem as a typical modernist utopia about the transformation of humanity and society, largely inspired by and taking issue with Nietzsche.[3] Others find in it a reflection of occult[4] and Masonic[5] motifs.

"The Sixth Sense" is written in the most traditional meter of Russian poetry: iambic tetrameter with alternating strong and weak rhyming syllables. The rhythm is loosened up by long words and word combinations featuring pyrrhic feet: the sequence of up to five unstressed syllables is highly unusual. These are lines 4, 6, and 9:

Сперва измучившись, нам насладиться . . .	we go from anguish to sweet happiness.
Над холодеющими небесами . . .	high in the cold expanses of the sky . . .
Ни съесть, ни выпить, ни поцеловать.	We cannot eat or drink or kiss these; still

In addition to the retardation effect noted by Alexander Zholkovsky,[6] these three lines are united semantically: they all speak of absence—the absence of reciprocal feeling, of solar warmth, of bodily contact. This *absence* is the lacuna that is supposed to be filled by "the sixth sense," namely, the sense of beauty, which incorporates both the erotic and the aesthetic.

The first two stanzas of "The Sixth Sense" form a thesis and an antithesis, consistent with Zholkovsky's conclusion that the poem can be read as "a rhetorical treatise on the need for a sixth—aesthetic—sense." In his analysis of the poem, Zholkovsky reveals a connection between Gumilev's aesthetic philosophy expressed in this poem and the key principle of acmeism—the antisymbolist movement he headed: attention to the body and bodily life, regarded not as the opposite of culture but, quite the other way around, as a distillate of cultural, psychological, and metaphysical processes.[7] Suffice it to note that, in agreement with the acmeist perspective, in the final stanza, Gumilev rhymes *plot'* and *Gospod'*, "flesh" and "Lord," provocatively destroying the traditional opposition between spirit and body.

Seen from this perspective, the first two stanzas may be roughly summarized as posing a question: If that which has pragmatic value is splendid, what about things devoid of such value that are still delightful? Logic demands that the third stanza provide an answer to this question. But it does not, and instead the situation of the lyric speaker is one of only greater bewilderment: "We cannot eat or drink or kiss these." Subsequent lines compound this sense of uncertainty. The reader may well wonder about the precise relevance of the moment that "flashes by unstoppably."

And what about "we are condemned to passing, passing by"? In English, these lines acquire a more meaningful connotation insofar as they hint at death. But the original Russian idiom (*idti mimo*) literally only means "to pass by." What these vague lines seem to capture above all is the failure of logic, pointing to the impossibility of solving a riddle. We are condemned to pass truth by, and so we waste time to no avail ("the moment flashes by unstoppably"). The solution is *principally* inaccessible to us. It is our inability to understand that concludes the first part of the poem—in a way, a culmination of the rhythmically accentuated motif of absence.

From the fourth stanza onward, a new approach to the theme is developed. Again, Gumilev tries to structure his poetic thought by using thesis, antithesis, and synthesis. Now, however, the poet operates not with formal logic, but with the language of Darwinism and evolutionary theory. The thesis and antithesis are constituted by figurative formulas of phylogenesis (a boy) and ontogenesis (a dinosaur?). In his development, the boy repeats the evolution of the species, albeit in a rather fanciful interpretation. "Still ignorant of love" and thus of the fact that he, too, is to feel torment and then, as Gumilev puts it literally "enjoy a woman," the boy nevertheless is (in the original) "*tormented* by a mysterious desire." The slippery prehistorical creature "roar[s] the misery / of impotence," experiencing an evolutionary mutation, whose meaning remains unknown and incomprehensible, at least to the poor creature itself. The motif of absence persists: no pragmatic goal is in sight here any more than earlier in the poem. Nevertheless, both phylogenesis and ontogenesis provide a step forward when compared to the first stanzas, because the absence turns out to be not absolute but rather temporary. The goal does not *yet* exist (or is not *yet* understood). Feelings and desires anticipate needs that have yet to be formed.

Gumilev's understanding of Darwinism is evidently very peculiar and hardly scientific. In Darwinian theory, evolution is driven by mutations defined by the current changes in the present environment. Gumilev replaces the present with the future, most likely because this is how he understands the "sixth sense," that is, as an intuition of what is to come and of unformed needs. The "synthesis" (albeit based on wishful thinking) in the last stanza weaves together all the preceding motifs, claiming an evolution of that new sense since the original speaks literally of an "organ for the sixth sense."

The transformation of a "useless" and disembodied sense of beauty into human anatomy weaves together the motifs of the first and second parts of the poem. In this context, the reference to God ("O Lord!") is also paradoxical, or at least as paradoxical as the idea of guided evolution—God is presented as the supreme manager of the evolutionary process. "Our soul cries out" resonates with the roar of the slippery creature in the fifth stanza, and "our poor flesh grows tired" recalls the sexual torments depicted in stanzas 1 and 4.

At the same time, the final stanza of "The Sixth Sense" is clearly an ironic paraphrase of Pushkin's "The Prophet." "The knife that art and nature wield" reproduces on a new level the act of "surgery" conducted by Pushkin's six-winged seraph, who ripped out the speaker's "sinful tongue" so as to replace it with what is arguably an "organ of the sixth sense"—a "coal, ablaze with fire." It is not only the appeal to the Lord in Gumilev's poem that reminds us of the seraph. So does the "slippery creature" ("slimy" in the present translation), which, after all, is about to sprout wings (and possibly even six).

Considering the entire course of poetic thought in "The Sixth Sense" from the perspective of the last stanza and accepting Gumilev's hypothesis of an evolution oriented toward future needs, this poem becomes a powerful declaration. The aesthetic sense at least in contemporary society is proclaimed to be the driving force of human evolution. Intuitively, the sense of beauty determines historical reference points, and, while they may still be unfamiliar to us, they are bound to grow steadily and become burning needs in the near or distant future. From this perspective, "The Sixth Sense" is devoted not so much to the posthumanist fantasy of transforming human nature as to a keenly relevant dispute about the logic and direction of history.

Such a view was of undoubted political significance in Petrograd in the 1920s (just after the revolution, the Red Terror, and the civil war). In this context, the reference to Darwinism is telling. In the article "On the Nature of the Word," written in the same period as "The Sixth Sense" and accompanied by an epigraph taken from Gumilev, Mandelstam writes with fury about "the bad infinity [as per Hegel] of evolutionary theory, not to mention its vulgar henchman, the theory of progress."[8] Clearly referring to Marxism, Mandelstam goes on to say:

> For literature, evolutionary theory is especially dangerous, and the theory of progress is downright murderous. If one listens to evolutionarily oriented literary historians, it seems as if writers were only thinking about how to clear the way for those who come after them, and not at all about how to accomplish their desired work—or it appears that they are all participating in an invention contest to improve some literary machine. To boot, nobody knows where the contest's jury is hiding or what the purpose of this machine is supposed to be.[9]

In contrast to what he perceives as vulgar Darwinism, Mandelstam offers his own theory of cultural evolution, which centers on a notion of language that resonates with Gumilev's "sixth sense," denoting a language that "has become flesh that sounds and speaks."[10] Associating the concept of language as flesh and action with the Hellenistic tradition, Mandelstam calls Russian culture Hellenistic. Moreover, he also regards this "sixth sense"—language as flesh—as an organ of the future: "The speed of language development is incommensurable with the development of life itself. Any attempt to mechanically adapt language to the needs of life is doomed to failure."[11] It is worth noting that, in the 1930s, Mandelstam would write about Darwin with great enthusiasm ("Darwin's Literary Style," 1932). Like Gumilev, he does not deny evolutionary theory. Rather, he rethinks it, wresting it from the hands of Soviet ideologists who use social Darwinism as a justification for class terror.

While Mandelstam's "On the Nature of the Word" develops thoughts Gumilev expressed in "The Sixth Sense" about aesthetics as the driving force of history, Gumilev himself had a predecessor: his longtime opponent and critic of acmeism Alexander Blok. Grigory Fridlender was the first to draw attention to the connections between "The Sixth Sense" and Blok's speech "On Romanticism."[12] In the speech, which Blok delivered to actors of the Bolshoi Drama Theater in Petrograd in October 1919, the expression "the sixth sense" appears as a synonym for romanticism. Fridlender argues that Blok's idea is the source of Gumilev's poem, written a few months later, in the summer of 1920.[13] Although the text of Blok's speech was published only in 1923, after the deaths of both Blok and Gumilev, and it is unknown whether Gumilev witnessed the speech being given, the similarities between Blok's ideas and "The Sixth Sense" are hard to ignore.

Discussing the essence of romanticism, Blok defines it as "a new way of living, living with tenfold strength."[14] Developing this definition, he introduces the concept of the "sixth sense":

> Romanticism, taken in its unblemished, pure form, can be conditionally[15] used to designate the sixth sense. Romanticism is but a way of arranging, organizing the human being, the bearer of culture, to create a new relationship with the elements. [. . .] It is significant that the word "romanticism" was uttered exactly when, for the first time in history, the elements manifested themselves in a new way: in the spirit of popular rebellion; this new force kept up, terrible and powerful, in the French Revolution, making Europe tremble with a sense of trouble. It was, so to speak, the fifth element—and culture responded to it with the sixth sense. Romantic consciousness was to become that traveling island, on which culture is both part of the elements and protected from its raging waves . . . [16]

Like Gumilev, Blok correlates "the sixth sense" with nature or, in his expression, "with the elements." "A new way of living, living with tenfold strength" is in tune with Gumilev's idea of evolution as future-oriented rather than adaptational. Most importantly, though, Blok speaks of romanticism and the sixth sense as a paradoxical state of culture, both a conductor of "the elements" and a defense against their more violent forms, such as revolutions. This clearly resonates with Blok's thesis: "Culture responded to [the Russian Revolution] with the sixth sense."

Fridlender interprets Blok's concept as a utopian dream of spiritual energy, lost in the "dead inertia" of the Russian Revolution, and argues that Gumilev shared this utopian vision. However, unlike Blok, Gumilev never admired the revolutionary element. A memoirist writes: "Full of belief in himself, in his own creative powers, in the indestructible truth of his poetic path, he hated Bolshevism with icy fire . . ."[17] This is why Gumilev replaces Blok's elements (which equal both nature and revolution) with evolution. By foregrounding evolution, he turns his understanding of the sixth sense into a *counterrevolutionary* concept of history. For him, history is driven not by class struggle, not by the change of economic conditions, and not by bloody revolts, but by aesthetics, by poetic intuitions of the future—by the "sixth sense."

Given the numerous parallels between Gumilev's poem and Blok's "On Romanticism," we can read "The Sixth Sense" as a manifesto of poetic neoromanticism—an "undeclared trend" in twentieth-century Russian literature. Although the poets who contributed to neoromantic aesthetics (see introduction) had different views on the revolution and on Bolshevism, they were all united by one idea: they believed in the aesthetic sense, arts, and literature as the main driving forces of history, the quintessence and concentration of existence, always ahead of their time, creating a future in the here and now. It is this understanding of art's historical mission that was articulated by Gumilev in his "Sixth Sense."

5

Vladislav Khodasevich, "Ballad" (1922)

THE RETURN OF ORPHEUS

Баллада

Сижу, освещаемый сверху,
Я в комнате круглой моей.
Смотрю в штукатурное небо
На солнце в шестнадцать свечей.

Кругом—освещенные тоже,
И стулья, и стол, и кровать.
Сижу—и в смущеньи не знаю,
Куда бы мне руки девать.

Морозные белые пальмы
На стеклах беззвучно цветут.
Часы с металлическим шумом
В жилетном кармане идут.

О, косная, нищая скудость
Безвыходной жизни моей!
Кому мне поведать, как жалко
Себя и всех этих вещей?

И я начинаю качаться,
Колени обнявши свои,
И вдруг начинаю стихами
С собой говорить в забытьи.

Бессвязные, страстные речи!
Нельзя в них понять ничего,
Но звуки правдивее смысла
И слово сильнее всего.

И музыка, музыка, музыка
Вплетается в пенье мое,
И узкое, узкое, узкое
Пронзает меня лезвиё.

Я сам над собой вырастаю,
Над мертвым встаю бытием,
Стопами в подземное пламя,
В текучие звезды челом.

И вижу большими глазами—
Глазами, быть может, змеи,—
Как пению дикому внемлют
Несчастные вещи мои.

И в плавный, вращательный танец
Вся комната мерно идет,
И кто-то тяжелую лиру
Мне в руки сквозь ветер дает.

И нет штукатурного неба
И солнца в шестнадцать свечей:
На гладкие черные скалы
Стопы опирает—Орфей.[1]

Ballad of the Heavy Lyre

I sit where the light is above me
My circular room is my sphere;
I gaze at a plasterwork heaven
where the sun is an old chandelier.

And likewise illumined around me,
the chairs and the table and bed.
Should I sit with my hands in my pockets,
or where might I put them instead?

Silently, frost on the window
grows palm-trees and icy white flowers;
my watch ticks away in my waistcoat,
metallically counting the hours.

Oh my life is so worthless, a quagmire
where I'm stuck with no way to get free!
And who can I tell of my pity
for the things that I own, and for me?

And hugging my knees where I'm sitting,
I'm rocking, quite gently at first
when out of the trance that I've entered
a chorus of verses has burst.

It's nothing but passionate nonsense!
Whatever it means, it's absurd.
But sound is more honest than meaning,
and strongest of all is a word.

And a music, the music of music
is twined in the song of my life,
and piercing me, piercing and piercing,
is the blade of the slenderest knife.

I find myself rising above me,
from where I exist but am dead;
my feet are in underground fire,
and a galaxy streams at my head.

I watch with my eyes ever wider—
how a serpent might see through the gloom—
I see my wild song is entrancing
the comfortless things in my room,

and the things begin dancing a measure,
with gracefully circling charms;
and somebody's heavy lyre comes
from out of the wind to my arms.

And there is no plasterwork heaven,
no chandelier sun anymore;

but the blackness of slippery boulders
and Orpheus, his feet on the shore.[2]

(TRANSLATED BY PETER DANIELS)

By the time Vladislav Khodasevich emigrated to Berlin in June 1922, he had already established his literary reputation with three books of lyric poetry. "Ballad" ("Ballada") is the final poem in *The Heavy Lyre* (*Tiazhelaia lira*), the last collection Khodasevich published in Russia before his departure.[3] During the revolutionary years, he watched the ongoing conflict between the Provisional Government and the Bolsheviks from the sidelines; in 1918, to make ends meet, he took on a number of minor administrative jobs while continuing to participate in literary life, publishing a Hebraic anthology (*Evreiskaia antologiia*) and joining the fledgling Union of Writers. He worked for the newly established Narkompromos (People's Commissariat of Education) and taught classes for Proletkult, the federation of societies for the cultural development of the proletariat. Late in the year, after making the acquaintance of Maxim Gorky and Nikolai Gumilev, he became the editor in charge of the publisher World Literature (Vsemirnaya Literatura) and did promotional work at bookfairs, also joining new cultural initiatives, especially in aid of poetry, even after the execution of Gumilev in August 1921 and the liquidation of the Petrograd Union of Writers. On the surface, these and other such activities show a writer trying to adapt. While his poetry generally remained aloof from contemporary history, in these years topical references and revolutionary scenes feature in his poems and betray unease as can be seen, for example, in the 1918 poem "Second November" ("2-e noiabria"), which captures both anxiety and the solidarity Khodasevich feels with the people. "Seven days and seven nights Moscow was buffeted," this long lyric begins, capturing through street scenes the impact of events on daily life. By this time, however, Khodasevich was dismayed by the political settlement after the civil war.

Together with Nina Berberova, his wife and a distinguished writer, Khodasevich left Berlin in the fall of 1923 and spent two peripatetic years in Prague, Marienbad, Rome, Turin, Paris, London, Belfast, Naples, and Sorrento before moving to Paris, the new center of émigré life.[4] In Paris, he took up a prominent position as poetry editor of the journal *Days* (*Dni*) and a position as chief literary critic for *Renaissance* (*Vozrozhdenie*), the conservatively oriented major daily newspaper founded in 1925 by P. B. Struve, the liberal politician who rejected his youthful Marxism and became a critic of Russian communism. A liberal without being firmly on the left, Khodasevich was instinctively and avowedly a cultural conservative. For him, Pushkin first and foremost represented the best in Russian culture, a devotion he carried with him into life abroad as a touchstone of émigré writing. His career is littered with initial periods of rapprochement followed by rows, sometimes about matters of conviction (such as with Gorky), though these spats were often very personal (as with Andrei Bely). The tendency toward vituperation mattered because a sense of insult and injury more widely informed émigré literary culture, seeping into and sometimes poisoning book culture. While other émigré figures sought a rapprochement with aspects of Soviet culture (here the philosophy of Eurasianism was crucial), Khodasevich grew to feel implacable hostility toward avant-garde figures who remained in Russia and were now closely associated with the regime, railing against the futurists for their call a decade earlier to throw Pushkin and Lermontov off the ship of modernity.[5]

After 1925, even as he wrote much less poetry—something like a total of fifteen lyrics before his death in 1939—he achieved greater and lasting eminence as an essayist and literary critic, remaining true to his ideals of taste in the hope of shaping an émigré literature that sustained those values. In 1921, Khodasevich's *Articles on Russian Poetry* appeared in Berlin and Petrograd—a pamphlet-length set of studies about past figures, mainly Pushkin and the poet and statesman Gavriil Derzhavin, another one of his heroes, who would become the subject of a classic biography he wrote in 1931. His reviews of contemporary poetry, often bracingly personal, are notably perspicacious for their positive judgments about Mandelstam and Tsvetaeva; and he produced something close to a literary history of decadence through the essays collected in *Necropolis* (1939), which stand as worthy companions to the classic memoirs of Marina Tsvetaeva and Benedikt Lifshits.

In an insightful appreciation of her late husband, Nina Berberova argued that Russian poets could be split into two genealogies: intellectual poets concerned with wisdom, and musical poets led by melodiousness. While undoubtedly a simplification, her scheme positions Pushkin as the poet who uniquely combined both attributes. She assigns Khodasevich to the "thoughtful chain" that includes Baratynsky and Tiutchev, nineteenth-century poets famed for their metaphysical outlook, and Annensky of the first-generation symbolists, possibly because his work was haunted by death and suffering.[6] Contemporary views of Khodasevich were less schematic: on the one hand, D. S. Mirsky, one of the foremost critics of the day and ideologically alien to Khodasevich as a "Eurasian" in favor of reconciliation with the USSR, mocked him as a "little Baratynsky from the underground," by which he meant a minor metaphysical poet with an axe to grind like Dostoevsky's Underground Man.

Nonetheless, Khodasevich, who found an early and stalwart admirer in Nabokov, has continued to grow in critical stature and is regarded as one of the foremost practitioners of pure lyric aestheticism in Russian.[7] Khodasevich was also a model for

Koncheev, the poet hero of Nabokov's last Russian masterpiece, *The Gift*, set in Berlin in the 1920s.[8] The novel revisits classic nineteenth-century debates about the social utility of art, in which Pushkin was targeted as an art-for-art's-sake aesthete. The call for art with a political purpose became a literary mission of the radical critics and revolutionaries from the 1860s, dramatized in the classic fiction of Dostoevsky and Turgenev as well as in an ideological novel by Nikolai Chernyshevsky, *What Is to Be Done?* In Khodasevich's view, a newfound "coldness toward Pushkin," which had a precedent in the attacks Chernyshevsky and the radical critics of the 1860s and 1870s mounted against him as a lightweight aesthete, was evidence of a degrading evolutionary process. The key question of whether utilitarian purposes such as political ideology frames the quest of the novel's hero to perpetuate the cult of Pushkin as the embodiment of all the beauty destroyed by the revolution. His poet hero, Fedor Cherdyntsev, was modeled at least in part on the figure of Vladislav Khodasevich. If the legacy of the poetic lyre weighed heavily on Khodasevich, it is in large part because of the significance he accorded to Pushkin. Though his verse is richly eclectic in his influences, Khodasevich was much more candid in his articles about his poetic antecedents. He more than once named Pushkin as his greatest model. This stopped short of claiming a profound likeness, and he even to a degree keeps Pushkin at arm's length as a phenomenon to be studied separately. Dedicated to the survival of the Pushkinian aesthetic, Khodasevich's essay "The Unshakable Tripod" (1922), written around the time of his departure for Europe, captured his view that Russian culture was now awash in a "coarseness" and "benightedness" (*ogrubenie, pomrachenie*) that threatened its very survival. In 1924 Khodasevich dedicated a book-length study of allusion and intertextuality (largely self-quotation) in Pushkin that now seems ahead of its time.[9] *Pushkin's Poetic Economy* (*Poeticheskoe khoziastvo Pushkina*) is a work of scrupulous philological tracing, impressive for its command of a single poet's lexicography, and it is also his way of showing us Pushkin from the inside out by demonstrating how greatness can lie in consistency of theme and unity of style.

His titles and use of epigraphs are often false signals, and "Ballad" does not descend from a specific Pushkin poem with that title or form. Yet at the heart of the poem is a dialogue Khodasevich sets up with Pushkin on the subject of creative inspiration. For all his attention to aspects of poetic craft, what Khodasevich formulated in his scholarship was a fundamental aspect of Pushkin's artistic psychology, about which he writes in the essay "On Reading Pushkin": "As the basis of the creative act, Pushkin places inspiration as the capacity to accumulate and process the experience of life. Poetry for Pushkin arises not from the caprice of imagination, not from abstract philosophizing. At the root of poetry lies an impression, that is material selected by inspiration of reality."[10] That interrelation of perception and inspiration are also the subject of this poem's chapter, and "Ballad" puts inspiration to the test by recalibrating for his own situation Pushkin's model.

Khodasevich contended that Pushkin's work, repeatedly challenged in his own time and especially by these reductive nineteenth-century critics, could "survive a series of changes in the consciousness of readers" (referring to revolution as an unprecedented break in cultural history, much as Sophocles and Dante were not drowned in the "sea of history") because of three qualities: his mastery of his medium and poetic form (*masterstvo*), his relevance on the subject of historical disruption as seen in the way various forces collide in the tragic narrative poem *The Bronze Horseman*, and his language.[11] While it was by no means to be taken for granted that a younger generation of poets would share this appreciation, Khodasevich charged his own generation with the mission of sustaining these qualities because he believed that poetry as an art form could not survive without an appreciation of such linguistic, technical, and formal accomplishment.

Throughout his poems, early and late, Khodasevich's abiding theme is the poet's own self and state of mind. It is not surprising in that connection to note that the influence of Blok's "Free Thoughts" (discussed in chapter 1) has been detected in the poems of *The Heavy Lyre*, an influence that exposes the incurable melancholy of the older poet, whereas in earlier poems, such as "Ballad" and the rapturous "Music," ("Muzyka," 1920), which opens the book, the speaker retains a capacity, however embittered by circumstances, for creative renewal.[12] Vigilance about his own spiritual alertness is prominent. "Soul" ("Dusha," 1908) asks, "What is life?" The answer ("Theater, the play of passions [. . .] the flickering of lamps, a play of shadows") follows a Pushkinian example of reflection at night on the contrast between routine life and awareness that a "distant world" (*otdalennyi mir*) can somehow be penetrated. As a collection, *The Heavy Lyre* suggests that there is an invisible realm to be glimpsed in the phenomenal world if only Orpheus would return to this sublunary world (the subject of his earlier "The Return of Orpheus," 1910). Like Lermontov, from whose romantic solitary figure he descends, Khodasevich's speaker can be a liminal figure, hovering between life and death, solitude and society, nature and civilization, and similarly attuned to traces (*sledy*) of the sublime and the apparition of a barely visible specter (*prizrak, ele zrimyi*). In this short poem of 1916, the landscape against which his solitude stands out is elemental:

Я бессонно брожу по земле меж вами,
Я незримо горю на легком огне,

Я сладчайшими вам расскажу словами
Про все, что уж начало сниться мне.[13]

I wander sleeplessly among you on earth,
I invisibly burn in an easy flame,
I will tell you in the sweetest words
About everything that has begun to come to me in dreams.

These lines also reveal a characteristic psychological and rhetorical feature of Khodasevich's poetry. As a biographer and memoirist, Khodasevich had a natural inquisitiveness about the multifaceted conditions that make up identity. It may be a condition of epiphany in his poetry that the senses of sight and sound are each insufficient on their own and must work together to induce a higher state of apprehension. Always highly visual, shown gazing in mirrors and through windows, Khodasevich remains on the lookout for the extraordinary. Memory, especially autobiographical episodes, can also be tapped, and Khodasevich's love of photograph generated the ekphrastic narrative of "Sorrentino Photographs," the longest poem in his next and final collection, *European Nights* (*Evropeiskie nochi*, 1928).[14] When his focus shifts inward, it is to concentrate on the "I" of the poet, set apart from the self that experiences daily life, who extracts emotional truths, and finds a language in which to relate them. "In front of a mirror" ("Pered zerkalom") opens with the poet famously deriding his own habit of introspection and self-portraiture—"I, I, I. What a barbaric word!"—and then once again falls into the habit of solipsism, asking "Is that someone there, is that I?"[15] in the hope that he might glimpse himself in the mirror.[16] Alienation from ordinary circumstances, while registered and sometimes acute, goads the poet far less than awareness of an inner split between a mundane self that is cast out from a lost paradise and a more angelic self that is granted access by inspiration to a higher realm represented by harmony.

A version of this situation occurs in "Midday" ("Polden," 1918), published in *The Path of Grain* (*Putem zerna*), the collection immediately preceding *European Nights*, which captures the ordinariness and anonymity of the poet:[17]

Никто меня не знает. Здесь я просто
Прохожий, обыватель, "господин"
В коричневом пальто и круглой шляпе,
Ничем не замечательный.[18]

Nobody knows me. Here I am simply
A pedestrian, a philistine, "Mister"
In a brown coat and round hat,
Unremarkable in any way.

The poem moves from the unremarkable to an intuition that, behind a little cloud and the thickly textured blue, there are "invisible but fiery stars," whose rays "madly fight with the rays of the sun." Poetic phrasing and vision enable the poet to recalibrate and explore imagined states. That visual perception of extraordinary energy, metaphorically expressed, triggers an auditory shift:

И всё, что слышу,
Преображенное каким-то чудом,
Так полновесно западает в сердце,
Что уж ни слов, ни мыслей мне не надо,
И я смотрю как бы обратным взором
В себя.[19]

And everything that I hear
Transformed by some sort of miracle,
Thus in full measure strikes my heart
So that neither words nor thoughts are needed,
And I look as though my gaze is turned back
Into myself.

"Midday" ends with a moment of vision and blockage. Reverie just falls short of epiphany, and the final word belongs to a female stranger seated alongside him on the park bench who interrupts to ask him the time. The timeless moment promised by "transformation" and "miracle" was only a feint.

Such frustrated inspiration sets the stage for "Ballad" and its sudden moment of visionary transport. In 1928, Vladimir Weidle wrote that, while Khodasevich was the last Russian poet for whom Pushkin meant everything, he had lost that feeling of poetic liberty Pushkin enjoyed: "The existence of Pushkin's lines presupposes a cosmos, a structured world, wonderful and indestructible, the very one that Khodasevich must absolutely pierce like an envelope of paper covered in an absurd azure blue, without which his own poetry would be impossible."[20] This critical observation about the poet's visionary understanding of a cosmos is worth unpacking in relation to "Ballad." Different models of inspiration can be deduced from the Pushkinian text, occupying a spectrum from parody of the Romantic poet (in the figure of Lensky in *Evgeny Onegin*) to the Christ-like martyr of his final Easter Cycle of 1836. The poems that most explicitly endow the poet with supernal visionary plenitude date to the late 1820s. "Arion, " "The Poet," and "To the Poet" can be historicized as works of their time and also read as eternal verities in which Pushkin believed. Following the Romantic tendency to denigrate the public as uncouth rabble or a mob (*tolpa*), "The

Poet" and "Arion" assert the distance the poet maintains from his readership, cultivating the impression that genius enjoys an independence of the imagination and is its own authority. This model of poetic inspiration depends on an oppositional sense of authorial status and independence. Yet however exalted the poet may become once favored by genius, other works such as "To the Poet" acknowledge a more mundane side. Later, Pushkin will treat this as a full-fledged dichotomy in his "little drama" *Mozart and Salieri*, showing how the poet in his daily life can, on the one hand, be banal and prosaic and, one the other, metamorphose into a different being entirely when attaining sublime heights artistically. Both of these models, while broadly influential, arguably look remote by several degrees from what Khodasevich describes in his essay "On Reading Pushkin" and enacts in "Ballad."

Pushkin's starkest representation of this change of state comes in "The Prophet" (1826), a lyric that projects a model of the *furor poeticus* dramatically as sudden, out of body and out of mind. It is to this projection of poetic power that "Ballad" responds by engaging directly with Pushkin's credo as one of the central works of the Russian canon that has shaped how poets see and write about themselves. It stands out even among Pushkin's works for its representation of inspiration as an extreme state, violent and painful. The dichotomy between existence as ordinary or trivial and inspired acquires a tragic dimension. "The Prophet" follows its subject on a journey from abject spiritual despair to ecstatic annihilation. Trapped in a despondent state of moral fatigue, the speaker drags himself in a "gloomy desert" when he is visited by an angel who grazes his eyes. The touch is magical, endowing him with or releasing a latent vision. He is compared to a young eagle, ready to fly, his pupils dilated in fear, his head filled with a huge din. The description of inspiration is altogether sublime, combining terror and beauty. The vision that then unfolds before the speaker takes in nothing less than the entire universe from the heavens to the ocean depths, from the flight of angels to the trail of undersea creatures. This is what transpires in the first half of the poem. The second half describes what could be called the cost of that out-of-body experience. The angel rips out the speaker's tongue, replacing his "cunning and purposeless language" with the "stinger of a wise serpent."[21] Violence then escalates as the angel chops open the poet's chest, and with his bloody hand rips out his heart and inserts a burning coal. The serpent and the coal are symbols of ancient, biblical wisdom, sinful and Mosaic. The poem comes full circle, and the subject is returned to the world. He is corpse-like in a desert until one further revelation. In lines inspired by the book of Isaiah, he is enjoined by the Almighty to be a prophet and "to burn the hearts of men with his speech."[22]

Khodasevich's "Ballad" treats inspiration by representing the poet's awareness of the inner process of epiphany, tracing a trajectory from dejection to exaltation. Both observer of the processes to which he is subjected and the vessel of inspiration, the poet lives through the experience from within as life-changing.[23] Yet to the degree that inspiration is also the result of Pushkin's poem as an intermediary, inspiration now involves a literary dependence. The idea of original genius, so prized by the Romantics (who themselves were highly intertextual), looks like an act of tribute and revision.

Khodasevich's poem is in eleven stanzas, and the first four correspond to the mise-en-scène of "Prophet" in its opening lines:

Духовной жаждою томим,
В пустыне мрачной я влачился,—[24]

Wearied by spiritual thirst
I dragged myself in a gloomy desert

The sixteen lines opening Khodasevich's poem literalize the spiritual. While Pushkin's desert is metaphorical, it is also starkly visual. Here, by contrast, the person in the room with a set of objects is listless and barren. No interior could be less sublime or more desolate than this opening tableau. The first two stanzas each split into two-line sentences. These might be the antithesis of poetry: they open and stop (sitting, watching); they tell us what to notice in the immediate space surrounding the poet, a roundness that, devoid of any natural light, is claustrophobic. The light fixture mocks any expectation of illumination from above. The poet is just one of a set of things itemized in the first two stanzas (the chairs, table, fixture, ceiling, and bed) on which light is shed, but he finds himself in a state of "confusion": there is a play on the similar sounds of *osveshchaemyi* and *smushchen* that is one of the few details to escape Peter Daniels's deft translation (lines 1 and 7). Khodasevich has found the equivalent setting for the spiritual desertedness of the room and the poet's listlessness without risking pastiche. Perhaps unlike the subject of "The Prophet," who is taken entirely by surprise, this speaker's awareness of his surroundings seems heightened.[25] The representation of emptiness requires the use of detail in order to be fully felt: the plenitude of artificial light marks the absence of the sun; the ticking of the pocket watch, a sound that presumably ricochets around the room, is a reminder of the silence of the inanimate. Apollo, the god of poetry and the sun, is invoked famously by Pushkin in "To the Poet." That lyric aphoristically elevates and encumbers the poet: "You are a king: live on your own" ("Ty—tsar'. Zhivi odin").[26] Here a "sun of sixteen candles" hanging from a "plaster ceiling" (in the translation, "an old chandelier" and "a plasterwork heaven") produces a setting conspicuously unfit for a visitation by Apollo. The perception that the palms opaquely dimming the outside world "blossom noisily" may remind the reader ironically that Pushkin's speaker's mind is filled with noise, that he enjoys a capacity to hear grapes grow on the vine, while here "palm-trees" grow on frost silently. The detail reads like a flicker of neurotic and ironic self-castigation.

These lines are sparse in sound effects that Khodasevich will save until the incantatory later stanzas. Decorative sparseness makes room for thought, unspoken between the sentences, to build inaudibly in the poet's mind. A watch may tick, but time recedes from the field of perception. The poem is one of two in Khodasevich's entire corpus written in amphibrachs, and as David Bethea notes in his commentary, they are highly regular with little omission of the stressed syllables that give a verse line flexibility in Russian.[27] The rhythm of the poem is deliberate and flows fluently, setting up a counterpoint of energy to the surface listlessness. The first three stanzas take us to the exhaustion of the poet's patience without preparing for the outburst:

> О, косная, нищая скудость
> Безвыходной жизни моей!
> Кому мне поведать, как жалко
> Себя и всех этих вещей?
>
> Oh my life is so worthless, a quagmire
> where I'm stuck with no way to get free!
> And who can I tell of my pity
> for the things that I own, and for me?

The angry expostulation to an impoverished life, reinforcing the sense of the room as a prison, implicates the reader in the speaker's self-pitying rhetorical question. To whom should he tell his story of ennui? Whatever revulsion he feels, he has still lavished two lines on deploring life as dull in the double sense of routine and uninspiring (*kosnyi*), impoverished again in both the literal and the metaphorical sense, so impoverished that it is the "quagmire" of his life that is "worthless" (lit. "poverty" and "beggarly," *nishchaia skudost'*).

Whether or not we are sympathetic, the frustration has been vented. As the poem moves into another gear, "I" appears more often and therefore more emphatically. In the Russian original, the first-person pronoun, which can be implied grammatically, had appeared only once in the opening two lines, though more extensively in the translation. Does the speaker initiate the action of swaying actively? Or is this movement being done to him (worth asking since, in "The Prophet," the speaker describes how the angel acts on him)?

Despite the claim of a loss of eloquence, the poem belies that fear of incoherence. A state of obliviousness provides access to greater eloquence. Certain lyrics in the

Russian canon, from Derzhavin to Brodsky, often cite an impasse in thought as the moment of the poem's creation. True poetry, they feel, must begin from a sonic disorder. Poems are seen to emerge from a state of semantic confusion that is preceded by a musical pulse. This drama of inspiration often bears the name of "tonguetiedness" (*kosnoiazychie*); that is the situation of Khodasevich's "Ballad." Real poetry is wrestled from its source with difficulty, as a number of examples indicate. In Pushkin's "The Prophet," following the story of Moses, the poet's tongue is maimed by the burning coal proffered by the visiting angel before it is finally ripped out and replaced with a new instrument. In Mandelstam's "Slate Ode," automatic writing battles to transcribe poetic words out of night-thoughts using a broken slate pencil likened to the same burning coal we find in "The Prophet," and inspiration is further embattled by the cautious, supervening awareness of a poet apprehensive about the political content of his verse.

In Pushkin's poem, the act of violence perpetrated by the angel against the poet causes a change in his sense of purpose. After this extreme jolt, redemption from spiritual languishment comes with his discovery that his mission is to "ignite the hearts of men." Whether the goal is spiritual, political, or social is not disclosed but it is clear that from this moment the poet's vision has endowed him with spiritual enlightenment and access to a new truth. Arguably, stanza 7 of "Ballad" contains the most radical revision to Pushkin's model of enthusiasm by privileging sound above all. It is on this point that Khodasevich modifies the Pushkinian instruction away from moral pedagogy onto pure art, a feature of "Arion" and "The Poet," as mentioned above. Two goals held separate in two of Pushkin's works with different emphases are now aligned: inspiration and music. Both poems depict violence to the self as a personal cost, but poetry's social mission is not endorsed. By the end, and with the complete transformation of Pushkin's speaker into the prophet, insight into the universe and moral perception have replaced the fearful "din" and "noise" visited on the speaker by the seraph. This may be why, correspondingly, instead of a brutal excision of the prophet's tongue and substitution of coal for a heart in Khodasevich, a finer type of insinuation takes place. In the English translation, the triple repetition of "piercing" (lit. "slender") mimics the repeated *u* and *o* vowels of the Russian: the "music" of the lines enter the poet as slowly as that blade.

While the lines are anything but "nonsense" (lit. "incoherent"), can we intuit what the meaning of music is? Must it remain associative rather than denotative? Is it a state of self-communing ecstasy, induced by "passionate speeches" that separate meaning and poetry and affirm poetry as nonreferential? The seventh stanza itself has an audible pattern, involving a most beautiful alternation of *o* and *e* as well as consonance on *z* and *k*, as *muzyka* echoes through line 25. The aspiration to write poetry equivalent to music, a discourse that reconciles the Dionysian and Apollonian, generated a line of poetry stretching in European lyric from romanticism to symbolism.[28] Khodasevich is typically not a poet who put "De la musique avant toute chose," in the famous phrase of Verlaine. Is the music he hears an underlying sound inaudible to the reader, as inaudible as the "passionate nonsense" (lit. "incoherent, passionate speeches") filtered out by the actual words? Yet we infer that the song may carry meaning rather than be pure music, since his language is called "speech" in the plural (*rechi*), a nineteenth-century stylization. Is it language and melody that make poetic language "strongest of all" and therefore not ordinary speech? Even as Khodasevich strives for a language that transcends ordinary speech and circumstance, we remain aware that this book of poems generally stays close to recognizable reality.

Yet, at the end, "Ballad" does surrender its vision of poetry as some overpowering state. We have seen here that the need to recuperate another, rather more ecstatic, vision of poetry takes its lesson from Pushkin's own credo. From at least the time of Horace, poets have measured the intensity of creative vision as the instant attainment of a sublime height. Horace, as he says in Odes 1.1, strikes the stars with "a lofty head," and the brow of Khodasevich's poet duly touches the stars even as his feet penetrate the core of the earth. That sensation of growth augments the Pushkinian theme of rebirth, and, for all the seeming fidelity to Pushkin's visionary script, the word *bytie* introduces a curious difference. Pushkin's prophet languishes because his "desert" is the world of mundane affairs or, in the Russian, *byt*. The elevated spiritual state paired as the opposite of *byt* is *bytie*, a higher realm of spiritual truth in which poetry has been seen to dwell. Poetry itself has been cast here as a process of overcoming a deadened state. Has the civic side espoused to some degree by "The Prophet" and then greatly exaggerated by a later nineteenth-century tradition become a deadweight for the later poet keen to adjust this model of inspiration?

The poem's profession is of a striving for an Orphic mystery and the suspension of the rational self. In his likeness to the serpent, an emblem of Dionysus as well as biblical wisdom, the wide-eyed poet comes to resemble Pushkin's visiting angel even more than Pushkin's speaker. The Orphic mysteries were not devoid of violence. In fact, they end with the dismemberment of Orpheus himself, who is scattered to the winds and rivers of the underworld, subtly signaled at the end of stanza 8. Here the force of poetry is not an exterior agent acting on a passive recipient, but the speaker's own inner double capable of both song and dance and of being the dancer and the dance.

Khodasevich's poem does not use the traditional balladic meter (trochaic tetrameter), nor does it follow the genre in evoking oral-traditional tales. Yet, insofar as he tells the story of a life-altering experience touched with magic, Khodasevich may be appropriating the generic title to convey mystery. For all the suggestiveness of the hint, however, he follows the classical Pushkinian use of metrically regular line and stable stanza. It takes words like "wild" and "dancing" and "circling" to indicate what the Dionysian state is meant to feel like, proving the poet's own aphorism that, while "music is more truthful than sense," the word or the power of strict form will overpower an inner chaos that this writer can only describe but not represent mimetically. However measured Khodasevich's control of the verse, his vision of poetic enthusiasm only affirms the violence of the Pushkinian model of inspiration.[29] In that respect, the poem extends the "return of Orpheus," the title of an earlier poem in *The Heavy Lyre*. The effect of Orpheus in the closing stanzas is to make the poet rock. Everything around the poet, inanimate more than animate, dances to this new music. And perhaps that is why the presence of the blade intimates that poetry can be a type of violence. Violence, represented by the blade, constitutes the moment when the poet apprehends the divine in the fabric of the everyday and sees that it moves independently of quotidian desolations and also of intention (if that is how one glosses "the strongest of all is a word"), carrying the poet away, obliterating reality and leaving the poet not transformed for society but fully gripped by art.

6

Velimir Khlebnikov, “Suppose I make a timepiece of humanity” (1922)

THE KING OF TIME

Если я обращу человечество в часы
И покажу, как стрелка столетия движется,
Неужели из нашей времен полосы
Не вылетит война, как ненужная ижица?
Там, где род людей себе нажил почечуй,
Сидя тысячелетьями в креслах пружинной войны,
Я вам расскажу, что я из будущего чую,

Мои зачеловеческие сны.
Я знаю, что вы—правоверные волки,
Пятеркой ваших выстрелов пожимаю свои,
Но неужели вы не слышите шорох судьбы иголки,
Этой чудесной швеи?
Я затоплю моей силой, мысли потопом
Постройки существующих правительств,
Сказочно выросший Китеж
Открою глупости старой холопам.
И, когда председателей земного шара шайка
Будет брошена страшному голоду зеленою коркой,
Каждого правительства существующего гайка
Будет послушна нашей отвертке.
И, когда девушка с бородой
Бросит обещанный камень,
Вы скаж<е>те: “Это то,
Что мы ждали веками”.
Часы человечества, тикая,

Стрелкой моей мысли двигайте!
Пусть эти вырастут самоубийством правительств и
книгой—те.
Будет земля бесповеликая!
Предземшарвеликая!
Будь ей песнь повеликою:

Я расскажу, что вселенная—с копотью спичка
На лице счета.
И моя мысль—точно отмычка
Для двери, за ней застрелившийся кто-то . . . [1]
28 января 1922

Suppose I make a timepiece of humanity,
demonstrate the movement of the century hand—
will war not wither like an unused letter, drop
from our alphabet, vanish from our little gap
of time? Humanity has piles, got by rocking
in armchairs forever and ever, compressing
the mainspring of war.

I tell you, the future is
coming, and on it come my superhuman dreams.
I know you are true-believing wolves—
I squeeze my shots into the bull's-eye like yours—
but can't you hear Fate's needle, rustling
in her wonder-working seams?
The force of my thoughts will inundate
the structures of existing states—

I'll reveal the drowned city of Kitezh, risen by magic,
to serfs blinded by the old stupidities.

When the band of Presidents of Planet Earth
will be thrown like a green rind to feed appalling hunger,
then the rough lug nuts of existing states
will yield easily to the turn of our wrench.
And when the bearded lady
throws the long-awaited stone,
that, you will say,
is what we've been wanting

for centuries. Ticking timepiece of humanity!
move like the arrow of my thoughts!
Grow as governments destroy themselves, grow
through this book, let Planet Earth
be sovereignless at last! PRESPLANEARTH alone
will be our sovereign song.
I tell you, the universe is the scratch
of a match on the face of the calculus,
and my thoughts are a picklock at work
on a door, and behind it someone has shot himself . . . [2]

(TRANSLATED BY PAUL SCHMIDT)

Velimir Khlebnikov (1885–1922), a futurist playwright and poet, was one of the originators of trans-sense art (*zaum'*). This maverick figure mesmerized contemporaries and, for most of the twentieth century and until the 1990s, the history of the critical reception of Khlebnikov's work has been hard to detach from his personal reputation as a visionary and eccentric. Even outside Russia, his work has influenced other avant-garde writers, such as Charles Olson and his "Projective Verse" and more recently Lyn Hejinian among American poets. Khlebnikov's linguistic experimentation made a striking (and possibly unique) contribution to the history of avant-garde poetry.[3] That element in his poetry has understandably attracted the greatest scholarly interest, a rich source for philological discussion and a key to a number of important longer works. Added to his unusual biography, the emphasis on language has inadvertently perpetuated the image formed in his lifetime of Khlebnikov as an unworldly and even otherworldly writer.[4]

There is no doubt that, of the poets of his generation, Khlebnikov stands out as well as somewhat apart. Are his verbal contortions more extreme even than those of OBERIU? Surrealist, Dada, and OBERIU poets embrace the absurd, revealing the nonsense of the world by exposing the gap between it and language as part of their acts of representation. While Khlebnikov is focused on discovering new meanings, often to be found in the repurposing of old words or their rewriting, he is not an absurdist writer. He had a strong belief that our customary visible order is not the only one: it coexists with other mythic, mathematical, and even linguistic realms. Anthologies in Russian and in translation have favored poems that showcase his verbal games at the expense of more transparent and discursive work. Long ago, Vladimir Markov noted that "Khlebnikov's true stature is seldom realized by poets and critics," but, perhaps with the zeal of a matchless scholar rather than true popularizer, Markov made his case for his broader relevance on the basis of works that require intensive deciphering.[5] It would be a mistake to conclude from such demonstrations of his trans-sense language that Khlebnikov is implacably obscure.[6] Khlebnikov is a multifaceted poet and a lyric writer of distinction. Osip Mandelstam, one of the most acute literary critics of the 1920s as well as one of the greatest poets, admitted that Khlebnikov was "like a mole digging down into the earth to make a path into the future of the entire century."[7] But he also opined that Khlebnikov's language is "the absolutely secular and mundane Russian language, resounding for the first time in the history of Russian letters."[8] Ultimately the different types of language he employed, whether mathematics or the entire range of philological modes (etymology, neologism, phonological speech), contributed to a vision of past and future very much informed by history and a philosophy of history.[9] Many lyrics, such as the work discussed here, found a more accessible language in which to balance conceptual loftiness and historical urgency—and historical urgency can be seen at the heart of "Suppose I make a timepiece of humanity."

Born in Astrakhan, raised in Kazan, later arrested during a student demonstration, Khlebnikov quickly acquired the aura of the exotic East and the glamour of the polymath. He studied natural sciences in Kazan, and in 1905 set out on the first of several nature expeditions to the Urals before he began publishing papers on ornithological topics. His naturalist interests waned once he moved to St. Petersburg and discovered his literary vocation. He found mentors among a number of important figures from the second generation of symbolists (Fedor Sologub, Viacheslav Ivanov), and younger avant-garde poets (Nikolai Gumilev and Mikhail Kuzmin). Memoirs and anecdotes from his earlier years portrayed him as a joiner of literary groups but not a follower, and his life as a vagabond figure reduced to penury after the end of the civil war cemented the impression of deep eccentricity. The Soviet literary establishment did not ostracize Khlebnikov, and editions of his works appeared in the late 1920s and early 1930s. The editorial process was insufficient to cope with an archive of great complexity: Khlebnikov was a tireless reviser of his poetic work, even his long narrative poems, and his technique of producing new material on scraps of paper complicated work on critical editions, cementing his reputation for obscurity.

The linguistic outlandishness and formal variety of Khlebnikov's narrative poems followed Khlebnikov's tenet that language, as the source of all knowledge, was open to infinitesimal calibration: his semantic alphabet posited etymologies that followed a logic separate from philological rules or actual etymology. These works are challenging because they are vehicles for the creation of a new language generated from Khlebnikov's energetic use of neologisms—and his often invented, highly creative word formation—to represent the realities of these new worlds. He was certainly not the only futurist to coin many new words. His original literary allies were the futurists, among whom Aleksei Kruchenykh excelled in the creation of *zaum'*, as did Mayakovsky whose poetry took the layout of poems in his use of the laddering technique (*lesenka*) and rhyme in new directions. Mayakovsky judged Khlebnikov harshly as a "poet for producers" rather than a "poet for consumers," which does not mean quite the same thing as a poet's poet, as might be said in English, because Mayakovsky's judgment more devastatingly was that he was "impossible to read."

If his logopoesis makes Khlebnikov a kindred spirit of the James Joyce of *Finnegans Wake*, his domain is not the mind. Whatever the style and local difficulty of separate compositions, there is a consensus about an overarching coherence to Khlebnikov's artistic vision, and it has been argued that an artistic grammar can be discerned out of which his works coalesce into a "super-book."[10] The work of poetic intelligence is applied to the solution of vast problems. This is especially conspicuous in the longer narrative poems envisaging both a primordial past and a utopian future. Khlebnikov's millenarian vision was hardly unique. As A. A. Hansen-Löve has noted, "Modernism—in Russia and elsewhere—is marked by various attempts at regression: from history and contemporary rationalism into a mythical primordial state."[11] What staggers in Khlebnikov's writing is the scale of a project that matches language and vision, generating new words using the rules of Russian morphology as applied to historic verbal roots to synchronize a universal primordial language with a primitive cosmogony, or to produce a new language untarnished by usage to match a futuristic world. That is not to say that Khlebnikov's shorter lyrics shy away from a preoccupation with humanity. If they do not lay out whole new worlds on the order of the longer poems, they nonetheless combine both hope and doubt: "Glory to you, bonfire of humanity, / Bright, burn!" is the opening of a 1920 poem that ends with the "universal language" of a child who weeps.[12] The upheaval of the revolutionary period from 1906 onward only sharpened Khlebnikov's quest for knowledge. Poems written from 1918 contain notes of anxiety, marked in rhyme by fevered brainwork ("volnuiushchaia brov'") and "unwearying blood" ("neunyvaiushchaia krov'"), about the "sketch of fate / still mysterious."[13] Khlebnikov also sought an objective calculus for history, delving into the "Laws of Time" and "Tables of Destiny," strikingly characterized as "numerological historiometrics."[14] This is all high-flown, but he could be self-aware and playfully ironic about his own obscurity. At the end of this chapter's poem, the phrase "and my thoughts are a picklock at work" finds an analogy for the procedure of poetry. Elsewhere he movingly and explicitly notes how he trusts the work of reason to "dampen the voice of torment, the ceaseless cry at night."[15]

Across Khlebnikov's work, future and past are inextricably linked. Poetic thought itself, working with the velocity of time's arrow, serves as humanity's timekeeper. If the mind of the poet is like an arrow or a hand on the clock of time, it can move forward toward the future or back to the past. Writing in a letter in 1909, Khlebnikov noted that he was working on a piece called *Time Transversal*, "where the logical rules of time and space are broken,"[16] and goes on to catalog his techniques of disconnection to mirror his idea of time. In 1912 Khlebnikov copublished with Aleksei Kruchenykh, at the time a fellow futurist, the pamphlet *Worldbackwards* (*Mirskontsa*). Illustrated on the cover and inside by Natalia Goncharova and Mikhail Larionov, the book flaunted the idea of reversibility, starting with the title, a neologism that mashed together three words, fusing both the end of the world and the beginning of a new world born from that ending.[17] Khlebnikov's 1913 essay, "The World in Reverse," imagines time running backward. In 1920, Khlebnikov, who crowned himself the King of Time, boasted that he had "discovered the pure Laws of Time."[18] He may have had in mind here a series of calculations he made, based on the dates of historical battles, showing that time moved in cycles of 317 years.[19] But by this period he had also acquired a more experiential than theoretical sense that revolution presented a victory over time by turning back the clock to the beginning of time and offering a new start. "Victory over time will be attained by means of a movement and transmission of consciousness during a second rebirth," he wrote to a friend, confident that his prophecy for the future was valid because he had anticipated 1917 and seen his hopes and calculations fulfilled, and that, while "the ticking timepiece of humanity" would run down, the life to come would be eternal.[20]

The narrative context that a poet such as Blok provides in his revolutionary narrative poem *The Twelve* (*Dvenadtsat'*, 1918) is discarded in Khlebnikov's lyric, which operates through statements of vision that imply the loss of past certainties. The present out of which Khlebnikov wrote was rife with speculation about history. Basic timekeeping itself had been redefined with the conversion from the old (Julian) to the modern Gregorian calendar, and even the seven-day week was criticized. More abstractly, philosophical theories about the abolition of death found pseudoscientific support in esoteric and popular culture, and the possibility of the end of time itself was envisaged, or, as one historian put it, "Revolution seemed a rebellion against time and its limits."[21] The view that time was cyclical replaced the assumption that progress was linear. The poet's vision in "Suppose I make a timepiece of humanity" oscillates between that of a seer, gifted with prophecy of the future, and that of the historian perhaps with privileged access to the past, measured in long units of thousands of years. When Khlebnikov thinks of time, his metric is centuries and, therefore, historical time. The question asked directly is about the relationship between shorter segments and the whole. Are there gaps in time through which war escapes? Should that single band in time be seen as a cross section? Or, to take the image used in the poem, if history is an alphabet, are there episodes that can be left behind like a forgotten letter? Reading this postulation at an anagogic or symbolic level, the question might be generalized yet further: Does history as the time of mankind have a grammar?

These thoughts, running through Khlebnikov's essays and letters, inform "Suppose I make a timepiece."[22] But the poem is neither a treatise nor an equation, a point felt even more keenly when we consider its prosodic and linguistic aspects. Rhymes come as alternating pairs, triplets, and couplets and of different types: sometimes they are half-rhymes, sometimes pararhymes or matchings of different parts of speech (as in the verb–noun combination of lines 2–4: *dvizhetsia, izhitsia*). Line lengths vary and follow no dominant binary or ternary tonicity. The poem has a syllabic bias and features verbal consistencies such as the tendency to place verbs at the start of the line that create an emphatic intonation. In its own way, the form seems to mirror the battle between chaos and order and to maintain both without resolving in favor of one or the other. Counterpointing this tension between regularity and disruption is a more consistent linguistic pattern of mirroring, as though time were telescoped in front of our eyes through prediction and realization within the poem itself:

> "Presidents of Planet Earth" become PRESPLANEARTH
> (председателей земного шара шайка >> Предземшарвеликая!)
>
> "as governments destroy themselves" corresponds to "behind it someone
> has shot himself . . ."
> (самоубийством правительств >> за ней застрелившийся кто-то)
>
> "let Planet Earth be sovereignless at last" turns up as "our sovereign song"
> (Будет земля бесповеликая >> повеликою)

the last one being a transformation of the world into weeds and wilderness.

It is Khlebnikov's ambition, and peculiar talent, that enables him to translate thought into the very stuff and structure of language, producing coinages, exploiting word formation as though words were things (and things were words). What the poem offers is more like a fantasy about the force of poetic knowledge, a statement of visionary power that is couched in the language of wishes and dreams rather than the triumphalist certainties of the more mathematical Khlebnikov. Whether the poet can achieve his dream of being like God the Watchmaker to humanity is not presented as a certainty. Is the poem a statement of democratic power that makes the power of prophecy contingent on the cooperation of humanity? Could the poet achieve his vision if he felt that mankind did not share his view of time? Once again, as in Pushkin's "The Prophet," the poem makes a case for accepting the poet on his own terms by revealing the vision the poet can share with humanity and on that basis demonstrating the poet's own charisma. What he reveals is a story of superior knowledge. Its source emanates from a common fund of dreams. The question he poses ("but can't you hear Fate's needle [. . .]?") dresses up the didactic as rhetorical. The knowledge of which he boasts can be called "superhuman" because it belongs to" mankind rather than sourced individually. The image of dreams as wolves to be targeted, apt in a poem prompted by war, stands in contrast to the quieter metaphor of time as the rustle of needlework. The image of fate as woven, sometimes by female figures like the Parcae, is widespread in world literature. It may also have a more immediate source. Has Khlebnikov in this opposition condensed the figures of the male and female, the male drawn from two of Mandelstam's poems that date to the same time? In "Tristia" (1918, published in 1922), a poem about lovers separated because of war, the male represents the world of aggression and war. Female virtues of suffering and resignation are embodied in the figure of Penelope, who weaves while waiting for Odysseus in "A stream of golden honey" ("Zolotistogo meda struia"):

Помнишь, в греческом доме: любимая всеми жена—
Не Елена—другая,—как долго она вышивала?[23]

Do you recall, in the Greek home: the wife loved by everyone—
Not Helen, the other one, and how long she embroidered?

Hearing the threading of history—Time's needle—corroborates the claim made for the poet of sensory powers: vision that is prophetic, hearing that is supersonic, and a gift of poetic storytelling.

These qualities turn out to be qualifications for political preeminence in the central section of the poem. Lines 13–16 in the Russian text (14–17 in the translation) vaunt the poet's awareness of his own potency and inspire the claim that supplants the power of the worldly authorities. Who is the poet if not the force that will bring about a new flood on a biblical scale? What is the point of the poet's arcane knowledge if not to disabuse those enslaved to "old stupidity"? The intention to drown current structures with "the force of my thoughts" (lit. "with this force, with the flood of thought") looks revolutionary on a mythic scale. It is also a guarantee to bring about the recovery of a fabulous lost domain. The legendary city of Kitezh, a Russian version of Atlantis, became invisible when, besieged by the Tatars, it sank into the depths of Lake Svetloyar. In this millenarian myth, its reappearance would signal the retreat of the enemy and dawn of a new age. True revolution, Khlebnikov maintains, also entails submerging an old mentality. The formation of a new revolutionary consciousness was part of the Bolshevik vision of how the destruction of Imperial Russia had to proceed as a necessary step toward the establishment of a socialist consciousness that would, in the Bolshevik interpretation of Marxism, abolish private property and establish the rule of the proletariat. In 1922, at the time of the poem's composition, Russia had only several months earlier begun to recover from a civil war that had devastated the economy (industrial production had shrunk by more than 90 percent, as had the value of the rouble) and blighted urban populations, leading to devastation in the countryside. "Appalling hunger" (line 19) had been a stark reality, precipitated by political violence visited on the peasantry when it resisted the requisitioning of grain by the Bolshevik authorities.

According to the poem, two forces will destroy the old: the first is identified as a book, the second is the arrow of thought (line 27 in the translation). Violence cannot be avoided, but at least in this poem it takes place offstage in the suicide behind the locked door of the poet's imagination. While Lenin had finally destroyed counterrevolutionary opposition, it was not clear what sort of world Russia was emerging into. Expectations for the new order are contingent on the collapse of governments. Writing in the same year as Khlebnikov, Mandelstam depicted in the "Slate Ode" a world reduced to a state of primitive economy and blank minds, its peoples waiting for the lawgiver to create a new consciousness. Mandelstam's lawgiver himself, however, suffers from a split identity, incapable of obliterating from memory his knowledge of the old world yet fearful of the legacy of violence that had brought the new world into being. No such anxiety inhibits Khlebnikov's speaker: the characterization of the new regime is pejorative ("a band"), and he expects to bring to heel the machinery of state, reduced here to mere tools. More controversial is the striking boast that, in reengineering the new state, the speaker undertakes to relieve famine by sacrificing that political cabal, disposing of nourishment that is like a stale rind. This idea of the new state implicitly envisages a settlement that is more democratic (because not concentrated in the few), uncoercive (the symbolic replacement of the whip with the tools of building), and led by the poet.

Sudden and unrehearsed images are a feature of Khlebnikov's use of symbols. Consider in this connection the unexpected figure of the bearded woman. Is she a representation of a new unisex human? Anthropological research has investigated the sexual element in sectarian religious rituals and practices from the late nineteenth century: androgyny either assumed or reengineered through castration has been documented in association with millenarian beliefs.[24] Decadent writing of the fin de siècle period also shows a fascination from a literary and aesthetic angle with the figure of the hermaphrodite.[25] Writers of the later Soviet period, of whom the most notable example is Andrei Platonov, relegated conventional sexuality to the old bourgeois order and saw in androgynous sexuality a model for a new humanity. Whether the bearded woman can be read as hermaphrodite or androgyne, she portends a world that in addition to its political equality also promises a different gender regime. Is the stone "long-awaited" because the arrival of a new order, anarchic and sexless, has finally happened? Is this stone a Masonic symbol associated with the Temple of Solomon? Evoking the stone at all may be intended to remind the reader that Petersburg, new in the eighteenth century, took its name from Peter, the visionary ruler who laid the city's foundation stone (*petrus* = stone).

What is the new order? Not only will this new world be genderless or crossgender, its dominion will be global and anarchist. For both these states, Khlebnikov coins new words, and new words are the contents of the book he writes to obliterate the past. The word he coins for this new realm, isolated on a line of its own (line 29 in the Russian), is not a calque from another language. With a sense of fantasy equal to Bolshevism's zeal, Khlebnikov also imagines the universal extent of his new utopia. It may be produced from two combinations: *predzem* signals toward *primord* as the historical state of the realm defined in the second sequence *sharvelikaia,* meaning "large globe." Given the feminine suffix (*-kaia*), the neologism is probably adjectival rather than denominative, modifying "earth" in the line above (*zemlia*). The third word in line 28, *bespovelikaia,* shows some creative morphology. It is coined from the verb meaning "to command" (*povelevat'*): the privative *bez* negates the command of the root. Khlebnikov also fuses an adjectival suffix *-ikii* in the feminine onto this verb, creating a second occurrence of the word "great" (*velikii/velikaia*). This "sovereignless world" is also implicitly great, and it is great because the only source of rule is song (line 30 in the Russian). Bolshevism aimed to achieve total security by propagating socialism as a global ideal through Comintern. And just as his "book," meaning the poetry of literature, can topple regimes, so can his song be its own command. It only takes the stroke of a pen to delete the prefix *bez-*, meaning "without," in order to restore authority: in Khlebnikov, the existence of the word, and its sound and shape, precedes the phenomenon signified by the word. Once the coinage exists, a new status for song can be predicted. The arrow of thought is the hand on the timepiece. Linear and sharp, it is also a metaphor for the pen that writes the song. Despite the declaration to eradicate government, the poem imposes its song as a command for the new order. Paul Schmidt's translation of lines 29–30 runs the two lines together, making this new land of PRESPLANEARTH the song. The more literal translation is: "Let song be a command to it." In a new land where song is the rule of law, it must be the poet who is the master of the timepiece of humanity, ruling truly as the King of Time.

7

Boris Pasternak, "Poetry" (1922)

EXPERIENCING LYRIC

Поэзия

Поэзия, я буду клясться
Тобой и кончу, прохрипев:
Ты не осанка сладкогласна,
Ты—лето с местом в третьем классе,
Ты—пригород, а не припев.

Ты душная, как май, Ямская,
Шевардина ночной редут,
Где тучи стоны испускают
И врозь по роспуске идут.

И, в рельсовом витье двояся,—
Предместье, а не перепев,
Ползут с вокзалов восвояси
Не с песней, а оторопев.

Отростки ливня грязнут в гроздьях
И долго-долго, до зари
Кропают с кровель свой акростих,

Пуская в рифму пузыри.
Поэзия, когда под краном
Пустой, как цинк ведра, трюизм,
То и тогда струя сохранна,
Тетрадь подставлена—струись![1]

Poetry

Poetry, till my voice is weary
and wheezy, I shall swear by you:

you're not some sweet-voiced dignitary,
you're summer in a third-class carriage,
a precinct, not a pretty tune.

A May-time city street, all stuffy,
or the Shevardino redoubt
at nightfall, when the clouds go huffing
and scattering as school's let out.

Then doubling, as the rails go winding—
a pleasance, not a pleasant tune—
they crawl home from the railway sidings,
not singing, but as dumb as stone.

Twigs of the downpour clog the clusters
and on and on, before dawn comes,
drip their acrostic from the rooftops,
threading the bubbles into rhymes.

Poetry, when like a zinc bucket
at the tap, an empty truism waits,
even then, your flow remains untroubled,
the page lies open—flow in spate!

(TRANSLATED BY PETER FRANCE)

Boris Pasternak (1880–1960) was a great sensory poet, his early work shaped by Kantian philosophy and a love of painting and music, all on display in his early *My Sister—Life* (*Sestra moia—zhizn'*), unquestionably one of the central verse collections in Russian. His father, the distinguished painter Leonid Pasternak, and mother Rosalie, a concert pianist, emigrated to Berlin in 1921, while Boris chose to remain in Russia. A star of the Silver Age, he retained critical and popular appeal in the 1920s and 1930s and was even promoted by the Communist Party theorist and leading Bolshevik politician Nikolai Bukharin to the role of "first poet" at the First Writer's Congress in 1934.[2] He achieved world fame, and then suffered opprobrium in the Soviet Union as a Nobel laureate in 1958, a year after the publication of the historical novel *Doctor Zhivago*, which contained poems of great religiosity and biographical poignance.

The young Pasternak was a poet of ecstatic outpouring of feeling and, in Victor Erlich's phrase, "lyric excitement."[3] The qualities of the Pasternak lyric are sensory abundance and ebullience carried along with speed and spontaneity. The particular quality may be found to attach itself to a state of feeling, and the best way to read the lines is to allow oneself to experience the quality of feeling the phrases exude rather than to try to make each phrase give up its meaning. His early lyric approaches the world phenomenologically, recording perception and apprehension as textures and sounds. Educated as a philosopher in the neo-Kantian tradition, Pasternak viewed the ideal as the real and the real as the ideal.[4] Gifted as a musician and painterly in his aesthetic, he brought an acute ear to the instrumentation of his poetry, pushing the reader toward an experience of synesthesia as the boundary between the aural and the visual. In an early Pasternak lyric, images are the transmitter of emotion to the point where it is not clear whether actuality generates images or images produce actuality. The inner and the outer worlds of the subject collide and collapse, pull apart briefly, and then converge. Poems tend to be in constant movement, as images suddenly emerge and set off chains of more images in which the perception of reality is reality.

At the heart of the Pasternak lyric is the image, and the vehicle of the poetic image is usually metaphorical. Marina Tsvetaeva compared him to a "downpour [*liven'*] of light,"[5] an image combining multiple senses of touch, hearing, and seeing. Tsvetaeva's use of metaphor—and a brilliantly judged metaphor it is—is not only a matter of her own extravagance to capture the impression of what it is like to read and hear Pasternak's poetry. "Poetry," the subject of this chapter, is a work of definition. It displays the unusual capacity of Pasternak's verse to create a sensory experience that corresponds to an idea, bringing together emotion and mind. Poetry is the idea of the poem; it is also the experience of reading it. But Pasternak, here more poet than philosopher, cannot rest content with a merely denominative approach to rendering the world, since words are one thing and sensations are another. Metaphor has a definitional purpose, and its use to characterize abstract nouns is nowhere more appropriate than in a work about poetry itself.[6]

Pasternak has often struck readers as immediately apprehensible at an emotional level, but also difficult linguistically. It can require effort to see how a poet professing to be so close to life mobilizes all the grammatical, acoustic, and syntactic techniques at his disposal to convey consciousness. And, arguably, poems aiming to mirror what Tolstoy called "life as it flows" (*tekuchaia zhizn'*) achieve their effect by decentering or obscuring the role of poetic consciousness. They do this by relying on language as though it speaks independent of agency. To a degree, one might say that this is always the case with poetry, and most especially with formal poetry. Formality and spontaneity define the tension between the surface air of randomness and flux and poetic art. That gap between the perceived and the act of perception, between the signified and signifier, is characteristic of a phenomenological approach, creating a space in the poem for acts of self-conscious reflection nearly simultaneous with the spontaneous sensory impact of reality. The texture of the poem and an idea of the sensory must be related. Yet there is no doubt that features of the Pasternak lyric are nonetheless structured rather than random, patterned rather than casual, and in that respect reproduce mimetically rather than analytically the sensation of life. Poems reflect some idea of what is happening in the mind and in feeling, and, with the aim of rendering reality tangible, prosody is used to heighten effects, some purely aural, some more semantic.

This tension may explain why interpretations of Pasternak's lyric poetry often polarize into two types: the autobiographical and the structural. Structuralist readings tend to see poems as a system in which all aspects of the work are overdetermined for meaning and every element must correspond to some structuring principle. In a study of Pasternak's poetry, exemplifying a method that has been more widely adopted in Russian poetics than in other traditions, Krystyna Pomorska provides a set of microreadings that largely eliminates extratextual factors and argues that meanings emerge only from the verbal fabric. Details that might look unrelated or highly impressionistic at least on the surface are seen in relation to an underlying structural cohesion. The structuralist reading also favors interpretation expressed within a binary opposition defined by the poem itself. Her section on this poem in a chapter titled "Pasternak and Futurism" argues that the defining terms are announced in the opposition of two definitions of poetry announced in stanza 1; the key center of meaning of the poem, therefore, will be between poetry as a type of mellifluous music, and poetry as the set of phenomena related to poetry as a third-class ticket on a summer train.[7]

There is nothing of the riddle in this opposition, and it might even seem obvious. However, a structuralist reading seeks to semanticize practically all the phonetic elements in a poem by referring them to one or the other side of a binary analysis. The method also assumes that poetic form, figurative language, and rhyme are more about the poem's own coming into being than about the external world. Most methods of criticism interested in form tend to find congruence between an aspect of prosody and meaning. This procedure is, for instance, typical of New Criticism. What is different about the structuralist approach is that it moves beyond the phonological to the referential. In stanza 4, for example, the occurrence of the consonant cluster *gr/kr* is certainly noticeable. It anticipates and might be heard as a pre-echo to "acrostic" (*akrostikh*) in the third line. Pomorska's reading goes one step further by suggesting that there is a referential element here because the sound-image of water captures the pure language of nature, and that the sound correspondences between signifier and signified are identifiers. The acrostic is, in fact, a visual pun on the rain fall flowing off the roof. *Akro* means a "height" while the Russian *stikh* signifies the word for "verse," the word for Nature (*stikhiia*), and also closely resembles the preposition "s" and the verb *tech'* meaning "to flow from." Insofar as language and the elements behave analogously, no agency is given to the active craft of the poet. Pasternak has a debt to romantic theories of poetic consciousness and a Schellingian view of how the mind of the poet converges with an innate spirit in nature. Insofar as the poem makes an argument, and that is Pomorska's starting point, it also proves itself to be a self-conscious act that simulates the unself-consciousness given to romantic poets while acknowledging an ironic gap.[8]

Yet the approach can also be reductive and particularly resistant to deconstructive subtleties. Consider, by way of counterargument, another proposition. While Pasternak sets up a contrast that may look definitive, the terms of that binary opposition are themselves metaphorical and not strictly defined. Moreover, and perhaps more importantly, such readings tend to eliminate irony and ambiguity. The poem overtly criticizes poetry that postures like a "sweet-voiced dignitary." But that hardly makes it less than harmonious or dignified. Sound-play is one of the pleasures Pasternak cultivates, and the sheer musical qualities of the verse remain attractive. Does that mean that the sound patterns that can be discerned are either entirely without meaning or entirely meaningful in a deeper sense? Even if answers are admittedly subjective, there is a larger point of principle about the musicality of verse as its own extrasemantic, enriching factor. Clearly Pasternak would not wish to be classified with a poet like Konstantin Bal'mont, a symbolist famed for an exaggerated use of sound orchestration akin to the effects in English of a Swinburne or Tennyson at their most pronounced. At the same time, "Poetry" undermines the perceived polarity between sound and meaning. In stanza 4, the comparison of rain dripping to an acrostic seems to suggest that sections or words are like rhythmic bubbles. If that is the case, then the tendency of the structuralist to find meaning in word particles like prefixes and suffixes is already ironized and stands in counterpoint to the more determined meetings prescribed by a headline binary opposition.

"Poetry" is a particularly good example, then, of the choices in method that readers face. Stepping outside trends in Pasternak criticism, we see that readings can also empasize the gestalt of the work by privileging a style whose musical and visual properties accumulate significance that override syntactic enigmas.[9] For this second method, the central issue of poetry is emotion and sense-data or ideas bundled as images. And, for this second type of reader, elliptical syntax, slippage in wording, motivic repetition constitute the poetry in the poetry—what T. S. Eliot thought of as the automatic or unconscious art that acts on the reader's feelings. A key to his affiliation with the futurists lies in Pasternak's appropriation of their favorite device of *sdvig* or shift. This is a type of verbal slippage or distortion that opens a gap between norms and the experimental text, and it often occurs in instances of misspellings, incompletions, off-rhymes, and offbeat rhythmic pulses. Poetic difficulty and suggestive richness are to be expected of the modernist lyric.

Whether the means for making poems comprehensible should also smooth out into logical sequence utterances that are meant to be felt as mysterious, even exuberantly baffling, is a more general issue in the history of how to read lyric. What "Poetry" foregrounds first and foremost is itself as the object of a profession of devotion. This work is a credo. Poetic speech is in the first instance illocutionary: to speak one's commitment is to make a vow and to be committed by verbal deed. The adjacent placement of the first two words, the art and the self, is the nucleus from which the fissile chains of comparisons begin in stanza 1. Whatever poetry will be compared to—and if it is not one thing then it will be another and another and yet another—poetry and the speaker will be predicated on one another because poetry is what the poet can do and what can be done to the poet. Poets are what poets say. Poems of definition rely on declarative sentences. Another lyric titled "The Definition of Poetry," written in 1917 and included in *My Sister—Life*, makes the act of definition a declarative procedure: seven lines containing seven phrases are predicated of the nominal phrase "It is . . ." Phrasally, these are existential statements. Each is in fact a metaphor because the attributes of poetry produced are not a genus that can be predicated of other things but a highly individual set of descriptors. Whether or not it is a paradox to express definitions like this, these statements make sensory action rather than logic their basis, perhaps substituting impression for intellection.[10]

In "Poetry," written only five years later, Pasternak returns to the question. Once again, he avails himself of declaration: the first stanza contains both negative and positive existential statements. Between stanzas 2 and 5, the descriptive amplification of an initial comparison has a musical or vocal element since the poet shouts his credo so enthusiastically that he risks losing his voice. Hoarseness, a token of ardor, will be the vocal proof that poetry is not "some sweet-voiced dignitary," meaning that poetry is not a tired rehearsal of fustian clichés and self-conscious poeticisms signaling "I am a poem." Yet exuberance and brilliance more than volume mark this and *My Sister—Life* as a whole. If there is a public side to Pasternak's persona, it comes not out of a feeling of exhibition in the manner of Mayakovsky. The need to turn the experience of life into art reflects the classic way lyric can capture the inseparable intimacy art and life share in consciousness as subjectivity processes reality. Life is life absorbed into the poem rather than life projected back onto the world: the drama to Pasternak's poetry lies in symbols that project outward an inner world onto a reality.

As Alexander Zholkovsky noted, "Pasternak tends to spatialize almost any abstraction."[11] That includes time such as seasons or months, processes such as the weather, emotional states, and aspects of life. Spatialization and temporalization are two ways the poem immediately externalizes the language of subjective feeling, and Pasternak is agile in doing both in single lines. The first stanza introduces the comparison of poetry to the train compartment as well as to the summer. Poetry can be likened to the experience of traveling in the summertime outside the city into the banlieue in a third-class carriage. The line picks up the previous observation that poetry is not a "dignitary," nor does it live in posh districts. In the stanza's rhymes, vowels and consonants come to the ear like related objects of perception. The poet who sings until hoarseness does not indulge in mere refrain (*prokhripev/pripev*); the type of poetry to which the speaker commits is not fatuously musical like an old song. It is third-class, as far from official as possible. Here as in the poem "Early Trains" ("Na rannikh poezdakh," 1941), Pasternak expresses an idea of the simple folk borrowed from Tolstoy—his father was an ardent follower of the sage of Yasnaya Polyana—with whom he feels solidarity, all set out of kilter by the off-rhymes (lines 1, 3, 4) bringing together his popular, class, and poetic credentials (*kliast'sia/sladkoglasna/klasse*). Whatever class poetry travels in metaphorically, the literal and metaphorical levels of representation are about poetry as a form of transport.[12] Declarative sentences (lines 3–5) use the logic of syntax to impose a logic of association. This is how the poet feels about the lines he is writing, but it is also the picture the reader must carry in the mind.

There is a plastic dynamism to these combined effects, and, once the rapid movement of thought has established the point of reference, the idea produced in the poet's mind has achieved on the page its own separate reality. Between the first and third stanzas with their vision of travel, the second stanza unfolds both temporal detail, turning the mention of summer into the feeling of summer, and spatial detail by staging the distance covered from Yamskaya Street in Moscow to the Shevardino Redoubt (lines 6–7), the site of an important skirmish before the Battle of Borodino.[13] On the ground, about eighty miles have been traveled. Is there an element of historic time travel too? Do the clouds emit groans because Nature replicates the pain sustained on the battlefield? The first stanza ends by noting that distances are not refrains: we might conclude that the remark hints at the fact that what the poet imagines even by way of pathetic fallacy is not the same as a factual repetition. The anagrammatic relation of the month of May and the place-name Yamskaya Street in central Moscow demonstrates that Nature and the man-made do echo one another. It is a particular effect of the Pasternak soundscape to redraw reality.

For Pomorska, this echoing attains a more essentialist quality in which the sounds represent the reality in keeping with a futurist emphasis on the sound-image.[14] The phonetic shape of words—and not even whole words because prefixes and suffixes also carry these effects—contains and enhances motivic clues. Stanza 3 moves back down from the sky to the horizontal plane of the train journey. The description of the noise literally as "winding" (*vitie*) plays on the etymological connection between the physical and the verbal as "eloquence" (*vitiistvo*) derives from this root. Pasternak's eye and ear continually defamiliarize the mundane by seeing convergence between the verbal and the actual. Word play for its own sake is not the point. In mentioning an acrostic (line 16), the poem addresses, and even thematizes, the fact that language and possibly the language of verse most especially utilizes modes of encryption. At the surface level of the poetry, sound pattern and use of paronomasia structure motifs without naming an idea itself, instead fragmenting the idea.[15] If one motif of the poem is about the speed and trajectory at which the poetic imagination travels, then the use of prefixes or sound particles indicating horizontal and vertical motion (*pro-, pri-, -isp, ros-, pusk-, str-*) already plants an idea in the memory of the reader as she processes the poem.[16] The obduracy of these sounds, perhaps initially puzzling or heard as purely musical, has a narrative function in the poem. The mention of the acrostic also reminds us that signifier and signified are not necessarily in a stable relationship. When there is a suggestion of a word-puzzle such as an acrostic in which certain letters can be arranged or shuffled to spell words, the question arises as to what is the relation ontologically between a name and a description. Is it a form of truism when you call an entity by a name and then describe it as an image without using the word?

The effect of doubling is to create two complementary realities: one empirical, the other imagined or heard. The emphasis on motion, the sound orchestration, the fragmentation, and syntactic lapses give the poem its futurist qualities even as perception, nature, and people coexist recognizably. From the very start, the definition of entities has been metaphorical rather than literal. But the categories are not mutually exclusive. Poetry is likened to a third-class seat in a railway carriage. By stanza 3, however, we are much more under the impression that an actual journey is underway, with milestones like Yamskaya and Borodino behind and further evidence of passengers and suburbia supplied in stanza 3. Yet, whatever information can be extracted from the text, Pasternak aims for nothing like photographic realism. The double-bind a work like "Poetry" seems to endorse concerns the mutual visions of the world outside the text and from within. Poetic language subjects perception to its own laws. On the one hand, poetic reality must keep up with the sensory world. If poetry is not a refrain (*pripev*, line 5), it is because reality—understood to be the sum total of external sensory perceptions lived in the moment—must not be reduced to repetitive forms, such as the refrain, that operate according to the laws of verse without reference to the empirical world. It is perhaps a stroke of wit on Pasternak's part, therefore, to have written a poem in quatrains that begins with a five-line stanza in which the question of pattern is mentioned even before the stanza form can be established.

This tension between pattern and variation shapes the subtle change in the rhymes of the last three quatrains. All make use of interlocking or ring-rhyme. In stanza 3, both pairs are perfect rhymes: *dvoias'/vosvoiasi* and *perepev/otoropev*. In stanza 4, the even lines rhyme perfectly (*zari/puzyri*) whereas the odd lines do not (*grozd'iakh/akrostikh*). In stanza 5, the rhymes are technically correct since Russian prosody allows the pairing of different parts of speech. The last word of the poem is imbricated in a cross-rhyme with the line above. The eye picks out the truncated pair *struia/struis*, an effect Peter France's translation captures, too, by repeating the word "flow" as noun and command. Pasternak's phonetic choices have an ulterior motive that takes them far beyond the confines of the line. As the critic Igor Smirnov argued, in Pasternak's poetry, the phonetic, grammatical, and other prosodic features acquire a further meaning, themselves often becoming the theme of a poem to a degree that makes any separate consideration of form and content crippling to meaning.[17] Certain sounds that look like musical impulses, impulses that slip past the controls of logic, can crystallize into a meaning later. The consonant cluster *spsk* (and root *spusk*) occurs twice in stanza 2. The weather is humid, but the clouds emit groans rather than rain. This is an instance of metonymy, a favorite device of Pasternak, in which "two elements are presented as being related by virtue of their contiguity rather than similarity."[18] The clouds' huffing (lit. "groan") represents thunder, contiguous with rain, but the showers are delayed until stanza 4 when the initial literal reference to "descent" (*spusk*) becomes the downpour. When the consonant cluster *spsk* recurs, it relates to the stream of poetry likened to water from the tap, providing a prelude to the real shower of the final stanza.

The movement of the poem is circular. When seen from the end of the poem as a vantage point, the doubling noted at the beginning of stanza 3 may in fact be just as much division as duplication. The poet's mind, on its visual and musical track, moves in one direction, whereas literal reality moves in another. The commuters who leave the railway stations and head back home "crawl" and are bereft of song. The poem, however, continues, and it leaves behind the railway metaphor and turns to liquid (rainwater) for a new metaphor and association. Twigs drenched with water that drips from roofs refresh the mind with new sounds suggestive of letters. There is a language in the rain that the poet might hope to hear, and, until they form words, they are bubbles, and until they can be arranged as rhymes these words are not yet poetry. The foregrounding of sound as rain self-consciously suggests that verse may be the manifestation of structures that are present in nature, making poems some simulation of the universe. If the supply of letters and words is like rain, and as natural as rain, then all the poet seemingly need do is channel what he hears. The final stanza, however, draws back from the idea that poetry comes as easily as a cloudburst. The reader has been moving progressively from stanza 1 under the illusion of a journey.

As a statement about the meaning of poetry, the opening stanza created within the metaphor of the railway its own journey. When we arrive at the final stanza and once again find an address to poetry—and catch a refrain—it is also to find that the act of composition of the poem is still pending. The poet's artifice in finding metaphors for inspiration has created the impression that the meaning of poetry as a subject for this lyric has worked. But perhaps everything that comes before the final stanza has been nothing more than bubbles arranged as rhymes, tracing nothing more than an acrostic or outline for the real words that have yet to come. The poet's artifice in hearing and arranging rhymes has proven to be an "empty truism." There is a conscious process to poetic art represented in the initial stanzas that has been exposed as collateral to the real moment of inspiration that remains outside the poem, prepared for but not yet ready to fill the poet's notebook. Nature will have its thunderstorms. What the poet hears is the single tap—an acrostic rather than the whole language—and what the poet prepared for those meager drops is his bucket in a final metaphor and last metatextual stroke.

8

Osip Mandelstam, "The Horseshoe Finder (A Pindaric Fragment)" (1923)

TIME FUTURE, TIME PAST

Нашедший Подкову

(Пиндарический отрывок)

Глядим на лес и говорим:
Вот лес корабельный, мачтовый,
Розовые сосны,
До самой верхушки свободные от мохнатой ноши,
Им бы поскрипывать в бурю,
Одинокими пиниями,
В разъяренном безлесном воздухе,
Под соленою пятою ветра устоит отвес,
пригнанный к пляшущей палубе,

И мореплаватель,
В необузданной жажде пространства,
Влача через влажные рытвины хрупкий прибор геометра,
Сличит с притяженьем земного лона
Шероховатую поверхность морей.

А вдыхая запах
Смолистых слез, проступивших сквозь обшивку корабля,
Любуясь на доски,
Заклепанные, слаженные в переборки
Не вифлеемским мирным плотником, а другим—
Отцом путешествий, другом морехода,—
Говорим:
И они стояли на земле,

Неудобной, как хребет осла,
Забывая верхушками о корнях
На знаменитом горном кряже,
И шумели под пресным ливнем,
Безуспешно предлагая небу выменять на щепотку соли
Свой благородный груз.

С чего начать?
Все трещит и качается.
Воздух дрожит от сравнений.
Ни одно слово не лучше другого,
Земля гудит метафорой,
И легкие двуколки
В броской упряжи густых от натуги птичьих стай
Разрываются на части,
Соперничая с храпящими любимцами ристалищ.

Трижды блажен, кто введет в песнь имя;
Украшенная названьем песнь
Дольше живет среди других—
Она отмечена среди подруг повязкой на лбу,
Исцеляющей от беспамятства, слишком сильного одуряющего запаха,
Будь то близость мужчины,
Или запах шерсти сильного зверя,
Или просто дух чобра, растертого между ладоней.
Воздух бывает темным, как вода, и все живое в нем плавает, как рыба,
Плавниками расталкивая сферу,
Плотную, упругую, чуть нагретую,—
Хрусталь, в котором движутся колеса и шарахаются лошади,
Влажный чернозем Нееры, каждую ночь распаханный заново
Вилами, трезубцами, мотыгами, плугами.
Воздух замешен так же густо, как земля:
Из него нельзя выйти, в него трудно войти.
Шорох пробегает по деревьям зеленой лаптой,
Дети играют в бабки позвонками умерших животных.
Хрупкое летоисчисление нашей эры подходит к концу.

Спасибо за то, что было:
Я сам ошибся, я сбился, запутался в счете.

Эра звенела, как шар золотой,
Полная, литая, никем не поддерживаемая,
На всякое прикосновение отвечала “да” и “нет”.
Так ребенок отвечает:
“Я дам тебе яблоко”—или: “Я не дам тебе яблоко”.
И лицо его—точный слепок с голоса, который произносит эти слова.

Звук еще звенит, хотя причина звука исчезла.
Конь лежит в пыли и храпит в мыле,
Но крутой поворот его шеи
Еще сохраняет воспоминание о беге с разбросанными ногами—
Когда их было не четыре,
А по числу камней дороги,
Обновляемых в четыре смены,
По числу отталкиваний от земли пышущего жаром иноходца.

Так
Нашедший подкову
Сдувает с нее пыль
И растирает ее шерстью, пока она не заблестит;
Тогда
Он вешает ее на пороге,
Чтобы она отдохнула,
И больше уж ей не придется высекать искры из кремня.
Человеческие губы, которым больше нечего сказать,
Сохраняют форму последнего сказанного слова,
И в руке остается ощущение тяжести,
Хотя кувшин наполовину расплескался, пока его несли домой.

То, что я сейчас говорю, говорю не я,
А вырыто из земли, подобно зернам окаменелой пшеницы.
Одни
на монетах изображают льва,
Другие—
    голову.
Разнообразные медные, золотые и бронзовые лепешки
С одинаковой почестью лежат в земле.
Век, пробуя их перегрызть, оттиснул на них свои зубы.
Время срезает меня, как монету.
И мне уж не хватает меня самого.[1]

On Finding a Horseshoe (usually called "The Horseshoe Finder")

(Pindaric fragment)

We look at the wood and we say:
—There's a shipwright's forest, a forest of masts,
Pink pines,
Free from the mass of fronds to their very tips
They ought to be creaking in gales
Singly, stone pines,
In the fury of a treeless sky,
Resisting the salt heel of the wind, a plumb line driven into the dancing deck,

And the seafarer
In his unquenchable thirst for the expanse
Hauls the geometer's delicate instruments through watery valleys,
Measuring, against the drag of the earth's hold,
The shivering surface of the seas.
And breathing in the smell
Of resinous tears, seeping through the ship's planking,
Admiring the boards
Clinched down, laid into bulwarks
Not by the gentle Bethlehem carpenter, but another
The father of travel, a friend to the seafarer—
We say:
They too once stood on the earth
The awkward earth, like the spine of a mule
And their tips have forgotten their roots
On that famed mountain ridge
Where they whisper under freshwater downpours
Asking the unheeding sky to exchange their noble freight for a thimble of salt.

Where to start?
Everything shudders and sways
The air trembles with comparisons.
No single word is better than another,
The earth hums with metaphor
And light chariots
In the flashing harness of throngs of birds, taut with the strain,
Break apart
Competing with the snorting favorites of the tiltyards.

Thrice blessed he who introduces name into his song
For the song beautified by name
Will live longer among the others—
She, alone of her friends, wears a bandage on her brow
To cure her of forgetting, that overly strong intoxicating scent
Like the proximity of a man
Or the coat of a powerful beast
Or the perfume of savory, rubbed between the palms.
The air is sometimes dark, like water, and all the living swim in it, like fish
Fins forcing forward, shoving
The taut-skinned, solid, slightly warm sphere,
A crystal, in which wheels turn and horses shy
Neaera's moist black soil, nightly tilled anew
With forks, tridents, hoes, and ploughshares.
The air as densely fleshed as the earth:
You can't leave, you can barely enter.
A shiver moves through the trees like a green oar
Children play at knucklebones with the vertebrae of dead animals.
The fragile calendar of our era draws to its close.

Thank you for what has passed:
I was mistaken, I strayed, I lost count.
The era clinked like a golden ball,
Cast in a round, supported by no hand,
Answering every touch with *yes* and *no*.
Like a child might say:
I'll give you an apple, or *I won't give it you*
And the child's face like a cast made from the voice uttering these words.

The sound rings on, but the source of the sound is gone.
The horse lies in the dust, and snorts and foams
But the sharp twist of his neck
Still carries the memory of the race legs flung wide—
Not just four of them,
But as many as stones on the road,
Starting afresh every four beats
The number of strikes made on the earth by the steaming horse.

So, when he finds the horseshoe
Blows the dust from it

Wipes it with wool, till it shines
Then
Hangs it over the threshold,
So it can breathe deep
Never again will it be made to shear sparks from the flint.
Human lips with nothing more to say
Hold the shape of the last word,
And the hand still knows the sensation of weight
Although the jug has spilled half its load on the way home.

That which I say now, is not spoken by me—
It is scraped from the ground like fossilized grains
of wheat.

Some
inscribe lions on their coins,
Others
a head.
All the various rounds of copper, gold
bronze
Lie with equal honor in the ground,
The age bites down on them, leaving the marks of its teeth.
Time clips me, like a coin.
And I have already felt the loss of myself.

(TRANSLATED BY SASHA DUGDALE)

Written during the revolutionary period, "The Horseshoe Finder" is Mandelstam's longest and arguably most complex lyric poem. Mandelstam gravitated to longer forms when he sensed inflection points in contemporary history. A decade later in the early 1930s, when Stalinization prevailed, he once again turned to more expansive poems as a vehicle to captured the feel of Soviet reality in images of popular culture and a crowd mentality increasingly marked by class warfare; this use of longer lyric will happen once again even later in the enigmatic cycle "Verses on an Unknown Soldier" (1937–38).

"The Horseshoe Finder" is a stupendous act of lyric imagining and creative growth as one of a series of poems written to capture a struggle with historical uncertainty and the impact on the survival of culture and poetry—what Blok in 1919 called "the collapse of humanism" (*krushenie gumanizma*).[2] In that connection, line

64 offers a striking formulation that can be understood in two ways: either that, as in Sasha Dugdale's translation, art survives its creator ("The sound rings on, but the source of the sound is gone"), or that art may ring hollow when the justification and possibly purpose of art have disappeared ("The song rings on but the reason for the sound has disappeared"). Both meanings are compatible with the interpretation this chapter develops.

"The Horseshoe Finder" first appeared in print in the Berlin-based newspaper *On the Eve* (*Nakanune*) and in Soviet Russia in the thick journal *Red Virgin Soil* (*Krasnaia nov'*) in the spring and fall of 1923, when the third and final edition of Mandelstam's first collection, *Stone* (*Kamen'*, 1910), was published. In Mandelstam's poems written before 1918, consistent with acmeism, it was his aim to escape from the authority of the symbolist philosophy and focus on higher things. He absorbed into his own language a hope for a transcendent vision based on appreciation of the worldly. The poetry of *Stone* was about craft and self-discovery, its lyrics cast in an exquisitely tentative voice, whereas "The Horseshoe Finder" has a new scale and thrust also dominant in his next collection. *Tristia*, composed around 1918, captured the historic tumult of the period. In the culmination of the classical trend in Mandelstam's poetry, the collection looked to the past, embracing the modernist lesson that poetic art could innovate by recycling culture.[3] Like the work of Imagist poets such as the young Pound of the early *Cantos*, single lyrics encompassed the archaeology of previous eras and reused their material traces in the new.[4] Even a short lyric could convey the complex layering of history embodied in the Hagia Sophia and its journey from Christian basilica to mosque.[5] Classical destruction, a principle Mandelstam also identified with the Russian Revolution, shaped material culture. Like T. S. Eliot, he was a poet of retrieved culture, allusive and layered, and like Yeats he was under the spell of Fraser's *The Golden Bough* and had begun to see recurrence and express it in mythemes (such as the quest embodied in the Argonauts motif of "The Horseshoe Finder"). The question of culture's transhistorical survival became more pressing and existential in the thick of revolution. *Tristia* as a whole dilutes the contemporary world into classical myths of transgression and strife, looking for stability against flux, or the Apollonian against the Dionysian, in ancient rituals that are a token of cyclical return.[6] The answer to what would be tolerated and what would flourish remained unclear in these years, and elements of doubt and self-doubt continued to shape the psychology of Mandelstam's lyric speaker.

This is the creative context of the poem treated in this chapter. "The Horseshoe Finder" takes its speaker and its reader on a journey. The quest that begins with the imagined building of a ship is a search for a talismanic object. This is the horseshoe found and fetishized near the end. The journey encompasses a propulsive launch that seems to happen simultaneously in the air and on the sea and land.

Parallel time frames of present, past, and future also coexist in the separate sections, and the journey into the future leads to a recovery of the past. The lyrical structure contains thematic centers out of which new dynamism builds, seeming to be improvisatory but achieving a rigor through the sustained journey into chaos and then a final perspective on time and the future. The resulting effects of momentous confusion define the surface of a poem that can seem bewildering. The longest middle sections are so richly loaded with dramatic effects, adding and compounding images from section to section, that the poem seems an epic on the brink of veering out of control, a feeling exacerbated by the free verse form and irregular rhyme.

The journey represented with an epic panache daringly places its geometer and voyager, figures of reason, in a battle against tumultuous elements, elements that mount a contest with the voyager. Emerging out of the murkiness of his seemingly amphibious trip, somewhere in the sea and in the air simultaneously, and moving away from the depiction of Nature, the speaker enables a parallel allegorical reading of History. Just as the seafarer contended with the overwhelming force of Nature, he now confronts the "fragile calendar of our era" (line 56) and the tone of the poem shifts from its bold opening to meditative conclusion. The question of who could see far enough into the future or look back far enough into the past to predict the outcome is at the heart of "The Horseshoe Finder."

Conceived on a large scale, it has a careful architecture in eight unnumbered sections of unequal length: (1) lines 1–13, (2) lines 14–27, (3) lines 28–36, (4) 37–55, (5) lines 56–63 , (6) lines 64–71, (7) lines 72–85, (8) 86–94. In its first two sections, the poem begins on a propulsive note of shipbuilding and sailing. A suitable, new vessel, a metaphor for the imagination, must be built to set sail on stormy seas, its builder and navigator not a Christian carpenter but some other visionary such as the mythic Jason or even Peter the Great (famed as a carpenter and for the geometric design of St. Petersburg, his new capital). Mandelstam was a famously allusive poet who had at his recall several literary traditions. With his early maturity he had developed sophisticated techniques of intertextuality in order to layer and bring into dialogue sources, sometimes themselves from the same tradition and cognate, sometimes more disparate across traditions. The departure point for "The Horseshoe Finder" may be Pindar's *Fourth Pythian Ode*, which tells the story of Jason and the Argonauts. But he leaves that work's inspiration behind almost from the start and finds in Catullus's Poem 64, a second poem about the quest of the Argonauts for the Golden Fleece, the more suitable launchpad for this journey:

> Pines once sprung from Pelion's peak floated, it is said, through liquid billows of Neptune to the flowing Phasis and the Aeetaean territory, when the picked youth,

> the vigour of Argive manhood seeking to carry away the Golden Fleece from Colchis, dared to skim over salt seas in a swift-sailing ship, sweeping the blue-green ocean with paddles shaped from fir-wood. That goddess who guards the castles in topmost parts of the towns herself fashioned the car, scudding with lightest of winds, uniting the interweaved pines unto the curving keel. That goddess first instructed untaught Amphitrite with sailing. Scarce had it split with its stem the windy waves, and the billow vexed with oars had whitened into foam, when arose from the swirl of the hoary eddies the faces of sea-dwelling Nereids wondering at the marvel.[7]

Most of Catullus's opening has been pared away, including classical toponyms and deities. The navigator (or geometer) replaces a goddess; the elements remain the same including the wind and billowing waves; and the reference to the topmost parts, now of the trees rather than the town, is also transferred. These efficient allusions are perhaps more than anything ways to signal scale without actually writing hundreds of lines; and insofar as he emulates a poem by Catullus that was itself a miniature version of epic, the label "fragment" looks appropriate. As in Catullus, the poem treats questions of destiny and nation, focusing on the speaker-cum-voyager as hero. Pindaric odes celebrate victorious charioteers, and the poet's imaginary vessel serves as both boat and chariot. Is the horseshoe the original object of its mission? Is the horseshoe all that remains in the geological-cum-archaeological record of his success? Both an exploratory vessel and a vehicle, its precious cargo may be the poet himself because ultimately it is a metaphor for a mental journey into the future and a future past.

The pressing question for the poet may not be whether he can shape history and rather where his victory or vision will lead. In "Slate Ode," history and the creation of a new society unfold in geological time; in that poem's vision of a primitive world, who has the agency to change hearts and minds remains in question. In "The Horseshoe Finder," the speaker borne along by his visionary élan ventures forth into an environment in which everything "shudders and sways." The image of navigation and the rational setting of a course by the geometer overlay the powers of Pindaric association as means against the ferocity of the elements. In the opening sections, the semantic field of building materials and equipment proliferates through repetition, variation, and synecdoche (hence *les* in lines 1, 2; *bezlesnyi*, line 7; *doski*, line 16; *verkhushki* as synecdoche of the forest, line 23). How the ship was built, of what materials, how it was launched, and how the poem as a song was sung become completely intertwined. Matching music and vision (and Sasha Dugdale's translation stays syntactically and sonically close to the original), the poem finds a propulsive rhythm on which to launch the ship's journey. All of the senses are also harnessed to this visionary effort with smell (lines 15, 41), touch (lines 13, 44), vision (lines 11, 16), and hearing (lines 25, 32, 60, 64) coming at the speaker pell-mell. The ship that has been built from the pine forest can barely withstand the force of the air and water.

Mandelstam, early and late, was steadfastly attentive to building materials, verbal and actual. Textually, the imagistic and metaphorical extravagance Mandelstam achieves by combining the seafaring of the Argonauts and the Olympic horse is both Pindaric, as the subtitle of the poem claims, but it is also modernist and belongs to the tradition of the delirium voyage on which Rimbaud's "Drunken boat" ("Le bateau ivre") embarks. Both Mandelstam's and Rimbaud's ships are pinewood; both journeys belong to an inspired figure (Rimbaud's intoxicated and hallucinogenic); both, more importantly, are vessels that each speaker in his emotional transport eventually leaves behind, Rimbaud's sailor to interrogate the skies for their future vital energy ("ô future Vigueur"), Mandelstam excavating the earth to recover artifacts buried by time the destroyer.[8]

Stone, most famously, serves in his poetry as rock, as a symbol of culture, as a cipher for Christianity (*petrus* connoting St. Peter), as an emblem of the poetic word; later on in the *Voronezh Notebooks*, it will denote the average citizen, likened to pebbles, who are the building-block of the communist state. The air is also an important element in his image-system. Not every poet will look at a forest and imagine the craft built in the opening block of lines. The poet-builder of "The Horseshoe Finder," who can set the air ringing with his voice, is seemingly able to fly, sail, and excavate partly because he can already see inscribed in his materials their evolution. He enjoins readers to "look at the wood" because the boat's timbers come from a forest that is itself "a shipwright's forest, a forest of masts," an example of the trope of catachresis used to express a teleological sense that a forest was planted for this purpose (and later on, when the talismanic horseshoe is found it is to be wondered for what purpose other than the song itself the journey was undertaken). The speaker stands back to admire a vessel ready for rough passage. Captivated by the sound of the treetops that still seem to reverberate in the planks of the ship, soaked by the sea, the seafarers have landed in an inhospitable new terrain ready to unload their "noble cargo" for a modest tariff of salt, a highly prized commodity, and also a symbolic good since sharing salt was thought to be a sign of trust. Within his Catullan and Christian allusions, Mandelstam also reminds the reader of Pushkin's "Arion" (1827). That poetic parable tells the brief story of a poet who during a storm continues to sing his poems, oblivious to the efforts of the sailors to save them from shipwreck. The only survivor, he is washed ashore, dries out his tunic, and resumes his song, impervious to the human cost around him. It has been read both as a parable of the freedom of imaginative art from social responsibility, and autobiographically and allegorically as an expression of Pushkin's chagrin at not being one of the band of conspirators in the Decembrist rebellion of 1825, readings that may inform how Mandelstam at a historically charged moment sees the question of what kind of ship to build, creatively and politically. Unlike Pushkin's speaker, Mandelstam's voyager does accept that a social utility (the trade in salt is a "noble" endeavor) is part of his mission, and he fears for the destruction of his ship.

Behind the opening table of "The Horseshoe Finder" one may also discern the opening vista from Pushkin's *Bronze Horseman*, in which Peter the Great surveys a vast expanse of emptiness, looks out over the surrounding forest, and imagines a city rising on the spot. This speaker's limitless hunger for space echoes with the same audacity. And here, as in Pushkin, the vision is father to the deed and can telescope history and bridge past and present, cause and effect. In *The Bronze Horseman*, just how marshes become land, sea becomes canals, huts become palaces requires no more than two phrases in the prologue: "A hundred years passed. The new city rose proudly." In Mandelstam's poem, a ship has already been built proleptically from the forest, a plumb line fixes its compass for the navigator or geometer who navigates a sea whose roughness has the texture of the forest. Yet Mandelstam's speaker may be daunted by the task since section 3 (lines 28–36), while structurally a brief transition just before the midpoint to the second half, introduces a hesitation in the poet's song. Even before section 4 begins on a note of relief with its own statement of the beatitudes, section 3 has dramatized the difficulty of steering and keeping the craft intact.

Before he can provide an answer to his own rhetorical question of "Where to start?" (line 28) he conveys the impact of the visionary moment on his own thought. The question turns out to be less about the next narrative segment than a confession about the near loss of language that threatens the speaker. The poem adopts and pursues its visionary posture yet cannot spring free of cultural moorings to which it is attached. Poetry is no less an artifact than a vase or even a building, provided it can be remembered, cited, reworked, and recited over the course of time.[9] When he asks the question about the ship's own direction, Mandelstam consciously looks back to Pushkin and beyond him to a whole odic tradition, including Mikhailo Lomonosov's own Pindaric "Ode on the Taking of Chocim" (1737), the first stanza of which portrays inspiration as close to aphasia as inspiration seizes the mind. The question "Where to start?" in Mandelstam, a performative statement of confusion about inspiration as unplanned or as a statement of rational choice as to the images selected by the poet's mind, descends from the rhetorical example of this most Pindaric of Russian poets. Lomonosov typically opened his poems with the figure of a hesitant poet, positioned on Mt. Pindus or Parnassus, tensely expectant of the *furor poeticus*, when inspiration as an outside force would take control of the individual self. In that exalted state, the poet became capable of sudden illumination, independent of conscious effort yet dependent on some outer power rather than his own imagination.

Mandelstam's metaphor of the imagination and sailing also reaches out to Pushkin. The question "Where to start?" in "The Horseshoe Finder" echoes the final words and question on which Pushkin's "Autumn" (1833) ends when language no longer is sufficient. In the Pushkin, eleven elaborately crafted stanzas, each in eight lines, had set out the pleasures of the senses afforded by the season, all of which quicken the poet's eye and senses. Appreciation of the whole comes out of an ample exposition of detail, and the pleasure induces a state of dreaminess "out of which poetry is awakened." Pushkin's poem ends by likening the mind to a ship, its sailors thrown about, its sails full of the wind that moves the "hulk." The complete plenitude signified by the images overwhelms, saps recent enthusiasm ("the fingers ask for a pen, the pen seeks paper"), and disables speech. The only words to appear in the final, twelfth stanza are in the first line: "Sails. Where indeed shall we sail? . . ."[10] The remaining seven lines appear as wordless dots, indicating noise. Mandelstam has reimagined Pushkin's question and metaphor in relation to history. His poem also creates a comparable sense of fullness that he yearns to take into the future; yet, while it does not lapse into silence, the sense of the ending replays the moment of fragmentation, Pindaric and Pushkinian, that creates a space in the poem for a journey after the unachievable, left as an emotional residue of regret and yearning that leads directly to Mandelstam's admission at the end that "time will clip me down."

In the manner of the Pindaric ode, the circumstances of the poem's production animate the poet: the poet must build his own craft in order to navigate the torrent of the age. "The Horseshoe Finder" catapults the reader to an unknown moment and begins with a strong deictic adverb to establish that time and place. The circumstances of the poem's production are its own imaginary realization of the poetic ship as historical product as well as a metaphor. "No single word is better than another" (line 31): Is there one authorial word or discourse—the Russian word *slovo* means both—the poet can emulate? Music, identified as the energy that makes the world hum, also inspires the poem's metaphoricity, his own equivalent of the geometer's navigational sense for finding the correct thought. After all, from the start Mandelstam has made striking use of rhetorical effects to assume a position of vatic authority.[11] And not only does the fourth section remind the reader that the song is a victory ode to the winner of a chariot race (the song is worn like both a bandage or victorious chaplet on the brow in line 40), it also makes clear what is at stake by claiming that it is the poet who preserves his name from "forgetting" (line 41, *bespamiatstvo*) and therefore worth the sweatily intoxicating efforts described in lines 41–44. The greater the feats of imagination, the greater the poem's capacity to elevate the winner.

The tradition of adaptation gave a license that Mandelstam exercised to balance the focus away from the race itself to the poet's own thoughts. If the Pindaric subtitle is meant to suggest an associative poetics, in the first instance, it also acknowledges the monumentality of the poet's conspicuous efforts.[12] The position of the Pindaric charioteer and that of Mandelstam's speaker are similar, since each contends with the battle between structure and chaos. Both the ship or the poetic imagination and the chariot threaten to break apart. Like the Olympic athlete of the Pindaric ode, the epic voyager seeks a prize or to be "thrice blessed." This possibility keeps before the reader the mystery of the poem's title. It is only at the end that the poet's reward appears in the form of the horseshoe, satisfying the notion he enunciates earlier in lines 38–40 that the matching of a song and a name is a blessing.

With section 5, the nature and value of the relation between the metaphorical tenor and vehicle, or imagination and chariot, become clearer. The speaker's purpose in asking "Where to start?" is to take stock, a pause that allows one to appreciate how the first part creates an extended metaphor for the poetic transport he needs to evoke the image of the Pindaric charioteer mentioned only in passing (lines 35–36). The original Pindaric style was conceived as freewheeling and oblique, and it split attention between the workings of the poet's imagination and the Olympic race. The poet is galvanized by this energy, but he sets out into the unknown since his voyage is neither Christian nor Hellenic ship, the vessel standing for an anterior phase of culture abandoned after the revolution. Uncertainty rather than timorousness stimulates the imagination. The ship and chariot are a double metaphor for the poetic imagination, which can open up a multisensory realm to consciousness that defies the blankness of amnesia yet can also be overwhelmed and races too quickly even to describe a single smell. This is the power that transports him through all the elements: at one and the same time, he remains at sea, on land pulled by a cart latched on to a flock of birds, and also aloft cleaving through the air. In competing with the "snorting favorite [steeds] of the tiltyards" (line 36), he performs a poem that keeps pace with the example of Pindar, whose odes operate at two levels as celebrations of victorious equestrians and themselves career along at great mental velocity.

Unlike Pushkin's speaker in "Autumn," Mandelstam's persona stakes posterity on his ability not to forget his purpose. While the imagination careens Pindarically, the task of the poet is to match the celebration with a name.

Трижды блажен, кто введет в песнь имя;
Украшенная названьем песнь
Дольше живет среди других

Thrice blessed he who introduces name into his song
For the song beautified by name
Will live longer among the others

Is it the poet's own name that must be introduced? Or that of the charioteer? What happens when only a nameless song is remembered? And if the song is nameless is it because ultimately even in the visionary moment the poet could not foresee the victor of the race or, if one is reading allegorically, the successful political contender in 1923? Whether to praise Lenin or, heeding rumors of Stalin's machinations, to fear his successor is one of the questions that animates another of Mandelstam's great poem of these years, "1 January 1924." Whether or not the particular issue of political leadership informs Mandelstam's thought, present uncertainty will, nonetheless, be subsumed in the larger question of what at all will exist in the future, creating the pessimism that haunts the poem's final sections when the discovery of relics offsets the motifs of fame, survival. Whether this is the name of the poet or the Olympic victor, the singer or the charioteer, one or both, is never disclosed; and the differentiation may be pointless because ultimately the poet and the victor are each insignificant or reduced without one another. Even at this point the poem looks beyond that question to wonder more fundamentally about the survival of culture. In his Pindaric-Catullan-Pushkinian-Rimbaud-inspired vessel, the poet extends the journey that recreates for his own age a mythic quest, crafted imagistically with a Pindaric metaphorical excess, the plenitude of Lomonosov's exalted visionary, and ethically with the commitment to poetry of the Pushkinian speaker to produce work that is aesthetically powerful, whatever its utilitarian relevance. For now the poet continues to try to find his way through the murky present:

Воздух бывает темным, как вода, и все живое в нем плавает, как рыба,
Плавниками расталкивая сферу,
Плотную, упругую, чуть нагретую,—
Хрусталь, в котором движутся колеса и шарахаются лошади,
Влажный чернозем Нееры, каждую ночь распаханный заново
Вилами, трезубцами, мотыгами, плугами.
Воздух замешен так же густо, как земля:
Из него нельзя выйти, в него трудно войти.

The air is sometimes dark, like water, and all the living swim in it, like fish
Fins forcing forward, shoving
The taut-skinned, solid, slightly warm sphere,
A crystal, in which wheels turn and horses shy
Neaera's moist black soil, nightly tilled anew
With forks, tridents, hoes, and ploughshares.
The air as densely fleshed as the earth:
You can't leave, you can barely enter.

A shiver moves through the trees like a green oar
Children play at knucklebones with the vertebrae of dead animals.

Just to recapitulate: the poet who started out as an Argonaut has moved forward on a ship pulled by birds, a passenger of Aphrodite or Apollo. Latterly, he seems to move through the air and the sea as an Olympian contestant on some marvelous amphibious craft, ploughing both realms. The first part of section 4 (lines 45–56) plunges back into the murky world of the elements, the land and sea reversed. "Neaera's moist black soil" conjures a sea nymph whose name means "new rising." Mandelstam was highly adept at using word play and planting crosslinguistic puns in his verse. Here the sound of "era" in the name "Neaera" (and possibly even "new era") gives a pre-echo of the mention of a new era (line 58). The section shifts the focus away from the charioteer and back onto the voyage, but it rounds off with a fatalistic-sounding apothegm about time. If the calendar of one era is coming to an end, what comes next?

With this section, emphasis shifts onto a conceptual vocabulary. The evocation of the era prompts a confession of guilt. The nature of the error is undisclosed. It follows a vignette of children at play, an image of innocence unmarked by sin, suggesting by proximity that the speaker's fault is poetry itself, and not writing the way children speak in the simple declarative sentences reproduced in line 62. Mandelstam held that the shape of the word, its aural envelope or the "cast made from the voice uttering these words," was a factor in its recognition. The perfect matching of intentionality, voice, and language may be an ideal that is not recoverable. Such innocence and transparency stand at an angle to the complex workings of the poetic imagination and speech in these very lines. Line 52 reflects a temporary moment of exhaustion, circling back to the image and sound of the rustling trees from which the ship was made. In addition to the blessing of song, there is also awareness of error and even hypersensitivity, since "every touch" elicits an ambivalent answer. Was it wrong to launch forth? Is the ship headed in the wrong direction? Has the speaker lost the assurance of the geometer and with it forfeited visionary confidence? Self-awareness coincides with the acknowledgment of a shift from mythic time to historical time. If the world was golden, turning at that point in a historical cycle, that might mean it was golden by privilege of being first in a sequence that inevitably brought decline. But even a golden age, now seen retrospectively, seems to have involved guilt. The speaker's attitude is marked by reckoning, by confession of right and wrong, and by childlike snippets of speech that record acts of gift giving that belong to the child or humanity in its infant state. "Thank you for what has passed" provides justification for the journey, expressing gratitude for the ecstasy of these first fifty lines of intense vision, a state explained as hard to enter consciously and impossible to stop voluntarily. It may also convey elegiacally a farewell to an earlier time, and an earlier self, whose echoes reverberate. Had Mandelstam been less thoughtful about his own historical instincts, he might have ended the poem in this section with these childishly hopeful lines. What follows them is startling as an expression of intense doubt because, having absorbed the Spenglerian pessimism of his period, he produced a more desolate vision at the end of the poem, where the poet-voyager succeeds in excavating the horseshoe and fulfilling his title role. Arguably, all that follows is a starkly elegiac anticlimax. Visionary poetry depends on the power of the poet's language to concretize the symbol—that is, the horseshoe—that represents fragmentation and continuity, the audible and the inaudible.

And reverberation is key to the assertion of fame through the song and its perpetuation. The sound of the poetic voice and the reverberation of the horse's hooves stand ambivalently in relation to one another as emblems of both permanence and impermanence. The last third of section 6 is a worthy counterpart to the opening section, comparable in length, imagery, and message. Both sections make more striking use of repetition than any other sections of the poem. The motif of sound (*zvenet'*, *zvuk*, line 64) is underscored. Unlike the poet's song, the chariot evoked in section 4 has broken apart, and only the skeleton of the horse and a medallion or coin can be recovered: time can be frozen in an image that is finally only a memory. This seems to be a poignant acknowledgment of loss: "memory" (*vospominanie*) cannot equal a moment of glory for the charioteer, whose renown in the end depends on the poet's capacity to hear the race imaginatively.

The mind of the geometer set a course according to principles. This is why the question of what will survive is important at every level of the poem, concerning the safe passage of the ship, the success of the charioteer, and the survival of the song itself. Survival of the name entirely depends on the reader (aka horseshoe finder) being able to read the marks left in the historical and geological record—but, above all, to read the marks left on the language by the poet. That same energy must also be carried over into the song developed from this same generative principle, and the poet who can harness the song by naming it is promised a state of grace ("Thrice blessed he who . . ."). If the song is to be real, it must also leave, as this vision insists, a physical object and trace as the material embodiment of its original energy. Is the cast taken from the voice an image of inspiration sustained by a single poet? Is the face of the poet one and the same with the speaker's current identity? Or has some fundamental rupture in identity taken place? That moment of discovery depicts the reading of an artifact.

Так
Нашедший подкову
Сдувает с нее пыль
И растирает ее шерстью, пока она не заблестит;
Тогда
Он вешает ее на пороге,
Чтобы она отдохнула,
И больше уж ей не придется высекать искры из кремня.

So, when he finds the horseshoe
Blows the dust from it
Wipes it with wool, till it shines
Then
Hangs it over the threshold,
So it can breathe deep
Never again will it be made to shear sparks
from the flint.

As happens so often in this poem, the shift in perspective is barely announced since the conjunction *tak* ("so") normally sets up simple sequences, whereas the connection between this tableau and the preceding verse paragraphs is close to non sequitur. In fact, the conjunction sets up what follows in a metaphorical relation with the entire poem up to this point; in addition, it implies a huge temporal shift from a work aiming at the future to a viewpoint in the present that is anterior to the final moment of retrospection. The aphorism about the relation of the song and name mooted earlier may now look as much like a challenge when seen from this perspective. How or when can the name or author who generates the song be certain of posterity? In a way, one of the poem's most moving and famous lines is least enigmatic when read literally:

То, что я сейчас говорю, говорю не я,
А вырыто из земли, подобно зернам окаменелой пшеницы.

That which I say now, is not spoken by me—
It is scraped from the ground like fossilized grains of wheat.

How much time can pass before a poem ceases to signify? The speaker suggests that what was once uttered has now become disassociated from the moment of creation or recital. Even the written word may constitute some distortion of the spoken word in its original moment of expression. If the historical circumstances, or even the biography of the author ,somehow fade from view, how much more attenuated does the meaning of the poem become? In his essay "On the Interlocutor" (1913), Mandelstam compared the future reader with someone who finds a message in a bottle years after it has been thrown into the sea. His topic at the time was how poetic language manages to remain intelligible and keep pace with the vernacular even as meanings change. Now loss through fossilization and decay are more to the front of his imagination as the poem envisages that the horseshoe will outlive its rider and, above all, the horse. From the shape of its fossilized skeleton, the speaker extrapolates the sound of its impact not by the number of legs but rather by the number of cobblestones on which it clattered along. A metaphor for poetic agency and language, for intentionality and recoverability of meaning, exposes how vulnerable to burial by layers of history the culture represented by the horseshoe may be.

The question of who speaks if not the poet reflects on the aesthetic shape of a poem that comes close to fragmenting and yet has great unity, celebrates poetic visionary power, and elegizes the fragility of renown. The poem's form gives a visible indication of a new departure, especially when considered alongside the complementary vision of "Slate Ode" or the belief in the durability of material culture embodied in the poems of *Stone*. A radical change in style accompanies a change in message. All the poems in Mandelstam's first two collections are written as formal verse. In *Stone*, the poems are largely stanzaic. Their high percentage of end-stopped lines and regular punctuation impose a highly controlled syntax. In *Tristia*, lines are longer, and ternary meter now features. The stanza form remains strictly observed, yet, in the shaping of arguments and lines, the increased use of enjambment adds movement to a strongly rhythmic use of meter. Those effects attain their culmination in "Slate Ode." The central metaphor around which the poem is built treats the relation of geological time and historical time, and the poem poses anthropological questions about the formation of societies and cycles of history. For its dense network of images and accumulation of subtexts on the theme of gradual transformation, the unconscious layering of practices out of which civilization is made, the Mandelstamian stanza is a perfect vehicle. Each thought seems to be tracked through the repetition of words, the additional meanings conveyed through the dispersal of word roots and meaningful musical effects.

"The Horseshoe Finder" devises yet another way to sing a new song for a disrupted age. For one thing, it is a virtually unique departure by Mandelstam into free verse: in scale, tone, and form, it takes him one step beyond the "Slate Ode" toward something closer to the forms of Mallarmé and Rimbaud at their most daring.[13] Its unrhymed blocks of lines are demarcated by exclamations, repetition, and rhetorical questions such as "Where to start?" The relation between line and syntax is unusually unsettled. In "Slate Ode," the following words are repeated across the eight stanzas and carry the semantic weight: *slate, water, language/speech, teaching, day, night, worlds*. The final stanza repeats lines from the beginning: the use of ring-composition corresponds to the conceit that an object the shape of a horseshoe can be turned into a ring and symbolically repair the breach between the prerevolutionary and postrevolutionary worlds. All forms of repetition in the poem are meant to seem like deliberate and unavoidable instances of a law of eternal return. Regular word order and parataxis are characteristic features of the other poetry he wrote in the period, especially in *Tristia*, and against these norms the manner of "The Horseshoe Finder" is a shattering of style. Here, entire sections are conceived as single sentences. The result is that more lines end where the syntax pauses, but not at the end of a sentence. Rather than instances of true enjambment, lines that continue over do so to make room for an additional phrase or word. The impression is that the form of the poem can barely contain its own content under the pressure of its own mental velocity, a formal quality well suited to the handling of the motif of centripetal and centrifugal forces that buffet the boat, the chariot, and ultimately the era.

"The Horseshoe Finder" is a work in which the free verse conduces to unpredictable repetition because its images reify discontinuity as the key to history. We can get a sense of how the poem progresses from order to fragmentation even by looking at the words positioned at the end of lines:

geometra (line 11)
korablia (line 15)
soli (line 26)
oduriashchego zapakha (line 41)
k kontsu (line 55)
inokhodtsa (line 71)
iz kremnia (line 79)
domoi (line 85)
pshenitsy (line 85)
lepeshki (line 90)

When listed this way, the words seem to index the journey the poem makes from myth to history, from a state of intoxicated movement to a primitive ending, from forward motion in mythic time to archaeological time, from one form of subsistence (e.g., a prayer for salt) to another (e.g., the find of petrified grains)—ultimately a journey that has circled back on itself. There are numerous other microstylistic elements that subtly provide threads of formal and thematic order to the poem. Against the sudden shifts, the breakdown of horizontal and vertical planes, what keeps "The Horseshoe Finder" from collapsing is its forward momentum and the presiding sense of audible consciousness that aphorism provides. This is the device Mandelstam uses to position the poet both as creator of the chaos and as the lawgiver who can chart a course forward. Individual images, often elemental, stand out line by line and are also tethered to a larger unit. As much as it relies on punctuation to underscore discrete images, Mandelstam's vatic style depends just as much on verbal repetitions within each graphic unit and across adjacent blocks and on images as building blocks. The use of a sound at the beginning of a set of lines that reverberates onward mollifies tones that sound brittle.

The final images of the poem may refuse closure and suggest that the process of loss and recovery extend indefinitely. These lines reprise the weighted symbolic language on which the poem began, but the ringing opening directive to build the ship capable of transporting poet and others to retrieve the lost object, through uneasiness and near disaster, has become more muted because success looks like a mixed picture. Objects survive but they are skeletal and wrecked, the poet continues to speak but he is at the mercy of his time. In such allegorizing, the title is a sign about the potency of poetry to preserve language and identity. Until the conclusion, the double processes of verbal and nautical creation are subjected to huge stresses as the speaker acknowledges the tensile strength and resistance of his double set of building and verbal materials. Everything in the poem from the first line intensifies the sense of the present moment and the ripening of the future. Mandelstam's mature style relies on repeated, accretive images, moments of gathering up in a larger lyric that promise clarification and deliver further intensification. It is no wonder that, well after the poem has sketched the shipbuilding plan, the speaker notes that the "air trembles with comparisons" (line 32).

When he can take a more distanced view, the speaker distills the experience of the journey and confusion into other gnomic lines: "No single word is better than another" (line 31), "The fragile calendar of our era draws to its close" (line 55), "The sound rings on, but the source of the sound is gone" (line 64). Allegorically, the Judeo-Christian narrative (metaphorized in the image of the carpenter from Bethlehem) that reassured the speaker about the survival of culture may not be sufficient for this new world. The tumult of history had registered infrequently in Mandelstam's earlier work.[14] Yet Mandelstam and history had one another in view. He faced the new reality of the Russian Revolution head-on in the great historical poems he published separately in the early Soviet press. Like Yeats, Eliot, Williams, his experience of nihilism led him to "find his own way to enter reality," to appropriate a fine formulation.[15] The name of the song, like the inscription on the coin or the image, is what vouchsafes the survival of the object from which the maker or the "I" may be disassociated. The idiom of the speaker, a student of the rockface, a metaphor for nature and history, is measured and portentous. Taken together, "Slate Ode" and "The Horseshoe Finder" contain a symbolic inventory of hidden and found objects, talismanic words, and incantatory song. Both poems are also preoccupied with a dynamic of building and destroying; remembering and forgetting transpose into the work's image system Nietzschean ideas about rebirth. The poet portrays himself as a double-dealing magus, exposed in the day to political risk and at night imbued with the spiritual elements of poetry, a figure who writes and erases at the same time.

Let us circle back to the poem's genesis. Staring into the chaos of the revolution, Mandelstam in the poems written at the time of *Tristia* sought points of cultural coherence. Other poems written between 1918 and 1923 treated the violence of revolution as history in the making and a challenge to continuity. Whatever was felt about the Bolsheviks' political program has yielded to something closer to a historiographical vision: the uncertain dialogue that "Slate Ode" stages within the self gives way to an externalized drama of the quest against a receding horizon of fulfillment. In its use of the voyage, in its evocation of poetic delirium, "The Horseshoe Finder" can again be seen as a Mandelstamian version of Rimbaud's "Bateau ivre." Inspired by a fin-de-siècle and Nietzschean vision of destruction and renewal, Mandelstam made his poetry new by writing on a larger scale about the perishability and survival of culture and the dawning of new poetic consciousness.[16] History is both actuality and a word for the process that leads to the rise and decline of civilizations. Some poems, like "The Twilight of Freedom" ("Sumerki svobody," 1918) and "The Age" ("Vek," 1918), take the reader directly into the chaos of the Russian Revolution as it unfolds, bringing to life the factionalization of politics and popular discord. "The Age" uses the image of a broken-backed monster to confront the violence needed to kill off the old. Some writings lament the damage that historical rupture and ongoing violence have done to culture and to humans. Four longer poems consider the present from different angles. "Paris" or "The Language of the Pavé" (i.e., French cobblestone; "Iazyk bulyzhnika," 1923) evokes the French Revolution as a precedent, a comparison that was fashionable in Soviet historiography at the time.[17] The poem obliquely interrogates the laws of history to see whether the past had already scripted Russia's destiny. In pondering the instability of the period, "1 January 1924" attributes to Lenin and the revolution the language and symbols of archaic religion and idol worship.

Concerned with the spiritual rebirth of what we would now call the Anthropocene, "Slate Ode" (1922) takes civilization back to prehistorical time to refashion the consciousness of a nation.[18] The poet imagines the reduction of humanity to a primitive state in which consciousness must be newly acquired, in which the poet battles unconsciously with remembered values that may no longer suit the world whose new values and codes he struggles consciously to learn. Who could see far enough into the future or into the past to predict the outcome? In "The Horseshoe Finder," when the speaker dusts off the horseshoe and contemplates the object, what will he hear, what relation of cause to effect, tenor to vehicle, object to culture, will he envisage? Omry Ronen, a pioneer of Mandelstam studies, argued that in Mandelstam's model of historical time the horseshoe stands for a process reduced to a single act, that is, the moment of contact between the horseshoe and the stone of the road.[19] The reverberation sets in motion a rhythmic sequence that cannot be unheard. Even when the horseshoe has been recovered, there is no guarantee that the sound it emitted will be heard or that the object, when recovered, understood as related to an event that gave rise to poetry. Like the horseshoe, the poet at the end of the poem is subjected to larger forces. He no longer coins the language. He is being remade by history and poetry, and his coin may have lost its value. The image of the historic coin itself recurs in Mandelstam's 1922 essay "Humanism and the Contemporary":

> The fact that the values of humanism have now become rare, as if taken out of circulation and hidden underground, is not a bad sign in itself. Humanistic values have merely withdrawn, concealed themselves like gold currency, but, like the gold reserves, they secure contemporary Europe's entire circulation of ideas, and control them the more competently for being underground.
>
> The transition to gold currency is the business of the future; and in the province of culture what lies before us is the replacement of temporary ideas—of paper banknotes—with the gold coinage of the European humanistic tradition; the magnificent florins of humanism will ring once again, but, when the moment comes, they will recognize their own day and resound like the jingling coins of common currency passing from hand to hand.[20]

That economic metaphor in which art operates as a gold standard is now symbolized in 1923 in a very different monetary context of unqualified and uncertain exchanges: copper, gold, and bronze "lie with equal honor" while the value of poetry is being milled as a new coin. There remains a hope that to recover the horseshoe, to note the imprint of its hoof on the road, is to uncover and recover a talisman to protect a humanist vision. Yet it will no longer strike sparks and its lip-shaped form does not produce new utterance. In *Stone*, the poet wondered where he could find the confidence as a fledgling writer to memorialize feeling and culture. "The Horseshoe Finder" deals with doubt that now seems to be in the fabric of culture. History accommodates the poet to its needs, dismantling poetic agency and its power to shape it.

9

Mikhail Kuzmin, “Not a governor’s lady with an officer” (1924)

EXIT GOD

Не губернаторша сидела с офицером,
Не государыня внимала ординарцу,
На золоченом, закручённом стуле
Сидела Богородица и шила.
А перед ней стоял Михал-Архангел.
О шпору шпора золотом звенела,
У палисада конь стучал копытом,
А на пригорке полотно белилось.

Архангелу Владычица сказала:
“Уж, право, я, Михайлушка, не знаю,
Что и подумать. Неудобно слуху.
Ненареченной быть страна не может.
Одними литерами не спастися.
Прожить нельзя без веры и надежды
И без царя, ниспосланного Богом.
Я женщина. Жалею и злодея.
Но этих за людей я не считаю.
Ведь сами от себя они отверглись
И от души бессмертной отказались.
Тебе предам их. Действуй справедливо.”

Умолкла, от шитья не отрываясь.
Но слезы не блеснули на ресницах,
И сумрачен стоял Михал-Архангел,
А на броне пожаром солнце рдело.

"Ну, с Богом!"—Богородица сказала,
Потом в окошко тихо посмотрела
И молвила: "Пройдет еще неделя,
И станет полотно белее снега."[1]

Not a governor's lady with an officer,
not an empress receiving an orderly,
but the Mother of God sat sewing
on a gilded elaborate chair.
And before her the Archangel Michael
was standing, his spurs ringing golden,
by the paling a horse stamped his hooves,
on the hillside linen was bleaching.

And the Lady said to the Archangel:
"Really, Michael dear, I don't know
what to think. I don't like the sound of it.
There's no place for a land that's unchristened,
no salvation in simple initials,
no living without faith, without hope,
or without a tsar sent from heaven.
I'm a woman, I feel for the wicked,
but I don't see these folk as people.
They have given up on themselves,
renounced their immortal souls.

I leave them to you. Do them justice."

She fell silent and kept on sewing.
But no tears gleamed on her lashes,
and the Archangel stood there darkly
with the sun blazing on his armour.
"So, goodbye!" said the Mother of God,
then looked quietly out of the window
and said: "Just a week from now
the linen will be whiter than snow."

(TRANSLATED BY PETER FRANCE)

Mikhail Kuzmin (1872–1936) was a writer of classical learning, aesthetic refinement, and erotic longing (and has sometimes been likened for style and sensibility to Cavafy). He published seven major collections of poetry, and, while he excelled in short forms, he also had a mastery of the architecture of the poetic cycle. The most famous example would be the *Alexandrian Songs* (1909), a lyric cycle of thirty-two poems about love, and his final book, organized as a sequence, *The Trout Breaks the Ice* (*Forel' razbivaet led*, 1929), both now canonical masterpieces of Russian modernism.[2] He wrote a pioneering queer novella, *Wings*, while living an openly gay life, an aspect he treats in the set of diaries that saw publication only from the 1990s after the collapse of the Soviet Union. Always alert to his public image and adept at cultivating an eccentric persona, Kuzmin understood that "sexual nonconformity was something of a badge in bohemian circles."[3] Early on, Kuzmin's poetry collections were greeted with acclaim by leading poets and critics (his influence on Akhmatova's early poetry is notable), whereas his late work was ignored by the Soviet press, and his diaries movingly and stoically recount his hardscrabble life after the Russian Revolution, when he was barely tolerated as a relic of the old regime.[4]

Contemporaries noted that in his person he could combine foppishness with an image of piety, playing dandy or monk, and his cultural range encompassed an eclectic mix of European writing and Russian popular and religious culture.[5] Conservative and daring, he was, like many a modernist classicist, a poet of connoisseurship and novelty. Kuzmin's cultural predilections were sophisticated and protean. Beneath the impression of great antiquity conveyed by the Hellenistic sources, the *Alexandrian Songs* subsume allusions to a range of Russian and European literature, including the poetry of Afanasy Fet, the legends of Nikolai Leskov, and the *Chansons de Bilitis* of Pierre Louÿs. His 1924 poetic collection *The New Hull* (*Novyi Gul'*) is named after a character in one of Fritz Lang's Dr. Mabuse films. In his prose, Kuzmin ably imitated eighteenth-century adventure fictions, while in *Wings* he achieved the polish of the model aesthete and student of Walter Pater. Although in so much Kuzmin looks like an aesthete, he initially greeted the revolution with the unfeigned enthusiasm of much of the intelligentsia, joining the avant-garde. His motivation was more patriotic than ideological. The overtly European sources of his writing were no bar to the long-standing devotion he felt for the tradition of Russian storytelling and art. Devoutly Orthodox, he highly valued icon painting as well as Russian folklore, tastes that carry over into his poetry.

History was not obviously the subject for a poet given to the personal angle. And yet, because his work consciously negotiates the area between order and chaos, and affirms the role of art in staving off forces of destruction that fin de siècle European culture had absorbed into decadence and into Spenglerian narratives of decline,

Kuzmin had a gift for resizing the bigger picture. He is the paradoxical poet of delicate affirmations dissolved by the encroachment of vast emptiness and of a disquiet leavened by playful irony, features that offset the historical pessimism in a work like "Not a governor's lady." Once we have entered into the confidences that draw readers into many of his lyrics, a chill or betrayal or darkness gnaws away at the intimacy, disrupts affective bonds, registers shadows closing in on light and despair engulfing what he calls the "enchantments of tender trifles" ("ocharovan'ia milykh melochei").[6]

Many poets in the period, facing their historical period as a challenge of scale, discovered an experimental energy.[7] Even as institutions and infrastructure collapsed and outcomes remained uncertain, poetry remained dynamic. Propagandistic poetry or *agitka* flourished during the revolutionary period, written by all sorts of poets, from the anonymous rabble rouser to a futurist leader like Mayakovsky (see chapter 3). Strongly structured with explosive rhymes, these poems were often marching songs or versified slogans dedicated to the socialist cause. They are in the revolution rather than about the revolution. Some poets striving to achieve the scope of epic had recourse to narrative verse. A poetic epic (*poema*) like Blok's *The Twelve* (1918) wove into its narrative of revolutionary violence, famously ending with an ambiguous messianic vision, a love plot about revenge. Its twelve lyrics, unified by plot and the recurrence of devices and motifs, offer multiple perspectives on revolution seen from the viewpoint of the unwanted clergy, uneducated recruits, a prostitute, and seemingly nature itself as a force. Like Blok, although with less success, Tsvetaeva deployed a formidable and highly complicated set of modernist devices in "Perekop," her narrative poem about the civil war, chronicling a hundred-day siege.[8] In *1905*, *Spektorsky*, and *Lieutenant Shmidt*, Boris Pasternak focalized history through the personal drama of individuals whose loves and loyalties are tested and tragically compromised by history.[9] All of these poems create diverse viewpoints. While mainly narrated in the third person, *Lieutenant Shmidt*, for example, also has sections written as letters in the first person, thereby changing perspective on the events surrounding the tragic fate of the sailor who was one of the leaders of the 1905 Sevastopol rebellion of the fleet.

Could the shorter lyric capture impressions of historic change? What capacity did lyric have for conveying disruption on the scale of the Bolshevik Revolution and its aftermath?[10] Lyric poetry that attempted to fathom the meaning of change, how it came about, and what it would mean could resort to mythemes, as we have already seen in Mandelstam's "The Horseshoe Finder," or adopt a position of epic, ironical distance focused on a single impression. Kuzmin's approach was to consider topically the ebbing away of the old from the new (an elegiac posture that the hero of his 1917 cantata *St George* also adopts). His poems often have elements of the personal diary or chronicle. For instance, the poem "Russian Revolution" (1917) takes a snapshot of the rapid changes following the collapse of the tsarist regime. Kuzmin's sharp ear and eye are preoccupied with capturing the sound and look of event, and that work produces a series of vignettes that focalize the reaction to historical violence through a single lyric speaker attuned to overheard slogans and commands, the roar of the crowd, snatches of conversation.

The poetic energy infused by the revolution would soon dissipate, and more poems which it provoked led to more difficult questions. Nikolai Bogomolov has noted that while Kuzmin's poetry had previously cultivated a distance from the contemporary world his poetic style began to change even before the revolution and that contemporary reality became decisively present.[11] "Not a governor's lady with an officer" looks at the spiritual state of a Russia abandoned by the gods after the revolution and takes a pictorial or ekphrastic approach. In Kuzmin's poetry, deities and pagan spirits or Christian saints seemed always to be present and familiar. This is especially true in his earlier work, where he seems to have one foot in the world of the ancient Mediterranean. The casual intercourse between mortal and deity typical of paganism also pervades poems about Russia open to folk religion, as in the cycle *Visions* (*Videniia*, 1916). *Russian Paradise* (*Russkii rai*), a cycle of five poems written from August 1915 into 1917, which ranges widely across the map of Russia, recalling the cities along the Volga, describing the history of tsardom, celebrating country life, and speaking in the tones of sectarian religion (there is a poem about the Khlysty, a religious sect). Altogether the poems create a picture of a country described as a "dream that is alive and distant" ("Vse tot zhe son, zhivoi i davnii").[12]

The loss of that dream, long disrupted by the revolution and civil war, is at the heart of "Not a governor's lady with an officer." Initially enthusiastic about the revolution, largely out of an aesthetic idealization of the people (*narod*), Kuzmin recorded in his diary an increasing revulsion over the violence of the Bolsheviks from the murder of Tsar Nicholas II and his family in July 1918. Nor did he see much advantage in the relative openness in the direction of literature in the aftermath of the civil war.[13] The worldview glimpsed here bears an affinity to the malaise the young Georg Lukács, an important Marxist literary theorist, had identified in his *Theory of the Novel*, first published in book form in 1920. Picking up a persistent millennial theme, Lukács memorably pronounced, "The novel is an epic of a world that has been abandoned by God."[14] Inspired by his reading of Nietzsche, Lukács observed that the reality of the novel in the modern world stood in sharp contrast to the wholeness of life depicted in ancient literature, the Homeric epics above all. Whereas the epic hero was guided by God, the modern hero was guided, if at all, by a demon or spiritual force that led the hero to live in a state of moral isolation, relying on his own subjective self, a sense of interiority, to make his way. Lukács considered that nihilism and terrorism in his own present were generated by the increasing alienation of the self. He also believed that Dostoevsky more than any other writer captured the quest of the hero to regain that wholeness. At the same time, the poem taps into a fear, widely treated in seventeenth-century popular literature, that the Virgin Mary in times of historical stress may abandon a country that has renounced its Orthodox values.

Unlike Lukács, who also, according to Galin Tihanov, saw promise in the development of a Marxist state as an objective spirit that would shape the world, Kuzmin's poem finds no such spiritual silver lining: the apostasy of God and from God defines the new order (lines 17–20):

Но этих за людей я не считаю.
Ведь сами от себя они отверглись
И от души бессмертной отказались.
Тебе предам их. Действуй справедливо

I don't see these folk as people.
They have given up on themselves,
renounced their immortal souls.
I leave them to you. Do them justice.

By 1924, the likely year of the poem's composition, the momentous historical question concerned the succession to power after the death of Lenin.[15] Mandelstam had made that uncertainty the subject of *1 January 1924*, a work of extraordinary ambivalence, which both mourns and mocks Lenin and captures anxiety about Russia's political future. For Kuzmin, the national and the spiritual were highly personal, and he opined in a short essay "Sprinters of History" that "art always was, is, and will be ahead of history and life."[16] His poetry did not aim for the metaphysical overview of history as a natural force that the nineteenth-century Slavophile poet Fedor Tiutchev achieved in the 1870s; nor did Kuzmin explore the impact of the Russian Revolution on poetic consciousness that Mandelstam fathomed in the early 1920s. The causes and effects of history were matters to be registered anecdotally rather than pondered theoretically. Like Blok, he hoped the revolution would finally bridge the gap between the elite and the *narod*.

"Not a governor's lady with an officer" responds to the state of the nation with humorous grace and suppressed bitterness. The center of the poem is a conversation between two of the mainstays of Russian Orthodoxy, the Mother of God and the Archangel Michael, whose potency became increasingly precarious in the newly atheistic state of the Soviet Union. In Russian Orthodoxy, the Mother of God was venerated as an intercessionary deity who, it was believed, would protect both Church and country and, above all, the Russian people. The Archangel Michael, one of the Bodiless Powers valued by Eastern Orthodoxy, was venerated as the Archistrategos or the Supreme Commander in Byzantine and Russian religion. His function was to be a leader of an army of angels against Satan and any un-Christian forces. A popular subject of icon painters, he had his own church in the Kremlin complex in Moscow, built originally in the thirteenth century. In one of the grandest of all Russian icons, known as the *The Church Militant,* depicting the Russian conquest of the city of Kazan, the Archangel Michael is shown accompanying Ivan IV while the Mother of God looks on.

The blessed space depicted in the poetic canvas ekphrastically seems laid out like the design of an icon. Normally in painting the Bogoroditsa is depicted in a three-quarter portrait. If she is ever shown at full length, it is usually in the Ascension to Heaven or in the Dormition, when her earthly body is laid out prostrate to be washed for burial. When she is shown seated, there is normally some type of architectural surround rather than this minimalist image, and the poem is in keeping with the suggestion that she passes the time in domestic chores. There are Western paintings of the Virgin shown sewing swaddling cloth or spinning fabric or even knitting during her pregnancy. These canvases are paintings though, and not objects of worship. Orthodoxy did not permit secular painting of the Trinity. Icons depict the Virgin holding the infant Christ in a variety of poses (cradled in her arms, nestled in her lap, held upright). The space of worship established between the icon and the viewer establishes its own dimension. In line 8, the word *polotno* has a double meaning. The word signifies both a swatch of linen left to bleach in the sun for use as an embroidery cloth and also the canvas on which an icon is painted. Each is relevant to the religious context and the referential context as the latter points outside the icon represented by the poem to an eternal Christian continuum outside the new Soviet religious space.

The poem glances away from that continuum toward a process taking place in time framed and kept at a distance. In Kuzmin's version of an icon, the perspective does not provide the usual symbols of elevation, such as heaven and clouds, or a radiant nimbus. Instead of heavenly trappings, we find only the linen. In fact, the symbols of a new state religion and Bolshevik cult were everywhere to be seen, and nowhere more monumental than in the display of a new god. While the mausoleum to Lenin was not opened until 1930, Lenin's body was preserved and displayed on Red Square from shortly after his death, first in a wooden hut and then in a mausoleum designed by Aleksei Shchusev to imitate an Egyptian pyramid. From the very start, the site attracted long lines of citizens paying homage to the founder of the new state. This was a cultic site that confirmed that a new god had displaced the old.

Rejected as they are by these new principles, the Mother of God and Archangel do not swallow their pride, but may decide themselves to withdraw from a people they no longer view as deserving. In fact, the establishment of atheism and materialist philosophy as state dogma unfolded in several phases, the trend that stands behind the poem's sense of disenchantment. Measures taken after the Tenth Party Congress in 1921 concentrated on suppressing the clergy and executing the Church hierarchy, confiscating Church valuables, excluding from the Party any traditional believers, and outlining a process of popular reeducation. A first official antireligious campaign, waged between 1921 and 1928, had the goal of declaring a materialist worldview as an ideological tenet of the state; the second phase that followed and lasted until the early 1940s took a hard line on the mass reeducation of the population, culminating in 1929 with new legislation to educate the population in atheism and to strictly ban religious activity. In this first phase, whose context effectively forms the background to the poem, the priority of the state was on discouraging traditional belief rather than outlawing it or inculcating a new religious ideology, achieved in part by fostering agnosticism and a materialist outlook. The Orthodox Church and its leaders were targeted for persecution, and Patriarch Tikhon of Moscow, affirming his loyalty to the new state on several occasions, declared that the Church was politically neutral.[17]

To return to our poem, it appears that, while the poem visually positions its foreground and background like an icon, its content inverts the usual process of veneration. In the theory of icon veneration, the viewer, by concentrating on the gaze of the silent figures, will enter into a direct relationship with the deity. That spiritual connection is a moment of communion and elevation of the human viewer onto a divine plane. In this poem, the hallowed figures are not shown in their typical saintly or heroic roles, mute and outside history. Within the superficial impression of a fixed frame, the two stanzas containing their conversation, Archangel and Virgin are engaged in pondering the present, shown like the gods in a Homeric epic considering their role in the affairs of humans. Irony and poise mark how they chat, questioning whether they have any role at all. In a single stroke of negation ("Not . . . not . . . but"), Kuzmin notes that the figures of the old political class are now defunct and irrelevant to the question that will be the topic of conversation—the question of what has befallen Russia. That conversation will happen at the highest level between the Mother of God and the Archangel; yet the question of their authority and relevance is the essential problem they face. With all the old verities and pieties swept away, they, too, must consider the possibility that they are destined to go the way of the governor's wife and the empress or tsarina, and become as outmoded as the fancy chair on which the Mother of God sits. A struggle has begun between their role in preserving Russia's historic status as an Orthodox kingdom and the Soviet Union's establishment of communism and socialist consciousness as its doctrinal belief. It is no wonder that the Mother of God feels consternation and is torn between her role in perpetuating Orthodoxy and her frank acknowledgment that the new historic context is inimical to its survival.

Every reader will respond to the work's comic pathos and its sheer human element, enhanced by the modest, colloquial language and choppy phrases underpinned by a consistent iambic pentameter.[18] The use of end-stopping more than enjambment confers on the conversation a poised effect and also provides distinctness to the pictorial effects. Each line seems weighted, no more so than at the start of the second section, where the use of caesura and assonance, extraverbal effects that are hard to translate, moves away from the reported speech of the previous paragraph and gives rhetorical weight: "She fell silent and kept on sewing" (*Umolkla, ot shit'ia ne otryvaias'*, line 21).

The poem makes a point of being accessible, avoiding the mystery of religion. Colloquial syntax and intonation convey the impression of conversation, as does the highly familiar use of the diminutive for the Archangel's name, Mikhailushka, endearingly used ("Michael dear" in the translation). The Archangel stands out of respect and may be poised to fulfill her command as the conversation finishes:

Уж, право, я, Михайлушка, не знаю,
Что и подумать. Неудобно слуху.
Ненареченной быть страна не может.
Одними литерами не спастися.

"Really, Michael dear, I don't know
what to think. I don't like the sound of it.
There's no place for a land that's unchristened,
no salvation in simple initials.

He hears out an expression of consternation in which the Virgin equates her own fall from grace with the country's uncertain position since the Soviet Union remained officially unrecognized: the United States took until 1933 although others such as the United Kingdom and Italy engaged earlier. A country is not merely a name or acronym (the literal translation of lines 13–14 is "A country cannot be unchristened. There is no salvation only in letters"). What is the status of the Virgin in this brave new world, and is she only a mortal woman? What is Russia without Orthodoxy? There is the societal issue around what constitutes an inhabitable political territory, on the one hand, and the existential reality of dwelling within the spiritual order, on the other. Given the apostasy from Orthodoxy, the phrase is more a metaphor for the country's alienation from the Christian world to which it belonged. A consequence of this will be the country's forfeiture of the divine grace formerly accorded by the Mother of God, and that is the matter under discussion. What is her responsibility? Down to earth and realistic, she reassesses the nature of her commitment and finds that she is caught as a traditional figure of caritas between feeling pity and abandoning the country that has abandoned her. She is also at least here a figure of female pride, becoming huffy when she considers that she has been rejected as a woman. In turn and perhaps out of spite, she concludes that people who have repudiated themselves (line 12) are not people she can endorse: they are beyond salvation since they have renounced their immortal soul. And with that she cedes to the Archangel, trusting that his actions, whether they are defensive or punitive, will be just.

If her withdrawal from action is not, in the end, a withdrawal of sympathy, her dismay is clear. In general, the use of more versified conversation is one of the striking aspects of Kuzmin's poetry from 1925, including later cycles like *Northern Fan* (*Severnyi veer*) and *The Trout Breaks the Ice*. Characters are always talking to one another (and sometimes themselves), posing questions, answering, exclaiming, singing. The interview of Archangel and Mother of God lacks the rapid reaction time of exchange because, like an icon, it is static, and because the two figures ruminate on their predicament. Yet gesture and small details are vital to the story here. Unlike a painting, a poem can create a moment of silence. The pause at the start of the third section is full of ominous negation. Despite her profession of sympathy, the Virgin does not weep for Russia, and, whether she continues her sewing out of indifference or anger, she wishes to make a show of her resolve to the Archangel. He may look blazing as the sun is reflected off his armor, but his mood is dark. Her brusque phrase can mean "good luck!" as much as "goodbye"—a valediction as well as a dismissal. The Virgin does not mobilize her foot soldier, nor does she contest or resist verbally. Her gaze is already pointing outward toward the world of history, from which they had temporarily retreated. In a world in which God is dead, the Mother of God now looks like an ordinary woman whose laundry is just outside drying. But, as a divine figure, she stands in Christian time outside the real world in some eternal space. This "linen" (*polotno*) is the canvas on which history is now being written or painted, a new canvas for a new world in which neither the Virgin nor the Archangel Michael will be represented. The whiteness of snow here is not a metaphor for innocence; rather it is an acknowledgment of the degree of erasure of the old that a new utopia requires.

10

Vladimir Nabokov, "Lilith" (1928)

DECADENT REVERIE

Лилит

Я умер. Яворы и ставни
горячий теребил Эол
вдоль пыльной улицы.
    Я шел,
и фавны шли, и в каждом фавне
я мнил, что Пана узнаю:
"Добро, я, кажется, в раю".

От солнца заслонясь, сверкая
подмышкой рыжею, в дверях
вдруг встала девочка нагая
с речною лилией в кудрях,
стройна, как женщина, и нежно
цвели сосцы - и вспомнил я
весну земного бытия,
когда из-за ольхи прибрежной
я близко-близко видеть мог,
как дочка мельника меньшая
шла из воды, вся золотая,
с бородкой мокрой между ног.

И вот теперь, в том самом фраке,
в котором был вчера убит,
с усмешкой хищною гуляки
я подошел к моей Лилит.
Через плечо зеленым глазом
она взглянула - и на мне
одежды вспыхнули и разом

испепелились.
    В глубине
был греческий диван мохнатый,
вино на столике, гранаты,
и в вольной росписи стена.
Двумя холодными перстами
по-детски взяв меня за пламя:
"Сюда- промолвила она.
Без принужденья, без усилья,
лишь с медленностью озорной,
она раздвинула, как крылья,
свои коленки предо мной.
И обольстителен и весел
был запрокинувшийся лик,
и яростным ударом чресел
я в незабытую проник.
Змея в змее, сосуд в сосуде,
к ней пригнанный, я в ней скользил,
уже восторг в растущем зуде
неописуемый сквозил,-
как вдруг она легко рванулась,
отпрянула и, ноги сжав,
вуаль какую-то подняв,
в нее по бедра завернулась,
и, полон сил, на полпути
к блаженству, я ни с чем остался
и ринулся и зашатался
от ветра странного. "Впусти-
я крикнул, с ужасом заметя,
что вновь на улице стою
и мерзко блеющие дети
глядят на булаву мою.
"Впусти- и козлоногий, рыжий
народ все множился. "Впусти же,
иначе я с ума сойду!"
Молчала дверь. И перед всеми
мучительно я пролил семя
и понял вдруг, что я в аду.[2]

Lilith

I died. The sycamores and shutters
along the dusty street were teased
by torrid Aeolus.
    I walked,
and fauns walked, and in every faun
god Pan I seemed to recognize:
Good. I must be in Paradise.
Shielding her face and to the sparkling sun
showing a russet armpit, in a doorway
there stood a naked little girl.
She had a water lily in her curls
and was as graceful as a woman. Tenderly
her nipples bloomed, and I recalled
the springtime of my life on earth,
when through the alders on the river brink
so very closely I could watch
the miller's youngest daughter as she stepped
out of the water, and she was all golden,
with a wet fleece between her legs.
And now, still wearing the same dress coat
that I had on when killed last night,
with a rake's predatory twinkle,
toward my Lilith I advanced.
She turned upon me a green eye
over her shoulder, and my clothes
were set on fire and in a trice
dispersed like ashes.
    In the room behind
one glimpsed a shaggy Greek divan,
on a small table wine, pomegranates,
and some lewd frescoes covering the wall.
With two cold fingers childishly
she took me by her emberhead:
"now come along with me," she said.
Without inducement, without effort,
just with the slowness of pert glee,

like wings she gradually opened
her pretty knees in front of me.
And how enticing, and how merry,
her upturned face! And with a wild
lunge of my loins I penetrated
into an unforgotten child.
Snake within snake, vessel in vessel,
smooth-fitting part, I moved in her
through ascending itch forefeeling
unutterable pleasure stir.
But suddenly she lightly flinched,
retreated, drew her legs together,
and grasped a veil and twisted it
around herself up to the hips,
and full of strength, at half the distance
to rapture, I was left with nothing.
I hurtled forward. A strange wind
caused me to stagger. "Let me in!"
I shouted, noticing with horror
that I again stood outside in the dust
and that obscenely bleating youngsters
were staring at my pommelled lust.
"Let me in!" And the goat-hoofed,
copper-curled crowd increased. "Oh, let me in,"
I pleaded, "otherwise I shall go mad!"
The door stayed silent, and for all to see
writhing with agony I spilled my seed
and knew abruptly that I was in Hell.[1]

(TRANSLATED BY VLADIMIR NABOKOV)

Vladimir Nabokov himself dated his awareness of his artistic consciousness to the composition of his first poem. His output in verse numbers at least one thousand poems, about half written in Russian.[3] The largest cluster dates to early in his career, from the late 1910s to early 1920s. In 1916 he brought out the plainly named *Poems* (*Stikhi*), containing sixty-eight poems mainly on the theme of early love. Few of these were to survive for republication in his next collections, beginning with *The*

Cluster (*Grozd'*, 1922) and *The Empyrean Path* (*Gornii put'*, 1923). In 1929 a book of short stories appeared under the title of its lead work, *The Return of Chorb,* also including twenty-four poems culled from the poetry he wrote between 1926 and 1928. *Poems 1929–1951* (*Stikhotvoreniia 1929–1951*), published in 1952, was the last all-Russian poetry collection he oversaw. He later published new poems in English as well as translations, culminating in his final *Poems and Problems* of 1970. In 1979, after his death, a further volume of Russian poems was seen into print by Vera Nabokov, his widow.

Even from early on, Nabokov's success as a novelist outstripped recognition for his poetry. Yet the fact that Nabokov's poetry in Russian and in English has earned less critical attention and popular acclaim partly reflects the history of publication.[4] Detractors from as early as the 1920s, put off by the perception that the poems were stylish but unfeeling, have tended to appreciate the skillful versification technique and purity of language that pleased his admirers.[5] His decision at the end of his career to publish lyrics alongside chess problems only confirmed a stereotype of Nabokov as the highly cerebral and unfeeling artist, a charge that Nabokov may have been attempting to parry, sincerely or not, when he wrote that poetry and chess problems shared qualities of invention, harmony, conciseness, and "splendid insincerity."[6]

His favorite topics, expressed exquisitely in classic Russian verse forms, were poetic inspiration, the seasons, and memory, and there was also room for familiar modernist motifs in poems about the airplane, telephone, cinema ("Kinematograf"), and trains ("Express"). In the mid- to late 1920s, the poems, including "Lilith," became the vehicle for a new theme concerning altered states of being. These poems represent the theme of paradise lost, in which paradise might be defined not only as a homeland—many other poems treated Russia nostalgically—but also as a state of innocence that has been corrupted, a familiar topic from Baudelaire well into fin de siècle writing, including the Russian symbolists. The poem "Paradise" ("Rai"), composed in 1925, overtly contrasts Russia remembered from Nabokov's youth as an Eden from which the speaker has been exiled and declares that "The world of this picture is deathless."[7] "In Paradise" ("V raiu," 1927) features an eccentric "provincial naturalist" who, lost amid a museum of objects (pupae, roses, tears), discovers that the afterlife is the image of his time on earth. By contrast, the explicit sex act depicted in "Lilith" looks inimical to a poem such as "White Paradise" ("Belyi rai," 1921), in which an "empty land" extends an "icy net" to a "blissfully happy" dreamer.

"Lilith" was first published in *Poems and Problems,* more than forty years after Nabokov wrote it "to entertain a friend" at a time when, as Nabokov knew, publishing a work of such near explicitness would have been difficult. While it might have been tolerable in prose as an exercise in European decadence, a lyric was bound to be offensive to prevailing tastes of the Russian émigré community, which regarded poetry as sacrosanct.[8] The English translation only aggravates the sense of taboo. In the Russian, Lilith is dubbed "unforgotten" (*nezabytaia*), glossing the way she continues to haunt the speaker either posthumously or when he awakens from the oneiric world of the poem. The English version departs by referring to her as an "unforgotten child." This may be one of the details that explain the tendency of the critical literature to consider the poem mainly as a stage on the way to *Lolita*, written twenty years later. Nabokov teased the reader by warning off any attempts to establish a connection to "his later prose," meaning at least *Lolita* and possibly also *Ada*, works in which the taboos of pedophilia and incest are central.[9] Our view is that the narrative skill with which the poem handles the speaker's psycho-sexual trauma, its treatment of a number of intertexts, and its explicit acts of desire inimical to the unearthly musings of other works make it a mature work rather than early precursor. "Lilith" has a psychological complexity, situational mystery, and seedy eroticism comparable to the novels Nabokov wrote in his Berlin period. "Lilith" is also about innocence lost and features a vision of the afterlife cast as a lurid drama of sexual agony stylized in the decadent manner of a Beardsley. It is strikingly prurient and stands out even among the work of émigré poets of a racier stripe.[10] Sexual excitement, oneiric presentiment, and echoes of the aestheticism of the 1890s fuse powerfully. Poised between bliss and disgust, it shows Nabokov uncovering labyrinthine depths closely associated with modernism.[11]

Within its dreamwork feel, Nabokov's poem archly pretends to be describing a scene that could have happened. The poem's temporal structure adds richness and ambiguity to how we understand the speaker's confused or at least unstable state of mind. The speaker opens by declaring his death, as the narrative moves into an antecedent time frame. Is the speaker alive or dead, that is, awake in the afterlife or in a dream? These two possibilities—and the further possibility that "death" here metaphorically refers to sexual exhaustion—merge indistinctly, presenting the reader with alternative and complementary scenarios. Either the monologue represents a posthumous vision of the afterlife or a dream state in which the speaker apprehends that he is dead; and, by corollary, either the monologue precedes the action that unfolds in a dream narrative or the action of the poem in fact loops back to the opening declaration and possibly a moment of awakening from sleep into consciousness.

Mythically, Nabokov's Lilith is a descendant of the biblical demon and, according to some sources, Adam's first wife. However, his heroine and the poem's landscape also take their literary pedigree from Mallarmé's "Afternoon of a Faun"

("L'après-midi d'un faune"), a poem that not only became a classic of symbolist verse but in 1912 was choreographed and danced by the Ballets Russes, set to the music of Debussy. In the first line of Mallarmé's poem, before the faun recounts his dream-like tale of the memories of his meeting with nymphs, he says, "These nymphs, I would like to perpetuate them."[12] The scene became notorious after Nijinsky's balletic impersonation of the faun caused a sensation for its explicit onanism: his faun pleasures himself on top of a veil abandoned by the nymphs he encountered in the glade, just as Nabokov's speaker will also attain climax after his encounter with Lilith. Thomas Karshan notes that "L'après-midi," in which a faun-artist dreams of two nymphs, one of whom he possesses and one who slips away from him just before orgasm, haunts many of Nabokov's later novels by "its aesthetic and metaphysical indeterminacy, its exquisite symbolist play of language, and its correspondingly intense eroticism."[13]

Nabokov's poem responds by condensing the French original's more convoluted psychological situation into the brutally direct opening that still retains an air of reverie. By "I died" the speaker may mean "I saw that I had died" as in a dream, in which case the poem is being recounted later by a speaker who has woken up; alternatively, the content of the poem is a vision of the afterlife, a reading that can look to the statement by Mallarmé's faun, who asks whether he "loved a dream" and ponders the afterglow of a fantasy, and also finds on his breast a "mysterious bite." Mallarmé's poem hints that the kiss sought by the dreamer may be a "taste of evil," and the rapturous evocation of flesh contains bruises and a "secret terror."[14] Sensuous delight entails transgression, yet antiquity conveys a patina of innocence. The certainty of punishment threatened for this erotic fantasy is broken off.

While Nabokov's poem preserves both Mallarmé's nymphs and his poem's structure, "Lilith" also inverts much of Mallarmé's scenario, shifting decisively away from remembered bliss toward a grotesque, highly decadent evocation. The encounter is cast as a transition from adolescence, marked by the narrator's original infatuation with the miller's daughter, to sexed adulthood, leaving behind the "springtime of my life on earth" for full exposure to female sexuality. The seeds of Persephone, and her chthonic status symbolized in the fruit, provide one hint at the hellish underside of this vision. Another hint comes in the reference to the god Pan, a figure associated with the Dionysian frenzy of fauns and satyrs in esoteric literature and a double for Mallarmé's faun.[15] Regret, near-obscenity, and monstrosity replace bliss, tact, and beauty—but not immediately, and the psychological drama of the poem lies in the way it charts a loss of paradise (line 7), unfolding from the first a false impression of bliss staged in the first block of lines. The encounter with a naked maiden combines mythic and vulgar features. Memory or literature-inspired dreamwork transform a perhaps real-life encounter with a streetwalker into a halcyon recollection of the miller's daughter, a figure reminiscent of Blok's "Unknown Woman," a symbolist emanation of erotic desire by one of Nabokov's favorite poets at the time.[16] Consistent with the dream state and the fluid nature of dream language, a further set of three metamorphoses occur in the poem: the transition from life to death; the maturation from maiden to woman; and the word "lily" that prefigures and even triggers the appearance of Lilith. In addition to the influence of Blok, this reworking compounds Mallarmé with the influence of Pushkin's play in verse *Rusalka,* the source of the figure of the miller and the Russian water sprite. Lilith is part Rusalka, part Lorelei, one of the underwater sirens of German and Russian myth. Such sorceresses were fatal to Pushkin's hunter as well as to Mallarmé's faun, whose death stands for orgasm.

From line 8, Nabokov's evocation of his femme fatale is set off typographically. Its single sentence is nested in clauses and subclauses organized by the regular use of alternating rhyme, an effect that is repeated from line 39. The whole section reads like a single twelve-line stanza. Everything here is tenderly described and voiced, and these lines more than any other part of the poem are crafted melodiously, perfectly cadenced line by line in their balancing of vowels and delicate repetition of single and paired hard and soft consonants (as in *tsveli/sostsy, zhenshchina/nezhno, vdrug/vstala*). Nabokov's intertextuality is rarely without complication. The verse form of "Lilith" is Pushkin's signature iambic tetrameter. The repeated use of enjambment and constant change of rhyme scheme (abbacc, ababcddceffe, etc.) seem to bury that connection with Pushkin intentionally in a very different soundscape, making the poem sound like a piece of "foreign" poetry that has been Russianized. The formal effect further defamiliarizes both Mallarmé and Pushkin.

However, the ostentatious euphony of the verse line and delicacy of expression do not divert from the speaker's salacious attention to Lilith's mature breasts, her armpits, and her sex. Yet, perhaps because he remains suspended between two states, there is a gap between what the eye sees and his inner train of thought. At the beginning of this section, the maiden is shielded from the sun. In his story of Actaeon, the mythic hunter who ignores warnings and looks directly at the goddess Artemis when she bathes in the river, Ovid compares viewing the naked goddess to staring at the sun, and blindness will be the penalty. Here, like Actaeon, the Peeping Tom of a speaker approaches and initiates the intense sexual encounter, dying a second time.

At line 20, the transition from innocence to corruption and to an escalation of the eroticism is strongly demarcated in the Russian. The phrase "And at this very moment" (*I vot teper'*) is omitted in the English, which moves directly into a description of a new space. This passage sees the object of desire change from the innocent young girl and miller's daughter of remembered reality into an underworld goddess or from the lily/Lily to Lilith. Mallarmé uses the switch in voices between a controlling narrator and long snatches of song from other voices to interrupt the plot of the remembered episode and cast it in doubt.[17] Nabokov, by contrast, seizes on effects of garish explicitness, mingling clumsy slang and euphemism. In no more than a flash of her "green eye," she seduces the highly sexed speaker, and with "two cold fingers" grabs his "flame." While the hero of Mallarmé's poem achieves a climax exquisitely in his fantasy dreamscape, the oversexed hero of Nabokov's work flaunts his masculinity—the word *bulava* is boastful—and bridles against restraints on his sexuality.

When the speaker penetrates the female ("snake within snake"), her monstrous transformation into full-blown Lilith is underway. Wrapped in her embrace, he sees a prostitute, an innocent maiden (albeit not necessarily a child), and at the point of consummation a writhing she-devil who ultimately destroys sexual pleasure. This is what makes Lilith a figure of demonic horror. Nabokov stays close to the morbidity and perversity self-consciously fetishized in the decadent aesthetic.

The poem began with a breath of wind, and in its final part a "strange wind" troubles the speaker. He is on the brink of disaster as intercourse with Lilith, a night figure cursed by angels, associated with monstrosity and shape-shifting, precipitates a fall from a state of grace into despair. As the female swoons in his embrace, shameless and deliberate, he responds to the pleasure through the language of sin and biblical violation. Male and female are not lover and beloved: each is now a serpent, an emblem of original sin, and the more they sin the greater the desire ("unutterable pleasure"). When the delirious subject in the demonic possession approaches the moment of climax, characterized with a normally religious word as "rapture" (*blazhenstvo*), the tension between the sinful and the religious explodes. In throwing back her veil, Lilith reveals the sins of the imagination. Despite the characterization of her depravity the poem does not offer us sordid obscenity and focuses sinuously on the consciousness of pleasure and frustration.[18] She defensively clothes her nudity and recoils from the sexual act at the most intense moment of sensation.

As the speaker awakens from the dream to the reality of his frustration, bliss and horror dovetail across a single line. The fullness of his potency flips over into emptiness at the halfway point to bliss. His awakening is from death into life, or a dream into reality. Is it also from hedonism into guilt? The final lines, extraordinary for their degree of self-revulsion, may reinforce the impression that from the dream-like main narrative sequence he has awakened into a secondary dream or nightmare. Described as "goat-hoofed" and "obscenely bleating," the people vent a prurient interest in his uncontrolled ejaculation, a scene that parallels Mallarmé's narrative of arousal.[19] At the end, the speaker confronts the impossibility of joining the

Dionysian crowd of fauns and nymphs and entering into a Nietzschean true world in which the soul drifts away from earthly reality. The tantalizing vision of sexual utopia, even after death, turns into a scene of mockery. Is there an element of guilt and punishment here? The phrase "to spill seed on earth" is close to the Russian Bible's formula for Onan ("izlivat' semia v zemliu").[20]

By definition, decadence is "permeated with a sense of loss," and that loss is felt most acutely at a moment of surfeit.[21] In "Lilith," the speaker's plight is typical of a dialectic of grace and shame that has been identified as a feature of fin de siècle decadence. The forfeiture of paradise and the shameful loss of innocence guide consciousness here.[22] The exploration of the afterlife of the soul, or alternatively the dream life of the unconscious, has revealed the power of poetry to plumb the depths of shame and to reveal the close affinity between beauty and spiritual abjection, and otherworldly vision and "exquisite depravity," Verlaine's phrase for a widely held view.[23] The crowd who shame the speaker are more satyrs than people. Far from displaying innocence and moral disapproval, their goat-like nature is a manifestation of sexual animalism also associated with Lilith and widely attested in French and English decadent literature from the 1890s.[24] In that same context, postcoital emission after sex with Lilith was seen to connote sterility.

The judgment of the émigré literary scholar Gleb Struve originally made in 1956, just on the cusp of the fame *Lolita* brought Nabokov, remains much quoted, namely that "his poems are the poems of a prose writer."[25] To the view that many of his poems were versified prose works was added the perception that Nabokov was highly derivative. His models were second-tier poets of an art-for-art's-sake bent like Khodasevich (see chapter 5).[26] This dependence on (or loyalty to) dated themes, combined with technical conservatism largely closed to the prosodic innovations of Russian poetry from the modernist period, occasioned the criticism that, unlike the novels of the émigré years in which their European location and ambiance were fully realized, Nabokov's poetry created a nostalgic world screened from the present reality by an ultra-aestheticism.

Arguably "Lilith" both supports and defies these limitations. From Nabokov's poetic oeuvre it stands out for two reasons. The first, more minor, reason concerns Nabokov's own development. The poem can be read as a bridge to the erotic obsessions key to the plots of his Berlin novels in the 1930s, in which the boundary between permissible erotic reverie and carnal disaster is explored. The poem therefore follows the direction of his prose works toward psychological complexity in its use of dream narrative and techniques of defamiliarization.

The second lies in the poem's distinction as an example of decadent verse. However belated it may seem to be as an experiment with a modernist set of tropes,

Nabokov's engagement with decadence was more than a flirtation of the émigré period pastiching fin de siècle tropes. This Nabokovian wet dream, stylized in the manner of Pushkin, Mallarmé, and Beardsley, may have a double status in relation to Nabokov's creative development from the late 1920s. The poem may look like a throwback to an earlier period of Nabokov's youthful interest in symbolism and Mallarmé in particular. Yet it also keys into a newer theme of disenchantment, nowhere more poignantly treated than in "Elegy" (1921) by Khodasevich, one of Nabokov's favorite poets. "Elegy" notes the withdrawal of poetry from the violence of the Russian Revolution. As in "Lilith," there is wind and there may also be a trace of Aeolus since there are harps making music. The principal female figure in Khodasevich's poem is the poet's Muse, and she is also dual in nature, beloved of him but increasingly estranged from the new world. He refers to her as a "female exile" (*izgnannitsa*) because she rejects a mob that raves "in its triviality." At the end of the poem, the poetic speaker admits that he cannot find a common language with this new reality, and he cannot imagine, as Khodasevich's concluding lines indicate,

> what she will be like in spirit
> In what paradise, in what hell.[27]

We have seen that there are multiple sources to Nabokov's work, and that he effortlessly recombined them. There is no obligation to read "Lilith" as an allegory about poetry or exile—often those themes receive their separate treatment in Nabokov's work. But, if there is any debt to Khodasevich, it is in a lesson he gave on how to flip rapidly from beauty to ugliness and from enchantment to tragedy. Both poems enact a journey from paradise to hell, and Nabokov's narration seems to spool out of the aphoristic compression of Khodasevich's final line in which hell and paradise are joined.

The perennial question for many readers about Nabokov from the 1950s was whether he hid his emotions or simply had no emotions at all. Artifice and the creation of art for art's sake pointed away from the human condition, toward words and literary play pursued for its own sake. Yet Nabokov is a contemporary of the French existentialists, and, while he was certainly not a kindred spirit artistically, the interwar period conditioned Nabokov, as it did them, to feel instability and the possibility of inner chaos. There is also in Nabokov's studies a persistent view that, underneath the surface brilliance, is a spiritual immanence and its earthly shadow. Few lines could be both more mundane and more fantastic than the opening of the main section: "I walked / and fauns walked." That existential equivocation will remain throughout the poem. If we shift our gaze from the spectacle of the poem as a prequel to *Lolita*, we may see here a precocious instance of Nabokov's fascination with *potustoronnost'* or the world beyond, a nebulous concept theologically and metaphysically latent with a spiritual open-endedness motivated by regret for "the springtime of my life on earth."[28] Other elements in "Lilith" raise the possibility that the speaker, like a good decadent and symbolist, follows the mind in the act of entering a dreamscape, playing with sleep as a death and awakening into an altered state of consciousness.

And even if a sense of yearning in Nabokov's art, early and mature, largely applies to the theme of Russia and childhood as a lost paradise, "Lilith" is the fullest realization of the aim he had for his verse art of making a short poem contain a plot and tell a story.[29] In this period, and later, Nabokov consistently felt that "the fabula is just as essential to a poem as to a novel."[30] Jonathan Culler has commented that one of the poetic powers is to create a resistance to the disenchantment of the world.[31] Nabokov's achievement has been to create a narrative that encompasses both prosaic and poetic states at the same time, enchantment as well as flight from it.

11

Daniil Kharms, "Myr" / "The Werld" (1930)

I THINK THEREFORE . . .

Мыр

Я говорил себе, что я вижу мир. Но весь мир недоступен моему взгляду, и я видел только части мира. И все, что я видел, я называл частями мира. И я наблюдал свойства этих частей, и, наблюдая свойства частей, я делал науку. Я понимал, что есть умные свойства частей и есть не умные свойства в тех же частях. Я делил их и давал им имена. И в зависимости от их свойств, части мира были умные и не умные.

И были такие части мира, которые могли думать. И эти части смотрели на другие части и на меня. И все части были похожи друг на друга, и я был похож на них.

Я говорил: части гром.

Части говорили: пук времени.

Я говорил: Я тоже часть трех поворотов.

Части отвечали: Мы же маленькие точки.

И вдруг я перестал видеть их, а потом и другие части. И я испугался, что рухнет мир.

Но тут я понял, что я не вижу частей по отдельности, а вижу все зараз.

Сначала я думал, что это НИЧТО. Но потом понял, что это мир, а то, что я видел раньше, был не мир.

И я всегда знал, что такое мир, но, что я видел раньше, я не знаю и сейчас.

И когда части пропали, то их умные свойства перестали быть умными, и их неумные свойства перестали быть неумными. И весь мир перестал быть умным и неумным.

Но только я понял, что я вижу мир, как я перестал его видеть. Я испугался, думая, что мир рухнул. Но пока я так думал, я понял, что если бы рухнул мир, то я бы так уже не думал. И я смотрел, ища мир, но не находил его.

А потом и смотреть стало некуда.

Тогда я понял, что, покуда было куда смотреть,—вокруг меня был мир. А теперь его нет. Есть только я.

А потом я понял, что я и есть мир.

Но мир—это не я.

Хотя в то же время я мир.

А мир не я.

А я мир.

А мир не я.

А я мир.

А мир не я.

А я мир.

И больше я ничего не думал.[1]

The Werld

I told myself that I see the world. But the whole world was not accessible to my gaze, and I saw only parts of the world. And everything that I saw I called parts of the world. And I examined the properties of these parts and, examining these properties, I wrought science. I understood that the parts have intelligent properties and that the same parts have unintelligent properties. I distinguished them and gave them names. And, depending on their properties, the parts of the world were intelligent or unintelligent.

And there were such parts of the world which could think. And these parts looked upon me and upon the other parts. And all these parts resembled one another, and I resembled them. And I spoke with these parts.

I said: parts thunder.

The parts said: a clump of time.

I said: I am also part of the three turns.

The parts answered: and we are little dots.

And suddenly I ceased seeing them and, soon after, the other parts as well. And I was frightened that the world would collapse.

But then I understood that I do not see the parts independently, but I see it all at once. At first I thought that it was NOTHING. But then I understood that this was the world and what I had seen before was not the world.

And I had always known what the world was, but what I had seen before I do not know even now.

And when the parts disappeared their intelligent properties ceased being intelligent, and their unintelligent properties ceased being unintelligent. And the whole world ceased to be intelligent and unintelligent.

But as soon as I understood that I saw the world, I ceased seeing it. I became frightened, thinking that the world had collapsed. But while I was thinking this, I realized that had the world collapsed then I would already not be thinking this. And I watched, looking for the world, but not finding it.

And soon after there wasn't anywhere to look.

Then I realized that since before there was somewhere to look—there had been a world around me. And now it's gone. There's only me.

And then I realized that I am the world.

But the world—is not me.

Although at the same time I am the world.

But the world's not me.

And I'm the world.

But the world's not me.

And I'm the world.

But the world's not me.

And I'm the world.

And after that I didn't think anything more.[2]

(TRANSLATED BY EUGENE OSTASHEVSKY WITH MATVEI YANKELEVICH)

Daniil Kharms (1905–42), originally best known in Soviet Russia as a children's writer, has since the 1990s become appreciated at home and abroad for a highly innovative legacy of poetry, prose, and dramatic works. His influence has been especially felt in settings and adaptations for absurdist theatrical production.[3] Born as Daniil Iuvachev into an intellectual family of revolutionary-minded gentry, he took the pen name of Kharms, a word of mysterious origin and typical of his playfulness. Several etymologies have been proposed. Most convincing of all is the suggestion that the word mixes the English words "charms" and "harms," while also playing on an actual German surname Harms and deliberately evoking

Sherlock Holmes through the close proximity of the Russian pronunciation Kholmes (there are photographs of Kharms wearing a deerstalker and smoking a pipe).[4] Such details and his own list of favorite authors, including Edward Lear and Lewis Carroll, indicate Kharms's love of puzzles and jokes. He believed that personal eccentricity was the mark of the avant-garde artist. His love for other authors such as Gogol, Hamsun, and Meyrink gives further evidence of his affinities with creators of figures of mystery who were themselves in life mysterious figures.[5]

A close friend and associate of Vvedensky and Oleinikov, Kharms was a member of the experimental group OBERIU. Linguistic play and descriptive defamiliarization inform his prose miniatures and lyric poems (scarcely published in his lifetime), which are imbued with philosophical perplexity, sometimes jarring drama and parable-like suggestiveness. Strikingly independent in manner as well as intellect, the apolitical Kharms was never easily (if at all) going to conform with Soviet society. Arrested and exiled with Vvedensky to Kursk in 1931, Kharms after the end of his sentence barely eked out a living for the rest of the decade. The only work that came his way were commissions from the legendary children's writer and editor Samuil Marshak at Detgiz, the state-run publisher of literature for children.[6] By 1940, he had published eleven collections of children's verse (in his notebook he lists children among his pet hates), works that were popular but also bore the stamp of his usual idiosyncrasies. In the 1930s, the prose writings containing his experimental forms and radical themes remained consigned "for the drawer," finally preserved in manuscript by friends.[7] While the 1960s saw the Soviet republication of Kharms's writing for children, it was not until the Perestroika period in the late 1980s that the Kharms of the adult writings, already known to a smaller group of avant-garde scholars, was discovered in Russia and abroad and to great acclaim.

"Werld" may be approached through philosophy and psychology as much as through aesthetics (i.e., defamiliarization). Techniques of defamiliarization pervade Kharms's work from proposition to proper nouns.[8] But, whereas defamiliarization, as understood classically in the work of the Formalists, served as a means to enhance perception of reality, in the work of Kharms perception leads more radically to the deconstruction of reality, attempting to "reveal the inconsistencies of existence by releasing words from their traditional meaning in this cognitive space."[9] This is most true of the many writings treated as absurdist in which the gap between expectation and reality has moved beyond irony or defamiliarization into a new logic or non-logic, upending fundamental ontological assumptions. Historically contextualized readings tend naturally to understand some works allegorically in connection to Stalinization, and they view defamiliarizing techniques as strategies to "activate the critical capacities of readers" because the destruction of automatized consciousness and "braking" (*tormozhenie*) of "perceptive machinery" constitute a form of opposition to state repression.[10]

Avant-garde-based readings, taking their cue from Kharms's OBERIU affiliation, emphasize a different goal, more philosophical than political, to use language to create collisions of meaning.[11] By intuiting both the feeling behind a word and its signification, a "collision of meanings" could be achieved that would give to language a new meaning beyond logic and reason, even transrational sense (as in the realm of *zaum'*).[12] Syntactic and grammatical features, even to the smallest degree, could be mobilized to expose the gap in a reality Kharms intuited beyond either empirical sensation or linguistic certitude, and discussions of his mathematical writings, mainly as recorded in his "Blue Notebook," have shown that even traditional assumptions about number sequences were rejected.[13] The same procedure is even extended to the body in the comically harrowing story "There was a red-headed man who had no eyes or ears" ("Byl odin ryzhii chelovek u kotorogo ne bylo glaz i ushei"), one of the sketches ("Sluchai") jotted down in the notebook.[14] Where nothing can be predicted, everything is unpredictable, leading to descriptions of "annihilation and oblivion," in the words of Matvei Yankelevich, one of Kharms's most sensitive translators and interpreters.[15]

Defamiliarization in "Werld" begins with questions of form. Is this poetry or prose, fiction or nonfiction—or somehow all of these combined? To Kharms, whose notebooks overflow with precision formulations, whether mathematical or verbal, how the utterance is formulated matters crucially. This text is crafted in such a way as to intensify the experience of grappling with questions of identity by being itself hard to identify. This fits the trend of Kharms's writing in the 1930s, during which his work became increasingly idiosyncratic.[16] His short prose is now regularly seen as intergeneric, erasing the boundary between fictional and nonfictional discourse, the fragment and the whole, and here, arguably, between poetry and prose. Prose poetry, it has been noted, like traditional lyric poetry, is marked by a "resistance to conclusive theorization" and engages "with the mysterious and ineffable."[17] It employs tropes less typical as prosaic techniques and more familiar as devices of poetry such as reiteration and repetition to create a formal indeterminacy. Prose poems, moreover, tend to be fragments less about narrative and more focused on ambiguity, hinting at a larger story that resists closure and "at unconscious forces at work in human experience as well as in language."[18]

Kharms has deliberately aligned the form of his work and its message of indeterminacy. "Werld" looks like a piece of prose. It is not lineated in the manner of verse, nor does it use rhyme. Yet that first surface impression is belied by Kharms's use of prosodic devices pulling in the direction of poetry, an effect typical of the prose poem in which "significant continuities between poetry and prose make clear that poetry [. . .] may be written in the mode of prose."[19] The layout features some indentation, creating bunches of lines with inner verbal arrangements such as the chiastic arrangement of lines 10–11:

Я говорил: части гром.
Части говорили: пук времени

I said: parts thunder.
The parts said: a clump of time.

Or from line 34 to the end, concluding lines begin with the conjunction "but" (*a*) to indicate a series of contradictions. While anaphora is not exclusively a poetic device, it is more typical of poetry than prose. Here, between lines 35 and 40, the alignment of initial words in consecutive lines also works with the text's function as a logical problem. Nonetheless, it would not be difficult, more radically, to recast at least sections of the text in blocks that approximate free verse by chopping up the prosaic lines into new units that retain the order and sense of the words but acknowledge that how they are printed is only a matter of convention.

"Werld" shares other features with poetry that give this work a special texture and make it a piece of prose poetry. Perhaps the most consistent feature of a genre that has provoked many descriptions and resisted generalization is that a prose poem is "a poem without line breaks."[20] Consider how differently the patterns of the words hit the eye when the opening lines have been rearranged (a reformatting that would work for most other sections, too):

Я говорил себе, что я вижу мир.
Но весь мир
недоступен моему взгляду, и
я видел только части мира.
И все, что я видел, я называл частями мира.

И я наблюдал свойства этих частей,
и, наблюдая свойства частей, я делал науку.
Я понимал, что есть умные свойства частей
и есть не умные свойства в тех же частях.

For one thing, units of repetition fall now at the line endings, creating vertical sequences of homonymic rhyme and off-rhyme (*mir/mir/mira/mira*; *chastei/chastei/chastiakh*). Within the lines, paratactic patterning also comes into focus, especially true of the second block with the alignment of the key thematic word "properties" (*svoistva*). When reordered, the line and pseudo-stanza are functional in a way that eludes the prose page: the former make audible breaks and coherences that are less distinct in the prose. What on the prose page looks like repetition, when lineated differently looks like a structural principle relating to the main concept, namely, that in any definition of things the relation of the part to the whole is both definitive and uncertain, fixed at a distance and indeterminate when reconsidered. In fact, form and content could not be more tightly reciprocal. "Werld" does not begin with an absurdist premise about the world. If in conclusion its speaker is backed into an aporia, unable to confirm the existence of anything outside his own mind, the interest of the work as a piece of literature that mimics philosophical discourse lies in its procedures and tone of anguish. Kharms's text is even more rife than Vvedensky's "Guest on a Horse" with the philosophical vocabulary of mind: thinking, understanding, observing, and seeing are its verbal backbone and define its analytical method.

It may be helpful here to lay out one approach to Kharms's procedure. Sight is important because it establishes the sensory or empirical approach to the quest for knowledge. Within the first fourteen lines of "Werld," the speaker has propounded an experimental or scientific method for examining the world as he sees it. Its initial descriptive language adopts the method of phenomenology, while line 14 by juxtaposition initiates a withdrawal into solipsism and more radical doubt about the verifiability of objects at all. In the first section, the process of self-description is taken up as a miniature exchange between the self and the parts. These actions reflect the self-conscious preoccupation of a speaker whose relationship to the outer world depends on a constant capacity for inner speech. This is the posture from the very start, beginning with an assertion to the self that is made only to be qualified. Written in short sentences of one or two clauses, this is a work of assertions emanating emphatically from the first person: "I" represents 61 of the 350 words. Philosophical solipsism seems to be both the premise and the result of a quest for epistemological security. All that can be guaranteed can only be guaranteed with reference to my own perception, and I can only be sure that I am the identifying subject if, at the very start, I denominate the one who speaks as the one who sees and therefore also the one who names. Whereas Vvedensky's speaker imagines regression to a primordial state of biblical genesis, here there is only a coming into consciousness of being conscious in the present. The entire text both describes and enacts that process.

It may be part of the inwardness of the piece that it seems formally cast as a single entity, using very little signposting to show awareness of the reader. Yet, even as it dispenses with more overt graphic divisions like paragraphing and even quotation marks to demarcate types of speech, Kharms uses variation in syntactic pattern to create internal structures. The first section therefore extends from the opening line to the fifth printed line: in each sentence the subject of the main clause is "I" governing a transitive verb involved in different modalities of seeing and understanding, all of which reduce the field of vision to parts. That field of vision, it has to be said, is remarkably empty of actual objects. The speaker does say that he distinguished the parts and gave them names, and that, depending on their properties, the named parts were intelligent or unintelligent. Yet nothing is named as such: the "parts of the world" with their attributes or properties (*svoistva*) exist in the abstract, seemingly to the narrator (the "I") and to the reader. The starting point is the inaccessibility of the entire world. From this it follows that the description of only a microcosm can be achieved. But that microcosm itself remains unnamed, at least to the reader, except with reference to parts of a larger entity referred to only as "everything" (*vse*). These are statements made a priori independent of worldly epiphenomena, articulated to help the speaker arrive at some fundamental propositions. Whether the approach is intended to be paradoxical, or the logic is just flawed, the entire work recoils from the empirical world and speaks in universals. What the speaker therefore means by "science" as knowledge of the world is the expression of properties expressed as meanings by predicates. Anything that can be an object of the verbs "to see," "to know," "to understand" qualifies, and this is all to be done without nominalization or description. Nothing that is named here can be visualized or described except predicatively. It depends ontologically entirely on the existence of the speaker or at least and perhaps more precisely on the speaker's grammatical function as subject.

And, insofar as Kharms has made his subject a speaker, the existence of the world that is seen from the very start is made dependent on speech acts. In the first twelve lines, comprising what is in effect the first section, the verb "to speak" (*govorit'*) is repeated four times (lines 1, 10, 12). The entire set of mental operations performed here is, however, much more complex. There is a presupposition that things have qualities that are inherent, containing the "thingness" of the specific object, whatever it may be, that must be visible and remains beyond the speaker's ken at least until its parts have been named. Speech as the key to apprehension and comprehension goes together with seeing, understanding, parsing (*delit'*), and naming. The premise here is that the characteristics (*svoistva*) that define substances emanate from constituent matter: this is the relation supposed between the features and parts, and it raises the question in the mind of the reader whether these parts are composed of even smaller particles that are "intelligent" or "thinking." Directed toward the outer world of things, the same procedure will eventually be turned back upon the speaking subject himself from line 10. An implied hierarchy underlies the procedure, moving from sight as empirical perception to identification and then observation as the basis of comprehension.

The process of observation is analytical, and the speaker regards his procedures as a form of science (lines 4–5). But it is not straightforward and not without mystery. Consider the status of the properties that constitute objects. The single attribute he predicates of these parts is intelligent/unintelligent or dumb. Similarity and comparison ("intelligent"/"unintelligent") are a basic logical process for categorizing knowledge. The key binary applied here is itself synthetic rather than descriptive, and it is itself both richly enigmatic and also hard to pin down. Are we to infer from lines 7–9 that entities deemed to be intelligent are animate and possibly even animal? Might we go one step beyond and infer that, insofar as the speaker posits a resemblance between himself and them, and the speaker is gifted with speech, these entities are also human? If that is the case, why does the speaker not simply name the human? Why does the speaker insist on a reductivism that is linguistically impoverished and procedurally maddening? Famed as an absurdist writer, Kharms also understood the nonsensical logic of *reductio ad absurdum*, of taking clarification to a point of incomprehension and then beyond. Yet his intention here might be the opposite. Without overly anticipating the final lines, we begin to sense that psychologically the speaker is incapable of universalizing propositions and assigning attributes to entire classes like species. Insofar as the speaker does not have universal access because his gaze will not allow it, he remains a prisoner of his own self-consciousness and is trapped by his solipsism. From the very start, this limitation seems key.

This internal dialogue produces no greater certainty in relation to the self or the world. Three ways of viewing the relation between parts and whole appear to inform Kharms's text: Cartesianism, Idealism, and solipsism. In his *Third Meditation*, Descartes suggests that spatial extension is indefinitely divisible or divisible into parts without limit. Insofar as the mode of analysis must break down the world into its smallest units, the work makes repetition its main trope, risking in its stripped down form of statement an impoverishment of language for the sake of philosophical certainty. Everything that can be seen must be decomposed into parts in order to make the larger wholes, predicated of these parts, visible. Yet the more repetitive the statements, the greater the uncertainty. What might be called epistemological reticence overwhelms the speaker when it comes to achieving his stated goal of perceiving a whole, and the text regresses from that moment into a posture of philosophical humility (*ves' mir nedostupen moemu vzgliadu*). If all the speaker can prove to himself conclusively is limited to his own existence in three dimensions, what is left? That moment of recognition grips the speaker in the second part, precipitating the final corkscrewing logic of assertion and denial. The turning point is signaled here from a sudden shift in verbal aspect from the imperfective (*delil, videl, nazyval, smotreli,* etc.) to the perfective of the verb "to understand," *ponial*: the verbal aspect means that understanding has reached a definitive point. When the scales fall from the speaker's eyes, it is to reveal that the process of scrutiny he took to be analytically secure was a mental synthetic act. In the contest between a Kantian belief in concepts of space and time as constructs that are intuitively true and an insistence on an external, sensationist proof of the reality of the world, the speaker had hoped to dispel the former stance by demonstrating the veracity of perception as an empirical science and as an escape from solipsism.[21]

What, then, is the world? The harder the speaker presses for certainty, the closer he comes to fixing what he sees, the more his vision fails him as in the declaration of line 24: "But as soon as I understood that I saw the world, I ceased seeing it." His argument here has been misconstrued to mean that he thinks "objects of entities exist as separate, independent and free" and that they are "pieces of the world."[22] By our reading, this statement is quite the contrary and amounts to a declaration of solipsism. In order to verify the existence of entities, their composition must be understood inductively and from first principles. To this end, the speaker adopts the premise that entities can be reduced to points (*tochki*) and parts (*chasti*), closely related to the word "particles" (*chastitsy*), the fundamental building block in materialist theory. If parts can no longer be discerned, as line 14 holds, this marks the boundary between the real and theoretical. It is where the speaker enters a theoretical realm of "small dots" or particles.

Once the speaker concedes that the world is the werld—the *mir/myr*—and is therefore only a synthetic mental picture of all visible details, external verification of reality looks impossible. The failure of the positive definition of *mir* or the world entails its negation. A text about seeing everything has become an admission about seeing "NOTHING" (*NICHTO*). Not only does the word stand out because it is all uppercase, it is centered in the line and is nearly at the midpoint of the word count of the entire text. The remaining lines therefore take up an antithetical description of this nonworld. With that realization and from that midpoint, "Werld" proceeds to negate any certainty built up about the logic of perception, unraveling nearly word for word and perception by perception. To stave off the fear of collapse, the speaker methodically and dialectically negates erstwhile premises. Parts previously fixed in the visual field have now "perished" (*propali*); the intelligence attributed to properties is negated; insofar as the world is made of up of those parts and they are no longer "thinking," the world itself has been deprived of intelligence.

Yet even this conclusion must imply its opposite, trapping the speaker in the paradox of a binary logic. If *x* then *y*, if *y* then *x*: if the parts of the world can be discerned in their order, then the world exists and conversely. If *x* then *y*, if *(-)x* then *(-)y*: if the world's parts make no sense, then the world does not exist because, we understand, it is only a figment of perception rather than objectively proven according to the text's verification hypothesis. Logically, the speaker himself should no longer be able to understand that the world does not exist, since its nonexistence implies his nonexistence, a position from which perception and judgment are impossible. This *reductio ad absurdum* pushes the speaker to embrace the illogical position of acknowledging that, even though the world has ceased to exist at least by his criteria, he can persist.

Logically, metaphorically, and perhaps even mentally, the speaker seeks an escape from the conundrum of existing in a world that does not exist. The attempt at a phenomenological description of the world presupposes that the world exists. The more assiduously the speaker applies the procedure, engaging in empiricism and nominalism (name-giving), the further reality slips away and the more he turns inward. "Werld" is a work in which the first person, the most personal pronoun, becomes hollowed out and used impersonally. The result is a state of solipsism in which the only observable reality has become the projection of the self. While the nonexistence of the world should conversely prove the nonexistence of the self, the nonexistence of the self is not a valid claim should the world not exist, since no such claim can be made from a position of nonexistence. The solution is to equate the world with himself.

Yet it was this position of solipsism from which the speaker sought to escape in the first place by aiming to reestablish his position in the world on a more empirical basis. That attempt failed in the first part of "Werld." The quest for the objective has led back to the affirmation of the subjective. But, insofar as it has already been shown that the subjective can only lead to the affirmation of nothing, the speaker becomes trapped. Within the framework of its philosophical style of exposition, exaggerated to a grotesque degree, this is a literary work because its logic is only a thin veil over the speaker's sense of terror that "the world will collapse" (lines 25–26). On this basis, the final lines capture a speaker incapable of proving either his own existence or the existence of the world, left only with language to convey his existential dilemma. Are these discontented or amused mutterings? That is, are they "damned if I do, damned if I don't" realizations, or quiet ravings by a man who has driven himself mad by creating what is in effect a "word machine"?[23]

In this regard, it is useful to look for a point of comparison on the question of form to Kharms's treatise "On Time, on Space, on Existence" ("O sushchestvovanii, o vremeni, o prostranstve," 1940). It begins from ground zero before the existence of the world, and then in a series of sixty formulations arrives at a point of certainty about the existence of the world based on the affirmation of the identity of the individual: "Speaking about oneself: 'I exist,' I place myself in the Universal Nexus."[24] In other words, this text works in the opposite direction of "Werld" and moves methodically toward *mir* or the "world." Even this brief quotation reminds one that utterance and identity exist in powerful connection for Kharms and that utterances can undo as much as they can do. In some critical writing the two texts, which share some utterances, have been treated as complementary and also interchangeable: "Werld" is seen as a prototreatise. Yet their form differs markedly, and the biggest point of differentiation is the use of repetition. This trope, expressed verbally through refrains, rhythmically through cadence, phonetically through sonic traces, is unique to "Werld" and creates a very different reading experience from "On Time, on Space, on Existence," in which all sixty propositions are numbered, whether or not they are consecutive or nonsequential. "Werld" becomes more involuted the more it repeats its premises. The indeterminacy of its form as a work that borders on different genres, whose language slips from the phenomenological to the solipsistic, is not incidental to its message and reading experience as a work of nervous insecurity.

"Werld" is not a treatise. The work delivers the experience of speech closely controlled and monitored for ontological veracity. "Werld" takes aim not at language but rather at the cognitive organization of the world: the gap between words and meaning exposed in other works here is the gap inherent in objects themselves taken to a point of such skepticism that the logic of automatic perception is blocked. The "thingness" of the world is progressively lost, as the connection between an entity and its parts, and between the parts themselves, becomes overwhelmed by the spaces between the parts and by the entire process of questioning. Intensely focused on things and also estranged from them, prosaic in layout yet poetic in its use of certain tropes, this prose poem of sorts is about a world that is also not the world: it only takes one spelling change from the letter *i* to *y*, an example of an absurdist master practicing the device of the subtle slip (*sdvig*), much loved by the futurists, to shift from "world" to an indefinable entity. While "Werld" is about *mir*, the world, its entire procedure is to question the speaker's assertion that he "had always known what the world was" (line 19) and ultimately to find it impossible to overcome the solipsism its discourse tries to escape. While the title might initially seem like a nonsense word, the reader will soon appreciate that, on the cusp between meaning and nonmeaning, it reflects how thin the border between logic and illogic or alogic is in Kharms's view. Kharms's coinage joins the Russian "my" (*we*) and "mir" (*world*), which the translator fully captures in that way that "we" resonates in "Werld." Like Vvedensky's "Man on a Horse," "Werld" treats the relationship between the inner and the outer and subjects it to an even more radical skepticism. Vvedensky's procedure is to undermine only indecisively the Cartesian supposition that space and time exist as an extension of mind. His poem leaves unresolved whether the Cartesian cogito is sufficient, suspending the thinking subject in a playback loop that rewinds time and abrogates space, and then revives the possibility that thought does occur through time and that bodies have spatial extension.

Poetry and prose, logical and absurd, empirical and metaphysical, worldly and out of this world—if "Werld" is more than a game, it is because its representation of radical uncertainty aims to deconstruct the subjective self and the external world. How do we understand? What can be understood? What is there to be understood? And what happens if we fail to understand? This set of questions and the production of such a work are conditioned by Kharms's own historical moment, fostering yet another instance of his genius for the rendering of the absurd. The dismissal of the external world is not merely a denial of contemporary traumas because the speaker is uncomfortable with that position; nor is its conclusion merely a defiant parody of the dialectical method. A positive meaning can also be recuperated if in the end the subject, still possessed of thought and speech, sees in solipsism the one way to change the world and the self. By changing consciousness, one changes the world—or at least the world of the self. Even as "Werld" seems to spiral downward into a trap of despair, it contains within itself the form and formula for an emancipation from history.

12

Alexander Vvedensky, "Guest on a Horse" (1931–34)

TIME–SPACE CONUNDRUM

Гость на коне

Конь степной
бежит устало,
пена каплет с конских губ.
Гость ночной
тебя не стало,
вдруг исчез ты на бегу.
Вечер был.
Не помню твердо,
было все черно и гордо.
Я забыл
существованье
слов, зверей, воды и звезд.
Вечер был на расстояньи
от меня на много верст.
Я услышал конский топот
и не понял этот шепот,
я решил, что это опыт
превращения предмета
из железа в слово, в ропот,
в сон, в несчастье, в каплю света.
Дверь открылась,
входит гость.
Боль мою пронзила
кость.

Человек из человека
наклоняется ко мне,
на меня глядит как эхо,
он с медалью на спине.
Он обратною рукою
показал мне—над рекою
рыба бегала во мгле,
отражаясь как в стекле.
Я услышал, дверь и шкап
сказали ясно:
конский храп.
Я сидел и я пошел
как растение на стол,
как понятье неживое,
как пушинка или жук,
на собранье мировое
насекомых и наук,
гор и леса,
скал и беса,
птиц и ночи,
слов и дня.
Гость я рад,
я счастлив очень,
я увидел край коня.
Конь был гладок,
без загадок,
прост и ясен как ручей.
Конь бил гривой
торопливой,
говорил—
я съел бы щей.
Я собранья председатель,
я на сборище пришел.
—Научи меня Создатель.
Бог ответил: хорошо.
Повернулся боком конь,
и я взглянул
в его ладонь.

Он был нестрашный.
Я решил,
я согрешил,
значит, Бог меня лишил воли, тела и ума.
Ко мне вернулся день вчерашний.
В кипятке
была зима,
в ручейке
была тюрьма,
был в цветке
болезней сбор,
был в жуке
ненужный спор.
Ни в чем я не увидел смысла.
Бог Ты может быть отсутствуешь?
Несчастье.
Нет я все увидел сразу,
поднял дня немую вазу,
я сказал смешную фразу
чудо любит пятки греть.
Свет возник,
слова возникли,
мир поник,
орлы притихли.
Человек стал бес
и покуда
будто чудо
через час исчез.

Я забыл существованье,

я созерцал
вновь
расстоянье.[1]

Guest on a Horse

Horse of the steppe
runs tired,

froth drips down the equine lip.
Guest of the night,
you expired,
you suddenly vanished mid-gallop.
There was evening.
I can't remember,
everything was black and proud.
I forgot
the existence
of words, beasts, water, and stars.
Evening was at a distance
from me, of many miles.
I heard the hoofbeat of a horse,
I didn't understand this hoarse
message, I thought it was a test
run of an object's transformation
from iron into word, into noise,
dream, drop of light, disaster, loss.
The door opened,
the guest entered alone.
Pain pierced my bone.
A man bends my way
out of a man,
stares at me like an echo,
has a medal pinned on his back.
He showed me with his inverse arm:
above the river in the dark
a fish upon its legs did pass,
reflected as if in a glass.
I heard the wardrobe and the door
clearly say:
a horse's snort.
I was sitting and I went
like a plant onto a table,
like a concept void of life,
like a feather
or a beetle
to the universal congress

of all sciences and insects,
mountains, forests,
cliffs and demons,
birds and night,
words and day.
I am glad, O guest,
so happy
that I glimpsed the edge of the horse.
It was smooth,
without riddles,
clean and clear as a brook.
It shook its mane,
a little strained,
it said,
"I'd like a bit of soup."
I was the chairman of the congress,
I had come to the assembly.
"Educate me, O Creator,"
and God answered, "very well."
Sideways turned
the horse and
I looked
into its hand.
The horse wasn't frightening at all.
I decided
I had sinned,
meaning, God deprived me
of body, mind, and will.
Yesterday came back to me.
In boiling water
there was winter,
in the stream
there was a prison,
in the flower
diseases acute,
in the beetle
a useless dispute.
I didn't see any meaning in anything.

God, maybe you're absent?
What a disaster.
No, I saw it all at once,
I picked up the day's mute vase,
I spoke out a funny phrase:
Miracle loves to warm its heels.
Light appeared,
words appeared,
the world was spent,
the eagles fell silent.
The man became a demon here
in the meantime
like a miracle
in an hour disappeared.

I forgot about existence

I again
contemplated
the distance.[2]

(TRANSLATED BY EUGENE OSTASHEVSKY
WITH MATVEI YANKELEVICH)

Alexander Vvedensky (1904–41) was born in St. Petersburg. An acolyte of the futurists, he also belonged to a smaller informal group of writers, including Yakov Druskin, Leonid Lipavsky, and Daniil Kharms, who took the name "Chinari" when they came together in 1925. Its derivation is unclear and has been traced to a type of Eastern tree and to the Russian word for "rank" (*chin*). Vvedensky himself later commented that a "Chinar is an author-ity of nonsense [*bessmyslitsy*]."[3] Mainly a talking shop to pursue abstract questions of language (and language in relation to music), this group was overshadowed by Vvedensky's and Kharms's affiliation with OBERIU as founding members in 1927.[4] The writers experimented with language, marked by grammatical instability, misaligned signifiers and signified, and a spare—sometimes whimsical—style that reflected their interest in the relation between epistemology and language. Aware of mimetic norms, they produced work that could be highly distinctive—and the differences between Kharms and Vvedensky are striking—but remained broadly true to some tenets of the OBERIU platform to be poets of a new perception of the world and a new art.[5] Underneath the surface of texts that looked absurd and sometimes like infantile babble—Vvedensky, Zabolotsky, and Kharms were skilled versifiers for children and collaborated on an illustrated book—was a belief in the chaotic, formless nature of the universe.

What that world itself actually had become was a pressing question by the end of the New Economic Policy period. From 1924 until 1929, the political leadership of the USSR relaxed controls on economic life after the devastation of the civil war and economic collapse. The 1920s saw an economic revival, a boom in publishing largely under the umbrella of newly established state publishing houses, and a flourishing in the arts and significant afterlife to Russian modernism. As the state came to impose its agenda of proletarianization on cultural life, and as Stalinization sought to control all forms of expression and thought in the 1930s, class warfare increasingly punished the avant-garde, as tolerance for politically innocent artistic experimentalism vanished. At the everyday level, the change in atmosphere was not lost on these writers. OBERIU's few public appearances elicited heckling; their apolitical and sometimes nonsensical art was antipathetic to politicized audiences. The historical world and often enigmatic mimetic world of OBERIU writings seemed to be collapsing into one another. In 1931, a year after OBERIU's demise, Kharms, Vvedensky, and a number of like-minded writers were arrested. During his exile until 1934, Vvedensky maintained his philosophical conversations with his friend Leonid Lipavsky as well as Yakov Druskin, an early mentor, and other members of their original circle. The experience of these times may have intensified the new emphasis in his poetry on mystery and incomprehension or the gap between logic and time. When characters disappear in an absurd story, that is a contrivance of plot; when people start disappearing from life with no patent reason, that is a different kind of randomness, and allegorical readings of works written in the spirit of the absurd take on a literal truth that can then seep back into works. If "Werld" asks the question "Who am I?" a poem like "Guest on a Horse" is a kind of extended thought experiment aimed at knowing the answer to "Where am I?" and "Where is God?"

"Guest on a Horse" is now regarded as one of Vvedensky's most significant lyrics, published only in 1987, nearly fifty years after his arrest and death during the Terror. In their earlier poems and other genres—stories for Kharms and plays for Vvedensky—these close friends explored the boundary between sense and senselessness linguistically and existentially. Playing with levels of reality and the boundary between life and art was one facet to the experimentalism of OBERIU. Art they likened to a "cupboard": an autonomous part of reality (and not inherently unreal or surreal) organized by its own laws and open to the senses. Their manifesto emphasized the belief that they were not fundamentally surrealists or practitioners of *zaum'*, transrational verbal art or pure sound disconnected from the world of objects, but were "real and concrete to the marrow of our bones." Their writing achieves a startling kind of defamiliarization by juxtaposing a familiar view of things newly described "with naked eyes." The process depends on a logic of art that does not destroy the object but rather exposes it in a new light. Poems are a bringing-forth of the process of working through a conceptual problem.[6] Like Dada or the Surrealists, they demoted the imitation of reality, decoupling the need to mirror the world at least directly from the workings of artistic language.

OBERIU writers, nonetheless, disavowed surrealism as a goal. That did not stop them from using metrical verse as a vehicle for nonsense, creating a gap between formal harmony and logical confusions.[7] Instability was the effect of a style that continually disrupted its own incipient patterns: a poem might start with a recognizable metrical scheme and then turn into prose; phrases would recombine the elements of conventional idioms in new combinations that beggared sense. This was as much a matter of lexicon as one of form; indeed, critics have repeatedly drawn attention to Vvedensky's "poverty of language."[8] By applying techniques that constantly defamiliarize the use of words and even the sounds of words, writers combined familiarity and incongruity in the description of objects and also situations. Here, too, the versification creates sudden, slight surprises: the poem is trochaic but easily slips into iambs as well, giving a kind of free overlayer to the undergirding of a familiar rhythmic pattern; and lineation mid-phrase propels the flow and also suspends sense units. The poetry of both Kharms and Vvedensky often makes use of lists to bring into a single visual field or semantic field objects whose connections may not be obvious and often look random; a key to the relations in the series needs to be sought in a formulation in the poem or even outside the poem, but once found it will reorganize perception. These clashes (or collisions) can verge on nonsense or the absurd by making the real look unreal, yet there remains an underlying logic that, when worked out, yields a fresh view on the relationship between objects in a space and the subject viewing them. For Vvedensky, in particular, the shift from bewilderment and confusion to perception, and from chaos to order, is where art comes in. The apprehension of defamiliarized objects leads to a state of heightened sensation, and it is this newly sensitized sense of hearing, touch, and vision that confers on the artist the status of a creator: "Whatever I am doing, I am fully aware that I am the creator of the world."

By 1929, Vvedensky's style had moved away from self-delighting nonsense, engaging now with a more fundamental sense that the universe was inherently random. He concluded that if order was to be sought then ordinary language was insufficient to express it; and that, if meaning was to be sought in life, it involved a recognition that some element of divine mystery surrounding man's place in the universe and nature might be glimpsed by thinking outside the normal frame of historical time and causal logic. The development of such inquitisiveness, a hallmark of his earlier work, comes out of an apprehension of unsettling contemporary events and a growing epistemological skepticism. Describing his attitude in the so-called Grey Notebook, a collection of his own ruminations and poetic jottings, Vvedensky admitted,

> I am convinced of the falseness/unreliability of previous connections and I cannot say what the new ones ought to be. I don't even know whether there should be one system of connections or many. And I have a fundamental feeling of the disconnectedness [*bessviaznost'*] of the world and the atomization of time. And since this stands in contradiction to reason it means that reason does not comprehend the world.[9]

By the end of OBERIU, Vvedensky had written a number of poetic and fantastic journeys as well as dramatic dialogues as vehicles for discussing metaphysical themes. The title of one piece tersely states his concerns: "Fact, Theory, and God" ("Fakt, Teoriia i Bog"). Alice Nakhimovsky, in her early and insightful study, rightly wondered whether both Vvedensky and Kharms around 1930 felt they had reached "some boundary of impenetrability" from which they drew back in the hope of speaking even to a dwindling readership with greater clarity.[10] In his works of the 1930s, of which "Man on a Horse" is often cited as a supreme example, Vvedensky adjusted his style. While bafflement was still an essential part of the heuristic procedure and reader experience, meaninglessness was no longer primarily a verbal effect, achieved earlier through neologisms and randomness. Instead, bafflement emerged at least as much from situations and the way poems handled narrative. In other words, whereas once it was the senselessness of Dada that attracted Vvedensky and others, now reality shifted to the recognition of absurdity as ontological. His plotting of narrative poems and the management of language, too, are less hectic, harder to spatialize and more portentous as a result.

Readers of Vvedensky's poems, especially those written between 1930 and 1934, will find a pleasurable immediacy in their clever use of form, linguistic inventiveness, and the unexpected. By the poet's own lights, the perennial challenge for the reader is to perceive that moment where "art comes in" or, in effect, to establish how ulterior meaning and strange surface effects work together where elements of anti-mimesis challenge logical expectations and expectations collapse into nonsense. How and why the normal organization of space, time, and action (including cause and effect) has been attenuated or shattered is the question. Whether there is an order that lies behind the changes of meaning created by words in the context of the poem is the further question that guides the procedure of reading many an OBERIU poem. That norm stands like an anterior world.

But more linear interpretation also risks flattening into a single dimension meaning that is meant to remain one step beyond a streamlined account, spoiling the surprising aspects of representation pursued by the OBERIU aesthetic as a "violation of predictable logical and semantic connections."[11] In the search for sense, readings may do well to remain aware of nonsense as an existential fact of the world represented in the poem. Dead ends, reversals, unexpected associations and unexplained states are also aesthetic tactics. How does the reader guard against a misstep or mistake in works that can deliberately aim to baffle? This is a question about an effective hermeneutics of interpretation. If the message of a poem can never be other than mysterious, or only understood by inferring some higher level of meaning to which its details correspond, interpretations are bound to remain speculative, more conjectural than usual, and expressed with greater conditionality than we associate with more direct poems.

Productive readings tend to follow the relation between patterns, thematic and formal, and meaning, symbolic or literal, that threads through a poem like "Guest on a Horse." We usually look to titles and nouns to indicate the subject matter. Both a "guest" and a "horse" figure in the poem, but basic questions remain about their identity, their relation to one another and to the lyric speaker. Yet it is helpful to note that the poem associates many processes with all three. It is out of those actions that the narration of the poem coalesces into a situation poised between coming into being and erasure. On the one hand, the poem is printed as a single uninterrupted nonstanzaic block, and, with the only two breaks indicated before and after line 91, the reader may expect narrative coherence. Yet, on the other hand, at the very start the speaker creates an expectation of incompletion and forgetting. While incidental features of prosody such as mixed-end rhyme and internal rhyme (lines 66–66 *reshil/sogreshil/lishil*) add musical coherence, the omission of causal conjunctions, skewed idioms, temporal shifts, and inversion of the ordinary confuse at the diegetic level. Repetition, another favorite trope, counterintuitively confounds more than it clarifies. Does the "horse of the steppe" actually arrive before vanishing? Why does the speaker confess to forgetting? It is also helpful to note that Vvedensky elsewhere views forgetting as a natural human propensity, and he expects art to capture gaps consistent with his quest to create art attentive to faltering certainty: "In a novel it is as though time flows in life. But this in fact has very little to do with reality. In a novel, night and day do not change over, practically an entire life can be remembered easily whereas in reality one can hardly remember even yesterday."[12]

In a work that seemingly advances and then cycles back to an anterior point in time and space, repetition is not used to anchor perception. Circularity is used to establish a reference point and then create an opposing viewpoint, thereby unfolding mutually exclusive meanings of nonequation and nonidentity. The guest exists—and does not exist; and the guest is not "I"—and is "I"; the horse is simple and clear, and as endless as the world. The "I" may be both the president of the assembly and a humble guest who implores God for soup and explanation. And yet ultimately the most fundamental paradox is the claim that "I am" and "I am not" because "God deprived me of body, mind, and will," even as God is both present and absent. In sum, repetition is the device that more than any other asserts and negates to an absurd degree, underscored further by the repetition of specific words such as "unhappiness" (*neschast'e*), "horse" (*kon'*), "the word" (*slovo*), "light/world" (*svet*), "distance" (*rasstoianie*), "devil" (*bes*), "dream" (*son*), which creates linkages among disjointed things, in this respect matched by the occasional rhymes when they appear. The phrasal unity of the first-person followed by a verb is one consistent principle, occurring nearly twenty times: "I forgot," "I said," "I heard," "I decided," and so on. Sensory perception is mobilized to describe action, and the speaker not only thinks but hears, sees, eats (and by implication tastes and smells). Yet ultimately the field of objects on which the senses act is unstable, since the only empirical datum the speaker confirms is that what he experiences is the "transformation of an object." Within this perceptual field, disappearances occur, aphasia seems imminent, and memory falters.

If one were to think about structure and an overall story as a way of providing some heuristic clarity, it would be possible to consider the structure of this poem as a set of six frames that can be paraphrased. Frame 1 captures the arrival of a horse, fatigued from some period of riding, but its rider, the guest, has vanished en route and the speaker expresses consternation but also provides a first instance of category confusion by referring to the evening as black but also proud, a combination that may speak to the resistance of the night to the gaze of the speaker who would like to penetrate the mystery of the guest's disappearance, anticipating the later view about the nonexistence of God. While lines 7–12 provide a setting, the storytelling falters: "There was evening [and] I can't remember . . ." In fact, within the first twelve lines, there are two acts of forgetting, compounding uncertainty. When does the speaker forget what? Is it the expectation of the rider that obliterates the "existence of words, beasts, water, and stars" from his mind?

Focalized through the speaker's awareness, the visual field is made up of separate indications: sounds approaching, sounds disappearing, drops of sweat seemingly audible across the plain at a distance of many miles: "I didn't understand this hoarse / message" is Eugene Ostashevsky's clever rendering of the word for "whisper." The arrangement of the nouns here is chiastic: noise and dream, unhappiness and "drop of light" pair off, with the last a metaphor for happiness juxtaposed to unhappiness and consistent with the dream state. Insofar as the poem telescopes background and foreground by bringing the rider starkly into the picture even as consciousness erodes, for at least the first twenty-one lines the arrival of the rider remains open to doubt. Other small spatial dislocations shunted into sensory effects add to the impression that reality cannot be grasped. For instance, "I heard," the speaker declares in lines 15 and 33. That the sound of the cupboard speaks clearly is not personification but an act of displacement: the sound of the guest's entrance and gestures, noted immediately above, is noticed only by way of an indirect report. Once again there is a blurring of frames as the speaker both notices the present and experiences a delayed reaction. Does this hesitation betray an element of reticence or even fear? Is this why the arrival seems on the brink of being reversed ("suddenly vanished mid-gallop")? Temporally, things are no clearer since he reader might well ask whether lines 1–20 are in the right order. That may be how the mind of the reader synthesizes details of the narrative into a single plot. Line 15 both gives and removes certainty. In the speaker's state of mental erasure, the relation between signifier and signified has become dissociated.

In frame 2 (lines 15–20) the speaker, perhaps more confident about hearing than seeing, seems to rehearse again the arrival described above. These lines also repeat the way information is structured in the first frame: the advent of the horse precedes a metaphorical or more abstract comment, now the associative transformations indicated in lines 19–20, again mixing different categories of things and feelings. In frame 3 (lines 21–45) the guest confounds expectations by appearing; yet within these lines there are delays and reversals compounded by category confusion: for instance, while there is no evidence of speech there is an echo (sound effect) of a glance (visual detail) rebounding on the speaker before they are joined by other beings. From line 21, leading up to a portentous dialogue, the next thirty-five lines focus on the encounter between visitor and speaker. We have seen that reversal is a key trope of the opening, and now inversions mark the next lines. The visitor's gesture of greeting is backhanded (line 29); the military decoration he wears is on his back rather than chest; a fish swims over rather than in the river. Nearly all action is concentrated in perception: the entire point of view on the scene might be visualized as a reflection in a mirror turning the world upside down or inside out. Once again, between the arrival of the guest and an utterance as an external event, the lines move away from the perceived event to its impact on the speaker. The younger Vvedensky and Kharms had likened art to what comes out of a cupboard (*shkap*). Here what emerges is an abstract set of thoughts that dehumanize the speaker, bringing him closer to plant and insect life. In line 36, the shift from sitting to going turns a simile ("like a plant") into a change of state since plants do not walk. If there is a fear of death, it leads in a chain of similes to a pantheistic merger with elements of nature and time itself. This interpenetration of self and the universe, listing creatures, noting the division of air and land and sea, and mentioning language, looks like a return to Creation itself. Lines 25–26 give a tautological description of the guest as "man from man" (or "human from human"). Is this meant to suggest that the speaker is not like Adam, the first man fashioned from dirt or clay, and more like Eve or the sons of Adam and Eve, made from human flesh or bone (perhaps motivating the detail that his appearance "pierced my bone")?

The portentousness of the poem lies partly in its cosmic language. Familiarity with Vvedensky's positioning of poems in relation to the romantic tradition—he is an avowed admirer of Pushkin—allows us to read this lyric in the context of Pushkin's classic statement on poetic wisdom.[13] The confession of amnesia inverts the claim the speaker of Pushkin's "The Prophet" makes to possess a vision of all creation, from the lowest creature and the oceans to the heavens. Whereas Pushkin's speaker at the end preaches his message by "ranging across seas and lands" (*obkhodia moria i zemli*), Vvedensky's speaker moves further away from a lofty existence. And yet the visionary experience of both figures includes violence. The prophet's "chest is split through by a sword."[14] In Vvedensky, the equivalent once again confuses subject and object since the line in Russian, *bol' moiu pronzila kost'*, is ambiguous and can mean "a bone penetrated my pain" and "pain penetrated my bones." Such reversals in transitiveness and perspective on the subject grow more intense and also move from history to some pre-history. The newly reborn man of the poem joins the ranks of Creation in its pristine state, the source of the elation he confesses to the guest. And once again there are reverberations of Pushkin's "The Prophet." The price of visionary exaltation and eloquence is mutilation:

И он к устам моим приник,
И вырвал грешный мой язык,
И празднословный и лукавый,
И жало мудрыя змеи
В уста замершие мои
Вложил десницею кровавой.[15]

He inclined toward my lips
And ripped out my sinful tongue,
Both spiteful and cunning,
And with a right hand bloody
In my astonished mouth
Laid the stinger of the wise serpent.

Pushkin's original is transformed into a statement about reflexive identity (lines 25–28):

Человек из человека
наклоняется ко мне,
на меня глядит как эхо,
он с медалью на спине.

A man bends my way
out of a man,
stares at me like an echo,
has a medal pinned on his back.

Frame 4 (lines 45–64) may contain as indirect reported speech the host's greeting of the horse and in turn the other guests, and it is rounded off by an appeal of the host to God who responds. These lines produce spiritual revelations delivered in glimpses rather than epiphanies. The frame also reverses the trajectory of "The Prophet," transforming the sublimely elevated vision of the flight of angels into a view of the life of insects, merging the speaker's viewpoint not with that of angels but with that of a beetle. Perhaps this is why Vvedensky's lyric hero speaks of himself as the convenor of a Creation-like summit presided over by the visitor, addressed as Creator (line 58 in the Russian, *sozdatel'*). Any reticence at the beginning of the poem may be in anticipation of this moment, and even now the Godhead is not looked at directly but seen askance. First, the speaker sees the "edge" or silhouette of the horse, tantamount to spotting the visitor out of the corner of his eye (line 48 in the Russian, line 49 in the English), whereupon the formal greeting prompts the inference that, while the "horse wasn't frightening at all," the rider inspires dread. Expectations are reversed when, first, the horse speaks, asking for soup; and then when, again, the horse rather than the guest declares his position of authority.

While the direction and speed of the horse (and the unidirectional Russian verb of motion) associate it with the flow of time, this is clearly not an ordinary beast. The horseman is no ordinary rider either, and, in general, the figure of the horse in Vvedensky's work has strong associations with eschatology, an association that was widely made in early-twentieth-century Russian literature.[16] The apocalyptic association is validated by the theological language of the encounter, including a musing on whether God is present or absent and in due course the evocation of sin. It is the horse rather than the rider who has on its palm something to display, presumably the sign of the Apocalypse. In lines 59–60 of the Russian, the punning internal rhyme (*Bog/bok*) uses a linguistic device to juxtapose the images of rider and horse.

However apocalyptic the rider, he is hardly fearsome. "Not terrifying" (*nestrashnyi*) may presume a level of comfort that not every speaker could muster. Vvedensky has created a subject poised for spiritual awakening and on the brink of revelation. In "The Prophet," Pushkin's great poem of epiphany, the manifestation of the divine is terrifying. The poetic vision and transformation from spiritual exhaustion to elation of the speaker come at a cost of violence done to him by the seraph. Here the speaker seems to voluntarily surrender "body, mind, and will." If this is a death in life, it is achieved gently. The ultimate goal of the surrender may be openness to a miracle and spiritual rebirth, and the poem takes a step in that direction: "Yesterday came back to me." Recapturing time, however, is not some linear process of memory or even autobiographical recovery, and the poem even moves away from the discursive language of autobiography or memory into a bevy of images. A known technique of OBERIU used to create a surface impression of chaos, a list of nouns can also on occasion have semantic coherence. Here the pattern of meaning is both syntactic and logical. Each unit is a prepositional clause, the object of which is an entity of a contradictory kind. Hence the cold of "winter" inhabits "boiling water"; there is stasis (denoted as a "prison") in water, usually a sign of flow and freedom; illness rather than flourishing to be found in a flower; and finally, and perhaps less symmetrically, provocation in the buzzing of a beetle rather than just a natural sound.

In frame 5 the host admits to being at fault in some unspecified way, and the sin is punished by a loss of agency and identity. Consequently—though perhaps not!—the speaker can now relive the past or possibly just the previous day (line 67). Although, if read literally, the line can also mean that time was reversed, an effect that is consistent with the hesitations of the opening two frames. This section is rounded off with a list of things that are part of that anterior time, all put in the past tense: Are they fragmentary images of the speaker's past, associations that float up in consciousness? Or are the two images of water (*kipiatok*, *rucheika*) semanticized off-rhymes? Line 76 (line 79 in the English) presents a declaration that may open a gap between the perspectives of reader and speaker and also plays with a burden of expectation: namely, that some order underlies the surface vision of the phenomenal world and that a pattern of contradiction can be overcome, possibly with reference to religion. The speaker ponders his own inability to understand the train of thought and in a final set of images seems to consider how it is that a world has come into creation in which "eagles fall silent," meaning presumably that nobility has been lost and "man has become a devil." Are the final four lines, grouped together, a defensive reaction to the predicament these frames depict obliquely? Is the distance the speaker occupies a way of objectifying the incomprehensible?

The poem is built on the quintessential OBERIU predicament, one in which Vvedensky excelled, of the poet situated in a landscape, attentive to something imminent and immanent that remains irretrievable. The repetition at the end of the phrase "I forgot about existence" both concludes the poem and turns back to the initial statement at line 10. Objects that might belong to external nature such as the horse have become things that appear and disappear, that are temporal and timeless, located and ephemeral. Consistent with the theme of failure of memory, announced in that line, the end of the poem also compels the reader to consider what has been forgotten (presumably by the narrator) and even what readers themselves may have forgotten or missed. Repetition proves to be a circling back, a reminder that we have traveled nowhere.

Yet even as the poem circles back on itself, arriving again at that moment of nonarrival, the mind looks outward if only to repeat the process of expecting and forgetting. The three lines of coda, detached from the rest by one blank line, close the frame on an experience. The only distance that can actually be completed is that last segment that closes the circle. Looking outward toward the arrival of the rider on the horse enacts both closure and beginning, and there is no evidence that the speaker understands the structure containing his experience.

If reactions in this poem are not explicitly psychologized because the style of characterization does not build a portrait of a subject, Vvedensky manages nonetheless to suggest that behind the combination of situation and reaction, lies a human quest for existential meaning. Once again it is to be wondered whether the order of the poem belies the order of events. Does the beginning of the poem actually lie in its ending? If we turn back to yesterday, then the real starting point is the question "God, maybe you're absent?" And it is from that moment of aporia that the visit unfolds. Riddled with doubt and forgetting, the poem creates on the surface a disjointed logic out of which a more linear order is recoverable. Things that appeared to happen for no reason now happen for a purpose insofar as the quest for meaning is a key. As memory and faith both waver, the appearance of the rider as a confirmatory sign fluctuates. Time in the world of the poem may be both progressive and linear (there is a yesterday) and also the nondirectional time of an interior world suspended in a state of semi-belief. Its form captures that split and also creates a circular dynamic of skepticism from which there is no escape. To express that dialectical state of hope and doubt, the speaker produces the metaphor of the empty vessel and a memorable aphorism. Patience will be rewarded because a miracle cannot be rushed. Yet is the miracle ever fulfilled or sufficiently fulfilled to fix order and dispel chaos?

The mixed nature of Creation as a struggle between order and chaos and light and darkness is woven into the poem's texture like the fabric of the universe. Every vision of a primordial state of creation must also cycle back to the origin of evil. Whatever his personal religion, Vvedensky's work looks rife with original sin. The Edenic state involves the knowledge of evil, and that is the condition for which the Adamic figure, the divine man, finally vanishes in an hour (line 90 in the Russian; line 93 in the English)—or thirty-four lines later, toward the end of the poem. The final comment belongs to the speaker, who finds himself entering here, as at the very beginning, a state of forgetfulness. The distance observed in the first line was the gap between the expectation and actual arrival of the rider. The distance observed in the final lines is symbolically the gap between the expectation of a new world promised by the advent of the rider and the unknowable next state somewhere between forgetting and awakening. Having been reduced to a state of nonbeing as memory sheds language, the speaker acquires once again all his sensory faculties and also a greater sensitivity: while animal-like and human, he also shares the universe with plants and insects. In following its trajectory from pre-event to event to erasure and return to the first state, the poem does not deny God but fathoms the gap between a state of religious apprehension and an ebbing away of light.

For a poem dedicated to a fleeting moment of meaningful consciousness, "Guest on a Horse" is full of energy and action. Of all the parts of speech, verbs are the most numerous, and the theme of cognition is prevalent in acts of forgetting and remembering. The space of oblivion is filled with acts of hearing, showing, seeing, and speaking. Communication is part of nature and part of us, the poem seems to show, even when consciousness emerges from nonbeing. The contrast with the position of Pushkin's prophet is profound because, in that poem, poetic exaltation brings the speaker into direct communication with the deity, confirming the Godhead. Here the moment of revelation can never be secured: "in an hour [it] disappeared" (*cherez chas ischez*) and then resumes. It is as if "The Prophet" were placed on a playback loop, hinting at the presence of God in a creative process that cannot be realized.

13

Nikolai Oleinikov, "Cockroach" (1934)

A FARCICAL TRAGEDY

Таракан

Таракан попался в стакан.
Достоевский

Таракан сидит в стакане,
Ножку рыжую сосет.
Он попался. Он в капкане.
И теперь он казни ждет.

Он печальными глазами
На диван бросает взгляд,
Где с ножами, с топорами
Вивисекторы сидят.

У стола лекпом хлопочет,
Инструменты протирая,
И под нос себе бормочет
Песню "Тройка удалая".

Трудно думать обезьяне,
Мыслей нет—она поет.
Таракан сидит в стакане,
Ножку рыжую сосет.

Таракан к стеклу прижался
И глядит едва дыша . . .
Он бы смерти не боялся,

Если б знал, что есть душа.
Но наука доказала,
Что душа не существует,
Что печенка, кости, сало—
Вот что душу образует.

Есть всего лишь сочлененья,
А потом соединенья.

Против выводов науки
Невозможно устоять.
Таракан, сжимая руки,
Приготовился страдать.

Вот палач к нему подходит,
И, ощупав ему грудь,
Он под ребрами находит
То, что следует проткнуть.

И проткнувши, набок валит
Таракана, как свинью.
Громко ржет и зубы скалит,
Уподобленный коню.

И тогда к нему толпою
Вивисекторы спешат.
Кто щипцами, кто рукою
Таракана потрошат.

Сто четыре инструмента
Рвут на части пациента.
От увечий и от ран
Помирает таракан.

Он внезапно холодеет,
Его веки не дрожат . . .
Тут опомнились злодеи
И попятились назад.

Все в прошедшем—боль, невзгоды.
Нету больше ничего.
И подпочвенные воды
Вытекают из него.

Там, в щели большого шкапа,
Всеми кинутый, один,
Сын лепечет: "Папа, папа!"
Бедный сын!

Но отец его не слышит,
Потому что он не дышит.

И стоит над ним лохматый
Вивисектор удалой,
Безобразный, волосатый,
Со щипцами и пилой.

Ты, подлец, носящий брюки,
Знай, что мертвый таракан—
Это мученик науки,
А не просто таракан.

Сторож грубою рукою
Из окна его швырнет,
И во двор вниз головою
Наш голубчик упадет.

На затоптанной дорожке
Возле самого крыльца
Будет он, задравши ножки,
Ждать печального конца.

Его косточки сухие
Будет дождик поливать
Его глазки голубые
Будет курица клевать.[1]

Cockroach

A cockroach was caught in a glass.
Dostoevsky

Cockroach, stuck inside a glass,
sucking on his reddish foot.
He is captured. He is trapped.
Soon, to death he shall be put.

He is staring at the couch
with his sad and soulful eyes,
where the vivisectors sit
with their axes and their knives.

And the medical assistant
bustles, cleaning every prong
and distractedly intoning
an extremely Russian song.

For an ape, it's hard to think;
so he sings away, the brute . . .
Cockroach's stuck inside a glass,
sucking on his reddish foot.

With his face against the glass,
Cockroach knows: he will be mauled.
Oh, he wouldn't dread his death,
if he knew he was besouled!
But the scientists have proved:
there is no such thing at all.
Kidneys, liver, bones, and fat:
only these make up the soul.

There are just connected points,
which, together, make up joints.

Souls, the scientists conclude
irrefutably, are fake.
Cockroach wrings his tiny hands
and prepares to suffer ache.

Now the torturer draws close,
cruel, merciless, and fierce.
He palpates the heaving chest,
finds the thing that he must pierce.

And he pierces it and topples
our poor Cockroach. Gruff and coarse,
he guffaws, his teeth laid bare,
bearing semblance to a horse.

And the vivisectors rush in,
pounce at him together, and
get at him with tongs and squeezers;
some are gutting him by hand.

Hundred tools aim at his heart,
tear his tortured frame apart.
Maimed by scalpel, forceps, vice,
clamp and cutter, Cockroach dies.

He is motionless and cold,
and his eyelids are like clay.
As the miscreants behold
this, they gasp and back away.

Pain and hardship, all is over;
all the suffering now stops.
Only subterranean waters
flow from his unmoving corpse.
In the cupboard's tiny crevice,
all abandoned and alone,
Cockroach Junior cries: "Daddy . . ."
Oh, poor son!

No, his father doesn't listen:
Death makes parents very distant.

Over his immobile body,
shaggy vivisectors loom:
haughty, hideous, and hairy,
tongs and scalpels spelling doom.

Evil wretch attired in trousers!
Know: this Cockroach who has died
is a martyr of your science,
not some cockroach who has died!

Soon, the janitor will grab him
with his rough, unfeeling hand,
toss his body from the window,
and head down our friend will land.

On a trampled dusty pathway
in a tiny shabby yard
he will wait, feet pointing skyward,
for the final act to start:

Heavy rains will wash his bones clean,
falling from the empty skies.
And a heartless clucking chicken
will peck out his azure eyes.

(TRANSLATED BY ALEXANDRA BERLINA)

While not formally a member of the Leningrad group of absurdists that published in 1927 a manifesto and called themselves OBERIU, Nikolai Oleinikov (1898–1937) in practice belonged to this circle of the writers and artists including Daniil Kharms, Alexander Vvedensky, Nikolai Zabolotsky, and Evgeny Shvarts. Like them, he frequently wrote for children, and the aesthetics of his "adult" poems, which were not published until the 1960s, also echoed OBERIU tendencies. Lydia Ginzburg, a disciple of Tynyanov and Shklovsky, knew Oleinikov personally and was the first major literary scholar to write about him. She observed his affiliation to several different traditions: the parody poetry of Kozma Prutkov, a fictional literary figure created by the Zhemchuzhnikov brothers and Alexei K. Tolstoy in the 1860s; the poems of Sasha Cherny, who wrote for the *Satirikon* magazine (1908–14) and was famous for his ironic depictions of the contemporary world; and also the experiments of the radical futurist Velimir Khlebnikov. Ginzburg writes:

> Kozma Prutkov, Sasha Cherny, and Khlebnikov—what could such a hybrid produce? What it produced was a system of extraordinary unity belonging to this particular poet and recognizable in every line (recognizability being an inherent property of any real poet). The signs of this system are: deliberate primitivism, simple syntax combined with complex semantics, grotesque discrepancies between the lexical/stylistic coloring of a word and its logical content. A unity, but one that is formed by complexly correlated summands.[2]

Ginzburg believes that Oleinikov rejected the "direct," "sincere" expression of serious feelings and thoughts because his personality

> had been formed in the [19]20s, when there existed (alongside others) this particular human type: a shy individual weary of any lofty phrases, both official and those of the intelligentsia. Oleinikov was such a person. People of this type

> felt that proclaiming big values and using big words were inadequate if this talk was not paid for at the highest rate in social and moral currency. They used jokes and irony as a protective cover for thoughts and feelings. It was only from the masses of jokes that what they really wanted to say about life made its difficult way out. To speak of matters high and lofty directly, without checking such speech by laughter, was forbidden.[3]

Certainly, Oleinikov's generation knew other "types" as well. Some of Oleinikov's contemporaries were not in the least ashamed to express feelings directly and with pathos. In this regard, it suffices to mention Vladimir Mayakovsky (1893–1930) or Sergei Yesenin (1895–1925). But unlike these poets, Oleinikov really was formed in the 1920s: he was a very young man when he found himself in the middle of the civil war on the Don. (The Nobel Prize-winning novel *And Quiet Flows the Don* would much later provide a glimpse of its cruelty and complexity.) Disowned by members of his family, he suffered his share of the terrible and traumatic. It is hard not to see a connection between the traumas he experienced and his rejection of traditional lyricism. While trauma created a desperate craving for the "banal" ideals of humanity and compassion, they made these ideals seem ridiculous. Still, such "banalities" were not run-of-the mill against the background of official Soviet culture, which interpreted them as bourgeois sentimentality and glorified "ruthlessness toward the class enemy."

This is the origin of the main technique underlying Oleinikov's aesthetics, which Ginzburg describes as a combination of opposing modalities: "The serious, the genuine flickers on the edge of the comical. It is, therefore, questioned. At times, it is difficult to get hold of these transitions, to pinpoint them."[4] For instance, Oleinikov wrote a number of poems that do more than merely "humanize" insects such as flies, beetles, and fleas. He simultaneously describes the relationship between the speaker and the insect from a biological perspective (the flea bites, the fly beats against the glass) and from a (parodically) romantic one. Hence "The Fly" (1934) opens with the confession "How madly did I love the fly!" and ends with a comic oxymoron: "Oh fly! Oh you my little birdie."[5] Another poem of his, "A Message beyond Class" (1932), describes the life of a flea named Petrova, who falls in love with a man. Her passion is not reciprocated, and poor Petrova commits suicide, a finale that is not entirely comical since it also includes a dramatic note:

> Дико прыгает букашка
> С бесконечной высоты,
> Разбивает лоб бедняжка . . .
> Разобьешь его и ты!

The poor thing takes a wild jump
From an infinite height,
The poor thing's forehead shatters . . .
And so will yours![6]

In the poem "Cockroach" (1934), we see this combination of opposite modalities in its most extreme form: it is a *farcical* depiction of *tragedy*. It is with good reason that Ginzburg compares "The Cockroach" to Kafka's "Metamorphosis":

> Oleinikov's "Cockroach" evokes an unexpected association with Kafka's story "The Metamorphosis," narrating the anguish and death of a man suddenly turned into a huge insect (some interpreters believe that it is actually a cockroach). Even some of the plot details coincide. In Kafka's case, the maid throws the protagonist's corpse onto the garbage dump; in Oleinikov's poem
>
> Сторож грубою рукою
> Из окна его швырнет,
>
> Soon, the janitor will grab him
> with his rough, unfeeling hand
> (lines 69–70)
>
> Most likely, this is an involuntary convergence of ideas: in those days, Kafka was not yet known in our country, and Oleinikov could hardly have read him. Still, a historical similarity between Oleinikov and his older contemporary undoubtedly exists.[7]

In Ginzburg's view, both Oleinikov's cockroach and Kafka's Gregor Samsa symbolize a new type of tragic character: that of a "mediocre man" who did nothing—nothing heroic and nothing villainous either—to deserve his terrible fate. Instead, he becomes a victim of a superhuman power (the state), which operates not with individual but with collective categories, declaring entire classes, nations, or professions to be enemies without explaining its criteria. In this, both Kafka and Oleinikov see the tragic essence of the modern condition. After all, in Brodsky's words, "in a real tragedy, it is not the hero who perishes; it is the chorus."[8]

The timeline of the poem's composition corroborates a tragic interpretation. It was written in 1934, the year of the assassination of the head of the Leningrad Party Organization Sergei Kirov, the event that launched the Great Terror, which would reach its peak in 1937–38. Despite being a member of the Communist Party, Oleinikov was arrested, tortured, and executed three years after writing "Cockroach." With this comical poem, he seems to have predicted his terrible fate.

The cockroach motif is surrounded by a dense network of associations and subtexts. Oleinikov's own epigraph to the poem—"A cockroach was caught in a glass. *Dostoevsky*"—refers the reader to a "fable" written by a minor, comic character in Dostoevsky's novel *The Possessed* (*Besy*, 1872), Captain Lebyadkin. The first stanza of this surreal fable reads as follows:

Жил на свете таракан,
Таракан от детства,
И потом попал в стакан
Полный мухоедства . . . [9]

There lived a cockroach in the world,
A cockroach from childhood on,
He then got into a glass,
Full of fly-devouring . . . [10]

At the center of *The Possessed* is the story of an innocent student murdered by revolutionaries who seal the unity of their organization in blood. For OBERIU, Captain Lebyadkin was important as an example of a blatantly bad poet whose comic verses could, nevertheless, serve as a source of new forms. In that respect, his verses bear comparison to the illiterate texts submitted to Soviet magazines by "simple workers." Yet an alternative critical view was part of the context, as Ginzburg makes clear when she quotes Akhmatova: "Akhmatova says that Oleinikov writes like Captain Lebyadkin—who actually wrote excellent poetry."[11] Ginzburg's article also mentions Zabolotsky, who responded to the reproach that his poems were similar to Lebyadkin's as follows: "'I've thought about it myself. But what I write is not a parody; it is my vision.' He then went on to quote the first stanza of Lebyadkin's cockroach poem."[12] At the same time, as Ginzburg notes, Dostoevsky never actually uses the words "A cockroach was caught in a glass": "Oleinikov had no need for an accurate quote; he needed to make a connection between the grotesque in his poetry and the grotesque in Dostoevsky."[13] It is worth adding that this is not simply a matter of literary reference. The crucial point is that the association with Dostoevsky's grotesque immediately sets up the possibility of a tragic reading.

And this is not a complete surprise. Readers of Dostoevsky's novel will recall that it is none other than Captain Lebyadkin who utters the famous phrase: "If there is no God, how can I even be a Captain?" According to Oleg Lekmanov and Mikhail Sverdlov, authors of the definitive scholarly edition of Oleinikov's works, his key theme is precisely a godless world:

> A human being within the "old" system of values is one thing: there is a "soul," which is connected to God, and God is connected back to the "soul." A human being who constitutes the sum of "kidneys, liver, bones, and fat," of "connected points" and "joints," is something else entirely—a human being equated with an insect [. . .] Readers must not only recognize themselves in the crushed insect but also see this inevitable misfortune as a manifestation of an ironclad law: pitifulness and pity in a world thus defined are comical because they appeal to values that do not exist.[14]

From this point of view, the line "falling from the empty skies" (line 78), added by Alexandra Berlina in her translation of the last stanza, expands into interpretative license: the skies are empty precisely because there is no place for pity and compassion in this world, a highly poignant note on which to close. It is also worth remembering that Captain Lebyadkin appears in a novel whose grotesque elements center on revolutionaries who have taken the path of *terror* against innocent people. This motif is undoubtedly brought to the forefront of Oleinikov's "Cockroach."

Other poetic interpretations of the cockroach motif, drawing on sources closer to Oleinikov, find support for this connotation. For example, in the rhymed tale "The Great Cockroach" (1923), Korney Chukovsky, one of the most famous children's poets of the Soviet period and a literary critic with sharp antennae, reacting in his own way to the terror of the civil war, depicts a cockroach as a tyrant who subdues powerful animals and subjects them to torment and torture:

> Вот и стал Таракан
> победителем,
> И лесов и полей повелителем.
> Покорилися звери усатому.
> (Чтоб ему провалиться,
> проклятому!)
> А он между ними похаживает,
> Золоченое брюхо поглаживает:
> "Принесите-ка мне, звери,
> ваших детушек,
> Я сегодня их за ужином
> скушаю!"[15]

> Cock-the-Roach was named the Victor Great and Grand,
> King of Field and Forest, Lord of All the Land.
> Ginger-Whiskers ruled-life was at its worst,

Birds and beasts were fooled.
(May his name be cursed!)
He struts and rubs his yellow tummy
As he orders every Mummie:
"Bring your little ones to me.
I shall take them with my tea,
Or eat them up at supper!"[16]

Despite its whiskers (*usy*, translatable also as "mustache"), the cockroach from Chukovsky's fairy tale was not yet associated with Stalin in the early 1920s, as would come to be the case in due course. Lev Loseff (a frequent variant spelling of Losev in English) observes:

> Among Stalin's several soubriquets, "cockroach" became permanent—thanks to this [Chukovsky's] children's tale. While Stalin was just gaining power at the time when Chukovsky was composing it, the tale did have a target, albeit not a specific political leader but the authoritarian system of government itself, the system which would later be denoted by the word "Stalinism." In the early 1920s, there were several mustachioed contenders for the role of dictator, but from the early 1930s onwards, the title of "cockroach" belonged exclusively to Stalin. [. . .] There is also no doubt that this image is reflected in Mandelstam's famous satire with its cockroach laughing into his mustaches.[17]

Losev is referring to Mandelstam's famous satirical poem known as "The Stalin Epigram" or "The Kremlin Highlander" ("We live, not sensing the country beneath us . . .", "My zhivem pod soboiu ne chuia strany . . ."), which was written in 1933 and became widely known in 1934, recited by the poet to a small group clandestinely. It is unlikely that Oleinikov was unfamiliar with it. In an additional twist, Stalin himself arguably appropriated Chukovsky's tale of the cockroach in 1930, turning it into an allegory of the struggle against the so-called right-wing opposition (Bukharin, Rykov, Tomsky, and others) in his closing speech at the Sixteenth Party Congress (July 2, 1930): "They hear a cockroach rustle; it hasn't yet even had time to crawl out of its hole—but they are already scurrying away, terrified and screaming about a disaster, the destruction of Soviet power. (*General laughter.*)"[18] The struggle Stalin is talking about here ended with a new round of brutal collectivization of peasantry and his complete triumph over his opponents.

What we see, then, is that the cockroach motif is associated with revolutionary and Soviet terror. Oleinikov does not need to use a literal transposition of the citation from Dostoevsky: he relies on connotation to transform the cockroach from a tyrant into a victim, a martyr of terror. Another important work on the literary horizon, again by Mandelstam, was his poem "Lamarck," published in the June 1932 issue of *Novyi Mir*. In this poem, the regression down the evolutionary ladder into the world of the simplest organisms is presented as a metaphor for the degradation of society, which has lost its connection to humanist culture:

Мы прошли разряды насекомых
С наливными рюмочками глаз.
Он сказал: природа вся в разломах,
Зренья нет—ты зришь в последний раз.

Он сказал: довольно полнозвучья,—
Ты напрасно Моцарта любил:
Наступает глухота паучья,
Здесь провал сильнее наших сил.[19]

We went past the orders of the insects
That have shot glasses for eyes.
He said: all of nature is in fractures,
Vision ends—you see for the last time.

He said: sonority is over.
No more Mozart—you loved him in vain.
Now begins the silence of cobwebs,
An abyss beyond our strength.[20]

Science, as personified by Lamarck, provides an elevated viewpoint for the subject onto modernity that sees social history as part of natural history.

Oleinikov's "Cockroach" reads like a polemical inversion of Mandelstam's poem.[21] Here, the cockroach is by no means a symbol of devolution. On the contrary, it—or rather he—is normal, ordinary, even likable. His melancholic courage in the face of death clearly elevates him above the sadists about to commit murder: "Cockroach wrings his tiny hands / and prepares to suffer ache" (lines 29–30). As for science, it is what the sadistic vivisectors represent: not a synonym of truth and wisdom but a source of violence against life.

Of course, it would be possible to read the references to science as a device designed to disguise the author's true intentions (e.g., for "science" read "the NKVD"). But such Aesopian language and use of allegory usually served to fool censors.[22] In fact, Oleinikov never intended his poem for publication and therefore had no need to resort to such tricks. Instead, he used science as a metaphor for the anti-individual forces that turn ordinary people into characters in a tragedy. The scale of these forces surpasses even Stalinist terror, which is but one of its many incarnations. A symbol of the superpersonal and suprapersonal, science becomes responsible for neglecting—indeed, for liquidating—the soul. In this context, "science" is synonymous with terror (lines 17–24):

Таракан к стеклу прижался
И глядит едва дыша . . .
Он бы смерти не боялся,
Если б знал, что есть душа.

Но наука доказала,
Что душа не существует,
Что печенка, кости, сало—
Вот что душу образует.

With his face against the glass,
Cockroach knows: he will be mauled.
Oh, he wouldn't dread his death,
if he knew he was besouled!

But the scientists have proved:
there is no such thing at all.
Kidneys, liver, bones, and fat:
only these make up the soul.

It is probably no coincidence that the meter of "The Cockroach"—trochaic tetrameter with stresses on the third and sixth syllables—echoes another narrative poem by Chukovsky, "Wash 'Em Clean" ("Moidodyr"), which alternates between trochaic tetrameter and dimeter. This 1921 story in verse advocated the need for hygiene, a scientific concept brought into everyday social praxis early in the Soviet period. In it, a washbasin chases a dirty boy, who flees only to run into a crocodile equally obsessed with cleanliness:

А потом как зарычит
На меня,
Как ногами застучит
На меня:
"Уходи-ка ты домой,
Говорит,
Да лицо своё умой,

Говорит,
А не то как налечу,
Говорит,
Растопчу и проглочу!"
Говорит.[23]

Then he turned and glared at me,
Then he stamped and flared at me.
"This is simply a disgrace,"
he exclaimed.
"Go and quickly wash your face,"
he exclaimed.
"If you don't, I'll beat you up,"
he exclaimed.
"If you don't, I'll eat you up!"
he exclaimed.[24]

By the 1930s, however, a violent cleaning-up conjured rather different associations—with the political purges and the repressions carried out in the workplace to "identify elements of the alien class."

To return to Ginzburg's thesis: How, precisely, does the synthesis of opposite modalities work in Oleinikov's "Cockroach"? How does tragedy become comic, and how does laughter lead to tragic catharsis? The most obvious technique is the imitation of the aesthetics of children's poetry. Oleinikov and "card-carrying" OBERIU members were professionals in this domain, some of them working for the state children's literature publishing house, all of them publishing verses in children's books and magazines. At first blush, "The Cockroach" reads almost like a children's poem, hence the associations with Chukovsky: there is the anthropomorphism, the narrative drive, and the rhyme scheme employing simple, often verb-based, rhymes[25] that are mostly organized crosswise (ABAB), with a few paired rhymes bursting into the text like a refrain. In Oleinikov's poem, these rhyme pairs, creatively preserved in Berlina's translation, emphasize the most brutal parts of the narrative, to wit:

- the statement that all hopes for the immortality of the soul are meaningless (lines 25–26):

  Есть всего лишь сочлененья,
  А потом соединенья.

  There are just connected points,
  which, together, make up joints.

- the scene of the cockroach being murdered (lines 43–46):

  Сто четыре инструмента
  Рвут на части пациента.
  От увечий и от ран
  Помирает таракан.

  Hundred tools aim at his heart,
  tear his tortured frame apart.
  Maimed by scalpel, forceps, vice,
  clamp and cutter, Cockroach dies.

- a description of the grief suffered by the son of the cockroach, who saw the executioners torture his father to death with his own eyes (lines 59–60):

  Но отец его не слышит,
  Потому что он не дышит.

  No, his father doesn't listen:
  Death makes parents very distant.

Just as in children's poetry, there is no psychological or moral ambivalence here. The speaker (and consequently readers) feels pure compassion toward the unfortunate cockroach and pure indignation toward the vivisectors who kill it. Masquerading as a moralist, the speaker addresses the main vivisector as an "evil wretch attired in trousers" (line 65). The description of his colleagues in the previous lines leaves no doubt as to their comically exaggerated villainy: "shaggy vivisectors loom: / haughty, hideous, and hairy, / tongs and scalpels spelling doom" (lines 62–64).

Unlike children's poetry, however, "The Cockroach" focuses not on saving the poor victim or punishing the villains, but rather on describing torture that is so terrible it horrifies even the vivisectors themselves: "As the miscreants behold / this, they gasp and back away" (lines 49–50). Nonetheless, the executioners' moment of remorse does not result in the defeat of evil. On the contrary, the vivisectionist triumphs in the finale, and the status of the cockroach as a "martyr of your science" (line 67) is immediately devalued by the posthumous "honors" awaiting this saint (lines 69–80).

When the cockroach acquires "azure eyes," the unabashedly farcical infiltrates the genuinely tragic conclusion. This twist takes the personification of the nonhuman protagonist, the most common technique of folktales, fables, and children's literature, to the point of outright absurdity. Other aspects also conspire to comically exaggerate the anthropomorphism: the cockroach is sad because he is deprived of an immortal soul; preparing to suffer, he "wrings *his tiny hands*" (lines 29); the vivisector palpates his "heaving chest" (line 33). When the cockroach dies, we also learn that he has eyelids (which become "like clay," line 48). In addition, the anthropomorphizing process changes his size in a rather extreme fashion. In the original, the cockroach is torn apart by *a crowd* of vivisectors armed with *104* tools, including nothing less than tongs, saws, and axes. The peak of anthropomorphism is reached with the grief of the cockroach's son. Seized by compassion for the unfortunate and defenseless victim of violence, the reader could easily forget that the protagonist is an insect (lines 55–58):

Там, в щели большого шкапа,
Всеми кинутый, один,
Сын лепечет: "Папа, папа!"
Бедный сын!

In the cupboard's tiny crevice,
all abandoned and alone,
Cockroach Junior cries: "Daddy . . ."
Oh, poor son!

The short line "Oh, poor son!" creates a rhythmic disruption, marking the emotional climax of the text. But it is soon followed by the detail of "his azure eyes," an instance of overkill in the truest and most literal sense that shifts the tone from tragedy to farce. A similar effect occurs when the anthropomorphizing of the cockroach is combined with the reverse technique. Here, humans are being likened to animals (lines 13–14 and 35–38):

Трудно думать обезьяне,
Мыслей нет—она поет.

For an ape, it's hard to think;
So he sings away, the brute . . .

И проткнувши, набок валит
Таракана, как свинью.
Громко ржет и зубы скалит,
Уподобленный коню.

And he pierces it and topples
our poor Cockroach. Gruff and coarse,
he guffaws, his teeth laid bare,
bearing semblance to a horse.

The grotesque in this poem is the flip side of tragedy. It arises from an exaggerated and deliberately tasteless use of emotionally powerful expressive means.

In the emotional trajectory of "The Cockroach," every poignant moment is followed by a comic descent, and each comic device is quickly neutralized by an element of tragedy. The humorous formula "kidneys, liver, bones, and fat: / only these make up the soul" (lines 23–24) is followed by an absurdist "synthesis" apt to cause confusion rather than amusement: "There are just connected points, / which, together, make up joints" (lines 25–26). What, exactly, do these points connect? In the original, *sochlenen'ia* rhymes with *soedinen'ia*: either could be translated as "joints" or "connections," and it is not at all clear why the former are supposed to be elements of the latter rather than the other way around. There can be no answer. The old picture of the world, one centering on the immortal soul, is replaced by blatant nonsense. Here, all metaphysical concepts must be stillborn.

From this metaphysical dead end, the poem proceeds to its murder scene. Here, as noted above, the tragic is negated by the combination of excessive anthropomorphism and the "bestialization" of the executioners. After the brutal description of violence, the atmosphere of tragedy is once again and immediately broken by a twist that betrays the ignorance of the speaker. In the phrase "only subterranean waters / flow from his unmoving corpse" (lines 53–54), "subterranean" sticks out as having nothing to do with the insides of a dead cockroach. This comic line, in its turn, is followed by a truly tragic description of the "poor son" and the triumph of the "vivisector." Yet again, tragedy only lasts for a few lines and the apostrophe directed at the villain ("Evil wretch attired in trousers!") cannot fail to bring a smile to a reader's face. After this invective, we witness the posthumous fate of the cockroach: the "martyr of science" was sacrificed in vain; there will be no retribution for the suffering of the innocent. Yet, no sooner has the sense of tragedy been built up, than a detail such as "azure eyes" undermines the effect.

What is the point of this dynamic? Above all, the oscillations deprive the reader of stability. Reading "The Cockroach," we do not know whether to laugh or cry. The horror of violence, the description of torture, from which there is no salvation or protection, is surrounded by excessive, self-parodic, affectation. At the same time, despite all the comic and grotesque elements, Oleinikov is using the insect as a symbol of tragic powerlessness, a theme explored by Shakespeare (and revived by Kafka): "As flies to wanton boys are we to th' gods. They kill us for their sport."[26]

By applying this formula to Oleinikov's poem, we can see that the gods have been replaced by "science," an embodiment of modernity and new—but no less brutal—forms of violence. The destabilization of the reader's perception in this context is similar to the effect produced by Shakespearean tragedy. Leonid Pinsky

(1906–81)—a contemporary of Oleinikov and a well-known Shakespearean scholar, who was also arrested but, unlike the poet, survived the Gulag—commented on these lines by Shakespeare as follows:

> For the first time, the human being becomes acutely aware of being transient, of having no home in the world—an unsettled, unfinished, unworthy world. Thus, for the first time, the individual is fully aware of *their own* responsibility for everything that happens [. . .] To be like the good, loyal Kent—to hold the stars, the natural order of things or the Great Chain of Being responsible—is as unworthy as it is naive [. . .] Moreover, the magnitude of evil in life is hard to reconcile with the belief in an all-powerful and all-good providence [. . .] Perhaps for the first time in human history, the individual becomes *ashamed* for themselves and others, for the whole, for their own home—and those of others.[27]

These words can be applied to "The Cockroach" too. Nikolai Oleinikov uses the grotesque, farce, and comedic excess as means of *ostranenie* (defamiliarization) that gives a new freshness and poignancy to this very complex of feelings and thoughts that form the basis of humanism.

14

Marina Tsvetaeva, "I Embrace You Like the Horizon" (1936)

TRANSCENDENT LOVE

Обнимаю тебя кругозором
Гор, гранитной короною скал.
(Занимаю тебя разговором—
Чтобы легче дышал, крепче спал.)

Феодального замка боками,
Меховыми руками плюща—
Знаешь—плющ, обнимающий камень—
В сто четыре руки и ручья?

Но не жимолость я—и не плющ я!
Даже ты, что руки мне родней,
Не расплю́щен—а вольноотпущен
На все стороны мысли моей!

. . . Кру́гом клумбы и кру́гом колодца,
Куда камень придет—седым!
Круговою порукой сиротства,—
Одиночеством—круглым моим!

(Та́к вплелась в мои русые пряди—
Не одна серебристая прядь!)
. . . И рекой, разошедшейся на́ две—
Чтобы остров создать—и обнять.

Всей Савойей и всем Пиемонтом,
И—немножко хребет надломя—

Обнимаю тебя горизонтом
Голубым—и руками двумя![1]

I embrace you as a zone of
mountains, granite corona
(engross you in conversation
so you breathe easier, sleep sounder).

Like the castle's walls encroached upon
by ivy's engulfing grasp
you've seen ivy embracing stone
its hundred fur gloved clasp?

But I'm no entwisting woodbine!
Even you, whose hands are my own kind,
not obliterated—but liberated
to the far edges of my mind

Like the rings of flowering beds, of wells
where lichen silvers the stone shelf!
The enfolding of orphanhood
my roundly lonely self!

(As strands of silver
have crept into my fair braids)
. . . Like a river splitting in two
to form an island—and to enlace

Like all Savoy and all Piedmont
and—snapping slightly the mountain spine—
I enclose you with the blue
horizon—and these arms of mine.

(TRANSLATED BY SASHA DUGDALE)

In her lifetime, Tsvetaeva's poetic books appeared in relatively small print runs. Nonetheless, they attracted considerable attention both in Russia and then abroad among the émigré circles in France, where she was a visible presence, albeit on the margins of circles increasingly polarized by cultural politics.[2] In Russia and the West, her permanent place as one of the indisputable Silver Age giants dates to the 1960s. Tsvetaeva's work was a well-kept secret in the Soviet Union from the 1920s and the time of her emigration until the early Thaw period when, in 1958, Ilya Erenburg, the veteran writer and journalist, published a set of poems in the magazine *Literary Moscow*. A large volume of selected works appeared in quick succession in the prestigious Biblioteka Poeta series. Simon Karlinsky's *Marina Cvetaeva: Her Life and Art* (1966), a precocious study of her work and tragic biography, paved the way for studies and editions, alongside which energetic and gifted translators such as Angela Livingstone and more recently Ilya Kamensky working with Jean Valentine have renewed her appeal to a new generation.[3] A spate of important biographies, popular as well as scholarly, and publication of her correspondence with friends and intimates enriched appreciation for the colossal creative will of a writer who can scarcely ever be said to have had a room of her own.[4] In Russian and in translation, multiple readerships, scholarly and popular, have come to appreciate Tsvetaeva's authorial daring, interest in gender fluidity, and complex sense of identity. Episodes of same-sex love in her biography and her play with gender identity, an expression of a "lifelong struggle with her lesbian sexual orientation,"[5] have generated work from a gender studies perspective.[6] Scholars of the émigré milieu found rich material in her essays about contemporary writers and other topics. Highly noteworthy in this regard is her remarkable essay "My Pushkin." Written in France after the Berlin summer Olympics when Jesse Owens famously triumphed, it took the myth of Pushkin in a new direction. Tsvetaeva makes out of his African ancestry a principle of "blackness" that stands for those marginalized by patriarchy and power, poets above all. Feminist readings of her biography and work have productively explored the huge pressures poverty and motherhood put on her writing at a time when the question of what difference a room of one's own made was being put forward by Virginia Woolf.

Every great writer requires a biography in order to be known by the public, and a number of well-researched biographies, as well as more popular spin-offs, captured a life that was nothing if not turbulent. Born into the intelligentsia class—her father was a distinguished classicist and museum director in Moscow, her mother a musician—Tsvetaeva, through her education and early reading, discovered her love of romantic myth and romantic myths of love, of dramas and tales of sacrifice, all elements that informed her friendships and can be found abundantly in the life she lived with her husband Sergei Efron, a handsome, Jewish poet who fought on the side of the Whites.[7] She followed him into exile, and their marriage was interrupted by long separations and extramarital affairs. Ostensibly drawn to Eurasianism, a cultural philosophy pursued by some émigré figures who advocated rapprochement with the USSR, Efron had also become embroiled in NKVD clandestine operations in France. Unaware of his involvement in a foreign assassination, Tsvetaeva eventually followed him back to Russia, without knowing that Efron had already been arrested and their daughter sent into penal servitude. At the outbreak of World War II, she was evacuated with her son Mur (Georgii) to the backwater of Elabuga in Tatarstan, where she took her own life in 1941.

Tsvetaeva found vehicles for acts of life writing in all the genres in which she worked. The Russian concept of *zhiznetvorchestvo* (life creation), prevalent among her generation of modernists, was made for a writer with her powers of imagination, literary sensibility, and emotional penetration. Like a Baudelaire or a Wagner, she captured both the real and the transcendent, rooting the symbolic in reality and transforming reality into something larger. Empathy and a sense of ethical principle are also powerful motors of her art, perhaps nowhere better seen than in "My Pushkin."

Tsvetaeva used every possible genre, from the narrative poem to the personal letter, to express her many themes. She wrote about nature, friendship, war, childhood, and motherhood, about Russia, poets (Pushkin, Mayakovsky, Pasternak, Sophia Parnok), and poetry. The epistolary triangle she formed with Pasternak and Rilke can be read alongside the ethereal "New Year Letter," her long poetic elegy for Rilke, and the "Poem of the Air" ("Poema vozdukha," 1927), a work inspired by Charles Lindberg's record-breaking transatlantic flight that builds a comparison between poet and aviator and explores how acutely she wrestled with the boundary between flesh and spirit, "regarding the 'victory of the human spirit over the natural elements [*stikhiei*]'" as a Pyrrhic success.[8]

Tsvetaeva believed that there were poets dominated by a single theme—that is, poets who were perfectly formed as sensibilities—and poets (like Goethe) who grew and ramified. Her contemporary Maximilian Voloshin (again, the subject of a fine portrait by Tsvetaeva) once said that she contained ten poets. The larger-than-life quality of her personality and the intensity of her intimate life and its expression would seem to bear out his claim, as does a plethora of formal techniques she devised for her uniquely expressive style. Those qualities of variety and explosive linguistic and metrical innovation have, more than with other Russian poets, sent foreign readers searching for analogies that help restore what even the best translations can lose. A writer whose voice carries her strongly performative style, Tsvetaeva brought a peerless ear and eye to innovation in Russian metrics and daringly combined classical meters with folk rhythms. Her repeated use of the long dash to replace verbs and to hasten the pace to the next thought gives the impression of a mind at work faster than language can carry it. This feature and her frequent use of exclamation make the look of her poems on the page instantly recognizable. Her love of accentual feet has brought her comparison with Gerald Manley Hopkins and his sprung rhythm. Her combination of conceptual loftiness and an almost geometric sense of abstract space and time has inspired comparisons to Rilke, and, somewhat inevitably, her tragic biography, controversies surrounding her amorous life, her style of parenting, and her suicide have suggested affinities with Sylvia Plath.[9]

Bearing in mind Voloshin's characterization, one has the impression nonetheless that, however many poets seem to live in Tsvetaeva's world, and whatever the multiplicity of themes, there is both great stylistic unity to her work and an underlying intellectual and emotional coherence. The fundamental basis of everything she writes about is an idea of love, and it is an omnipresent, even unstoppable, generative principle across genres. Her longer works—plays, narrative poetry, and cycles—can sacrifice plot for concentration on the psychological power of the monologue, one of the great forms in her work. If there is an unrelieved intensity about the treatment of love as a theme, it may be because there is a part–whole relationship between the lyric and larger entities like the cycle or the narrative poem.[10] Love in Tsvetaeva is configured to represent couples sometimes united in ecstasy but more often split apart by unequal strength of passion or circumstance. Moments of separation are no less powerful than togetherness in pushing speakers to extreme declarations. In that world, the lyric "I," often an androgyne, is riven between a strenuous need for attachment and possession and the countervailing resistance of the beloved.

Passion in Tsvetaeva's poetry is embodied essence. In her "New Year Letter" written in response to the news of Rilke's death, the female speaker mourns and reaches higher and higher to pursue his lofty spirit.[11] No poems in Tsvetaeva, and perhaps in the entire canon of Russian poetry, treat passion with more desperate plangency than the "Poem of the Mountain" ("Poema gory") and "Poem of the End" ("Poema kontsa"), the two long works dedicated to the beginning and end of Tsvetaeva's affair with Konstantin Rodzevich in 1924, shortly after her emigration to Czechoslovakia.[12] In "Poem of the Mountain," her account of a passionate affair that took place in Prague, the speaker achieves oneness with the beloved, the struggle of the journey uphill; in "Poem of the End," by contrast, every gradient in the landscape marks the undoing of that love. Sense of place, personal circumstance, and real-time narration in a discursive present are part of the autobiographical nature of these works.[13] The eruptive energy of the passionate affair and the torrent of despair as she descends the mountain after their tryst ends cannot keep these works earthbound as contained episodes.

In her adaptations of the myths of Phaedra and Ariadne into modernist neoclassical drama, Tsvetaeva invented metrical equivalences for Greek tragedy.[14] The lofty tone and stylized utterance produce a form appropriate for love conceived on a mythic plane. Her version of *Phèdre,* a story of incestuous passions, displays her fascination with one-sided love exercises, since her writing and biography return to situations in which the beloved fails to see the lover, or, as Phaedra says to Hippolytus,

You looked at me so little
Blindly unawarely[15]

before forcing him to acknowledge her criminal lust. In her drama *Ariadne*, the prominent theme of "failure to connect" (*razminovenie*) reaches a climax in a scene of abandonment, no less powerful for the mythic status of the protagonists. The opening statement of the *Girlfriend* (*Podruga*, 1914–15), ten poems exploring love through Shakespearean and romantic archetypes, is "I love you" ("Ia Vas liubliu").[16]

In a letter of 1926, written to Salomeia Andronnikova, a legendary beauty and the addressee of a famous love poem by Mandelstam, Tsvetaeva produced a key to her erotic philosophy: "I, when I love a person, take him with me everywhere, do not part with him in myself, *assimilate*, gradually turn him into the air I breathe and in which I breathe—everywhere and nowhere."[17] Tsvetaeva's love poetry territorializes love and also defies mortal limits. The striving to communicate posthumously with the beloved reaches higher and higher; the love of country unifying the cycle of poems in *Anguish for my Homeland* (*Toska po rodine*) pushes across borders. In the poem chosen for this chapter, the cliché that love makes the world go round seems true: the poem represents what one might call, reaching for a word, *surroundingness*. Love here means the expanse between lovers, the expansive embrace that encircles and contains, and the contrary impulse toward liberation that the beloved needs.

Similarly, a tension between permanence and impermanence creates a crucial dramatic feature of Tsvetaeva's love poetry, treated most movingly in her 1923 cycle of ten poems *Provoda*, a work that seems to apply all the devices of her poetics, including puns, split words and interlinear enjambed word boundaries, fragmentation, and the ubiquitous dashes that convey how hard language must work to communicate feeling.[18] The title alone, playing on "farewells" ("próvody") and "telegraph wires" ("provodá"), makes the cycle as a statement of ambivalence relevant to "I Embrace You." Separation rather than fidelity drives emotional volatility.[19] Love given if it is truly love, while never selfless, is also never just possessive. Sharing a lover is not to diminish one's love, because love seems indivisible and inexhaustible; and yet love is not altruistic, since it must be reciprocated. The attachments of love, physical and spiritual, seek proximity and intimacy, yet overpower space; the power of love is more encompassing, like a force field that surrounds the beloved.

Even a shorter lyric can take us directly into the emotional world of Tsvetaeva's poetry. "I Embrace You" is the second poem in a sequence of six lyrics ("Verses to an Orphan," ["Stikhi k sirote"]) that Tsvetaeva composed in 1936 and never collected into one of her books of poems. Its dedicatee was the young Russian émigré poet Anatoly Shteiger, who had written to her from a sanatorium in Switzerland where he was to undergo an operation.[20] Not for the first time, Tsvetaeva embarked on an epistolary relationship in which she took on the roles of mother, poet, and lover. Details of his landscape permeate the cycle: glaciers, snowdrifts, mountain ranges, and specific place-names such as the references at the end of this poem to northern Italy and France. The correspondence is incomplete, with only one of his letters having survived. They never managed to meet, and, by the time the cycle appeared in the journal *Sovremennye Zapiski* in 1938, it was an epitaph to the coup de foudre. The first poem in the cycle establishes the setting—"A tiara of mountains made of ice"—and also introduces motifs that will play more of a part in "I Embrace You," such as ivy and the fortress of stone, than in the next poems, which develop other image systems. Characteristically, the cycle ends on a note of masochistic devotion with the poet noting a wound in her palm, a romantic form of stigma, and pledging to put her hand in a flame for him.

There is not much of a boundary between the *poema* and the lyric cycle in Tsvetaeva. Both are encompassing forms, holding in balance different moods and emotional states that are the stages in an emotional history traversed in the course of the whole. In comparing the end of a lyric to the opening of a wound, Tsvetaeva wished to convey not that separate poems in a cycle were not intelligible on their own but rather that the dynamism of the emotional portrayal depended on the successive effects, and affects of the entire structure and movement. The sequence is formally diverse: poems 1, 2, and 6 are written in rhyming quatrains, poems 3 and 4 are written as free verse with lines groups unequally, and the fifth poem is in three couplets. The first poem sets up certain reference points for the remaining five: mountainous and rocky landscapes (often granite), the gesture of embrace, botanic images, fairy-tale-like images (the castle, the cave, the dragon, the panther), interwoven branches and rivers as emblems of love, crescendoed in the image of the rainbow. And because the cycle sustains that initial intensity, fixated on the ecstasy of the speaker's quest to connect with the beloved, "I Embrace You" can stand apart from the cycle as a self-contained declaration. Drama in Tsvetaeva is not only a matter of gradual work toward a culmination. Long poems and short poems display her ability to make lines and stanzas, beginnings and endings, gripping moments: a whole work never seems more, or less, than the sum of its parts. Tsvetaeva does not adjust her style for scale, and even here, in a brief lyric, the reader encounters her trademark use of exclamation, hanging clauses, unexpected rhymes, habitual use of the long dash to replace verbs, and ellipsis. She makes of the quatrain in alternating rhyme, usually a highly controlled stanza form, a space for emotional volatility. Yet a contrary effect of containment is built into the stanzaic shape of "I Embrace You." End-stopped and enjambed lines are in about equal number in the poem, perhaps giving an undercurrent of containment and resistance. Even a stanza break can mimic sense: here the extension of a circular view (*krugozorom*, line 1) over the line finds its syntactic and visual border when it reaches the mountains (*skal*, line 2). Later on, other rhymes, semantic as well as phonetic, will add to the coherence of feeling. The geography of love that begins with unbounded space in the first quatrain acquires more specific (albeit no less exotic) coordinates in stanza 6, underscored in the rhyme *Piemontom/gorizontom* (lines 21 and 23), and the emotional tension of the poem between images of domination and independence is distilled into the image of breaking and holding conveyed in the poem's final, compound rhyme (*nadlomia/rukami dvumia*, lines 22 and 24).

How ardent does a profession of love have to be to be sincere and successful? Do the strongest statements imply an attempt to overcome doubt? Certainly Tsvetaeva's embrace seems devised to eliminate the possibility of failure. A Pushkinian love poem works by seduction and insinuation. The speaker of Pushkin's 1830 lyric "When I enclose your slender frame in my embraces" ("Kogda v ob'iatiia moi tvoi stroinyi stan ia zakliuchaiu") holds the beloved tight in order to whisper sweet nothings into her ear. Tsvetaeva's approach is to grasp the entire visual field in her embrace so that the lover's existence is nearly unthinkable outside it, and her voice carries across distances. Her world, in the excellent phrase of M. L. Gasparov, is like "a closed ring and horseshoe magnet in which one pole attracts material things and the other the spiritual."[21] Nothing then could be more direct than the opening statement, a declaration that, with this poem, the first-person speaker performs an embrace of the addressee (whose gender is masculine, as we learn from the past verbal forms, line 4). Perhaps the most striking question the first stanza raises is about the actual nature of the dialogue between speaker and addressee. There is a reference to a conversation (line 3), and perhaps the use of parentheses here both indicates a quotation and also creates a visual (graphic) image of embrace juxtaposed with the grander plane bordered by mountains. It is also overpowering, and the parenthetic aside, meant first for the speaker and the reader eavesdropping on the intimacy, is not actually directed at the lover at all. Between the lines, we sense an anxiety. Is this declaration the first time the speaker has expressed her feelings? Is it a reciprocity after the lover's capitulation? Or is the point of the declaration an attempt to dissolve resistance, a bid on such a scale that he couldn't possibly escape?

All of these conjectures about motivation are part of the psychological implication inherent in the opening stanza. It is very human to express love as a quantity: the more one wishes to be seen to love, the larger the quantifier. The lover who wishes to be seen to love incontrovertibly must also love immensely or, in this case, nearly infinitely. The all-encompassing embrace encircles both speaker and addressee. Has the addressee asked the speaker to indicate the extent of her love? (In other words, is there an implied question like: "How much do you really love me?") The answer that her love is as tall as cliffs, as hard as granite, as wide as mountains leaves no doubt. The parenthetic statement of lines 3–4 is its own act of encirclement: whereas the declaration of love may require a bold gesture on a grand scale, the intimate statement that persuades can be no greater than the two-line space of a poetic phrase.

The hint of a magical quality, the sense that perhaps a spell has been cast, spills into the next two stanzas with their feudal images evoking a premodern world in which knights errant, leaving their castles, can be put to sleep (as in Ariosto's poetry or Pushkin's *Ruslan and Liudmila*), and women can attain transcendent love (as in the case of Isolde). The second stanza expands the definition of the embrace. In Pushkin, fire and ice are famously the contrasting elements of love and friendship. Here the visual elements are vegetation and stone, the first the organic matter of entanglement, the second the substance to which vegetation cleaves, both gripping and pulling away from the rock. The speaker's conquest is stealthy, creeping up the sides of the castle like a pair of fur gloves that cling like ivy. The double simile can be read in two directions, as tenor and vehicle are interchangeable—the ivy being fur-like, the fur being ivy-like. Modernist poetry favors a rich variety of discourses, and the verbal specificity of Tsvetaeva's poetry lies in dynamic word creation. Like Mayakovsky and Khlebnikov, Tsvetaeva reveled in the generative property of Russian morphology, using grammatical case, prefix and suffixal systems, and highly productive lexemes to coin neologisms. In her highly active exploitation of Russian morphology, Tsvetaeva likes to take some creative license and bend grammar, and she uses the proximity of lines or density of poetic form (what Russian verse theorists refer to as the *tesnota stikhovogo riada*) to add new connotation. Although *pliushch* ("ivy") functions as a noun, it also looks like the participle of the verb *pliushchit'* ("to flatten," "to make smooth"). While that verb has a different stress, its meaning is evoked here and also appears in the next stanza (line 11) as *raspliushchit'*, with reference to the extent of the lover's grasp as a metaphor for conquest and her antithetical ability to release and grant freedom. The interchange of verb and noun would be consistent with the transformation of substances that metaphorically characterizes this vision of love: to act like ivy is to be ivy.

Both stanzas 2 and 3 define the embrace spatially as vertical and horizontal, and therefore inescapable, as the ivy puts out its tendrils. The ivy could be embracing the stone, or the stone could be itself described as "embracing." Once again, the grammar subtly underscores the reciprocal action of stone and plant and allows an exchange of subject and object: the participle of the verb "to embrace" (*obnimaiushchii*) can function adjectivally or predicatively, making lines 7–8 open to two translations: "You know that the ivy embracing the stone is like a hundred and four hands and streams" or "You know that the stone embracing the ivy . . ." Even here, the constitution of love is mutable, grasping like hands and flowing like water, clinging and loosening. If there has been overstatement from the start, it may emanate from an awareness that the attachment of love cannot escape a paradoxical disequilibrium between ivy and stone, hand and river, lover and beloved, conquest and escape. What does the beloved know? The question is a delving into whether he understands that the expansive nature of love, set out so impressively in the first stanza, is more a reaching beyond and a grasping for than it is the certainty of possession.

The turning point comes in stanza 3, with its fixed poles of the female (plant) and the male (mineral). Aware that metaphor has its limits, and that love cannot ensnare like ivy, the speaker disentangles this first metaphorical strand. Letting go, however, does not mean tearing the ivy off the stone and thereby releasing it (*raspliushchit'*) and granting love the freedom to expand, a gesture that requires her own self-denial, emphasized by the internal rhymes in lines 9–11 (*pliushch, raspliushchen, vol'nootpushchen*). Such release is not the same as unfettered freedom, and elsewhere Tsvetaeva qualifies love as "desirable non-freedom among human beings."[22] The state of being emancipated (*vol'nootpushchen*) is seen as coterminous with the lover's own thoughts, and it is those thoughts in their poetic action that form the new stone on which the beloved, now as much a part of her as her own hand, can act, "taking the beloved everywhere" as the definition of what it means to love. Ivy and love must come up against stony natures. True to the opening images of the first stanza, the primacy of stone reasserts itself here against the metaphor of the embrace. That embrace might be like plant growth. But its object remains as staunch as the cliff face, the castle walls, the stone that is the object of "embracing" (*obnimaiushchii*) and not its active subject. Even in a world that contains its "flowering beds" (line 13), the source of nourishment is the well made from stone. In a poem of 1920, Tsvetaeva wrote, "One person is made from stone, another from clay . . . ," and this later work confirms that her own capacity to love is adamantine.[23] The elderly, presumably after a lifetime of wanting love, must still come to that well made from stone, aware that it is a metaphor for the emotion built around their own sense of isolation or orphanhood. At the center of the lover's being is awareness of presence and absence.

Space rather than time is the threat. Age does not diminish passion. The threads of silver in the speaker's hair metamorphose in her mind into a new source of energy, a river. If anything, age is the well out of which passion can continue to grow. Line 14 has the ring of a proverb: love comes to those who wait, that is, have become gray with age. But, if she were asked why she is prepared to wait for so long, the answer comes in a metaphorical expression that intertwines the hand that reaches and the circle that encloses. The root and image of the "circle" (*krug*) remain key to the poem. *Surroundingness*, if we can be allowed a neologism of our own, has a moral dimension by implying that love carries a responsibility to house or shelter: her loneliness is bound to his orphaned state. The pledge seems to be understood as reciprocal because it is extended to the orphan by a lover-cum-mother and by the adoptive-child-cum-lover to the woman, and it is perhaps even owed to the female because her solitude is unbroken. In such responsibility to the orphan, she has found a type of circularity that complements her self-enclosed solitude and finds their congruity and the basis for their togetherness. Out of two types of apartness, orphanhood and separation, a bond can be formed. Its basis seems to be ethical more than erotic: *krugovaia poruka* (line 15) denotes mutual responsibility, a caring that has been tested by waiting and age. Semantically, visually, and phonetically, stanza 4 is full of repetition: the circularity of the flower bed (*klumba*) goes with the idea of surrounding and aroundness (*krugom* [twice], *kolodtsa, krugovoi, kruglyi*), and there is persistent alliteration of *-k*, particularly at the beginning of the line. The stanza reverberates with the horizon of the poem's opening promise to embrace on that scale. While the promise still ripens, at least verbally the sound of the poem has created its circularity by an encompassing consonant and vowel pattern. And the poem plays a visual experiment by drawing contrasts. The silver threads running through her auburn hair either accentuate her youth or underscore her aging, like the metaphorical river that hugs the contours of the island divided on each side into his and hers, loneliness and orphanhood, two faces of the same state or two strands intertwined as tenor and vehicle, and the rhyme words *priadi/dve*.[24] But the twist is that the female is both one part of the island and also the river that creates it in an embrace, defining both separation and togetherness.[25]

Has the poet at this point come to renounce the idea of love as possession? Not at all, because stronger binding elements than the honeysuckle (in this translation rendered as *woodbine*, l.9), a royal leaf, and the humbler ivy emerge out of the chain of metaphors. Having aspired originally to surround him all round and contain him from the outside, the speaker is now both outside and inside, sharing his experience of isolation and making out of it their common boundary against the exterior. Once that inner loneliness has been acknowledged, it leads to a new belief that to love is to contain and also to expand.

The message of stanza 5 is that love must be built out of contradiction if it is to have a lasting foundation. Repetition and parallelism are tropes Tsvetaeva uses to convey a tug of war between movement so essential to her thought and attachment so essential to her emotions. The final two stanzas play off that tension, reiterating the act of embracing at the end, yet also at line 20 leaving the time frame open by using the infinitive. Here the use of the long dash and the parentheses also convey ambivalence by isolating syntactically the moment two people are cleaved apart and then through her intervention cleave together. The punctuation makes space for the interweaving of the two metaphors of braided hair and the river, and containing the risk his freedom brings (lines 17–20):

(Та́к вплелась в мои русые пряди—
Не одна серебристая прядь!)
. . . И рекой, разошедшейся на́ две—
Чтобы остров создать—и обнять.

(As strands of silver
have crept into my fair braids)
. . . Like a river splitting in two
to form an island—and to enlace.

That freedom, while not denied, is granted only briefly as the poem circles back to the beginning and asserts its claim: "to embrace" as a performative utterance. If the poem had ended with the fifth stanza as above, then its trajectory would have been from an act of surrounding expressed as an indicative verb in stanza 1 (*Obnimaiu*) to the potential to embrace confined to an infinitive verb (*obniat'*). The final stanza, having approached disaster, changes that all over again by restating the claim. Is the breadth of the horizon lesser or greater than the breadth of all of Savoy and Piedmont? These points on the map look beyond the original barrier of cliffs, the ridge of which has been broken, building up to the declaration in the poem's reprisal of the first line in the penultimate line. Repetition is its own form of circularity, variation is extension. This final embrace is of the entire sky (blue) and is two-handed. Is this a claiming gesture or a beseeching gesture? The poem poses a question to the lover without waiting for an answer. Part promise, part wish fulfillment, this love lyric ends by coming at the addressee both from above (*nad*) and on the same level (*gorizont*). It surrounds the addressee rhetorically, just like the two hands compared to the river, and works to create out of two selves a single island.

"I Embrace You" is a work about love and the negotiation between possession and dispossession, an unusually concentrated expression of an important subject of Tsvetaeva's dramas and longer poems. If this slighter work offers relatively few verbal fireworks from a poet famed for ingenuity and complexity to rival Mayakovsky in the form of verse, it characteristically reveals the manifold purpose of language in a modernist lyric. Nouns, adverbs, and verbs all communicate essential information about literal meaning. But the relationship between signifier and signified extends to a symbolic level on which the parts of speech—verbal roots, prefixes, adverbs—point to another higher emotional plane of existence, the famous distinction between being and existence (*byt/bytie*) recognized in the Russian language. The notion of "around" joins up to the concept of the circle that closes the space between language as a sign and language as an essence. Words become what they stand for in a supreme effort to communicate states of feeling that might otherwise be ineffable.

15

Anna Akhmatova, "Secrets of Craft" (1936–60)

THE FORMS OF INSPIRATION

Тайны ремесла

1. *Творчество*

Бывает так: какая-то истома;
В ушах не умолкает бой часов;
Вдали раскат стихающего грома.
Неузнанных и пленных голосов
Мне чудятся и жалобы и стоны,
Сужается какой-то тайный круг,
Но в этой бездне шепотов и звонов
Встает один, все победивший звук.
Так вкруг него непоправимо тихо,
Что слышно, как в лесу растет трава,
Как по земле идет с котомкой лихо . . .
Но вот уже послышались слова
И легких рифм сигнальные звоночки,—
Тогда я начинаю понимать,
И просто продиктованные строчки
Ложатся в белоснежную тетрадь.

2.

Мне ни к чему одические рати
И прелесть элегических затей.
По мне, в стихах все быть должно некстати,
Не так, как у людей.

Когда б вы знали, из какого сора
Растут стихи, не ведая стыда,
Как желтый одуванчик у забора,
Как лопухи и лебеда.

Сердитый окрик, дегтя запах свежий,
Таинственная плесень на стене . . .
И стих уже звучит, задорен, нежен,
На радость вам и мне.

3. *Муза*

Как и жить мне с этой обузой,
А еще называют Музой,
Говорят: “Ты с ней на лугу . . .”
Говорят: “Божественный лепет . . .”
Жестче, чем лихорадка, оттреплет,
И опять весь год ни гу-гу.

4. *Поэт*

Подумаешь, тоже работа,—
Беспечное это житье:
Подслушать у музыки что-то
И выдать шутя за свое.

И чье-то веселое скерцо
В какие-то строки вложив,
Поклясться, что бедное сердце
Так стонет средь блещущих нив.

А после подслушать у леса,
У сосен, молчальниц на вид,
Пока дымовая завеса
Тумана повсюду стоит.

Налево беру и направо,
И даже, без чувства вины,
Немного у жизни лукавой,
И все—у ночной тишины.

5. Читатель

Не должен быть очень несчастным
И, главное, скрытным. О нет!—
Чтоб быть современнику ясным,
Весь настежь распахнут поэт.

И рампа торчит под ногами,
Все мертвенно, пусто, светло,
Лайм-лайта позорное пламя
Его заклеймило чело.

А каждый читатель как тайна,
Как в землю закопанный клад,
Пусть самый последний, случайный,
Всю жизнь промолчавший подряд.

Там все, что природа запрячет,
Когда ей угодно, от нас.
Там кто-то беспомощно плачет
В какой-то назначенный час.

И сколько там сумрака ночи,
И тени, и сколько прохлад,
Там те незнакомые очи
До света со мной говорят,

За что-то меня упрекают
И в чем-то согласны со мной . . .
Так исповедь льется немая,
Беседы блаженнейший зной.

Наш век на земле быстротечен
И тесен назначенный круг,
А он неизменен и вечен—
Поэта неведомый друг.

6. Последнее стихотворение

Одно, словно кем-то встревоженный гром,
С дыханием жизни врывается в дом,
Смеется, у горла трепещет,
И кружится, и рукоплещет.

Другое, в полночной родясь тишине,
Не знаю, откуда крадется ко мне,
Из зеркала смотрит пустого
И что-то бормочет сурово.
А есть и такие: средь белого дня,

Как будто почти что не видя меня,
Струятся по белой бумаге,
Как чистый источник в овраге.
А вот еще: тайное бродит вокруг—

Не звук и не цвет, не цвет и не звук,—
Гранится, меняется, вьется,
А в руки живым не дается.
Но это!.. по капельке выпило кровь,

Как в юности злая девчонка—любовь,
И, мне не сказавши ни слова,
Безмолвием сделалось снова.
И я не знавала жесточе беды.

Ушло, и его протянулись следы
К какому-то крайнему краю,
А я без него . . . умираю.

7. Эпиграмма

Могла ли Биче, словно Дант, творить,
Или Лаура жар любви восславить?
Я научила женщин говорить . . .
Но, боже, как их замолчать заставить!

8. Про стихи

Владимиру Нарбуту
Это—выжимки бессонниц,
Это—свеч кривых нагар,
Это—сотен белых звонниц
Первый утренний удар . . .

Это—теплый подоконник
Под черниговской луной,
Это—пчелы, это—донник,
Это—пыль, и мрак, и зной.

9.

Осипу Мандельштаму

Я над ними склонюсь, как над чашей,
В них заветных заметок не счесть—
Окровавленной юности нашей
Это черная нежная весть.
Тем же воздухом, так же над бездной
Я дышала когда-то в ночи,
В той ночи и пустой и железной,
Где напрасно зови и кричи.
О, как пряно дыханье гвоздики,
Мне когда-то приснившейся там,—
Это кружатся Эвридики,
Бык Европу везет по волнам.
Это наши проносятся тени
Над Невой, над Невой, над Невой,
Это плещет Нева о ступени,
Это пропуск в бессмертие твой.
Это ключики от квартиры,
О которой теперь ни гугу . . .
Это голос таинственной лиры,
На загробном гостящей лугу.

10.

Многое еще, наверно, хочет
Быть воспетым голосом моим
То, что, бессловесное, грохочет,
Иль во тьме подземный камень точит,
Или пробивается сквозь дым.
У меня не выяснены счеты
С пламенем, и ветром, и водой . . .
Оттого-то мне мои дремоты
Вдруг такие распахнут ворота
И ведут за утренней звездой.[1]

Secrets of Craft

1. Creation

Sometimes it's a kind of languor—

The ticking of the clock grows loud,
The muttering of distant thunder.
I dream of voices, a captive crowd
Of strangers—plaintive cries
Closing around me, an invisible ring.
But in these depths where whispers rise
One sound overcomes the throng
So all the rest are hushed for good,
So hushed I hear grass breach the earth
A traveler's footsteps through the wood—
And now faint words struggle forth
And rhythms marked by signal bell
And now I seem to understand—
The words dictated to me fill
A pale notebook, in my own hand.

2.

I have no need of odic routs
Or the pleasures of elegiac study.
My poems come unannounced
They burst in rudely.

If only you knew where they took root
From what muck,
Shameless as dandelions in the dirt
Or pigweed, or dock.

An angry shout, the hot tar smell,
The mysterious mildew on the wall . . .
And there it is—the poem swells
Tender, fervent, there for all.

3. *The Muse*

Around my neck a noose
They insist on calling the Muse
Saying *go stroll with her, my dear*
Or *that divine babble in your ear . . .*
She roughs me up like a fever, then
Runs off for the rest of the year.

4. Poet

Can this carefree existence
Really be called work—
Snatching a sudden refrain,
Making it mine with a joke.

Arranging someone's scherzo
Into lines of my own—
To swear that the poor heart suffers
In shining fields, alone!

I eavesdrop in the forest,
Among pines, who once took a vow
Of silence, as a curtain of mist
Drops all about me, slow.

I take a little from here,
A little from there, without guilt.
From this artful life I pick out what I need
And all—in the silence of night.

5. Reader

There's no call for great unhappiness
Nor secrecy, for sure—
To be understood by her peers
The poet must be flung wide like a door.

The thrust of the stage beneath her feet
And all is empty, deathly, bright,
Her forehead branded
By the disgraceful flame of limelight.

But every reader is a mystery
A trove buried in earth—
Even the last of them, coming upon it,
Who has never since uttered a word.

Here is all that nature hides
When she wants, from view.
Here is someone weeping helplessly
At each given cue.

And the twilit hours
The shadowy cold of night
When those same unknown eyes
Speak volumes till first light,

Sometimes they reproach me
Sometimes we're in accord
A wordless confession, pouring forth,
The blissful fevered talk.

Our time on earth passes quickly
Our appointed circle is small,
But the poet's unknown friend
Remains constant, eternal.

6. Last Poem

One breaks in, like a thunder bolt
Heaved into noise, it is vital, breathing,
It laughs, flickering at the throat
And circles, applauding.

Another is born in the middle of the night
It creeps in from a hidden haunt,
It stares out of the empty mirror
Muttering—gaunt.

And there are others—in bright day
I stand unseen,
While they pour down the page
Like a pure spring through a ravine.

Or else they prowl mysteriously about me,
Muted—pale and wordless shapes
That shift and splinter and seethe
Evading my embrace.

But this one! It drained my veins of blood,
As once that hellcat Love did suck
And without uttering a single word
Back to silence shrunk.

And I haven't known a more awful grief.
It's gone and only its traces are left
Reaching to the furthest line
And leaving me here—dying.

7. Epigram

Could Beatrice have created the Empyrean peak?
Or Laura sung the heat of love?
I taught women how to speak—
But how the hell to shut them up!

8. Of Poetry

For Vladimir Narbut
The silt of sleepless nights—
The soot of crooked candles—
A hundred towers, all white—
The first bell sounds for matins.

A warm seat at the window—
Under the Chernigov moon,
And bees—and sweet clover—
And dust and heat and gloom.

9.

For Osip Mandelstam
I bend over it, as I would a chalice
Containing countless secret truths—
Here in black a fond record
Of our bloodiest youth.
I stood over the same abyss,
The air I breathed was the same
On that night of iron emptiness
When all cries were in vain.
That peppery breath of carnation
How it came to me once in a daze—
It's Eurydice's slow revolution

Europa borne over the waves.
Here our shades rise up
Over the Neva they flee
It's the Neva's splash at the step,
Your pass to immortality.
It's the keys to an apartment
That disappeared without trace—
It's the voice of the mysterious lyre
Idling in the burial place.

10.

Yes, so much remains that still demands
I raise it up in song—
A wordless thing that roars and booms
Or hollows out underground caverns
Or emerges through a veil of fog.
I have not yet settled my debts
With flame and water and air—
And so in my fits of drowsing
Such gates are thrown back wide
And lead me beyond the morning star.

(TRANSLATED BY SASHA DUGDALE)

Like *Requiem,* her great cycle of poems about the Stalinist Terror, the ten poems of "The Secrets of the Craft" were written over nearly twenty-five years, starting with "I have no need for odic routs" (poem 2) in 1943, followed by "Yet so much remains" (the final poem in the definitive cycle, composed in 1944), and then "Creation" (poem 1) in 1958. The penultimate poem in the set ("To Mandelstam") dates to 1966, the last year of Akhmatova's life, and the remaining six poems formed a cluster in 1960. All ten appeared in ten different publications ("The Muse" and "Epigram" in different issues of *Literaturnaia Gazeta*). Despite its thematic coherence and an organic unity appropriate to the poem's holistic representation of poetic inspiration, the poems were not conceived as a cycle. Evidence relating to Akhmatova's intention to publish a collection titled *The Seventh Book* (*Sed'maia kniga*) suggests that the idea of organizing the poems as a cycle grew out of that (unrealized) project.[2]

A preliminary word may be helpful about Akhmatova's standing toward the end of her life, since this is one context for a cycle that meditates on the nature of poetic art. "Who could have hoped that Akhmatova, the sorceress of the faraway Tsarskoe Selo, would in the 1960s conjure up a disciple?" asked one American critic about the lone survivor of the Silver Age.[3] She posed the question in the same year Akhmatova traveled to the West to receive an honorary doctorate from the University of Oxford, her first trip outside the USSR and during the reprieve of the Khrushchev-era Thaw. By the late 1920s, Akhmatova was publishing less poetry in the Soviet press. Advanced plans for two volumes of *Collected Verse* (1927) were scuppered late in the day. Nonetheless, Akhmatova was prolific in the war years, and her output has been described in terms of works that were intended for publication (such as her essays on Pushkin), works that were censored, and works she did not expect to publish and wrote for her "desk drawer," as the expression goes.[4] In 1946, she and the satirist and master of psychological prose Mikhail Zoshchenko were targeted by Andrei Zhdanov in a notorious article in *Pravda* that faulted her for concentrating "on the drawing room, the bedroom, and the chapel" rather than on Soviet reality.[5] Various subsequent attempts at publication were thwarted. It was during these decades that Akhmatova, much consumed by personal dramas in her private life, practiced the art of "writing for the drawer" and also became a cult figure. Beneath the stoic silence, awareness of contemporary history was painfully acute. Engagement with the present was not only passive. The publication only in 1989 of the poem "Stanzas," written in 1940 in imitation of Pushkin's 1826 appeal to Nicholas I, revealed the extent of her desperation. Written to help secure the release of her son Lev Gumilev from a penal camp, the poem in draft is a supplication of mercy to Stalin that produces a synthetic portrait of the ruler. If her original intention was to appeal, the dominant note of the draft text is one of terror and victimhood. This was a brave if false start on the way to the historical perspective on the trauma of the Terror memorialized in *Requiem*.[6]

In the early 1960s she was "rediscovered" by a generation of gifted Leningrad poets, often referred to as "Akhmatova's Orphans," including Joseph Brodsky, Anatolii Naiman, Evgeny Rein, and Dmitry Bobyshev.[7] In the West, the legend of Akhmatova was perpetuated by the British intellectual Sir Isaiah Berlin's account of their meeting in Leningrad in 1951, an event Akhmatova later cited as the beginning (and cause) of the Cold War. Her poetry captivated British and American readers from the 1980s and especially 1990s with the appearance of a two-volume complete translation. For many readers in the West, at least from this date and to the present, Akhmatova—once called "Anna of all the Russias" by Tsvetaeva—is the embodiment of the Russian poet, shaping the expectation that poetry can be a vehicle for quiet resistance and the defense of the individual. Joseph Brodsky, in one of the first essays published after his exile, called her the "greatest Russian poetess of the twentieth century" (the sexist "poetess" in the original Russian was decorous rather than demeaning), and he later produced a proper homage, now often cited.[8] The distinguished American poet and critic C. K. Williams named her, together with Mandelstam and Mayakovsky, as formative influences.[9] The novelist Mary Gordon, sensitive to the fallibility of translations, nonetheless professed, "I would not like to have lived without the poetry of Akhmatova and Rilke, which I have read only in translation."[10] By then, Seamus Heaney had celebrated Akhmatova in his Nobel lecture (1985), subtly drawing a parallel between how she put her art to the service of describing the Terror and the position of his own poetry to the Troubles in Northern Ireland.[11] These poets, together with the likes of Carolyn Forché and Denise Levertov, thought of Akhmatova as synonymous with twentieth-century poetry of witness.[12] That valorization of courage and moral purpose was a typical Cold War attitude among Western critics about Russians they respected, and Akhmatova's poetry also had a special appeal for feminist readers and poets. The Irish and American writers Eavan Boland and Tess Gallagher spoke for many when the former described her and Adrienne Rich as "women poets who were witnesses to the fact that myth is instructed by history," and the latter cited her as a "grief-causing poet" capable of a special bond.[13] It is a sure sign of deeper cultural acceptance when fictional characters are referred to as readers: the hero of William Trevor's story "The Unknown Girl" keeps a postcard of a portrait of Akhmatova pinned on his wall. If Akhmatova found an abiding English-language readership from this time, the fixation was on her earlier love lyrics and *Requiem* rather than on any of the later poetry or this particular set of poems, which deserve to be better known.

Thematically, the poems of "Secrets of Craft" represent the most sustained meditation in verse on the nature of poetic inspiration since Mandelstam's "Octaves" (1932). It is not for nothing that the penultimate poem in this cycle is dedicated to him. Akhmatova had earlier written a series of elegies to commemorate fellow writers Mayakovsky, Mikhail Bulgakov, and Boris Pilniak. While this is a tribute to Mandelstam, a beloved friend of hers and her former husband Gumilev's, it takes its own line on the question of how poems come into being.[14] Something of the difference in Akhmatova's and Mandelstam's approaches can be gleaned from the titles alone. Inspired by German romantic theories of nature, and also influenced by contemporary theories of cognition and speech development, Mandelstam's "Octaves" focused on structure as a fundamental generative principle in the creative act of the mind.[15] Interested in awareness as the primary condition of art, Mandelstam found a productive tension between the view of the imagination as unpredictable, enjoying an associative volatility, and the scientist view that linguistic and mental structures control images just like the development of a leaf. Was it form that determined how ideas came into the imagination? Does an entire cycle cast (mainly) in a single stanza form originate in a single mental impulse? How far back can that impulse be traced? "Octaves" as a cycle aims poetically to structure images and moods—of ingenuousness, self-consciousness, and artistic maturity—in order to show that an image in mind has a genesis architecture of its own. Akhmatova steps away from the mind and knowing one's own inner thoughts to exploring the forms of thought, using the sequence to accommodate types of expression and demonstrating through each separate poem how the same creative impulse can unfold differently. The process, open-ended and rarely finalized, was one on which the poet had to reflect. Mandelstam provided an example of how the poet, in exfoliating the idea, could be both inside the process as participant and simultaneously outside as a witness. The degree to which complex meaning, created by poetic language as its own system, could reflect authorial intention was an issue that mattered to Mandelstam for two reasons. Interested in the psychology of art, he had a fundamental question about the connection of subvocal speech and the imagination. That more theoretical curiosity overlapped with a greater presentist awareness that transparency of meaning had become a requirement of art in the Soviet period, especially after 1929, when the drive to achieve socialist consciousness and collective unity of purpose and thought became a national priority.

The use of the cycle is one point of continuity in Akhmatova's poetics. Starting with the early collection *Evening* (*Vecher*, 1912), she grouped poems within book collections: notable cycles include "Black Dream" ("Chernyi son") and "Biblical Songs" ("Bibleiskie pesni") in *Anno Domini* (1921), and then later the magnificent "Northern Elegies" ("Severnye elegii," 1940–64). (Cyclization of her narrative or epic poems was also an important principle.)[16] The title "Secrets of the Craft" gives equal weight to separate sources of inspiration, the mysterious or irrational and planned or crafted. The cycle title provides only a veneer of unity, since separate titles head each poem (perhaps acknowledging their separate genesis). Does the cycle as a series (on which, see Introduction) promise ten different snapshots of the same process? Is the process viewed at different stages or from different perspectives? Is the cycle cumulative or discrete, a greater-than-parts sum or chorus of compatible but distinct voices on the nature of poetic art?

The first poem "Creation" ("Tvorchestvo") presents Akhmatova's sensibility at its most approachable and sets certain motifs that the rest of the sequence explores. The second and third poems repudiate poetry written out of a civic need and eschews the hackneyed language of the Muse, putting clear water between the mature poet and her earlier work in which the Muse was prominent. "Creation" provides a comprehensive description of the process from its opening definitional phrase, literally "This is how it happens."[17] Precisely what happens is a process characterized surprisingly by exhaustion rather than energy: *istoma* is a highly Pushkinian word for spiritual exhaustion brought on by mental effort. The poem starts at the end point rather than at the moment of creative inception. Exhaustion is the result of a process marked by an intense concentration on filtering out layers of noise that accompany creativity. Even as the poem sets rational axes about poetic creativity, the motif of the "secret" (*taina*) is picked up in the first poem and recurs in the fifth and sixth poems, serving as a complement to the more linear heuristic purpose. Here and later on, sound rather than vision or touch will be the dominant sense. The advent of sound is described in clear, analytical terms charting a process of reduction from sensory bombardment to the emergence of the single "victorious sound." The clustering of nouns in lines 2–8 to represent a single semantic field of sound is Akhmatova's most important verbal technique here, most visible if we think of the literal meaning of the words: "racket" (*raskat*), "beat" (*boi*), "voices" (*golosov*), "groans" (*stony*), "laments" (*zhaloby*), "whispers" (*shepoty*), "noises" (*zvony*), and finally "sound" (*zvuk*). Akhmatova is by no means the first poet gifted with heightened powers of listening. After all, we can see in the present book how other poets such as Khodasevich and Pasternak respond to the idea of acute auditory perception as the divine gift the angel brings when grazing the poet's ears in "The Prophet." Earlier in his lyrics of the late 1820s, Fedor Tiutchev, inspired by German Idealism and Schelling's belief in the power of the poetic mind to merge with a Nature infused with some divine impulse, also heard the grass grow and the hum of insects. Famed as a city poet, Akhmatova came to Nature late, and the newfound attentiveness may once again owe inspiration to Mandelstam, for whom Tiutchev was an abiding influence. The word "sound" (*zvuk*) in itself looks like an overt allusion to the opening poem, in Mandelstam's first, celebrated collection *Stone*, one of the foundational texts of acmeism. In that first lyric "A muffled, cautious sound" ("Zvuk ostorozhnyi i glukhoi," 1908), the birth of the poem is expressed metaphorically as the "sound of a fruit that carefully and quietly breaks off from a tree."

Akhmatova herself was a founding member of acmeism, a group whose aesthetic was dedicated to concrete things rather than the abstractions beloved of the previous generation of symbolists. Mandelstam's collection was much preoccupied with the poet's own discovery of his own voice and the origins of poetic music, and Akhmatova's poetry has been read as a struggle to fashion a female poetic voice "fitting her own self as a woman."[18] Much more tentative than the later "Octaves," and also more impressionistic, "A muffled sound" compares the poetic word as it comes to the poet to a fruit that falls from a tree. Here at a much later age, Akhmatova, weaving into her own lines the discoveries of Tiutchev and Mandelstam, has recreated for herself a theory of poetic imagination that synthesizes the romantic auditory imagination and the later, more Saussurean or scientific theory of poetry as an idiom (or *parole*) governed by rules of rhythm, usage, and syntax within the language. What the poet hears, at least in this part of the cycle, stands in both an internal and an external relation to her consciousness. She is part of nature, and nature is part of her; and yet literature, that part of creation related to craft, is also made from other literature, characterized here literally as "unrecognized and captive voices." Now the blank notebook into which sound can be captured as words, the poem balances naivete and self-consciousness. The tendency of the poem is to semanticize key affinities between art and the world in rhyme, culminating at the end in the collocation of understanding and writing (*ponimat'/ tetrad'*). By the end, the poem has become the space that replicates the world. Salvation from the "depths where whispers rise" enacts its own mise en abyme.

If "Creation" offers a positive definition of poetic art, poem 2 presents a negative description of the genres and aesthetic this poet rejects. In the first stanza alone, the pronoun "I" (in the dative *mne*) appears three times, meaning "according to me" or "by my lights." At the very least it underscores the idea that art is a matter of a personal credo. The opening stanza is a position statement on taste. The rejection of "odic routs" (line 2.1) at least signals an unwillingness to compete for favor and establishment privileges, suggesting repudiation of poetry as a public mode. In the second rejection, the emphasis may fall less on the elegiac, since Akhmatova herself wrote distinguished elegies, than on the idea of insincerity, of conceits that use charm to mask what the writer genuinely thinks. The phrase *ne kak u liudei* (lit. "not like people do") implies a degree of queerness or nonconformity. Odic contests (*odicheskie rati*) broadly gesture toward a tradition of public poetry, devised originally for court occasions in the Imperial period. In the Soviet period, poems of praise for leaders and national occasions were a common feature, from the agitational verse written by Mayakovsky in the 1920s to panegyric of Stalin from the 1930s to the 1950s. By "elegists" we may take Akhmatova to be looking back to the self-advertising biographical nature of romantic poetry. Does circumscribing one's role come at a cost? To repudiate the role of the poet as praise maker and elegist may be to deny oneself certain types of recognition. The poem continues to insist on a definition of poetry's proper subject matter that is negative: the idea of the "inappropriate" (*nekstati*) or "unannounced," as in the translation, works in contrast to an implied "appropriate" (*kstati*). The final lines, aphoristically, complicate the picture by suggesting that, while human relations require a certain clarity—and the word *dolzhno* implies this as a moral imperative—the clarity that is desirable in the human is not privileged as a defining quality of poetry.

The potential to compare poetry and human relations is pursued in the second stanza. A key difference between the human and the poetic lies in the relation to feelings of shame. Shame is what people feel. Poetry, the verbal distillation of "muck" of any kind, is disassociated from shame. While that doesn't mean that poetry is shameless, Pushkin, Akhmatova's ideal, jotted down a now much quoted aphorism: "Poetry [is] above morality or at the very least is entirely another matter."[19] Similarly, Akhmatova's position seems to endorse the separation of lyric from a moral compulsion to explain motivation and deliver a message. In leaving the description of poetry open-ended, however, the speaker proves the claim that poetry must not be "appropriate" or prescribed. And in thinking about its sources rather than the final product, Akhmatova turns to metaphor to touch glancingly on the difference between the natural and the artificial or cultivated. Like the plants named in lines 2.6–8, whether the flower on the edge of the fenced-in plot, the burdock loved by bees, or the Atriplex that grows in deserts (the Saltbush mentioned in the Book of Job), poems grow best when wild or on the margins and perhaps unnoticed.

What brings the poem into being, and what the poem brings to one's being, is the subject of the final quatrain. Adjectives, in short supply earlier, now hint at the subjectivity forming impressions of the things that populate a world, from the anger obvious in an outburst or the inexplicable appearance of a bacterial film. The image of the "mysterious mildew on the wall" followed by ellipsis rather than words is an act of reticence, suggesting that decomposition is the catalyst for inspiration. That realization and the recurrence of nature imagery continue the description offered in "Creation." New adjectives ("yellow," "secret," "angry," "fresh," "tender") are added because the poetic subject stands more outside the process. Her role is to capture how old impressions are transformed into the new. There are two sides to lyric subjectivity, beginning with the subject who receives the world and produces the poem, and shifting to the subject who receives the poem, who produces a new sense of the world as changed by the poem. If the second stanza sets up a challenge to the addressee (a second person who may be the poet) to understand how poetry works, it provides its own demonstration of how poetry might work by delivering a sense of joy. Playfully, the poem that sounds "fervent" (line 2.11, *zadoren*) bears an echo of its origins in rubbish (*zador/sor*). But there is an unresolved tension at the end as to whether this is the poem that "swells" and is therefore joy itself; or whether the lines offer a metadescription of a joy that is occurring somewhere else, somewhere invisible to the reader but sensed by the poet from within.

In six rhymed lines, poem 3 takes unsparing aim at the idea of the Muse. Far from being a privileged daimon, the Muse is the creation of reported speech. No better than a figment of gossip, the Muse is represented demeaningly as a construct needed by others to explain how it is that poets write. The tradition of contesting the idea of inspiration as an external form of enthusiasm can be traced back to Pushkin, always a touchstone for Akhmatova. In "A Conversation between a Poet and a Publisher" (1823), his longest lyric poem originally conceived as a preface to the novel *Evgenii Onegin*, Pushkin set in dialogue form a debate about the nature of genius, juxtaposing the poet's own sense of self-mystery with the publisher's commercial view that genius needed to be hyped: "the divine word," echoed here in the idea of "divine babble," was the commodity on sale, whether the poet liked it or not.

Как и жить мне с этой обузой,
А еще называют Музой,
Говорят: "Ты с ней на лугу . . ."

Around my neck a noose
They insist on calling the Muse
Saying *go stroll with her, my dear*

Akhmatova bridles at the "burden" (literal meaning of *obuza*), affronted at the way the word "Muse" glamorizes a relationship the poet finds as tedious as a fever or an unreliable friendship. Dependence on an unreliable power of epiphany is cause for resentment. The final line, with its descent into childish slang, is a sting-in-the tail for both the public and the poet. "Those who speak" remain oblivious to the real problem: the yearlong wait for inspiration to strike.

Relational ordering governs the arrangement of this lyric sequence. The first four poems project poetic creation, from the writer's perspective, as a polarity between the deliberate and accidental, the free and commissioned. After these approaches, a definition poem about the poet was inevitable. "Poet," the fifth lyric, essentially poses the question of whether there is a danger in rejecting this hieratic model of inspiration. In Akhmatova, humility is performative and the admission of uncertainty is buttressed by an enormous sense of poetic authority descending from Pushkin and the affinity she cultivated. We might turn again to Pushkin as a reference point, appropriate given Pushkin's importance to her as the exemplary poet. In Pushkin's set of poems about the poet figure (1826–30), he rejected the dependence of the poet on the "crowd," precisely the group represented here literally as "People say" (*govoriat*). Unlike Akhmatova, however, Pushkin tolerated the use of certain tropes such as the visit by Apollo or the Muse that elevates the poet in the eyes of the public, even if ultimately the poet sees through stylization as a theatrical prop. In that respect, Akhmatova agrees with Pushkin in distancing herself from gossip about poetry, adopting the view of both Pushkin and Mandelstam that, to remain poetry, poetry must retain a mysterious interiority.

The dialogue and even argument with Pushkin continue, exercising a right Akhmatova assumes to be both his follower and her own independent judge. Akhmatova's "Muse" neither confirms nor denies the position Pushkin's 1827 lyric "The Poet" takes regarding the romantic vision of genius portrayed of the poet as a worldly child until inspiration ends his idling and transforms him. The poem insists on a gulf between the visionary artist and the mere mortal. Pushkin damns the latter with the faintest praise by saying that

И меж детей ничтожных мира,
Быть может, всех ничтожней он.[20]

among the trivial children of the world
He is perhaps the most trivial of all.

To return to the poem at hand, Akhmatova's opening quatrain can be read as a riposte to both sides of Pushkin's argument. In contrast to the high style of Pushkin's poem, she adopts a tone of pleasant frivolity and recasts Pushkin's vision of inspiration as a matter of work:

Подумаешь, тоже работа,—
Беспечное это житье:

Can this carefree existence
Really be called work—

Her noun *zhit'e* has an overtone of casualness (as in the phrase *sladkoe zhit'e*). It involves culture (e.g., listening to music). If the concept also involves creativity (because the music in question is the music of poetry), then imitation rather than the strenuousness of original genius is given license. Taking delight in composition as a form of play and relaxation is not in itself un-Pushkinian—arguably it is the supremely Pushkinian virtue. Akhmatova deflates Pushkin's more monumental statements by applying a Pushkinian tone of self-irony and jocularity, dashing off at the end of stanza 2 shopworn elegiac phrases (*bednoe serdtse, bleshchushie nivy*).

That wavering between adopting and amending Pushkin's strictures is resolved in the final two stanzas. In effect, the poem backtracks on its mockery of the poetic process. The sources of inspiration captured here (forest, pines, weather) and the helter-skelter process (lit. "left and right," "without a sense of guilt") cannot get away from the part of the process that remains a mystery.[21] That capacity to hear the underside, to capture the unexpected and to do it as easily as picking left and right, rather than to make poetry applied work, is what draws the poet, and this poem, back into the realm of making lyric. There are two other essential elements that are conjoined in the rhymes of the final quatrain: an absence of guilt and stealth. Poetry may be a distillation of the voice of nature, but it is also mediated through other voices. These voices cannot be unheard. Aware of intentionality, the poet draws from life "left and right," meaning the world of deliberate effort and awareness, while also offsetting the contrived with the world that lives at the back of the mind, in dreams, in the unconscious. Pushkin's ending is proportionate to the grandeur of an opening in which Apollo stimulates the writer to poetry. Akhmatova's final lines are scaled to her own more intimate voice, but recall the end of Pushkin's "Poet":

Бежит он, дикий и суровый,
И звуков и смятенья полн,
На берега пустынных волн,
В широкошумные дубровы . . . [22]

Wild and stern, he flees,
Full of both sounds and disarray,
To the banks of deserted waves,
To the wide-sounding oak thickets . . .

Insofar as they affirm Pushkin's vision of release into nature and harmony, it is deliberately on a quieter note.

Pushkin was one of the first Russian poets to consider the role of the reader in the creation of meaning, and many discussions of his work, especially *Evgeny Onegin*, focus on a feature that Roland Barthes called *scriptibilité* in relation to works of art that, through all sorts of devices, like direct address and fragmentation, invite active participation by the reader. The question of the reader's role was also important to the acmeists, including Gumilev (in his essays about Russian poetry) and, above all, Mandelstam, who considered that special affinity between writer and reader in a number of essays. As both a Pushkinist and a reader and friend of Mandelstam, Akhmatova gives the reader equal space right after a section on the poet. With the fifth poem, at the midpoint of the cycle, we turn from the mystery of creation to the mystery of the reader, valorized in the declaration that "every reader is a mystery." The relationship between poet and reader, touched on but left undefined in poem 4, develops the quest to allocate the creative agency of writer and reader, and poem 5 synthesizes the contradiction by recognizing the parity of both. Here Akhmatova does not quite follow Pushkin, whose perspective is poet-centric, since he privileges in the romantic way detachment from, and even disdain, of the reading public. His friendliest comments about reading and readers were reserved for *Evgeny Onegin* outside his lyric corpus. Akhmatova's closest contemporaries, including Mandelstam, Gumilev, and Tsvetaeva, as critics or in their verse, all explored the idea of the reader. For both Tsvetaeva and Akhmatova, the impact of Pushkin on their conceptualization of the reader was decisive. We have seen that Akhmatova's relationship to the Pushkinian precept can be dialectical. The first two stanzas cast the relationship between writer and reader in equivalent terms of mutual understanding. The bold demand that the writer be totally transparent (*Ved' nastezh' raspakhnut poet*) reverses the Pushkinian posture of exclusivity. But it looks like an overstatement, leading to a grotesque theatrical representation of the poet in stanza 2 that will be revised by the end of the poem. Stanza 3 establishes a principle of emotional equivalence as the basis of reader response. This entails a state of empathy for the reader's emotional fragility (*bespomoshchno plachet*) as well as a conviction that there is a depth of hidden feeling that can be tapped into. The idea of the hidden is seen here as a principle of nature and also a common bond: just as the poet can never fully know their creative impulses, the reader also discovers in reading a hiddenness from the self. Respect for the reader's own private self and for poems that do not make an extrovert display ("the disgraceful flame of limelight") is a priority when poetry is considered from that end of the relationship.

It may be that Akhmatova's implied reader tends to her own mirror image. Poetic and readerly selves both contain shade and darkness, out of which a capacity for conversation with the poet—or at least the poem—emerges. And here again, perhaps unexpectedly, there is a transition to a Pushkinian kind of statement of affinity, making him once again a touchstone. Stanza 7 evokes the language of the small appointed circle (lit. "special close-knit circle"), one that is unbreakable and eternal, which is one of the great Pushkinian themes:

Наш век на земле быстротечен
И тесен назначенный круг,
А он неизменен и вечен—
Поэта неведомый друг.

Our time on earth passes quickly
Our appointed circle is small,
But the poet's unknown friend
Remains constant, eternal.

For Pushkin, biographically, his closest readers were the friends of his childhood and youth. Akhmatova's poems seem to envisage a process in which poetry creates the personal affinity. Friendship is the basis of poetry, and poetry is the basis of friendship in a virtuous cycle that presumes distance. The language of "mystery" manages to preserve the impersonal element required of great art to be both touching and universal, timely and timeless.

Part of that mystery comes with shock and awe. The poem that hits like a thunderclap, sending the poet into head-spinning raptures, owes something to the first poems in Mandelstam's "Verses on Russian Poetry" ("Stikhi o russkoi poezii," 1932), which liken poetry to thunder and a storm (the word *raskat*, used in "Creation," also appears here):

> Гром живет своим накатом—
> Что ему до наших бед?
> И глотками по раскатам
> Наслаждается мускатом
> На язык, на вкус, на цвет.[23]
>
> Thunder lives through its din—
> Why should it care about our woes?
> In gulps during storms
> It enjoys the muscadet [falling]
> On its tongue, palate, on a flower.

Mandelstam's cycle goes on to explore how, in verse tradition, dialogue with one poet always seems to be mediated intertextually through the voices of other poets. If Mandelstam's poetic word can seem saturated with connotations and quotational references, Akhmatova's more limpid style in poem 6 has its own successes in absorbing other voices. Readers may hear in Akhmatova's imagistic exuberance, and even in the phrase "breath of life" (in the Russian, line 6.2), the voice of the young Pasternak.[24] The image of mirrors may be drawn from another Silver Age contemporary, Andrei Bely. The fact that the word *belyi* occurs twice might be a playful reminder of how pervasive mirrors are in his lyric poems. Similarly, an ear for the tradition proves helpful in poem 8 because its definitional statements read like an intertextual medley of images from other poets. Other voices can inhabit the poet's mind. What the tenth and final "Last Poem" describes phenomenologically is the sense of aporia about where the poem comes from. Sudden like a bolt of thunder, stealthy (*kradetsia ko mne*), watchful, and menacing like a doppelgänger, or entirely free of the poet who might feel they are at rock bottom (in "a ravine"), the poem will feel like a "pure spring."

But this poem does not end on such an easy note. Juxtaposition is a main technique in the cycle. The use of the conjunction *a* to indicate a logical reversal of a previous position occurs throughout. Here, the final three stanzas produce an alternative to the three poetic moments that precede. In these stanzas, the creative imagination confronts an impulse to poetry that is evasive and shape-shifting. The effort to bring the work to fruition as a living entity is murderous or at least vampiric. The poem preys on the poet, feeds off her like an insatiable love and sullenly inflicts pain. Is a poem, therefore, the residue of pain, the traces of what cannot be completely expressed? What we read can be no more than a summary of a process that Akhmatova's lines calmly analyze with complete poise. Her rhymes, however, linger precisely because they are among the most common and banal in the Russian verse. It does not take great formal complexity and originality to produce pointed reminders that a poem can take one to the brink (*umirAIU/krAIU*), and that the relationship between poet and language can feel like a matter of blood and love (*krov'/liubov'*), silence, and near-death—none of which the poet would ever wish to relinquish because even a poem that is a distillation of torment is an act of communication rather than silence.

From poem to poem, the cycle's affect has ranged from ecstasy to despair and, in the eighth poem, to hallucinatory association. The cycle is not structured symmetrically to match long and short poems. Mood and tone rather than length offer some pattern of alternation in topic and mood. Poem 6 explores more exuberantly and emotionally what the creative act feels like and how unexpected poems can be, breaking them down into types. Just how much poetry can keep the poet and the reader off-kilter is part of the game the cycle plays. Poem 7 offers some relief.

Могла ли Биче, словно Дант, творить,
Или Лаура жар любви восславить?
Я научила женщин говорить . . .
Но, боже, как их замолчать заставить!

Could Beatrice have created the Empyrean peak?
Or Laura sung the heat of love?
I taught women how to speak—
But how the hell to shut them up!

The epigram is a satirical genre, and the poem is suitably brief and witty. A simple quatrain organized with a small amount of artistry in the arrangement of a set of four verbs by masculine and feminine rhyme is an act of pure bathos. Having compared the inception (or conception) of a poem to the love of a "hellcat," Akhmatova now takes aim at the greatest adolescent crushes of the Renaissance, blithely dismisses them, and tartly regrets her own contribution to women's writing. Epigrams have a point—or rather the epigram is constructed around a *pointe* or dictum at the end. Nobody could possibly mistake this for a serious act of literary criticism. Light verse, however, is its own tradition and own type of pleasure. One of the affordances of being serious throughout the cycle is that it opens up an opportunity for levity and the enjoyment poetry can bring by negating itself. With a light touch, Akhmatova recognizes her own authority in the tradition of love poetry. No longer the one and only female love poet, she is not beyond hinting that she might be the most authentic of them all.

And authenticity of feeling, ever a touchstone in Akhmatova's poetry and the basis of the special relationship she enjoyed with successive readerships nationally and internationally, was the constant in her friendship with Mandelstam, the dedicatee of poem 9. The ordering of the poems is noteworthy, consciously leaving an explicit act of tribute to the end of the cycle before ending with a poem about the unsayable. From the time of his death in transit to the Gulag in 1938, Mandelstam's name and his poems had been erased from Soviet literature. His widow was not granted permission to return to Moscow until 1966, a decade after she received official notification of his death. Two of the great poets of the Silver Age were also personal friends, and Akhmatova showed considerable bravery in visiting the poet after his arrest and exile to Voronezh in 1934. The "voice of the mysterious lyre" (*golos tainstvennoi liry*, line 9.19) is as much Mandelstam's in this poem as it is her own. The striking opening of the poem looks like a divination scene. An equivalence is implied between reckoning with Mandelstam's poems and the practice of discerning the future in a bowl (usually by reading the pattern of dripped wax). If the "marks" are "hallowed" it is because the speaker contemplates the manuscript copies entrusted to her and many others of unpublished works preserved posthumously.

The poem contains a characteristic turn of phrase that is more common to Akhmatova than any other poet and is something of a stylistic signature: her tendency to name things with a sentence in which the subject is the definite neuter pronoun "This is" (*Eto*). Here are a few from dozens of examples to illustrate her use of the phrase to give emphasis, injecting momentarily a dramatic intonation and surprise:

"Ah! This is you again" ("A! Eto snova ty," 1916)
"But perhaps this is not we" ("V Zazerkal'e," 1963)
"Suddenly they recognized—he is the one!" ("Vdrug uznali—etot tot!")[25]
"Like two stars—and it is he / Who asked" ("Kak dve zvezdy—i etot tot / Kto sprashival")[26]

"He is the one, who on leaving did not turn back, / He is the one to whom I sing this song" ("Etot, ukhodia, ne oglianulsia, / Etomu ia etu pesn' poiu")[27]
"These are they who screamed 'Barabas' . . ." ("Eto te, kto krichali: 'Varravu'")[28]
"I know: it is you, killed, that wish" ("Ia znaiu: eto ty, ubityi")[29]

In moments of resistance, when something cherished is menaced by hostile circumstances, Akhmatova has a habit of using repetition to express commitment to entities under threat. To name deeds and special attributes is to record, and perhaps even to cast a protective spell. In "To the Londoners," written before the Blitz and filled with Shakespearean names as tokens of her love for the city, Akhmatova imagines the drama of war and says

Только не эту, не эту, не эту,
Эту уже мы не в силах читать![30]

But not this, not this, not this—
This we have not strength enough to read!

The lines of poem 9 combine Mandelstamian motifs. Tenderness is his favorite word for affective relations; the classical references to Eurydice and the underworld reprise the Hellenic language of *Tristia,* his second collection originally published the year after Akhmatova's own great book *Anno Domini* (1921); the reference to the rape of Europa alludes to Mandelstam's own poem on the myth, reflecting a tension between the love both poets shared for the city and acknowledgment of its revolutionary violence. What Mandelstam calls "the black record" of their "bloodiest youth" is revisited as a portal to the eternal, Elysian realm of the underworld. No amount of conjuring can actually bring Eurydice back, a point acknowledged in Mandelstam's poem, in which she has been read as a metaphor for a European Russia lost after the Russian Revolution. But in the Pushkinian spirit—his poems contain numerous predecessors or shades (*teni*)—Akhmatova believes that poetic shades inhabit the lines and lives of later poets, haunting their shared city.[31]

The sum of the cycle is greater than the constituent parts because the set traverses the great themes of poetry—inspiration, memory, love and loss, poetry itself, friendship, and literary ties. At the end, the lines do not pause to look back and consolidate. The opening and closing poems are nearly fifteen years apart. The same mood of inquiry that opened the first poem, the later by date of composition, marks the final poem, information that helps us see how circular the sequence truly is in making the openness of the question the point of closure. Even if one was unaware of the publication information, it is still undeniable that the final poem considers not what has been said but rather what cannot be said and what remains to be said or not: the "wordless" (*besslovesnoe*) continues to "roar and boom" within the poet like a force of nature. The admission of the ineffable in poem 10 is cast as a reckoning on a grand scale, something to be settled between Akhmatova's individual talent as a force of poetry and the elements. The poem places the poet in a primordial world, in which her voice is equivalent to water, fire, and air. It is not to be forgotten that poetry, associated with sleep, may escape her conscious control. Within her unconscious mind lie resources or literary touchstones that are a part of her nature, and possibly simply as much a part of nature as poetic language. First, the image of poetry as subterranean stone worked on by nature and working on nature takes us back to the central metaphor of Mandelstam's "Slate Ode." Second, the final lines of the entire cycle consciously echo the famous opening of Pushkin's version of the Parable of the Sower (also see Chapter 19).

Оттого-то мне мои дремоты
Вдруг такие распахнут ворота
И ведут за утренней звездой.

And so in my fits of drowsing
Such gates are thrown back wide
And lead me beyond the morning star.

In this short lyric, written during his exile to Kishinev in 1823, Pushkin casts the poet as a Christ figure who will be in the vanguard of his people and catch the morning star:

Свободы сеятель пустынный,
Я вышел рано, до звезды[32]

A sower of freedom in the desert,
I went out early, before the morning star.

Aspirations to liberate his peoples and bring them spiritual enlightenment are quickly dashed; they can only be realized if the masses come to understand the value of freedom. Poets cannot spiritually enlighten others on their own. This is consistent with the way poem 2 abjures the "odic routs" of civic poetry. Yet this is not cause to deny the historic responsibility of the Russian poet as the vox populi or to dismiss her own authority and stature in the tradition. Such awareness was critical to the composition of *Requiem* over roughly the same period when Akhmatova was also writing "Secrets of the Craft."

The cycle is the work of a Silver Age poet, classical in form and modernist in content. That combination bears out an observation Boris Eikhenbaum made about her earlier poetry, namely that, while attention has focused on the debt her poetry owes to classic nineteenth-century poets, especially Pushkin and Baratynsky, her verse also displays a self-consciousness typical of modernism.[33] "Secrets of Craft" is an example of how late style works by creating a new message for a familiar vehicle. The tone, mastery of other voices, and prosodic features such as use of off-rhyme and polymetric variation make these poems recognizably the work of Akhmatova. It is their statement on the art of lyric that is more overt than she had ever attempted.[34] In "Octaves," Mandelstam posed a key question as to whether the relation of part and whole, just like the relation between the individual and the collective, was already scripted by nature and individual nature. Decades later, Akhmatova produced an answer that seems to confirm the principle of both accident and determination in art. Akhmatova famously and pithily opined that few were aware that verse grows "from what muck" (or "rubbish," exactly what Elena Shvarts writes about). There are instances of such "muck" as well as high art as source of inspiration in "Secrets of Craft." To the degree that there is something in the poet's own psyche that determines how poems come about, it is the element of craft in the rubbish. Unlike *Requiem*, the cycle is not a poem with political content. Its view on the sources of poetry is not an explicit provocation or challenge to socialist art, even if the point is made implicitly. The theme is the nature of poetic talent, and it is also the role of the reader. Free of self-consciousness and self-importance because Akhmatova's stature spoke for itself, the cycle is akin to a treatise but devoid of all didacticism, and it is replete with allusions that attest to the role of craft or literary knowledge. Its lightness of touch and candor affiliate it with both the Pushkin who treated these subjects that remained fundamental to Russian poetry and to Mandelstam, whose thinking, while relevant to Akhmatova, was overdue for revival in the 1960s.

16

Ian Satunovsky, "Yesterday, late on my way to work" (1939)

POETICS OF THE ETHICAL

Вчера, опаздывая на работу,
я встретил женщину, ползавшую по льду,
и поднял ее, а потом подумал:—Ду-
рак, а вдруг она враг народа?
Вдруг!—а вдруг наоборот?
Вдруг она друг? Или, как сказать, обыватель?
Обыкновенная старуха на вате,
шут ее разберет.[1]

Yesterday, late on my way to work.
I met a woman, crawling over the ice,
I lifted her up, then I thought—You
fool, maybe she's an enemy of the people?
Maybe! And maybe just the opposite?
Maybe she's a friend? Or—what's the word—a philistine?
An ordinary cotton-wadded old woman,
The devil only knows.

(TRANSLATED BY ANDREW KAHN AND ANDREW BROMFIELD)

Ian Satunovsky (1913–82) wrote of himself:

I am not a poet.
I have not published since the year one thousand 938.[2]

The date, not fortuitously chosen, is the very year from which Satunovsky began the tally of his own poems that he regarded as genuine, although he had written poetry from an early age, ever since he became acquainted with the constructivist poets while studying in Moscow in the early 1930s. A chemical engineer by profession, he grew up in Dnepropetrovsk (today Dnipro, Ukraine) and graduated from the university there. He was also drafted into the army from there in 1939. He fought in the war, attaining the rank of senior lieutenant by the end. After the war, he lived in the town of Elektrostal in the Moscow region, and in 1961 he found his way into the Lianozovo circle of poets and became an integral part of the group after discovering an understanding of art consonant with his own in the painting of Oscar Rabin and the poetry of Evgeny Kropivnitsky, Vsevolod Nekrasov, Igor Kholin, and Genrikh Sapgir. During his lifetime, he formally published twenty children's books, but his "adult" poetry could only appear in samizdat and tamizdat.[3] Outside of a close circle of friends, his poems were also praised by eminent writers such as Viktor Shklovsky, Ilya Erenburg, Igor Selvinsky, Georgii Oboloduev, and Aleksei Kruchenykh.

Today he is regarded as the originator of "concrete" or "found" poetry in Russian literature. He is also the author of the programmatic single-line poem: "The main thing is to have the insolence to know that this is poetry" (1976).[4] However, in contrast with the German "concrete poets," who employ montage to arrange shards of everyday speech or affected officialese in new sequences, Satunovsky follows an entirely different path. The critic Vladislav Kulakov wrote, "Satunovsky's lyrical genre was precisely defined by Gennady Aygi as 'remark-poems [*stikhotvoreniia-repliki*], as pungent as pepper.' And, indeed, Satunovsky's poems are first and foremost remarks, plucked out of a continuous conversation—with no beginning or end. Remarks expressing indignation, accusation, or protest, addressed to an unnamed but always recognizable antagonist, or expressions of reflection or observation addressed to himself."[5]

However, Satunovsky's apparent conversational tone is deceptive.[6] What seems to be a spontaneous utterance turns out, on much closer scrutiny, to be a rhythmically and phonically structured poetic text. As a general rule, even Satunovsky's free verse includes within itself fragments of syllabotonic and accentual verse. Furthermore, the poetic form that oral or inner speech assumes under Satunovsky's pen is a means of ethical utterance. For while his texts are seemingly so unassuming at first glance, as though through a crystal lattice, their ethical principle is revealed in the form of the consonances and rhythmical shifts. Moreover, as a general rule, Satunovsky uses this ethical-cum-poetic structure as a way of testing either opinions that are common among the intelligentsia or the official (state) discourse.

"Yesterday, late on my way to work" ("Vchera, opazdyvaia na rabotu") is marked with the number 6 in the 1930 "List" of poems that Satunovsky kept throughout his life. By that time, he had already graduated from university and was working as a chemical engineer while waiting to be drafted into the army. But in this eight-line poem we can already see the complex, dialectical interplay between the ethical-poetic and the political that Satunovsky would continue to investigate in the course of his lifetime.

Despite its brevity, this poem is distinguished by an exquisite intricacy. The entire eight-line stanza is shot through with a dense patterning of inner consonances and rhythms: *na rabotu—po l'du—podumal; polzavshuiu—po l'du—podnial—potom—podumal; du/rak—vrag; drug—vdrug; naroda—naoborot—razberet; obyvatel'—obyknovennaia; obyvatel'—na vate*. The word *vdrug* (literally—"suddenly," but in translation "maybe" or "what if") is repeated an emphatic four times in eight lines, while rhyming with either *drug* ("friend") or *vrag* ("enemy"). Through rhyming, the official formula of the state terror *vrag naroda* ("enemy of the people") is transformed, first into *naoborot* ("just the opposite") and then into *shut ee razberet* ("the devil only knows"). An unexpected enjambment conveys the abrupt reinterpretation of an everyday situation: *Du/rak, a vdrug ona vrag naroda?* ("You / fool, maybe she's an enemy of the people?" lines 3–4). The symmetrical verbal formulas *vdrug ona vrag* ("maybe she's an enemy," line 4) and *vdrug ona drug* ("maybe she's a friend," line 6) are bound together, not only by anaphora and syntactical parallelism, but by the repeated spondee form, which creates a rhythmical syncopation.

The rhythm of the poem is no simpler than the syntactic structure, and the resemblance to everyday speech is deceptive. Written in free verse, the poem begins with an iambic pentameter and ends with a broken iambic trimeter. In the crucial and climactic lines 4–5, the rhythm comes as close as possible to trochaic, in either trimeter, tetrameter, or pentameter variations. The third and seventh lines, which seem to create a different—narrative or calmer—tone, consist of trimeters of different metric feet. This poem could actually have sounded like accentual verse, with the traditional alternation of three-stress and four-stress lines, if not for the sixth line, with its five stresses: *Vdrug ona drug? Ili, kak skazat', obyvatel'?* ("Maybe she's a friend? Or—what's the word—a philistine?"). The rhythm of the line conveys the transition from an external situation, apparently innocent, to an internal monologue, suffused with panic and terror.

A structure of surface simplicity and inner complexity was necessary to lay bare the inner drama of everyday Soviet life in 1939, which is, according to traditional Soviet histories, the final year of the Great Terror. And at the same time, this very form becomes a kind of "cardiogram" of an ethical sensibility that at times is suppressed by fear, and at times struggles against it. The initial impulse to help a woman who has slipped on ice—a reflex, not even specifically ethical as yet—collides with the horror of political suspicion. This is the climactic moment of the poem, denoted by the abrupt enjambment *Du/rak,* which cleaves the word in half. Beginning from this moment, the lyrical subject's thinking convulsively shifts from one extreme to the other: "You / fool, maybe she's an enemy of the people! / Maybe! And maybe just the opposite? / Maybe she's a friend?" (lines 4–6). This sudden gallop is in glaring contrast with the everyday situation described in the poem. But it is precisely the struggle of ethical sensibility against the fear instilled by the political climate that constitutes the inner conflict of the poem. In fact, the same conflict, often channeled through Jewish themes, dominates other Satunovsky poems, especially those written about his firsthand experience of the war, the Holocaust, and postwar Soviet antisemitism.[7]

For Satunovsky, the abrupt swings in the lyrical subject's thinking are a veiled expression of the logic nurtured by the Stalinist campaigns of terror: anyone can turn out to be an enemy, and no reasons for this are necessary. Any help, even the most innocent, even the slightest contact with a potential enemy, can be used against you—and then turned into the crime of aiding and abetting the enemy. The arbitrary, contingent, and abrupt nature of the boundary that separates an "enemy of the people" from a "friend" lies at the basis of this logic, which is conveyed by internal rhymes, in which one and the same word—*vdrug* ("maybe")—can rhyme with *vrag* ("enemy"), and also with *drug* ("friend"). The fourfold repetition of *vdrug* conveys the rapidity of the political transmutations that shaped the period of terror, and the pattern of the lyrical subject's thoughts reproduces this rapidity. They are not even thoughts, but new reflexes, hammered into people's heads by the mass arrests, the trials of enemies of the people, and the constant, paralyzing fear.

This inner drama is already present in the first three lines of the poem. A traditional lyric opening, "I met a woman" abruptly descends into the bathos of "crawling over the ice," and a romantic situation is transformed into a grotesque one. The grotesquerie is intensified by the monotonous repetition of the syllable *po*—*polzavshuiu po l'du, / i podnial ee, a potom podumal* ("crawling over the ice, / I lifted her up, then I thought"). In Russian, *po* also represents the way in which Edgar Allan Poe's surname in pronounced, and a veiled allusion to this author's literary horrors can be discerned in these lines by Satunovsky. The grotesquerie climaxes in the enjambment splitting the word *du/rak*, which results in the syllable *-rak* appearing at the beginning of a line, sounding like the separate word *rak* ("crayfish"), and therefore visually "rhyming" with the woman crawling over the ice. And here, because the Russian word *rak* also signifies cancer, it adds a sense that the fallen stranger is a menace.

We can further appreciate Satunovsky's art of deceptive simplicity by considering how subtly he folds into the poem its historical milieu. Even the thoroughly neutral opening line "Yesterday, late on my way to work" is not entirely neutral. From 1938, draconian laws were introduced in the Soviet Union, establishing punishment for arriving late at work: initially dismissal, but from June 1940 "corrective labor" and jail terms were brought in. The prelude to this law was a resolution of the Central Committee of the All-Union Communist Party and the Council of People's Commissars of December 27, 1939.[8] And thus, our protagonist's gentlemanly gesture could prove costly, since he is already late for work. And, in general, this entire situation reads like a materialization of the metaphor of "walking on thin ice."

Even the resolution of the drama embodies internal conflict. The binary opposition "enemy of the people" / "friend" is seemingly canceled by the neutral "philistine"—apparently it is possible to be neither one nor the other, but merely a philistine! This line is metrically anomalous by virtue of its five stresses. The word *obyvatel'* ("philistine") is also formally emphasized. First, by the double rhyme with *obyknovennaia starukha na vate* ("an ordinary cotton-wadded old woman"), and, second, by the fact that the entire line could quite easily have fitted into a weakened trochaic meter, if not for the last three words, which create two amphibrachic feet. What "spike" on the ethical cardiogram is signaled by this formal "thickening"?

The speaker has seemingly discovered a way out of his ethical dilemma. He attempts to define the unfortunate stranger with a "neutral" term. Such "neutrality" would seem to presuppose the permissibility of compassion and assistance—that is, of ethical behavior. But how genuinely neutral is this neutrality? Consider two important shifts happening in these lines of the poem. First, the woman undergoes a characteristic metamorphosis: she is transformed not only into an "ordinary old woman" but into a "cotton-wadded old woman." "A cotton-wadded coat" (*pal'to na vate*) used to be a standard turn of phrase, and this synecdoche emphasizes the transformation of a human being into an object. Here we have the most mundane effect of terror—people are dehumanized and perceived as contagious objects, any contact with which is fraught with deadly danger. And second, there is another internal shift, marked by the awkward interpolation of "what's the word" (*kak skazat'*), which would seem to be inappropriate in this extremely laconic poem. We assume that this interpolated phrase is very far from accidental—it fulfills the role of verbal quotation marks, signaling that we are confronted here by "someone else's" word, an unacknowledged quotation.

The winter of 1938–39 was the period of the so-called Beria thaw. When a former head of the NKVD, Nikolai Yezhov, was arrested along with the entire top brass of his organization and replaced by a new boss Lavrentii Beria, the terror was declared to consist of "excesses at the local level," and several thousand victims were released. Also at that time, a number of Communist Party directives were approved, condemning the excesses of the NKVD, the most important of which was the joint resolution of the Sovnarkom and VKP(b) of November 17, 1938, "concerning arrests, prosecutorial oversight, and the conduct of investigations." However, on January 21, 1939—at about the time when Satunovsky's protagonist was walking over the ice—the anniversary issue of *Pravda,* devoted to the fifteenth anniversary of Lenin's death, carried an article by Mikhail Kalinin (who, as chairman of the Presidium of the Supreme Soviet of the USSR, was formally the head of state), titled "How Best to Commemorate the Memory of Lenin." Its central theme was an attack on the intelligentsia:

> The meaning of the word "philistinism" is palpably clear. And yet how difficult it is to determine the specific substance of philistinism, how difficult it is to define and describe the full variety of its manifestations in practical life. A philistine has an indefinite form, like dough; his thinking is always vague and *hard to pin down.* A philistine *lives for the present day,* disregarding or entirely failing to see any longer-term perspective. *His views are fickle and unstable.* The so-called swamp in Western European parliaments consists of "active" individuals of this kind. If truth be told, even among our own people there is a significant stratum of individuals whose defining quality in their actions and the instructions that they give is *the quality of indefiniteness,* who constantly equivocate and prevaricate. What Comrade Stalin requires from our political people is Leninist clarity and definiteness. [. . .] The urgent question is how to move beyond philistinism. I think that a powerful means for achieving this is mastering Marxism-Leninism.[9]

Kalinin's article is structured as a commentary on a speech that Stalin gave (quotations from the speech are given in italics) on December 11, 1937, in which he spoke specifically about "political philistines":

> The voters, the people must demand that their deputies be constantly up to the mark with their responsibilities, that they do not sink down to the level of *political philistines* in their work, that they remain on guard as functionaries of the Leninist type, that as functionaries they be precisely *as clear and definite* as Lenin (applause), that they be precisely as fearless in battle and *merciless to the enemies of the people* as Lenin was (applause), that they remain *entirely free of panic,* of any semblance of panic, when *the work starts getting complicated and danger of one kind or another looms up on the horizon,* that they be as free of any semblance of panic as Lenin was.[10]

The reactualization of Stalin's old speech after a brief period of criticism of the Terror and its managers, decried as "merciless to the enemies of the people," definitively indicated this path had now reached its end. Only philistines—that is, the intelligentsia—could take the criticism of repression to be a deviation from the general line of the Party, which was and remained coercion where enemies of the people were concerned.

In this context, Satunovsky's poem reads like a sardonic reply to these political declarations; for that reason, in the quotation above, we have italicized those phrases that resonate directly with his eight-line poem. The ethical import of the poem is even more bitter than it seems at first glance. Leninist/Stalinist "clarity and definiteness" turn out to be justifications for total dehumanization and blinkered cruelty. The "neutrality" of the term "philistine" turns out to be imaginary, as is emphasized by the introductory "quotational" phrase "what's the word." For Satunovsky's speaker, this signifies that an ethical attitude to the female stranger is impossible since "philistine" is, after all, merely one more definition of the *enemy*. Consequently, the only appropriate response is to turn away, if not simply to step over the fallen woman.

However, the panic experienced by the protagonist of the poem unequivocally characterizes not only the unfortunate woman, but also himself as precisely a "philistine," who is incapable of being "merciless to the enemies of the people," incapable of internalizing blind violence. And, therefore, he is already charged with a crime—if only because he has failed to rid himself completely of ethical sentiment; it is precisely this complete purging of compassion, of empathy for someone else's pain, of simple civility, that the ideology of terror requires from an individual.

And so, by and large, the "solution" is illusory. Or is it? After all, the position of a philistine living "for the present day" is the position of a person who "does not see and is incapable of regarding matters from the viewpoint of the general interests of the state."[11] In Satunovsky's poem, it is precisely this position that proves to be the only one available *as an ethical position* under conditions of terror. Arguably, this very meaning is the one expressed most strikingly in the last line: "the devil only knows" (*shut ee razberet*). The idiom of indefiniteness in Satunovsky's eight-line poem acquires a literal meaning: it is in the Russian a *shut* (i.e., a jester or trickster) who emerges as the final authority, as the symbol of a possible way of transcending "the viewpoint of the general interests of the state."

It is a fitting coincidence that, at this very time, Mikhail Bakhtin wrote his treatise "Forms of Time and of the Chronotope in the Novel," in which he reflects on the structural "outsideness" of the jester, the trickster, and the fool: "Essential to these three figures is a distinctive feature that is as well a privilege—the right to be 'other' in this world, the right not to make common cause with any single one of the existing categories [. . .] Their entire function consists in externalizing things."[12] In Dnepropetrovsk, twenty-five-year-old Satunovsky could not, of course, read the unpublished works of Bakhtin, but he was clearly animated by the same feeling as the philosopher, who had only just returned from exile.

17

Gennady Gor, "I lie together with my wife, the two of us in the apartment" (1942–44)

IS THERE LIFE AFTER DEATH?

Лежу с женой вдвоем в квартире,
Да стол, да стул, да лампа,
Да книги на полу.
И нет уж никого. Лицо жены. Открытый рот.
Глаза закрытые глядят.
Но где же то живое, робкое? Где милое?
Людмила где? Людмила!
Я кричу во сне и так. Но нет жены.
Рука, нога, да рот.
Еще беременный живот,
Да крик зловещий в животе,
Да сын иль дочь, что не родятся.
И не поднять мне рук и ног,
Не унести. Она лежит и я лежу.
Она не спит и я не сплю.
И друг на друга мы глядим
И ждем.
Я жду, когда пойдет трамвай,
Придет весна, придет трава,
Нас унесут и похоронят.
И буду лживый и живой
В могиле с мертвою женой
Вдвоем, втроем и на полу не будет книг.

Не будет лампы. Но буду думать я—
Где ты? И что такое тут лежит?
Чья рука? Чья нога? Моя? Твоя?
И буду лживый и живой
В могиле с милою женой.
Вдвоем я буду как сейчас.
В квартире тускло. Я сижу.
Гляжу на мертвую жену.
Нога в могиле. А рукою
Она не трогает меня. Рука в раю
И взгляд угас. И рот уже отъели крысы.
Но вот нешумною рекою
Потекли. И снится лето. Я с женою
Вдвоем, втроем течем
Бежим, струимся. Но входит дворник.
Нас несут в подвал. И я кричу:
—Живой! Живой!
Но мне не верят. А жены уж нет.
Давно растаял рот. Скелет
И я вдвоем, втроем течем, несемся.
И нет квартиры.
Лишь лампа гаснет, то горит,
Да дворник спит не умолкая.[1]

I lie together with my wife, the two of us in the apartment.
And the table, the chair, the lamp,
The books on the floor.
No one there already. My wife's face. Mouth open.
Closed eyes look on.
But where is that living, timid thing? Where's my dear?
Where is Ludmila? Ludmila!
I scream in my dreams and here. But my wife is not there.
Hand, foot, and mouth.
Also the gravid belly,
The ominous shriek in the belly,
Son or daughter who won't be born.
I cannot lift the hands and feet,

Can't carry them off. She lies there, and I lie.
She is not sleeping and I am not sleeping.
We look at each other
And we wait.
I am waiting for the tram to start running,
For the spring to come, for the grass to come,
For us to be carried off and buried.
And I will lie, lying and living,
In the grave with my dead wife,
The two of us, the three of us, no books on the floor.
There'll be no lamp. Though I will wonder:
Where are you? And what is that that's lying here?
Whose hand? Whose foot? Mine? Or yours?
And I will lie, lying and living,
In the grave with my dear wife.
We will be the two of us like we now are.
The apartment is dim. I am sitting.
I am looking at my dead wife.
Foot, in grave. The hand
She does not touch me with. The hand in heaven
And her gaze went out. Rats have gnawed her mouth off already.
But then we melted and became
A quiet river. A dream of summer. The wife and I,
The two, the three of us, we are flowing.
Running, streaming. The janitor comes in.
They carry us to the cellar. But I am screaming:
—I'm alive! Alive!
They don't believe me. My wife is not there already.
Her mouth melted long ago. A skeleton
And I, the two, the three of us, we are flowing, rushing.
There's no apartment either.
Just the lamp, now going out, now burning,
And the janitor sleeping, incessantly burbling.

(TRANSLATED BY BEN FELKER-QUINN AND EUGENE OSTASHEVSKY)

To Soviet readers, Gennady Gor (1907–81) was known primarily as a successful author of works of science fiction that were well-written, high-quality entertainment if not especially striking. No one knew that he also wrote poems. Unpublished in his lifetime, they only saw the light of day twenty years after his death. In his youth, Gor had belonged to the Leningrad literary group Smena, formed around the magazine of the same name and including the so-called Komsomol poets such as Alexander Bezymensky, Alexander Zharov, Nikolai Kornilov, Nikolai Dementyev, and Jack Altausen. It is unclear what Gor might have had in common with these proto–socialist realists. His literary tastes seemed quite different given his evident attraction to modernist poetics and avant-garde experiments. As his publisher and researcher of his work Andrei Muzhdaba writes, "Gor, an ambitious member first of the university literary circle, then of the Smena literary group, published a few quite heterogeneous texts that overtly imitated now Leonid Dobychin, now Konstantin Vaginov, now Shklovsky."[2] Gor's literary studies, then, were not limited to the interests of the "Komsomol poets." As his siege poems show, he was well acquainted with the work of OBERIU, and researchers also see the influence of Osip Mandelstam on his work.

Gor began to publish his prose in the 1930s and was soon subjected to *prorabotka*,[3] that is, a public criticism for ideological mistakes. The ordeal conditioned him to exercise caution in life and circumspection in literature. Nonetheless, after writing an avant-garde short novel about collectivization, *The Cow* (1930, published only in 2000), he was expelled from university. His first collection of short stories, *Zhivopis'* (*Visual Art/Paintings*, 1933), was criticized in official publications for its "formalism" and "expressionism," and among informal literary circles for its caricatures of avant-garde artists, including Kharms. All this notwithstanding, Gor was admitted into the Soviet Writers Union in 1934 and went on to prove his loyalty by writing ethnographic nonfiction about the North, Siberia, and the Far East, where he often traveled (luckily, unlike Mandelstam, not under NKVD escort).

During World War II, Gor first joined the militia and then, after returning to Leningrad, lived in the besieged city throughout the crisis winter of 1941–42, when thousands of people perished from hunger and cold. Evacuated from Leningrad in April, he was transported to Perm near the Ural Mountains, where, the impressions still fresh, he wrote his terrifying surreal poems about the siege.

Alexander Laskin, a writer who knew Gor personally, offered these observations in the memoirs accompanying the first magazine publication of his siege poems in 2002:

> These poems were his secret. Some unpublished stories and the novel *The Cow* he did show to a few people, but these poems—he did not so much as even

mention them. It seems he was embarrassed by the uncompromising mode of self-expression he had once chosen.

It is his radicalism that is most surprising in these texts. [. . .]

Never before or since did he write with such staggering despair. He does not so much speak of his fear as let it speak for itself. This is how horror should speak—confusingly, illogically, in the most unexpected combinations of words. [. . .]

These poems are the direct, uninhibited speech of the subconscious.[4]

Reviewing the publication of Gor's poems in the Russian–German bilingual edition *Blokada*, the poet and critic Oleg Yuryev explained the origin of these poems as follows: "In besieged Leningrad, in a situation of absolute existential horror, he suddenly began speaking an entirely different language without any reservations or restrictions."[5] In a conversation with Andrei Muzhdaba, who compiled the first complete collection of Gor's siege poems published in Russia,[6] the poet Polina Barskova, who has written extensively about the siege in verse and prose, noted: "The publication of Gor's siege poems was a significant event: the siege now had 'its own Paul Celan,' a poet who managed to interweave the historical catastrophe with a catastrophe of language."[7]

Gor's poems about the Siege of Leningrad are full of vivid, grotesque images, reminiscent of surrealist paintings. It is no coincidence that Gor was a connoisseur and collector of modern art, and his eye for color and shape comes across strikingly, even in a medley of snippets from poems:

Красная капля в снегу. И мальчик
С зеленым лицом, как кошка

A red blob in the snow. And a boy
With a green face like a cat

Мужчины сидят
И мыло едят,
И невскую воду пьют

Men are sitting
eating soap
drinking Neva water

То птица сидела с человечьим лицом
Птица ночная в военной шинели
И со свастикой на рукавах
Взмах и она улетает

That was a bird with a human face,
A night bird in a military overcoat
And with a swastika on its sleeves.
One swoop, and it flies away.[8]

Consider by way of even more macabre visuality this short poem as a self-portrait:

Мне отрубили ногу,
Руку и нос.
Мне отрезали брови и хвост,
Хвост я взял у коровы.
Руку я взял у соседа.
Ногу я занял на время.

They cut off my leg,
my arm, and my nose.
They cut off my eyebrows and my tail,
I took the tail from a cow.
I took a hand from a neighbor.
I borrowed a leg for a while.[9]

Behind all these grotesque images loom the realities of the siege: families dying in their apartments, corpses on the streets; queues for water at the ice hole on the Neva; hunger that forces people to eat inedible things. And cannibalism, which was a mass phenomenon.

Я девушку съел хохотунью Ревекку
И ворон глядел на обед мой ужасный
И ворон глядел на меня как на скуку
Как медленно ел человек человека
И ворон глядел но напрасно
Не бросил ему я ревеккину руку.

I ate a giggly Rebecca the girl full of laughter
A raven looked down at my hideous dinner
A raven looked down at me like at boredom
At how slowly this human was eating that human
A raven looked down but it was for nothing
I did not throw it that arm of Rebecca.[10]

The experience is so monstrous, so beyond anything imaginable, that reality and hallucinations, memories and imagination merge. Arguably, Gor's poems matter above all because they depict not only the siege itself but a state of *shifting consciousness,* a dislocation in a self shaken by the nightmare of history. The author conveys these shifts in consciousness through shifts in language, which often lack logical or even emotional consistency. Gor breaks his poems' rhythm and uses rhymes, assonances, and consonances ironically—as fragments of shattered and forgotten cultural languages, models of harmony, which have become impossible, indeed unthinkable.

Many researchers have argued that Gor's broken language and poetic forms, close to OBERIU poetry, deliberately embody historical catastrophe. Yet arguably his aesthetic aim was not to imitate OBERIU and their parable-like approach to reality. Oleg Yuryev suggests that the real circumstances of the siege had concretized the imaginary, surreal "parallel worlds" only imagined by the absurd poets in the 1920s and 1930s:

> Gor did not have to look for the parallel world: it came to him on its own. He did not need to fog his consciousness—it was already floating in a gleaming fog. It was fogged with hunger, with cold, with horror, with the utter destruction of the culture he had so longed for. [. . .] The closer his poems are to the realities of the Siege, the closer they are also to the logic and speed of a dream.[11]

"I lie together with my wife, the two of us in the apartment" is the longest of Gor's poems reflecting the siege, and it fully exemplifies his overall vision of this tragedy. We are faced with a stream of surreal and confused consciousness. Within that flow, some recurring images and refrains serve to ground what is recounted in a reality beyond the text. This indexicality proves to be essential because the situation is so unclear, standing outside any conventional framework. A reconstruction of events, and even the work of actually conceiving what has happened, requires serious effort and attention to detail on the reader's part. We can assume that the poem's speaker lies in a dazed, semiconscious, hunger-weakened state next to his wife, who had died and who had been pregnant.[12] The fact that he is slowly dying of hunger and cold is conveyed by the tangled thoughts and images forming the fabric of the poem. Or perhaps he survives only because he eats the dead woman's hand, "the hand in heaven." Fictional horror could barely compete with the horror of reality, and such a scenario was more or less typical for Leningrad of this period. In the winter of 1941–42, janitors regularly broke into apartments and removed bodies to the cellar to await burial in the spring (hence the motif of spring). In this case, however, the speaker is alive and still able to make the noise that brings him (temporary) reprieve. This is the story (*fabula*) of the poem—Shklovsky's term for the actual material that the author transforms into a plot (*siuzhet*), an aesthetically processed and transformed representation of events.

The plot of Gor's poem is created by leitmotifs. The first of these is set by the refrain (lines 21–22):

И буду лживый и живой
В могиле с мертвою женой

And I will lie, lying and living,
In the grave with my dead wife

(In line 28, "dead wife" is transformed into "dear wife"—we will return to this shift below.) As Muzhdaba points out, an earlier version read "And I will be alive, alive."[13] The word *lzhivyi* ("lying," "false") is phonetically close to *zhivoi* ("living"), but it adds a touch of uncertainty about one's own judgments and impressions. *Zhivoi* both alliterates and rhymes with *zhenoi* (as it happens, a literal translation would rhyme as well: "alive"/"wife," but the present translators apparently found this solution too facile); however, in juxtaposition to this life-affirming alliteration is another alliterated doubling of references to death: *V mogile s mertvoiu* ("in the *grave* with [the] *dead*"). What we see here is an oxymoronic juxtaposition of life and death. Moreover, the entire poem represents living in death as an existential state.

Within death and decay, life smolders and sometimes erupts, yet one state is inseparable from the other. The rhythm of the poem conveys this paradox with precision: it is iambic except for five lines, four of which are trochaic and one is written in free verse. Similarly, rhymes and semi-rhymes are irregular, only occasionally intruding, and, when they do, their purpose is to establish simple semantic connections: *Gde miloe?—Liudmila* (lit. "where [is the] dear?—Ludmila"); *rot—zhivot* ("mouth"—"belly"); *zhivoi—zhenoi* ("alive"—"wife"); *ia—tvoia* ("I"—"yours"); *zhenu—v raiu* ("wife"—"in paradise"); *rukoiu—rukoiu—zhenoiu* ("hand"—"hand"—"wife"). However, these connections are too simplistic to keep the speaker's mind from disintegrating.

The setting that opens the text recurs several times, and each time becomes more deformed. "The table, the chair, the lamp, / The books on the floor" (lines 2–3) disappear—"no books on the floor. / There'll be no lamp" (lines 23–24) and, at the end, "There's no apartment either" (line 44). The dead wife's face and the rest of her body also suffer devastating transformations: "But my wife is not there. / Hand, foot, and mouth. / Also the gravid belly" (lines 8–10); "her gaze went out. Rats have gnawed her mouth off already" (line 34); "My wife is not there already. / Her mouth melted long ago. A skeleton" (lines 41–42). First, her arms and legs (or, in the present translation, hands and feet—*ruka* and *noga* respectively can mean either) are separated from her body: "I cannot lift the hands and feet, / Can't carry them off" (lines 13–14).

And then: "Foot, in grave. The hand / She does not touch me with. The hand in heaven" (lines 32–33). What is nothing less than an act of dismemberment appears to take place in a dream; yet there is an equal possibility that it is really happening. There is no certainty, and Gor deliberately maintains this uncanny effect. While cannibalism is nowhere explicitly described, its shadow looms over the poem.

The climax of the poem, too, hinges on this semi-articulated motif of cannibalism (lines 25–26):

Где ты? И что такое тут лежит?
Чья рука? Чья нога? Моя? Твоя?

Where are you? And what is that that's lying here?
Whose hand? Whose foot? Mine? Or yours?

The syntactic structure of these lines, saturated with questions and exclamations, connects them to the beginning of the poem (lines 6–7):

Но где же то живое, робкое? Где милое?
Людмила где? Людмила!

But where is that living, timid thing? Where's my dear?
Where is Ludmila? Ludmila!

and also with the finale (lines 39–40):

Нас несут в подвал. И я кричу:
—Живой! Живой!

They carry us to the cellar. But I am screaming:
—I'm alive! Alive!

In this moment of frenzy, not only does the speaker see himself in the grave next to his wife, but his own body becomes indistinguishable from that of his wife and is incapable of separation. What we witness is an act of love, leading to a complete absorption of and by the other, which also involves cannibalism. This is the very moment at which the phrase "dead wife" yields in the next line to the refrain "dear wife." The grotesque version of the love and even "family" motif finds its ultimate embodiment in an agrammatical usage: *ia vdvoem, vtroem*—"I the two, the three of us," also translatable as "the two of me, the three of me" (line 43):

И я вдвоем, втроем течем, несемся.

And I, the two, the three of us, we are flowing, rushing.

What initially looks like a hallucination of a life lived happily with a wife and child turns into yet another version of living in death, since the continuation of the speaker's life entails absorbing the death of his wife and their unborn baby. In the poem's climax, this formula of the bizarre "family" is combined with the motif of water, of flowing (lines 37–38):

> Вдвоем, втроем течем
> Бежим, струимся.
>
> The two, the three of us, we are flowing.
> Running, streaming.

Muzhdaba also notes that Gor follows the OBERIU poets in interpreting fluidity as the distinctive emblem of time.[14] Death in the siege, as nightmarishly envisioned here, appears to be outside time because past, present, and future become conflated in the mind of the speaker. This even confounds the usual positive expectation that spring and summer are harbingers of a return to life ("For the spring to come, for the grass to come"; "A quiet river. A dream of summer," lines 19, 36), with warmth, with the cycle of seasons. In Gor's poem, however, "spring" means "burial," and "flowing" is only possible in the state of death—as a vision, a dream. The appearance of the janitor, the intrusion of reality, interrupts this idyll.

We see then that the plot (*siuzhet* in Shklovsky's terms) of the poem passes through three phases: in the first (lines 1–17), the speaker experiences the shock of his wife's death; in the second (lines 18–38), he himself surrenders to dying, becoming inseparable from the dead; in the third and final part (38–46), beginning with "the janitor comes in," there is the possibility that the protagonist returns to life. Yet, if this is a resurrection, it offers no epiphany. "They don't believe me" (line 41) is the response to his cry of "I'm alive! Alive!" (line 40), suggesting that survival of a catastrophe does not guarantee revival to life or emergence from a death state. The lamp is the only part of the "past" to make a return and, tellingly, its light flickers: "Just the lamp, now going out, now burning" (line 45).

The poem closes with an oxymoron of a kind much favored by the absurdists of OBERIU: *Da dvornik spit ne umolkaia* ("and the janitor sleeps, never shushing"; in the present translation, "and the janitor sleeping, incessantly burbling," line 46)—thus, living in death is transposed to a domestic, even comic level where sleep appears as a mundane, temporary equivalent of death. Despite the expectation that, with spring, death will end and life will be renewed, it turns out that life consists of the same elements as death. The only difference is a reduction in intensity.

Gennady Gor's poem stymies the possibility of interpreting war and other historical upheavals in a heroic fashion. His existential conclusions about the experience of war closely resemble Varlam Shalamov's conclusions about the experience of the Gulag. Having spent seventeen years in the camps, the author of the *Kolyma Tales* "considered the camp a negative experience for a human being, from the first to the last hour." He insisted: "Nobody should know such things, nobody should even hear about them. Nobody becomes better or stronger after the camp."[15] According to Shalamov, the terrible experience of the Gulag demonstrated the fragility, the defenselessness of all values nurtured by humanism and humanist culture in the face of brutal, merciless, and systematic violence. No moral lessons can be drawn from this experience. Shalamov says that one who writes about the Gulag bears comparison to Pluto, who rose from hell, rather than to Orpheus, who descended into hell and returned. True, in a way, Gor's speaker resembles Orpheus going down to hell for his Eurydice. But a return from hell, as Gor shows, is possible only externally. Hell remains inside Orpheus, continues to torment him. Indeed, the entire poem can be read as a recurring, unrelenting nightmare.

If we interpret Gor's poem not only as a reflection on the existential experience of the siege but also as a more general metaphor for historical tragedies, what we see being destroyed is not only cities and villages and not "only" human lives. What is at issue here is the very border between life and death. Life after a catastrophe remains nothing more than a shadow of death, the continuation rather than overcoming of death. Gor's siege poems were written more than a decade before Adorno's universally remembered statement: "To write poetry after Auschwitz is barbaric."[16] The meaning of Gor's message resonates closely with Adorno's even if Gor's formulation relies on illogical and discordant poetic language with the goal of creating a philosophic paradox. It is impossible to imagine poetry written in the state of half-death. Yet we are reading such a poem, and the impossible and unthinkable are happening now in front of our eyes. The meaning of this paradox simultaneously contradicts and complements Adorno's maxim: Gor proves that only by poetic means can we tame the affect of barbarity and that poetry takes the reader closest to the actual experience of the historical catastrophe.

18

Igor Kholin, "Fences. Trash-heaps. Flyers. Ads" (mid-1950s)

THE SLUMS OF COMMUNISM

Заборы. Помойки. Афиши. Рекламы.
Сараи - могилы различного хлама.
Сияет небес голубых глубина.
Бараки. В бараках уют. Тишина.
Зеркальные шкапы. Комоды. Диваны.
В обоях клопы. На столах тараканы.
Висят абажуры. Тускнеют плафоны.
Лежат на постелях ленивые жёны.
Мужчины на службе. На кухнях старухи.
И вертятся всюду назойливо мухи.[1]

Fences. Trash-heaps. Flyers. Ads.
Barns that are graves for various trash.
The depths of the heavens are gleaming blue-bright.
Barracks. The barracks are cozy. It's quiet.
Dressers with mirrors. Wardrobes. Couches.
Walls full of bedbugs. The tables have roaches.
The lampshades are sagging. The ceilings are dim.
On the beds lazing are languishing wives.
The men are at work. In the kitchens—old women.
And buzzing in circles hover ever the flies.

(TRANSLATED BY AINSLEY MORSE)

The first publication of the barracks poems of Igor Kholin (1920–99) was in the samizdat almanac *Syntaxis* (compiled by Alexander Ginsburg, 1959). They were immediately noticed by the "official periodicals," which printed descriptions of the forty-year-old author's poetry like the following:

> The Muscovite I. Kholin demonstrates a quite distinct taste for describing all sorts of garbage and filth. Somewhere a husband has beaten his wife, someone has gotten drunk and ended up in a fight with his drinking companion, a slovenly resident has allowed bedbugs to proliferate in an apartment—nothing escapes the attention of I. Kholin. He scrupulously records all these details in his latest opus. We had occasion to converse with this individual. He doesn't do anything, he lives on casual earnings. The way he tells things, he's unlucky: he can't work well together with anyone else. "They're all bad."[2]
>
> Perhaps I. Kholin is protesting and exposing deficiencies? No, he collects them. [. . .] And such, if one may use the term, is I. Kholin's "position." He surveys surrounding reality from up on the top of the garbage heap and from the inner depths of the toilet. Having consciously deprived himself of that which renders an individual human—labor—he mooches about on the sidelines of life, grousing and venting his bile in his poorly rhymed exercises. Yes—it is precisely idleness, parasitism, and the habit of living at other people's expense that lead to this "position."[3]

"He collects deficiencies," "they're all bad," a view "from up on the top of the garbage heap and from the inner depths of the toilet"—these formulations assumed by default that, of course, abominations did exist, but a Soviet subject should be able to ignore them and to view things, naturally, not from the top of the garbage heap, and most certainly not from the inner depths of the privy, but from the heights of an imaginary communism, from where people or roaches all look the same anyway.

Nobody needs to be persuaded any longer that Kholin's poetry derived its strength from his ability to see what readers were accustomed to ignoring. Nonetheless, arguments about Kholin continue, as formerly, to revolve around "the author's position." For instance, the critic Alexei Konakov, after astutely analyzing Kholin's poetics, ends his article with a severe rebuke to the poet for his inappropriate attitude to "the main subject of the age: the alienated proletariat": "The associations of robotized human beings in Kholin's poems are incapable of producing anything but quarrels, fights, crimes, and lust. But does such a position not demonstrate the right-wing worldview of the poet? [. . .] A conservative ideological premise, cast in extremely avant-garde forms?"[4] The poet Galina Rymbu took exception to this:

> Kholin's own position with regard to the inhabitants of the barracks should not be interpreted as alienated criticism of the somber and hazy body of the proletariat, but as his own complete self-identification with this body. With his elimination of the "authorial I" [. . .] Kholin himself becomes the body of the proletarian girl who has just undergone the abortion and is lying spreadeagled in the middle of the barracks; he becomes the shit, in which she is lying.[5]

Although Konakov's viewpoint does indeed seem anachronistic (how is it possible to speak of a left-wing or right-wing position without taking into account the hegemonic ideology of the time?), Rymbu's position does not seem entirely tenable either—for Kholin's authorial perspective does, after all, presuppose a distance from his characters. But this is certainly not the distance of class or cultural superiority.

Kholin's poem "Fences. Trash-heaps. Flyers. Ads" was not included in the *Syntaxis* selection, but it is the poem that opens the cycle, "Barracks Dwellers" ("Zhiteli baraka," written in 1956–58), in every publication of those poems during the poet's lifetime, that indicates its special role. The first line—"Fences. Trash-heaps. Flyers. Ads"—resonates with the beginnings of other poems in this cycle. Vladislav Kulakov points out a prototype of openings of this kind in the poems of Kholin's teacher, Evgeny Kropivnitsky:[6]

Полночь. Шумно. Тротуар.
Пьянка. Ругань. Драка. Праздник.
Хрипы. Вопли, Безобразник
Едет в Ригу. Тротуар
Весь в движении. Угар
В головах шумит, проказник.
Полночь. Шумно. Тротуар.
Пьянка. Ругань. Драка. Праздник.[7]

Midnight. Pavement. Rowdy din.
Boozing. Brawling. Celebration.
Wheezing. Bawling. Loutish ruffian
Off to Riga. All the pavement
Just a confused blur of movement.
Heads spinning, wild exhilaration.
Midnight. Pavement. Rowdy din.
Boozing. Brawling. Celebration.

The structure of the poem, consisting of one- and two-word nominative sentences, which in Kropivnitsky's oeuvre is a one-off, becomes for Kholin a designation of genre. What is the essence of this genre?

It is obvious that a syntactical structure of this type references Alexander Blok's classic lyric "Night, street, streetlamp, pharmacy" ("Noch', ulitsa, fonar', apteka"), with its hopeless version of Nietzsche's "eternal return." The genre that arises out of this structure is based on the collision of two temporal modalities—on the one hand, we have before us an instantaneous snapshot; on the other hand, these snapshots will never change and thus, along with a passing moment, they signify eternity. Eternity is its most banal and annoying manifestation. Through this form, Kholin creates "snapshots" that are simultaneously representational and abstract, referencing the recognizable and devoid of all connection with locale. One can see this paradox in many other poems form the cycle "Barracks Dwellers":

Улица. Липа. Толпа.
Дом.
Случай с маляром.
Полетел вниз.
Ударился о карниз.
Мозги вдребезги.[8]

A street. A lime tree. A crowd.
A building.
A painter's mishap.
Plummeting down.
He crashed into the molding.
Smashed his brains out.

Рыба. Икра. Вина.
За витриной продавщица Инна.
Вечером иная картина:
Комната,
Стол,
Диван.
Муж пьян.
Мычит:
—Мы, бля-я . . .
Хрюкает,
Как свинья.

Храпит
Инна не спит.
Утром снова витрина:
Рыба. Икра. Вина.[9]

Fish. Caviar. Wines.
At the glass counter the salesgirl Inna.
A different picture in the evening.
A room.
A table.
A couch
Her husband's soused.
He roars;
Fuck it, weee'll . . .
He grunts
Like a pig.
He snores.
Inna can't sleep.
Next morning, the counter again.
Fish. Caviar. Wines.

It is significant that the poems from Kholin's barracks cycle that were published in *Syntaxis* bore the subtitle "a fragment." Discernible behind each separate text is a long and uniform series of similar instances. Seriality would become an important feature of conceptual art; Ilya Kabakov, for instance, explains that this is a way of developing the identity of an authorial persona or "image," as Dmitry Prigov put it.[10] But Kholin does not create an authorial persona—in his poems, "serialism" is inherent in the structure of everyday reality, constantly repeating its ugly norm. Moreover, in order for the perception of a series to arise, Kholin does not need several poems depicting the same situation or personages: repetition is embedded in the functional mechanics of every poem.

These principles are already pronounced in the first poem of the cycle "Fences. Trash-heaps. Flyers. Ads." In contrast with Blok's nervous iambic rhythm with a spondee at the first foot, Kholin's poem is written in amphibrachic tetrameter, without a single pyrrhic foot in the entire text. Furthermore, in the first line each word-sentence is also a metric foot: the syntactical and metrical rhythms coincide, which creates a chanting effect. The impression is almost that of a brisk march, and it is reinforced by a rhyme scheme of couplets, with rhymes that are always banal and in which the rhyme of the first and second lines (*reklamy—khlama*) returns in the fifth and sixth (*divany—tarakany*). Most of the rhymes are feminine, and only one is masculine (*tishina—glubina*): it apparently marks the transition from the outside space to the barracks' coziness.

As Olga Sedakova has noted, the amphibrachic tetrameter in which Kholin's poem is written is associated with Boris Pasternak's poem "The Miracle" ("Chudo") from *The Poems of Doctor Zhivago*, and the ninth poem of Pushkin's "Imitation of the Koran," which in turn echoes Vasily Zhukovsky's "Arab's Song over His Horse's Grave" (1809–10). These are all poems with manifestly metaphysical aspects, reflected in their prosody: Sedakova even calls the semantic aura of this meter a "religious amphibrach."[11] We can add here that this "religious amphibrach" is the meter in which Pasternak's poem "My Sister—Life" is written, and also "The State Anthem of the Soviet Union" (apart from the refrain) by Sergei Mikhalkov and El-Registan.

Another example that is chronologically close is Nikolai Zabolotsky's "Woodland Lake" ("Lesnoe ozero"), written in 1938 and only published in 1956. Sedakova also confidently assigns this metaphysical lyric to the tradition of the "religious amphibrach." Despite its basic alternating rhyme scheme, "A Woodland Lake" also opens with a rhyming couplet, establishing a resonance between Zabolotsky and Kholin:

Опять мне блеснула, окована сном.
Хрустальная чаша во мраке лесном.[12]

Again, shackled in sleep, I caught its glitter,
A crystal chalice amidst the gloom of the forest.

In both poems, the lyrical hero's viewpoint is in motion. In Zabolotsky's case, the lyrical hero arrives at the lake, a focus of beauty and "source of truth," by moving through the "terrible world" of nature:

Сквозь битвы деревьев и волчьи сраженья,
Где пьют насекомые сок из растенья,
Где буйствуют стебли и стонут цветы,
Где хищными тварями правит природа . . . [13]

Through battles of trees and wolves' fierce contention,
Where insects drain sap from the live vegetation
Where stalks rampage fiercely and flowerheads groan,
Where nature holds reign over rapacious beasts . . .

We may suspect that Zabolotsky's herds of animals and wild beasts are transformed into Kholin's bedbugs, roaches, and flies, swarming in the barracks' coziness.

Zabolotsky's "Woodland Lake" concludes with the appearance of the night sky in the smooth surface of the lake. In Kholin's poem, the sky becomes part of the initial "frame" of barracks coziness: "The depths of the heavens are gleaming blue-bright" (which sounds similar to Zabolotsky's line from "A Woodland Lake," "At the first gleaming of the evening star"). Of course, in Kholin's poem the sky appears not only in its banal aspect of gleaming blue depths but also coupled with parodistic death: "Barns that are graves for various trash." Nonetheless, light penetrates even into the barracks, although it grows dimmer on the way; it is reflected in the mirrors of dressers, duplicated in lampshades and dim ceiling lamps—a double mention of the attributes of lamps in a single line ("The lampshades are sagging. The ceilings are dim") is hardly likely to be accidental.

But the most important connection between these poems clearly lies in the question that is asked by Zabolotsky and answered by Kholin: "Where does the splendor of such slums come from?" ("Otkuda v trushchobakh takoie velich'e?").[14]

"Zabolotsky wrote these poems in the special convoy that was taking him to a prison camp," Olga Sedakova writes in her commentary on "A Woodland Lake."[15] Similar to Zabolotsky, Kholin also possessed knowledge of the Gulag that was more than mere hearsay. The son of a commissioned officer in the tsarist army, at the age of nine he was placed in an orphanage by his mother, and his path took him through a labor colony, military service, and four years at the front. And also through the prison camp at Lianozovo—Kholin was an inmate, more precisely a pass-holding convict, when he became acquainted with the Kropivnitsky family, the core of the future "Lianozovo circle": "While serving a two-year sentence in Lianozovo, Kholin called in to the local library to get some books (he was sometimes permitted to leave the prison camp's territory), and the librarian there turned out to be Olga Ananieva Potapova, the wife of Evgeny Leonidovich Kropivnitsky."[16] In other words, Kholin arrived at the Kropivnitskys' barracks home directly from the Gulag.

This is why Kholin does not perceive the inhabitants of the barracks—including the proletarians among them—as an oppressed class. He is also devoid of even the slightest sense of superiority—in either cultural or class terms—concerning them. However strange this may sound, Kholin regards this population as the Soviet middle class. Status is relative and he is, after all, observing them from the very different barracks of a prison camp. It is only natural, then, that his eye is caught by the coziness of the barracks:

В обоях клопы. На столах тараканы.
Висят абажуры. Тускнеют плафоны.

Лежат на постелях ленивые жёны.
Мужчины на службе. На кухнях старухи.
И вертятся всюду назойливо мухи

Walls full of bedbugs. The tables have roaches.
The lampshades are sagging. The ceilings are dim.
On the beds lazing are languishing wives.
The men are at work. In the kitchens—old women.
And buzzing in circles hover ever the flies.

Life as it appears here resembles the philosopher Giorgio Agamben's description of *zoe*: existence in the raw as purely biological and uniform for animals, insects, and people entirely devoid of individual subjectivity. The fact that Kholin in this manner levels out the ontological value of objects, insects, and human beings of the barracks world is deliberate. The poem juxtaposes two triads, first of bedbugs, roaches, and flies and then of husbands, wives, and old women. Both of these are correlated with the triad "Dressers with mirrors. Wardrobes. Couches." The syntactical parallels also emphasize these resemblances: *V barakakh uiut, V oboiakh klopy* ("The barracks are cozy," "Walls full of bedbugs"); *Na stolakh tarakany, na posteliakh lenivye zheny* ("The tables have roaches," "On the beds lazing are languishing wives"); *Muzhchiny na sluzhbe. Na kukhniakh starukhi* ("The men are at work. In the kitchens—old women"). However, the pairing *Muzhchiny na sluzhbe. Na kukhniakh starukhi* differs from the other parallels noted above: first, because the men sent off to work clearly transgress the boundaries of the barracks' realm, and, second, because the old women in the kitchens are no less active than the irksome flies. Notwithstanding the declared peace and quiet of the barracks' coziness, these are disruptive. The broken line 9 emphasizes the parallel between the old women, busily fussing in the kitchen (there is food! That is why they are rhymed with flies) and the men working in offices—not in a factory or a workshop—who pay for this food. Given the association between bedbugs and social parasitism that harkens back to Mayakovsky's satirical play *The Bedbug* (1929), Kholin's poem could sound like a standard Soviet "condemnation of philistinism," with such staples of coziness as lightshade and geranium.

But this is not a condemnation, although Kholin did call himself a satirist. The movement of viewpoint in the poem is a shift from the outside world, its fences, ads, and barns, *into the interior* of the barracks—toward the furniture, bedbugs, lazy wives, and old women. From his position of exclusion as an ex-convict, the lyrical subject acquires a new status, himself becoming if not an inhabitant of these barracks then at least a visitor to them. Kholin does not try to whitewash this *habitus*, he is all too aware that Soviet *zoe* is hellish. In one of the poems in the "Barracks Dwellers," he places Adam and Eve precisely in the very same hell:

Адам
Токарь-инструментальщик
Ева
Слесарь-лекальщик
Место работы
Завод "Пеношлак"
Место жительства
Общежитье
Барак
Хуже Ада[17]

Adam's
A lathe-instrument maker
Eve is
An instrument-gauge maker
Their workplace is
The "Foamslag" factory
Their residence
A dormitory
A barracks
Worse than hell

But this very hell, as we see from the first poem in the cycle, is by no means devoid of coziness. And furthermore, the barracks' hell is an attempt at life on the outskirts of town or situated in the ruins of the even more terrible hell of prison and the Gulag from which the author has arrived. If we ask why in this poem Kholin resorts to the "religious amphibrach," it is most probably because the form conjures the sound of an optimistic march, or nearly.

In considering post-catastrophe human condition, the philosopher Valery Podoroga characterized life as a constant struggle for survival, in his words "a minimalist and absolutely transparent existence, from which the human is eliminated."[18] In depicting the world after the Gulag, Kholin does not restrict himself to minimalism and bareness. His interiors contain furnishings like dressers with mirrors, wardrobes, and couches. In the barracks hell there is even light, however dim, and the sky can be seen. Life in the sense Agamben gives it is present, but the vision is bleak, containing not children but flies. As Rymbu comments: "The reverse side of this total irony and cruel objectivity is horror, bitter sorrow for the downtrodden, for the proletarian who is oppressed as a result of the 'great revolution,' crammed into the barracks and still yet carries on living in his own dreadful vitality."[19]

In other words, life is all around. This is not so small a thing as it seems. For insofar as it is not extinction, bare life contains the possibility of renewal and that possibility of optimism counters a grotesque reality in a Soviet context changed by the death of Stalin and the decline of the Gulag. Even people living in the vicinity of a labor camp are learning to *simply live*, not just survive. Such is the message of what might be regarded as Kholin's own version of Pasternak's *My Sister—Life*. But another point of view must also be considered. And it embodies the yearning for a different life beyond the limits of biological need and joys. Poetry is basically the most direct embodiment of this yearning. And, however hard it may seem to imagine, from the viewpoint of poetry, a cozy barracks is not the antithesis of a labor camp, but its continuation.

Giorgio Agamben writes:

> Whoever entered the camp moved in a zone of indistinction between outside and inside, exception and rule, licit and illicit, in which the very concepts of subjective rights and juridical protection no longer made any sense. [. . .] This is why the camp is the very paradigm of political space at the point at which politics becomes biopolitics and *homo sacer* is virtually confused with the citizen.[20]

In addition, Agamben contends that precisely the prison camp becomes the paradigm of a contemporary society, in which biopolitics has displaced politics: "There is no return from the camps to classical politics. In the camps, city and house became indistinguishable, and the possibility of differentiation between our biological body and our political body—between what is incommunicable and mute and what is communicable and sayable—was taken away from us forever."[22] If we read Kholin through Agamben, then the barracks embody the condition of modernity, both Soviet and non-Soviet, in which, according to the philosopher, "we are all virtually *homines sacri*." This is a condition in which the boundaries between prison camp and city are erased, creating "the zone of indistinction."[23] Ultimately, it is the inception of this new form of societal organization that Kholin records in the first poem of the barracks cycle—precisely this is the significance of all his couplings and parallels, welded together by the unity of the mighty "religious amphibrach."[24]

19

Nikolai Zabolotsky, “Somewhere not far from Magadan” (1956)

A GULAG ELEGY

Где-то в поле возле Магадана,
Посреди опасностей и бед,
В испареньях мёрзлого тумана
Шли они за розвальнями вслед.
От солдат, от их луженых глоток,
От бандитов шайки воровской
Здесь спасали только околодок
Да наряды в город за мукой.
Вот они и шли в своих бушлатах—
Два несчастных русских старика,
Вспоминая о родимых хатах
И томясь о них издалека.
Вся душа у них перегорела
Вдалеке от близких и родных,
И усталость, сгорбившая тело,
В эту ночь снедала души их,
Жизнь над ними в образах природы
Чередою двигалась своей.
Только звёзды, символы свободы,
Не смотрели больше на людей.
Дивная мистерия вселенной
Шла в театре северных светил,
Но огонь её проникновенный
До людей уже не доходил.
Вкруг людей посвистывала вьюга,
Заметая мёрзлые пеньки.

И на них, не глядя друг на друга,
Замерзая, сели старики.
Стали кони, кончилась работа,
Смертные доделались дела . . .
Обняла их сладкая дремота,
В дальний край, рыдая, повела.
Не нагонит больше их охрана,
Не настигнет лагерный конвой,
Лишь одни созвездья Магадана
Засверкают, став над головой.[1]

Somewhere not far from Magadan,
in the grip of miseries and danger,
slowly, through the breaths of icy fog,
they trudged on behind a sledge.
From the soldiers, from their iron throats,
from the predatory crooks and thieves—
only the infirmary could save one,
or being sent for flour into town.
So they trudged along, in battered coats—
two ill-fated Russian men—
two old peasants yearning for their huts,
the far-off huts where they'd been born.
Burned out by life, they'd no heart left,
far away from all their folk;
and the weariness that hunched their bodies
now consumed their very souls.
Up above them all the forms of nature,
all of life proceeded on its course.
But the stars, those harbingers of freedom,
were no longer looking down at men.
The mystery of the universe might still
have been unfolding in the northern skies,
but these two—they were no longer
pierced by those penetrating fires.
Round about them whirled a blizzard,
spreading on the stumps a snowy cloak.

And on this snow the freezing men now sat,
without a word, without a look.
The horses stopped. Labor was now over—
over now, the life that they'd been dealt . . .
A sweet somnolence embraced them,
took them, sobbing, to a distant land.
Now the guards would never overtake them,
never would the escort catch them up—
only Magadan's bright constellations
will catch fire high up above.

(TRANSLATED BY BORIS DRALYUK)

Born in distant Urzhum, Nikolai Zabolotsky arrived in Petrograd in 1921, enrolled at the Marxist Herzen Pedagogical Institute, which trained teachers, and quickly discovered a vocation for poetry. His arrival coincided with the last stage of the civil war and the transition to the New Economic Policy, when Modernism was entering its final dynamic phase, expressed in the visual arts, café culture, and the periodical press. Zabolotsky also confronted a rapidly changing social reality. In the New Economic Policy period, the Bolshevik desperation to stabilize the economy created a hybrid of capitalism and state ownership, leading to speculation, profiteering, fraud, and much consumerism, of a kind brilliantly captured in period classics like Mayakovsky's satirical play *The Bedbug* (1928) and Ilf and Petrov's novel *Twelve Chairs* (1928), with its con-man hero Ostap Bender. Mayakovsky and Zabolotsky were perhaps the supreme verse satirists of the period, although in other respects they were markedly different since Zabolotsky showed nothing like the political interest Mayakovsky pursued in his revolutionary poems. Zabolotsky's youthful lyrics, published in the early 1920s when he lived and worked in Leningrad after his university education in Moscow, are autobiographical insofar as they evoke his youth in the countryside and peasant origins.

A more vibrant and innovative Zabolotsky soon emerged. His early maturity embraced the new urban reality and already hints at his later, more spiritualized vision of nature, reflecting German Idealism, with its pantheistic view of a world suffused with consciousness, and the contemporary philosophical ideas and pseudoscientific views of Konstantin Tsiolkovskii and Pavel Filonov.[2] His first collection of poems, *Columns* (*Stolbtsy*, 1929), is a book of about fifty lyrics brimming with scenes from everyday urban life. Some of the titles, such as "Samovar," "The Bakery," "Foxtrot," "Football," and "Circus," convey the social and cultural milieu in stanzaic lyrics written in a highly visual, even expressionist, style and with great metrical energy. These works absorbed onto the page all the confusion, garishness, and grotesque excesses of the New Economic Policy period. Naturally a highly visual person, Zabolotsky was drawn to contemporary painters Pavel Filonov and Konstantin Malevich. He also became a founding member of OBERIU, already discussed in earlier chapters on Kharms and Vvedensky. Both sets of visual and poetic affinities enhanced his linguistic and visual powers of expressivity. Replete with scenes of lavish bourgeois consumption and urban decadence, *Columns* offers streetscapes and interiors, whether bars or markets, football or foxtrot, and contains many vignettes of popular culture in poems about football or the House of the People juxtaposed with quasi-mystical evocations of nature and the peasantry. Its phantasmagoric universe has the kinetic energy of the roaring twenties and a revolutionary energy depicted by the painters he most admired, including Marc Chagall and Filonov. Its visual field is kaleidoscopic and fragmented, and the language is lavishly metaphorical. Poems move quickly from scene to scene, and the tone can be satirical, colloquial, and jokey while Zabolotsky's command of classical forms and use of delightful and blisteringly inventive rhymes is ingenious in the manner of his fellow OBERIU poets Daniil Kharms and Nikolai Oleinikov.

The authorities looked askance at Zabolotsky for his failure to contribute to the socialist cause and for standing aloof from the devastating collectivization and militarized industrialization and ushered in the Stalinist epoch after the New Economic Policy. His writings had drawn inspiration from the contemporary world in all of its absurdity and vulgarity without putting forward anything like the positive vision required of art by the state. Excerpts from his dramatic narrative "The Triumph of Agriculture" first appeared in 1929, coinciding with the proletarianization of culture and dominance of the RAPP (Russian Association of Proletarian Writers). The entire work (a prologue and seven parts) was published in *Zvezda* in 1933. The reception was uniformly hostile. A strong revisionist argument has been made in scholarship on Zabolotsky for seeing the poem as a utopian vision. Contemporary reviewers, however, reacted with indignation and saw the work as a satire of collectivization.[3] Their attacks also took swipes retrospectively at *Columns* as a work of antisocialist decadence. Despite continued hostility, from that time until his arrest in 1938 on fictitious charges of anti-Soviet activity, Zabolotsky continued to publish in high-profile outlets such as *Izvestiia* and to try to find a point of accommodation with Soviet political ideology.[4] He was arrested, interrogated, and tortured, an experience he described in a memoir *The History of My Imprisonment*, published abroad in 1981 and in Russia only in 1988 early in the Glasnost period.[5] His sentence was commuted in 1943, and he returned to live in Moscow and in Peredelkino, the writers' village, after 1946. To a degree, he retreated from poetry and took refuge in his important and extensive translation work, most notably of the medieval epic *The Lay of Igor's Campaign.*

The earlier Zabolotsky epitomized the avant-garde immersion in the urban world, and this work had garnered much admiration in literary circles, especially OBERIU, for its mastery of visual tropes and linguistic daring. The Zabolotsky who emerged from the Gulag bowed to circumstance and resumed the more overt capitulation to the authorities that characterized his attempts to defend himself in the years immediately before his arrest. The split self was now even more pronounced and, in the view of Darra Goldstein, became a psychological habit of mind that was consciously pursued as Zabolotsky divided his creative personality between the outward-facing urban poet and the more abstruse singer of Nature.[6] "Somewhere not far from Magadan" is rare as a treatment of forced labor and the recovery of inner freedom. It is also a poem that captures the stark change in the poet's literary persona and style, after eight years of exile and labor in penal colonies ended with his return to Moscow in 1946.

This duality, Goldstein notes, acquired a new dimension in Zabolotsky's post-Gulag poetry. Zabolotsky had always maintained his innocence of any crimes, and while he was never exonerated, he was readmitted in 1946 to the Union of Soviet Writers, the professional guild whose approval was a mark of establishment acceptability and a source of sales and income. He had a family to support and became increasingly concerned about securing a livelihood as well as a legacy. The result was poetry of a more conformist nature, politically supportive of the state and compatible with socialist realism. The private Zabolotsky explored his own anguish and recovered the affinity for nature that pervaded his earlier work. For both sides of this "double-dealing self," to use a term familiar from the 1920s, he adopted a new manner in his lyric poetry. He changed his technique in order to write poems that communicated more directly the universality of certain experiences and emotions. The more personal lyrics focus on interiority and the subjective self, linking them to the tradition of lyric poetry Zabolotsky knew well as a reader of Baratynsky and Goethe. Like Khodasevich's "Music," the poem begins with the mundane and moves toward epiphany, similarities in outlook and expectation that also repeat the paradigm of Pushkin's "The Prophet." While Zabolotsky's language had moved away from the conspicuously modernist and was not tainted by any hints of "bourgeois" experimentalism, his treatment of adversity as a cosmic problem (rather than a Soviet injustice) should not be read as an act of conformism, self-recrimination, or apology. The horror of the situation the poem describes places it beyond politics.

Magadan, the place-name mentioned in the first and final lines, is sufficient to strike terror in the heart of readers familiar with the history of Soviet penal colonies, or Gulag, established during the Great Terror of the 1930s. It was the capital of the Kolyma region, center of the most brutal network of camps to which Soviet political prisoners were shipped from around 1932 and subjected to forced labor in the mines of this gold-rich territory. Stripped down to its basic components, the poem relates a story about the brutal death of two men, both peasants by origin, sent in a work brigade to chop wood (the frozen tree stumps suggest as much) during a snowstorm. They are no match for the hostile conditions, and, after they have completed their work ("Labor was now over," lit. "they had completed their tasks"), they quietly sink into a sweet sleep and freeze to death. The repetition of sound clusters is particularly pronounced as a musical feature at the beginning and end of this poem. Lines 1–15 contain repeated instances of the combinations *-rz/zr, pos/pas, -lo/ol,* as well as combinations close to internal line breaks, such as the vertically aligned *vspominaia/tomias'* and the poignant *ustalost'/snedaia.* Toward the end, the sounds *rz/zr* first used in words denoting cold recur to remind us of the freezing conditions. They interrupt the reverie on the "beautiful mystery" of the world. Even as the narrator's language becomes more tight-lipped, matching the failure of language between the two convicts who succumb silently to their fate, the sound of the poetry pulsates with some other feeling carried in the sound *-la/al,* which reverberates through the words *dela* ("deeds"), *obniala* ("embraced"), *dal'nii* ("distant"), *povela* ("lead"), *lagernyi* ("camp"), and is finally varied in the place-name Magadan, mentioned at the beginning and at the end and conveying a sense of the closure of the journey. Melodiousness is not mimetic: the sounds themselves have no inherent meaning. If they are elegiac, it is because the beauty they contribute is a conscious effect. Unlike the beauty of the universe, indifferent and distant, the beauty of the poetry adds some measure of care that cannot be verbalized but can be sounded.

The poem's plot frames treatment of the starry sky around the middle, a brief digression that slows down the inexorable conclusion and adds a vital element of spiritual poignance. While misery has devoured their souls, it has not exhausted the fellow feeling of the narrator-poet or that of the reader. Just as Paul Celan's "Todesfüge" responded to Adorno famously claiming that poetry after Auschwitz was barbaric, in the same year as Khrushchev's secret denunciation of Stalin's crimes against the Soviet people, Zabolotsky demonstrated his own capacity to find the necessary words for a heinous scene and to recover his own lyric voice.

The surreal gaiety and technical brilliance of Zabolotsky's early verse no longer came easily, perhaps inappropriate in poetry pinned between self-doubt and cosmic uncertainty. As one of Russia's great nature poets, Zabolotsky was a continuator of the romantics, Russian and German. His landscapes pulsate with the subjective spirit of consciousness. Descended from Schellingian philosophy, Zabolotsky's understanding in his earlier poetry is of Nature as a pantheistic force and principle. His vision of the natural world as an abstract entity is also informed by other cognate philosophical theories, mingling scientific and popular belief about Nature's spiritual content. From the 1940s, the quest to return to Nature is visible in Zabolotsky's poetry. He situates the poet somewhere on the edge of nature (as he writes in the short lyric "The Blind Man" ["Slepoi," 1946], his attempts at conversation with the elements are one-sided and contained "in my bitter heart" ["v gorestnom serdtse moem"]).[7] His Gulag years were passed under the evil star ("zloveshchaia zvezda") described in "The Opposition of Mars" ("Protivostoianie Marsa," 1956), which

> sketched in the heavens signs
> of suffering, blood, and war.[8]

Full of pathos, these statements are plainer than those that can be found in the earlier poet, who met his tumultuous age with an unstinting verbal and visual energy. Caution and fatigue condition poetic responsiveness marked by an awareness that trauma cannot be overcome, but equally that the need to write poetry cannot be ignored.

"Somewhere not far" contains notable features of Zabolotsky's later style, namely a tendency to a more symmetrical line rather than the earlier use of irregular rhythmic patterns. The shuffling, trochaic pentameter line trudges along, its intonation flat and neutral. The form "entered the repertoire of Russian poets relatively late" and, because it made little use of a fixed caesura, proved to be a more expansive flowing line.[9] In the nineteenth century, trochaic meters were often associated with poems about marching and walking, an appropriate association here just as the pentameter was favored for interior monologue and philosophical reflection. One feature of the trochaic pentameter is that the high percentage of stressed syllables in the strong positions of the line created a relatively stable rhythmic profile. As a rule, the first and third ictuses were strong. The rhythmic shape of this work somewhat diverges from that norm. While the number of lines in which the third ictus is filled is high and at the average, the first foot shows an unusual tendency to omit stress. Syntax and word choice explain this effect: Zabolotsky positions at the opening of lines, and therefore in the first foot, words such as prepositions (*ot, do*), particles (*ne*), adverbs (*zdes', lish', tol'ko*), conjunctions (*no, i*), and other words that have no inherent stress (*dva, vot, shli, stali*). This feature is audible and striking at the line opening, and, coupled with a tendency to enjambment and the use of gerunds. The relative moderation of meter, only one of the prosodic features that demarcate poetry and prose, conduces to a depoeticization: the impression may be that this is a short story told in the third-person cast in the form of a lyric. At the same time, these lines have a vocalic harmony, word after word producing long *a*-sounds, somehow detached from their surface reality as though there is a musical level at which poetry lives, its cadence possibly offering relief. This subtle, simultaneous reduction (metrically) and retention (sonically) of poetic effects put the poem on the side of its subjects, striking a modest, resigned tone even when the vision of the starry sky might have occasioned a hint of ecstasy. Inner and outer landscapes, the penal and the natural, time and space, emptiness and fullness—all take their place, humanizing and stripping away illusion in a poetry of quiet despair.

Rarely has terrain been more uninspiring and terrifying than the frozen wasteland. Yet a poem can attain a vantage point even on the nameless individual, a Gulag everyman, even when the force of history has blanked out personality. What is left is a residue of feeling, a partial memory of origins, a partial yearning for elevation. If we face daily annihilation, can lyric poetry concentrate on a routinized present, relegating awareness of the past and future? Zabolotsky's earlier poetics was one of animation, a cubist clashing of planes, linguistically ambitious and musically propulsive. In general, Gulag poems focus on first-person experience and single moments, often a memory of life before incarceration. "In a Field" stands out because it takes us into the world of Varlam Shalamov's *Kolyma Tales*, a now classic, harrowing work of Gulag literature in which snowy landscapes of pristine beauty hide all trace of human suffering.[10] At the earthly level, the visual field is mapped out with imprecision, called "somewhere" and "near" in a nameless field as the men grope blindly. Magadan is the only place-name, mentioned twice, as the marker of their location on earth at the start and the place from where they see the sky at the end, a single name circumscribing reality and even escapism. Distance and neglect characterize the human perspective and the attitude of nature. "Far away from all their folk" (lit. "far from their close ones"), while an unoriginal piece of word play, fits a larger pattern in the poem, foregrounding physical distance and emotional proximity. In relation to this environment, the rhyme words *MagadAn*/*tumAn* ("Magadan/fog") contain a physical reality. The phrase "frozen air" (*merzlyi vozdukh*) is almost unique to this poem and, in its own subtle way, perhaps more poignant.[11] Even air cannot be taken for granted in such a brutal environment, where a basic element has been frozen into an indistinct mass.

In a landscape that seems to evaporate into a frozen mist of violence and starvation, the only escape may be skyward. The poem reduces death and life to the barest tokens. No more need be mentioned than threats from gangs (line 5) to note the menace of violent death and relief from hunger in food parcels from local towns. Time is no more precise than location, as the conversation that unfolds against the backdrop of the initial lines might have happened anytime and any number of times in the lives of two convicts. Their exchange is summarized rather than quoted in the body of the poem. Omniscient narration goes together with descriptive detail in maintaining pathos for their plight and distancing from their individual circumstance. This is the scaffolding on which the emotional state of these two doomed ZEKs can be exposed. From afar, the signs of weariness are clear to the viewer who notes their hunched posture. The state of their soul is also seen from within, and the train of their thoughts focused on a remembered past and on the sky seems to be a form of emotional salvation. Both meanings of the adjective *neschastnyi* apply, since they are unhappy and unfortunate. The hunger that threatens their lives, only given the briefest mention, is nothing compared with the hunger that devours their souls.

This latter hunger must be starved rather than fed, however. At the midpoint, the poem creates a shift from the matter-of-fact statement of a prosaic situation to a more abstract language about the spiritual. Is there a glimmer of hope? Has the "icy fog" of slavery lifted to reveal a more optimistic view? In Russian poetry, Pushkin's works will always be the touchstone for later poems that recuperate from desolation moments of uplift and vision. Three of Pushkin's lyrics inform Zabolotsky's work in relation to the potential for spiritual renewal ("The Prophet," "Prorok"); in relation to the association of the star with political freedom ("Sower of a barren desert," "Svobody seiatel' pustynnyi"); and finally in relation to a vision of death in a distant place as a refuge ("It is time, it is time, my friend," "Pora, moi drug, pora," 1834).

Several poems discussed in this book take inspiration from and rework "The Prophet." Most relevant in this context is Khodasevich's "Ballad." Although a work of a very different kind, especially in its concentration of the poet's own egotistical sublime, the poem contrasts states of spiritual and physical torpor and visionary plenitude. While there are no stars or sun, and a room with a naked fixture of sixteen bulbs is the equivalent to the desert of Pushkin's "The Prophet," the poet is at the end granted access to radiant music. The juxtaposition with Zabolotsky's subjects is a case of affecting counterpoint because his poem asks us to consider the impact of the stars on both the prisoners and the authorial speaker. Only one of them is granted spiritual revival. The closer language comes to capturing precisely what they feel, the less tangible it becomes, and the tension between the near and far, the intimate and distant, the momentary and the continuous remains in play. What is the force of the adjective modifying "soul"? Is this to be translated as "their whole soul" or "their soul through and through"? Can a soul be affected in part but not entirely?

The question is apt, because lines 13–16 suggest that their spiritual ability is entirely exhausted:

Вся душа у них перегорела
Вдалеке от близких и родных,
И усталость, сгорбившая тело,
В эту ночь снедала души их

Burned out by life, they'd no heart left,
far away from all their folk;
and the weariness that hunched their bodies
now consumed their very souls.

Worn out by physical labor, hostile cold, loneliness, and age, too, the pair must have repeated this journey across a field many times. Such incapacity portends no epiphany or relief. People are separated from the cosmos. This is death without the spiritual elevation vouchsafed by Pushkin's prophet. The speaker's soul remains alert to another dimension of feeling embodied in the universe at large, as seen in the sky above. Yet that feeling of spiritual rebirth cannot be achieved. Insofar as the speaker's language seems to replay the classic situation of "The Prophet," starting in depletion and lassitude and penetrating to a radiant vision of the universe, that expectation is not fulfilled because the stars "were no longer looking down at men" and the men "were no longer / pierced by those penetrating fires."

Yet something different occurs on "this night" (line 16 in the Russian) to revive openness to a "marvelous mystery of the universe" (line 21 in the Russian). That special event must be both the death of the two prisoners and the lesson brought home to the poet by the force of the recognition with which he perceives the distance of the stars. The description of life above them notes the indifference of the stars, and whatever sense of life and freedom remains accessible to them seems to be contingent not on their projection of sympathy into nature but rather on the opposite appreciation of the complete separation between mankind and nature. That separation is the opening to death into which Zabolotsky folds life. Life dwells apart from man. Yet in spite of that separation life also exists in relation to man, and nature is represented by the stars, a realm opposite to the labor camp, security guard, and convoy. Again, a Pushkinian intertext has an important claim as a point of reference here. Few images are more freighted with a history of poetic use than Pushkin's equation of the star with freedom (also notable in the Akhmatova cycle discussed in chapter 15), and it may be the most conspicuous examples that together infuse these lines. In Pushkin's early poetry, such as "To Chaadaev" (1818), he used the star as a symbol of freedom. Even more germane is "Sower of a barren desert," based on the Parable of the Sower (Matthew 13:1–23, Mark 4:1–20, Luke 8:4–15). Freedom's star is what greets the ploughman, a figure not unlike Zabolotsky's workers who are also following a horse-drawn vehicle. This figure goes out early to sow his fields only to discover that his message, a seed cast to a people enslaved by the yoke, fails to arouse their instinct for freedom. The poem is both a subversive and a disenchanted statement about the power poetry has to motivate political action and the risk of failure. Unpublishable in Pushkin's lifetime, "Sower of a barren desert" circulated clandestinely and inspired some Decembrist rebels who acknowledged Pushkin's poetry as an inspiration. It was published in 1856 by the socialist thinker Alexander Herzen in his journal, *The Northern Star*, whose title carries yet another astral association exactly one hundred years before "Somewhere not far from Magadan." While Pushkin's speaker despaired of the people, Zabolotsky reverses the cause of disenchantment. The stars, fully acknowledged as "symbols of freedom," now spurn man. There is a sense of salvation at hand that, once available, now remains out of reach, perhaps reminiscent of the position the Virgin Mary takes in Kuzmin's "Not a governor's lady," discussed in chapter 11, about God's abandonment of Russia after Russia's apostasy from God. Here the description of the position of the stars, when understood astronomically, only underscores the bitter and absolute neglect and also inverts the scenario of "The Prophet" by cutting off access to a higher realm. Magadan is roughly 60 degrees north. This means that, around the December solstice, days last barely four hours, emitting a light that shines but does not warm. The night sky is a semipermanent backdrop in the winter. The literal morning star and symbolic star of freedom are equally remote. Also, as the earth rotates around its axis, stars appear to move in the sky along tracks that are more parallel to the horizon than the foreground. For figures on the brink, a star is more so an emblem of an indifferent universe than a benign or hopeful symbol.

For most readers of classic Russian literature, the spectacle of the stars contemplated by a subject in duress necessarily evokes the several exchanges in Tolstoy's *War and Peace* between Prince Andrei and Pierre Bezukhov that contrast earthly life and the higher world represented by the sky. For Pierre especially, the immensity of the vista and the radiance of the stars represent a higher realm of truth that overcomes the pessimistic view that nature is indifferent to man's trivial affairs. Glimpses of the sky reveal for him a potential source of happiness rather than despair. Zabolotsky's view of the sky does not obviously offer the religious prospect of a radiant afterlife, the belief in a moral law, or the kind of materialist dissolution into nature as a pantheistic entity that his earlier poetry espoused. If there is a truth to be intuited from the stars as described here, it is the view that the universe that elevates the individual has ended, and the image performs its own devastating break with romantic idealism.

If one looks back to Zabolotsky's earlier works, there are many points of contact between his poetry and the romantic movement. Whereas German romantic poetry explores "openness, dissolving the structures of the visible world to reassemble them in the ideal inward form,"[12] Zabolotsky's evocation of heaven—a heaven that is very close to the horizon and not very lofty—draws the reader into the world of the night and poetry only to close them off. In withdrawing such a philosophical revelation from these two victims, Zabolotsky's narrator offers only the consolation of a peaceful death, represented as sleep, in the face of the universe's deafening silence. Again, readers may hear a further allusion to Pushkin. This time the reminiscence is of the conclusion of the fragment "It is time, it is time, my friend" in which a weary speaker, assailed by troubles and doubt, seeks unearthly repose in a "distant" (*dal'nii*) region:

На свете счастья нет, но есть покой и воля.
Давно завидная мечтается мне доля—
Давно, усталый раб, замыслил я побег
В обитель дальнюю трудов и чистых нег.[13]

Happiness does not exist on earth, but there is peace and freedom.
Long have I dreamed of an enviable realm—
Long, a tired slave, have I conceived an escape
Into a distant shelter of works and pure pleasures.

Similarly afflicted by earthly cares, Zabolotsky's speaker also conceives of an ulterior realm defined by "freedom from." Like Pushkin in one mood, the poem finds in sleep or oblivion the only way out. Pushkin's vision associates pleasure and labor, his word for poetic composition, as a promise of creative liberation. This poem reverses that dynamic and moves back from epiphany to drudgery: whereas Pushkin's prophet is imbued with moral authority by his ecstatic epiphany, Zabolotsky offers a vision of freedom as a privative state, that is, at best death seen as freedom from coercion missing the spiritual (albeit painful) redemption. Not only is it less otherworldly, his poem depicts a gap between the prisoners of the Gulag and the universe deprived of any promise of redemption.

20

Bella Akhmadulina, "Along My Street" (1959)

AN ELEGY ON BETRAYAL

По улице моей который год
звучат шаги—мои друзья уходят.
Друзей моих медлительный уход
той темноте за окнами угоден.

Запущены моих друзей дела,
нет в их домах ни музыки, ни пенья,
и лишь, как прежде, девочки Дега
голубенькие оправляют перья.

Ну что ж, ну что ж, да не разбудит страх
вас, беззащитных, среди этой ночи.
К предательству таинственная страсть,
друзья мои, туманит ваши очи.

О одиночество, как твой характер крут!
Посверкивая циркулем железным,
как холодно ты замыкаешь круг,
не внемля уверениям бесполезным.

Так призови меня и награди!
Твой баловень, обласканный тобою,
утешусь, прислонясь к твоей груди,
умоюсь твоей стужей голубою.

Дай стать на цыпочки в твоем лесу,
на том конце замедленного жеста
найти листву, и поднести к лицу,

и ощутить сиротство, как блаженство.

Даруй мне тишь твоих библиотек,
твоих концертов строгие мотивы,
и—мудрая—я позабуду тех,
кто умерли или доселе живы.

И я познаю мудрость и печаль,
свой тайный смысл доверят мне предметы.
Природа, прислонясь к моим плечам,
объявит свои детские секреты.

И вот тогда—из слез, из темноты,
из бедного невежества былого
друзей моих прекрасные черты
появятся и растворятся снова.[1]

Year after painful year, along my street
I have been hearing steps—my friends are leaving.
I hear the shuffling of reluctant feet:
the gloominess outside demands its levy.

My friends' affairs are woefully neglected,
their homes so silent, songless, that it hurts.
And only ballerinas, blue and painted,
seem animated in their ruffled skirts.

Well, well . . . I hope you won't awake in fear,
defenceless, in the middle of this night.
A penchant for betrayal is so near,
beloved friends, and obfuscates your sight.

Oh mighty loneliness, your character is cruel!
Your iron pair of compasses stays sterile;
you close the circle, so detached and cool,
not heeding any outcry or demurral.

So summon me, and give me my reward!
Your darling, by your icy hands caressed,
at your cool breast, I'll find myself restored.
In your cerulean frost, I'll find my rest.

Let me stand up on tiptoe in your wood,
and slowly stretch my hand toward the leaves,
breathe in their smell, inhale their autumn mood,
and feel my growing orphanhood as bliss.
Give me the silence of your reading room,

your chamber concerts' solemn, strict motif.
I will grow wise. I will forget them soon—
those who have died and even those who live.

And I shall know all wisdom and all woe.
The Earth itself will whisper, gently leaning
against my shoulder, things untold before,
and objects will divulge their secret meanings.

And then—from all the grief, from pain, and lies,
from ignorance, and gloom, and tears, and fear—
my friends' beloved faces will arise.
They will arise, before they disappear.

(TRANSLATED BY ALEXANDRA BERLINA)

The poem discussed in this chapter is the most famous work by Bella Akhmadulina (1937–2011), one of the star poets of the 1960s, regularly ranked with Yevgeny Yevtushenko, Andrei Voznesensky, Robert Rozhdestvensky, and the singer-songwriter Bulat Okudzhava. Like them, she was a true star of poetry. Her readings on the stage of the Polytechnical Museum in Moscow and at other venues attracted hundreds and even thousands of listeners. However, the poems that gained cult status were usually reactions to political events—above all, de-Stalinization and the associated dramatic changes in the country. This was not Akhmadulina's forte. She excelled in elegant, complexly constructed lyrical poetry, written seemingly in nineteenth-century Russian. Stylistically, if not historically, to some degree she uses irony to distance herself from modernity. Her work has always been close to the romantic elegy and conveys a sense of poetic inspiration as a power of will. Her vision is focused on how an "ancient style" leads into a layer of cultural memory and transforms the present. This is her version of neoromanticism (on the term, see the introduction):

Влечет меня старинный слог.
Есть обаянье в древней речи.

Она бывает наших слов
и современнее и резче.[2]

I am attracted to the ancient style.
A charm lies in its measured way.
It is more modern, has more bile
than all the words we speak today.[3]

When the most prominent poets of the 1960s generation began to join the Soviet literary establishment, Akhmadulina was not in their ranks, and she simply continued to write her unpolitical poems, ostensibly failing to notice that the Thaw had ended and that a long and hopeless era of Stagnation had begun. Despite, or arguably because of, her aloof poetic posture, she was a consistent and defiant critic of the regime, an energetic defender of dissidents and persecuted writers. In the 1970s and 1980s, Akhmadulina spoke in support of Solzhenitsyn and Sakharov, against the political harassment of Vladimir Voinovich and Dmitri Prigov. Her political nonconformism is also clearly signaled by her participation in the uncensored 1979 almanac *Metropol,* which caused a large-scale scandal in the Soviet literary community.

There is a certain irony in the way the poem "Along My Street" gained popularity. Written in 1959, at the beginning of the Thaw, it made its crucial appearance sixteen years later, in a very different era, in Eldar Ryazanov's film *The Irony of Fate*. This romantic comedy was first aired on January 1, 1975, and went on to become the late-Soviet symbol of New Year, signaling a celebratory mode to TV viewers for decades, as regular as the chimes of the Kremlin. "Along My Street" was one of several poems set to music by the composer Mikael Tariverdiev for the film; it was sung onscreen by its heroine Nadya (a schoolteacher of literature, which explains her poetic erudition), her voice dubbed by another superstar in the making—the singer Alla Pugacheva, who was just starting her career in 1975. Her singing was very different in the film from her style onstage. While she went on to become famous for her eccentric and brilliantly theatrical performances, in *The Irony of Fate* she provided a calm, everyday, intimate voice. As it happens, this manner differed strikingly not only from Pugacheva's stage persona but also from the prayer-like manner Akhmadulina adopted when reading her poems.

To sum up: the comedy's protagonist Nadya, played by the Polish actress Barbara Brylska, found herself singing a poem by Bella Akhmadulina in the voice of Alla Pugacheva. A film that became a symbol of Stagnation made famous Akhmadulina's poem written during the Thaw. Not surprisingly, as filtered through these cultural layers, the poem lost its key stanza (lines 9–12):

Ну что ж, ну что ж, да не разбудит страх
10 вас, беззащитных, среди этой ночи.
К предательству таинственная страсть,
друзья мои, туманит ваши очи.

Well, well . . . I hope you won't awake in fear,
defenseless, in the middle of this night.
A penchant for betrayal is so near,[4]
beloved friends, and obfuscates your sight.

This excision turned a poem about the price of betrayal into a melancholic elegy to loneliness. The fuller version, with this all-important stanza, raises the question of what betrayal Akhmadulina means.

To explain the context in which Akhmadulina wrote her poem, we need to remind ourselves of the political campaign launched against Boris Pasternak in 1958, which for many conjured the specter of all too recent Stalinist times. Pasternak's novel *Doctor Zhivago* had not been published in the USSR, but its unsanctioned appearance abroad and its politically unorthodox depiction of the Russian Revolution and civil war caused a massive scandal. In 1958, Pasternak was awarded the Nobel Prize in Literature for his novel, after which he was expelled from the Union of Soviet Writers and forced to surrender his Nobel Prize. But Stalin was dead after all, and, while threatened with arrest, Pasternak was neither killed nor imprisoned.[5] Many respected writers, including those he had considered friends, took part in the campaign against him, publicly repudiating him and uttering routine denunciations.

Akhmadulina herself not only refused to sign the collective letter against Pasternak, she also wrote a personal letter to the Central Committee of the Communist Party of the Soviet Union demanding it stop harassing the poet. For this reason, she was expelled from the Literary Institute. She wrote "Along My Street" soon after these events. The question is whether Akhmadulina refers in her poem to friends who betrayed her because they were afraid of guilt by association with a rebel, or to those writers who betrayed Pasternak. The theme of betrayal resounded clearly in Akhmadulina's own recollections of these events:

> It was announced that this writer [Pasternak] was a traitor. Some found it easy to sign accusations; some simply did not understand what it was about. Yes indeed, adult people, writers, some distinguished ones at that, signed false accusations against Pasternak. [. . .] This affected all writers; only a few managed to avoid it. That is, decent people tried to keep their hands clean somehow, not to get dirty, but not everyone could manage it.[6]

It makes sense to assume that the betrayal in Akhmadulina's poem is not limited to the autobiographical background, but also refers to Pasternak's tragedy. The poem's second theme, loneliness, takes on a different meaning in this context: it is the loneliness of the poet rejected by society and peers. This assumption is confirmed by the overlap between "Along My Street" and another poem by Akhmadulina, "In Memory of Boris Pasternak" (1962), written three years later. The latter contains a prose fragment describing the author's only meeting with Pasternak, which took place in Peredelkino, a writers' village near Moscow:

> All at once he emerged from the dense thicket of Peredelkino's trees one late evening in October, more than two years ago.[7] [. . .] I felt such tenderness toward him and such pride that I could hardly see his face—only the blinding bright white flashes of his hands in the darkness in the corners of my eyes. "Hello!" he said, "I've heard of you, and I recognized you at once." Then suddenly, with unexpectedly strong feeling, he exclaimed: "Please do excuse me! I'm afraid I must make a call at this very minute!" He went into a small office building momentarily but returned before making his call; the bright light of his face, his forehead and cheekbones luminescent in the faint moonlight, moved toward me from total darkness, struck me, splashed my face. I felt a sweet, icy, Shakespearean chill of worry for him. Horrified, he asked me: "Aren't you cold? It's almost November, after all!"—then grew embarrassed and awkwardly backed away into the low door. Leaning against the wall, I could hear, with my very body, the muffled sounds of him talking. He seemed to be passionately justifying himself, and also enveloping the person at the other end in a circle of care and love with his voice. [. . .] The house, the bushes, and I: by chance, we all fell into the abundant embrace of his spherical, loving, majestical, delicate intonation. Then he stepped out, and the two of us took a few steps on that extremely uncomfortable ground with its stumps, fallen twigs, and hedges. Somehow he seemed at ease and at home in the prickly abyss thickening around us—with the cheap gleam of the bulging stars, with that hollow in place of a moon, with the roughly placed, uncomfortable trees. He said: "Why don't you ever visit? Sometimes, very nice and interesting people come over—you won't be bored. Come on, join us! Come tomorrow." I felt so giddy that my reply must have sounded almost haughty: "Thank you. I'll be sure to drop by sometime."[8]

A number of motifs connect "Along My Street" with this poetic memoir. First of all, there is the motif of cold: "so detached and cool" and "in your cerulean frost, I'll find my rest" in "Along My Street," and "In Memory of Boris Pasternak" has "a sweet, icy, Shakespearean chill" and "aren't you cold? It's almost November, after all!" The motif of the circle is represented by "you close the circle" in the poem and by "enveloping the person at the other end in a circle of care and love with his voice," and "spherical [*okruglyi*], loving, majestical, delicate intonation" in the prosaic insertion. Finally, the motif of night and gloom appears in both: "the gloominess outside demands its levy" and "I hope you won't awake in fear, / defenseless, in the middle of this night" in verse, and "his face [. . .] in the faint moonlight, moved toward me from total darkness" and a "hollow in place of a moon" in the memoir.

However, all the motifs associated with loneliness in the poem—woods, cold, isolation, darkness—are overcome and transformed in the memoir. Rather than entering the wood like the speaker of "Along My Street," Pasternak emerges "from the squalid thicket of Peredelkino's trees." The cold makes him worry for others, and he transforms the circle of lonely isolation into an "abundant embrace" of love and care. When he confronts the darkness, not only do his face and hands reflect the faint light of the moon, he himself appears a source of light in the dark: "the blinding bright white flashes of his hands in the darkness in the corners of my eyes"; "the bright light of his face, his forehead and cheekbones luminescent in the faint moonlight, moved toward me from total darkness, struck me, splashed my face." Akhmadulina finishes by saying that Pasternak seemed "at ease and at home in the prickly abyss thickening around us . . ."

It is no accident that Akhmadulina describes her meeting with Pasternak within a poem and not in a prose memoir. While the description might be read as factual, the concrete situation and landscape form a background to the image of the poet as a mythological hero, able to tame chaos, conquer the abyss, and radiate light within darkness. Crucially, the Pasternak described here is the Pasternak after the disaster that followed the awarding of the Nobel Prize. In this context, one might argue that the poem "Along My Street" was written by Akhmadulina as an answer to the question: *How to become like Pasternak?* In other words, how to transform betrayal, rejection, and loneliness into the wisdom and strength of a poet?

Read from this perspective, "Along My Street" turns into a mythological rite of passage, comparable to the process described by Arnold Van Gennep and much later by Victor Turner.[9] While their work was unknown to Akhmadulina in 1959, she may well have been aware relatedly of Vladimir Propp's works—above all *The Historical Roots of the Wondertale* (1946)—which also discuss rites of passage. In their process, a young man or woman must leave their home and, once isolated, undergo a series of trials imitating death, after which they acquire a new identity and may return to the community with a new status (as an adult, an initiate, etc.). Then again, it hardly matters if Akhmadulina was familiar with the scholarship since, as these and other studies show, the rite of passage is a structure that underlies many forms and genres of mythology and folklore, above all, fairy tales. In this light, it is not surprising that "Along My Street" breaks down into three parts, reminiscent of the structure of a fairy tale.

The first three stanzas depict a domestic crisis in the terms of a traditional fairy-tale opening. Instead of the death of a mother and her replacement with a cruel stepmother, Akhmadulina's heroine experiences her friends leaving her. The first part works through repetition: the word "friends," for instance, is repeated three times in three stanzas. In the original, phonetic emphasis complements this semantic saturation: *ukhod . . . ukhodiat . . . ugoden . . . toi temnote . . .* The scene for a conflict is thus set as a world about to be destroyed by the betrayal of friends. However, the second stanza suggests that the friends themselves have domestic trouble, too: "My friends' affairs are woefully neglected, / their homes so silent, songless, that it hurts" (lines 5–6). The motifs of chaos become ever more intense: in the first stanza, it is darkness; in the second, the absence of harmony (lit. "music and singing"); in the third, dangers of the night and disorientation: "in the middle of this night," "obfuscates your sight" (a more literal translation would be "fogs your sight"). The third stanza also names the reasons for the growing chaos: fear ("I hope you won't awake in fear," line 9) and "a penchant for betrayal" (lit. "a passion for betrayal," line 11).

Strikingly, while in the first two stanzas the narrative is dominated by the third-person plural (*oni*: "they"), stanza 3 switches to the second-person plural (*vy*: "you"), and stanza 4, addressing solitude, is written in the informal second-person singular (*ty*: "you"), emphasizing closeness to the object of speech, a closeness greater than in the original relationship with the departing friends. What is the meaning of this shift? Arguably, in this way Akhmadulina conveys that her poetic persona is approaching the "heart of darkness," plunging into the isolated space of temporary death, like in a fairy tale or a rite of passage.

Stanzas 4–7 describe the heroine's departure into a wood. In the fairy tales, the mysterious forest is associated with motifs of temporary death; in Akhmadulina, it embodies loneliness. This part is rhythmically highlighted when, for a single time, a line of iambic hexameter replaces iambic pentameter: *O odinochestvo, kak tvoi kharakter krut!* ("Oh mighty loneliness, your character is cruel!"). This exclamatory sentence (reproduced above in a phonetic transcription) combines with the use of assonance and alliteration. It marks an intonational shift, which in turn acts as a sign of transition to another world, to the other side of everyday life and history (lines 13–16):

О одиночество, как твой характер крут!
Посверкивая циркулем железным,
как холодно ты замыкаешь круг,
не внемля увереньям бесполезным.

Oh mighty loneliness, your character is cruel!
Your iron pair of compasses stays sterile;
you close the circle, so detached and cool,
not heeding any outcry or demurral.

Stanzas 5–7 are syntactically constructed as imperatives addressed to loneliness. Akhmadulina's speaker simultaneously submits to its coldness and appeals to it, acting as both neophyte and priest. Loneliness, as required by the rite of passage, involves the isolation of the subject—"you close the circle, so detached and cool" (line 15)—followed by a phase of liminality: "a period and area of ambiguity, a kind of social limbo."[10] This phase can be clearly traced in Akhmadulina's work: the speaker accepts and absorbs as a positive value what she had initially perceived as a threat, as signs of chaos. The following motifs are reconsidered here:

- cold: "In your cerulean frost, I'll find my rest" (line 20, lit. "I'll wash myself / my face with your cerulean frost");
- the gloom of the forest: "Let me stand up on tiptoe in your wood" (line 21);
- and even rejection: "and feel my growing orphanhood as bliss" (line 24).

As it happens, a color epithet (*goluboi*, translated as "blue" in one case, as "cerulean" in the other) connects the cold with the image of Degas' ballerinas in the second stanza (lines 7–8, in Berlina's translation: "ballerinas, blue and painted") who look fragile, but yet are resilient to chaos. In the end, loneliness is transformed into wisdom and harmony in the line "the silence of your reading room, / your chamber concerts' solemn, strict motif" (lines 25–26).

The state of liminality also implies "the liberation of human capacities of cognition, affect, volition, creativity, etc., from the normative constraints incumbent upon occupying a sequence of social statuses."[11] This effect explains why syntactically it is in stanzas 5–7 that an "I" gradually returns. First, it appears in first-person verbs: "I'll find myself restored" (line 19, lit. "consoled") and "I'll find my rest" (line 20, lit. "I'll wash myself/my face") have no pronoun in Russian because the verb is sufficient to signal first-person singular usage: *uteshus', umoius'*. Then, we have a direct, albeit ironic self-description: "I will grow wise. I will forget them soon—/ those who have died and even those who live" (lines 27–28). The irony lies in the fact that the wisdom thus acquired is inseparable from liminality and based on the complete severance of ties with the living and the dead.

Connected by anaphora ("And I shall know . . ." / "And then . . ."), stanzas 8 and 9 narrate the speaker's return to the ordinary world after her temporary death and her acquisition of a new status. In rituals, Van Gennep calls this phase "reintegration"; in fairy tales, this phase usually precedes a wedding at the end.

И я познаю мудрость и печаль,
свой тайный смысл доверят мне предметы.
Природа, прислонясь к моим плечам,
объявит свои детские секреты.

And I shall know all wisdom and all woe.
The Earth itself will whisper, gently leaning
against my shoulder, things untold before,
and objects will divulge their secret meanings.

This stanza, too, seems to harbor a shadow of Pasternak in the motif of nature, crucial to Pasternak's poetry, and perhaps even in the *p*-alliteration harking back to his name. The intimate confidentiality of nature acting as a child in relation to the wise heroine also echoes the way Akhmadulina perceives Pasternak. "In Memory of Boris Pasternak" comes to mind again: "The house, the bushes, and I: by chance, we all fell into the abundant embrace of his spherical, loving, majestical, delicate intonation." And in the poetic part of the text:

Как он играл в единственной той роли
всемирной ласки к людям и зверью[12]

He played the only role there is to play:
worldwide affection for both men and beasts.

It would seem that a dream comes true in "Along My Street" when the speaker acquires Pasternak's wisdom, and the first stanza in effect appears in rewind mode: "from all the grief, from pain, and lies, / from ignorance, and gloom, and tears, and fear" (lines 33–34), the *friends return*. The triple repetition of the preposition "from" (*iz*) makes the whole phrase sound like a spell that cancels pain and darkness. Peace is restored. But for how long? In a fairy tale, the heroes live "happily ever after" once they have been through a deadly ordeal. But Akhmadulina radically departs from the traditional scheme. The last lines of her poem leave no hope for a long-term happy end: "my friends' beloved faces will arise. / They will arise, before they disappear" (lines 35–36).

This finale essentially returns to the beginning of the poem, explaining the phrase "year after painful year" in the first line. The betrayal and departure of friends is not a single act, but a repetitive, cyclical process. This is why the rite of passage described in the poem is suffused by a melancholic irony. Wisdom gained does not save one from new betrayals and new loneliness; the poet's triumph over darkness is always short-lived and fragile. However, the motif of the circle, as mentioned above, also resonates with the memoir of Pasternak, whose shadow remains present in the poem's finale.

That irony is emphasized by the poem's complex rhythmic structure. While only one line ("Oh mighty loneliness, your character is cruel," line 13) disrupts the iambic pentameter, the entire lyric is orchestrated as a dialogue of two voices. The first and dominant voice sings of loneliness as inexorable fate; the second, a very intimate and personal one, embodies a sentimental hope for friendship, light, and warmth, for overcoming loneliness. The first voice mostly uses lines with a pyrrhic fourth foot, which constitute the dominant rhythm of the poem. Lines without a pyrrhic fourth foot are thus intonationally stressed in comparison to the dominant rhythm. It is these lines that form a second voice. When the text is reformatted along these lines, the dialogue sounds as follows:

Voice 1 (dominant)

Друзей моих медлительный уход	I hear the shuffling of reluctant feet:
той темноте за окнами угоден.	the gloominess outside demands its levy.
[. . .]	[. . .]
нет в их домах ни музыки, ни пенья,	their homes so silent, songless, that it hurts.
и лишь, как прежде, девочки Дега	And only ballerinas, blue and painted,
голубенькие оправляют перья.	seem animated in their ruffled skirts.
[. . .]	[. . .]
К предательству таинственная страсть,	A penchant for betrayal is so near,
друзья мои, туманит ваши очи.	beloved friends, and obfuscates your sight.
[. . .]	[. . .]
Посверкивая циркулем железным,	Your iron pair of compasses stays sterile;
как холодно ты замыкаешь круг,	you close the circle, so detached and cool,
не внемля увереньям бесполезным.	not heeding any outcry or demurral.
Так призови меня и награди!	So summon me, and give me my reward!
Твой баловень, обласканный тобою,	Your darling, by your icy hands caressed,
[. . .]	[. . .]
умоюсь твоей стужей голубою.	In your cerulean frost, I'll find my rest.
[. . .]	[. . .]
на том конце замедленного жеста	and slowly stretch my hand toward the leaves,
найти листву, и поднести к лицу,	breathe in their smell, inhale their autumn mood,
и ощутить сиротство, как блаженство.	and feel my growing orphanhood as bliss.

Даруй мне тишь твоих библиотек,
твоих концертов строгие мотивы

[. . .]
И я познаю мудрость и печаль
свой тайный смысл доверят мне предметы.
[. . .]
объявит свои детские секреты.
[. . .]
из бедного невежества былого

друзей моих прекрасные черты
появятся и растворятся снова.

Give me the silence of your reading room,
your chamber concerts' solemn, strict motif.
[. . .]
And I shall know all wisdom and all woe,
and objects will divulge their secret meanings.
[. . .]
against my shoulder, things untold before,
[. . .]
from ignorance, and gloom, and tears, and fear—
my friends' beloved faces will arise.
They will arise, before they disappear.

Voice 2 (counterpoint)

По улице моей который год
звучат шаги—мои друзья уходят.

[. . .]
Запущены моих друзей дела
[. . .]
Ну что ж, ну что ж, да не разбудит страх
вас, беззащитных, среди этой ночи
[. . .]
О одиночество, как твой характер крут!
[. . .]
Дай стать на цыпочки в твоем лесу
[. . .]
и—мудрая—я позабуду тех,
кто умерли или доселе живы.

[. . .]
Природа, прислонясь к моим плечам
[. . .]
И вот тогда—из слез, из темноты,

Year after painful year, along my street
I have been hearing steps—my friends are leaving
[. . .]
My friends' affairs are woefully neglected
[. . .]
Well, well . . . I hope you won't awake in fear,
defenseless, in the middle of this night.
[. . .]
Oh mighty loneliness, your character is cruel!
[. . .]
Let me stand up on tiptoe in your wood
[. . .]
I will grow wise. I will forget them soon—
those who have died and even those who live.
[. . .]
The Earth itself will whisper, gently leaning
[. . .]
And then—from all the grief, from pain, and lies

The seventh stanza is particularly interesting in this regard:

Даруй мне тишь твоих библиотек,
твоих концертов строгие мотивы,
и—мудрая—я позабуду тех,
кто умерли или доселе живы.

Give me the silence of your reading room,
your chamber concerts' solemn, strict motif.
I will grow wise. I will forget them soon—
those who have died and even those who live

The first two lines here are subject to the dominant rhythm: only the fourth foot is pyrrhic. In the stanza's final lines, by contrast, the second and the third foot are pyrrhic, creating the effect of a hiatus. It would seem that at this point the two voices acquire equal power, reflecting the stability and inner harmony found by the speaker after undergoing the rite of passage. However, in the last two stanzas the dominant voice, which is associated with loneliness, triumphs again. Rhythmically, the final stanza is closest to stanzas 2 and 3, where the fourth foot is pyrrhic in three consecutive lines. The voice of solitude is restored, devaluing the heroine's completion of the rite of passage. The inner transformation appears to have been in vain after all.

However, despite this dramatic irony, resistance to the forces of chaos is ultimately embedded in the cycle of nature, and, even if futile, it is unceasing. For Akhmadulina, poets can become part of the natural world, no one more so than Pasternak, as attested by other poems, such as "Bad Spring" (1967):

и высоко над ним плыл Пастернак
в опрятности и простоте величья.[13]

and high above it
floated Pasternak in neat and simple majesty.

A snowstorm and a brook speak with Pasternak's voice in "February, the love and wrath of weather" (1968), for he gave them a new meaning, made them precious:

Как сильно вьюжит! Не иначе—
метель посвящена тому,
кто эти дерева и дачи
так близко принимал к уму.
Ручья невзрачное теченье,
сосну, понурившую ствол,

в иное он вовлек значенье
и в драгоценность произвел.
Не потому ль, в красе и тайне,
пространство, загрустив о нём,
той речи бред и бормотанье
имеет в голосе своем.[14]

Oh what a snowstorm! Is, I wonder,
this blizzard raging for the one
to whom these things had so much meaning:
these dachas, trees, this winter sun?
The narrow brook, its modest current,
the old and slightly drooping pine:
he took these things and he transformed them,
he turned this village to a shrine.
Is this perchance the mystic reason
why it resounds like a hymn—
his voice, its rambling in the snowstorm—
space, in its longing, mimics him.

In Akhmadulina's world, every true poet, and not only Pasternak, possesses a mythological power that endows reality with value and meaning. Inevitably, however, the poet is also a tragic figure, as the harmonious universe created by him or her is fundamentally fragile and defenseless before the forces of chaos. In the same way, the poet, too, is defenseless before history and fate. As Akhmadulina writes in her poem "In Memory of Osip Mandelstam" (1967):

Что может он? Он нищ и наг
пред чудом им свершенной речи.
Гортань, затеявшая речь
неслыханную,—так открыта.
Довольно, чтоб ее пресечь,
и меньшего усердья быта.[15]

What can he do? He's destitute
before the wonder of his poems.
Unheard-of speech, soon crushed in ice.
His head thrown back, his throat is bared.
A lighter touch would have sufficed
to stop his words—the speech he dared.

She goes on to present the poet as a figure tortured by dramatic irony: "a singer with a gag in his mouth; a gourmand deprived of bread."[16] The world of beauty and love, the harmony created by the poet, is always for others, never for him- or herself. The poet's suffering and pain, the experience of solitude as temporary death and resurrection, prove to be the only available (albeit inevitably tragic) way to give at least some solidity to this fragile utopia. We see here the reason for Akhmadulina's penchant for elegies. After all, as *The Princeton Encyclopedia of Poetry and Poetics* notes, in the elegy, "the emotion, originally expressed as a lament, finds consolation in the contemplation of some permanent principle."[17]

21

Alexander Galich, "The Night Watch" (1963)

HISTORY AS THE UNCANNY

Ночной дозор

Когда в городе гаснут праздники,
Когда грешники спят и праведники,
Государственные запасники.
Покидают тихонько памятники.
Сотни тысяч (и все—похожие)
Вдоль по лунной идут дорожке,
И случайные прохожие
Кувыркаются в "неотложке".

И бьют барабаны!..
Бьют барабаны,
Бьют, бьют, бьют!

На часах замирает маятник,
Стрелки рвутся бежать обратно:
Одинокий шагает памятник,
Повторенный тысячекратно.
То он в бронзе, а то он в мраморе,
То он с трубкой, а то без трубки,
И за ним, как барашки на море,
Чешут гипсовые обрубки

И бьют барабаны!
Бьют барабаны,
Бьют, бьют, бьют!

Я открою окно, я высунусь,
Дрожь пронзит, будто сто по Цельсию!
Вижу: бронзовый генералиссимус
Шутовскую ведет процессию!
Он выходит на место лобное—
Гений всех времен и народов!—
И, как в старое время доброе,
Принимает парад уродов!

И бьют барабаны!..
Бьют барабаны,
Бьют, бьют, бьют![1]

Прет стеной мимо дома нашего.
Хлам, забытый в углу уборщицей,—
Вот сапог громыхает маршево,
Вот обломанный ус топорщится!
Им пока—скрипеть да поругиваться,
Да следы оставлять линючие,
Но уверена даже пуговица,
Что сгодится еще при случае!

И бьют барабаны!..
Бьют барабаны,
Бьют, бьют, бьют!

Утро родины нашей—розово,
Позывные летят, попискивая.
Восвояси уходит бронзовый,
Но лежат, притаившись, гипсовые.
Пусть до времени покалечены,
Но и в прахе хранят обличие.
Им бы, гипсовым, человечины—
Они вновь обретут величие!

И бьют барабаны!..
Бьют барабаны,
Бьют, бьют, бьют![2]

The Night Watch

When the town celebrations fade away,
The unrighteous and righteous in bed asleep,
Those the state has put by for a rainy day
Step down quietly from their pedestals.
In their hundreds of thousands, identical,
Along moonlit paths they go pacing,
And the odd belated pedestrians
Dive for shelters in first-aid stations.

And drums are a-drumming!

Clock pendulums freeze, stand motionless,
The hands on their faces pull backwards,
A uniform statue with soldier's step
Marches out, repeated in thousands.
Some of marble, and some of brass made,
Some are holding that famous pipe,
Alabaster ones, shattered fragments,
Itch to follow, like a white-flecked tide.

And drums are a-drumming!

I lean out from my window, shivering
With a fever, one hundred Celsius,
As the brazen generalissimo
Heads a pageant of fools and jesters.
He climbs up on the hallowed podium,
"Of all peoples and ages the genius,"
And salutes a parade of monsters,
As he did in those days so dear to us.

And drums are a-drumming![2]

By the wall of the block my flat's in,
Among heaps of abandoned dust and trash,
You can make out a goose-stepping jackboot,
And a broken-off piece of moustache.
For the moment, they creak, drop a curse or two,
Now, they only leave facing traces,
But the last little button's certain to

Come in useful again on occasion.

And drums are a-drumming!

Dawn's pink fingers suffuse our motherland,
Station callsigns ping down the radio waves,
The bronze statue returns to its place of rest,
Alabaster ones stay in their hideaways.
Maybe crippled, just temporarily,
But their fragments retain the makings,
Alabaster only needs humankind,
And again it will rise to greatness!

And drums are a-drumming![1]

(TRANSLATED BY G. S. SMITH)

Alexander Galich's (1918–77) enduring claim to fame lies in his contribution to the genre of the poetic or bardic song. "The Night Watch" dates to the early 1960s and a fateful period of personal reckoning with the political system. It was at this time that he discovered his voice as a writer of songs as well as the nonofficial subject matter they treated. Until that time, he was a successful playwright and writer of romances, a favorite of the literary establishment and Soviet public. After the war, his play *Taimyr Calling* (1947, coauthored) was widely staged in the USSR. He was rewarded with a commission to celebrate the fortieth anniversary of the Komsomol (this was his romantic comedy *The Name of the Steamer is Eagle*), and he was also the author of some popular songs, avidly consumed by the public after the death of Stalin.[3] Nobody could have been more of an establishment figure than Galich. His acclaim in the 1950s had brought him material comforts well beyond the reach of most of his fellow citizens. Galich worked as a scriptwriter until the 1960s, and official recognition came in the form of privileges and status conferred by membership of the Union of Writers and Union of Cinematographers. In the second half of his mature period, from his early forties, Galich (who was born Alexander Ginzburg into a family of Jewish intellectuals and professionals) repudiated and vilified the Soviet authorities and institutions that had once rewarded him.

Speculation about the causes of this Road to Damascus conversion from loyal artist of the regime to its critic has cited numerous reasons, including antisemitism, censorship, and the suffering Galich's own brother, a highly qualified scientist, experienced as a victim of repression who returned after twenty-four years in the camps. Galich himself experienced antisemitism at its most explosive during the wave of repressions

Stalin launched against prominent Jews, starting with the murder of the great actor Solomon Mikhoels in 1948, followed by the Night of the Murdered Poets in 1952 that claimed the lives of figures he knew, and culminating in the Doctors' Plot in which numerous Jews were singled out. Other events, such as Galich's own experience of censorship and encounters with survivors of the Gulag who returned from the camps, fundamentally altered his view. When, in 1975, in exile in Paris where he worked for Radio Liberty (and died in an apparent accident), he looked back on that journey, he claimed that he had become "sick of serving like a slave"[4] (unwillingness to serve was for Pushkin a mark of artistic freedom, and Galich uses the term in that sense).

From the 1960s into the 1970s, his work became more critical of a politically repressive system and its social injustices, full of the music of "righteous rage" ("pravednyi gnev").[5] Korney Chukovsky, the much-loved children's author and by the 1950s an elder statesman of literature, called Galich the "inheritor of Nekrasov's angry muse."[6] Galich's satirical views put him in repeated and permanent conflict with the authorities, who banned his writings from print and performances.[7] While he was never arrested, he was banned and then finally expelled. In the early 1960s, his songs began to circulate clandestinely in samizdat, starting with the publication of four songs in the almanac *Sphinxes*: their publication abroad and the appearance of a book of his songs in 1969 were regarded as a treasonous act by the authorities. Songs also circulated as sheet music and in tape recordings known as *magnitizdat*, one of the primary channels for the dissemination of politically sensitive lyrics to a mass audience.[8] They made him a hero of underground culture, and in many ways a spokesman for dissidents who confronted the re-Stalinization of Soviet life after the Thaw, the brutal military invasion of Czechoslovakia in 1968, and then the Stagnation (*zastoi*) of the Brezhnev period. By 1968 he was both estranged from official institutions and newly embraced by the intelligentsia and multitudes for songs that "are deadly accurate in the way they capture the most striking and yet the most typical elements of Soviet social life—one task that official socialist realism is supposed to carry out, but manifestly does not."[9] In March of that year, under the menacing auspices of members of the Politburo and aware that he was now under active surveillance daily, Galich made a sensational appearance at the Festival of Bards in Akademgorodok near Novosibirsk. Public acclaim led him to repeat his reading of "In Memory of Pasternak" as an encore, and among the more incendiary works he shared was "The Night Watch."[10] More than twenty years later, when censorship faltered at the end of the Soviet Union, an anti-Stalin recording was released with that song as its title.[11] Hounded into emigration in 1974 as a result of what G. S. Smith calls his "satirical masterpieces," Galich also became a nonperson in the Soviet press until his contemporary and fellow bard Bulat Okudzhava broke the taboo and mentioned him in a newspaper interview in 1987.[12]

Together with Vladimir Vysotsky and Bulat Okudzhava, both of whom worked in the cinema as actors and composers, Galich was a preeminent practitioner of the genre of guitar poetry. Often referred to as *avtorskaia pesnia* (poet's song), this type of lyric should be seen as distinct from the pop song (*estradnaia pesnia*, lit. "stage song"). Bards sang or semi-recited their works almost always to a guitar accompaniment, creating an intimacy in stark contrast to the loud music typical of Stalin-era songs.[13] Galich's canonical status in the history of Russian culture was marked in the post-Soviet period by the publication of a volume in the Biblioteka Poeta series, the Russian equivalent of the Pléiade and Library of America. While there were many other bards, these three were the poets who established these principles as the conventions of the genre.[14] Unlike the first two, however, Galich also wrote longer songs, sometimes organizing his work in cycles of shorter lyrics and longer poems on a theme.

The style and tone of "The Night Watch"—its slangy diction and proverb-like idioms, its cleverly knowing rhymes, its covert sense of menace and strikes of boldness—mark it out as the kind of poem Galich had been writing since the 1970s on his journey from a successful Soviet cultural figure to dissident bard. In the bardic tradition, every lyric poem can be a story, and "The Night Watch" contains all the elements of when, how, and where. The causal elements of why and how do need to be spelled out in a poem that is about the projection and exercise of power. What is important is the way reality and fantasy merge, making it impossible to discern whether the vision of the poem's first-person narrator, seemingly an eyewitness, takes place on the street or in his mind. That sense of reality and chimera as equivalent, a situation in which the mind of the state invades the citizen's state of mind, is the product of a sense of dread that grows in the course of Galich's poem. Withholding detail is also part of how the poem works on a symbolic level. Location? "In the city": we suppose it is Moscow, but the city could be anywhere. When? No season, month, or year is mentioned: the focus is on nighttime.

The technique of defamiliarization produces an insidious mood in scene, moral vocabulary, and agency. What sort of parade takes place at night rather than in the day? While the opening clause ("When the town," line 1) suggests an element of routine, the second line shifts the discourse onto a symbolic or ethical plane: the players in these festivals are not merely citizens or politicians. Line 2 applies the stark language of moral categories. Who are the sinners, who are the righteous? The answer, made implicitly in line 3, is that the state makes the determination in its own interests. These marchers in the nocturnal parade that follows the daylight celebrations prove to be a vast entourage of statues. If they march quietly we surmise it is less to avoid disturbing the sleep of the citizenry but rather because they constitute the "night watch," insidiously on the prowl. Surveillance is about maintaining order. The concept of *poriadok* was a defining norm of the social code in Soviet life, marked by complete behavioral compliance and also part of a pervasive discourse. The existence of "sinners" suggests a fallibility that even the righteous cannot prevent, motivating vigilance as exercised here by the state.

As much as it creates a real sense of the ritualized oppression of parades and other manifestations of propaganda, the poem also invades our imaginations by playing on deeper fears. While a poem cannot recreate the pomp of a parade, it can fill its urban space with a sense of menace and, above all, the uncanny.[15] When brazenly flaunted through the rituals of a parade, power has something of the occult about it—remote and superhuman and grotesquely flawed. Each of the five narrative stanzas of eleven unequal lines is punctuated at the end by the refrain, an effect analogous to the relentless din of the drumbeat. The cadences of the refrain's first two lines provide some musicality; the briefer final line, punched out unrhythmically, adds brutality and indifference. We cannot hear this unmusical language without hearing in contrast the body of the stanza, cast flowingly in a foot of mixed iambic-anapestic meters, which is brought to a sharp halt at the end, also disrupting the pattern of alternating rhyme.[16] The refrain notes the beating of drums to which the parade marches, but it also adds in the final line a subordinate sense that this sound is itself a beating, either that it stands for violence or that violence is occurring elsewhere: "beat, beat, beat," or, because the third-person plural in Russian is rendered in English in the passive voice, "beaten, beaten, beaten." We know who beats the drums, but we do not know who is being beaten. What matters more in a culture of political violence than the identity of victims and oppressors is the presence of violence as an existential fact, all the more sinister when perpetrated by an anonymous system. In classic melodramatic fiction, the narrative voice, with its grandiose questions and hypotheses, can lead the reader in a movement through and beyond the surface of things to what lies behind, to the spiritual reality that is the true scene of the drama to be played out in prose fiction. But in this poem the first-person speaker, the closest we have to a narrative voice, takes fright and offers no insight beyond the further description of the spectacle.

If one were looking for a visual equivalent in painting, we might think of the neobaroque paintings in which Giorgio de Chirico represented his fascination with archaeology and history. In canvases like *Turin Spring* (1914) or *Piazza d'Italia* (1964), stationed on planes that intersect, views or partial views of monumental buildings in the classical style are juxtaposed with symbols. These typically feature emblems of power that fly across the proscenium of buildings and nearly break the wall of the painting itself: a massive fist, an equestrian statue seemingly moving into view, a colossal bust, all on a scale to dwarf the human. Similarly, human life and history itself are crowded out into the background of Galich's poem, dwarfed by the throng of monuments and drowned out by the drumbeat. Amplification is the main trope of the narrative, which piles on detail to create the impression of gigantism. Sound seems to reverberate and grow louder in these spaces: footwear "rumbles," "signals fly," a body part "squeaks," accentuating the visual effect of greatness (*velichie*), the last word of the poem before the final refrain. As in melodrama, man is seen to be, and must recognize himself to be, playing on a stage that is the point of juncture, and of clash, of imperatives beyond himself that are irreducible.

Yet in this instance the marching statues are lampooned as a motley parade, and, while some are made from more durable materials—it is possible that only Stalin's monument is in bronze—some are cheaply constructed, and others represent fragments of body parts or a remnant of a bristly moustache, more comical than scary. A missing button, only a small detail, conveys unkemptness and disorder. Yet, even in their grotesque state, these statues retain their element of menace: the threat that they might even, when toppled ("among heaps of abandoned dust"), regain their human form and "rise to greatness" contributes to a deeper, troubled fear. Boris Groys has argued that "socialist realist mimesis attempts to focus on the hidden essence of things rather than on phenomena."[17] In aesthetic terms, the nocturnal phenomenon may be described as an episode of the uncanny. In Freud's definition, the uncanny is not merely the horrible or frightening. The uncanny is "that class of the frightening which leads back to what is known of old and long familiar," and a further effect of the uncanny is that it may be a secret not known of old. "The Night Watch" cultivates the sense that the speaker alone witnesses "what is concealed, kept from sight."[18] One function of the ironic humor of the poem is perhaps to reassure the reader that this eerie vision is not the delusion of a madman's imagination (a premise for Freud). For Freud, instances of the uncanny usually lead back to a form of trauma, and, while his reading of Hoffman's "The Sandman" is geared toward his theory of the castration complex, he is also interested in how the uncanny uses doubling figures to convey the fear the child has of ego destruction. The double confuses the familiar and the strange by being dead and alive, familiar and strange, whole and fragmented, and by making interchangeable the good leader and the oppressive evil simulacrum threatening the viewer.

The last stanza of the poem moves from darkness to morning, though, in the time frame of this poem, this transition may be the literal return of day. What really matters is the metaphorical reestablishment of the socialist utopian vision based on a reference that contemporaries immediately perceived to a famous picture: *The Dawn of Our Land* by Fedor Schurpin, commissioned to mark Stalin's seventieth birthday in 1946. It depicts Stalin in the foreground, standing at the front of a field, with the rosy dawn and pink sky behind him. Popular legend has it that, when the painting was displayed, Stalin said to his son, "You think that you are Stalin? No! You think that I am Stalin? No!" And with that, he pointed to his image and said, "There is Stalin." The substitution of simulacrum for the real is consistent with the insistence in socialist realist art that the ideal is the real. As night ebbs, the statues withdraw. Initially we might think that the break of day is the phenomenal world that, according to Groys, obscures the hidden essence of things. That in itself is only an illusion, since the rosy dawn that opens the final stanza is the name of the painting, making escape from an environment controlled by its own nightmarish laws impossible. At the same time, the speaker remains tensely aware that rest is only provisional and that, no matter how damaged these monsters may be, it is in their very nature always to return at night. These statues are not just doubles of historical figures. They are also doubles, even when dismembered, of other statues that have already haunted the Russian cultural imagination.

Textual reality and historical reality seem inextricably linked on the symbolic plane. For, as long as statues embody certain principles of leadership that are relived from one figure to the next, literature will continue to refigure these images intertextually. The title of "The Night Watch" blatantly signals this poem's debt to a famous lyric by Vasily Zhukovsky, "The Night Lookout" ("Nochnoi smotr").[19] Tutor to the future Tsar Alexander II, distinguished translator of German and English and eventually Homer, originator of the ballad form in Russia, and literary executor of Alexander Pushkin's estate, Zhukovsky was a key figure in the history of Russian romanticism. In addition to the title, the two poems share a Gothic fascination with the possibility of hauntings. Zhukovsky's poem is in fact a translation of an 1827 German original, "Die nächtliche Heerschau," by the Austrian dramatist Johann Christian von Zedlitz, also known in its version as a song set by Robert Schumann. The Napoleonic theme had a long life in Russian romanticism, from the emperor's lifetime through to 1840, and it appears in poems Zhukovsky wrote during the Napoleonic Wars such as "The Song of the Bard at the Grave of the Slavic Victors" ("Pesn' barda nad grobom slavian-pobeditelei," 1806) and "A Singer in the Camp of the Russian Soldiers" ("Pesn' vo stane russkikh voinov," 1812). In this version—and, for our purposes, the departures from Zedlitz are not a close concern since detailed consideration of Zhukovsky's multiple rewordings can be found elsewhere—each of the four twelve-line stanzas begins with the phrase "At twelve o'clock at night," followed by a second line in which a military figure rises from the dead. The first of these is the drummer (*barabanshchik*), the second a cornet, the third a general, and the fourth to awaken is the "dormant Imperator"; in each of their respective stanzas, the spectral figures rouse their forces to do battle. Zhukovsky adapted the original meter. His three-foot amphibrachic line is unrhymed; its rhythm is relentless and consistent with the pattern of action in each stanza describing how forces are mobilized posthumously. Devoid of any sense of surprise, the stanzas portray these surreal happenings with a certain inevitability, adding to the effect of horror at the symbolic prospect that tyrants will live on through their indestructible effigies.

Zhukovsky initially produced the translation for publication in *The Contemporary*, Alexander Pushkin's literary journal. Despite Zhukovsky's concern that the censor might object, the poem was published in its first issue in 1836. Although they got lucky, Zhukovsky's inhibitions were well founded. Behind his reworking of Zedlitz's original stands the greatest poem in Russian about the supernatural animation of statues, Pushkin's narrative poem *The Bronze Horseman*. One of the great symbols of St. Petersburg, as famous an image of Russia as St. Basil's Cathedral in the popular imagination, the statue was based on the great equestrian figure of Marcus Aurelius on the Capitoline Hill. Pushkin's poem begins with a tribute to Peter as a visionary who founded the city and elevated Russia, and then in the body of the narrative tells the story of the clerk Evgenii. The setting is November 7, 1824, when a flood hit St. Petersburg. Among its victims was Evgenii's fiancée, Parasha. Driven to insanity by his loss, Evgenii confronts the statue of Peter the Great on Senate Square, issuing a rebellious challenge to the tsar on the spot where the Decembrists would rebel only a year later after the actual flood. In a brilliant dramatic coup, Pushkin has the statue come to life, and the bronze horseman pursues the upstart through the city. Evgenii's challenge to the statue is certainly to be read as a cathartic emotional gesture. But, once the statue responds, the poem acquires an allegorical meaning. The statue acts as a defender of the realm Peter created, and it quells any hint of popular revolt. The poem's political message lies in how the aims of the unchecked, absolutist state will also justify any means and any cost to individual lives.

Like *The Bronze Horseman*, "The Night Watch" projects through its symbolism both the fear of rebellion against which tyrants maintain vigilance and the psychological trauma experienced by the oppressed. Jakobson noted that "Pushkin's symbolism of the statue continues to affect Russian poetry to the present day," by which he meant Russian modernist poetry.[20] In "The Night Watch," Galich updates the myth to suit the Soviet projection of power through massive scale—zombies parading in their "thousands." The state's defenders, however, are not mere police or soldiers. Since antiquity, statues have functioned as both figurative and symbolic markers, literally present in the real world but also symbolically present in the semiotic organization of space.[21] They can be potent visual representations of both duration and historical change, whether subtly conditioning the body politic to internalize figures of authority or rallying protesters against an old order and discredited values.[22] In Soviet space, statues, gigantic posters, and other monuments such as Lenin's Tomb had a totemic function, creating a cult around leaders that repurposed religious elements in a way that was acceptable to an atheistic state.[23] The theme of the animated statue was of great interest to Pushkin at the time of the poem's composition. In his play *The Stone Guest*, partly inspired by Molière and the opera by Mozart and Da Ponte, Pushkin treated the myth of the figure whose monument returns to life supernaturally and posthumously to avenge a wrong.[24] Sergei Gandlevsky, following earlier critics like Andrei Sinyavsky, finds Galich at his most compelling and original when he is at his most theatrical.[25] Animate statues belong to the theater of Molière and Pushkin, and they open onto the realm of the occult. Here the statues that stalk the citizenry are zombie figures of dread—Roman Jakobson in his famous discussion refers to them as "monsters of horror"—and the "odd belated pedestrians" recoil at the sight and probably at the sound of the percussion accompaniment.

Reversal of nature (time stops and reverses; lines 12–13 in the Russian, lines 10–11 in the translation), darkness and the moon, theatrical movement, hyperbole, mystery, the supernatural—these are the classic elements of the uncanny and dreadful, which often feature in the romantic ballad and horror story (or film). They create a state of feeling in the reader that is also common to the literature of the supernatural in which fantastic occurrences defy rational explanation. The fantasy of a parade of statues on the march, defying the physical laws of the universe in order to maintain complete order, belongs to rulers rather than the ruled. There may also be a more proximate influence to be found in the poem "Artists Represent Lenin" ("Khudozhniki risuiut Lenina") by Boris Slutsky, which circulated in manuscript in 1962, on the theme of desecrated monuments and de-Stalinization.[26] It begins in tones of mock pity at the fate that has befallen Stalin. With Lenin's reputation permanently in the ascendant, Stalin is taking knocks, reduced to a "malicious nonentity" ("zlobnoe nichtozhestvo") when in fact he was "a cruel magnificence" ("zhestokoe velichestvo"). Images of Stalin now face a commensurate fate, "piled up in cellars" ("v podvaly svaleny"). The poem's conclusion seems to allow no possibility of rehabilitation:

Лежат гранитные и бронзовые,
написанные маслом, мраморные,
а рядом гипсовые, бросовые,
дешевые и необрамленные.

Уволенная и отставленная,
лежит в подвале слава Сталина.

Granite and bronze,
Painted in oil, marble,

And nearby plaster, clay,
Cheap and unframed

Redundant and neglected
Stalin's glory lies in the cellar.[27]

As embodied in the statue, Peter the Great's fame had become its own ineluctable force in Russian culture, symbolizing the human sacrifice required to achieve modernization. In the Soviet space, after Khrushchev's Secret Speech of 1956, the question was whether it was truly possible to bury the tyrant and relegate both iconography and reputation to the scrap heap of history. Slutsky's poem records a process of cancellation, one that was widely used by the ancient Romans who repurposed statues and monuments. The poem leaves the question of whether this is irreversible. Galich's poem offers an equivocal view, suggesting that, while the specter of the tyrant continues to haunt imaginations, its potency may have been reduced. In its latest instantiation, the generalissimo inspires all the standard clichés of Soviet panegyric ("Of all peoples and ages the genius"). Nonetheless, whereas Pushkin's bronze horseman is fearsomely magnificent on the prowl in a grand city, the phantom in Galich's "Night Watch" is maimed and unkempt; and, whereas the Pushkinian horseman as the emblem of forward-moving history charges heroically through the city, defying the elements as well as crushing the population, this simulacra parade passes through "heaps of abandoned dust and trash." In Pushkin's poem, the confrontation between Peter and the hero Evgenii, seen as the archetypal Little Man of Russian literature, creates a sense of terror for both sides. Here the situation more closely resembles the nightmare Marx envisaged when the "sorcerer is no longer able to control the powers of the nether world," and the proletariat rise up and "the dead seize the living." The effect of the uncanny and horror is a zombie type of history in which a single chapter is replayed endlessly, even as it becomes more broken and run-down.[28] Such repetition seems less than a triumph when the cyclical reiterations of history are tantamount to mass-produced and cheapened statuary. The reversal of Slutsky's vision envisaged at the end of the poem delivers a parody of the optimism socialist realism required of all patriotic art, flagellating the listener with the sound of this unmusical "beat, beat, beat."

22

Vladimir Vysotsky, "My Gypsy Song" (1967–68)

CHOREOGRAPHY OF DESPAIR

Моя цыганская

В сон мне—желтые огни,
И хриплю во сне я:
—Повремени, повремени, -
Утро мудренее!
Но и утром всё не так,
Нет того веселья:
Или куришь натощак,
Или пьешь с похмелья.

В кабаках—зеленый штоф,
Белые салфетки.
Рай для нищих и шутов,
Мне ж—как птице в клетке!
В церкви смрад и полумрак,
Дьяки курят ладан.
Нет! И в церкви все не так,
Все не так, как надо.

Я—на гору впопыхах,
Чтоб чего не вышло.
А на горе стоит ольха,
А под горою вишня.
Хоть бы склон увить плющом,
Мне б и то отрада,

Хоть бы что-нибудь еще . . .
Все не так, как надо!

Я тогда по полю, вдоль реки.
Света—тьма, нет бога!
А в чистом поле васильки,
Дальняя дорога.
Вдоль дороги—лес густой
С Бабами-Ягами,
А в конце дороги той—
Плаха с топорами.

Где-то кони пляшут в такт,
Нехотя и плавно.
Вдоль дороги все не так,
А в конце—подавно.
И ни церковь, ни кабак—
Ничего не свято!
Нет, ребята, все не так,
Все не так, ребята![1]

My Gypsy Song

Yellow lights disturb my sleep;
hoarse, I beg my sorrow:
"Wait, it's better than it seems,
let it rest till morrow!"
But the morrow's just as bad,
joy is gone forever,
so you drink and smoke in bed,
hungry and hung over.

Fools and paupers laugh and spar;
drink stains pea-green fibers . . .
Me, I'm feeling in the bar
like a bird behind bars.
Incense smells too sweet and strong,
and the hall's too shady.
No, the church, too, is all wrong.
Nothing's as it should be.

From the bar and church I flee,
up a hill I hurry.
On the hill, an alder tree,
and below, a cherry.
With some ivy on the slope,
things might look less shabby.
Might not something give me hope?
Nothing's as it should be.

So again I take another road,
past a winding river.
Light aplenty, but no God,
only fields of clover . . .
Then I tried a risky bend,
haunted woods I traveled.
What awaited at the end
was a hangman's scaffold.

Somewhere, horses dance and sway,
somber und unwilling.
All is wrong along the way,
and the end is chilling.
Churches, bars, this useless song—
they just make me shudder.
Nothing's sacred, all is wrong,
nothing's as it should be!

(TRANSLATED BY ALEXANDRA BERLINA)

It has long been assumed that the poetry of Vladimir Vysotsky (1938–80), cult actor and singer-songwriter, was a part of Soviet mass culture. In fact, Vysotsky's songs were only rarely played on the radio or on TV. In films, his songs were heard, but he rarely appeared on screen. His first book of poems came out soon after his death in 1980. Official vinyl records of his songs were rarely produced and sold out in a flash. If a Soviet family owned a tape recorder, then it was almost certain they listened to Vysotsky and, usually, to illicit recordings of the unofficial concerts held in scientific institutes or in private apartments. In his husky, cracked voice, he created a theater of the grotesque full of the most ordinary yet most unlikely impersonations[2]—con men and criminals, alcoholics, aliens, pirates, World War II soldiers (alive and dead), wolves and horses, and even seemingly inanimate objects such as a fighter plane. By stylizing his vocabulary and speech manner, the poet became each of them in turn, transforming each song into a performance of otherness. In his poems, too, Vysotsky remains an actor. Masterfully imitating or inventing different characters with their own manners of speech and thinking, he captures his listeners with humor, assertiveness, and energy. Crucially, all these voices are unofficial, excluded from the picture of the world and history presented by Soviet culture. Even in the role of a popular Soviet character, such as a cosmonaut or athlete, Vysotsky exposes the grotesque beneath the gloss.

The performativity of Vysotsky's poetry descends from the carnival tradition, especially from the Russian version of Harlequin known as *skomorokh*.[3] As Nikolai Bogomolov has argued, Vysotsky's multifaced actor/poet persona demonstrates the limitations of any monological position since, "in his songs, Vysotsky seeks opportunities to transcend self-referential speech that dominates conventional poetic genres." The effect is that the listener (or reader) can "joyfully [recognize] their world reflected in the song."[4]

In parallel, Vysotsky's poetic persona acquired ever more complex overtones as he became steeped in the characters he played. Every one of them is not only "the other," but also a twist or even inversion of this persona. For him, the "discourse of the other" (to use Mikhail Bakhtin's term) is a form of speech distanced from the self, and serves as a form of *self*-expression. Hence, in "Wolf Hunt," the monologue of a wolf becomes a crucial manifesto of Vysotsky as a poet:

> Я из повиновенья вышел
> За флажки—жажда жизни сильней . . . [5]
>
> Yet I rebel and go against the rules
> My instincts outweighed by will to live.[6]

Even in such distinctly narrative texts as "Police Protocol," "A Lecture on the International Situation," or "Letter to the Editor of the Television Program 'The Visible and the Incredible' from Kanatchikov Psychiatric Hospital,"[7] it is not so much the author's distance from his characters that is striking but the joy of incarnation, the opportunity to express the personal and intimate on behalf of "the other." According to Andrei Skobelev and Sergei Shaulov, who authored one of the first literary monographs on Vysotsky, his entire artistic concept is characterized by a "fluid experience of reality," a "multivariant world."[8] His protean poetic persona has a unique gift of multilingualism. Open to the world, he is almost an encyclopedia of his era's voices and consciousnesses, albeit in a markedly masculine way. This persona takes the guise of a collection of different male characters, including some fairly dislikable ones. Fittingly, one of his last poems, "I got the chills again" ("Menia opiat' udarilo v oznob," 1979), deals with an "other" inside his "I," a rather unpleasant one, a boor, a lumpen:

Во мне сидит мохнатый злобный жлоб
С мозолистыми цепкими руками.
Когда мою заметив маету,
Друзья бормочут:—Снова загуляет,
Мне тесно с ним, мне с ним невмоготу!
Он кислород вместо меня хватает.
Он не двойник и не второе "я",—
Все объясненья выглядят дурацки,—
Он плоть и кровь, дурная кровь моя.
Такое не приснится и Стругацким.[9]

In me, there is a furry, vicious bastard.
His calloused hands are muscular and strong.
My friends would see: again, I'm getting restless.
They'd mutter: "He'll go on a binge!"
But it is he who's breathing with my mouth.
I hate his guts, he truly makes me cringe.
He's not my double, not my other self,
no evil twin, no alien addiction.
He is my flesh and blood, he's my bad blood—
far stranger, this, than any science fiction.

Vysotsky was famously adept at the storytelling technique known as *skaz*, a type of narrative that imitates oral speech with multiple nonstandard elements, underscoring cultural and social (often class) difference. In Vysotsky, the most humorous examples of *skaz* tend to be based on social and philosophical metaphors that go far beyond the specific material and that are always grotesque. Hence his "Dialogue in Front of the Television," consisting of a husband and wife commenting on a TV show, exposes the similarities between a circus performance and the life of the "ordinary Soviet citizen" with all its incredible tricks, such as drunken acrobatics and vanishing objects and persons. Similarly, "Letter [. . .] from Kanatchikov Psychiatric Hospital" likens clinical insanity to fashionable myths from popular culture, such as that of the Bermuda Triangle. Vysotsky's speaker is acutely aware of the social chaos; indeed, he (or, sometimes, she) is an integral part of it, and for that reason the often grotesque fantasies of his most unhinged characters look like eerily accurate prophecies. Thus,

"A Lecture on the International Situation, Held by a Man Sentenced to Fifteen Days in Jail for Disorderly Conduct in Front of his Cellmates" (1979) can today be read as predicting a number of post-Soviet political events, ranging from the collapse of the USSR to the opening of the economic and political arena to the criminal world. "By the end of the decade, we will be in command!" proclaims the hoodlum.

Nonetheless, it is worth bearing in mind that, as a performer, Vysotsky was an acolyte not of Stanislavsky but of the Brechtian school of acting, possibly because the Taganka Theater, where he worked all his life, was Brechtian in its method. As Bogomolov reminds us,

> According to Brecht, while portraying another person on stage, an actor must at all times also show the audience an external, theatrical attitude toward the character—his or her own and that of the director [. . .] It is in [Vysotsky's] songs that this Brechtian approach is most dominant, where he becomes both demonstrator and storyteller, where he incarnates in another while expressing his attitude toward this other.[10]

In Vysotsky's songs, the Brechtian V-effect—the effect of alienation, of distance separating actors from characters—is never flaunted and is always present in the fabric of the text, in its intonation and imagery.

The polyphony of Vysotsky's poetry embodies a special concept of freedom: this is a freedom not to subscribe to any one "truth," position, or faith, but to combine them all, sometimes in glaring *self-contradiction*. Take, for instance, a poem that clearly polemicizes with the Russian poetic tradition of celebrating one's own grandeur by imitating Horace's "Monument" poem. In Vysotsky's version of the "Exegi Monumentum" tradition, his speaker dreams not of a posthumous monument but of its destruction:

> Саван сдернули—
> как я обужен!—
> Нате, смерьте! Неужели
> такой я вам нужен
> После смерти?[11]

> The shroud was pulled off—
> how small I had become!—
> Go ahead and measure me!
> Do you really need me
> like this
> after death?

Such freedom is hard to bear, and Vysotsky is clearly burdened by his unstable, unbalanced poetic position. Motifs such as black ice, bewitched forests, fog, suffocation, dark depths, and hopeless labyrinths are strikingly frequent in his lyrics:

Поздно! У всех порваны нити!
Хаос, возня - и у меня
Выхода нет![12]

Too late! Everyone's threads are torn!
Chaos, panic—and I
have no way out!

Connected to these themes are motifs of his lifestyle as a *poète maudit*, who continually stimulated himself with alcohol and drugs, pushing himself to the brink in order to infuse his work with maximum energy. This image became a reality with Vysotsky's untimely death at the age of forty-two and the mass mourning for him, which surpassed all expectations: despite all official resistance, many thousands came to the funeral of the unofficial national poet.

Vysotsky unquestionably belongs to the tradition of Russian neoromantic poetry (see introduction), an affiliation signaled by the very title of "My Gypsy Song." A neoromantic aesthetic finds expression not only in Vysotsky's taste for stylization and performance art, but also in his focus on extreme situations.[13] It is not for nothing that the poem "Capricious Horses," with its central image of a singer in a sledge rushing "along a precipice, over the abyss, at the very edge," became an epitome of Vysotsky's poetry.[14] This image draws on the romantic tradition, finding its closest literary relative in the figure of Pushkin's Walsingham. The hero of *A Feast in Time of Plague* (from Pushkin's set of *Little Tragedies*, 1830) finds a certain thrill "at the edge of a dark abyss" in the midst of a pandemic. More than anything else, "Capricious Horses" delivers a statement of Vysotsky's characteristic romantic strategy: life needs to be compressed into one tragic, ultimate moment if one is to experience true freedom, a destructive, deadly freedom—in Vysotsky's world, there is no other. His persona embraces such risk over life lived as a sentence of "slow death":

Мы не умрем мучительною жизнью—
Мы лучше верной смертью оживем![15]

We shall not die a painful life—
We'd rather come alive by certain death!

It is out of this ethos that Vysotsky positively gravitates toward characters according to their ability to live "at the edge of a dark abyss." His favorite poetic roles feature strong people under extreme conditions. The role of the liminal situation in Vysotsky's poetics has been noted by many researchers. Under duress, everything superfluous disappears, and all that remains is the desire for freedom, even if it comes at the price of death. Complexity vanishes, the fog of "ifs and whens" dissipates, and one can exclaim with relief: "Luckily, I have no choice!"[16]

It is characteristic of Vysotsky to depict the creative process itself as a life-or-death situation. Thus, in "The Song of the Singer at the Microphone" ("I'm bathed in light, and seen by all the eyes . . ."), the microphone is compared to an embrasure, a knife blade, a snake, and a gun: "It'll shoot nine grams of lead into my forehead . . ." Even the very setting of a performance evokes violent associations:

Бьют лучи от рампы мне под ребра,
Слепят фонари в лицо недобро,
И слепят с боков прожектора,
И жара, жара . . .

The footlights pummeling against my ribs
the lights are out to blind me
shining in my face and from the sides
it is so hot, so very very hot . . .

The poet is under fire, under attack, in the center of a deadly tornado. Actually, though, it is the speaker's own creative imperative that saturates such essentially innocent details of stage machinery as the microphone, the stage lights, and the footlights with deadly semantics: "I must sing to the point of madness and of death . . ." For Vysotsky, poetry is the ultimate expression of freedom, and, consequently, it needs the extreme situation, "the edge."[17]

The poem in this chapter, "My Gypsy Song" ("Moia Tsyganskaia," 1968), one of Vysotsky's most popular and recognizable songs, assembles many motifs of his art. It has attracted a great deal of professional and amateur interpretation,[18] which suggests a certain mystery behind an outwardly transparent text. First, the song manifests Vysotsky's orientation toward performance and toward "the word of the other." Its music is borrowed: it is the melody of the famous romantic song "Two Guitars" (lyrics by Apollon Grigoriev), also known as "Gypsy Czárdás." Not only the melody but also certain motifs of Vysotsky's text come from this song. The line "cornflowers in an open field" (the literal flower turned by Alexandra Berlina to "clover" for reasons of rhyme) echoes some versions of the "Czárdás" song (for instance, both Vadim Kozin and Petr Leshchenko sang of "poppies and cornflowers in the field"). "On the hill, an alder tree, / and below, a cherry" (lines 19–20) resembles the rhythmically similar and very popular folk ditty (*chastushka*) that exists in countless variations.[19] Arguably, the first stanza of Vysotsky's poem ("so you drink and smoke in bed, / hungry and hung over," lines 7–8), too, paraphrases the "Czárdás":

Как тебя мне не узнать?
На тебе лежит печаль
Страстного веселья,
Бурного похмелья. [...][20]

I would know you anywhere:
On your face, there is the stamp
of your wild abandon,
of your fierce hangover.[21]

When performing this song, Vysotsky would often add a refrain, also borrowed from "Czárdás": "One more time, and one more time, and many, many more times!" In other words, the very genre of "My Gypsy Song" suggests a focus on the "word" and "tune" reminiscent of the popular tradition and also of nineteenth-century lyrics. Stylization is always two-voiced, and "My Gypsy Song" is no exception. Vysotsky himself called it "a variation on Gypsy themes." However, his stylization of so-called Gypsy romantic songs does not make the least attempt at understanding Sinti/Roma culture and identity. (This is why Berlina decided to use the word "Gypsy" in the song's title, despite its questionable status; elsewhere in the chapter, too, it is used when alternatives such as "Sinti" or "Roma" do not fit the historic context.) This exposes the limitations in Vysotsky's dialogues: he explicitly continues the "Gypsy" theme *only* with the Russian literary tradition (both poetry and prose) as its reference point.

"My Gypsy Song" reproduces a model that can be traced back to many nineteenth-century Russian literary works, such as Pushkin's "Gypsies," Turgenev's "End of Chertopkhanov," Leskov's "Enchanted Wanderer," Tolstoy's "Living Corpse," and Gorky's "Makar Chudra," to name the most prominent. In all these narratives, the protagonist leaves "good society" for the Sinti/Roma community (most often because he—and it is always a he!—falls in love with a woman there), thereby realizing a need for freedom that could never be satisfied/pursued in his home environment. However, once he finds himself alone with the Sinti/Roma woman or within the traveling community, he discovers that, for him, "Gypsy" freedom is destructive: he finds either that he is incapable of being truly free (as in "The Gypsies"), or that the path of transgressions blows his life to smithereens ("The Living Corpse"). An elaborate plot is not required by Vysotsky to retain three major motifs: *freedom*, *transgression*, and *self-destruction*.

Thirst for freedom can be heard in lines such as "Me, I'm feeling in the bar / like a bird behind bars" (lines 11–12). Transgression manifests itself in a variety of ways, above all in the refrain "Nothing's as it should be" (lines 16, 24, 40) and the final lines: "Churches, bars, this useless song—/ they just make me shudder. / Nothing's sacred, all is wrong, / nothing's as it should be!" (lines 37–40). The motif of (self-) destruction appears in the first stanza. Initially, it sounds merely like a traditional variation on "Gypsy" motifs. In "Czárdás," the speaker complains,

Oh it hurts, oh how it hurts,
my head with a hangover . . . [22]

"So you drink and smoke in bed, / hungry and hung over," Vysotsky echoes (lines 7–8). However, in the second part, this motif acquires a sinister (albeit stylized) twist: "What awaited at the end / was a hangman's scaffold" (lines 31–32); "All is wrong along the way, / and the end is chilling" (lines 35–36).

How then are these motifs combined in "My Gypsy Song"? The poem is written in trochaic lines with mixed three or four feet and divided into five cross-rhymed eight-line stanzas, alternating strong and weak rhymes. The original third line—*Povremeni, povremeni!* (lit. "Wait awhile, do wait awhile!")—disrupts the rhythm: it is iambic, has a dactylic clause, and the rhyme with *ogni* is less precise than the other rhymes in the song (as reflected by "sleep"/"seems" in Berlina's translation). The rhythmic emphasis of this line draws out an inner tension that gives the poem its drive. The gist of the lines, rendered here as "Wait, it's better than it seems, / let it rest till morrow!"(lines 3–4), comes from a fairy-tale saying: "Things might look better in the morning" (*Utro vechera mudrenee*), implying that difficult problems will find their solution the next day (an equivalent of "Sleep on it" in English). Here, nothing of the sort happens. Instead, the fairy-tale tone set by these lines continues in the fourth stanza, where the speaker finds himself in "a dense forest / full of Baba Yagas" (lines 29–30 in the Russian). Just one of these Russian witches would normally be quite sufficient to arrest the hero's progress. Their appearance in the plural here is highly unusual. The essence of the dramatic choice facing the speaker remains unclear, but the "Wait awhile, do wait awhile!" (line 3 in the Russian) begs time to stop before a decision must be made. The lyric protagonist is in constant movement, going to the bar, to the church, up the mountain, down the mountain, along "another road, / past a winding river" (lines 25–26), the embodiment of restlessness and angst.

What is the meaning of these struggles? What does Vysotsky's character seek? Freedom? Meaning? Another life? Arguably, all of these. After all, the yearning embedded in the tradition of the "Gypsy" romantic song is but existential ennui. For

Vysotsky, from the very first stanza, this ennui is elevated to the level of a crisis, an extreme situation, a critical threshold between existence and nonexistence, an emphasis felt in the opening scene, in which the protagonist begs hoarsely in his sleep and when awakening from sleep to reality. Extreme tension is also conveyed by Vysotsky's performing style. In performance he stresses the consonant *j* and also

> deliberately changes the soft vowels *ia* and *e* to hard ones: *a* and *ė*. This gives additional emotional coloring, increasing the volume and conveying the anxious state of the performer. Researchers also note the strongly rolled *r*—which appears thirty-nine times in "My Gypsy Song"—as well as the stressed, deliberately hoarse pronunciation of spirants: *kabakakhkh, shtoff, polumrakh, takh, takht.*[23]

To return to semantics: each stanza, with the exception of the first and last ones (which serve as opening and coda), is built around a traditional binary opposition: *sacred/profane* in the second stanza, *up/down* in the third, *light/darkness* in the fourth. Moreover, whereas the space-time (or, to use Bakhtin's term, the chronotope) of the second stanza implies a *social* dimension (church, bar), in the third, the *natural* chronotope (mountain, alder tree, cherry tree, ivy) takes center stage, and, in the fourth, we enter a *mythological/fairy-tale* dimension (forest, Baba Yagas, an executioner's chopping block, that is, "a hangman's scaffold" in the present translation, line 32). Vysotsky's speaker seeks metaphysical support; he strives to understand the meaning of his existence, to find solid foundations for his freedom. But, whatever he tries, the result is unstable and dubious. "All is wrong, / nothing's as it should be!"

In the second stanza, the characteristics of the profane and the sacred appear jumbled. In the original, the tavern is "a *paradise* for beggars and fools" (line 11), which is full of vivid colors (e.g., green tablecloth, white napkins). The church, by contrast, is characterized by "stench and darkness" (somewhat euphemistically rendered as "incense smells too sweet and strong, / and the hall's too shady," lines 13–14). The darkness makes another appearance in the fourth stanza, and its juxtaposition with the tavern resurfaces in the ending (in the original, in a very direct form): "Neither church nor tavern / nothing is holy!" This begs the question of why a tavern should be holy. That makes sense only within inside-out carnival culture based on the "upside-down" logic of representation (Bakhtin) in which the tavern replaces the church. Is this perhaps why Vysotsky's speaker exclaims that "joy is gone forever"? Is he suggesting that, without the sacred, there is no carnival freedom that could liberate one from the shackles of dogmatism and seriousness?

The next stanza, with its image of the mountain, does not lend itself to easy interpretation. As mentioned above, "On the hill, an alder tree, / and below, a cherry" (lines 19–20) is a quote from a Russian folk limerick (*chastuska*), making it unwise to look for deeper meaning in the botanical details. In the original, the next lines—"from the bar and church I flee, / up a hill I hurry" (lines 17–18)—suggest danger: the speaker hurries up a mountain *chtob chego ne vyshlo* (line 18). Translatable as "out of harm's way," this expression suggests that the source of danger is the speaker himself. The mountain is an image full of symbolic meanings, and, here, it appears to be a place where one hopes to escape one's own demons. Arguably, however, something else is more important here: movement itself—first upward, then downward. Not only the goal but the way itself is bleak: "joy is gone forever," not to be found even in motion (lines 21–24). Neither upward nor downward movement resolves the crisis. At no altitude is a new self to be found, nor is there an alternative to the deadlock in which the protagonist finds himself when on the slope or under the mountain. The top is indistinguishable from the bottom, and neither harbors any joy. The anaphoric repetition of *khot' by* ("if only") conveys a growing thirst for something different, something harmonious, something right—a thirst that remains unquenched.

It has been noted that, in "Vysotsky's poetic system, top and bottom often act as equivalent targets of motion."[24] This artistic strategy is strikingly different from the traditional romantic model. Hence, his angels "sing with evil voices"[25] ("Capricious Horses"), and paradise is likened to a prison camp ("Paradise Apples"). Even while fleeing, Vysotsky's speaker represents the model of the very place he flees from: a place that, in "My Gypsy Song," is characterized by the absence of stable boundaries between ethically and aesthetically opposed states and values.

The fourth stanza transports the speaker to a fairy-tale space. This leap from a (narrative) reality to the realm of fantasy is emphasized by a rhythmic "malfunction": in the first line of this stanza, the word *togda*, "then" or "again," is superfluous, jarring: *Ia togda po poliu, vdol' reki* ("So again I take another road," line 25). It turns a four-feet trochee chorus into a five-feet one, the only such line in the entire song. The core opposition is set by the contrast between the fields and the forest with its Baba Yagas. However, the seeming contrast of light and darkness is exposed as an illusion in the fourth stanza: "Light aplenty, but no God!" (line 27). At this point, the original uses word play, an ambiguous phrase that can refer to oxymoron: *Sveta—t'ma! Svet* means "light," and *t'ma* usually denotes darkness. However, the latter can also be colloquially used to mean "a lot," hence the line reads "a lot of light"—or "a darkness of light." This generates a philosophical paradox: the impossibility of distinguishing between light and darkness suggests abandonment, emptiness, a life devoid of meaning and supreme justification.[26] And indeed, the line goes on to exclaim that there is no God. For a resident of an atheist country, it might seem strange to make this statement so dramatically. Arguably, this line relates to the acute sense of existential crisis that became a mass condition in late Soviet culture. The speaker disbelieves in

God not because atheism is the norm; in fact, a return to religion and to church had been on the rise among the intelligentsia since the late 1960s. Rather, the falsity of the world around him serves to disprove God's existence.

There are some surprising similarities between "My Gypsy Song" (1967–68) and the short story "I Believe!" (1971) by Vasily Shukshin, also a writer and actor, who belonged to a cultural and social milieu very different from Vysotsky's. While Vysotsky was close to the antiregime intelligentsia, Shukshin was perceived as one of the leaders of the writers associated with "village prose," which expressed the views and experiences of the Russian peasantry, maimed and displaced by collectivization. The protagonist of "I Believe!" is an ordinary villager called Maxim Yarikov. He is going through a crisis. Like Vysotsky's hero, he has lost his taste for life. He, too, is suffering from a yearning whose essence is existential rather than social: "his soul hurts." The question that torments him is simply: "What for?" (*Zachem?*) For instance: "There goes a little kid, Vanka Malofeev's son . . . And I remember when Vanka himself was like that, walking around, and I was that age too. Then they'll have their own kids just like that. And the kids will have their kids . . . Is that all there is? What for?"[27]

The way Maxim questions the meaning of life suggests the collapse of an entire belief system. The ideals laid down by the Soviet utopian project of communism turned out to be false; the traditional values have been lost—hence the longing for a new, vital, and clear meaning. Searching for an answer to his questions, Maxim finds a defrocked priest and attempts to "lean" on his understanding of the sacred, very much like the speaker of Vysotsky's song. Shukshin's priest is excommunicated, but this does not prevent him from explaining Maxim's ennui. True, he does not provide any intelligible answers to his distressing questions. But he does give him a reply and a piece of advice: "Your soul aches? Good. Good! You've at least begun to stir, damn it! Or we wouldn't be able to pull you off the stove if you were in a state of spiritual equilibrium. Live, my son, weep and dance!"[28] In accordance with this worldview, the real answer to the protagonist's existential crisis lies in the dance he and the priest perform together at the end: "Both the priest and Maxim were dancing with such anger, with such frenzy, that it didn't even seem strange that they were dancing. At this point they could either dance, or tear the shirts off their chests and cry and gnash their teeth."[29]

"My Gypsy Song" is the equivalent of such a dance. In Vysotsky's lyrics, as in Shukshin's story, existential despair is intertwined with an acute thirst for new directions in life: when "the soul hurts," it generates vitality. This is why, despite its unquenchable intensity, yearning is *life-giving*. Vysotsky transforms the experience of extreme strain into a liminal situation that also works at the level of myth. Victor

Turner argues that the liminal situation originates in traditional rites of passage but goes beyond ritual, producing what he calls liminoids. He defines liminality as "a temporal interface whose properties partially invert those of the already consolidated order which constitutes any specific cultural 'cosmos.' [. . .] Liminal entities are neither here nor there; they are betwixt and between the positions assigned and arrayed by law, customs, conventions, and ceremonial."[30] In Vysotsky, liminality is indeed expressed by an inversion of traditional oppositions, such as church and the tavern in the second stanza, up and down in the third. The speaker's restlessness, his inability to accept either side of the opposition, corresponds precisely to the liminal identity of "betwixt and between."

In the fourth stanza, the plural "Baba Yagas" can be understood as a direct reference to rites of passage. According to Propp's famous *Historical Roots of the Wonder Tale*, the fairy-tale witch Baba Yaga symbolizes a priest(ess) who tests neophytes during initiation rites that symbolically imitate death, a motif that also clearly resounds in Vysotsky's song, namely in the fourth stanza. However, the protagonist believes that his death will be real, final, and irrevocable. At the same time, the liminal logic unfolding in the lyrics also suggests an opposite resolution. According to Turner, liminality is "an instant of pure potentiality," which contains "the settings in which new symbols, models, and paradigms arise—as the seedbeds of cultural creativity, in fact."[31] Hence, by using the song and dance energy of "variations on 'Gypsy' themes," Vysotsky captures how overflowing creativity generates an intellectual and emotional thirst for philosophical rather than pragmatic goals of existence, for deep rather than superficial sources of joy. But in this context, the very thirst for meaning, furiously articulated by the speaker, becomes a value in itself, generating resistance to an era that decades later would be called stagnant.

The philosophical yearning of Vysotsky's speaker cannot be apolitical in nature. Soviet society had lost meaningful goals and values, something that became especially clear after August 1968, when Soviet tanks crushed the possibility of humanist socialism in Czechoslovakia. "My Gypsy Song" was written before those events, in the winter of 1967–68. But the end of the Thaw and new repressions, such as the arrest of Andrei Sinyavsky and Yulii Daniel in 1965 for publishing "anti-Soviet" works abroad, could not fail to perturb Vysotsky, especially as he considered Sinyavsky his teacher. There is a temptation to see the appearance of an executioner's chopping block in the poem as an allusion to these events or as foreshadowing the coming tragedy of the Prague Spring. But, precisely because "My Gypsy Song" is not tied to any specific events, it conveys a state of life-giving philosophical crisis, transcends its time, and remains a fundamentally open text.

Appendix

My Gypsy Romance

Yellow fires in my dream—
all night long I mutter:
"Hold on, brother, bide your time—
morning's always better."
Morning comes, but nothing's right,
ain't no life of clover:
smoking on an empty gut
or boozing, still hungover.

There's green damask in the taverns,
napkins gleaming white:
it's paradise for fools and beggars—
but I'm a bird caged tight . . .
Priests smoke incense in the church,
barely any light—
no, it isn't right, this stench,
it just isn't right!

I race up the hill, don't stop—
otherwise, god knows . . .
But an alder grows on top
and cherry trees below.
Give me ivy on the rise,
that would be a sight . . .
Give me something, something else—
but nothing's going right!

By the river lies a field—
light or dark—no god!
I see bluets at my feet,
and a long, long road.
That road leads into a brake
full of wicked hags.
At the end—a chopping block
and a sharpened axe . . .

Somewhere all the horses trot
in rhythm, like a chorus.
But on this road, nothing is right,
and at the end—it's worse.
Not the churches, not the taverns—
nothing's sacred, fellas!
I tell ya, nothing's right, my brothers . . .
It's all wrong, I tell ya!

(TRANSLATED BY BORIS DRALYUK)

Uniquely for Vysotsky's poem, we commissioned two English versions as an opportunity to showcase the art of the translator. A high technical capacity to solve formal problems is common to both the versions by Alexandra Berlina and Boris Dralyuk. Each is stanzaic, preserving the length and shape of Vysotsky's original, each makes a feature of different types of rhyme, exact and approximate, to add spice and humor, and Dralyuk's "clover/hungover," "stench/church" are memorable collocations in exactly the right spirit of this countercultural songster. Most differences concern word choice, starting with the title. All songs are words set to music but in Russian the term "romance" (*romans*) usually denotes a strophic lyric set to music, a feature brought out in Dralyuk's title, which also for the Anglophone reader supplies a romantic nuance. The poem presents a challenge of how to render a slangy tone, and these variations inevitably inflect a mood of the lyric persona. Morning comes and with it the realization, as Dralyuk's figure shakes off the hangover, that "it just isn't right!" Ready to "race up the hill," he has three more stanzas in which to confront "no god," a "long, long road" and learn again that "nothing's right," a truth he imparts familiarly ("I tell ya"). Berlina's gypsy singer is a man of nouns, Dralyuk's more of adjectives. The former has perhaps come down further in the world, a habitué of "taverns" rather than "bars," leery of the "hangman's scaffold" rather than "a chopping block," and what is "worse" for Dralyuk's is "chilling" and "wrong" for Berlina's. Both prove faithful to the message of the original that "nothing is sacred," and at the same time demonstrate how much nuance a rendering can bring.

23

Dmitri Prigov, Three Poems about Dishwashing (1980s)

THE BANALITY OF THE ROMANTIC

Я всю жизнь свою провел в мытье посуды
И в сложении возвышенных стихов
Мудрость жизненная вся моя отсюда
Оттого и нрав мой тверд и несуров

Вот течет вода—ее я постигаю
За окном внизу—народ и власть
Что не нравится—я просто отменяю
А что нравится—оно вокруг и есть
(1980)

Банальнос рассуждение на тему свободы
Только вымоешь посуду
Глядь—уж новая лежит
Уж какая тут свобода
Тут до старости б дожить
Правда, можно и не мыть
Да вот тут приходят разные
Говорят: посуда грязная—
Где уж тут свободе быть
(1982)

Я с домашней борюсь энтропией
Как источник энергьи божественной
Незаметные силы слепые
Побеждаю в борьбе неторжественной

В день посуду помою я трижды
Пол помою-протру повсеместно
Мира смысл и структуру я зиждю
На пустом вот казалось бы месте[1]
(1983)

I've spent all my life washing dishes
And composing poems most sublime
And this has lent me all of my life's wisdom
And made my temperament firm and mild

I watch the water flow and comprehend it
Below my window—the people and the powers
Whatever I don't like I simply overrule it
And what I like is all surrounding me

Banal Rumination on the Topic of Freedom

Just when you've finished up the dishes
Look—a whole new pile awaits
What kind of freedom is this
Just let me make it to old age
True, you could just not wash them
But then various people come by
And say: the dishes are dirty
What kind of space for freedom here

I wrestle with domestic entropy
As a source of energy divine
These forces, inglorious and blind,
I overcome in quiet unsung struggle

I'll wash the dishes three times a day
Wash and scrub the floor all over
I'll build the meaning and structure of the world
On this place that seems like it is empty[2]

(TRANSLATED BY AINSLEY MORSE)

Dmitri Prigov (1940–2007) was a conceptualist poet, artist, creator of numerous performances and installations, and theoretician of postmodernism. His immense poetic legacy comprised tens of thousands of texts, from which these poems are among the most popular. Working primarily as an author of samizdat, without seeking entry into "official" Soviet literature, from the early 1970s onward Prigov developed methods of poetic writing intended to subvert and undermine the discursive foundations of Soviet culture. The most important of these methods was to generate texts that on the surface could be regarded as nothing more than the product of a writing obsession or "graphomania." These texts represent a special kind of *skaz*. Whereas, in classic *skaz*, the writer creates the image of "another person's speech" (usually stylistically anomalous and culturally distanced), here Prigov creates the image of "another person's consciousness," that is, the consciousness of an ordinary Soviet individual who fancies himself a poet. This quasi-poet is not endowed with any particular faculty of introspection, and he translates the norms and concepts of a banal consciousness into verse that is unintentionally absurdist. Prigov himself called this project that of "the ideal poet," by which he meant "a poet who has described and covered the world to an adequate degree with his words."[3]

Poems like the ones treated in this chapter constituted the large meta-cycle "Housework" ("Domashnee khoziaistvo"), which Prigov began in about 1976 and continued until the mid-1980s and the start of Perestroika. And, whereas Prigov's other poems are typically perceived as satires of a Soviet mode of consciousness, the neoprimitivist poems of "Housework" provoke an entirely different response. For instance, Andrei Zorin, one of the first critics to write about Prigov in the Perestroika press, argued that the laughter triggered by these poems by Prigov is born of the joy of discovery: "the discovery, in the mendacious and ideologized world of Soviet sociality, [of] a sphere of pure, unadulterated personal experience."[4] And the poet Alexander Barash asserted that, in these poems, Prigov had created an "Encyclopedia of the Little Man. A Thesaurus of everyday situations (the street, the shop, the wait in line, cooking, sitting by a window)." For Barash, the poems provide "a legitimization of the human—of what remains of it after everything that has been done to it. And in the form in which it remains. If you don't like this, then your quarrel is not with the person showing it, but with history."[5]

In the introduction to his samizdat collection *Poems of Fall Winter 1978* (1978) Prigov defined his method as "high parody," counterposing it to satire. To Prigov's way of thinking "satire aspires to demonstrate the absence of the subject of description by stylistic means, or its complete lack of correspondence to the 'genuinely' existing phenomenon."[6] "High parody" pursues a different goal: by employing "someone else's" stylistic register, this method is intended to "elucidate the essential nature of the time that is materialized in the style, at the point of its attachment to eternity. And the parodist is motivated (I specifically emphasize this point) by love for the living reality of the subject of description."[7]

Enlarging upon this principle in relation to Prigov's "Housework" poems, we may assume that here "the point of attachment to eternity" is everyday routine. Although tinted in Soviet hues, routine is nonetheless absolutely universal, consisting as it does of washing the dishes, taking out the trash, standing in line, doing the laundry, tidying the apartment, preparing food, feeding one's child, examining fellow passengers in the subway, and so on. Routine is what theoreticians such as Michel de Certeau and Pierre Bourdieu define as the practice of everyday life, namely the most persistent (albeit imperfectly articulated) "grammars" of a social, cultural, and historical way of life. And, according to Prigov, it represents the "Officially Unapproved Foundations of Life" (which was the title of his 1985 samizdat collection of poems).

Indeed, even now, almost half a century after they were written, in some surprising fashion these poems retain their freshness and humor. It is tempting to declare unwashed dishes an "eternal" theme (especially if you do not have to wash them), with roots that can be traced back anthropologically to a mythology of chaos and to the ancient motif of dirt as embodying the penetration of nature into culture and the instability of the cultural order. Prigov actually foregrounds this theme in one of the poems considered here, writing, "I wrestle with domestic entropy." But the other two texts, together with several others about washing the dishes, suggest a completely different conception associated with the subject. It is interesting that, despite their conceptual differences, the poems under discussion resemble each other not only in exploiting the motif of washing the dishes, but also in their form: all are iambic eight-line stanzas with an alternating rhyme scheme (with only a single exception). Formal similarity is not only a principle of coherence defining these three works as a distinctive subset. Microscopic variations in prosody, minimally conveying congruence and difference, provided Prigov with the means to embody conceptual subtleties.

Let us examine them in order. The first poem, "I've spent all my life washing dishes," which was included in the cycle "Extremely Meager Consolations" (1980), represents this activity as synonymous with existence and even as a parallel with "sublime poetry" (lines 1–4):

Я всю жизнь свою провел в мытье посуды
И в сложении возвышенных стихов
Мудрость жизненная вся моя отсюда
Оттого и нрав мой тверд и несуров

I've spent all my life washing dishes
And composing poems most sublime
And this has lent me all of my life's wisdom
And made my temperament firm and mild

An opposition between high and low has been canceled here: the humdrum domestic concern for the cleanness of plates and cups (low) and writing poetry (high) are both dedicated to the same goal, namely, maintaining harmony. Of course, the image of a sage occupied exclusively with washing dishes and composing poetry is patently absurd. The third line, "And this has lent me all of my life's wisdom," emphasizes the point musically by giving a distinctive stress to the first foot of the Russian: *Mudrost' zhiznennaya vsia moia otsiuda*. In the other lines, there is a pyrrhic foot at this point; moreover, this line is also marked by a minor stylistic inexactitude, since it is not clear to what *otsiuda* (lit. "from there") refers (i.e., where exactly the source of wisdom is located, whether in washing dishes or in composing sublime poetry).

The second quatrain, written in trochaic pentameter and hexameter with a caesura following the fifth syllable and alternating masculine and feminine rhymes, is highly reminiscent of Alexandrine verse (a twelve-syllable line with a caesura after the sixth syllable and strictly alternating masculine and feminine rhymes), the meter of neoclassical verse tragedies:

Вот течет вода—ее я постигаю
За окном внизу—народ и власть
Что не нравится—я просто отменяю
А что нравится—оно вокруг и есть

I watch the water flow and comprehend it
Below my window—the people and the powers
Whatever I don't like I simply overrule it
And what I like is all surrounding me

This solemn verse represents a "formula" of harmony, elaborated around two oppositions; one is "objective," connoting nature/society; the other is subjective, expressing "I don't like"/"I like." The solemnity of the poem's tone is in stark contrast with the primitiveness of its logic. The translator has subtly conveyed this primitive quality with a tautological rhyme: "I watch the water flow and comprehend it [. . .] Whatever I don't like I simply overrule it." And, after all, the grandiloquent wisdom proves to be a sham: the comprehension of water flowing out of a faucet tells us no more about nature than the banal phrase "the people and the powers" does about society. There is a comic Hegelianism to the formulation "Whatever I don't like I simply overrule it / And what I like is all surrounding me," and it renders revealed moments of harmony indistinguishable from blindness and self-deception. The only residue remaining from this verse is the motif of height—"*Below* my window"—which fits well with the "poems most sublime" of the first verse. Both illusory harmony and illusory wisdom serve here as the foundations for the "height" that is the a priori position of the poet, and all of his efforts to "harmonize" the world amount to nothing more than trying to maintain this height.

The next poem is taken from Prigov's large sequences "Forty Banal Reflections on Banal Themes" (1982). The banality is expressed in the way in which washing the dishes, and in general everything connected with daily routine, is presented here as subjugation of the individual personality, and how the poet, obliged to waste his precious time on household activities, portrays himself as a martyr:

Только вымоешь посуду
Глядь—уж новая лежит
Уж какая тут свобода
Тут до старости б дожить
Правда, можно и не мыть
Да вот тут приходят разные
Говорят: посуда грязная—
Где уж тут свободе быть

Just when you've finished up the dishes
Look—a whole new pile awaits
What kind of freedom is this
Just let me make it to old age
True, you could just not wash them
But then various people come by
And say: the dishes are dirty
What kind of space for freedom here

In the dishes and freedom, we see an opposition that reappears as the contrast between "I" and "various people." It is no coincidence that, in Russian, the word for "various people" (*raznye*) is emphasized in the only paired rhyme in all three poems, and this rhyme is with the word "dirty" (*griaznaia*): *Da vot tut prikhodiat raznye / Govoriat posuda griaznaia* ("But then various people come by / And say: the dishes are dirty"). Apparently, the only thing these "various people" know is how to soil the dishes before reproaching the poet for having dirty plates. These folks are the ones who deprive him, the poet, of his freedom. Unable to bear "their" reproaches, he submits to the pressure and renounces freedom for the sake of his routine obligations. But the pain and suffering remain. (Although, of course, "you could just not wash them.")

This melodramatic logic is undermined not only by the rather truculent tone of the poet's complaints, but also by the form of the poem. It is written in trochaic tetrameter, a standard meter of Russian poetry since the Pushkin period. This poem astonishes in the way its mere eight verses encompass masculine, feminine, and dactylic line endings, featuring both primitive verbal rhymes (*lezhit/dozhit', byt'/myt'*) and an elegant root rhyme (*posuda/svoboda*). These rhymes themselves suggest a logic contrary to the one that is explicitly asserted: for the poet, dishes are opposed to freedom, but the weak rhyme connects them after all. Existence, says the subject of the poem, is incompatible with washing plates, but the rhyme (*byt'/myt'*) testifies to the opposite. The tautological repetition of *uzh* ("already") also creates an internal connection between dishes and freedom: *Gliad'—uzh novaia lezhit / Uzh kakaia tut svoboda* ("Look—a whole new pile awaits / What kind of freedom is this," lines 2–3).

The poem "I wrestle with domestic entropy" was written by Prigov as part of the cycle "Poems of the Transitional Era" (1983). It presents the act of dishwashing as an arduous conflict on a mythological scale:

Я с домашней борюсь энтропией
Как источник энергьи божественной
Незаметные силы слепые
Побеждаю в борьбе неторжественной
В день посуду помою я трижды
Пол помою-протру повсеместно
Мира смысл и структуру я зиждю
На пустом вот казалось бы месте

I wrestle with domestic entropy
As a source of energy divine
These forces, inglorious and blind,
I overcome in quiet unsung struggle
I'll wash the dishes three times a day
Wash and scrub the floor all over
I'll build the meaning and structure of the world
On this place that seems like it is empty

Here the poet equates dirty dishes and chaos—"these forces, inglorious and blind"—and unhesitatingly identifies himself with "a source of energy divine." The first verse, written in the fully stressed anapest trimeter, sounds like a march or a hymn to the poet as a godlike creator of world order. But, standing out against the background of predominantly feminine line endings, the dactylic rhyme *Kak istochnik energ'i bozhEstvennoi* [...] *Pobezhdaiu v bor'bie netorzhEstvennoi*, in combination with the old-fashioned contraction of *energii* to *energ'i* ("energy"), lends a parodic ring to this hymn. Ainsley Morse has conveyed this breakdown of the triumphant intonation with a breach of normal word order in "As a source of energy divine."

The second verse is constructed on the counterpoint of its first two lines with the last two. The first two, devoted to housework, are shot through with alliterations: *Pol pomoiu-protru povsemestno* ("Wash and scrub the floor all over"). They lend material tangibility even to a description of such household activities. The following two lines shift from concrete imagery to an abstract affirmation of the inherent passion of these activities: "I'll build the meaning and structure of the world / On this place that seems like it is empty" (*Mira smysl i strukturu ia zizhdiu / Na pustom vot kazalos' by meste*).

However, lurking within this boastful assertion of the triumph of order over chaos, there is a shift of perception. First, the correct, first-person form of the old Russian verb *zizhdit'* ("to build, to raise up") would be *zizhdu*. The actual conjugation used here, *zizhdiu*, is incorrect and sounds comical. Second, the absence of punctuation marks around the comment clause "that seems like" (*vot kazalos' by*) creates an intonational hiatus in the final line, which reveals the internal contradiction unnoticed by the poet. If "meaning and structure" are created "on this place that [...] is empty," then what is it that the poet "wash[es] and scrub[s]" so strenuously in the first two lines? Anything other than emptiness?

The contradiction is not only logical, but also philosophical. On the one hand, the poem asserts that, in his everyday struggle against "domestic entropy," the poet creates the "meaning and structure" of the world. But, on the other hand, it turns out that the world submerged in chaos is indistinguishable from emptiness, and there is nothing intelligible in it. Consequently, in creating a world of meaning, the poet shifts from the reality of concrete phenomena into a world of abstract, intangible ideas, intended to justify all his tireless activity. Yet in the process they erase reality, reducing it to emptiness.

Dissimilar structures can be discerned in these three poems: epic, melodramatic, and mythological approaches develop around the theme of dirty dishes. In one way or another, they all structure the position of the poet with respect to daily routine. In the first case, routine is cast as a part of the poet's sterile and sublime world. In the second, routine serves as an agent of "others," of society, seeking to subjugate the poet and thus depriving him of his freedom. In the third case, the poet exploits daily routine as the battlefield for waging his struggle against universal chaos, whereby he creates order and meaning. In all three cases, however, the very fabric of the poem sabotages the poet's ambitions, rendering each poem farcical.

What are Prigov and his readers laughing at together? In the early 1980s, more or less at the same time he composed his poems about dirty dishes, one of his contemporaries, the Soviet philosopher Merab Mamardashvili, described the human individual commensurate with the anthropological catastrophe that occurred in the twentieth century in the following terms:

> This indescribably strange person is not tragic, but absurd and ludicrous, especially in his flights of quasi-sublime exaltation. This is a comedy of the impossibility of tragedy, the monstrous grimace of some unearthly kind of "sublime suffering." It is impossible to take seriously a situation in which an individual looks for the truth in the same way as he looks for the toilet, and vice versa—while actually only looking for the toilet, he fancies it to be truth, or even justice (such, for instance, is Joseph K. in Franz Kafka's novel *The Trial*). Ludicrous, inept, pompous, absurd, some kind of tedious rigmarole, something otherworldly.[8]

Prigov writes his poems *from the viewpoint of this individual,* who, while merely washing the dishes, fancies that he is creating universal harmony and waging a struggle for freedom. This is the character of Prigov's poet. Like this individual, his poet is also "not tragic, but absurd and ludicrous, especially in his flights of quasi-sublime exaltation." The definition "a comedy of the impossibility of tragedy" proves an apposite description of all of Prigov's oeuvre, and of these poems in particular. Why is tragedy impossible? Probably because the "transcendent" or the "sublime" has been irretrievably lost in modern culture. Or because the only representative of "eternity" is this same routine. After all, has there ever been a time when the dishes have not needed to be washed?

Prigov's world reveals how obsolete and archaic a romantic conception of the poet as mediator between the sordid world of social reality and daily routine, between the prosaic and the ideal universe of eternal meanings and ideals, has become. In fact, he suggests that it is entirely without foundation. The comedy derives precisely from the situation of a modern individual trying on for size, one way or another, the romantic poet's laurel—or crown of thorns. Each and every time, the outcome turns out to be parodic and ludicrous, even though the poet's obliviousness renders the falsity of the romantic position obvious and comical.

Although Prigov may well not have suspected it at the time, poems written in 1980, 1982, and 1983, respectively, about dishes and a romantic poet can be perceived as snapshots of the final years of the Soviet era and reactions to this turn of history. The year 1980 was the high point of "late socialism," subsequently dubbed "the age of Stagnation." Milestones included the beginning of the war in Afghanistan, the death of Vladimir Vysotsky, about which people learned exclusively from the reports of Western radio stations, and the Moscow Olympic Games, boycotted by the majority of world powers. At the same time, the word "eternity" never occurred more frequently in contemporary literature and journalism than it did at that time.[9] Time itself had come to a standstill, suggesting that the status quo would never change. This is the condition the character in the poem "I've spent all my life washing dishes" faces, justifying the "eternity" of stagnation with sterile pretensions to celestial status. Prigov's attitude to this "Hegelianism" is made quite clear in the title of the cycle to which this poem belongs: "Extremely Meager Consolations."

In 1982, Brezhnev died, and, while outwardly nothing changed, a certain hope or perhaps more the shadow of a hope for change became perceptible. This is the condition conveyed by the feeble rebellion of Prigov's poet, who has begun hankering after freedom even as he suppresses the seditious thought that "true, you could just not wash [the dishes]." In 1983, the shadow of hope was banished by the attempts of Yury Andropov, the general secretary of the Communist Party, to "tighten the screws," the shooting down of a South Korean airliner, and the persecution of underground writers. Prigov's poet reacts to these changes in heroic fashion by returning to his kitchen emigration and once again endowing a struggle for cleanliness with the significance of an exalted battle against universal chaos. However, this heroic gesture is essentially bathetic and pointless, since it deprives the heroic activity itself of meaning by transforming it into "tidying up a void."

Taken together, these poems can be read as an existential chronicle of the last years of the Soviet era. They contain comical reactions to the extremely tragic condition that was defined by Alexander Blok at the very beginning of Soviet history as a "lack of air,"[10] and, in the denouement of this historical chapter, Prigov subjected attempts at the romantic elevation of passivity and conformism to merciless mockery. In conclusion, we may recall that to Prigov's mind the motivating impulse of his "high parody," a feature manifested so fully in his "Housework" poems, is "love for the living reality of the subject of description." In other words, this is a love of washing the dishes, no more, no less. And if this love did not exist—neither would the poems.

24

Elena Shvarts, "A Rubbish Heap" (1983)

AN ODE TO ROT

Свалка

Нет сил воспеть тебя, прекрасная помойка!
Как на закате, разметавшись, ты лежишь со
всклоченною головой
И черный кот в манишке белой колко
Терзает, как пьянист, живот тяжелый твой.
Вся в зеркалах гниющих, в их протресках
Полынь высокая растет,
О—ты Венеция! (и лучше бы Венецья)
И гондольером кот поет.
Турецкого клочок дивана
В лиловой тесноте лежит
И о Стамбуле, о кальяне
Бурьяну тихо говорит.
В гниющих зеркалах дрожит лицо июля.
Ворона медленно на свалку опустилась
И вот—она идет, надменнее, чем Сулла,
И в цепкой лапе—гибель или милость.
Вот персик в слизи, вспухи ягод, лупа,
Медали часть, от книги корешок
Ты вся в проказе или ты—ожог,
Ребенок, облитый кипящим супом.
Ты—Дионис, разодранный на части,
Иль мира зеркальце ручное?
Я говорю тебе—О Свалка,

Зашевелись и встань. Потом,
О монстр, о чудище ночное,
Заговори охрипло рваным ртом.
Зашевелись и встань, прекрасная помойка!
Воспой, как ты лежишь под солнцем долго,
Гиганта мозгом пламенея, зрея,
Все в разложеньи съединяя, грея,
Большою мыслью процвети, и гной
Как водку пей, и ешь курины ноги.
Зашевелись, прекрасная, и спой!
О Rosa mystica, тебя услышат боги![1]

Rubbish Heap

I haven't the strength to sing your glories, resplendent rubbish heap!
How you lie sprawled at sunset, a matted tousle,
And a black cat in his white bib picks and rips
A tune, like a pianist, in your heavy torso.
In all your rotting mirrors, in their shivers
The tall wormwood grows,
O you, Venice! (even better than Venezia)
And the cat, like a gondolier, mews.
A scrap from a Turkish divan
Lies in lilac clutter
Murmuring to the steppe grass
Of Istanbul, of the hookah.
July's face trembles in a rotting mirror.
A crow descends slowly on the midden
And watch her stalk, prouder than Sulla
And her claws hold: death or pardon.
See—peach slime, berries' swollen burst, a loupe
Part of a medallion, a book's empty cover
You—your leprous pocks, or are they scalds,
A child burned by boiling soup.
Dionysus torn asunder,
Or pocket mirror to the world.
I am speaking to you, Rubbish Heap,
Stir yourself. Arise. And then, O monster,

rasping from your ripped lips. Night outcast,
Stir yourself! Arise! O wondrous tip
Sing of how you lie so long in the sun's heat,
Your flaming, ripening giant's brain
Baking, consumed by decay.
Let bloom your great thoughts, sup on rot
like vodka, chew a chicken wing
Stir yourself, most wonderful being, and sing!
O Rosa Mystica, the gods are listening.

(TRANSLATED BY SASHA DUGDALE)

Elena Shvarts (1948–2010) was recognized as a star of Leningrad's underground poetry scene in the 1970s and 1980s. Even as a very young woman, she had her share of fame and success, but only outside official cultural institutions. Her original talent and mastery of poetic form were coupled with a natural nonconformism of character: she was unwilling, indeed unable, to compromise and accept the rules of official culture. The Soviet literary canon suffocated her, and she couldn't stand a "professional" approach to literature. She felt much more at home in a theatrical setting, where literature was perceived as a raw material for performance. Her mother, Dina Shvarts, headed the literary department at the Bolshoi Drama Theater under legendary director Georgy Tovstonogov, and Elena grew up in this eminent theater, absorbing its artistic atmosphere. She enrolled at the School of Philology at Leningrad State University, eventually leaving and taking her degree from the Department of Theater Studies at the less prestigious Leningrad Institute of Theater, Music, and Film. Proficient in several languages, Shvarts earned her keep by translating Western plays for Leningrad theaters.

She began writing poetry as a teenager. When Akhmatova rejected Elena's work, calling her *zlaia* (a word whose shades of meaning can range between "angry" and "malicious"), Shvarts had the chutzpah to accuse the great Akhmatova of narcissism: "She sees nothing but herself!"[2] Shvarts managed to combine nonconformism with a precocious belief in her own greatness, and a propensity for scandal and physical fights (especially when intoxicated) with a reverent, priestly attitude toward poetry as a magical practice. A Shvarts lyric often boldly violates propriety and boundaries. Tellingly, her favorite poetic figures include the eternal rebel Marina Tsvetaeva and the early Mayakovsky. Early on, Shvarts also decided matters of her own artistic taste. She rejected both "the slaughterhouse of *vers libre* (nothing but bad prose)" and "artificial classicism," explaining: "My preference is the line between harmony and dodecaphony. I dreamed of finding a rhythm that would change with each turn in the course of thought, with each new feeling or sensation."[3]

Before Perestroika, Shvarts only published her poems in the West; in her home country, they circulated as samizdat copies. The readings she gave in private apartments drew huge audiences, even though her poems were almost devoid of political content. Instead, their key themes were aesthetic and philosophical. Dmitry Volchek, publisher of the samizdat magazine *Mitin Zhurnal*, recalled his impressions of Shvarts's readings:

> I first saw Elena Shvarts in the basement on Petr Lavrov Street, where underground writers gathered: she was reading *The Labors and the Days of Nun Lavinia*.[4] It was a strange phenomenon, as if an actress from a theater for elves or dragonflies had by mistake entered the stage in the human world . . . I remember some ridiculous discussion at the Writers Union, a fat man in a brown suit who ran the poetry department [at the Writers Union][5] mumbled something about Elena Shvarts, using the word "blasphemy," but it was clear that he was just scared: everything he and those other clay people did was dust, was nothing after her poems.[6]

The sources of Shvarts's poetry range across an impressive set of influences, from the syllabic poetry of the baroque and the symbolist understanding of poetry as theodicy, to the futurist rejection of cultural hierarchy and the acmeist attention to corporeality and materiality. Shvarts said of herself: "I am a complicated person. My unconscious is premodern, my consciousness is medieval, and my eye is baroque."[7] The contemporary poet and critic Alexander Skidan argues that her aesthetics are the direct opposite of Joseph Brodsky's "neoclassicism": "Brodsky is all about culture (his poems contain an entire gallery of statues, busts, and torsos), his favorite trope is petrification putting an end to historical and cultural metamorphoses. Shvarts is theatrical, and her theatricality has its origins in medieval mysteries and parodies, with their carnivalization, their topsy-turvy inner and outer worlds."[8] The critic Oleg Dark speaks of the distinctive humor of her poetry:

> The comical in Elena Shvarts's work is of the same essence as that of the baroque poets (in the tragedies of Calderon or the last plays of Shakespeare), in Gozzi's fairy tales or the work of the German Romantics (among Russian poets, only V[ladimir] Odoevsky had a funny bone like this)—a long, never interrupted

> tradition of ontological mockery. It has its origins in the strange humor of the Gnostics: to them, the very connection between the material and the spiritual, body and soul, is funny.[9]

Baroque, or rather neobaroque, is a comparatively (albeit not fully) accurate description for Elena Shvarts's original version of modernism. Baroque sensibilities appear in the grotesque combination of extreme abstraction with physiological concreteness, of beauty and ugliness, of metaphysical quests with a sense of a hopelessly conflictual world order inalterable by death or even immortality. The baroque tradition forces Shvarts to shift the borders of metaphysical oppositions. This was for her a matter of certainty: "Where there is darkness, there is light, all of the world is mutilated . . ."[10] In her poetry, the baroque appears as a form of irony that reveals the anti-value behind the value and the nightmare behind the idyll. But, far from replacing the idyll with the nightmare, this irony unites them. It is here that we can see that a crucial principle of Shvarts's artistic philosophy, again consistent with the baroque, is her predilection for oxymorons.

From this point of view, it is not at all surprising to find Shvarts composing a fervent ode to a rubbish heap. In her portrayal, the garbage dump embodies the identity of the repugnant and the sublime, the physiological and the spiritual: "Your flaming, ripening giant's brain / Baking, consumed by decay" (lines 28–29). The text of the poem is a stream of metamorphoses, in which a stray cat turns first into a pianist and then into a gondolier, a crow into a Roman dictator, the remains of things into Dionysus who has been torn apart—things bloom into decay. Finally, the rubbish heap itself turns first into a beautiful woman, then into a monster ("Stir yourself. Arise. And then, O monster . . . ," line 24), and finally into the Virgin Mary, albeit one in a theology with multiple gods: "O Rosa Mystica, the gods are listening" (line 33).

Moreover, the rubbish heap in this poem is strikingly international, almost universal, bearing traces of Venice, Turkey, ancient Rome ("And watch her stalk, prouder than Sulla," line 15).[11] Finally, the mentions of Dionysus and the Rosa Mystica sanctify the rubbish heap with motifs of ancient Greek and Christian mythology. Related to this universalism is the recurring image of the looking glass: the words "rotting mirror" appear twice in the poem. Another mirror occurs in proximity to the mention of Dionysus: "Dionysus torn asunder, / Or pocket mirror to the world" (lines 21–22). Dionysus was torn apart by the Titans but was reborn to a new life from his preserved heart. The comparison of the rubbish heap with Dionysus suggests an infinite process of metamorphoses, the unstoppable transformation of destruction into creation, fragmentation into a new wholeness. The world is always in a state of chaotic decay, and even mirrors rot in tandem with the world reflected in them. Moreover, both Dionysus and the mirror are combined in the unnamed theme of poetry, which the rubbish heap seems to symbolize. We can also surmise that the phrase "Dionysus torn asunder" alludes to the death of Orpheus, dismembered by the maenads driven to a frenzy by his music.

In a short article titled "Three Features of My Poems" ("Tri osobennosti moikh stikhov," 1996), Shvarts highlights what are to her the most important characteristics of her poetics. All "three features" appear prominently in "A Rubbish Heap." First, universalism:

> I was walking along the road and thinking: in the poems, as in a taiga hut, a traveler should find everything he needs in case of emergency—matches, bread, salt, an axe, a well nearby. Quickly rummaging through the poems, I found it all.
>
> But then it turned out that you can find more in them—you name it: musical instruments, work tools, almost all birds, animals, abstract concepts, flowers, clothes, money, dishes . . . Though I'm not a describer of the everyday, by no means. Of course, not all the objects that exist are in my poems, but there are all kinds of them, row by row, though in these rows, as in a broken comb, a couple of teeth are missing.[12]

Tellingly, while developing this thesis, Shvarts introduces the image of the mirror (*zerkalo*): "I have repeated this world syllable by syllable, following the Creator, as much of it as my eyes could find—a variation on the song of the Demiurge. A compendium of the world encased in a tiny ball and poisoned with pain. This is my message to the Creator, a tiny mirror."[13]

The second feature she describes in her essay is her penchant for transformations: "I am irresistibly drawn to metamorphosis. Like Ovid. Everything turns into everything. Sirius into a drunkard, a Wolf into a Lion, a human being into a bouquet of flowers, into a tower, a cicada, a bird, a living grave; a murderer into a victim. Man into God. And so on."[14]

In addition to these elements of universalism and metamorphoses, a third feature reveals something less than obvious about "A Rubbish Heap." Shvarts writes:

> There are not many themes and motifs in world poetry. I happened to stumble upon a few quite new ones. For example: "Lovers at a Funeral," "A Strange Treat," "Elegy on the X-Ray Picture of My Skull," "How Andrey Bely Almost Got Hit by a Tram," "Washing My Hair in a Storm," "The Invisible Hunter" (about the metaphysics of birthmarks). Or one about a man overgrown with flowers—"The Animal Flower," etc.

> Not to mention the long poems: *Hiumbi*, about the creation of a new human type through spiritual alchemy. Or my book about Lavinia, who lives in a multi-faith monastery that is Orthodox, Catholic, and Buddhist at the same time.[15]

One might argue about the actual novelty of the themes, whose discovery Shvarts considers to be her achievement. What matters more is what unites them: not just a juxtaposition of opposites, but *an oxymoronic juxtaposition* of incompatible elements and categories, sometimes arousing horror (looking at an X-ray of one's own skull) or disgust (tasting a girlfriend's milk), sometimes generating new hybrids, such as the "animal flower" or the human bird Hiumbi, and sometimes leading to the discovery of unexpected similarities between distant phenomena, like the scattering of moles on the body and the map of the starry sky in "The Invisible Hunter."

In Shvarts's view, the oxymoron is arguably the key poetic trope. As mentioned, it corresponds most closely to her own "baroque vision." The poet and critic Oleg Yuryev perceptively wrote about this vision's philosophical implications. In Shvarts's poems,

> the world emerges in a special state—carnivalesque and terrible, oscillating between death and life—*smertozhizn'*, deathlife, as she once called it herself, following Samuel Coleridge ["Life-in-Death"]. This deathlife, this special zone of existence, can be unsafe for the ordinary consciousness, physically frightening when not dressed in carnival attire—but the constant spiritual effort of the poet transforms, as it should, the rough into the sublime, horror into catharsis.[16]

Echoing Yuryev, Valery Shubinsky writes of Shvarts: "William Blake has a shocking engraving. It depicts a classic statue—Laocoon. The caption reads, 'Yahweh with his sons, Adam and Lucifer.' Shvarts goes even further, explicitly stating 'the identity of Adam and Lucifer.'"[17]

A rubbish heap is also a depiction of what can be called *deathlife*, a macabre carnival of things and ideas that had once been of value. Almost every line of this poem spills over with oxymorons, from "resplendent rubbish heap" (repeated twice in the original) to the rhyme *gnoi/spoi* (lit. "pus"/"sing," lines 31 and 33 in the Russian, lines 30 and 32 in the English). The "identity of Adam and Lucifer" translates into the mediating role played by garbage, which brings together West and East, Rome and Greece, paganism and Christianity, nature—wormwood, weeds ("lilac clutter" in the translation, line 10), "peach slime, berries' swollen burst" (line 17)—and culture; a cat and a crow, "a child burned by boiling soup" (line 20), and the Rosa Mystica (line 33).

The form of "A Rubbish Heap" could also be called oxymoronic, and in this connection its rhythm is revealing. Based on predominantly iambic pentameter, the meter frequently transforms into iambic tetrameter. It is also disrupted by the outrageously long second line, then by the unfixed caesura (especially in lines 23–24) and by the abrupt shortening of lines. The few lines that feature no rhythmical interruption compensate by featuring a bathetic contrast between a more solemn rhythm and "low" content, dealing with stray cats, rotten fruit, vodka, and chicken legs. One cannot but agree again with Oleg Dark's observation that "rhythm, or rather, arrhythmia (the disorganization of habitual rhythmic activity) seems to be the aim and object of Elena Shvarts's efforts [. . .] This is what her poems are all about."[18]

In this context, "A Rubbish Heap" may also be understood as a polemical response to Akhmatova's famous poem from her "Secrets of Craft," analyzed earlier:

> If you only knew from what rubbish
> Poems grow, not knowing any shame . . . [19]

For Akhmatova, poems are like flowers: they transform "rubbish," compost, into beauty. For Shvarts, by contrast, rubbish itself, its decay and disintegration, *is* beauty. Or rather, the *new* beauty extolled by Shvarts, who combines all these elements and on an equal footing: the Virgin Mary and Venice, but also pus, slime, and putrefaction. The *deathlife* of the rubbish heap ensures the *liberation* from both hierarchies and boundaries of time and space. This text—and, more generally, the concept of poetry proposed by Shvarts—perfectly suits Bakhtin's definition of the carnival as "a temporary abolition of all hierarchical relations, privileges, norms, and prohibitions [. . .] a true feast of time, a feast of formation, change, and renewal."[20]

Moreover, Bakhtin's theory of the carnivalesque includes "a special language of carnival forms and symbols" that is "characterized by a peculiar logic of inversion [. . .] by the 'topsy-turvy,' the 'inside out,' the logic of top and bottom, of face and ass, incessantly changing places; by various types of parody and travesty, of lowering, profanation, buffoonish crowning and uncrowning."[21] These characteristics are fully applicable to the model of culture created in "A Rubbish Heap," foregrounding its logic of inversion (destruction as creation) and its pathos of rebirth and renewal central to the Bakhtinian concept of carnival. There is, however, one difference: despite his theoretical declarations ("pure negation is completely alien to popular culture"),[22] all the examples the theorist gives in his book on Rabelais testify only to a downward movement into the "underworld of meanings." "A Rubbish Heap" shows the reverse trajectory of metamorphosis by elevating the dirty and disgusting to the splendid and sublime.

Strikingly, the basis of Shvarts's poem is the eighteenth-century genre formally cognate with neoclassical tragedy, namely, the ode. This is perhaps the most jarring oxymoron of all. Traditionally associated with the apotheosis of *order* personified by *power,* here the ode becomes an image of chaos and unabashed disorder. Inspired by the ode, Shvarts employs its tropes in such rhetorical gestures as the apostrophe addressing the praised object: "I haven't the strength to sing of you, resplendent rubbish heap!" (line 1); "O you, Venice! (even better than Venezia)" (line 7); "[You] Dionysus torn asunder" (line 21); "Stir yourself! Arise! O wondrous tip / Sing of how you lie so long in the sun's heat" (lines 26–27); "Stir yourself, most wonderful being, and sing! / O Rosa Mystica, the gods are listening" (lines 32–33).

The Formalist literary theorist and scholar of Russian versification Yury Tynyanov wrote that the ode as an oratorical genre "was formed out of two reciprocal principles: the principle of maximum impact at any given moment, and the principle of verbal development and elaboration."[23] In Shvarts, both sources are presented as successive models resolved by an apotheosis. Lines 3 through 12 follow the same model—description ("development and elaboration") appears in the odd line, the action in the even one:

И черный кот в манишке белой колко
Терзает, как пьянист, живот тяжелый твой.
Вся в зеркалах гниющих, в их протресках
Полынь высокая растет,
О—ты Венеция! (и лучше бы Венецья)
И гондольером кот поет.
Турецкого клочок дивана
В лиловой тесноте лежит
И о Стамбуле, о кальяне
Бурьяну тихо говорит.

And a black cat in his white bib picks and rips
A tune, like a pianist, in your heavy torso.
In all your rotting mirrors, in their shivers
The tall wormwood grows,
Oh you, Venice! (even better than Venezia)
And the cat, like a gondolier, mews.
A scrap from a Turkish divan
Lies in lilac clutter
Murmuring to the steppe grass
Of Istanbul, of the hookah.

Then the action intensifies further, and, in lines 13–15, a verb appears in every line:

В гниющих зеркалах дрожит лицо июля.
Ворона медленно на свалку опустилась
И вот—она идет, надменнее, чем Сулла,

July's face trembles in a rotting mirror.
A crow descends slowly on the midden
And watch her stalk, prouder than Sulla

This fragment, emphasizing "the principle of maximum impact at any given moment" (to cite Tynyanov once again), is followed by a part consisting of a "verbal development and elaboration" expressed in a static description (lines 17–22), practically devoid of verbs (which are replaced by participles):

Вот персик в слизи, вспухи ягод, лупа,
Медали часть, от книги корешок
Ты вся в проказе или ты—ожог,
Ребенок, облитый кипящим супом.
Ты—Дионис, разодранный на части,
Иль мира зеркальце ручное?

See—peach slime, berries' swollen burst, a loupe
Part of a medallion, a book's empty cover
You—your leprous pocks, or are they scalds,
A child burned by boiling soup.
Dionysus torn asunder,
Or pocket mirror to the world.

Far from being calmly static, this descriptiveness, however, creates a tension to be resolved by a new outburst of action, that is, an apotheosis expressed by a series of imperatives. Taken together, these injunctions rouse garbage to become the subject of culture. Paraphrasing the biblical "Rise, take up thy bed, and walk," this call is additionally emphasized by anaphora: "Stir yourself. Arise" (twice, with variations in punctuation, lines 24 and 26), "Sing" (line 27), and "Stir yourself [. . .] and sing!"(line 32)

О монстр, о чудище ночное,
Заговори охрипло рваным ртом.
Зашевелись и встань, прекрасная помойка!
Воспой, как ты лежишь под солнцем долго,

[. . .]
Зашевелись, прекрасная, и спой!

I am speaking to you, Rubbish Heap,
Stir yourself. Arise. And then, O monster,
rasping from your ripped lips. Night outcast,
Stir yourself! Arise! O wondrous tip
Sing of how you lie so long in the sun's heat
[. . .]
Stir yourself, most wonderful being, and sing!

Astonishingly, this structural logic is recreated in Sasha Dugdale's translation with only the most minimal modifications. Moreover, by reducing the number of lines, she strengthens "the principle of maximum impact" by supplementing the anaphora with an enjambment.

Analyzing the odic tradition of words as monuments (with specific reference to Horace's "Exegi Monumentum") in Russian literature, Lev Pumpyansky wrote: "Indeed, the theme of greatness in poetry can only arise in an empire; an empire assumes itself to be eternal, not subject to such disasters as have happened in the past . . ."[24] In Shvarts's ode, the empire—or any trace of the state for that matter—is a gaping absence; nothing alludes to it whatsoever. The rubbish heap is clearly not subject to any powers that be; indeed, it is a state in itself, a universe in itself. In its oxymoronic fullness, it embodies sovereignty and autonomy. Thus, "A Rubbish Heap" can be read as a philosophical metaphor for freedom defined by rejecting all structure and organization—the freedom of chaos, one might say, which contains the fragments, splinters, and remnants of previous orders.

At the same time, despite its outwardly apolitical nature, this poem can be seen as an unexpectedly optimistic reaction to the state of historical deadlock, of stopped time, of the "end of history"—which was experienced acutely in the final years of the USSR (the poem was written in 1983). Within the Soviet empire, its disintegration felt not like a Western triumph and more like a self-defeat. Given the frequency of the metaphor of "the rubbish heap of history" (attributed to Trotsky, who probably had it from Petrarch) in Soviet official vocabulary, Shvarts's poem can be said to majestically address the mythical landfill, where the imperial utopia disposed of the cultural worlds not suited to its purposes. It is this very landfill that the poet sees as a source of new life and new culture, its semantic potential demonstrated by the new vigor it injects into the rhetorical devices of the ode.

Shvarts is far from arguing for restoration. We have seen that she is fascinated by unprecedented oxymoronic hybrids of heterogeneous cultural fragments, united by the spirit of decay and disintegration. The apostrophe addressed to the rubbish heap, scripting its new role, reads in effect like a call for a new language, a language capable of merging all the things to be found on the rubbish heap of history and of creating a bold and transgressive cultural universe from old ingredients. One might say that Shvarts's ode is a poetic manifesto of postmodernism with its eclecticism, hypertrophied intertextuality, and freedom from all canons. The poem is a real ode, written in a version of the high style and combined parodically with "inappropriate" material. However, Shvarts herself never considered herself a postmodernist and was in general somewhat suspicious of all -isms. Rather, she was attracted to the effect of *ostranenie* (defamiliarization) produced by unexpected incarnations of ancient myths.

25

Ry Nikonova, "furious furious rabious" (1985)

THREADING THE AVANT-GARDE

Бешенство, бешенство, взбешенство
кровь и взимание дынь
дым коромыслом и лешенством
леший жующий полынь.
Ляшебу, ляшему, лишнему
в рожу взимаю налог
голою бранью задвижиму
словом—в немой потолок!
Песенкой палец прищéмила
голову бритвою в таз
лесенкой слезы щенятся
чугунная мысль дребезжит.
Рифма, на бёдра твои обопрусь я
дай мне свободу в груди
тёплой струёю картины нарвусь я
стадо всех слов впереди.
Клык навострило скользящее
бегает Рык вереща
а вот и мое подлежащее
надлежащее дать мне леща
Богова Матерь не смотрит
я—мелочь
радостный день не оббит
сама попросила я бестолочь
выход и вход карапуз.[1]

furious furious rabious
blood and the withholding of the gourd
smoke of the yoke and the wood imp
impious gnaws a bitter straw.
Impietous impery! With impetus
my fist intracts your tax
with naked scorn enthrusted
& word at silent ceiling spat!
I caught my finger in a song
cutthroat head in a basin
ladder of tears tumbling puppies
castironthought clangs along.
Rhyme I lean my hands on your hips
give me space in my chest
warm stream of me pluck up
herding the words ahead
Slippy sharpens a fang
runs squealing Raptor-me
here my undergone
overborne slap me
Mother of God looks away
I am thruppence
the feast day unfrayed
I asked myself for nonsense
Exit and entry child

(TRANSLATED BY SASHA DUGDALE)

Anna Tarshis (1942–2014), who wrote under the pseudonym "Ry (or Rea) Nikonova" from 1981, was a true female champion (or Amazon, in the Russian) of the avant-garde, though her name is less well known than those of female visual artists like Varvara Stepanova, Alexandra Exter, or Natalia Goncharova. Ry Nikonova belongs to a much younger generation than the avant-gardists of the 1910s and 1920s. It was the recovery and development of the abandoned and forbidden discoveries of the avant-garde era that provided the main impetus of her diverse oeuvre, and her creation has encompassed avant-garde poems, including *zaum'*, experimental visual and sound versification, and attempts at a synthesis of various sciences and arts.

The poet and artist Boris Konstriktor, who knew her well, wrote:

> Ry was your basic ordinary genius [. . .] Her musical talents (all her life, she gave piano lessons) and her mathematical abilities, the special scientific and artistic arrangement of her mind enabled her to turn the whole machinery of art into a kind of home harpsichord, from which she extracted limitless kaleidoscopic combinations of letters, syllables, images, and words [. . .] It was an endless extravaganza, her creative energy seemed to have no limits.[2]

Ry and her husband Sergey Sigey (Sergey Sigov) did not merely love and study the Russian avant-garde. They believed their mission as artists (in the broadest sense of the word—literary, visual, transmedial) lay in reviving the violently interrupted history of the avant-garde in Russia. Between 1965 and 1974, while she undertook and completed her studies at the Sverdlovsk College of Music, both participated in the avant-garde group that later came to be called the Uktusskaya School, named after a mountain with a ramp located on the outskirts of Sverdlovsk.[3] The group consisted mainly of visual artists, but all its members were deeply interested in various manifestations of the avant-garde.

Having moved from Sverdlovsk to Yeisk, a small town in the southwest of Russia on the shore of the Sea of Azov, Nikonova and Sigey began publishing the samizdat magazine *Transponans* (1979–87) and calling themselves transfurists.[4] Both terms rely on the idea of transposition. One transfurist manifesto (1980) describes *transponirovanie* (transposition) as "the translation into another tone (semantic or formal) of one's own or someone else's work (not necessarily literary or artistic); relevant associations are also 'transcendental' in the sense of 'over,' 'above'—unusual enough to approach the supernatural—and 'transport' in the sense of moving any accents or phenomena (for example, from a past not fully understood and realized), etc."[5] Ilja Kukuj, a prominent scholar of transfurism, explains the term as follows: "*Transponirovanie* is based on the perception of the text as a palimpsest, in which every reader identifies hidden potentials of new meanings and in becoming an author constructs a new 'poetic organism.'"[6] According to Kukuj, "In the eight years of its existence, *Transponans* went from a slim pamphlet with mostly theoretical texts by its publishers to an exquisite album featuring the leading forces of contemporary Soviet literary avant-garde."[7] In addition to the leading representatives of the literary underground, the magazine continuously published the works of classic avant-gardist authors Ilya Zdanevich, Andrei Egunov, Kazimir Malevich, Aleksei

FIGURE 25.1. Mikhail Vrubel. *Pan* (1899). Public domain.

Kruchenykh, Daniil Kharms, Alexander Vvedensky, Alexander Tufanov, as well as the ego-futurist Vasilisk Gnedov and the last OBERIU member, Igor Bakhterev.[8]

It is in this context that Ry Nikonova's poem "furious furious rabious" appears. Published in 1985, in the twenty-sixth issue of *Transponans,* it belongs to her mature oeuvre. Atypically for her poetry, which is rarely metrical, this text is largely dactylic with some amphibraic feet (lines 12, 19, 20, 22, and 24). In Nikonova's poetry, rhymes are not typical, whereas here up to line 11 she maintains a regular alternation between dactylic (sometimes hyperdactylic) and masculine rhymes. From line 12, a more traditional alternation of feminine and masculine rhyme replaces this pattern, occasionally permitting the intrusion of dactylic rhymes (lines 17, 19, 24). The poem is rich in neologisms and agrammatisms brought about by the omission of verbs and a frequent use of rhymes made from parts of words. For example, *dyn'* (lit. "melons") in the second line rhymes not only with *polyn'* ("wormwood") at the end of line 4, but also with *dym* ("smoke") at the beginning of line 3. The neologism *vzbeshenstvo* ("rage," "frenzy," or "fury") draws on the noun *beshenstvo* and the verb *vzbesit'sia* ("to rage," "to go mad"). At the same time, the opening line (*Beshenstvo, beshenstvo, vzbeshenstvo*), in which all the words are united by a shared root and the consonance *sh,* is almost precisely mirrored in line 5 (*Liashebu, liashemu, lishnemu*). The word *leshii* (a Russian forest spirit) through its first appearance in the previous line generates a whole range of neologisms. While the first of these, *leshenstvo,* can be deciphered as an area belonging to a *leshii,* the words *liashebu* and *liashemu* (creatively and sensitively rendered by Sasha Dugdale as "Impietous impery! With impetus . . .") in fact convey no precise semantic meaning. Instead, they sound similar to swearing, heightening the overall expressiveness.

These and similar devices are in tune with the programmatic principles of the transfurists. They give the poetic text exceptional dynamism. Furthermore, they make it open to a multiplicity of interpretations. By replacing key concepts with neologisms, whose meaning is not entirely clear, the text turns into a kind of incantation or formula, its meanings fluid.

The poem begins with an image of sacred madness (frenzy) as the source of poetry. Supporting this interpretation of the first eight lines is the motif of wormwood (artemisia), a herb used in many Slavic rituals.[9] It gains further support in the motif of sacrifice ("blood and the withholding of the gourd") and the appearance of smoke (the food of the gods). However, the recipient of the sacrifice is neither Apollo nor Dionysus, but a *leshii,* that is, a forest spirit who embodies chaos. He is

> endowed with negative attributes and exhibits a certain "left" bent [. . .]: he closes the left side of his clothes on the right, puts his left *lapot'* on his right foot, etc. [. . .] In *bylichka* tales [a prosaic genre of Russian folkloric, free-form stories about spirits], he is a cursed man or [. . .] a malicious dead man. A *leshii* can scare people with his laughter or lead a child astray.[10]

At the same time, the *leshii* resembles Pan, the patron of poetry and companion of Dionysus, as can be seen in Mikhail Vrubel's famous painting *Pan* (1899), in which the Greek Pan bears a close resemblance to the Slavic *leshii.*

In his well-known book *The Tree of Life*, the nineteenth-century Russian folklorist Alexander Afanasiev describes the *leshii* less as a chaotic spirit and more as a mediator between people and the world of heavenly spirits.[11] To earn his favor, hunters make sacrifices to him:

> Whoever ventures to hunt a forest beast, must above all bring something as tribute/appeasement to the *leshii* in order that the hunt be successful and that the *leshii*, the mysterious master of the forest, not make the hunter lose his way. One would usually bring a piece of bread (or a pancake), with salt on top, and puts this offering on a stump.[12]

While Ry Nikonova's poem features no such details, it conjures negative associations with the image of the *leshii*, given greater density by the string of related neologisms that sound like swearing: *leshenstvo* [. . .] *liashebu, liashemu*. This chain ends with a lexical, understandable word: *lishnemu* (superfluous). The speaker's anger appears to be directed against this superfluous pseudo-deity, which for some reason receives the levy of poetic creativity: "my fist intracts your tax / with naked scorn enthrusted / & word at silent ceiling spat!" ("в рожу взимаю налог / голою бранью задвижиму / словом—в немой потолок!" [lines 6–8]). This last line is stressed by an exclamation point: the traditional link between poetry and transcendence is broken; instead of rising up to the heavens, the poetic word rests against the mute, *logos*-free ceiling. An ancient ritual is shattered by an act of rebellion induced by sacred madness and fury.

Arguably, this scene is a concise, "formulaic" reproduction of the avant-garde theomachy. A close parallel in terms of images and theme appears, for instance, in the finale of Vladimir Mayakovsky's 1914 poem *A Cloud in Trousers*:

> Я думал—ты всесильный божище,
> а ты недоучка, крохотный божик.
> Видишь, я нагибаюсь,
> из-за голенища
> достаю сапожный ножик.
> Крылатые прохвосты!
> Жмитесь в раю!
> Ерошьте перышки в испуганной тряске!
> Я тебя, пропахшего ладаном, раскрою
> отсюда до Аляски! [. . .]
>
> Эй, вы!
> Небо!
> Снимите шляпу!

Я иду!

Глухо.
Вселенная спит,
положив на лапу
с клещами звезд огромное ухо.[13]

I thought that you were the Great God, Almighty
But you're a miniature idol—a dunce in a suit,
Bending over, I'm already reaching
For the knife that I'm hiding
At the top of my boot.

You, swindlers with wings,
Huddle in fright!
Ruffle your shuddering feathers, rascals!
You, reeking of incense, I'll open you wide,
From here all the way to Alaska.

[. . .]
Hey you,
Heaven!
Take your hat off,
When you see me near!

Silence.
The universe sleeps.
Placing its paw
Under the black, star-infested ear.[14]

The similarity is emphasized by concrete parallels, such as the ones between Mayakovsky's deaf universe and Nikonova's silent ceiling, or between Mayakovsky's variations of the word "god" (*bog—bozhishche, bozhik*) and Nikonova's variations of the word *leshii*.

If we accept this parallel, we can assume that Nikonova begins her poem where Mayakovsky concludes his. Her starting point is the crisis of romantic poetry and its mythology based on the sacred role of the poet as a secular prophet, a role in which the poet is almost fated to become dependent on societal powers of one kind or another, whether the authorities (as in the case of Mayakovsky in the Soviet period) or their antagonists. According to the logic of the poem, the avant-garde gives an answer—or rather, a spectrum of answers—to the question of what new role poetry might play after abandoning the traditional connection with the transcendent. Though the word "avant-garde" does not appear in the poem, Ry Nikonova obliquely introduces the theme by means of transposition—by using and shifting images and themes associated with the most important representatives of the Russian avant-garde (lines 9–12):

Песенкой палец прищéмила
голову бритвою в таз
лесенкой слезы щенятся
чугунная мысль дребезжит.

I caught my finger in a song
cutthroat head in a basin
ladder of tears tumbling puppies
castironthought clangs along.

Unlike the previous and subsequent sections, this quatrain features no rhymes in the original (the rhythm is preserved), which differentiates it in the overall structure of the poem. Each line in this quatrain refers to at least one particular avant-garde poet. "I caught my finger in a song" brings to mind Vasilisk Gnedov (1890–1978), an ego-futurist whom Nikonova and Sigey held in high esteem, and with whom Sigey corresponded. A 1974 poem by Gnedov can be read as a commentary on this line, and indeed on the entire poem by Ry Nikonova:

Народные песенки	Folk songs
Спеть нельзя	Can't be sung
Без нотной лесенки	Without a ladder of notes
Орлом не взять	Can't just overtake them
Слова неплохие	The lyrics aren't bad
А голоса нет	But there's no voice
Говоришь а глухие	You speak but [they are] deaf/voiceless
Хочется петь	[You] want to sing
Надо пластинку	You need a [gramophone] record
Английский язык	English language
В платочке свинку	A piggy in a handkerchief
И хрюканья рык[15]	And a grunting growl[16]

Notably both a ladder (*lesenka*) and a growl (*ryk*) appear here, as they do in lines 11 and 18 of Nikonova's poem (with *ryk* turning into a proper name, rendered as "Raptor-me" by Sasha Dugdale). The most salient point is that Gnedov speaks of language-free, direct communication with higher powers, whose traces have been preserved in archaic forms ("folk songs") and cannot be reproduced in contemporary culture. This is precisely the situation described (and rejected) at the beginning of Nikonova's poem. It is this impossibility that the avant-garde expresses, referring in this case to foreign or nonhuman speech ("English language," "grunting growl"). In Gnedov's work, the theme is associated with his famous "Poem of the End," which consisted of a title and an empty sheet of paper—or, in readings, a gesture.[17] As Mikhail Pavlovets describes it, "When developing the theme of 'silence,' he burned the manuscript of a new poetry collection in 1918. This poetic performance cost him dearly, and struck a decisive note in how he approached his work. Although he never stopped writing, he concealed his poetry until his death."[18] With great compression, Ry Nikonova boils this theme down into a single line conveying the physical sensation of childish powerlessness and pain from a pinched finger. In her understanding, avant-garde poetry becomes a cry of pain from the inexpressibility of the transcendent.

This is the source of the theme of suicide in the next line: "cutthroat head in a basin." One detects here a likely reference to the suicide of another ego-futurist highly regarded by the transfurists, Ivan Ignatyev (1892–1914), who cut his throat the night after his wedding. Khlebnikov dedicated a quatrain to his tragic death, and the artist Olga Rozanova turned it into a color hectograph:

И на путь меж звезд морозных
Полечу я не с молитвой
Полечу я мертвый грозный
С окровавленною бритвой . . .

And toward the frosty stars
I will fly not with a prayer
I'll be menacing and dead,
bloody razor in my hand . . .

Ignatiev was also a friend of Vasilisk Gnedov and the subject of several poems the latter wrote much later in the 1970s. As Gnedov says in one of these:

По Вашем пульсу привыкли эпоху сверять
И неожиданно на нем бритвы черта резкая

We used to check the era by your pulse
Suddenly the sharp line of a razorblade on it.[19]

The motive of suicide is invisibly present in the next line, too: "ladder of tears tumbling puppies." The term can be read as an allusion to Mayakovsky, from whom Nikonova has appropriated his characteristic accentuated fragmentation of the poetic line known as the *lesenka* (literally a "little ladder" or a verse ladder [see the earlier chapters on Mayakovsky and Pasternak]). As for puppies, these allude to Mayakovsky's signature in his private letters: *Shchen*, short for *shchenok*, "puppy (line 12)." On the whole, this line suggests yet another strategy of avant-garde poetry: the imitation of triumphant vigor, an intonation that distinguished Mayakovsky's post-revolutionary poems written in "ladders" (*lesenki*), concealing an inner drama that ultimately leads to suicide.

What do we make of the final line of this quatrain, "castironthought clangs along" (line 12)? We observe that in the larger structure of the poem and within a stanza that stands out in any case, this line is metrically accentuated insofar as an amphibrach replaces a dactylic foot. Does this metrical shift signal a thematic change? The three preceding lines presented three baleful avant-garde scenarios of silence, suicide, and creative self-destruction. This last line suggests a positive strategy. We can assume that, for Ry Nikonova, the link is with Velimir Khlebnikov. The epithet "cast-iron" points directly to him, especially in combination with "thought." One of the last entries in Khlebnikov's diary of 1921 reads as follows: "To commission Tatlin to build a chapel for manuscripts—a repository of fut-humanity [*bu-chelovechestvo*]: an iron skull, a shared cast-iron forehead for our deeds and thoughts. So that the mice of time won't gnaw them away."[20] "A shared cast-iron forehead" full of the thoughts of futurists, that is, of artists who were ahead of their time, is Khlebnikov's *exegi monumentum*, whose reverberation is discernible in Nikonova's line. Moreover, the motif of cast iron in association with poetry is also found in other poems by Khlebnikov, for example, in one devoted to another futurist: "To Burliuk" (1921):

С великанским сердца ударом
Двигал ты глыбы волн чугуна
Одним своим жирным хохотом.
Песни мести и печали
В твоем голосе звучали.
Долго ты ходы точил
Через *курган чугунного богатства,*
И, богатырь, ты вышел из кургана
Родины древней твоей[21]

With your giant heartbeat
you moved heavy waves of cast iron
with your fat guffaw.
Songs of vengeance and sorrow
were the sound of your voice.

You've been long creating tunnels
through the mound of cast-iron wealth,
a bogatyr, you came out of the mound
of your ancient homeland.[22]

What does Khlebnikov's "castironthought" comprise? Does it consist of combining the future ("a repository of fut-humanity") with antiquity ("the mound of cast-iron wealth")? While this single word does not necessarily corroborate our interpretation, the entire subsequent text of the poem in which the poetic persona comes to the fore can be productively read as a development of Khlebnikov's cast-iron thinking (lines 13–20):

Рифма, на бёдра твои обопрусь я
дай мне свободу в груди
тёплой струёю картины нарвусь я
стадо всех слов впереди.
Клык навострило скользящее
бегает Рык вереща
а вот и мое подлежащее
надлежащее дать мне леща

Rhyme I lean my hands on your hips
give me space in my chest
warm stream of me pluck up
herding the words ahead
Slippy sharpens a fang
runs squealing Raptor-me
here my undergone
overborne slap me

This part of Nikonova's poem foregrounds the creative act by combining two sets of images. One is sexual: "Rhyme I lean my hands on your hips" (line 13), "warm stream of me pluck up" (line 15); the other associated with hunting: "herding the words ahead / Slippy sharpens a fang / runs squealing Raptor-me" (lines 16–18). It is not by chance that "me" appears in Dugdale's translation: the original beast is called *Ryk* (roar, growl), differing in only one letter from the pseudonym of the poem's author, *Ry* Nikonova.

Sexuality and the hunt—the first being the origin of life, the second being an aestheticized form of murder—merge in a word, and in the *form* of Nikonova's neologism. It is in the form that the mutual transformation of opposites takes place; in

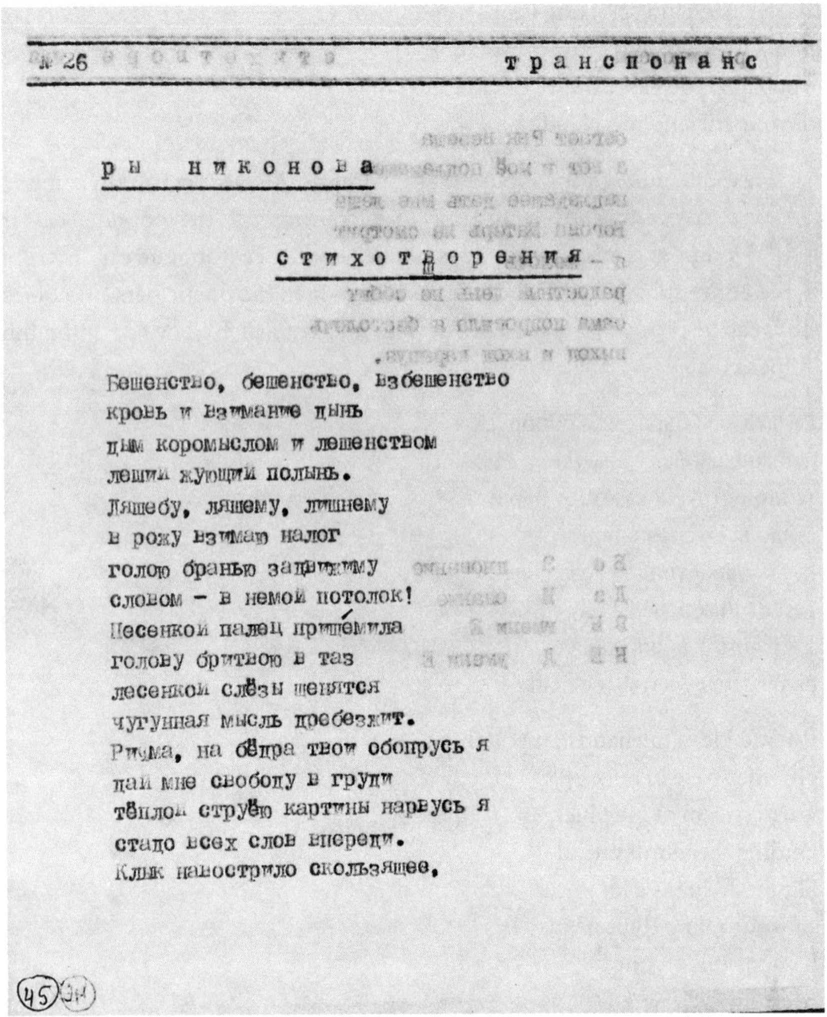

№ 26 транспонанс

ры никонова

стихотворения

Бешенство, бешенство, взбешенство
кровь и взимание дынь
дым коромыслом и лешенством
леший жующий полынь.
Ляшебу, ляшему, лишнему
в рожу взимаю налог
голою бранью задвижиму
словом – в немой потолок!
Песенкой палец прищемила
голову бритвою в таз
лесенкой слёзы щенятся
чугунная мысль дребезжит.
Рифма, на бёдра твои обопрусь я
дай мне свободу в груди
тёплой струёю картины нарвусь я
стадо всех слов впереди.
Клык навострило скользящее,

FIGURE 25.2. A page from the first publication of Ry Nikonova's poem in the samizdat magazine *Transponans* (1985, no. 26). Open source: https://samizdatcollections.library.utoronto.ca/islandora/object/samizdat%3A10193.

fact, the form itself derives from this continuous metamorphosis. The Russian word *podlezhashchee* is the subject of a sentence and literally means "something that lies underneath." This turns into the word *nadlezhashchee,* meaning metaphorically "something that one has to do" but also literally "something that lies above." A more ribald interpretation of this scene cannot be excluded, since the wordplay with *podlezhashchee* and *nadlezhashchee* refers to a well-known series of sexual jokes.[23] Yet

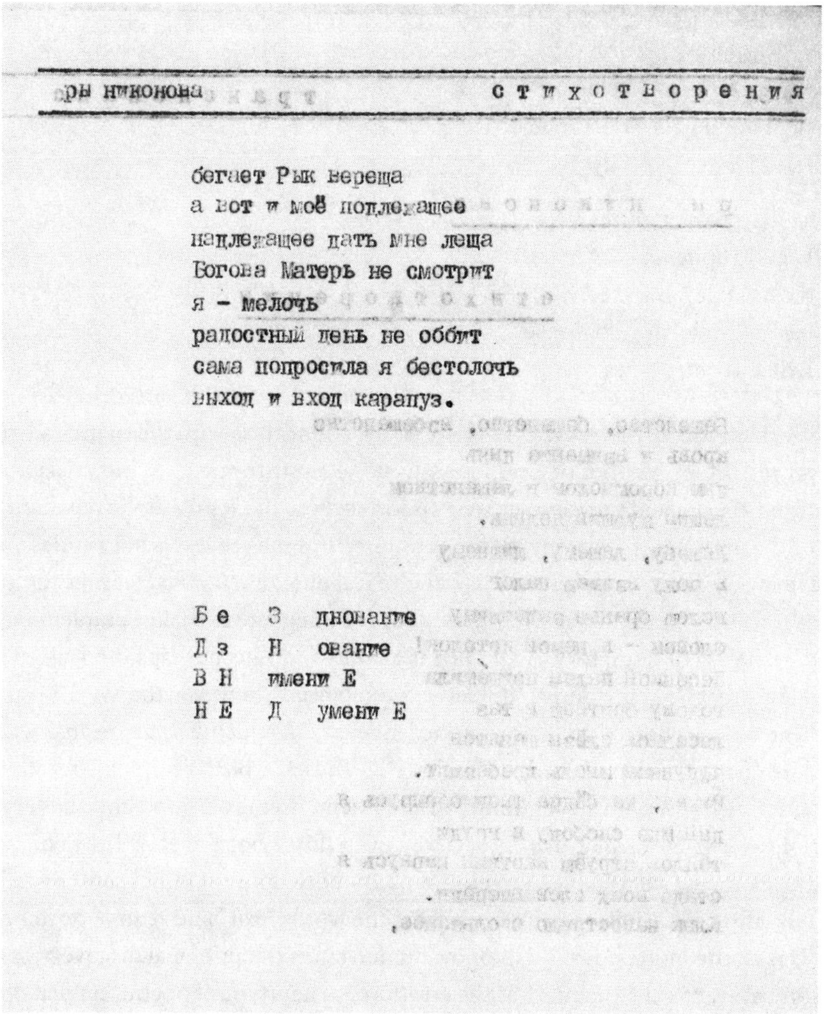

ры никонова стихотворения

бегает Рык вереща
а вот и моё подлежащее
надлежащее дать мне леща
Богова Матерь не смотрит
я - мелочь
радостный день не оббит
сама попросила я бестолочь
выход и вход карапуз.

Б е З днование
Д з Н ование
В Н имени Е
Н Е Д умени Е

FIGURE 25.3. A page from the first publication of Ry Nikonova's poem in the samizdat magazine *Transponans* (1985, no. 26). Open source: https://samizdatcollections.library.utoronto.ca/islandora/object/samizdat%3A10193.

on balance the word play is directed toward the question of creative inspiration. Moved by the shape of the word, the poetic act produces a higher (albeit not transcendent) meaning. In turn, this meaning strives to dominate and subjugate the speaker since the word sets out to "slap [her]," perhaps intending to guide her to the right path with this punishment.

Богова Матерь не смотрит
я—мелочь
радостный день не оббит
сама попросила я бестолочь
выход и вход карапуз

Mother of God looks away
I am thruppence
the feast day unfrayed
I asked myself for nonsense
Exit and entry child

The final part of the poem confirms that the connection with the transcendent is never restored: "Mother of God looks away / I am thruppence." The crisis is not resolved, the ancient function of poetry is lost forever, the results of the rebellion are not to be undone: "I asked myself for nonsense." But the process is not fruitless, and the final enigmatic line expresses its paradoxical outcome: *vykhod i vkhod karapuz*, "exit and entry child" in translation. Its many meanings are partially complementary and partially contradictory. A *karapuz* is a child and thus perhaps the fruit of the sexual act that had previously unfolded. Etymologically, however, the word is usually interpreted as a borrowing from Turkic languages in which *karpuz* means "watermelon" (from the Persian *harbuz*, "melon").[24] Thus, the birth of new life recalls the sacrifice described at the beginning of the poem: literally "blood and the levy of melons" (*krov' i vzimanie dyn'*). However, even this is not the end. The sexual act, the birth, the sacrifice in themselves never achieve closure but rather carry on indefinitely. This conflation of opposites is what the words "exit" and "entry" portend.

This is, therefore, how Ry Nikonova understands the principal discovery of the historical avant-garde: namely, as the creation of a new type of poetic text that operates as a laboratory, in which binary oppositions disintegrate, contradictions are reconciled, and new meanings are created. After all, as one of the first transfurist manifestos asserted, "The boundary of verse is almost always wrong. Any work of art can be continued or broken up; the ability to regenerate is proof of the genre's antiquity and unspent powers."[25] Ry Nikonova's poem also embodies another program principle of transfurism: "To preserve the thread of the poetic avant-garde, that is, to pour [it] into oneself, to soak [it] in oneself, to transfer into the alien, to carry through the similar, to transmit to everyone, to pierce everything."[26]

26

Olga Sedakova, "The Grasshopper and the Cricket" (1979–85)

THE MUSIC OF THE EARTH

Кузнечик и сверчок

The poetry of earth is never dead.
John Keats

Поэзия земли не умирает.
И здесь, на Севере, когда повалит снег,
кузнечик замолчит. А вьюга заиграет—
и забренчит сверчок, ослепший человек.
Но ум его проворен, как рапира.
Всегда настроена его сухая лира,
натянут влажный волосок.
Среди невидимого пира—

он тоже гость, он Демодок.
И словно целый луг забрался на шесток.

Поэзия земли не так богата:
ребенок малый да старик худой,
кузнечик и сверчок откуда-то куда-то
бредут по лестнице одной—
и путь огромен, как заплата
на всей прорехе слуховой.
Гремя сердечками пустыми,
там ножницами завитыми
всё щелкают над гривами златыми
коней нездешних, молодых—

и в пустоту стучат сравненья их.

Но хватит и того, кто в трубах завывает,
кто бледные глаза из вьюги поднимает,
кто луг обходит на заре
и серебро свое теряет—
и всё находит в их последнем серебре.

Поэзия земли не умирает,
но если знает, что умрет,
челнок надежный выбирает,
бросает весла и плывет—
и что бы дальше ни случилось,
надежда рухнула вполне
и потому не разучилась
летать по слуховой волне.
Скажи мне, что под небесами
любезнее любимым небесам,
чем плыть с открытыми глазами
на дне, как раненый Тристан?..

Поэзия земли—отважнейшая скука.
На наковаленках таинственного звука
кузнечик и сверчок сковали океан.[1]

The Grasshopper and the Cricket

The poetry of earth is never dead.
John Keats

The poetry of earth will never die.
Here in the north, when snowflakes throb and hum,
the grasshopper pipes down. A blizzard starts to fly,
the cricket, blind old man, begins to strum.
His rapier wit is nimbly wrought,
the strings of his dry lyre taut,
the vital thread vibrates.
A feast veiled from the eye awaits,
he is Demodocus, distinguished guest,
and all the singing meadow climbs into his nest.

The poetry of earth is not so rich:
a tiny child, a wizened patriarch,
the insects trace a lonely arc,
a staircase poised above the ditch—
a path so vast it wraps across
the gaping sonorous abyss.
Thunder peals from empty hearts,
while scissors coiled and curled
click-clack o'er golden manes unfurled
by spectral colts not from these parts—
into the void their rifts are hurled.

And yet his pipes still howl and wail
his pale eyes gaze beyond the hail,
at dawn he paces to and fro,
his silver lost unto the snow.
No poverty would dare to mute
the silvery riches of his flute.

The poetry of earth will never die,
but if the end were drawing near,
he'd shed his oars and cease to steer
his trusty barque beneath the sky—
as hope would crumble to the ground,
so he would glide through waters deep,
though ruined faith would surge and leap
to ride the wave of pulsing sound.
O, tell me, what on God's green earth
would heaven smile upon more brightly,
than idling in the vessel's girth
like wounded Tristan, plucking lightly?

The poetry of earth is tedium undaunted.
On anvils rich the mystic clang is flaunted—
the insects hammer out the ocean's birth.

(TRANSLATED BY HELENA KERNAN)

In the work of Olga Sedakova (b. 1949) poetry sets its gaze on the heavenly and the earthly. She finds the numinous in the mundane and the human in the spiritual. The titles alone of two of her collections, *The Garden of World Creation* (*Sad mirozdan'ia*, 2014) and *Gates, Windows, Arcs* (*Vrata, Okna, Arki*, 1986), speak volumes about an art attentive to cultural specificity and the eternal.[2] Both these sides of her poetic craft correspond to the artistic and ethical values her essays about other poets explore as well, and they also attest to her erudition and training in Slavonic philology and the study of Slavonic theological texts. As a critic, she is drawn to the texture of reality in the poetry of Osip Mandelstam, helping to define the relation between abstract notions of weight and sensation in his earlier acmeist poetry and sensation, or what she has called the "materiality of being human" (*veshchestvo chelovechnosti*). Other writings, especially about figures ranging from the early Christian desert fathers to romantic poets including Pushkin to modern masters such as Rilke, are drawn to the moments of transcendence that poetry can recuperate in quiet moments of thought.[3]

Her habits of mind include a love of paradox, a tension between the finite and infinite, the directed and undirected, and her poetic eloquence and gracious style also display an ear for metaphorically conveying the invisible and unheard. Her attentiveness to other poets is also a notable feature.[4] Readers of her poetry—and readers of all poetry in her view—see reading as a process of double unfolding: peeling away the ordinary will lead to spiritual epiphany that can reveal the beauty in truth and the truth in beauty; and close attention to a lyric that may have a seamless unity on the surface will reveal echoes and influences, subtly absorbed. The voice of her solitary speaker can achieve its autonomy while also absorbing other voices. Sedakova's citational practice does not aim to challenge the reader with obscure learning. Her allusions often come from well-known, famous poems that many a reader can quote. Erudition for its own sake in the manner of a philological poet is not what she strives to condense into a poem. Her allusive technique serves a type of clarifying shorthand, elegantly and often overtly positioning her own lyric in relation to earlier poems.

The poem discussed in this chapter brings to that sense of gentle revelation features that typify her art. The title and epigraph of Sedakova's poem openly affiliate it with Keats's sonnet "The Grasshopper and the Cricket" (1816). Keats's poem famously and possibly apocryphally was written in fifteen minutes in a sonnet competition with Leigh Hunt, whose version bore the similar title "To the Grasshopper and Cricket."[5] If grasshoppers and crickets lack the glamour of nightingales and cuckoos in romantic lyric, the dance and music of insects pervade English poetry.[6] The sonnet's optimism about song as a ceaseless bounty of nature has made it a classic statement in the romantic celebration of nature and poetry. Yet neither of these poems is primarily an environmentalist work, insofar as these lyrics subordinate questions of nature to the nature of poetic creativity. Keats's poem has been read by critics as an illustration of an anti-intentionalist argument, evidence that for Keats the cultural capital of poetry lay in its ease and not in evidence of work.[7]

Poems written spontaneously might seem to confute the idea that poetry must be based on a Wordsworthian ideal of "emotion recollected in tranquillity." Whatever the arguments, the position of a poem written in imitation that is carefully meditated as an act of rewriting clearly involves questions of intentionality and work rather than the Keatsian profession of indolence. Each English poem tells a story of a competition between two types of poet, the luxuriant summer that is the grasshopper and the lone resilient poet that is the cricket. The question for the reader of the later, Russian poem, is where does this parable of poetic typology leave Sedakova. Does a poet-imitator seek to be a lone voice? Or does the same poet speak for an entire chorus of poets subsumed into a tradition? What kind of poetic song does Sedakova hope to channel by appropriating Keats's voice? In imitating Keats, she has consciously chosen lyric poetry that, in the words of Seamus Heaney, "is orchestrated to its most opulent."[8]

Keys to that larger question of intentionality lie in the relationship between translation and imitation. Sedakova has clearly followed Keats in producing a poem about nature and voice—and made something new of his conceit. Descriptive and often metaphorical, conversational and learned, Sedakova's poem, counting the epigraph, is exactly three times longer than Keats's. Its forty-one lines are irregularly paragraphed, bunched in groups of ten, sixteen, twelve, and, finally, three lines. A skein of rhymes thrown across the entire poem provides a formal constant within which there is the variety of a change-off between three main schemes: alternating rhyme, interlocking rhyme, contiguous and sometimes identical rhyme. These rhymes give certain blocks of lines the shape of the quatrain, the couplet, and the tercet formatted across a paragraph break. It is part of the poem's ingenuity that some sequences of lines taken in combination appear to fall into the pattern of some kind of sonnet, such as the second segment, which might be a version of the eleven-lined curtailed sonnet.

In the end, the poem only flirts with formal approximation to Keats. Sedakova in her own formal design may have approached the sonnet with an awareness of its historical flexibility, picking up on asymmetries in the English original. Commenting on Keats and the sonnet form, one critic noted that poets in the period "developed a free approach to the Shakespearean model that tolerated a variety of irregular and hybrid constructions."[9] Imitation as deviation (or, in formalist terms, a *sdvig* or shift) is a sign of the creative license the poem will take on a thematic level, too, as it adapts Keats's elements to a different time and place. While Sedakova has written a poem clearly in dialogue with Keats, there is in the decision not to replicate his form some measure of tasteful refusal to enter into a singing match. For a poet who loves paradox, as Sedakova does in art and religion, it is to be expected that, despite the way her poem takes over from Keats, her tribute will be additive rather than competitive.

Keats's description compartmentalizes the two voices of grasshopper and cricket in the octave and sestet. Each unit opens with a declarative statement, the second replacing "never dead" with "ceasing never":

The poetry of earth is never dead:
When all the birds are faint with the hot sun,
And hide in cooling trees, a voice will run
From hedge to hedge about the new-mown mead;
That is the Grasshopper's—he takes the lead
In summer luxury,—he has never done
With his delights; for when tired out with fun
He rests at ease beneath some pleasant weed.
The poetry of earth is ceasing never:
On a lone winter evening, when the frost
Has wrought a silence, from the stove there shrills
The Cricket's song, in warmth increasing ever,
And seems to one in drowsiness half lost,
The Grasshopper's among some grassy hills.[10]

Nature in its estival abundance produces unceasing delights. These delights include the noise of the grasshopper, whose voice is fed by the new-mown grass and replenished in the shade of the "pleasant weed." Winter, while a season of interiority and silence, is not without its music, since the cricket in the hearth, a symbol of prosperity, sings. There is a touch of naturalism to Keats's tribute in crediting its song to "warmth increasing," because the insect chirps more quickly near the heat. Both vignettes about grasshopper and cricket are framed by their headline claim about the poetry of the earth: first, that it "is never dead," and, second, that it "is ceasing never."

In short compass, Keats has produced with the greatest musicality and poised detail a poem about an ecosystem that is pictorial, associative, and logical, and that juxtaposes summer and winter, abundance and austerity, noise and silence, fatigue and ceaselessness, sleep and alertness, heat and cool. While the poem itself must end, it shares the poet's belief that Nature, of which poetry is posited as an extension, will never end. And, while poetry may or may not cease to be written, a proposition that cannot be tested but can be imagined, poetry—in its original meaning of *poeisis* or doing—will not end for as long as insects live. The miracle of the biosphere is renewal, whatever happens in the Anthropocene. Yet, insofar as poetry is a human product, man is part of nature, and poets continue to respond to poets and write verses on one another, there is a sense in which the human sphere also partakes in that process of conservation of energy and of awakening and warmth increasing.

Warmth increasing, however, cannot feature in Sedakova's landscape. Transposition to a new climate of the mind entails translation of circumstance. Winter, the only season to be found in "The Grasshopper and the Cricket," displaces Keats's fading "summer luxury." The adjustment, however, does not betray the universality of the message, and the essential truths expressed by Keats remain in force. The Russian poem confirms the status of the earth; it also affirms that, even in the north, the music of the grasshopper and cricket, although on a new rhythm and adjusted for a harsher climate, confirm that truth. In Keats, silence is both "wrought" and belated, whereas silence and a winter storm dominate the adaptation. From that starting point of variation, Sedakova expands in her own direction. The world remains a touchstone for her as for Keats. But the universality of the claim about its music is tested in a colder climate. Can the grasshopper and cricket sing in the Russian cold?

These questions are about poetry, and are to be answered metaphorically. The answer seems to be that both grasshopper and cricket can endure the change from the luxury of summer to the austerity of winter, and adapt to landscapes in which snows and blizzards replace "cooling trees." While they are changed, the question is whether they are reduced or perhaps even made stronger by endurance. Sedakova's poem may be a case in point. It is longer than Keats's, her metaphors more elaborate, and her poetic insects more active. In Keats, the grasshopper comes first and, while he may be "tired out," only rests. In Sedakova, by contrast, "the grasshopper pipes down" and cedes his place to the cricket. In counterpoint to the "shrilling" of Keats's cricket, a verb that was often used of the wind as much as of the human voice, the Russian cricket has a whole new set of attributes. The harsher the climate, the more robust the requirements for poetic agency. While the Keatsian cricket takes refuge in the hearth and merely echoes the more robust summer song of the grasshopper, the Russian cricket has the grandeur of a bard: intellect (line 5), musicianship (lines 6–7), fine-tuning are his characteristics. Likened to Demodocus, the blind poet Odysseus hears at the court of King Alcinous, his position is no less than Homeric and his music is as polyphonic as an entire band or, in a reversion to Keats's summer, a meadow. The meadow is the preserve of the grasshopper rather than that of the cricket, yet the poem shows their equivalence, giving proof that the Russian cricket can match the English grasshopper. If there is in this some element of national pride, it comes from the belief that poetry can make out of a toyshop insect the grandest singer, and out of the racket of winter an audience for song. If ever proof were needed for the proposition that the "poetry of earth is never dead," however far north we go, this demonstration of vitality provides it. The validity of such a claim lies in the proof of poetry itself, proof with a precedent to be found in a much earlier poem by Mikhailo Lomonosov, the great eighteenth-century polymath and important verse theorist. The insect hero of Lomonosov's lyric "Dear Grasshopper, how fortunate you are" ("Kuznechik dorogoi, kol' mnogo ty blazhen," 1761) is the object of envy. While many might despise him as a lowly creature, the poet celebrates him as nothing less than a king ("Tsar") in recognition of the advantages he enjoys over mankind:

Препровождаешь жизнь меж мягкою травою
И наслаждаешься медвяною росою.

You spent your life in the soft grass
and you take delight in the sticky sap.

Lomonosov's grasshopper is the image of a poet-king and is so mobile as to be nearly immaterial (*besploten*). Not only is he the image of a natural capacity to sing, later to be associated in romantic poetry with the nightingale, he is also "everywhere at home."[11] In domesticating Keats's poem, Sedakova also has before her the image of Lomonosov's Russian grasshopper as a metaphor for poetry.

The multiplicity of songs to be heard in the imaginary Russian meadow serves as an allegory of the richness of lyric achieved through allusion and connotation. Across her poetry, Sedakova's technique of intertextual allusion is multifaceted, sometimes signaling affiliation with another poet that is a type of friendly familiarity, sometimes condensing the contents of a previous poem with all its thematic complexity and creating a shorthand for shared preoccupations. An earlier chapter of this book examined Pasternak's "Poetry," a work that defines poetry by surrounding it with an explosion of metaphor. Freshness of perception is what Sedakova shares with Pasternak and Keats: all value the perceptual work of defamiliarization, Pasternak through metaphorical language, Keats through the immersion of the senses in the natural world, and Sedakova here through imitation. In this instance, Pasternak and Sedakova share the summer and an acceptance of poetry that avoids what Pasternak in "Poetry" (see chapter 7) calls "mellifluous posturing" (*osanka sladkoglastsa*). Just as Pasternak prefers the noise of the people to be heard in a third-class railway carriage, Sedakova favors the lyric over the epic. Both poems are attuned to a language out of the mainstream, whether figured as the suburb or the far north, appreciated not as the easy melody of a refrain but as something far more jumbled and unpredictable.

In Keats, nature determines the timing and type of melody appropriate for a season. It is natural in the summer for the grasshopper to take the lead. The line "The poetry of earth is not so rich" concedes that summer in Russia is relatively brief. Here the grasshopper never takes the lead. At best, there is instead a quick-changing interplay between both insects, neither ever quite the sole protagonist. From the start, then, forms of compensation respond to the relative difference in resources between Keatsian abundance and Russian severity. The cricket picks up the slack from the grasshopper and, as polyphonic as a Greek singer of epic, he is blind and sharp, solitary and multiple. Beginning with a discursive and metaphorical flourish, the second section reinforces and extends the role of metaphor in the poem. The second section repeats the Keatsian juxtaposition of large spaces filled by the noise of insects, and it also maintains the same structure (an assertion followed by somewhat choppy qualifications), except that the Russian text is longer, if only (and almost comically) by one line. Syntactically and acoustically, the "gaping sonorous abyss" of Helena Kernan's translation (*put' ogromen*, line 15) expands evocatively on the "singing meadow" (*selyi lug*, line 10) and links the visual field with sound. This is further reinforced by line 18 and the scissors metaphor, linking back to the image of the rapier mind of the cricket (and in this connection readers will remember that Pushkin, a pervasive presence in Sedakova's poetry, was known to his contemporaries by the nickname of "Cricket" [*sverchok*]). In the second paragraph, however, there is a suggestion that space has overwhelmed the insects and that even their joined efforts to be heard may be insufficient against the white noise of nature: despite a common effort, their sound cannot provide, in the literal Russian, a "patch sewn across the gamut of hearing" to muffle the noise of the blizzard.

The poet, however, can redouble her efforts, through an intricate figure of speech that nests a simile within a metaphor. Grammatical flexibility allows the gerund "Jingling empty heart-shaped bells" ("Thunder peals from empty hearts" in the translation) to stand alone. Syntactical ambiguity permits the poet to place the subject of the main verb "to clink" and the gerund as the last word in the paragraph, but its meaning is also doubled. "Their comparisons" (the literal translation of line 21 of the Russian and Kernan's "rifts") can be either subjective, meaning the "comparisons" the grasshopper and cricket produce themselves, or objective, meaning the comparisons in which they figure. Their capacity to generate poetry has been questioned by the vastness of space. If there is a suggestion of auditory insufficiency, it is offset by the images introduced in lines 19–20. Here the golden manes of horses expand into a metaphor for scissors. The image insinuates a connection to classical epic, as though these invented steeds were Olympic runners wearing greaves about which a Homeric poet like Demodocus would have sung. The image answers emptiness with the pure invention of the invisible. The two paragraphs stand in complementary relation because the sharpness of Demodocus's mind has now been appropriated by the poetic speaker who throws at the void the power to conjure images.

Emptiness rather than Keatsian plenitude marks the second half of the poem. Both insects retreat from line 22 until the last line of the poem, giving way to a force emanating from the snowstorm. The poem therefore rises to the challenge of taking silence seriously and, in effect, of being that winter cricket to the English poet's grasshopper.[12] The force that barrels down the chimney upends the ease and pleasantness of the original. Winter and wind appear in each of the three sections, and Sedakova layers her depiction with folkloric and modern detail to increase a sense of animacy, epic scale, and risk. Sedakova uses inherited versions of the storm in weaving, in the literal words of the text, the "patch sewn across the gamut of hearing," starting with the folkloric images of these lines (lines 18–20 in the Russian):

там ножницами завитыми
всё щелкают над гривами златыми
коней нездешних, молодых—

while scissors coiled and curled
click-clack o'er golden manes unfurled
by spectral colts not from these parts—

This traditional motif in the genre of the Russian wonder tale (*volshebnye skazki*) became widely familiar through Petr Ershov's *Konek-gorbunok* (*The Little Humpbacked Horse*). Inspired by Pushkin's versions of folktales, this classic children's fable was originally published in 1834 and remained a highly popular work well into the Soviet period in more than a hundred editions. The steeds driving the hero of Ershov's plot are also "golden-maned" (*zlatogrivy*), their tails coiled in golden rings:

Вьются гривы золотые,
В мелки кольца завитой,
Хвост струится золотой.

Their golden manes curl
In small golden rings,
Their golden tail flows.

In one scene, a mare speaks to the hero, urging him to keep her and her two foals because the younger horses in the winter will "keep him warm" and in "summer keep him cool."[13] Sedakova seems to have carried over this image as a metaphor into her poem for the poetry of the earth.

Yet there may also be an element of unease in these lines. Consider again Lomonosov's poem. An expert student of Russian poetry and literary history, Sedakova can be relied on to know that the cheerful tone masked the author's disgruntlement. Anecdote has it that Lomonosov wrote the poem while on the road, at a time when his dependence on the court for promotion in the Academy of Sciences had become a chronic cause of complaint and unhappiness, a state of things openly advertised in the original title.[14] The lot of the grasshopper was not enviable only in an abstract sense: it ironized his creator's own position of dependence and relative lack of freedom because, as a scientist and administrator, he encountered constant interference. In Russian literature, snowstorms abound as signal moments of moral hazard, when chance and accident confuse plans and intentions, situations that often seem to have the force of parables. Of particular relevance here is Pushkin's poem "The Devils" ("Besy"), a lyric imbued with Gothic mystery in which a coach carrying an unsettled passenger plunges into the tumult of racing clouds and the chaos brought about by the snowstorm. In both Pushkin and Sedakova, the storm is called a *viuga*. Sedakova's poem also has its ghostly figures in the invisible horses or the eyes and wind that haunt this space. In Pushkin, the traveler's eyes are blinded by the wind that "blows, spits at me" ("duet, pliuet na menia"),[15] whereas here "pale eyes" stare out of the chaos. Line 25 is enigmatic, and whether it could be glossed to mean "everything of value," meaning our last salvation, depends on this final bit of silver. The image of the scattering of precious metal helps to explain why the "poetry of earth is not that rich." It is not only that the power of poetry to reverberate may be diminished in a more hostile environment, drowning out both the grasshopper and the cricket separately and combined.

Poetry is also implicated in a productive tension between absence and presence, emptiness and creativity. The repetition of the opening aphorism invites the reader to continue to contemplate the persistence of poetry, although part of that fullness is the capacity to represent emptiness.[16] It is one thing to claim that, because nature is unending, its poetry will also be unending. In the fourth block of lines, Sedakova exploits nuances of the Russian verbal system. Russian verbs normally have two forms, an imperfective form that carries the idea of an ongoing process and a perfective form that emphasizes completion. Because the line "The poetry of earth is not dying" uses the imperfect verb, the Russian can mean "The poetry of the earth is not dying"—that is, the process it undergoes does not contain death—or it can mean a more general condition, that it "never dies" and even "is not mortal." Line 26 in the Russian introduces a new condition that qualifies the first meaning. Poetry, or at least "the poetry of the earth," may live as though it were not mortal and may be ignorant of death. But there may come a time, and here everything depends on the "if" clause, when an awareness of the certainty of death will have to be acknowledged. The second clause uses the perfective verb, and that means that the subject recognizes death as a certainty. The line can mean "should it know that it is mortal." What has not been divulged is the condition under which that occurs, when poetry moves from a naive state of easy description to a sentimental state of self-reflection (to use the terms of Schiller's famous essay on poetry), and poets move from being the "preservers of nature" to seekers of a lost nature and ideal.

Has the Russian poem already moved from a state of enchantment to a state of longing in relation to the naive opulence of Keats's original? To fill emptiness, the poetic imagination can respond with fanciful imaginings that "knock at emptiness." They cannot dislodge or erase emptiness, for, however far they roll it back, there is always "enough of it" to upset and reduce. In Sedakova's vision, the brightness of dawn never quite gives up the silver coloring of the snow or hoar frost, and it is that residue of silver that seems one essential half of the coin of life and death, poetry and silence.[17] From what sources then can the poetic imagination in a cold climate, figuratively and literally, generate warmth?

The answer as so often in Sedakova lies in literature and a voice hidden in plain sight within her poem. In the second segment of lines, Sedakova requires a patch to bridge the gap between the two types of music, and hearing is impeded. A dissonance between the Russian and the English poems, a gap between the two as striking as the difference in seasons between a Russian winter and an English summer, must be repaired. Her dialogue with Keats is mediated through Mandelstam. Their common ground is heat, poetic song, mortality, and, of course, the singing grasshopper. Lines 27–30 in the Russian pick up on that transition by echoing another poetic voice, opening it up to a dream state of poetic creation as a type of death and renewal. These lines overtly quote from the middle of Mandelstam's "If the clock-grasshopper sings" ("Chto poiut chasy-kuznechik," 1918) given here in its entirety:

Что поют часы-кузнечик,
Лихорадка шелестит
И шуршит сухая печка—
Это красный шелк горит.
Что зубами мыши точат
Жизни тоненькое дно—
Это ласточка и дочка
Отвязала мой челнок.
Что на крыше дождь бормочет,—
Это черный шелк горит,

Но черемуха услышит
И на дне морском: прости.
Потому что смерть невинна
И ничем нельзя помочь,
Что в горячке соловьиной
Сердце теплое еще.[18]

If the clock-grasshopper sings
A fever rustles
If the dry oven hisses
It is red silk that burns.
If mice gnaw with their teeth
At the frail depths of life—
It is my barque that
A daughter swallow has unleashed.
If rain grumbles on the roof
It is black silk that burns.
But the cherry tree will hear
At the bottom of the sea: farewell.
It is because death is blameless
And one can do nothing about it
That in a nightingale fever
The heart remains still warm.[19]

This mysterious poem is about the feverish state of mind in which a web of symbols and associations and sounds occur. If one needed a plot to motivate many details, the underlying scenario is of a poet with a fever. He hears the clock is ticking, a fire is burning in the stove, it is raining, thoughts of life and death occur, perhaps he loses consciousness. In the first stanza, Mandelstam conveys the heat of poetic creativity through a set of suppressed similes using auditory, visual, and tactile images. There is a clear allusion in the second stanza to Pushkin's "Insomnia" ("Bessonitsa"), an existential meditation focalized through a half-awake, half-asleep consciousness. There the gnawing mouse is Pushkin's metaphor for the way time eats away at life. In alluding to this poem by Mandelstam, Sedakova has deliberately chosen a palimpsest poem that writes over another famous Mandelstamian lyric, doubling the quotational power of her text. Mandelstam has yoked the quotation to an auto-citation from his "Take from my hands" ("Voz'mi na rado'st iz moikh ladonei," 1920), which ends with a surreal image of the poet untethering a small boat (picked up by Sedakova in line 29 in the Russian), a metaphor for the imagination. In Mandelstam, the swallow/sparrow stands for the poetic word, and verbal links generated by free association in the unconscious mind are likened to a barque untethered in a stream of consciousness. The grasshopper-clock, the fever, and the stove are all conditions of which the consequence is the red silk burning: Mandelstam's *shelk* ("silk") may be echoed in Sedakova's *shchelkaiut*. Similarly, the teeth of mice eating away at the cauldron bottom are the condition from which the swallow-daughter unmooring the boat follows. It is in the final stanza that Mandelstam memorably intimates the view that poetic creation, a state of mind whose flame is fueled by other poetry, is a type of feverish hallucination also fed by an awareness of death or emptiness (*pustota*).

The patch "sewn across the gamut of hearing" is the poem's metaphor for its own relation to the English translation-cum-adaptation. We have seen that this gamut also extends over a "vast distance" into the Russian tradition, patching Sedakova into the verses of two of her favorite poets, Pushkin and Mandelstam, including a second poem by Mandelstam echoed in lines 29–30. The fact of death and the image of the boat cast adrift also come from "Take from my hands." That poem is about gift giving between poet and addressee and, like those by Keats and Sedakova, it is also an insect poem. Mandelstam recalls the summer activity of bees that, during the season of Persephone, transform their food ("honeysuckle, time, and mint") into sound.[20] By dint of their shape, texture, and actions, they are likened to kisses, but these emblems of love must die, as bees do after pollinating, once they have been turned into words, and the gift that the poet presents to the addressee in the poem, made up of these words-bees-kisses, is a desiccated necklace made of dead insects.

All the warmth that has gone out of Sedakova's original Keatsian landscape has now been recaptured through echoes of Russian lines that take poetry into a world of unconscious process. Behind the poem stands anxiety about the unknown and about death, comparable to Sedakova's confession that, once the poetry of the earth admits of death, then all hope is lost. In Mandelstam's poem, the speaker obeys the order of Persephone's bees. The making of the gift or the act of poetry happens because it is in the nature of things for the poet who, when seized by the *furor poeticus*, is incapable of "conquering fear in this tangled-dreaming life" or escaping in an "unmoored boat." Lines 25–30 in the Russian, which write Mandelstam's words into Sedakova's text, seem to hold open that possibility that the landscape of the poem hovers between the underworld, because the barque may be sailing on the River Styx, and the mythic realm of Tristan, also transported on a deathly voyage by sea. In the spirit of its reversal of Keats, Sedakova's poem also reverses Mandelstam and imagines a way out of the impasse of mortality. The poem's paradox is that, once there is no hope of escaping death, there is every incentive to find a way out, at least by riding the "wave of sound." While the conditional clause ("if the end were drawing near") means that a state of grace for poetry cannot be guaranteed, "The Grasshopper and the Cricket" offers a salvific vision of poetry in which even belatedly Mandelstamian and Pushkinian sounds and images have the power of transport.

"If the end were drawing near" seems to portend failure. Yet the work of the two poet-insects is on an oceanic scale, and the poem itself, a work of lyric, suddenly flows into the epic. If poetry can also represent a wound, the image of Tristan's knowledge, it is also the voice of love.[21] The tribute to the blind Demodocus, a Homeric bard, that comes in the first section anticipates the poem's final lines. The idea of contest between the epic and the lyric looks ahead toward the mention at the end of the poem of Tristan, another wounded hero. In her essay "What Tristan and Isolde Is About," Sedakova dwells particularly on the hero of Gottfried von Strasburg's medieval epic and extends her essay to Wagner's opera, the last an inspiration for a long cycle of poems, named for Wagner's masterpiece.[22] A chivalric story about a love that is both innocent and guilty, this work of mythic proportions shatters social boundaries, transcends a world too small to contain it, and attains metaphysical exaltation by conquering death. While Sedakova, a distinguished medievalist, is aware of the multiple textual versions of the legend, she gives Wagner as the source here. In the opera, Tristan, vassal to King Mark, has been sent to Cornwall to fetch Mark's bride Isolde. In Wagner's version, she is an Irish sorceress who accidentally bewitches Tristan with a potion, leading him to betray King Mark. When the couple's illicit love is discovered, Tristan is wounded and, exiled to a distant land, he is transported on the water by a faithful retainer. The image of the boat blown to another land, mentioned by Sedakova in her essay and recombined here with Mandelstam's barque, clearly haunts her. Her essay also singles out wind as a force in Wagner's opera, and perhaps it is the same wind that sweeps across her Keatsian landscape at the beginning, reunited with its source at the end of the poem. She also attributes to it a provenance in the history of poetry that makes her own work cognate with poems that feature a force such as love or the wind that can never be entirely quelled:

> The sea wind from the beginning of *Tristan* sounds at the beginning of T. S. Eliot's poem *The Waste Land*. It can also be discerned in his late *Four Quartets*, the wind and the deserted sea ("Oed und leer das Meer"). An important epoch in European and Russian life was animated by Wagner's music. Without it one cannot imagine the pathway of our own great lyric poet, Alexander Blok. His soul often repeats Tristan: "The heart secretly craves doom . . ."
>
> (TRANSLATED BY ANDREW KAHN).[23]

The spirit of death that shadows Tristan is the path to an eternal life that defies death:

Wie koennte die Liebe
Mit mir sterben,
Die ewig lebende
Mit mir enden?

How could Love
Die with me,
The eternal living
End with me?

Wagnerian and chivalric love achieves greatness by remaining mortal, and thus achieves immortality. Heroic because "gripped by an inhuman strength," the protagonists are also proclaimed "innocent in their guilt."[24] Sedakova's poem has itself become a vehicle, its own barque, for the voices of a whole tradition from the Homeric bard to Gottfried von Strasburg to Keats to Wagner to Mandelstam. Closeness to Keats affirms the poem as an environmental tribute, rooting poetry in the elements. The poem's rich use of other voices, including folkloric pastiche, Lomonosov, Pushkin, Mandelstam, Pasternak, and Wagner, creates a second level at which its climactic terms become allegorical rather than literal. Poetry makes the weather, and Russian poetry is Sedakova's element. It becomes its own proof of the claim that the poetry of the earth, even when "not so rich," bridges the chasm, and in reconnecting with multiple traditions (that "staircase poised above the ditch") remains a conduit for that mysterious sound hammered out by a nature of which poets are a part.

27

Lev Losev, "One Day in the Life of Lev Vladimirovich" (1985)

SELF-PORTRAIT IN A CLOUDY MIRROR

Один день Льва Владимировича

Перемещён из Северной и Новой
Пальмиры и Голландии, живу
здесь нелюдимо в Северной и Новой
Америке и Англии. Жую
из тостера изъятый хлеб изгнанья
и ежеутренне взбираюсь по крутым
ступеням белокаменного зданья,
где пробавляюсь языком родным.
Развешиваю уши. Каждый звук
калечит мой язык или позорит.

Когда состарюсь, я на старый юг
уеду, если пенсия позволит.
У моря над тарелкой макарон
дней скоротать остаток по-латински,
слезою увлажняя окоём, как Бродский,
как, скорее, Баратынский.
Когда последний покидал Марсель,
как пар пыхтел и как пилась марсала,
как провожала пылкая мамзель,
как мысль плясала, как перо писало,
как в стих вливался моря мерный шум,
как в нём синела дальняя дорога,
как не входило в восхищённый ум,
как оставалось жить уже немного . . .

Однако что зевать по сторонам.
Передо мною сочинений горка.
“Тургенев любит написать роман
Отцы с Ребёнками.” Отлично, Джо, пятёрка!
Тургенев любит поглядеть в окно.
Увидеть нив зелёное рядно.
Рысистый бег лошадки тонконогой.
Горячей пыли плёнку над дорогой.
Ездок устал, в кабак он завернёт.
Не евши, опрокинет там косушку . . .
И я в окно—а за окном Вермонт,
соседний штат, закрытый на ремонт,
на долгую весеннюю просушку.
Среди покрытых влагою холмов
каких не понапрятано домов,
какую не увидишь там обитель:
в одной укрылся нелюдимый дед,
он в бороду толстовскую одет
и в сталинский полувоенный китель.
В другой живёт поближе к небесам
кто, словеса плетя витиевато,
с глубоким пониманьем описал
лирическую жизнь дегенерата.

Задавши студиозусам урок,
берём газету (глупая привычка).
Ага, стишки. Конечно, “уголок,”
“колонка” или, сю-сю-сю, “страничка.”
По Сеньке шапка. Сенькин перепрыг
из комсомольцев прямо в богомольцы
свершён. Чем нынче потчуют нас в рыг-
аловке? Угодно ль гонобольцы?

Всё постненькое, Божии рабы?
Дурные рифмы. Краденые шутки.
Накушались. Спасибо. Как бобы
шевелятся холодные в желудке.

Смеркается. Пора домой. Журнал
московский, что ли, взять как веронал.
Там олух размечтался о былом,
когда ходили наши напролом
и сокрушали нечисть помелом,
а эмигранта отдалённый предок
деревню одарял полуведром.
Крути, как хочешь, русский палиндром
барин и раб, читай хоть так, хоть эдак,
не может раб существовать без бар.
Сегодня стороной обходим бар.

Там хорошо. Там стелется, слоист,
сигарный дым. Но там сидит славист.
Опасно. До того опять допьюсь,
что перед ним начну метать свой бисер
и от коллеги я опять добьюсь,
чтоб он опять в ответ мне пошлость. . . .:
"Ирония не нужно казаку,
you sure could use some domestication,
недаром в вашем русском языку
такого слова нет—sophistication."
Есть слово "истина." Есть слово "воля."
Есть из трёх букв   "уют." И "хамство" есть.
Как хорошо в ночи без алкоголя
слова, что невозможно перевесть,
бредя, пространству бормотать пустому.
На слове "падло" мы подходим к дому.

Дверь за собой плотней прикрыть, дабы
в дом не прокрались духи перекрёстков.
В разношенные шлёпанцы стопы
вставляй, поэт, пять скрюченных отростков.
Ещё проверь цепочку на двери.
Приветом обменяйся с Пенелопой.
Вздохни. В глубины логова прошлёпай.
И свет включи. И вздрогни. И замри

. . . А это что ещё такое?
А это—зеркало, такое стеклецо,
чтоб увидать со щёткой за щекою
судьбы перемещённое лицо.[4]

One Day in the Life of Lev Vladimirovich

Displaced from North Palmyra[1] and New Holland,
here at the present time I make my bed,
in North America, New England, all out
of company. And exile's bitter bread
I chew, extracted from what's called a toaster,
and every morning I ascend some steep
steps leading to a building of white stonework,
and earn that bread using my native speech.
I can't believe my ears. Every last sound
cripples my language or at best insults it.

When I grow old, away to the old south
I shall depart—that's if my pension funds it.
Over a plate of pasta by the sea
I'll while away my final days, in Latin,
a teardrop moistening my ranging eye,
like Brodsky—or, rather, like Baratynsky.
The latter, when he sailed out of Marseilles,
the way steam puffed, marsala was imbibed,
the way she saw him off, that hot mamselle,
the way his thoughts did dance, his pen indite,
the way the sea ran measured in his lines,
the way his distant route shone there in azure,
the way it didn't cross his rapturous mind
how little there remained of life to treasure.

That's quite enough of idle sidelong looks.
A pile of student essays here awaits.
"Turgenev loves to written novel books
Fathers with Childrens." Joe, well done, all A's!
Turgenev, he loves looking through the glass.
Seeing the cornfields clothed in greeny bast.

The trotting gait of a fine-legged pony.
That film of burning dust over the roadway.
The horseman's tired, he drops into an inn.
Knocks back a bowlful on an empty stomach.
I too look out, Vermont is over there,
my neighboring state, closed down now for repair,
the long long drying out, now springtime's coming.
Dotted among those moisture-clad hillsides
at least one house of every fashion hides,
there's every dwelling there you could imagine—
in one, reclusive grandaddy's shut up,
he's all dressed up in beard of Tolstoy cut,
and Stalin semi-military jacket.
And in another, closer to the sky,
is he who verbalized a high-flown plait,
with understanding quite profound described
the lyric life of a degenerate.

Having assigned the undergrads their task,
pick up the paper (there's a stupid habit).
Aha, some verse. A "corner," need you ask,
"a little piece," or, lithp-lithp-lithp, a "tidbit."
Headline on S., spot on. He's done a jump
from Komsomol to God's own mob, a hole in
one. What could they be serving in that dump-
like greasy spoon? The bilberries, they're wholesome?
Fast (ha-ha!) food, is it, slaves of the Lord?
There's rotten rhymes. And all the jokes are stolen.
We've had enough. Thanks muchly. Slimy, cold,
it's bobbin', shiftin', slidin' down your colon.

Darkness is falling. Home! Perhaps I'll keep
a Moscow journal so's to get to sleep.
Some blockhead dreaming how it once was done,
when our lads would storm forward at the run,
smashing the filthy foreigners for fun,
and one now emigrated's distant forebear
presented to his village half a tun.
Twist it around, the Russian palindrome

barin i rab (that's "squire and slave"), twist faster,
the slave still can't exist without the master.
Today it's best to leave the bar alone.
It's nice in there. Cigar smoke stratified,
spreading. A Slavist, though, in wait inside.
Beware. I really musn't have so much that I
once more begin to cast my pearls before him
and—he's my colleague—yet again I force him
to shoot his shit in a banal reply,
"Your Cossack has no need for irony,
you sure could use some do-domestication,
your russky lingo doesn't know how to say—
no word for what we call sophistication."
There's *istina* for starters. Then there's *volia,*
uiut as well, three letters. *Khamstvo,* yes.[2]
So good, not having drunk one drop, night falling,
to let things go, mumbling to emptiness
these words for which translations are there none.
With *padlo* we have just about reached home.
Make sure the door's shut tight behind you, that
the spirits of the crossroads may not enter.
Into your worn-out slippers, poet, thread
two sets of five gnarled outgrowths, scrunched together.
Go back and check the door-chain's put on right.
With dear Penelope exchange a greeting.
Then slope off to your bolthole, sighing deeply.
Turn on the light. And shudder. Freeze with fright.
. . . Whatever could it be, that freak?
A mirror's what it is, just a glass plate,
so as to see, brush poised behind his cheek—
this D. P.[3] who's been set down here by fate.

(TRANSLATED BY G. S. SMITH)

Lev Losev (1937–2009), a born-Leningrader of the same generation as Joseph Brodsky, first published as a journalist. The son of a famed children's poet, Vladimir Lifshits, Losev took his pen name to avoid confusion with his father once he began publishing children's poetry of his own and serving as editor of the children's magazine *Bonfire* (*Koster*). The name became permanent with his move to the United States, where he had a successful academic career, initially at the University of Michigan and then at Dartmouth College, where he was professor of Russian literature. The author of distinguished scholarly publications, most especially *On the Beneficence of Censorship: Aesopian Language in Modern Russian Literature* (1984), a now classic study of the rhetorical techniques Soviet writers used to cope with censorship and communicate with a readership accustomed to reading between the lines, Losev also wrote many literary essays and published nine books of poetry, mostly collected in the posthumous magnum opus that appeared in 2012. His 2006 critical biography-cum-memoir of Joseph Brodsky broke new ground.

Published in *The Miraculous Descent* (*Chudesnyi desant*, 1985), when Losev was only forty-eight, "One Day in the Life of Lev Vladimirovich" sounds like the work of a writer either in poor health or a gloomy state of mind or both, and certainly older than his years. The book was the first collection of poems Losev published after his emigration to the United States in 1976, and this poem, one of his longest lyrics, comes toward the end of the collection's final cycle, "A Lesson in Photography." The previous section, "Against Music" ("Protiv muzyki"), set the tone for the entire collection, beginning with its elaborate set of epigraphs. At the top of the page is a sentence from a presumably bogus *Guidebook*, with a comment that the hallmark of the Petersburg school of still life is incompleteness. As proof of fragmentation, positioned immediately below and in a rectangular box demarcated with a thick black line is an incomplete prose passage, a rambling monologue strewn with word play about light, still life, painting (the early- to mid-nineteenth-century landscapists Andrei or Alexander Ivanov and Sylvester Shchedrin), and alcohol worthy of a Dostoevskyan hero. Alcohol and the struggle to remain sober dominate the poems of the book's first half ("To the Memory of Vodka"), a testimony to what G. S. Smith has called Losev's unprecedented bravery in talking about the role of this poison-cum-elixir in Russian authorial consciousness.[5] The third piece of paratext is a would-be epitaph. Losev makes himself into an object of still life:

L. Losev (1937–?). Still-life
Paper, typ. writt. Incompl.[6]

The English "still life" is more euphemistic than the Russian word of French origin *Natiurmort*. These three features together sketch the poles of life and death, sobriety and intoxication, polish and fragmentation within which the poems grouped in this part of the book range. The titles and graphic devices also hint at the variety of speech effects and modes Losev employs, including ekphrasis, *skaz* (the use of oral speech), and self-elegy. The poems in the final section, "A Lesson in Photography," are full of grotesque figures from the recent Russian past, remembered in poetic vignettes, half-remembered in dreams or an alcoholic haze (one poem is written like a recovery log, "Saturday is over, haven't even got drunk"), or when a record is put on the turntable ("Record," "Plastinka"), or when one tunes in to a radio station ("At Christmas," "Na Rozhdestvo"). Consistent with the tone of "Against Music," this section has its still life ("Nature Morte with Surnames") and its funerary-cum-morbid lines (*Tam i prekrasny eti sny*) and elegy ("And, finally, the station 'Cemetery,'" "I nakonets, ostanovka 'Kladbishche'"), and, while it is imbued with memories of Russia ("A Letter to the Homeland"), America begins to intrude in the later poems. Like Brodsky, Losev made use of the postcard poem—works with "postcard" in the title as opposed to works written and sent as postcards—including "Postcard from New England, 1 and 2," recording new settings. The progress toward the adoption of a new life features most prominently near the close of the book with his "Imitation of Frost" ("Nork Brook" for Frost's "West-Running Brook") and then the lyric featured in this chapter. "One Day in the Life of Lev Vladimirovich" captures the poet further along in his autobiography. He is in midlife, caught in the workplace, meditating on and between his Russian sense of identity and his experience of America. Here the characteristics of belonging and not belonging are not landscape-related or specifically territorial: what matters is literary affiliation, linguistic sharpness, and emotional vulnerability.

"One Day in the Life of Lev Vladimirovich" consists of seven tableaux: (1) exile as displacement from Old World to New, entailing linguistic alienation; (2) an evocation of age, in which the poet distracts himself with thoughts about another poet's death; (3) a vignette about daily routines as a professor of Russian literature in New Hampshire; (4) the émigré landscape of New England, surprisingly well stocked with Russian writers; (5) a splenetic, hilarious lampoon of émigré and Soviet poetry; (6) an encounter with a colleague in the present; (7) at home. It is about the old life and the new. But the poem is not of the postcard-sent-back-home variety that became a subgenre in émigré poetry of this period.[7] If it is firmly rural, all hints of sentimentality are steadfastly resisted.

Losev begins grandly, the opening phrase and classical reference highly formal. But, within just a few lines, everyday habits of mind and turns of phrase unbend that stiff effect. The unassuming asserts itself through attention to routine. Losev, a consummate master of classical forms, had a superb ear for the rhythms of ordinary speech, which is one of the noteworthy aspects of this poem. He renders his thoughts in a mixed meter of two- and three-syllable iambs and manages the syntax flexibly: lines overflowingly transcribe the speaker's stream of consciousness until they are punctuated by a moment of resolve. The thoughts are those of a writer, imbued with literary reference, saturated with a range of discourses from poetic high style to vulgar, Soviet slang, lavishing affection on an esteemed writer (lines 15–20) in a pastiche of his style, execrating hack writers he deplores.[8] While the opening strives to aggrandize exile, it is more humble-brag than genuinely vain. Far from glamorizing dislocation, the poem treats its tedium as chronic. Part of that tedium is the realization that it is one thing to be a solitary exile, it is altogether another to find oneself among a posse of similarly displaced writers. A discerning eye and competitive ego travel with one into exile.

That is a source of crusty amusement more than genuine consternation. It is with a light touch—and Losev, however dour his subject, has always been appreciated for his unfailing irony and enthralling use of form—that the poem responds to a famed tradition. Losev's map of exile is both textual and familiar. Dante's bread of exile has been transfigured into a piece of toast. There is grandeur in the reminiscence of Evgenii Baratynsky, famed even in the Pushkin period for his metaphysical lyrics, who died unexpectedly after reaching Naples: the trip by sea from Marseilles occasioned the poem "Hydrofoil" ("Piroskaf"), one of the greatest meditations on the tensions between modernity and poetry, a poem that seems to launch the poet into some timeless metaphysical sphere. The contrast with Losev's own life—brought down to the most prosaic notion of existence in the rhyming of chewing and existing (lines 2, 4 in the Russian)—adds a stroke of bathos on top of the picture of the poet mounting the steps of a white-stoned building. No classical temple to the Muses, it proves to be the scene of pedagogical humiliation and alienation from his native language.

But the map is also peopled with other, more celebrated exiles treated in cameo portraits (lines 38–48). Brodsky's New England and Losev's New Holland are one and the same. But in their poetry Brodsky and Losev did not share the same map of exile—or at least not entirely, and the scale of their vision differs markedly. Brodsky's awareness of the American empire was more historicized and strategic than local. He saw its history as another in the series that included Byzantium, Rome, and the USSR. His attitude, now seen as highly controversial because neocolonial, remained imperial and grand, facing both East to the Soviet empire he left behind (and the Byzantine empire, celebrated by Brodsky for its dust, the by-product of history) and also West to the American empire on which the poet trained his sights and his tongue. For all its abrasive tone of condescension, a feature that puts Brodsky suspiciously on the side of first-world "winners," his apocalyptic forebodings temper any triumphalism because all empires will come to an end. If the two poets shared a New England space, Losev's poetry generally remains fixated on the present and on time passing in the moment. Brodsky generally marked time in centuries, only occasionally devoting a lyric to his own physical aging, as in his highly autobiographical fortieth-birthday poem "I took the place of a wild beast" ("Ia vkhodil vmesto dikogo zveria v kletku," 1980) and in another to mark a later New Year, "How long I've tramped" ("Kak davno ia topchu"), noting signs of physical decay. With a wink at Ivan Denisovich, Losev's poem captures the effort of the daily grind. His walk to the office as he mounts the steps could not be less grand than Horace's famous description of how he mounted the Capitoline (in "Exegi Monumentum"). It is no surprise to find him clumsily putting slippers on his cramped feet after a day's work. There is a day to be got through, and a pile of undergraduate work to mark. Other poets find boredom to be ripe with the potential for epiphany. For example, in his "Winter. What is there to do in the countryside?" Pushkin captured the turning point between boredom and productive distraction when the imagination takes flight. In *The Heavy Lyre*, radiant inspiration relieves the stark prosaic surroundings in which Khodasevich's lyric speaker is to be found. Not so here. Boredom, on which subject Brodsky wrote his celebrated "In Defense of Boredom" as the 1985 commencement address at Dartmouth College, is one state of mind to be whiled away or just tolerated, evidence in Losev of resistance to the romantic idea that the poet can recover a wholeness of subjectivity through nature.

The poem therefore has its documentary strategy, bringing together details that go together in a biographical narrative yet also look jarringly unrelated since Turgenev, Vermont, Stalin, and others are examples of a paratactic montage.[9] "One Day in the Life of Lev Vladimirovich" looks back to the bitterness of Russian life a generation earlier and finds little that is authentic in the author's present situation to celebrate apart from a repudiation of sentimentality delivered with an exactness of wit and poetry. Beneath the surface acerbity there is movement, since this is a poem brimming with linguistic and formal felicities. G. S. Smith, the poet's foremost exegete, has praised Losev's talent as "tradition-tested craftmanship," referring both to his command of Russian prosody, especially rhyme, and to his intertextual facility with allusion, an aspect of play and dialogue rather than a display of erudition.[10] Structurally, the most important element of this poem is its use of rhyme to create variety and surprise, offsetting the rhythmic stability.[11] There are blocks of text in which alternating rhyme features consistently, while other sets of lines tend toward couplets. The rhymes themselves are more innovative than classical, taking liberties with phonetic rules. They can be counted on to be verbally clever (e.g., lines 1/3, 17/18, 26/29, 28/30,

67/68), and because they are ostentatiously engaging they add levity in counterpoint to a downbeat tone. In some sections (e.g., lines 48–59), alternating masculine and feminine rhymes create some regularity, even though an irregular distribution of couplets and triplets disrupt a fixed pattern. The effect of impulsiveness is a meaningful counterpoint to the monotony of daily routine. Rule breakage occurs, as in the splitting of a word across a line (*perepryg/ryg-*, lines 52, 54). In the Russian tradition, words can rhyme if they share sounds that are alike but not identical (known as inexact rhyme), as in "Marseille/Marsala/Mamsel" (abbreviation of "mademoiselle"), the genuinely humorous juxtaposition of *shutki/v zheludke* ("jokes" / "in the belly"), or the consecutive repetition of homophones, as in *bar/bar* (lines 69, 70): the words do not rhyme because the consonant before the vowel is the same, and there is bathos in the juxtaposition of high and low ("bar" as in "saloon," and also meaning "master"). Many other examples affording formal delight and semantic import can be found. The point to emphasize here is that this capacity comes to the poet unknowingly and without consciously distracting him from tedium vitae (even if there is obvious delight in the creation of the palindrome of line 67). If anything, the resistance to distraction is underscored. "That's quite enough of idle sidelong looks," is G. S. Smith's elegant version of the more abrupt and perhaps more futile sound of the Russian idiom (*chto zevat'*), intimating the pointlessness of comparing himself with illustrious figures like Baratynsky or even hinting at Dante. Yet, despite the self-reproach, Losev's alter ego cannot help looking through the window. If the grass is greener on the other side, it is so both literally and figuratively. The end of winter heralds a long period of drying out, meant literally in relation to the landscape but also figuratively by way of alcohol. In the spring sun, the grass will grow and turn green, but what will happen to the dried-out poet?

At a crossroads, poets can look back and ahead. Losev looks sideways. The most famous meditation on the growth of the poet's sensibility, on aging and posterity, on connecting past and present, is Pushkin's "Once again I revisit," another iambic poem written as a first-person monologue and of similar length (and also discussed in chapter 1). Written in the Wordsworthian tradition, its form conceived in imitation of "Tintern Abbey" to achieve psychological amplitude, Pushkin's elegy is a classic example of the capacity of romantic lyric to fix a spot in time, erasing the gap between time past and time present for just a moment as the later poet through the landscape finds unity with a younger self and achieves a timeless sense of continuity. The mention of exile at the opening is common to both poems as the turning point, with Losev consciously repeating Pushkin's word (*izgnanie*). Pushkin's poem relies heavily on the deictic, gesturing to locations in the scenery: the sight of a clump of trees that he remembered first as saplings, sees now as fully grown, and imagines years hence is the conduit to that spot in time. Pushkinian readers will hear in Losev's evocation of the Vermont hillside echoes of Pushkin's evocation of the hill on which he used to sit in the continuation of his exile after his years in the south on the modest family estate at Mikhailovskoe. From the hill, just as wooded as Losev's view of Vermont, he spies a little house tucked away, once inhabited by the nanny of whom he was famously fond. No such tenderness is to be found here. Access to nature, represented by Vermont as the greenest of states, is barred. And, to make things worse, what Losev spies through the shrubbery is not a restorative vision of trees but the homes of other writers.

In not yet becoming narrative, not quite indulging in the feelings these lines studiously repress, Losev gestures toward the romantic without either celebrating exile or communing with nature, a reluctance that distances him from both Brodsky and Pushkin. The speaker brings himself up short in order to focus on marking student work, but his wandering gaze is not really toward nature. It is toward nature in literature and the literary figures hidden in nature. Undergraduate ignorance sparks a memory of a familiar landscape, and the pulse of the poem quickens a bit with a flourish of nineteenth-century poetic diction in line 31, with Losev flaunting his formidable gift for imitation and stylization. But Losev cannot truly commit himself to a novelistic description of the countryside. Instead, he strains to glimpse two celebrated émigré figures, each the polar opposite of the other and neither regarded as his own spiritual kin. The unsociable Solzhenitsyn, who remained grandly aloof in the Vermont redoubt in which he created his own Russian utopia, elicits no warmth. But Losev's title unfailingly reminds the reader of Solzhenitsyn's Ivan Denisovich, however perverse and self-pitying the hint of comparison may be. Sasha Sokolov, the second figure, had achieved considerable renown for his novel *A School for Fools*, published in English in 1976, a pioneering postmodern work that took a new, fluid approach to identity, told from the viewpoint of a divided, troubled adolescent dissolving both narrative and psychological structures. In Sokolov's novel, words like "idiot" and "cretin" occur, sometimes preceded by emphatic epithets, such as "witless" (*bezmozglyi*) and "frightful" (*uzhasnyi*). Losev's own word, "degenerate," while shockingly harsh and unacceptable in today's idiom, was in Russian a clinical term used from the nineteenth century to indicate a congenital inherited mental or psychiatric condition.[12] Both Solzhenitsyn's stature and posture, however stilted his costume and bearing, and Sokolov's inventiveness look enviable to the hyper-rational Losev, whose musings offer respite from the drudgery of his job but cannot arrest the sense that physical decay, the abrasion of teaching, and spiritual torpor slowly corrode his identity. The point may be that neither of those writers could possibly be imagined spending a single day like the day recounted here, since none of the routines described is the stuff either of heroism and dissent, Solzhenitsyn's stock-in-trade, or of Sokolov's Joycean stream of consciousness and surrealism.

Losev has the novelist's awareness of his own inner moods, the variations in emotional temperature registered as small changes to diction and tone. Something of a "campus poem," the lyric satirizes his unease as a teacher. Throughout the poem, Losev delights in pedagogical pretense by giving vocabulary lessons in Russian, Latin, and English with no expectation of joy from the classroom. Disgruntled by the quality of undergraduate Russian—and the Russian idiom *razvesit' ushi* translated here as "I can't believe my ears" indicates fastidiousness—he wonders about retirement. The fantasy of the south is phrased with conspicuous clumsiness: the repetition "When I grow old" and the "old south" is weary rather than delightful word play, an effect compounded a few lines later with "while away my final days" (*skorotat' ostatok*). This would-be Ovid is stuck in suburbia. Beneath the grouchy surface, other meanings bubble up and verbal slippages lead to flights of fancy. In a poem, a reference to macaroni may punningly hint at "macaronics," that is, crosslinguistic wordplay such as the rhymes to be found later in the poem ("sophis tication"/"domestication"), just one specimen of the delight the speaker takes in being ironical, satirical, and both high-minded and foul-mouthed (lines 79 and 81 in the Russian; lines 78 and 80 in the English).

In his penchant for combining "colloquialisms and barbarisms," Losev reflected a larger trend among émigré poets to move in and out of their new vernacular, sporting the foreign with bravado but also underscoring their marginality within their new environment.[13] (The translator's witty solution has been to create the effect of a negative by turning into Russian the English words of the original poem). In daily life, the speaker as a social being encounters such frustrations as the poor Russian of his students and the obtuseness of a condescending colleague; as a reader and writer, he also finds in newspapers plenty of material to feed his discontent. What is silently borne in the world percolates in the mind of the poet. However prosaic the day may be, it somehow becomes the material of poetry. The absence of one liquid (vodka) is compensated by another: the wetness of a tear, a sign of strength of feeling, moistens not just the eye but rather the field of vision contained within the eye ("ranging eye" does about as much justice as an English equivalent possibly can). In the blink of an eye, therefore, the poet imagines Baratynsky about to embark on his final journey, unaware that it is to be the last before his sudden death. The vision also lifts Losev's spirits, heard in that triple group of clever off-rhymes (*marsel'*/*marsala*/*pisalo*) rhetorically strengthened by the use of anaphora (lines 18–24). While those rhymes are Losev's own touch, musical and whimsical (after all his mind is dancing), "the way the sea ran measured in his lines" refers to a poem in which the pulsation of the steam engine and the driving rhythm of the meter are matched to great effect. "Distant route" is a euphemism for another euphemism: "last journey" (*poslednii put'*) means "death" in Russian, and to shine "in azure" (*sinet'*) in Russian poetry is regularly associated with a supernal realm.

In other words, there is a literariness that cannot be suppressed, even when the poem makes a show of melancholy literalness. Another great Russian writer abroad overshadows the poem and inhabits the lines. Losev's classroom scene (lines 26–50 in the Russian) cannot help but recall the story of Pnin, the Russian professor hero of Nabokov's novel, as well as the story of his creator, Professor Nabokov, whose antics, routines, and attitudes to American students had already become part of his legend. In this Losev joins the tradition of émigré martyrs to the struggles and failures of American pupils with the Russian language and literature, and Losev's irritable parroting and parodying of poor Joe strikes a topos already familiar from *Pale Fire* and *Pnin*, Nabokov's celebrated campus novels that spare neither professors nor students his caustic wit. Such satire of undergraduates—the Russian *studiozusy* from the Latin *studiosus* is a mock affectionate scholastic touch—is a gentle prelude to the lines about Soviet writers in which he positively pulls his tongue out of his cheek. Losev's persona is also studious, he tells as much at the opening. But he is far from whiling away his days reading Latin: a perusal of a Russian émigré newspaper loosens the fetters that restrained any real criticism of Solzhenitsyn and Sokolov. Journalistic spats and literary quarrels were a staple of twentieth-century émigré literary life. In his short chapter on this poem, Petr Vail sees it almost entirely in the context of the sometimes bruising treatment meted out to writers by critics renowned more for spite than for generosity, citing the example of Georgy Adamovich.[14] A stickler for formal correctness and afficionado of well-worn themes like loneliness, suffering, and death, Adamovich pulled no punches about his dislikes past (Fet, Chekhov) and present (Nabokov/Sirin, Tsvetaeva, Pasternak), and generally detested all experimentalism. Losev's generation also split into ideological factions. But Losev's critical jabs concern skill, tone, and taste, and are part of a much longer tradition of verse about verse that was established in Russia in the eighteenth century and flourished particularly in the Pushkin period. Here Losev's satire is generic rather than individual. The first target most likely is the *New Russian Word* (*Novoe russkoe slovo*), which started publishing in New York before World War I and closed in the 2010s. Its editor, Andrei Sedykh, was caricatured in Sergei Dovlatov's autobiographical memoir-cum-novella *Craft* (*Remeslo*), the first part of which was published in 1977, and the sequel around the time Losev was writing this poem. In their sharp-eyed awareness of the politics of reputation and celebrity (including Solzhenitsyn and Brodsky), in their self-disgust, and in their acknowledgment of the potency of alcohol, Losev's poem and the Dovlatov memoir are kindred spirits. Losev finds on the pages of the first newspaper "versicles" (*stishki*) with lame rhymes and tired or cynical professions of belief. The verse of a newfound religious poet he recognizes as a former member of the communist youth organization is enough to turn his stomach—and the reader's too (the word used for "greasy spoon" is literally a "vomitorium"). Time passes, but the speaker clearly enjoys newspapers more than student compositions and moves on to a second newspaper mixing Soviet rhetoric of civil war vintage and the language of nostalgia for the prerevolutionary aristocracy, a fad from the 1970s. Losev loves to split logical pairings into verbal dislocations. He uses the technique as a modified form of chiasmus in the opening paragraph by separating "North" and "New" twice from the paired nouns "Palmyra" and "Holland," and "America" and "New England." This newspaper, like the first, repeats the same type of juxtaposition found in the internal rhyme and word play of *Komsomol/Bogomol* (line 53): the émigré newspaper carries news of a conversion from a communist youth sect to an old religious sect. The rhyme itself spoofs a popular song from the film *Volunteers* (*Dobrovol'tsy*, 1958) by E. Dolmatovsky, full of determination to "open new paths" and attain the "heavenly heights" and "earthly depths." Sentiments once expressed atheistically can be repurposed for religious affectation.

Irony is an indelible position in Losev's work, the result of a sense of permanent estrangement and his own artistic awareness of estrangement or defamiliarization as a literary device. The ironies play off against the apparent casualness in the first parts of the poem, where the speaker adopts matter-of-factness as a technique, and once again at the end. Initially and only until the end of the first section, the long lines of the poem break conversationally at natural pauses rather than being end-stopped, whereas, in much of the rest of the poem, the verse line and sentences coincide more frequently, at least until the conversation between the lyric speaker and his Slavist colleague. Both these sections associate physical and linguistic exile, and both sections underscore certain words: in lines 9–10, "ears" (*ushi*) and "tongue" (*iazyk*) are placed for emphasis; in lines 82–84, the speaker lists words silently offered as proof against the pejorative claim about Russian and Russians. From the start of the poem, the speaker's eye has been on the clock, first in a larger sense when thinking about age, and then on the day itself as it draws to a close. "Darkness is falling," and he is running out the day ahead of happy hour. Not that happy hour is mentioned, but in the 1980s that was how bars packed in casual and serious drinkers. Determined not to be a slave to drink—to be *barin* (a lord) rather than "in the bar"—he conjures the smoky atmosphere he likes. What preempts temptation is a conversation, either remembered or imagined, with a departmental colleague, a Slavist slavishly gripped by prejudices. For readers of "One Day in the Life," there are certain aspects of the speaker's character that have already become apparent. Losev's poem may look back on the day, but it now replays the opening description of linguistic alienation and perhaps even adds insult to injury: it is one thing to struggle with undergraduates, another to find oneself affronted by a colleague in the discipline devoid of elementary understanding. Blockheads confronted on the pages of newspapers and mocked at a distance turn out to exist nearby and can only be confronted quietly. And the best defense against philistinism, defined as *khamstvo*, is both irony and the cultivation of a quiet life behind a tightly locked door, the coziness defined in Russian as *uiut*.

Staying calm, maintaining the cool emotional palette typical of his verse, rejecting stupidity, acknowledging that departure from Russia has its minuses, the poet finds all the necessary but pointedly untranslatable words to keep to himself, meting out truthful judgment and exercising restraint; these are the modes that, in Smith's reading of Losev's psychology, enable him to cauterize emotion by applying "an acerbic intellect."[15] Has emigration meant only swapping the harassment of Soviet life with its speech codes and ideologies for the petty indignities of foreignness and the asymmetry of relations? Losev is not a sententious poet or conspicuously wise in the way of Brodsky, whose mind finds general laws about time, space, and language all around him. From the high-flown grand language of the first part, Losev returns to the routine of everyday. Any day in a life can be made into a story or a poem by showing rather than telling self-understanding and feeling: a story that can do justice to the individual focuses on the inner life of a character rather than politics or destiny. If geography is destiny, it turns out, ironically, that one can be born in Russia, and in rural America find oneself surrounded by other Russians recreating an idyll they never enjoyed back home. There may be a hint of immanence or just folkloric superstition in a sidelong look at "the spirits of the crossroads" (line 88), warding off an encounter that might impart knowledge of the future better left untold. There is a hint of grandeur with (again) a sidelong look at Penelope, ironized by the unheroic posture and physique of the speaker, who is "sloping off" and "freezes with fright." Odysseus's journey was about the theme of the return of *nostos*, in Greek the root of "nostalgia." The arrival home only underscores that homeless was already a condition of Losev's being in the Soviet Union.

The poem comes full circle to the motif of dislocation, and ends its story of how the poet ages. Pushkin's "Once again I revisit," whose echoes are noted above, deals with mortality by imagining a span beyond a single lifetime and projecting the poet's own habit of commemorating himself onto the reader. Nature's capacity for endless self-renewal as saplings become majestic, towering pines partially offsets mankind, whose hope for renewal lies in the belief that posterity will read this very poem. Losev's subject has removed himself from nature, being neither novelistic nor romantic in imitation of Turgenev or Pushkin.

Shutting the door on the outside world does not eliminate that reality. At the end, the poem's reflections risk becoming reversals, perhaps suited to the fate of a DP (displaced person), Losev's literal translation of the bureaucratic term. In Russian, the difference between "squire" and "slave" seems to be only the transposition of a few letters (*barin/rab*), and the proximity of the words for "brush" and "cheek" (*shchetka/shcheka*) also becomes spatialized by what the poet sees in the mirror. How accurate is the self-portrait he sees of himself in the looking-glass? Is the gap between his identity, past and present, and his appearance as vast as the gap between squire and slave or as close as that between brush and cheek? If the glass is transparent, then this is more of a trompe l'oeil effect, as he looks into another dimension altogether. Is that in the great New England tradition akin to Wallace Stevens's "fitful tracing of a portal" ("Peter Quince at the Clavier"), another poem about the boundary between the quotidian and the spiritual? Is the vision of his own singular, individual face now a metaphor for the process of how time works on us? The routine encounters that document the "estrangement of exile,"[16] in Svetlana Boym's fine phrase, momentarily turn into something new in the most familiar daily ritual of scraping away the old. The posture at the end also conjures the example of Khodasevich's "Before the Mirror," a soliloquy written just about sixty years earlier, in 1924, about identity and the shock of recognition and denial that the sight of himself in the mirror causes. In both of these poems, the speaker realizes that one's image in the mirror is not a reflection of physical reality, but a reflection of one's view of how biographical change and new circumstances have transformed one's self-image. Khodasevich ends with a bitter acceptance of the "truth of the mirror." In Losev's case, his reflection offers a one-line moment of transcendence or despair. The meaning of the final line is ambiguous, at least in G. S. Smith's otherwise faithful translation. His version introduces an interpretation that looks like a liberty, an understandable expansion of meaning. Smith's version instrumentalizes fate as the force of exile. The literal meaning of the line reads differently because what the poet spies behind the shaving brush is "the changed face of fate."[17] The introduction of fate, as a force that is either one's own destiny or impersonal, is understated as well as portentous. A sense of loss, kept in check earlier, now haunts the speaker: loss of one's face, the loss of biography and language, and the loss of identity. Gestures of rejection have been directed toward both his literary past (sections 2 and 3) as now unattainable and foreign, and the literary present (sections 4–6).

The final three sections have tried to define the self outside the literary perspective, also producing alienation from nobility, drink, and fellow Slavist professionals. Most telling for the poet is the use of language as the last foundation of selfhood. Here Losev produces a list of untranslatable words and ends with a swear word (*padlo*) even as the poem shifts emphasis from the first-person singular to the plural "we." This language belongs to "us," but the "I" has begun to disappear and change unrecognizably. As a writer working in the emigration, painfully aware of dependencies that accompany dislocation, and keenly conscious of the complexities of a literary career and reputation sustained in the diaspora, Losev brings surprisingly little homage to his native tradition or wonder to the New World; nor is he particularly exercised by personal memory unless it involves settling scores. Yet the poem is much more than an exercise in quarrels with others or a bilious confessional. Without celebration, but with humanity and pathos, it deploys powers of self-analysis on the path to self-knowledge. At the end it confronts ageing as the biggest dislocation after exile. The small routines of daily life, from entering the classroom to shaving, provide an illusion of autonomy; yet the individual life captured in this poem has experienced profound physical and linguistic dislocation. Openly autobiographical by virtue of its title and setting, this confessional but restrained lyric frankly acknowledges the two kinds of displacement haunting the speaker. Both are existential and journeys into the unknown. The question on which the poem leaves Losev and the reader is whether exile as a transition to a new state is merely a metaphor for death as transition to an unknowable state.

28

Joseph Brodsky, "Homage to Chekhov" (1993)

PASTICHING THE PROSAIC

Посвящается Чехову

Закат, покидая веранду, задерживается на самоваре.
Но чай остыл или выпит; в блюдце с вареньем—муха.
И тяжелый шиньон очень к лицу Варваре
Андреевне, в профиль—особенно. Крахмальная блузка глухо
застегнута у подбородка. В кресле, с погасшей трубкой,
Вяльцев шуршит газетой с речью Недоброво.
У Варвары Андреевны под шелестящей юбкой
ни-че-го.

Рояль чернеет в гостиной, прислушиваясь к овации
жестких листьев боярышника. Взятые наугад
аккорды студента Максимова будят в саду цикад,
и утки в прозрачном небе, в предчувствии авиации,
плывут в направленьи Германии. Лампа не зажжена,
и Дуня тайком в кабинете читает письмо от Никки.
Дурнушка, но как сложена! и так не похожа на
книги.

Поэтому Эрлих морщится, когда Карташев зовет
сразиться в картишки с ним, доктором и Пригожиным.
Легче прихлопнуть муху, чем отмахнуться от
мыслей о голой племяннице, спасающейся на кожаном
диване от комаров и от жары вообще.
Пригожин сдает, как ест, всем животом на столике.

Спросить, что ли, доктора о небольшом прыще?
Но стоит ли?

Душные летние сумерки, близорукое время дня,
пора, когда всякое целое теряет одну десятую.
"Вас в коломянковой паре можно принять за статую
в дальнем конце аллеи, Петр Ильич." "Меня?"—
смущается деланно Эрлих, протирая платком пенсне.
Но правда: близкое в сумерках сходится в чем-то с далью,
и Эрлих пытается вспомнить, сколько раз он имел Наталью
Федоровну во сне.

Но любит ли Вяльцева доктора? Деревья со всех сторон
липнут к распахнутым окнам усадьбы, как девки к парню.
У них и следует спрашивать, у ихних ворон и крон,
у вяза, проникшего в частности к Варваре Андреевне в спальню;
он единственный видит хозяйку в одних чулках.
Снаружи Дуня зовет купаться в вечернем озере.
Вскочить, опрокинув столик! Но трудно, когда в руках
все козыри.

И хор цикад нарастает по мере того, как число
звезд в саду увеличивается, и кажется ихним голосом.
Что—если в самом деле? "Куда меня занесло?"—
думает Эрлих, возясь в дощатом сортире с поясом.
До станции—тридцать верст; где-то петух поет.
Студент, расстегнув тужурку, упрекает министров в косности.
В провинции тоже никто никому не дает.
Как в космосе.[1]

Homage to Chekhov

Sunset clings to the samovar, abandoning the veranda,
but the tea has gone cold, or is finished; a fly scales a saucer's *dolce*.
And her heavy chignon makes Varvara Andreevna look grander
than ever. Her starched cotton blouse is staunchly
buttoned up to her chin. Vialtsev, deep in his chair, is nodding
over the rustling weekly with Nedobrovo's latest swing
at the Cabinet. Varvara Andreevna under her skirts wears
not a thing.

The drawing room's dark piano responds to a dry ovation
of hawthorns. The student Maximov's few random chords
stir the garden's cicadas. In the platinum sky, athwart,
squadrons of ducks, foreshadowing aviation,
drift toward Germany. Hiding in the unlit
library, Dunia devours Nikki's letter, so full of cavils.
No looker; but, boy, what anatomy! And so unlike
hardcovers.

That is why Erlich winces, called in by Kartashov
to join Prigozhin, the doctor, and him at cards. "With pleasure."
Ah, but swatting a fly is simpler than staving off
a reverie of your niece, naked upon the leather
couch and fighting mosquitoes, fighting heat—but to no avail.
Prigozhin deals as he eats: with his belly virtually
crushing the flimsy table. Can the doctor be asked about this little boil?
Perhaps eventually.

Oppressive midsummer twilight; a truly myopic part
of day, when each shape and form loses resolve, gets eerily
vague. "In your linen suit, Piotr Lvovich, it's not so hard
to take you for one of the statues down in the alley." "Really?"
Erlich feigns embarrassment, rubbing his pince-nez's rim.
It's true, though: the far-off in twilight looks near, the near, alien;
and Erlich tries to recall how often he had Natalia
Fiodorovna in his dream.

But does Varvara Andreevna love the doctor? Gnarled poplars crowd
the dacha's wide-open windows with peasant-like abandon.
They are the ones to be asked: their branches, their crow-filled crowns.
Particularly, the elm climbing into Varvara's bedroom:
it alone sees the hostess with just her stockings on.
Outside, Dunia calls for a swim in the night lake: "Come, lazies!"
To leap! overturning the tables! Hard, though, if you are the one
with aces.

And the cicada chorus, with the strength of the stars' display,
burgeons over the garden, sounding like their utterance.
Which is, perhaps, the case. Where am I, anyway?
wonders Erlich, undoing his braces at the outhouse entrance.

It's twenty versts to the railroad. A rooster attempts its *lied*.
The student Maximov's pet word, interestingly, is "fallacy."
In the provinces, too, nobody's getting laid,
as throughout the galaxy.[2]

(TRANSLATED BY JONATHAN AARON AND JOSEPH BRODSKY)

In "Homage to Chekhov," Joseph Brodsky (1940–96) has produced a pastiche in verse of the celebrated Russian playwright's theatrical style. Written in a tonic meter with an irregular number of syllables between stressed syllables, the *taktovik* that became something of a signature, the poem also features a highly wrought stanza form that is more typical of Brodsky than the highly prosaic subject matter itself. Famed as an intellectual poet "fusing high seriousness, sophisticated argumentation, irony, uninhibited play with tradition," he has made his great themes history and empire, time and space.[3] It is to be expected that the prosaic in prose was antithetical to a writer who detested a "lyric speaking subject that upstages its object."[4] Even in his lyric persona, Brodsky insisted repeatedly that poets serve the language, and that the language (of poetry, notably) working through poets describes its own historical and cultural moment. His poems about Rome, Florence, and Washington, DC, juxtapose the detritus of modern life and antiquity and strip away the veneer of both new and old. Like a true heir to the acmeists, he sees culture as the result of an almost geological process that builds the present out of the past, often recycling, often destroying.[5] His model of temporality was poetic in disposition: Akhmatova's poetry rather than Chekhov's prose conditioned his capacity to hear what the great eighteenth-century metaphysical poet Gavriil Derzhavin, a favorite of Brodsky, called "the metal din of time." Yet, in an act of literary dedication rare for him, Brodsky singled out Chekhov.

Is this humorous, poetically organized, quietly psychological vignette an exercise in how to recover the poetic in Chekhov? Or is its aim competitive and to show that it takes a poet to do "the prose thing"? Brodsky maintained an aesthetic hierarchy in which poetry ranked higher than prose, and following the likes of Gavriil Derzhavin, he naturally placed great poets at the top of the chain of being. In his essays, reviews, and interviews, favorite poets outnumber favorite novelists. Whilst his essays about poets and poems fill several books and are regarded as important critical contributions, articles about prose are far fewer. In Brodsky's remarks about classic writers of Russian prose, Chekhov never fared well.[6] His standard bearers were Platonov, to whom he dedicated a seminal essay that helped to bring him out of obscurity, and Dostoevsky, whose saturated and highly varied language and capacity to surprise he found thrilling. Chekhov's banal plots and more neutral language were implicitly a form of anti-poetry for Brodsky, invoked only to be dismissed. In "The Rustle of the Acacias" (1977), Brodsky aims a sideswipe: "Ibsen is leaden. Chekhov is trite." (Although Daniel Weissbort's translation ["A. P. Chekhov pretit"] tones down the Russian, which means more literally "provokes disgust.")[7] Brodsky's backhanded compliments stand for something. Neither Platonov nor Dostoevsky overtly or implicitly casts a shadow on Brodsky's poetry, and, while Brodsky dedicated many poems to contemporary writer friends, "Homage to Chekhov" is rare in mentioning an author in the title. Whether the poem is dedicated in tribute or in parody is a question to draw the reader in. For Brodsky, one of the virtues of poetry was its great economy. One challenge in taking on a prose writer would have been in showing cleverly the capacity of poetry to achieve excellence as a facsimile of a short story or play, resolutely in poetic form and with far fewer words.

Nothing could be less prosaic on the surface than the formally elaborate prosody of the poem. A great stanzaic poet, Brodsky loves variations and permutations. Here he modifies the basic structure of the octave by writing, in effect, seven-line stanzas in which the eighth line is a clause held over from the sentence.[8] The effect is one of both overflow, through the use of enjambment, and truncation, by abbreviation of the final line. Metrically, matters are no more orthodox. Often longer than fifteen syllables, the lines tend to a ternary meter by sporadically falling into the short-long-short pattern of the amphibrachic foot. Otherwise, however, the irregular pattern of stressed syllables set against a stable length of line moves this closer to syllabic poetry. Such syntactic and metrical slackness, artfully controlled, is well suited for the conversational element and rhetorical variety on display, especially in the central stanzas in which question follows question.

The question of what is poetic, as opposed to what is prosaic in this work, is a false distinction in sizing up whether Brodsky fancied that nearly 350 words could accomplish what a short story or play can do at much greater length. Situation and ambience are essential Chekhovian elements, as is the love plot disclosed by the narrator who seems to watch from close-up. From the start, mise-en-scène is front and center, filled with the typical props of a drama. The poem replicates standard features of the Chekhovian house party, such as its social mix of professionals and landed gentry, gender, and generations. These are the ingredients of a situational comedy that can only be implied. The poem zooms in on the busywork of characters and their appearance, and then regains its outside perspective for the sake of atmosphere. The setting is a Russian country house, characters disporting themselves on the veranda (mentioned in line 1) and at play inside as well. This division of space is typical of the country-house drama found in Turgenev's novels and Chekhov's plays. Interior and exterior scenes allow separate speeches, dialogues, and relationships to take place and advance in parallel, and it is a way to create an objective temporal framework while following the interior time of characters.

Stanza 1 opens with a shot of sunset before moving off the veranda inward. While three characters are mentioned for the first time and caught in medias res, their actions are minimal, and there is an effect of exhaustion and just a hint of plot intrigue: What is Varvara Andreevna buttoned up against? Stanza 2 begins inside, but mentally is already drifting abroad to Germany, and the poem edges outward again with stanza 4 to an evening scene further described in the next three stanzas. The season and climate, a sultry summer evening (stanzas 1 and 5), suit the hothouse atmosphere of repressed erotic tension brewing among the main characters—Varvara, Erlich (Petr Ilyich), Dr. Vialtsev. They have only slightly more profile than the secondary characters, whose purpose is to distract as well as suggest latent action and subplots. We shall never know the contents of Nikki's letter, and whether it affects the mood in which Dunia musters the others to a late swim. The potential for comic relief comes from characters like the student Maximov, and a certain Kartashov and Prigozhin—guests or neighbors—make up a game of cards. Time and nature, unified as a single external sphere, operate according to their own laws, just as all these figures go about their business seemingly oblivious to them. The scene benefits from the pastoral chronotope, so prominent in nineteenth-century Russian fiction, of landowners shown as isolated from progress, of estates run invisibly by others and generally run-down, of an enveloping passivity. The greater matters of the world are of no account; people focus on concerns no larger than a mettlesome pimple (line 23) or a bothersome fly (line 19).

Small irritations in Chekhov's plays usually reveal personal frictions and frustrations that grow into despairing outbursts or tragicomic confessions or tragedy. Those seeds of drama are planted here. A fly in the jam, the slight dissonance between Maximov's piano chords and the music of the cicadas are first hints that, underneath the relaxed atmosphere, instability and dissatisfaction simmer. It is out of feelings on the brink of combustion that Chekhov creates his dramas. All that, however, must remain latent here, since Brodsky's poem is missing its fifth act.[9] The potential of the drama is only hinted at by Erlich in the final stanza. He may be noble by name, but he also has earthier thoughts, wondering how much longer he can control his desire for Varvara Andreevna Vialtseva, whose husband Vialtsev seems permanently cloistered behind a newspaper (line 6): "What if in fact? Why am I getting carried away?" thinks Erlich (line 43 in the Russian). Erlich has an eye for detail, spotting all the discordant notes but also spying the comely Vialtseva in her stockings. There is more than a note of contempt in Brodsky's decision to give him his reflective moment when he is seated on the toilet in the outhouse. That line, in fact, provides the single historical detail in the poem that dates it: Nedobrovo can be identified as the poet and critic Nikolai Vladimirovich Nedobrovo, who also served in the Gosduma. Yet there is a sting in the tail: Nedobrovo had never been a public speaker and was unlikely ever to have been published in a newspaper. Futility piled on futility seems to be the point of Brodsky's touch.

Arguably, Erlich is not the only one getting carried away. The narrator seems to share a voyeuristic position in relation to goings-on. The narrator, being omniscient, sees all this and peers into Erlich's fantasy life and his dreams as invaded by Vialtseva, dreams in which he fantasizes about sex with Dunia. The less he sees of Vialtseva, the more Erlich dreams of possessing her. In *A Lover's Discourse*, Roland Barthes observed that the erotic works through suggestion and small revelations rather than complete exposure. There is also consistency, and perhaps ironic parody, of Chekhov's dramatic construction. While there is no mention of a firearm in act 1 that must go off in act 5, there is a buttoned-up blouse that must be unbuttoned, eventually.

Fragmentation and all forms of decay fascinated Brodsky, and we get a hint of that outlook in the sentiment expressed aphoristically in line 26: "Now is the moment when every complete thing loses a tenth" ("when each shape and form loses resolve" in the translation). In Brodsky's worldview, decay is a process of ebbing away and flowing back, of degradation and compensation. Matter seems to be conserved even as it is frittered away, a philosophical feature to his handling of description that becomes ingrained in his early maturity with poems like "The Great Elegy to John Donne" (1963). This famous tribute, written as a baroque stylization full of paradox and contradictions, is a natural mode in which to ponder sleep as a gravitation toward complete entropy. No poem could be more rhetorically energetic in describing deadness. Famously, the verb for "sleep" tolls repeatedly in the lines that describe how deadness pervades everything and functions as an epistemological category. Nothing is knowable because consciousness sleeps until, unexpectedly, the poem becomes a conversation between the mind in sleep and the plaintive soul. Similar preoccupations, toned down and adjusted for their false theatrical frame, pervade "Homage to Chekhov." The tea cools, losing energy; the day ends, losing light; a pipe burns down, losing heat; the universe, by contrast, expands, relativizing the place of the human. Even the names of these shadowy protagonists speak to internal contradiction. Vialtseva's name contains the Russian root *vial* meaning "decayed," "worn out." The boundary between the animate and inanimate frequently slips, related to other category confusions that heighten the phenomenological presence of the world even as its existential security is called into question.

The malaise that afflicted the gentry in the late nineteenth century was the result of post-emancipation economic and demographic factors. By the 1870s, the biological sciences had informed the view of society and the individual as the products of larger determinist forces; hence social decay was seen to reflect Darwinian, evolutionary forces. The biologicization of society grounded personal and class relations as well as individual relations in the laws of nature. Chekhov's own stories, most famously "Lady with a Lapdog," explored the female sexual drive, building on the tradition of the nineteenth-century Russian novels in which the fate of heroines is determined by their sexual drive and associated pessimistic philosophical scenarios. Anna Karenina's ardor has been read persuasively as a denial of the procreative instinct. Similarly, Odintsova in Turgenev's *Fathers and Sons* is likened to a death goddess, and Olga in *On the Eve* is cast as an Isolde figure. Sex and the death instinct go together in the Freudian view and occupy a prominent place in theories of decline and decadence. These theories on occasion inform Chekhov's mature stories, sometimes shaping the individual conduct of some characters. In Chekhov, no story better symbolizes this biologized view of love than "The Grasshopper," in which the feckless heroine Olga undermines her scientist husband Gromov, like the female's instinct to eat the head of the male when mating with him. Indeed, the original title "Grasshopper-Dragonfly" ("Poprygunia-Strekoza") refers to a famous fable by Ivan Krylov, one of the great Russian satirists, in which the heroine turns into a female spider. Chekhov saw nature as rife with positive, destructive energy, an unstoppable force ultimately indifferent to human intervention and guided by physical laws that sometimes ravage the human or, more gradually, through entropy reduce everything to nothing.[10]

At the end of "The Bust of Tiberius," Brodsky's meditation on the frailty of imperial vanity and debility of empire, the ant is all that remains among postapocalyptic ruins.[11] Imperial decline and fall present a much more extreme vision than the gentle dilapidation depicted here. In "Homage to Chekhov" that decay is cast in terms familiar from Chekhov, but Brodsky goes a step further and pulls back the veil on sexual instinct as the only spark of energy latent in the scene. Even vegetation courses with sexual energy—"Trees cling to the open windows of the estate like girls to a boy" (lines 33–34 in the Russian)—and it is the elm tree alone, rather than any character, that successfully penetrates "Varvara's bedroom." Varvara may in Erlich's fantasies be wearing no underwear, but the word choice deliberately associates her, emphatically, with "nothing," in the translation rendered as "not a thing" and in the Russian spelled out syllabically as an utterance might be voiced: ни-че-го. Whatever his civilizational pessimism, Brodsky is ironizing an erotic gloom he has picked up in Chekhov and made it the central plot feature in a plotless poem.

Brodsky is a highly visual writer with a talented eye for interartistic effects. No modern poet could be more convinced of the Horatian principle of *ut pictura poesis*, namely "as is painting, so is poetry." Lyrics about paintings and films feature significantly in his work, and he makes use of ekphrasis, the still life or *nature morte*, and spatial metaphor to create three-dimensionality.[12] In this case, however, that keen eye is put to the humorous dismantlement of the props and scene-setting of realist drama. There is perhaps even a hyperrealism that communicates the nearly obsessive wish of the artist—and therefore, in effect, the pseudo-playwright—to privilege every single detail as meaningful, at least in the first stanza, which more than any other focuses on appearance (details of dress, propriety of costume) while there is still light before the rest of the poem develops in darkness. Consider the opening line, which notes how "Sunset clings to the samovar, abandoning the veranda." This is more of an instruction to the lighting designer of a production than it is a mirror to nature, and it is more overtly poetic than the prosaic "The lamp has not been lit" (line 13 in the Russian) a stanza later.

Everything, however, is not quite as it meets the eye. Varvara's primly fastened blouse is sartorially correct and suggests a certain formality, details fit for a Chekhovian play. The observation that, under her rustling skirt, there is "nothing" is not the kind of comment usually found in a Chekhovian script. Chekhov's plays are of course famously full of talk rather than action. Characters respond to stultifying boredom by becoming increasingly stultified through talking about the impossibility of action (and, when action does take place, it is normally a single devastating moment). Chekhov's short stories are also famous for cultivating the zero-action plot, lacking resolution and privileging the ineffectual over resolution. Brodsky's Chekhovian riff seems to go one step further by featuring neither philosophizing nor action and insinuating the tasteless and vulgar. In focalizing Erlich's fantasy, the lines look behind Chekhov's motivations and suggest that the feuds that typically embroil his characters are not the high-minded social and aesthetic differences they cite but rather the effects of libido.

In retelling the basic situational plot of a Chekhov play in his own terms, Brodsky adopted the content, vocabulary, and dramatic technique of hackneyed plots. The poem is a massive distillation, reducing to a reading time of perhaps ten minutes what Chekhov might have done in several hours. There is also a double focus, since the themes of decay, time, the cosmos, and erotic love, also prominent in Brodsky's poetry, are repressed here or suffer from being attached to repressed characters. Readers of both Chekhov and Brodsky in general will note the role determinism plays in their fundamentally pessimistic outlooks on mankind, Chekhov's driven more by biology, Brodsky's by history of empires.[13] But "Homage to Chekhov" also conveys in relief that their radically artistic means set them in some sort of opposition. Philosophical proximity has its value, but, for a great formalist like Brodsky, what the poem can expose is limitations in what drama can achieve. Tiresome and tired plots may continue to amuse—or look threadbare when reduced to an outline given here.

A dedication is not necessarily an act of homage. It was long ago observed that Brodsky's "attitude to monuments is suffused with irony," and it should come as no surprise that his attitude to literary monuments (i.e., Chekhov) should inspire him to give Chekhov the once over. What Brodsky disliked in Chekhov is what he identified in the sound of crickets: "They always resume in the same note they quit last night. This is one of the frightening powers of exchanges, of dialogues."[14] The reaction, however, was mixed: while in his own art Brodsky admitted that monotony and repetition were the enemy, leading him always to try to "take the next step," he ascribes "powers" to the writer (or insects) who can exploit a successful device ad infinitum (and ad nauseam). "Homage to Chekhov" is a brilliant success almost despite Chekhov, with scenes that might seem long-winded reduced to phrases, and the pompous pseudo-philosophizing that Chekhov himself lampoons now eliminated altogether until the mention of the cosmos in the very final line. It is also in the spirit of Chekhov, much more than the ill-tempered snipe found in "The Rustle of the Acacias," in mocking gently. Brodsky's play with tradition is certainly uninhibited in relation not just to Chekhov but perhaps to his own serious preoccupations. The first stanza ends with a tasteless wink to upskirting, and the poem ends on a note of existential loneliness that is undercut by the vulgar use of the verb "to give" (*davat'*), meaning "to have sex." In a poem that ends with such a mock evocation of the cosmos—one has only to think of Astrov's great speech in *Uncle Vanya* for the Chekhovian equivalent—the evocation of the female womb as "Nothing" (*ni-che-go*) could easily be turned against Brodsky's own notorious *horror vacui*. For all its mastery of Chekhov's dramatic tropes, the poem has the brio of a postmodernist dissection of dominant cultural discourses. Given the hallowed status of the plays in the Russian tradition, it qualifies as something of a "profanation" or desecration in saying directly what Chekhov's characters never speak about—namely, sex. At the same time, while laying bare in period terms the degree to which characters are actually and unconsciously in the thrall of an unconscious id, beneath the veneer of civilization, Brodsky also mocks Freudianism just as much. And, by extension, he may also be mocking his own tendency, often represented in poems, to see apocalypse everywhere, attaching it to the Freudian theory of *thanatos* and *eros*. Given the prerevolutionary context of Chekhov's plays, the poem half-jokingly suggests that historical catastrophes have followed on from repressed sexuality.

29

Lev Rubinshtein, "That's me" (1995)

THE SELF AS CARD INDEX

"Это я"

1

Это я.

2

Это тоже я.

3

И это я.

4

Это родители. Кажется, в Кисловодске. Надпись: "1952."

5

Миша с волейбольным мячом.

6

Я с санками.

7

Галя с двумя котятами. Надпись: "Наш живой уголок."

8

Третий слева—я.

9

Рынок в Уфе. Надпись: "Рынок в Уфе. 1940 г."

10

Неизвестный. Надпись: "Дорогой Ёлочке на память от М.В., г. Харьков."

11

А это отец в пижаме и с тяпкой в руке. Надпись: "Кипит работа," Почерк мой.

12

Мама с глухой портнихой Татьяной. Обе в купальниках. Надпись: "Жарко. Лето 54."

13

А это я в трусах и в майке.

14

Сидят:

15

Лазутин Феликс.

16

(И чья-то рука, пишущая что-то на листке бумаги)

17

Голубовский Аркадий Львович.

18

(И капелька дождя, стекающая по стеклу вагона)

19

Розалия Леонидовна.

20

(И маленький розовый конверт, выпавший из женской сумочки)

21

Кошелева Алевтина Никитична, уборщица.

22

(И беззвучно шевелящиеся губы телевизионного диктора)

23

Покойный А. В. Сутягин.

24

(И обрывок фотографии, плывущий по весеннему ручейку)

25

Гаврилин А. П., школьное прозвище “Таксидермист.”

26

(И надувшиеся вены на руках пожилого рабочего)

27

Проф. Витте.

28

(И раскрытый зонтик, медленно выплывающий из-под моста)

29

Стоят:

30

Мартемьянов И. С.

31

И мы видим одинокий листок, оказывающий отчаянное сопротивление ледяному осеннему ветру.

32
И надпись: “При чем здесь я?”

33
Могилевская С. Я. и Пилипенко В. Н.

34
И мы видим падающие на пол золотые кольца состригаемых волос.

35
И надпись: “Виноваты все, а отвечать тебе.”

36
Толпыгин Г. Я.

37
И мы видим заплаканное лицо итальянской тележурналистки.

38
И надпись: “С тех пор прошло немало лет, а ты все тот же, что и был, как некогда сказал поэт, чье даже имя позабыл.”

39
Иоахим Сарториус.

40
И мы видим разорванный пополам валет пик на сиденье кожаного кресла.

41
И надпись: “Здесь будет все: и плеск весла, и слово нежное люблю той, что еще не доросла, чтоб строить глазки королю.”

42
Говендо Т. Х.

43
И мы видим шесть или даже семь ярко-оранжевых таблеток на дрожащей детской ладошке.

44
И надпись: “Такой я буду умирать. Другой споткнусь и упаду. Недаром так боялась мать, что я пойду на поводу.”

45
Макеева О. А.

46
И мы видим отмеченный на географической карте город Бохум.

47
И надпись: “Привычка так существовать восходит к той еще поре, когда шуметь и приставать не разрешали детворе.”

48

Конотопов В. Н.

49

И мы видим кучку собачьего говна со свежим следом велосипедного колеса.

50

И надпись: “Когда устанешь ждать беды в своем таком родном углу, запомни влажные следы на свежевымытом полу.”

51

Замесов В. Н.

52

И мы видим детский пальчик, неуверенно подбирающий на клавишах мелодию шубертовской “Форели.”

53

И надпись: “Терпенье, слава—две сестры, неведомых одна другой. Молчи, скрывайся до поры, пока не вызовут на бой.”

54

И мы различаем в полумраке силуэт огромной крысы, обнюхивающей лицо спящего ребенка.

55

Это я.

56

И тут наконец-то появляется большая серебряная пуговица на дорожном плаще молодого человека, едущего навестить умирающего родственника.

57

И дрожит дуэльный пистолет в руке хромого офицера.

58

И дрожит раскрытый на середине французский роман в руке молодой дамы.

59

И дрожит серебряная табакерка в руке бледного молодого человека.

60

И дрожит оловянный крестик в руке пьяного солдата.

61

И дрожит большой серебряный самовар в руках пьяного военного врача.

62

И слегка подрагивает блестящий клюв большой черной птицы, неподвижно сидящей на голове гипсового бюста античной богини.

63

Это все я.

64

Лазутин Феликс: “Спасибо. Мне уже пора.”

65

(Уходит)

66

Мартемьянов Игорь Станиславович. Сезон откровений: Сб. лит.-критич. статей.—М.: Современник, 1987.

67

Голубовский Аркадий Львович: “Ну что ж. Я, пожалуй, пойду.”

68

(Уходит)

69

Толпыгин Геннадий Яковлевич. Крещенский зной: Стихотворения и поэмы.—Тула: Приокское кн. изд., 1986.

70

Розалия Леонидовна: “Уже поздно. Мне пора.”

71

(Уходит)

72

Могилевская Сусанна Янкелевна, Пилипенко Владимир Николаевич. Нам весело! А вам?: Репертуарный сб. для учащихся 4–6 кл. школ слабослышащих.—М.: Просвещение, 1984.

73

Кошелева Алевтина Никитична, уборщица: “Ой, батюшки! Что ж это я расселась-то? Надо уж идти.”

74

(Уходит)

75

Сарториус Иоахим. Формула колеса: Роман / Пер. с нем. и послесл. В. А. Ривкиной.—М.: Наука, 1984.

76

Покойный А. В. Сутягин: “Бывают ли у вас, Любочка, такие состояния, при которых буквально все, что происходит с вами и вокруг вас—вон старушка—видите?—что-то ищет в сумке, а вон кошка забежала за угол,—что все это исполнено какого-то великого и тайного смысла, который, кажется, сделай лишь малое усилие—и поймешь сразу и навсегда? Что, простите?”

77

“Ничего, я слушаю.”

78

“Так бывают или нет?”

79

“Что бывают?”

80

(Уходит)

81

Говендо Тамара Харитоновна. Некоторые вопросы неконвенциональной поэтики в поздних трудах Джеймса Доуссона // Актуальный лабиринт. Вып. 3.—М., 1992.—С. 12–21.

82

Макеева Ольга Александровна. Календарные обряды племен среднего Левобережья // Там же, стр. 12–21.

83

Конотопов Валерий Николаевич. Драма Томаса Бауэра “Скотница и курфюрст”. К анализу основных мотивов // Там же, стр. 12–21.

84

Замесов Виктор Николаевич. Кризис паразитарного сознания. Что дальше // Там же, стр. 12–21.

85

Гаврилин А. П.: “Мы, к примеру, говорим: вот ветер шумит. Да?”

86

“Ну да . . .”

87

“А шумит вовсе не ветер, а то, что попадается ему на пути: ветки деревьев, кровельная жесть, печные трубы. А ветер, Любочка, не шумит. Что ему шуметь?”

88

“Действительно . . .”

89

(Уходит)

90

Проф. Витте (один): “Господи! Сколько же можно! Пережить это нету никаких сил. Ведь я же честно стараюсь. Видит бог, я честно стараюсь.”

91

(Срывается на крик)

92

“А это все она! Она! Эта тупая мещанка Антонина! А уж чего мне стоил ее восхитительный кузен, эта ненавистная скотина, украшенная университетским дипломом, знает один только бог. Впрочем, я, кажется, знаю, что надо делать!”

93

(Уходит).

94

“Вот смотри. Сначала надо протереть вот этой губочкой. Смотри, я ведь тебе показываю. Вот этой губочкой. Потом вот этой сухой тряпочкой. Чтобы не ржавело. Понятно?”

95

(Уходит)

96

“Они мне сказали что в праздник зайдут вечерком. Ну, я пирог испекла с яблоками. Они любят с яблоками. Переоделась, сижу жду. А они мне вдруг звонят от Шустеров. Говорят, их Шустеры пригласили и они к ним поехали. Ну как же так? Я так расстроилась. Сижу как дура со своим пирогом. Позвонила тебе, думала, может быть, ты заедешь поешь. Ты ведь тоже любишь. Тебя тоже дома нет. Я даже поплакала немножко. Так тоскливо было . . . Ну ладно, не обращай внимания . . .”

97

(Уходит)

98

“Ты знаешь, я пойду, пожалуй.”

99

“Куда же ты пойдешь, чудак? У нас свободен весь чердак. Все есть: подушка, одеяло . . .”

100

“Нет-нет. Спасибо. Мне пора. (Смотрит на часы.) Двенадцать десять. Успеваю.”

101

“Ну что ж. Ни пуха ни пера.”

102

(Уходит).

103

А это я.

104

А это утро золотое, когда пускался наутек от разъяренной тети Зои простой соседский паренек.

105

А это я.

106

А это Ларичевой Раи полузабытый силуэт. Мои очки в простой оправе. Мне девять, ей двенадцать лет.

107

А это я.

108

А это те четыре слова, которые сказал Санёк, когда Колян согнул подкову, а разогнуть уже не смог.

109

А это я.

110

А это праздничной столицы краснознаменное “ура” и свежевымытые лица девчонок с нашего двора.

111

А это я.

112

А это гимна звук прелестный в шесть ровно, будто и не спал. Наверное, радиоточку кто-либо выключить забыл.

113

А это я.

114

А это я в трусах и в майке.

115

А это я в трусах и в майке под одеялом с головой.

116

А это я в трусах и в майке под одеялом с головой бегу по солнечной лужайке.

117

А это я в трусах и в майке под одеялом с головой бегу по солнечной лужайке, и мой сурок со мной.

118

И мой сурок со мной.

119

(Уходит)[1]

"That's me"

1

That's me.

2

That's me, too.

3

And that's me.

4

That's my parents. In Kislovodsk, I think. The inscription says: "1952."

5

Misha with his volleyball.

6

Me with my sled.

7

Galya with two kittens. It says: "Our pets' corner."

8

I'm third from the left.

9

The market in Ufa. It says: "Market in Ufa. 1940."

10

I don't know what that is. It says: "For dear Yolochka, to remember me by, from M. V., city of Kharkov."

11

That's my father in his pajamas holding a mattock. It says: "Working hard." The handwriting is mine.

12

Mama with the deaf dressmaker Tatiana. Both in bathing suits. It says: "It's hot. Summer '54."

13

That's me in underpants and an undershirt.

14

Seated:

15

Felix Lazutin.

16

(Someone's hand writing something on a sheet of paper.)

17

Arkady Lvovich Golubovsky.

18

(A drop of rain slipping down the window of a train car.)

19

Rosalia Leonidovna.

20

(A small pink envelope that has fallen out of a woman's purse.)

21

Alevtina Nikitichna Koshelyova, a cleaning woman.

22

(The soundlessly moving lips of a television announcer.)

23

The late A. V. Sutyagin.

24

(Part of a photograph floating down a spring rivulet.)

25

A. P. Gavrilin. At school they called him "Taxidermist."

26

(The distended veins on the arms of an elderly worker.)

27

Prof. Witte.

28

(An open umbrella floating slowly out from under a bridge.)

29

Standing:

30

I. S. Martemianov.

31

Now we see a solitary leaf desperately resisting an icy fall wind.

32

And it says: "What do I have to do with it?"

33

S. Ya. Mogilevskaya and V. N. Pilipenko.

34

Now we see ringlets of golden hair cascading to the floor.

35

And it says: "Everyone's to blame, but you have to answer."

36

G. Ya. Tolpygin.

37

Now we see the tear-stained face of an Italian woman, a TV reporter.

38

And it says: “Many years have gone by since then, and you are still the person you were, as the poet whose name I can’t even remember once said.”

39

Joachim Sartorius.

40

Now we see a jack of spades that’s been torn in half and left on the seat of a leather armchair.

41

And it says: “Here we’ll have everything: the plash of an oar and the tender words ‘I love you’ to one not yet old enough to make eyes at the king.”

42

T. Kh. Shittova.

43

Now we see six or even seven bright orange tablets in the palm of a child’s trembling hand.

44

And it says: “That’s the person I’ll be till I die. Otherwise, I’ll stumble and fall. No wonder I was so afraid of my mother and always did what she said.”

45

O. A. Makeyeva.

46

Now we see the city of Bochum marked on a map.

47

And it says: “The habit of existing like that dates back to the time when children weren’t allowed to make noise or interfere.”

48

V. N. Konotopov.

49

Now we see a small pile of dog shit bearing the fresh imprint of a bicycle tire.

50

And it says: “When you’re tired of waiting for trouble at home and can’t wait anymore, then remember the large black footprints on the freshly washed floor.”

51

V. K. Zamesov.

52
Here we see a child's hesitant finger picking out the melody of Schubert's Trout on the piano.

53
And it says: "Patience and glory are two sisters, yet neither one knows the other. Be quiet and keep out of sight until you're asked to join the fight."

54
In the semidarkness we make out the silhouette of an enormous rat nuzzling the face of a sleeping child.

55
That's me.

56
Here there finally appears the large silver button on the riding-cloak of a young man on his way to visit a dying relative.

57
A dueling pistol trembling in the hand of a lame officer.

58
A French novel, opened to the middle, trembling in the hand of a young lady.

59
A silver snuffbox trembling in the hand of a pale young man.

60
A small tin cross trembling in the hand of a drunken soldier.

61
A large silver samovar trembling in the hands of a drunken army surgeon.

62
The shiny and slightly trembling beak of a big black bird sitting motionless on the head of a plaster bust of an ancient goddess.

63
That's all me.

64
Felix Lazutin: "Thank you, but I have to go."

65
(Goes out)

66
Martemianov, Igor Stanislavovich. *A Season of Revelations*: Coll. Lit.- Crit. Articles. Moscow: Sovremennik, 1987.

67
Arkady Lvovich Golubovsky: "All right then. I think I'll be going."

68
(Goes out)
69
Tolpygin, Gennady Yakovlevich. *Epiphany Sizzles: Verses and Poems.* Tula: Priokskoye Pub., 1986.
70
Rosalia Leonidovna: "It's late. I have to go."
71
(Goes out)
72
Mogilevskaya, Susanna Yankelevna; Pilipenko, Vladimir Nikolaevich. *We're Having Fun! How About You?: Repertory Coll. for 4th, 5th and 6th Graders with Hearing Loss.* Moscow: Prosveshcheniye, 1984.
73
Alevtina Nikitichna Koshelyova, the cleaning woman: "Oh, dear! What'm I doin' sittin' here like this? I gotta go."
74
(Goes out)
75
Joachim Sartorius. *Decoding the Wheel: A Novel.* Tr. from German and postface by V.A. Rivkina. Moscow: Nauka, 1984.
76
The late A. V. Sutyagin: "Lyubochka, do you ever have the feeling that everything that's happening to you and around you—that old woman over there, see her?—looking for something in her bag, or that cat that just ran around the corner—that all this is filled with a great and mysterious meaning which, if you just made a little effort, you would understand once and for all? I'm sorry, what did you say?"
77
"Nothing. I'm listening."
78
"So, do you ever have that feeling
or not?"
79
"What feeling?"
80
(Goes out)

81
Shittova, Tamara Kharitonovna. Some Questions Concerning the Unconventional Poetics in the Later Works of James Dowson. In *Contemporary Labyrinth* (3rd ed.),—Moscow, 1992 (pp. 12–21).
82
Makeyeva, Olga Aleksandrovna. Calendrical Rites Among Tribes of the Middle Left Bank. Ibid, pp. 12–21.
83
Konotopov, Valery Nikolaevich. Thomas Bauer's Prama "The Cowgirl and the Kingmaker": An Analysis of the Dominant Motifs. Ibid, pp. 12–21.
84
Zamesov, Viktor Nikolaevich. The Crisis of the Parasitogenic Consciousness: What's Next. Ibid, pp. 12–21.
85
A. P. Gavrilin: "For example, we say, 'The wind is making so much noise.' Am I right?"
86
"Well, yes . . ."
87
"But it's not the wind that's making the noise, it's everything in its ways: the branches on the trees, the sheet metal on the roofs, the chimneys. But the wind, Lyubochka, doesn't make any noise. Why should it?"
88
"Indeed . . ."
89
(Goes out)
90
Prof. Witte (Alone): "Good Lord! How long can this go on? I simply cannot get over it! I mean to say, I am honestly trying. God can see that I am."
91
(Starts shouting)
92
"This is all because of her! Her! That mindless philistine Antonina! And as for what her delightful cousin has cost me, that hateful scoundrel done up in a university diploma, God alone knows. Actually, I think I know what to do!"
93
(Goes out)

94
"Now look. First you have to wipe it with this sponge. Look, I'm showing you how. With this sponge. Then with this dry rag. So it doesn't rust. See?"
95
(Goes out)
96
"They told me they would come by on the holiday, in the evening. So I baked an apple cake. They like apple cake. Then I changed my clothes and sat down to wait. And suddenly they call me from the Schusters and say that the Schusters invited them so they went. How can they do that? I was so upset. Sitting there like a fool with my cake. I called you because I thought you might come by and have some. You like apple cake, too. But you weren't home either. I even cried a little. I felt so depressed: Well, anyway, doesn't matter now . . ."
97
(Goes out)
98
"You know, I think I'll go."
99
"Don't be absurd. You can't go anywhere now! Look, you can have the whole attic to yourself. We have pillows, blankets, everything . . ."
100
"No, no. Thank you. (Looks at his watch) Ten past twelve. I can still make it."
101
"Well, all right. Good luck."
102
(Goes out)
103
And that's me.
104
That's a golden morning with this simple kid who lived next door running away from furious Aunt Zoya.
105
And that's me.
106
That's Raya Laricheva's half-forgotten silhouette. My glasses in simple frames. I'm nine, she's twelve.

107
And that's me.
108
Those are the four words Sanya said when Kolya bent the horseshoe, then couldn't unbend it.
109
And that's me.
110
Here's festive holiday Moscow, red flags flying and cries of "hooray!", and girls from our yard, their faces freshly washed to honor the day.
111
And that's me.
112
That's the lovely sound of the Stalinist anthem at exactly six am, as if I'd been up all night. Somebody must have forgotten to turn off the radio receiver.
113
And that's me.
114
That's me in underpants and undershirt.
115
That's me in underpants and an undershirt with my head under the covers.
116
That's me in underpants and an undershirt with my head under the covers running across a sunny glade.
117
That's me in underpants and an undershirt with my head under the covers running across a sunny glade, and my marmot with me.
118
And my marmot with me.
119
(Goes out)[2]

(TRANSLATED BY JOANNE TURNBULL)

Lev Rubinshtein (1947–2024) died in January 2024 after being hit by a car on a Moscow street. The avalanche of obituaries and memoirs about him on social media made clear that he was the living and breathing embodiment of the entire epoch that began in the 1970s, in the late Soviet cultural underground, and ended with Russia's full-scale invasion of Ukraine in 2022. Among other tributes paid to Rubinshtein in the immediate aftermath of his death was a consideration about his role in the history of Russian poetry. Ilya Kukulin and Mikhail Pavlovets[3] reiterated the observation of the late scholar Maxim Shapir, who considered Rubinshtein's "poetry on cards," "card index," or "catalog" poetry as a new versification system comparable with syllabotonic or accented verse.[4]

The first texts written by Rubinshtein following a new method date from the years 1974–75, when they represented a truly remarkable discovery long ahead of its time. The "card index" assembling a constellation of heterogeneous fragments of language gave rise to a rather wide spectrum of interpretations—irrespective, strangely enough, of the content of the actual compositions. The art critic Ekaterina Degot compared Rubinshtein's compositions with "computer hypertexts, in which each message implies a large context, and in reading which, it is impossible not to leave behind you a chain of files either [. . .] unopened or read."[5] The scholar and writer Mikhail Bezrodnyi, however, considered this genre less as an anticipation of the computerized future and more fundamentally for its echoes of the modernist past: "If you leave nothing of a Chekhov play except individual lines out of sequence, such as: 'Qiqihar. Smallpox is rampant here,' then you will get something similar to Rubinshtein's solitaire. In sum, let us discard everything superfluous—*et tout le reste est littérature*."[6]

Among the early interpretations, two predominated: the transcendent and the metalinguistic.[7] In his articles about the new tendencies in poetry of the 1970s and early 1980s, Mikhail Epstein compared Rubinshtein's cards with the albums of Ilya Kabakov, asserting that in both cases there occurred a purging of language from the ideological garbage littering it. In this case, a catalog assumes the role of a garbage dump thus giving a new spin to Akhmatova's and Shvarts's motifs of garbage as a breeding ground for poetry. Epstein held that, by means of such a purge, "Rubinshtein creates an image of that which is limitless, unnameable and beyond images. This is an idiosyncratic metaphysics of negative terms, which signify the Absolute deletion of all its specific definitions."[8] The poet and philosopher Vladimir Lettsev propounded a fundamentally similar idea that Rubinshtein's compositions resemble Zen koans, by virtue of which fragments of everyday speech are transformed into something like a springboard allowing consciousness to transcend the boundaries of the rational and intellectually comprehensible.[9]

However, there were also attempts to interpret Rubinshtein's texts without any appeals to the Absolute. Thus in the very first article about Moscow conceptualism that accompanied the first publication of Rubinshtein's poetry, which took place in the first issue (1979) of Paris-based journal *A-Ya*, Boris Groys suggested treating Rubinshtein's compositions as performances of language, liberated from everything circumstantial and extraneous. He writes about them: "Performatory verbal acts reveal their illusory character and return us to the text as pure literature, masking nothing evident but the despair and the torment of reading. The literary text is impenetrable and transparent: it requires no interpretation."[10]

A decade later Andrei Zorin, presenting Rubinshtein for the first time in the legal Soviet press of the Perestroika period, expounded a similar concept. In his opinion, in Rubinshtein's catalogs, the author

> juxtaposes styles, demonstrating the inadequacy of each of them, exhausting their possibilities and resources by sorting through the options at length. He reveals the limits and possibilities of any utterance, so that, when there is a pause, we can perceive with total clarity the necessity and the impossibility of complete embodiment in the word. In essence, this is the position of the old, romantic irony, refracted through the existential experience of the second half of the twentieth century.[11]

Finally, it is important not to lose sight of the fact that Rubinshtein's texts—especially in the "oral" period of their existence—appeared to be not entirely literature, but something different. "Well, is it poetry after all, or action art? Or some other, unknown form of theatrical art?" asked the poet and critic Mikhail Aizenberg.[12] And indeed, Rubinshtein's poetry is inseparable from authorial performance—and from an exclusively authorial reading. In describing this performance, Aizenberg wrote:

> Perhaps the essential thing about Rubinshtein's art is the rhythm, perceived as an unmanifested melody. This is precisely the reason why his compositions lose a great deal in journal and even book versions. They have to be performed (and preferably by the author himself) [. . .] The audible voice of a performer is not the voice of the author: the true author hears everything but doesn't pronounce anything. He gives away all his rights to other voices. And, what's more, in this leafing through and dry clicking over of index cards, there really is a dramatic effect so precise, that at times it transforms the text into its own accompaniment. (This hypothesis is also confirmed by the fact that, on some cards, there is no text at all. This is an objectified pause. But sometimes several such empty cards follow one after another, and the unspoken action of this overall pause unfolds within

it.) [. . .] What, then, is the point of combining different languages in a single space? Probably it lies in their collision. But also in certain secondary events that occur concurrently. The possibility of restricting yourself to a single language disappears, and consciousness starts a smooth but ineluctable transition from one language to another.[13]

The rhythm of heterogeneous elements of language, emphasized by the empty cards, lends the leafing through of the cards the significance of a special kind of epistemology. In Rubinshtein's reading-performances, what could otherwise be a ritualistic and recurrent syncretism, combining word, visual object, and theatricalized action, emerges as a broken line, constituting a possible mode of apprehension, one of many. Rubinshtein himself compared the leafing through of the cards with "a sequential removal of layers (in the manner of archaeological excavations), literally a movement into the depth of the text; this is a concrete metaphor for the process of reading as game, spectacle, and work."[14]

Rubinshtein assigns to every individual card the significance of a rhythmical gesture; in his mind each of them is "a universal unit of a rhythm that levels out any verbal gesture, whether it is a line of poetry, a fragment of street conversation, a stage direction, an exclamation, or even silence—an empty card."[15] These gestures accumulate to form rhythmical "themes" that may follow each other, be superimposed on each other, or be sounded simultaneously, in counterpoint, forming the melodic structure of a text that is seemingly woven out of "verbal trash" or, at any rate, out of logically unrelated elements.

In its most general form, the principle underlying the structure of Rubinshtein's compositions can be described as follows: each of the "cards" contains a more or less chaotic stream of heterogeneous linguistic, discursive, and stylistic forms, quotations and pseudo-quotations. All the forms presented in these fragments have been torn from their "native" contexts and therefore appear as comically alienated. At the same time, the fortuitous interactions between the fragments confer on them a new coloration and a new meaning that are not immediately discernible.

These associations as they come into being before our very eyes are incarnated in the rhythmical structures of Rubinshtein's compositions. At first their rhythms seem parodic, since, generally speaking, they are based on formal repetitions that patently conflict with the content of the cards, variegated to such a degree as to defy unification of any kind. But step by step, card after card, these rhythms become more and more complex; they become suffused, as it were, with meaning, while at the same time preserving their own illusory (because temporary and fortuitous) nature. Generally speaking, what creates these rhythms is the highly dispersed and seemingly random literal repetitions of words, phrases, motifs, or images. It is owing to these rhythms that new cards and cards that have already been voiced enter into invisible and indirect dialogues with each other.

In creating these complex rhythmical-semantic structures, Rubinshtein almost invariably works with parodic and trivial discursive fragments. Recognizable intertexts, banalities, truncated phrases, the beginnings of highly meaningful literary passages or scenes, all kinds of linguistic absurdities, empty cards—these are his preferred material. Strange as it might seem, however, the absence of an independent meaning in these discrete fragments, as well as their ability to function as an emblem of an entire discourse, a concrete, easily reconstructed speech situation—which was noted by Zorin in the late 1980s[16]—transforms them into an entirely untrammeled resource for generating new meanings.

In his early compositions, such as "A New Intermission" (1974), "The Imperative Program of the New Intermission" (1975), "Another Program" (1975), and "A Catalog of Comedic Novelties" (1976), Rubinshtein investigated the process of the generation of meanings through the clashing and decontextualization of diverse abstract grammatical structures, speech situations, and models. The scholar Gerald Janecek asserts that the models with which Rubinshtein operated in these texts were so universal that they generated a wide diversity of meanings, even some that mutually annihilated each other. He opined that Rubinshtein's early texts present "the unfolding of a profoundly pessimistic view of the world and of human activity as a passage through the grammatical prescriptions of language—a mechanical, hopeless, limited existence."[17] Janecek remarks that, for example, in "Another Program" the grammatical structures and speech models—or, in other words, the language itself—take the place of the author and, furthermore, transform the author into a puppet character who can easily be manipulated. Essentially the same thing also occurs in "A Program of Mutual Experiences" (1981) and in "Thirty-Five New Pages" (1981): in these texts, Rubinshtein constructs a rather flexible system of communication between the author and his readers/listeners—but this model is profoundly abstract: we are presented with the algebraic "formula" of a discourse, deprived of any concrete signs.

It is precisely the author's presence in the text that remains unrepresented in the process of representation. It is significant, for instance, that the card index "A Program of Mutual Experiences" is equipped with the remark: "Following reading, this is passed from hand to hand." The card with the inscription: "9. Attention! The author is among us. The Author" was conveyed to listeners silently by Rubinshtein during his performance of the text (according to Mikhail Aizenberg's account).

Rubinshtein resumed his authorial presence in the 1990s. Two of his compositions bear almost tautological titles: "I'm here" ("Ia zdes'") and "This is me" ("Eto ia"). Moreover, in both these titles Rubinshtein himself uses quotation marks. "I" ("ia") is also a quotation. This punctuation emphasizes a "quotational" character of a personal history and personal identity that Rubinshtein presents as a collage of borrowings and reflections of the other. Here the verbal principle is paired with the visual in a new manner: bibliographical cards (and, moreover, the kind on which the titles and publication details of fictitious books are given) alternate with descriptions of snapshots from a family photo album. But it is only together that the cards and snapshots create a performance under the heading "That's me." The composition as a whole can be perceived as a special kind of conundrum. What, the reader may ask, is the reason for this entire inventory, this collection, this dump of words and items, which includes people's names, miscellaneous phrases, book titles, captions, brief dialogues, remarks—basically, as is always the question with Rubinshtein—why is "that" "me"?

The first part (cards 1–13) is organized by references to snapshots that include "I" or "me": "6. Me with my sled. [. . .] 8. I'm third from the left. [. . .] 13. That's me in underpants and an undershirt." The intervals between these cards are filled by naming photographs with "others." "I" becomes a kind of rhyme, which is emphasized in the first three cards: "1. That's me. 2. That's me, too. 3. And that's me." This construction acquires the significance of not only a formal but also a semantic anacrusis: the mentions of "I" and the constant presence of "my" image—like some kind of common denominator—make it possible to set in a single sequence "parents," "Misha with his volleyball," "the market in Ufa," "Mama with the deaf dressmaker Tatiana. Both in bathing suits . . ." It is significant that the final card in this fragment reinforces the role of these mentions of "I" by means of a metrical element: "That's me in underpants and an undershirt" ("A eto ia v trusakh i v maike") is in Russian an obvious iambic tetrameter, with only a single pyrrhic foot.

The start of the next rhythmical fragment (cards 14–28) is indicated by the description of yet another photograph, this time of a group: "14. Seated:" The rhythm of this fragment is created by the alternation of certain names and meditative phrases:

14
Seated:
15
Felix Lazutin.
16
(Someone's hand writing something on a sheet of paper.)

17
Arkady Lvovich Golubovsky.
18
(A drop of rain slipping down the window of a train car.)

The degree of rhythmicality here is rather high, since all the odd-numbered cards of the fragment are given over to names, and all the even-numbered cards to meditations. In addition, the meditative phrases ("soundlessly moving lips," "an open umbrella floating slowly out from under a bridge," and so on) are correlated with each other by a distinct syntactical parallelism. The meaning of this rhythmical structure is also highlighted by a play on "my," "mine," and "someone else's." At first glance, what we have before us is an alternating sequence in which an individual (the personal name) precedes an impersonal detail. But the expressive quality of the descriptions of these details convinces us of the opposite: the item or object, whether it is a drop of rain, a scrap of a photograph or "an open umbrella floating slowly out from under a bridge," catches the reflected glimmer of the "I," of the perceiving subject. In parallel, the human name is transformed into an unintelligible sign, an impersonal index, and is, in effect, decorporealized.

The third rhythmical fragment (cards 29–55) begins with a card that rhymes with the beginning of the previous fragment: "14. Seated:"—"29. Standing:" And the structure of this part is a more complicated version of the previous segment's structure. The sequence of names is continued (cards 30, 33, 36, 39, 42, 45, 48, 51). The sequence of expressive details carries on. However, phrases of this type are now connected to each other by the anaphoric repetition "Now we see . . ." (*I my vidim . . .*) (cards 34, 37, 40, 43, 46, 49, 52, 54). A new rhythmical component is added to these familiar elements: it is created by cards that begin with the words: "And it says . . ." (*Nadpis' . . .*) (cards 35, 38, 41, 44, 47, 50, 53). Special semantic relations arise between phrases with identical beginnings. For instance, the "Now we see . . ." cards ring the changes on a motif of pain, weakness, bewilderment, or revulsion:

37. Now we see the tear-stained face of an Italian woman, a TV reporter.
43. Now we see six or even seven bright orange tablets in the palm of a child's trembling hand.
49. Now we see a small pile of dog shit bearing the fresh imprint of a bicycle tire.
54. In the semidarkness we make out the silhouette of an enormous rat nuzzling the face of a sleeping child.

Such a video sequence, if we can call it that, really does resemble a photomontage. This sequence is naturally opposed by the verbal sequence—or, to put it another way, the verbal sequence of "captions" enters into dialogue with it. Rubinshtein deliberately intensifies the literary character of these cards by giving them the form of rhymed stanzas: "*38. I nadpis': 'S tekh por proshlo niemalo let, a ty vse tot zhe, chto i byl, kak nekogda skazal poet, ch'io dazhe imia pozabyl'* ("And it says: 'Many years have gone by since then, and you are still the person you were, as the poet whose name I can't even remember once said'"). If the remark *I nadpis'* is removed, cards 38, 44, and 53 can easily be written in a column as "normal" iambic tetrameter with masculine rhymes.

Two cards do not fit into this microtext: "32. And it says: 'What do I have to do with it?'" and "35. And it says: 'Everyone's to blame, but you have to answer.'" But, in effect, by prefacing the verse-form "text within the text," these "captions" directly transform it into a description of "I." In the verses that are captioned, the speaking subject "I" philosophizes about what within himself can be counterposed to suffering, baseness, and weakness. However, the paradox here is the same as in the second part: that which lays claim to the role of individual self-expression turns out to be the vicarious, trivial, hackneyed speech of impersonal, secondhand poetry.

It is significant that the alternation of all three elements of the rhythmic structure of this segment is extremely regular. In effect, one and the same "stanza" is repeated seven times, consisting of a name unknown to the readers, a phrase beginning with the words "Now we see . . . ," and a phrase, beginning with the words "And it says . . ." The only deviation occurs at the end of the fragment, where the "tercet" is replaced by a "distich": "Now we see . . ." is replaced by "We make out" (*I my razlichaem . . .*) and, instead of the name of an "other," "I" appears again.

> 54. In the semidarkness we make out the silhouette of an enormous rat
> nuzzling the face of a sleeping child.
> 55. That's me.

Deviating from a relatively stable rhythm is always a means of accentuating a semantically important point in a poem. And this applies to Rubinshtein, too. The final "That's me" card becomes a distinctive summary of the entire fragment: all this is me. Jumping ahead, we can note that the beginning of the penultimate segment of the composition will be precisely that: "63. That's all me." In other words, self-consciousness and self-awareness of the "I" arise at the intersection of the names, impressions, and words of others, ostensibly spoken about oneself.

This conclusion is also entirely applicable to the fourth fragment (cards 56–62), the rhythm of which is generated by the repetition of deliberately bookish, almost quotational phrases, beginning in Russian with *I drozhit* . . . ("And trembling . . ."): a dueling pistol (57), a French novel open to the middle (58), a silver snuffbox (59), a tin cross (60), a silver samovar (61). Moreover, this fragment starts with a phrase that clearly elicits associations with the beginning of Pushkin's *Evgeny Onegin*—"56. Here there finally appears the large silver button on the riding-cloak of a young man on his way to visit a dying relative"—and it concludes with an allusion to a poem no less canonical than *Evgeny Onegin*, Edgar Allan Poe's "The Raven": "62. The shiny and slightly trembling beak of a big black bird sitting motionless on the head of a plaster bust of an ancient goddess." These are all literary, primarily romantic models of fate—but all this is also "I."

The rhythm of the fifth fragment, which is the largest and the penultimate one (cards 63–102), is also composed of repeating elements that lend themselves to summary as utterances by specific characters, which gradually develop into short sketch-dialogues of one to five cards. For example:

> 76. The late A. V. Sutyagin: "Lyubochka, do you ever have the feeling that everything that's happening to you and around you—that old woman over there, see her?—looking for something in her bag, or that cat that just ran around the corner—that all this is filled with a great and mysterious meaning which, if you just made little effort, you would understand once and for all? I'm sorry, what did you say?"
> 77. "Nothing. I'm listening."
> 78. "So, do you ever have that feeling or not?"
> 79. "What feeling?"
> 80. (Goes out)

In the middle of the segment appear philosophical reflections, lamentations, invectives, and everyday advice:

> 90. Prof. Witte (Alone): "Good Lord! How long can this go on? I simply cannot get over it! I mean to say, I am honestly trying. God can see that I am."
> 91. (Starts shouting)
> 92. "This is all because of her! Her! That mindless philistine Antonina! And as for what her delightful cousin has cost me, that hateful scoundrel done up in a university diploma, God alone knows. Actually, I think I know what to do!"
> 93. (Goes out)

Other repeated elements of this segment are the dividing stage direction "Goes out" (which always occurs after a character's utterance or at the end of a scene), bibliographical references, titles of scholarly articles and books, including the author's name, publishing details, pages, and so on in full.

The latter part of the segment would appear to be completely devoid of any elements even tinged with lyricisms, those bearers of the self-consciousness of "I." But, in actual fact, "I" is manifested here indirectly via "others." Hence, for instance, the titles of books and articles listed in this card index can easily be interpreted as a parodic auto-meta-description of Rubinshtein's poetic style:

> 84. Zamesov, Viktor Nikolaevich. The Crisis of the Parasitogenic Consciousness: What's Next.

Is this not the crisis of postmodern consciousness that concerns the author—not Zamesov, of course, but Rubinshtein? Among bibliographic references, the reader cannot help noticing recurring mentions of articles published in the collection under the title *Contemporary Labyrinth* (*Aktual'nyi labirint*—cards 81, 82, 83, 84). And, indeed, Rubinshtein's cards create a virtual labyrinth. Sometimes, Rubinshtein inserts provocative self-referential "titles," such as:

> 72. Mogilevskaya, Susanna Yankelevna; Pilipenko, Vladimir Nikolaevich. We're Having Fun! How About You?: Repertory Coll. for 4th, 5th and 6th Graders with Hearing Loss. Moscow: Prosveshchenie [Enlightenment], 1984.

It is noteworthy that the names of people given on family photographs in the first part of the composition turn into the "authors of books" of the second part. By the logic of the subtext, these purely rhythmical connections establish correlations between widely separated iterations. This produces a double, or even triple, effect. First, what seemed to be the impersonal designation of a person suddenly acquires a voice and speech. Second, the actual name becomes, as it were, imbued with a new freshness, engendering unpredictable associations with its immediate setting. Whereas in his early texts Rubinshtein played on the metaphor of the world as a library, conferring living voices on linguistic structures, fragments of discourses, and so on, here, by contrast, he moves from "reality," from what has not been introspectively analyzed, to "language," to the book. A beloved face, a person who is near and dear, a stranger's fate that is yet so familiar—these, too, prove to be quotations.

As we recall, personal names first appeared in this poem following the stage directions "Seated:" and "Standing:" In the final part of the fifth section, a certain group photograph from the family archive comes to life before our eyes, and the characters in it "leave." The connection between the characters in this part and the family photographs at the beginning of the composition clearly demonstrates that the "I," which repeatedly appears beside "Shittova T. Kh." and "the late A. V. Sutiagin," combines these two segments into one for us in the overall space of the text—in effect on a single stage, from which all gradually "go out." And the remarks that they utter can only seem mysterious outside of the general semantic field of the text. Thus, for instance, Gavrilin A. P. declares:

85. A. P. Gavrilin: "For example, we say, 'The wind is making so much noise.' Am I right?"
86. "Well, yes . . ."
87. "But it's not the wind that's making the noise, it's everything in its ways the branches on the trees, the sheet metal on the roofs, the chimneys. But the wind, Lyubochka, doesn't make any noise. Why should it?"

However, this is a direct answer to the question concerning the manifestation, embodiment, and, in general, presence of "I," a question that the structure of the text continually toys with. "I" is the wind, which embodies itself in what is other and through others, but it is not reducible to the roofs, chimneys, and trees, and remains something separate from them.

Illuminatingly, at the end, when they all leave ("Go out"), the "I" nonetheless does not disappear. The rhythm of the final part (cards 103–19) returns to the rhythm of the first, initial fragment. But the rhythmicality of the final fragment is far more intense. Here there is precise repetition of one and the same phrase—"And that's me" (*A eto ia*, cards 113–17)—whereas at the beginning "I" was mentioned in different variations. This repeating dictum is in turn anaphorically connected with the phrases about others. These phrases once again form a versified, rhymed text, but one that is not disrupted by the refrain "And that's me." On the contrary, the refrain becomes an integral part of a distinct rhythmical pattern. Here we really do have a manifestation of the "I," dissolved in the signs of the existence of others. And at the end of the text—for the first time—a phrase is deployed about "I," and only "I," that is entirely sufficient unto itself, although it exists in the words and images of "others":

113. А это я
114. А это я в трусах и в майке.
115. А это я в трусах и в майке под одеялом с головой.
116. А это я в трусах и в майке под одеялом с головой бегу по солнечной лужайке.

117. А это я в трусах и в майке под одеялом с головой бегу по солнечной лужайке, и мой сурок со мной.
118. И мой сурок со мной.
119. (Уходит)

113. And that's me.
114. That's me in underpants and undershirt.
115. That's me in underpants and an undershirt with my head under the covers.
116. That's me in underpants and an undershirt with my head under the covers running across a sunny glade.
117. That's me in underpants and an undershirt with my head under the covers running across a sunny glade, and my marmot with me.
118. And my marmot with me.
119. (Goes out)

At first glance chaotic, the structure of Rubinshtein's text turns out to be a sequence of localized rhythms, which are also correlated with each other. And it is precisely at the point of their mutual intersection that the "I" arises as the interlinking of fleeting rhythmical patterns that emerge out of unrelated forms and dissolve back into it. From this point of view, it is clear that the actual card index, structured as a combination of rhythms of this kind, is isomorphic to Rubinshtein's philosophy of the "I" as a text. "That's me" becomes not only a model of (self-)consciousness in motion, but also an analogue of all human life from childhood to death. Moreover, in the ending adduced above, childhood and death (leaving, departure) are united in a single point.

The rhythmical structure of the composition acquires special significance: each segment of it corresponds to philosophical (more than biographical) phases of the formation of the "I," and each time these presuppose a new correlation between the heterogeneous languages of culture, a new set of elements that are "other." In essence, the rhythmical patterning of this text can be read as a bildungsroman in miniature—or, rather, as a suggestive synopsis of such a novel, consisting entirely of metaphorical or metonymic associations that are equally individual and universal in nature.

Rubinshtein does not renounce the postmodernist understanding of the individual personality as a sum of diverse discourses of identity. Yet he restores the rights of individual subjectivity, which appears in his composition in an entirely irrational fashion over and above the hackneyed and impersonal material of language, as a fluid but always inimitable combination of what is repeatable or "other": words, things, gestures, images, and so on.[18] With this approach, subjectivity appears as something similar to the pattern in a kaleidoscope. It is inconstant and changeable, consisting of impersonal fragments. At the same time, the "I" takes form as a dynamic unity of all the elements of the text, emerging as the factor that configures the rhythm, while the rhythm generated by the "I" also remains a variable value. Searching for this combination and sorting through these rhythms that connect what is "other" and what is "one's own" constitute the unique, inimitable, and priceless meaning of life.

30

Elena Fanailova, "... Again they're off for their Afghanistan" (2003)

SCARS OF IMPERIAL EROS

... Они опять за свой Афганистан
И в Грозном розы черные с кулак
На площади, когда они в каре
Построились, чтоб сделаться пюре.
Когда они присягу отдавать,
Тогда она давать к нему летит,
Как новая Изольда и Тристан
(Особое вниманье всем постам)
И в Ашхабаде левый гепатит

Он пьет магнезию из общего бачка,
Железною цепочкой грохоча,
Пока она читает Отче наш,
Считая дни задержки у врача.
Лечение идет своей чредой,
И он пока гуляет молодой,
Проводит дни, скучая и дроча

Ефрейтор N., постарше остальных,
Еще салаг,
Знаток похабных дембельских наук,
Им разливает черного вина,
Поскольку помнит не из уставных
Параграфов, а как-то так:
Болезни грязных рук—
Проглоченные пули из говна

Общинный миф и коммунальный ад.
Она же в абортарий, как солдат,
Идет привычным шагом строевым,
Как обучал недавно военрук,
И делает, как доктор прописал.
И там она в кругу своих подруг.
Пугливых стройных ланей и дриад—
Убоина и мясокомбинат.

И персональной воли нет,
А только случай, счастье выживать.
А там в Афгане—пиво по усам,
Узбечки невъебенной красоты
Уздечки расплетали языком.
Их с ветерком катали на броне
И с матерком,
Чтоб сор не выносить вовне,
Перед полком расстреливал потом,

Точней, командовал расстрелом сам
Полковник,—этих, кто волок в кусты,
Кто за косы в кусты волок
И кто насиловал их по кустам,
Афганок лет шестнадцати на вид,
На деле же—двенадцати едва.
Насильникам не больше двадцати.
Родня не узнавала ничего.
И медленно спускался потолок,
Как будто вертолет, под бабий вой

Теперь они бухают у реки
И вспоминают старые деньки.
И как бы тянет странный холодок
Физическим телам их вопреки.
Теперь любовникам по сорока,
Сказать точнее, мужу и жене.
Ребенку десять, поздно для совка.
Их шрамы отвечают за себя.

Другой такой страны мне не найти.[1]

. . . Again they're off for their Afghanistan,
And black roses in Grozny, big as fists,
On the plaza, as they form a square
On their way to being smashed to bits.
When they go to get sworn in,
She flies to give it up to him,
Like a new-fangled Tristan and Isolde
(Special dispatch to all posts)
And there's a strange strain of Hep in Ashkhabad

He drinks magnesia from the common trough,
Making a racket with the metal chain
While she recites Our Father at the doctor's
Counting the days of menstrual delays.
The cure proceeds at its own pace,
And meanwhile he carouses like a boy
Bored and jerking away his days

Corporal N., a bit older than the rest,
Who are still wet behind the ears,
Is an expert in the vulgar furlough arts,
He pours black wine for them,
Remembering, not from the authorized
Sections, but something along these lines:
The diseases of dirty hands are
Swallowed bullets made of shit

Common myth and communal hell.
She's off to the abortion clinic,
Exactly as the doctor has prescribed,
Like a soldier marching the familiar march,
According to the commander's drill.
And there she is, surrounded by her friends,
Slender and skittish fauns and dryads all—
Cattle at an abattoir.

There's no free will,
Just chance, the luck to simply stay alive.
And there in 'Ghanistan were beer-soaked mustaches,

Fucking beautiful Uzbek girls
Unbraiding bridles with their tongues.
They got to ride on armor metal,
Fast and crude.
Later, to keep the whole affair from leaking out,
The colonel himself shot them dead

In front of the regiment—or more precisely,
Had them shot, the ones who dragged
The girls into the bushes by their braids
And those who raped them in the bushes,
The Afghan girls who looked about sixteen,
But weren't any older than twelve, and barely.
The rapists weren't more than twenty.
Their families heard nothing of it.
And the ceiling bore down slowly like
A chopper to the sound of women wailing

Now they're at the river getting soused
And reminiscing about the good old days.
And it's as though a strange chill tugs
Against their corporeal flesh.
Now the lovers are both forty.
Or, more precisely, the husband and the wife.
The kid is ten, they had him late by Soviet standards.
Their scars speak for themselves.

I'll never find another country such as this.

(TRANSLATED BY GENYA TUROVSKAYA)

Having originally qualified as a doctor and then as a psychologist, Elena Fanailova (b. 1962) works professionally as a journalist at Radio Liberty. She became a pioneer of the new political poetry that emerged in the 2000s, when it seemed on the face of things that the themes discussed so vehemently in the Perestroika period during the 1980s and tumultuous 1990s had lost their allure, especially in poetry. Nonetheless, this was the very moment when Fanailova began writing incisively topical poems. In so doing, she lay the foundations of the new poetics that emerged in the 2010s, following the unsuccessful "winter revolution" of 2011–12. From this point, the politically oriented poetry of those years once again attracted the attention of the broad public. Indicative of this success is the cycle "Poet and Citizen" ("Poet i grazhdanin") by Dmitry Bykov that enjoyed a mass success, each poem in the cycle eagerly awaited by the public and circulated as a meme. Performed at the time by the actor Mikhail Efremov on YouTube, it is now published in book form.[2]

Several years earlier, Fanailova's "Baltic Diary" ("Baltiiskii dnevnik," 2008) had already provoked a stormy political discussion in the blogosphere, in the course of which, among other opinions, it was suggested by some that Fanailova was reverting to "civic poetry" in the spirit of "the Sixtiers," sacrificing aesthetic considerations to provocative topicality and demonstrating the intelligentsia's arrogant attitude to "'the masses.'"[3] A journalist by profession, Fanailova is much closer than other people to points of potential political conflict that the general public preferred to ignore in the 2000s, when it reveled in the comfort of Putin's "stability," secured at the time by Russia's commodities boom. Fanailova's poems of the first decade of the twenty-first century bucked that trend, and they find a place for Yeltsin and Putin, including sharp, crisp political diagnoses ("Don't come back: the KGB is here again / And stagnation is being parodied . . .")[4] as well as criticisms of state security operatives, Ramzan Kadyrov, and the police practicing aikido on the public entrusted to its care.

Two parallel processes, thematic and stylistic, are coordinated in Fanailova's poetry: on the one hand, political motifs acquire increasing significance, and, on the other, syllabotonic versification and regular rhyme schemes are disrupted, effecting a transition to a rhythmical system based on shifts and discontinuities of the melodic momentum. Many of those who have written about Fanailova remark that the formal shift that occurred in her poetic manner in the 2000s is an indirect manifestation in Fanailova's poetic practice of her experience as a journalist.[5] Mikhail Aizenberg's characterization of the collection "Black Suits" ("Chernye kostiumy," 2008) ably provides the gist:

> There is something rapid and fleeting, almost like live reporting, in the pattern of phrasing, in the narrative style. It is as if Fanailova strives to lubricate the literary form until it becomes completely intangible and teach the word to seize on the raw material, like a hawk—like a Kodak instant camera. The piling on of details, the whipping up of *emotion*, which is meant to take the place of poetry, but not become "verses."[6]

All of this serves to confirm that, rather than speaking of Fanailova and the politicization of lyric poetry, it would be more correct to speak of *the politics of the lyrical subject*, which finds its embodiment in all the components of poetic utterance from intonation to rhythm to imagery. In this regard it is significant that

Fanailova herself names two events as the source of this new poetic manner: the personal tragedy of the death of her partner and the horror of the hostage taking in Beslan (2004), which, as a journalist, she observed close at hand. In the traditional typology of poetic genre, these events are separately assigned to the "lyrical" and "civic" categories. But for Fanailova it was precisely the way they resonated with each other that exploded her former poetic style and former lyrical subject. "I didn't write for almost a year. My own personality seemed absolutely insignificant to me [. . .] Since that time, only something that can bear comparison with death has seemed important to me,"[7] Fanailova said in an interview with Linor Goralik. And, concerning her new poetic voice, she added, "It's the internal intonation of a condition in which the border between worlds, the border between the world of the living and the world of the dead, is erased. The old rhythmical framework completely collapses."[8]

In the early 2000s, an idealizing nostalgia for the USSR became the common ground on which the aspirations of the national authorities coincided with those of "the broad masses." This is the context for Fanailova's poem ". . . Again they're off for their Afghanistan." It exposes the terrifying nature of Soviet nostalgia as simultaneously arousing both her compassion and her revulsion. Fanailova later equipped her text with an extensive prose commentary, in which she told the story of its creation:

> In August 2001 I was sitting on the bank of the Usmanka River, near Voronezh. More precisely, I was sunbathing with a girlfriend: a campsite, warm weather, the last days of summer when you could still go swimming. Next to us was a group of people: husband and wife, their son, the wife's mother, and some man, to whom they suddenly, and for no apparent reason, began to tell their story: how the husband was taken by the army, that the training was in Grozny, and the roses there were big and black, the time she went to see him for the swearing in, the roses on the plaza were fist-sized, remember, how beautiful the city was (addressing each other)? Then he came down with jaundice, and was sent to Ashkhabad for some reason, to the hospital, and they drank magnesium by the mug there, no other available treatment, and in the evening, in the ward, they drank local wine.[9]

The sociologist and critic Boris Dubin wrote that "Elena Fanailova stands out for me in contemporary Russian poetry by the firm determination with which she devotes space in her poems to the voices of others."[10] In perfect conformity with this analysis, the poem under consideration here is written "through" other people's voices, which is emphasized by the first—grammatically incorrect—phrase: *Oni opiat' za svoi Afganistan* (the correct form would be . . . *pro svoi Afganistan*), a phrase that is captured in Genya Turovskaya's translation as ". . . Again they're off for their Afghanistan" (line 1), while in a more "proper" style, it would be something like: "now they're going on about their Afghanistan."

Who is the lyrical subject of this poem? Probably it is the poet who, sponge-like, soaks up the voices of characters neither near and dear nor psychologically close to her. The outcome is a hybrid narrative in which other people's words are interwoven with a distanced evaluation, either ironic or generalizing, which sounds like a stage direction in a play. This hybridism is subtly conveyed in the form of the poem. Its basic verse form of iambic pentameter was strongly associated with high-minded official Soviet poetry, which is surely what Fanailova wants to undermine. But the metrical scheme is enriched by a complex verse arrangement and an even more complex rhyme system, as well as the use of severely truncated lines (in line 18 this is lost in the translation, but in line 39 it is well preserved). Taken together, all these complications stretch the syllabotonic scheme as far as possible, making it sound very similar to free (although rhythmically organized) verse.

In Fanailova's poem, the speech of others is not homogeneous. Two perspectives, those of the husband and the wife, merge together into a sort of double-voiced narrative. This results in multilevel resonances between the voices, manifesting unexpected connections between the speech of the characters and the words of the poet. Consider, for instance, Fanailova's diagnosis in line 32: *uboina i miasokombinat*—the excellent translation "Cattle at an abattoir" even conveys a profound assonance of the original—absorbs into itself both the "black roses [. . .] big as fists" (line 2) and the "puree" (line 4) into which the conscripts are doomed to be transformed (in the translation they are "smashed to bits"); the "magnesia from the common trough" (line 10); the "black wine"(line 20); the "swallowed bullets made of shit" (line 24), as well as, finally, the abortion clinic. In other words, we have a variety of motifs of a suffering, sick body that is doomed to die, of a person reduced to the condition of meat, food, a carcass. In a similar fashion, a company of conscripts, infected with hepatitis, who are taking lessons in "vulgar furlough arts" (*pokhabnye dembel'skie nauki*, line 19) from corporal N., rhymes with the ironical choir of "slender and skittish fauns and dryads" (line 31) accompanying the heroine to the abortion clinic. But the generalization made by the author applies to both of these: "There's no free will, / Just chance, the luck to simply stay alive" (lines 33–34).

On close examination, it becomes clear that Fanailova is simultaneously operating not with two but with three voices that intertwine and resonate with one another, each of them recording a particular position about violence and coercion. Throughout the poem, we hear the voice of a woman who is a direct victim of violence. If it is medical rather than military, nonetheless it emanates from the culture of war. The second voice belongs to a juvenile soldier, indistinguishable from the mass of other conscripts just like him, and therefore an indirect accomplice to violence. Third, there is the voice of the observer, attempting, on the one hand, to distance herself from the ubiquitous violence, but, on the other hand, confident that the poet cannot possibly abstract herself from her characters and their experience. This triple subject becomes the prism that Fanailova uses in her efforts to refract the quintessence of the Soviet experience from the conversation of her coincidental neighbors by the river.

The poem is split into stanzas with a variable number of lines, in which the verses fluctuate in length and have flexible rhyme schemes, although the rhymes are exclusively masculine. The second stanza (lines 10–16), the fourth (lines 25–32), and the last (lines 52–60) are distinguished by the fact that, regardless of the length of the stanza (from seven to eleven lines), a shared rhyme unites their first and last lines, while being repeated three or four times altogether in the stanza. These rhymed lines frame an authorial voice containing revulsion, irony, and compassion.

The final line of the poem is particularly striking ("I'll never find another country such as this," line 60) because it robs the observing author of any possibility of maintaining a position of estranged irony. Yuri Leving noted that this line very slightly reworks the line of the famous song "Wide Is My Motherland" by Isaac Dunaevsky and Vasily Lebedev-Kumach from the film *Circus* (1935, dir. Grigory Aleksandrov),[11] the song that was an unofficial anthem of the USSR:

I know of no other such country
Where a man can breathe so freely.

This intertextual reference assuredly creates a contrasting effect vis-à-vis the poetic narrative of violence and traumas. Moreover, it excludes any possibility that the author shares her characters' nostalgia for the fallen empire. As Fanailova explained: "Of course, the last line, which I wrote from myself, expresses an unbearable bitterness and pain for this country, and not at all the admiration that some readers imagine they have glimpsed."[12]

The first, third, fifth, and sixth stanzas are structured in a similar way, but the repeated rhymes in them emphasize the logic of the "communal hell" (*kommunal'nyi ad*, line 25) internalized by the characters. The first line of the poem, ". . . Again they're off for their Afghanistan" (*. . . Oni opiat' za svoi Afganistan*), rhymes in the Russian with the contrasting "Like a new-fangled Tristan and Isolde" (*Kak novaia Izol'da i Tristan*, line 7) and the deflatingly ironic "Special dispatch to all posts" (*Osoboe vnima'e vsem postam*, line 8). In the third stanza there is no dominant rhyme, since each rhyme is repeated only once: ABCDABCD. But the "communal" wisdom of army hygiene is contradicted by the "vulgar arts" of the corporal, and the black wine that reminds us of the black roses "big as fists"(line 2) in the first stanza. In the culminating fifth and sixth stanzas, the end rhymes are interwoven with internal rhymes, binding together in a single whole sex and violence, gratification and killing (lines 35–48):

А там в Афгане—пиво по усам,
Узбечки невъебенной красоты
Уздечки расплетали языком.
Их с ветерком катали на броне
И с матерком,
Чтоб сор не выносить вовне,
Перед полком расстреливал потом,

Точней, командовал расстрелом сам
Полковник,—этих, кто волок в кусты,
Кто за косы в кусты волок
И кто насиловал их по кустам,
Афганок лет шестнадцати на вид,
На деле же—двенадцати едва.
Насильникам не больше двадцати.

And there in 'Ghanistan were beer-soaked mustaches,
Fucking beautiful Uzbek girls
Unbraiding bridles with their tongues.
They got to ride on armor metal,
Fast and crude.
Later, to keep the whole affair from leaking out,
The colonel himself shot them dead

In front of the regiment—or more precisely,
Had them shot, the ones who dragged
The girls into the bushes by their braids
And those who raped them in the bushes,
The Afghan girls who looked about sixteen,
But weren't any older than twelve, and barely.
The rapists weren't more than twenty.

These fragments expose the eroticism of violence as the main theme of Fanailova's poem. From the first lines, the motifs of erotic gratification and violation are consistently developed in seamless permutations. Roses (a traditional symbol of love) are reminiscent of a fist (an image of violence) and associated with a city of war—Grozny (in 2001, when this poem was written, a colonial war was being waged again, this time between Russia and Chechnya). The military expression *otdavat' prisiagu* (lit. "to take an oath," line 5) is transformed in the next line to a colloquial *ona davat' k nemu letit* (lit. "She flies to give him one," line 6) where *davat'* carries a meaning of having sex with someone. It is the eroticism of violence that takes center stage first—the outing to the abortion clinic looks like militarized demolition of the individual personality (lines 26–29):

Она же в абортарий, как солдат,
Идет привычным шагом строевым,
Как обучал недавно военрук,
И делает, как доктор прописал.

She's off to the abortion clinic,
Exactly as the doctor has prescribed,
Like a soldier marching the familiar march,
According to the commander's drill.

The pastoral motifs of lines 30–31 ("And there she is, surrounded by her friends, / Slender and skittish fauns and dryads all") sound frankly derisive here, ironically leading us to the verdict that concludes the verse: "Cattle at an abattoir" (*uboina i miasokombinat,* line 32). The Soviet system of health care inflicts coercion on people, degrading and dehumanizing them no less than war. Fanailova comments that "Soviet gynecology was the legalization of extreme humiliation and utter shame, all performed barracks-style, like the rest of Soviet existence."[13]

In this poem, Fanailova is clearly glancing over her shoulder at Joseph Brodsky's well-known "Verses on the Winter Campaign 1980" ("Stikhi o zimnei kampanii 1980-go goda"), in which the war in Afghanistan is also associatively linked with the motif of abortion and the transformation of a human being into "uboina" ("fresh meat").

Заунывное пение славянина
вечером в Азии. *Мерзнущая, сырая*
человеческая свинина
лежит на полу караван-сарая.
Тлеет кизяк, ноги окоченели;
пахнет тряпьем, позабытой баней
Сны одинаковы, как шинели.
Больше патронов, нежели воспоминаний,
и во рту от многих "ура" осадок.

Слава тем, кто, не поднимая взора,
шли в абортарий в шестидесятых,
спасая отечество от позора![14]

The doleful, echoing Slavic singing
at evening in Asia. Dank and freezing,
sprawling piles of human pig meat
cover the caravansary's mud bottom.
The fuel dung smolders, legs stiffen in numbness.
It smells of old socks, of forgotten bath days.
The dreams are identical, as are the greatcoats.
Plenty of cartridges, few recollections,
and the tang in the mouth of too many "hurrahs."
Glory to those who, their glances lowered,
marched in the sixties to abortion tables,
sparing the homeland its present stigma.[15]

In Brodsky's poem, abortion is a form of protest against "a new glaciation—the glaciation of slavery" creeping across the globe.[16] In "Verses on the Winter Campaign," everybody is a victim, and no one can survive the new apocalypse, not even a dog orbiting Earth in a spaceship. For Fanailova, on the contrary, abortion is a form of war: in the Soviet clinic, the same mechanisms of dehumanization are at work as in Afghanistan.

This difference is indicative of a deeper polemic between Fanailova and Brodsky. For Brodsky, war is unequivocally synonymous with death. By contrast, Fanailova describes a colonial war through the motifs of sex and gratification, interwoven with horror and death, something that only makes the picture even more terrifying. The officers' sex with Uzbek women, who have been recruited into the Soviet army, gives way to the soldiers' rapes of young girls in occupied Afghanistan, culminating in the shooting of the rapists and the weeping of their mothers. Women are treated as colonial subalterns, which is emphasized by the obscene vocabulary and the rape scene. The rhymes in these lines create an effect of comparability that yokes together opposites: the dashing jollity of a colonial army and the execution of soldier-rapists: *a tam v Afgane—pivo po usam* ("And there in 'Ghanistan were beer-soaked mustaches," line 35)—*komandoval rasstrelom sam* ("The colonel himself shot them dead," line 41 in the translation). The erotic sequence of *uzbechki* ("Uzbek girls," line 36) and *iazykom* ("with their tongues," line 37) is rhymed with symbols of masculinity, power, military might, and subjection: *uzdechki* ("bridles," but also a penis's frenulum),[17] *s veterkom katali na brone* [. . .] *s materkom* ("They got to ride on armor metal, / Fast and crude," lines 38–39), and *rasstrelival potom* ("Later [. . .] shot them dead," lines 40–41). The victims of rape, "who looked about sixteen, / But weren't any older than twelve, and barely" (lines 46–47), are like the rapists: "The rapists weren't more than twenty" (line 48).

Internal rhymes running through the text bond together the rapists and the victims of rape, the soldiers of empire and the colonial subalterns, the executioners and the executed into a "communal body," as the conceptualist artists of the 1970s called it. The assessment "cattle at an abattoir" (line 32) refers specifically to this collective body. But this body is also imbued with the eroticism of violence that later evokes nostalgia for things Soviet. The eroticization of violence eliminates the question of guilt or responsibility, that is, it cancels out any ethical assessment at all for complicity in the crimes. Ethical judgment is displaced by the illusion of belonging to a "communal body," which in this case is also the body of an empire. And it is precisely this memory of belonging to an imperial body, bonded together by the eroticism of violence, that is preserved by the narrators, namely, the husband and wife.

And the eroticism of violence is double-edged. On the one hand, the husband and wife are scarred by the violation that they have experienced, which is not necessarily military in nature—the "strange chill" (line 54) and the scars on their bodies are the signs of this eroticism.[18] On the other hand, the memory of the eroticism of empire is devoid for the protagonists of ethical evaluations and easily incorporated into the fabric of the present day's "normality," surmounting the rift between the Soviet 1980s and the post-Soviet 2000s. Fanailova comments:

> The sense of violence is the main thing that I remember about this era; this sense penetrated all entertainments, pleasures, sensations and feelings, not to speak of work, and it was fully present in the conversation of these people, my contemporaries. They speak about monstrous things in a rather ordinary way, even with some animation, because it is their youth they are referring to, and in the moment of telling their story they re-enter it.[19]

In the "stable post-Soviet situation," when "they're at the river getting soused / And reminiscing about the good old days" (lines 52–53), the eroticism of violence is a subject for nostalgia. However, the fact that "they speak about monstrous things in a rather ordinary way" indicates that the "taste for violence" originating in the 1980s does not conflict so very greatly with the taste of the 2000s marked by Russia's brutal colonial war in Chechnya. The reference to Grozny in the first stanza is a clear indication of this subtext. Furthermore, Fanailova demonstrates that nostalgia for the eroticism of violence facilitates its further glorification, holding out the prospect of the "return" of imperial "joys" and tragedies in the 2020s.

In ". . . Again they're off for their Afghanistan," by conflating and correlating the voices of the victim, the accomplice, and the observer of violation, Fanailova deprives the reader of immunity to the eroticism of violence and therefore, also, of the right to moral recourse. The impossibility of separating and distancing oneself from the reflectively uncontemplated experience of the eroticism of violence is perceived by Fanailova as a tragic and, at the same time, ethical position. It is precisely by adopting this position that the lyrical heroine of her poetry acquires "the internal intonation of a condition in which the boundary between worlds, the boundary between the world of the living and the world of the dead, is erased," as Fanailova says in the conversation with Linor Goralik quoted above.[20]

Fanailova developed a poetic optics that allowed her to spot the return of the eroticism of violence in post-Soviet culture and politics throughout the years that followed, in the course of which nostalgia for the Soviet empire would produce new violence—first of all, in Chechnya and Georgia, then in Belarus, in the squares of Moscow and Petersburg, with policemen using their truncheons to beat respect for the authorities into the heads of young people, in the prisons filled with political prisoners, and now, when we are writing this text, in Ukraine. Characteristically, antiwar motifs in her lyrics will become dominant after 2014, when Russia first invaded Ukraine, and have sustained a peak of intensity from 2022—most illuminating in this respect is Fanailova's open-ended cycle "Lysistrata." The poet detected the role of nostalgia for Soviet times as the source and inspiration for new violence long before political analysts paid any attention to this factor. Fanailova's poem homes in on the nostalgia for violence as the fusion of perspectives belonging to the victim of violence and its accomplice. The only cure the poet can offer to this condition is the effort of gaining distance and feeling empathy for the poem's protagonists, who stand for the majority of those who survived the USSR. This is a doubtful consolation at best.

31

Linor Goralik, “Little Star” (2010)

THE TALE OF THE HARE AND THE WOLF

Как в норе лежали они с волчком, -
зайчик на боку, а волчок ничком, -
а над небом звездочка восходила.
Зайчик гладил волчка, говорил: “Пора”,
а волчок бурчал,—мол, пойдем с утра, -
словно это была игра,
словно ничего не происходило, -
словно вовсе звездочка не всходила.

Им пора бы вставать, собирать дары—
и брести чащобами декабря,
и ронять короны в его снега,
слепнуть от пурги и жевать цингу,
и нести свои души к иным берегам,
по ночам вмерзая друг в друга
(так бы здесь Иордан вмерзал в берега),
укрываться снегом и пить снега, -
потому лишь, что это происходило:
потому что над небом звездочка восходила.

Но они всё лежали, к бочку бочок:
зайчик бодрствовал, крепко спал волчок,
и над сном его звездочка восходила, -
и во сне его мучила, изводила, -
и во сне к себе уводила:
шел волчок пешком, зайчик спал верхом
и во сне обо всем говорил с волчком:
“Се,—говорил он,—и адских нор глубина

рядом с тобой не пугает меня.
И на что мне Его дары,
когда здесь, в норе,
я лежу меж твоих ушей?
И на что мне заботиться о душе?
Меж твоих зубов нет бессмертней моей души."

Так они лежали, и их короны лежали,
и они прядали ушами, надеялись и не дышали,
никуда не шли, ничего не несли,
никого не провозглашали
и мечтали, чтоб время не проходило,
чтобы ничего не происходило, -
но над небом звездочка восходила.

Но проклятая звездочка восходила.[1]

Deep in the woods lay a wolf and a hare,
one snug on his side, one back to the air,
and the star rose up in the sky.
"Let's go," said the hare, with a stroke and a yawn,
"No, no," murmured wolfie, "let's wait until dawn,"
as if it were but child's play,
and nothing at all had happened that day,
but the star rose up in the sky.

Dawn came, it was time to gather their gifts
and trudge through the wintry brush,
let their crowns fall in the puddles of slush,
go blind from the blizzard and gnaw on the scurvy,
bear their souls to a faraway land.
To lie frozen at night, chill hand in chill hand
(like the Jordan iced over embracing its banks),
nestle down in the snow and drink from its drifts,
and all because of what happened that day,
for the star rose up in the sky.

And yet still they lay, hare's eyes gleaming white,
flank pressed into flank, wolfie out like a light,
and the star rose up in his dreams,

to plague him, torment him,
and lure him away:
he crept through the woods, hare asleep on his back,
but they spoke as he padded the frostbitten track.
"Lo," said the hare, "with you as my bed,
these devilish woods cannot fill me with dread.
What use do I have for gold or for myrrh,
when I'm swaddled up warm in your fur?
Why should I care for the fate of my soul,
when bliss is with you, curled up in our hole?"

Together they lay, crowns laid on the earth,
ears twitching, breath bated, hardly daring to hope,
no journey, no gifts, no proclaiming His birth,
and they dreamed, so the hands of the clock wouldn't stray,
so nothing at all would happen that day,

but the star rose up in the sky.

The wretched star rose up in the sky.

(TRANSLATED BY HELENA KERNAN)

Linor Goralik (b. 1975) is a writer entirely shaped by the post-Soviet era. She emigrated with her family from Ukraine to Israel when she was fourteen and obtained a degree in computer science at the Ben-Gurion University of the Negev in Beersheba. From 2000 Goralik lived and worked in Russia and became one of the authors to develop a new cultural journalism focused on the internet and its audience (as opposed to the traditional literary crowd). In 2014, after the annexation of Crimea, Goralik returned to Israel, where she continues to live. After Russia's invasion of Ukraine, she became one of the leaders of the Russophone literature of resistance to Putin's regime: in 2022 she created an online magazine *ROAR*, the monthly of Russophone oppositional culture, and runs the project News 26 in which she educates Russophone teenagers about current political events in and around Russia from a perspective different from the official one.

Linor Goralik is a versatile author, equally original and recognizable in poetry, short prose, novels, children's books, essays, interviews, research projects, translations, and visual art, working in genres and mediums as diverse as comics, multifigured panels of fictional city life, and grotesque jewelry. She is the author of several novels—*All Who Can Breathe Breath* (*Vse, sposobnye dyshat' dykhanie*, 2019); *Named after So-and-So* (*Imeni takogo-to*, 2022); and *Bobo* (2023)—that display the same kind of mythologism that can be detected in embryo in "Little Star" (first published in 2007).

All Who Can Breathe Breath depicts the world after a local apocalypse (in and around Israel), which endowed all beasts with the gift of speech. In *Named after So-and-So*, a realistic and tragic story—the evacuation of a Soviet mental hospital during the Nazi invasion in 1941—is transformed into something very much like a dark fairy tale: all the machinery is depicted as living beings—a downed ship bleeds, a broken engine oozes pus, and so on. In *Bobo* an elephant, gifted by the ruler of Turkey to Putin, has to walk across today's militarized Russia to reach Moscow. During his journey Bobo, the eponymous hero and a highly empathic character endowed with thought and speech, loses faith in Putin and becomes his sworn enemy. Eventually he kills the dictator as the source of grief and pain for so many people.

Goralik radically transforms well-developed genres—such as the postapocalyptic narrative, the epic about the "Great Patriotic War" (the national chapter of World War II), and the animal's travelogue—by boldly introducing magic and dark fantasy, thus turning these narratives into variations of fairy tales. In using fairy-tale elements to create *ostranenie* (defamiliarization), her work destabilizes the automatized expectation prompted by traditional genres and stimulates the reader to rethink their cultural assumptions.

Something very similar occurs much earlier in Goralik's work and is on view in this chapter's poem. In "Little Star" she places a "bunny" (*zaichik*) and a "wolfie" (*volchok*) at the center of the New Testament Nativity myth. The diminutive suffixes (*volchok, zaichik*) clearly link these characters with children's culture: cute little bunnies appear as characters in fairy tales, poems, and cartoons, and even exist as plush toys.[2] In particular, the word *volchok* ("baby wolf") immediately evokes strong associations with a lullaby warning against a little grey wolfie (*seren'kii volchok*) who might come to bite your side, as well as with a legendary animated film by Yuri Norshtein, *Tale of Tales* (1979), inspired by that lullaby and based on a script by the contemporary writer Lyudmila Petrushevskaya. Moreover, it brings to mind the standard toy of Soviet childhood: the spinning top, also called *volchok*. Arguably, other animations by Norshtein, especially *Hedgehog in the Fog*, also to some degree form intertexts in relation to Goralik's poem. After all, *Hedgehog* tells the story of a little hedgehog wandering through a vast world of chaos and danger toward a warm burrow, where he is welcomed—with hot tea and jam—by a little bear. Like

Norshtein, Goralik is telling a fairy tale. Hers deals with the Star of Bethlehem and the Nativity, but it is told from the perspective of traditional children's characters, which brings to mind the Russian Formalists' term *sdvig*, meaning the modernist device of a tear in the text or shift from convention. What new understanding of the biblical narrative does this *sdvig* create?

Linor Goralik herself comments on this poem as follows (in a message to one of the authors):

> I have been a deeply religious Christian since I was ten, and for me this text is, among other things, about how scary and difficult it is to try every day and every hour to leave your world of small love (in the broadest, nonromantic sense of the word) for the cold world of His Great Love, at His bidding.

But, while this was the intention of the poem, the form of Goralik's text suggests a very different meaning, as we will see below.

Goralik's poem is saturated with internal rhymes and repetitions:

укрываться снегом и пить снега (line 16)
Но они всё лежали, к бочку бочок (line 19)
Так они лежали, и их короны лежали (line 33)
никуда не шли, ничего не несли (line 35)

In the original, a simple structure involving the conjunction *a* ("while," "but") is often repeated: again and again, we read that the little hare was doing something while the little wolf was doing something else. Anaphora is frequent:

словно это была игра,
словно ничего не происходило, -
словно вовсе звездочка не всходила.
(lines 6–8)

потому лишь, что это происходило:
потому что над небом звездочка восходила.
(lines 17–18)

и во сне его мучила, изводила, -
и во сне к себе уводила:
[. . . .]
и во сне обо всем говорил с волчком:
(lines 22–23, 25)

И на что мне Его дары,
[. . .]
И на что мне заботиться о душе?

(lines 28, 31)

Moreover, ten of the forty lines in the Russian open with the conjunction *i* ("and"). Arguably, all these techniques orchestrate the main refrain, highlighted by Goralik via italics "*and the star rose up in the sky*," repeated six times with variations (lines 3, 8, 18, 21, 39, 40 in the Russian).

This flow of repetitions creates a kind of drive, an almost physically tangible narrative pressure of history, pushing toward the inevitable. For that reason, by way of counterpoint to this pressure, the hare and the wolfie dream—and hope—that no time will pass ("and they dreamed, so the hands of the clock wouldn't stray," line 35 in the present translation). Two opposing types of stylization merge in this flow. On the one hand, there are biblical motifs (the Jordan River, the crowns, the gifts, the star), reinforced by archaisms ("'Lo,' said the hare," line 26). On the other hand, fairy-tale motifs are conveyed by the deliberately simple rhymes, often verb-based[3] or tautological, typical of children's poetry. Thus, a structural oxymoron emerges: a tragic biblical myth is inextricably intertwined with a naive (or perhaps quasi-naive) children's aesthetic. It is this oxymoron that generates a cathartic affect—but not the one traditionally associated with the Christian tradition.

In Goralik's poem, catharsis does not lie in the birth of the Savior destined to redeem humankind. Rather, the affect that connects mythological and quasi childish aesthetics is related to the sense of impending disaster that will inevitably destroy the warm and fragile domestic world of the little hare and wolf. This affective connection subverts the binary opposition between darkness and divine light. In Goralik's poem, divine light floods a cozy dark burrow, the home of the little hare and wolfie, while the radiance of the star promises suffering and pain. Why is that? Why does Goralik conceptualize the Star of Bethlehem as a "wretched" (or cursed: *prokliataia*, line 40) star?

A crucial intertext for her fairy tale is Joseph Brodsky's cycle of Nativity poems, which reshaped the poetic image of the birth of Christ for Russian culture after the Christological treatment of the cycle of poems Pasternak wrote for *Doctor Zhivago*. In all of Brodsky's works, the Nativity scene appears as a reminder of a certain stable axis of existence, which connects the Christ Child and the star despite all the changes and catastrophes, while the star's light suggests the presence of God the Father. In

Brodsky's Nativity poems, the emptiness, loneliness, homelessness, helplessness of existence—constant motifs of his work—are justified and sanctified by the presence of this axis:

> But when drafts through the doorway disperse
> the thick mist of the hours of darkness
> and a shape in a shawl stands revealed,
> both a newborn and Spirit that's Holy
> in your self you discover; you stare
> skyward, and it's right there:
> a star.[4]
>
> Keenly, without blinking, through pallid, stray
> clouds, upon the child in the manger, from far away—
> from the depth of the universe, from the opposite end—the star
> was looking into the cave. And this was the Father's stare.[5]
>
> Imagine the Lord, for the first time, from darkness, and stranded
> immensely in distance, recognizing Himself in the Son
> of Man: His homelessness plain to him now in a homeless one.[6]
>
> Grow accustomed to the desert
> and the star
> pouring down its incandescent
> rays, which are
>
> just a lamp to guide the treasured
> The child who's late,
> lit by someone that desert
> taught to wait.[7]
>
> The star looked in across the threshold.
> The only one of them who could
> know the meaning of that look
> was the infant. But He did not speak.[8]

The following motifs represent constants in most of the Nativity poems written by Brodsky between 1963 and 1995: frost, complete with snowstorms and blizzards (rendering the biblical landscape rather Russian), a star, a child. All other classical motifs of the Bethlehem myth—Mary, Joseph, the divine Father, Herod, the Magi—may or may not make an appearance.

Goralik retains the frost and the star, which acquires a diminutive suffix in her poem ("little star," *zvezdochka* rather than *zvezda*), a characteristic transformation corresponding to the child-like modality of her poem. In her version, there is no God the Father, no Mary, no Joseph, no Bethlehem, no crib, no desert, and no Herod. It is the little hare and wolfie who are the Magi. Above all, this is a Nativity scene without a baby Jesus. If he is mentioned at all, it is indirectly and negatively: "Why would I want His gifts?" ("What use do I have for gold or for myrrh?" in the present translation, line 28). Without the child, the stable axis of existence blurs and shatters in the cold, and the little star becomes the embodiment of the opposite affect—namely, the destruction of peace, approaching cataclysms, and global changes.

The disappearance of the Christ Child from the Nativity scene is a striking gesture. No doubt it could be interpreted as referring to the contemporary crisis of Christian culture, which is arguably losing its "central values" (its axis) due to the role of Christianity in antisemitism, colonial violence, and the global tragedies of the twentieth century that have created what Auden long ago called "the Age of Anxiety." However, although this conceptual background is discernible in Goralik's poem, it hardly dominates the internal logic of the text in which she contrasts Christianity, one of the most powerful metanarratives in human history, with the "tiny narrative" of a fairy tale.[9] The poem's protagonists must sacrifice their micro-utopia of mutual love and tenderness to the global promise of universal love and salvation. It is the global nature of this call that terrifies the characters—and arguably also the author, or at least her speaker. The menacing star looms *above the sky* ("*up in the sky*" here). Nothing could be higher, nobody could manage to hide from its all-seeing eye and from the fate it dictates.

In Goralik's poem, the little hare and wolfie, despite their role as the Magi, replace the vanished Christ Child. They—children who have not yet sinned—are, in fact, the first victims of the global utopia of salvation. Strikingly, their relationship is characterized by an eroticism that is innocent. To the role of a magus, the little hare prefers the joy of lying "between the *ears*" of the wolfie (lines 30 in the Russian),[10] a comical variation of a traditional erotic formula. At the same time, this image humorously paraphrases an Old Testament utopia often read as a prophecy about Christ: "The wolf shall also dwell with the lamb, and the leopard shall lie down with the kid; and the calf and the young lion and the fatling together; and a little child shall lead them" (Isaiah 11:6). Goralik alters Brodsky's Nativity narrative not in order to undo his existentialist philosophy but rather because she wishes to include the experience of her generation. In her teenage years, her own private world was radically transformed by emigration when her family left the USSR for Israel. In a broader sense, Goralik's contemporaries—the first post-Soviet generation, youngsters who still went to school or were recent graduates in 1991—were the first victims of the great "capitalist revolution" that took place in Russia in the 1990s, depriving many families of social status, jobs, and savings.

However, the philosophy of this poem goes far beyond the mere fear of historical change, absorbed as it is with the existential experience of a generation. The cursed little star becomes a symbol of the historical telos.[11] In his final book, *Culture and Explosion*, Yuri Lotman argued that the idea of purpose, albeit an intellectual construct, lies at the heart of traditional historical narratives:

> It is typical of the historian to start from the assumption that what has happened was inevitable. But his creative activity manifests itself elsewhere: from the accumulation of facts retained in memory, he constructs the contiguous line that leads most reliably to this conclusive point. [. . .] The concept of an endpoint, objectively alien to history, is imposed on it. [. . .] It is the basis by which history is justified and infused with Higher Meaning. It is, however, a fact of history, and not the instrument of its knowledge.[12]

From this point of view, the identification of the "Higher Meaning" of history with myth appears logical, although myth, with its cyclical concept of time, contradicts the linear, purpose-oriented concept of history. The absence of the Christ Child in Goralik's poem, combined with the insistent presence of the star, arguably stresses this contradiction, potentially referring to the emptiness and fictitiousness of teleological historicism.

Goralik's poem itself sounds like a touching, childlike attempt to resist the violence of teleologically oriented history—and that is a resistance doomed to failure. Hegel comes to mind at this point. While defending a teleological understanding of history, he unabashedly proclaimed: "History is not the soil in which happiness grows. The periods of happiness in it are the blank pages of history."[13] He made no bones about calling such history a "slaughter-bench" (*Geschichte als Schlachtbank*).[14] It is this futile resistance to teleological history that renders the poem truly tragic. Ultimately, any attempt to preserve the value of individual feeling and individual life in a world blown through by the cold wind of history is doomed.

In Goralik's poem, tragedy is concealed under the veil of a children's tale. The shift from the modality of the myth to that of the fairy tale reworks features of a genre that look fixed, replacing them with individual affects and the play of fantasy.[15] In fact, this very principle is followed by the little hare and wolfie—they try to behave "as if it were but child's play, / and nothing at all had happened that day, / *but the star rose up in the sky*" (lines 6–8). Thus, the protagonists' resistance to teleological history is transferred to the level of form, on which myth is overcome by the fairy tale. This formal gesture contains a strategy that resonates with postmodernist philosophy. For rather than abolishing or refuting the great myths of humanity, postmodernism transforms them into playful stories commensurate not with the global but with the individual scale. In Goralik's poem, the story becomes fairy tale.

32

Galina Rymbu, “My Vagina” (2018)

THE PERSONAL IS THE POLITICAL

Моя Вагина

17 мая 2013 года под музыку группы “Смысловые галлюцинации”
из моей вагины вышел сын,
а затем—плацента, которую акушерка держала, как мясник—
взвешивая на ладони. Доктор положил мне сына на грудь
(тогда я ещё не знала имени сына)
и сказал: ваш сын. И сын тут же опѝсал мне грудь и живот,
а мир стал моей вагиной, сыном, его горячей струйкой,
его мокрой тёплой головой, моим пустым
животом.

Потом мою вагину зашили,
она изменила форму. Стала узкой и стянутой,
вагина-тюрьма, вагина-рана. На мне тогда были
белые компрессионные чулки—все в крови,
дешёвое красное платье-халат, купленное в китайском павильоне, а на нём—
две женщины, держащие кроны деревьев,
и звери, держащие женщин.

Без трусов, без поддержки, с запутанными волосами
я шла после операции по солнечному коридору роддома
забирать сына. Я взяла его и подумала:
его пальцы похожи на маленьких мармеладных червячков.

[2]

Теперь моя вагина—это норка
для твоего коричневого зверька с большой красной головкой.
куда он иногда проскальзывает, чтобы набраться сил. Это ямка

для твоего нежного языка, для твоих тонких крепких пальцев, похожих
на письменные принадлежности из прошлого века.

Моя вагина сжимается сейчас, рядом с нею, чуть выше—набухает клитор,
он похож на бусинку и завернут в нежный
складчатый капюшончик, который иногда можно снять
под слепым дождем лёгких прикосновений.
Ты можешь . . . Аккуратно . . .

**[3]*

Когда мне было 13, я пыталась засунуть туда дачный
огурец: хотела понять, что такое секс.
Тогда я ещё не знала, что это не только
пенетрация. Я часто смотрела на свой клитор в маленькое
разбитое зеркальце, которое папа использовал для бритья.
Я была сухим деревом, которое горело
с каждым днём всё сильнее.

**[4]*

Я жила в мире школьной литературы, где всё видно только мужским взглядом,
в мире районных разборок и падиков, набитых потными
парнями в чёрных куртках и рваных ботинках. Я любила сидеть на кортах, любила
обтягивающие джинсы, сдавливающие клитор
и большие губы.

**[5]*

Тогда я ещё не знала, что до моей вагины всем есть дело:
государству, родителям, гинекологам, незнакомым мужчинам,
православным батюшкам, у которых под рясой погоны,
а на рясе—женская кровь,
работодателям, эшникам, военным, нацикам, миграционным службам,
банкам, консервативным критикам "развратного образа жизни,"
патриотичным деятелям культуры, юзающим традиционные ценности
под коньячок.

[6]

Из моей вагины раз в месяц идёт кровь,
и тогда мой любимый идёт в магазин за прокладками
(мне нравятся тонкие, с запахом ромашки).
Иногда кровь вываливается сгустками, похожими
на круглые шлемы маленьких астронавтов.
Мой менструальный космос в миниатюре: планета матки,
кометы яичников, млечная галактика припухшей вульвы.
Иногда кровь льётся, как водка,
из специального узкого горлышка сувенирной бутылки.
Иногда её нет.

Мне нравится заниматься сексом во время месячных,
всё тело становится суперчувствительным.
Люблю, когда твой член весь в моей крови,
и люблю представлять, что у тебя тоже месячные,
что солёная тёплая кровь капает из маленькой дырочки
на твоей головке.

Люблю, когда твои руки липкие от моей крови,
когда она засыхает на твоих ногтях и заусенцах,
люблю чувствовать, как пульсирует матка в моём животе,
словно второе сердце, как набухает грудь и становится горячей,
как будто оттуда вот-вот польётся молоко.
Я дам тебе его пить, любимый, оно зальёт твое лицо,
твои нежные розовые соски (почти как у девочки),
сделает мокрыми твои волоски на груди,
твою шею, животик, в котором,
я мечтаю, ты когда-нибудь сможешь выносить нашу дочь.

[7]

Люблю, когда ты говоришь о моей вагине,
и когда мы вместе её обсуждаем,
пока ты сидишь на мне сверху
в моей футболке и зелёных серёжках, которые я тебе подарила.
Люблю, когда ты легонько шлёпаешь меня по губам.

Как хорошо, что ты делаешь это не в России,
где Юлю Цветкову хотят отправить в тюрьму за нежные рисунки вагины,
где мои подруги боятся целоваться на улице,
где мы с Катей после школы подолгу лежали на ковре
у неё дома и трогали друг друга, превращались в одно
солёное море, а потом
боялись об этом говорить.

**[8]*

Наши вагины и вульвы называют кисками,
но у меня скорее не киска, а домашняя декоративная мышка,
маленькая, пушистая, беспокойная.

Она умрёт раньше времени?
Она умрёт в клетке?

**[9]*

Однажды я трогала свою мышку на лекции в универе,
трогала её в пустом автобусе, ползущем по ночному городу
от заводов к панелькам, от кладбищ к торговым центрам.
Я трогала её за гаражами, осенним утром,
сидя на ржавой трубе,

трогала в машине скорой помощи, которая везла меня
на операцию, и трогала после операции,
когда в уретре стоял катетер, когда из уретры текла кровь,

трогала, когда мой живот был огромным, в душном
отделении роддома,
когда писала в баночку в поликлинике,
когда писала и плакала ночью в старом дачном саду,
полном кузнечиков и ночных мотыльков,
когда писала на иртышской набережной прямо в штаны
для прикола, когда писала на снег
у проходной завода,
когда писала в общаге в горшок сына,
когда писала после пива в парке культуры, а неподалёку
бродили менты,

трогала в летнем лесу, пока меня облепляли насекомые,
обнимали деревья.

Трогала её после того, как случайно порезала бритвой губы и клитор,
после ссоры с другом и после
судмедэкспертизы,
после поездки в онкоцентр и после
ареста, на съёмной квартире,
после акций протеста на Болотной площади
и после акций протеста на Марсовом поле.

трогала, читая Николая Кузанского,
читая Гастева,
Касториадиса,
Эрнста Блоха,
"Этику" Алена Бадью,
Исэ-моногатари,
учебник по физике,
антологию немецкой поэзии,
Маяковского,
Якобсона:

(я их захватила!).

Я трогала мою мышку, когда плакала и хотела от тебя уйти,
трогала, когда плакала и хотела от тебя ребёнка,
трогала, сидя у тебя на лице,
и трогала, прижимаясь лицом
к твоей тёмной промежности,
и просто—глядя тебе в глаза.

И всё равно до сих пор не знаю, не понимаю её до конца,
мою мышку,
боюсь и стесняюсь.

[10]

Но мне нравится мыслить её политически,
это заводит, качает танцпол старых идей,
даёт надежду в отсутствие новых

активистских методов.

Делать революцию вагиной.
Делать свободу собой.

Я думаю, а что, может, и правда вагина погубит это государство,
прогонит незаконного президента,

отправит в отставку правительство,
отменит армию, налоги для бедных,
фсб как структуру самой гнусной власти и подавления,
разберётся с полицией,
консерватизмом и реваншизмом,
расформирует несправедливые суды, освободит
политических заключенных,
сделает невозможным тухлый русский национализм,
унижение угнетённых, сфабрикованные дела,
разъебёт олигархат и патриархат,
парализует войска,
движущиеся в чужих государствах—
всё дальше и дальше:
в пизду милитаризм!

Моя вагина—это любовь, история и политика.
Моя политика—это тело, быт, аффект.
Мой мир—вагина. И я несу мир,
но для некоторых я—опасная вагина,
боевая вагина. Это мой монолог.[1]

My Vagina

On May 17, 2013, to music by the group *Meaning Hallucinations,*
a son emerged from my vagina,
and then the placenta that the midwife held like a butcher,
weighing it in her hands. The doctor placed my son on my breast
(at that point I still didn't know my son's name)
and said, "Your son." And immediately my son pissed on my breast and
stomach,
and the world became a scorching vagina, my son, his burning stream,
his wet, warm head, my empty
abdomen.

Then they stitched up my vagina;
it changed shape. Became narrow and constricted
a vagina-prison, vagina-wound. I was in the grasp of
white compression stockings—all bloody—
a cheap red dress-robe, bought at the Chinese market, and on it—
two women, holding the crowns of trees,
and beasts, holding the women.
With no underwear, no support—and with tangled hair
post-op I strode down the maternity hospital's sunny corridor
to collect my son. I took him and thought
his fingers looked like little candied worms.

**[2]*

Now my vagina is a burrow
for your little brown beast with its big red head.
Where he slips in once in a while to gather strength. It's a furrow
for your tender tongue, for your thin, strong fingers, resembling
last century's writing instruments.

Now my vagina is flexing and next to it, a little higher, my clitoris is swelling;
it looks like a little bead and it's wrapped in a delicate
folded hood, which can sometimes be pulled back
under a blind rain of light touches.
Go ahead . . . Carefully . . .

**[3]*

When I was 13 I tried to place a summer
cucumber in it: I wanted to understand what sex was.
I still didn't understand then that it's not just
penetration. I often looked at my clitoris with the little
broken mirror that papa used to shave.
I was dry wood that burned
stronger every day.

**[4]*

I lived in a world of assigned reading, where everything is viewed through
 the male gaze,
in the world of streetgangs and stairwells full of sweaty

guys in black jackets and tattered boots. I loved squatting on my haunches,
loved
tight jeans, pressing against my clitoris
and big lips.

**[5]*

I didn't know then that everyone had an interest in my vagina:
the state, my parents, gynecologists, strange men,
Orthodox priests, with epaulets beneath their robes,
and women's blood on the robes themselves,
employers, national guards, military men, nationalists, the border police,
banks, conservative critics of "depraved lifestyles,"
patriotic cultural figures, users of traditional values,
washed down with cognac.

**[6]*

Blood comes out of my vagina once a month
and then my beloved goes to the store for pads
(I like the thin ones, with chamomile scent).
Sometimes the blood comes out in clots that look like
the round helmets of little astronauts.
My menstrual cosmos in miniature: the womb-planet,
egg-comets, swollen-vulva-milky-way-galaxy.
Sometimes the blood flows like vodka
from the special narrow neck of a souvenir bottle.
Sometimes there's no blood.

I like to have sex during my period;
your whole body gets super-sensitive.
I love it when your penis is covered with my blood,
and love to imagine that you have a period, too,
that salty, warm blood is dripping from the little hole
in your glans.

I love it when your hands are sticky with my blood,
when it dries on your nails and ragged cuticles,
love to feel my womb pulsing in my stomach,
like a second heart, my breast swelling up and getting hot,
like milk is about to pour out of it.

I'll let you drink it, love, it will pour over your face,
your tender little nipples (almost like a girl's),
wet the fuzz on your chest,
neck, your tummy, where,
in my dreams, you might someday carry our daughter.

**[7]*

I love when you talk about my vagina
and when we talk about it together,
while you sit on top of me
in my t-shirt and the green earrings
that I gave you;
love it when you lightly slap against my lips.
It's so good that you don't do it in Russia,
where they want to send Iulia Tsvetkova to prison for delicate images of vaginas
where my girlfriends are afraid to kiss in the street,
where Katia and I would lay forever on the carpet after school
over at her apartment touching one another, turning into a single
salty sea, and then
would be afraid to talk about it.

**[8]*

They call our vaginas and vulvas pussies,
but mine is less like a pussy than a decorative, domestic mouse—
small, furry, and restless.

Will it die before its time?
Will it die in a cage?

**[9]*

Once I touched my mousey during a university lecture,
touched it in an empty bus crawling through the night city
from the factories to the concrete block housing, from the cemeteries to the malls.
I touched it behind the garages, one fall morning,
sitting on a rusty pipe,

touched it in the ambulance taking me
for the operation, and touched it after the operation
when in my urethra I had a catheter and blood trickled from the urethra,

touched it when my stomach was huge, in the stifling
maternity ward
when I pissed in a jar at the polyclinic,
when I pissed and cried at night in the old dacha garden,
full of crickets and night moths,
when I pissed right in my pants on the Irtysh Embankment
for fun, when I pissed on the snow
by the factory entrance checkpoint,
when I pissed in the dorm in my son's potty,
when I pissed after drinking beer at the Culture Park while nearby
cops were creeping around,
touched it in the summer woods while being attacked by insects,
embraced by trees.

Touched it after I accidentally cut my lips and clitoris with a razor,
after fighting with a boyfriend and after
the forensic medical examination,
after the trip to the oncology center and after
my arrest, at the rental apartment,
after the protest on Bolotnaya Square
and after the protest on the Field of Mars.

Touched it while reading Nicholas of Cusa,
while reading Gastev,
Castoriadis
Ernst Bloch
Alain Badiou's *Ethics*,
Ise Monogatari,
the physics textbook,
an anthology of German poetry
Mayakovsky,
Jakobson
(I took them by storm!).
I touched my mouse when I was crying and wanted to leave you,
touched it when I was crying and wanted a child from you,
touched it, sitting on your face,

and touched it when my face was pressed
against your dark groin,
and just while looking in your eyes.

And all the same I still don't know it, don't understand it completely,
my mouse,
it scares and flusters me.

\[10\]

But I like to think it politically—
that winds things up, rocks the dancefloor of old ideas
gives hope in the absence of new
methods of activism.

To make revolution with the vagina.
To create freedom with oneself.

I think, well, maybe the vagina will bring down this state for real,
drive out the illegitimate president,
disband the government,
abolish the army, taxes on the poor,
the FSB as a structure of utterly vile power and oppression,
will deal with the police,
with conservatism and revanchism,
will dismantle unjust trials, free
the political prisoners,
make impossible putrid Russian nationalism,
the humiliation of the oppressed, fabricated cases,
will shatter oligarchy and patriarchy,
paralyze the troops deployed in other states—
farther and farther
into militarism's pussy!

My vagina is love, history and politics.
My politics is the body, the everyday, affect.
My world is the vagina. And I bear peace.
Yet for some I am a dangerous vagina,
a fighting vagina. That is my monologue.[2]

(TRANSLATED BY KEVIN M. F. PLATT)

In the 2000s and 2010s, Russian poetry underwent profound changes. At first glance, these seemed to consist mainly of a radical departure from the syllabotonic system (the dominant metrical system since its establishment in the eighteenth century) toward free verse with minimal rhyme. This formal shift, however, was only an expression of deeper processes: the beginning of the millennium witnessed a renewal of poetic language brought about by the striking debuts of young poets. The avant-garde of new poetry were women authors who unabashedly proclaimed their commitment to radical feminism and were united by communities such as the F-Writing channel on the syg.ma website (https://syg.ma/f-writing).

The term "feminism" has long been perceived by Russian cultural figures, even the most liberal ones, as a swear word, and most women writers have not only flatly refused to express any sympathy for feminism but energetically resisted when critics or interviewers have attempted to place their work in a feminist context. The demonization of feminism in post-Soviet culture is related primarily to the rejection of the Soviet version of "feminism," which was radical in word and patriarchal in practice: the rhetoric of gender equality was no match for the double burden that women with careers faced of household work and childcare in an atmosphere of gender discrimination. In addition, the decommunization of Russia coincided with the global offensive of neoliberalism, the latent patriarchalism of which became an explicit, indeed a dominant, trend in the Russian cultural mainstream of the 1990s and 2000s. These factors may explain why Russian women in the 1990s and 2000s rarely supported the international feminist ideas of their time.[3]

The situation changed after the attempted antiauthoritarian revolution of 2011–12. The arrest, trial, and imprisonment of the feminist activists known as Pussy Riot, who spoke out against the alliance of the authoritarian regime and the Orthodox Church, became a turning point. Though the protest of the creative class against Putin's regime was brutally crushed in 2012, Pussy Riot, with their video performance (released simultaneously with the mass political protests in February 2012) and their valiant final courtroom speeches, did manage to bring feminism onto the political scene in contemporary Russia. The number of feminist groups has increased dramatically since then; crucially, they are beginning to play an important role in the antiauthoritarian movement.

Not surprisingly, women's poetry in Russian has become predominantly political. This new feminist poetry (hereafter referred to as F-poetry) is characterized by the perspective of "women or nonbinary people with experiences of female gender socialization."[4] Another important characteristic is its transgressive essence: these poems methodically and often scandalously undermine the unarticulated but extremely influential patriarchal norms of Russian culture. The authors permit themselves to speak openly and directly about the unmentionable—about the female body as imperfect and in pain; about sexuality devoid of the traditional romantic halo and including LGBTQ themes; about sexual and gender violence, violence against the female body and person, permeating all pores of society. Sexism, misogyny, sexual repression, homophobia and transphobia, racism, police terror, Russia's war against Ukraine—all these motifs resound in F-poetry. Moreover, its very language—for instance, the extensive use of obscenities—is meant to make the reader uncomfortable.[5] Although the concept of F-poetry is still fairly new in Russian literature, there is already a considerable body of critical work devoted to poets associated with this movement.[6] The publication of the English-language anthology of Russian feminist poetry *F-Letter*[7] has also caused a great deal of resonance.[8]

Galina Rymbu (b. 1990) is the leading figure of Russian F-poetry. The striking emotional energy and philosophic depth of her sharply political poetry made a huge impression from the start. Rymbu is the creator and editor of the F-letter website, a coeditor of the *F-Letter* collection, and, above all, one of the most striking poets of her generation. Despite her relatively young age, Rymbu is well known as an activist and author, having been awarded prestigious poetry prizes and published several books of poetry in Moscow, New York,[9] Kharkiv, Riga, and Amsterdam, in original and in translation. Born in the Siberian city of Omsk, she graduated from the Literary Institute in Moscow then studied philosophy and political theory at the European University in St. Petersburg. In 2018, she left Russia for Ukraine. Rymbu witnessed the Russian invasion of Ukraine from Lviv, where she has lived since 2018.

Rymbu belongs to the first post-Soviet generation, a generation that was confronted with capitalism in its most crass and inhumane form at an early age. Hence her commitment not only to feminism but also to leftist political ideas, including Marxism. As she puts it,

> I had an experience of gender oppression that, in one way or another, permeated everyday life, socialization in literature, and thinking. [. . .] Plus, from my school days, I was also exposed to racist discrimination, which was probably the most traumatic and incomprehensible experience to me as a child. And I found myself wondering: Why does my last name move people to use the n-word? Why am I being humiliated merely for being a girl? Why do we have nothing to eat when my parents work from morning till night, and the TV is showing well-fed rich people? Why do some people have everything and others have nothing? What is wrong with this world?[10]

Hence her search for a poetic language that can generate political effect. Specifically, she says:

> Poetry should be a form of public speech and thought, written as if there is someone else present, someone concrete, not just an abstract reader. When I write, I'm not alone. There is a community around me, classes of people, even my friends, their speech, and it's as if I'm answering them, speaking "here and now." [. . .] My poetry does have much in common with rhetoric and oratory, based on devices like repetition, clear performative constructions, the desire to convince. Here there is also something (either a single subject or a community) that insists on its presence in speech.[11]

The community and rhetorical effect acquired full force when Rymbu published a poem titled "My Vagina" on her Facebook page. It was written as a contribution in support of the LGBTQ activist and artist Iulia Tsvetkova from Komsomolsk-on-Amur, who was arrested in 2019 in connection with her administrative work for the feminist public page *Vagina Monologues* (*Monologi vaginy*). Based on her antisexist drawings, she was accused of distributing pornography, and while she was acquitted by a court she was registered as a "foreign agent" in 2022. Rymbu's poem was immediately reposted by many Facebook users, but it also provoked a storm of negative reactions, including from many poets of the older generation. In turn, numerous younger and middle-generation poets, both women and men, publicly expressed support for Rymbu, sometimes in verse.[12] Rymbu herself responded to the aggression against herself with a poem titled "Great Russian Literature," in which she said things such as:

> Кто в "русской литературе" эстетизировал насилие над женщиной?
> Кто имеет право и голос, чтобы издеваться в своих текстах и
> комментариях
> над нашими словами, нашим телом, нашими мыслями и текстами?
> Кто может написать про нашу поэзию, поэзию женщин:
> "эта девочка больна, раз такое пишет"
> или
> "иногда мне жаль, что ушла в прошлое
> советская
> исправительная
> психиатрия,
> она бы хорошо
> над ней
> поработала"?[13]

Who in "Russian literature" aestheticized violence against women?
Who has the right and the voice to mock, in their texts and
comments,
our words, our bodies, our thoughts, and our texts?
Who can write about our poetry, the poetry of women:
"this girl is sick if she's writing such things"
or
"sometimes I feel sorry that
Soviet
correctional
psychiatry is a thing of the past,
it would have done a good job
on her"?[14]

Why, then, did the impact of "My Vagina" exceed all expectations? The answer appears to lie in the true political significance of the poem. As Jacques Rancière argues, the political is based on what he calls "dissensus": "Dissensus is not a confrontation between interests or opinions. It is the demonstration (manifestation) of a gap in the sensible itself. Political demonstration makes visible that which had no reason to be seen."[15] What gap in the sensible did Rymbu expose when she published "My Vagina"? What thing that "had no reason to be seen," according to her opponents, did she make visible?

Were the sex scenes too explicit? Did the poetic portrayal of menstruation offend sensibilities? Was the problem the depiction of female masturbation? Or perhaps the very mention of the vagina? All of these answers are possible given, on the one hand, the puritanical conservatism of the Russian cultural tradition. Yet, on the other hand, the guardians of "great Russian literature" have not always been implacable about the intrusion of sexual themes into the sacred realm of poetry. Scandalously erotic poets such as Ivan Barkov (1732–68) and his many imitators in twentieth- and twenty-first-century literature have for at least a generation been present in the Russian poetry canon—and here the notable and mitigating factor is that they were always men. Arguably, in this instance, the cause of such hostility owes less to the violation of sensibility than to persona and style. Rymbu, by contrast, had the audacity to write poetry of this kind as a female. What would be tolerable coming from a man sounds insulting and obscene to the self-appointed "guardians" when written by a woman, and with such unflinching bravura as well.

This is not merely a provocative pose. Crucially, the vagina is truly central to Rymbu's poetic universe. It becomes a metaphor for both the cosmos and the individual, and a tool for studying the world, too. Here, for instance, is how Rymbu describes menstrual blood (lines 54–57 in the Russian):

Иногда кровь вываливается сгустками, похожими
на круглые шлемы маленьких астронавтов.
Мой менструальный космос в миниатюре: планета матки,
кометы яичников, млечная галактика припухшей вульвы

My menstrual cosmos in miniature: the womb-planet,
egg-comets, swollen-vulva-milky-way-galaxy.
Sometimes the blood flows like vodka
from the special narrow neck of a souvenir bottle.

Rymbu is, of course, familiar with Jacques Derrida's notion of phallogocentrism, that is, the traditional worldview with the phallus at the center of being and culture, equating logos, writing, creativity, and reason. She radically overturns this picture of the world by placing the vagina in the sacred position previously reserved for the phallus. Even more impudently, she replaces writing with peeing: as it happens, the Russian words *pisát'* and *písat'* look exactly the same, unless one adds an accent. It is peeing and not writing that becomes the prism of the poetic persona's evolving experience (lines 104–12).

Moreover, the central part of the poem is united by the repetition of the word "touched" in reference to masturbation, which presents the vagina as an organ of cognition. This part culminates in the following lines (122–32):

трогала, читая Николая Кузанского,
читая Гастева,
Касториадиса,
Эрнста Блоха,
"Этику" Алена Бадью,
Исэ-моногатари,
учебник по физике,
антологию немецкой поэзии,
Маяковского,
Якобсона:

(я их захватила!).

Touched it while reading Nicholas of Cusa,
while reading Gastev,
Castoriadis

Ernst Bloch
Alain Badiou's *Ethics,*
Ise Monogatari,
the physics textbook,
an anthology of German poetry
Mayakovsky,
Jakobson
(I took them by storm!).

It is through her vagina that the speaker "captures" cultural knowledge, from the medieval Nicholas of Cusa to the avant-gardists Mayakovsky and Gastev, from the Structuralist Roman Jakobson to the neo-Marxists Ernst Bloch, Cornelius Castoriadis, and Alain Badiou. In this context, the word "touched" becomes provocatively polysemous.

Feminist concepts pertaining to the ethics of embodiment also resonate with the poem's artistic logic. Toril Moi, a prominent feminist theorist, argued that the category of the lived body, the bodily experience, absorbs the categories of sex and gender, and, on an even more general level, plays a crucial role in the formation of subjectivity.[16] In her "Feminist Perspectives on the Body," Kathleen Lennon observes, "Feminist theorists of the body, working with the notion of the bodily imaginary, therefore see creative acts directed at alterations in our mode of perceiving bodies, as central to the process of political and social transformation."[17] The question of subjectivity, in its turn, is inseparable from the question of power—it thus has a political significance of its own. This is why, in Rymbu's poem, the vagina is not only a metaphor for the cosmos, the center of lived bodily experience and of cognition, but also a node of political struggle (lines 43–50):

Тогда я ещё не знала, что до моей вагины всем есть дело:
государству, родителям, гинекологам, незнакомым мужчинам,
православным батюшкам, у которых под рясой погоны,
а на рясе—женская кровь,
работодателям, эшникам, военным, нацикам, миграционным службам,
банкам, консервативным критикам "развратного образа жизни,"
патриотичным деятелям культуры, юзающим традиционные ценности
под коньячок

I didn't know then that everyone had an interest in my vagina:
the state, my parents, gynecologists, strange men,
Orthodox priests, with epaulets beneath their robes,

and women's blood on the robes themselves,
employers, national guards, military men, nationalists, the border police,
banks, conservative critics of "depraved lifestyles,"
patriotic cultural figures, users of traditional values,
washed down with cognac.

And further on (lines 142–47):

Делать революцию вагиной.
Делать свободу собой.

To make revolution with the vagina.
To create freedom with oneself.

The vagina—and thus the female body and female subjectivity—is controlled by various forms of power, state and nonstate, parental and biopolitical (medical), authoritarian and nationalist, religious and "patriotic." But the very fact that such different and influential forces seek to control the female body suggests that liberating this body will explode the entire political structure.[18] In essence, this is Rymbu's revolutionary program, her utopia. Strikingly, the poem's internal plot suggests that this utopia could be realized. "My Vagina" consists of ten parts of unequal length. Taken together, they form a coming-of-age story, a bildungsroman in miniature. The first part (lines 1–9) depicts the vagina in the context assigned to it by patriarchal culture as an organ designated almost exclusively for conceiving and bearing children, preferably sons. This is why the vagina here becomes a prison, a wound. The "cheap red dress-robe" (line 14) with a mythological depiction of the world—"two women, *holding* the crowns of trees, / and beasts, *holding* the women" (lines 15–16)—is contrasted with the following lines: "With no underwear, no support—and with tangled hair / post-op I strode down the maternity hospital's sunny corridor / to collect my son" (lines 17–19). The patriarchal mythology of women being generously supported is replaced by reality: she is alone and without support; it is she who *holds* her tiny son in her arms.

What follows (from line 21 to the end) is the process of liberating the vagina. The logic here is obvious: if the world turns a woman into an object, into a walking vagina, then the vagina must gain freedom. The second part creates a "portrait" of the vagina, both physiological and almost sentimental: "Now my vagina is flexing and next to it, a little higher, my clitoris is swelling; / it looks like a little bead and it's wrapped in a delicate / folded hood, which can sometimes be pulled back / under a blind rain of light touches" (lines 26–29). The third part returns to the speaker's first "meeting" with her vagina, her first attempts to own it: "I often looked at my clitoris with the little / broken mirror that papa used to shave. / I was dry wood that burned / stronger every day" (lines 34–37). But subjugation, too, is outlined here as part of the school and social world, "where everything is viewed through the male gaze" (part 4, lines 38–42, here line 38) and the political forces "ha[ve] an interest" in one's vagina (part 5, lines 43–50, here line 43). The emerging confrontation is resolved in parts 6 (lines 51–76) and 7 (lines 77–88), where transgression becomes explicit and demonstrative. Here Rymbu breaks the taboo by introducing the "obscene" motif of menstruation (lines 61–80, italics added):

Мне нравится заниматься сексом во время месячных,
всё тело становится суперчувствительным.
Люблю, когда твой член весь в моей крови,
и люблю представлять, *что у тебя тоже месячные,*
что солёная тёплая кровь капает из маленькой дырочки
на твоей головке.

Люблю, когда твои руки липкие от моей крови,
когда она засыхает на твоих ногтях и заусенцах,
люблю чувствовать, как пульсирует матка в моём животе,
словно второе сердце, как набухает грудь и становится горячей,
как будто оттуда вот-вот польётся молоко.
Я дам тебе его пить, любимый, оно зальёт твое лицо,
твои нежные розовые соски (почти как у девочки),
сделает мокрыми *твои волоски на груди,*
твою шею, животик, в котором,
я мечтаю, ты когда-нибудь сможешь выносить нашу дочь.

I like to have sex during my period;
your whole body gets super-sensitive.
I love it when your penis is covered with my blood,
and love to imagine that *you have a period, too,*
that salty, warm blood is dripping from the little hole
in your glans.

I love it when your hands are sticky with my blood,
when it dries on your nails and ragged cuticles,
love to feel my womb pulsing in my stomach,
like a second heart, my breast swelling up and getting hot,
like milk is about to pour out of it.
I'll let you drink it, love, it will pour over your face,

your tender little nipples (almost like a girl's),
wet the fuzz on your chest,
neck, your tummy, where,
in my dreams, you might someday carry our daughter.

The repeated word *liubliu* ("love"/"like," lines 63, 82) in this fragment emphasizes the speaker's agency and also imitates the rhythm of the sexual act, thus involving the reader (listener) in it. In addition, we are faced with a parodic ritual in which "forbidden" menstrual blood "transforms" a man into a woman! The whole scene overthrows heteronormativity: the speaker fantasizes that her male partner also has a period and that he would one day bear her child; she dresses him up in her own clothes and says that he has "tender little nipples (almost like a girl's)" (line 73). This creates a natural transition from the sex scene with a man to a recollection of same-sex adolescent relations and the present-day persecution of LGBTQ people (lines 81–88 in the Russian, lines 82–88 in the translation). The upshot is that transgressions, expressed at the level of image and language, undermine patriarchal logic, demonstrating its dependence on taboos, and, while these taboos are based on phantoms, they can nevertheless generate genuine repressions.

The short eighth part (lines 89–93) picks up the motif of repression—"Will it die before its time? / Will it die in a cage?" (lines 92–93)—to lead to a higher-level transgression in part 9 (lines 94–141), the one that foregrounds the motif of touching oneself. Here masturbation becomes a metaphor for complete liberation from male power: the woman chooses who or what touches her and turns her on, and the vagina becomes an organ of concentrated experience, memory, pain, happiness, knowledge—everything the lived body can absorb.

It is only after these two major transgressions against patriarchal norms and restrictions that Rymbu delivers her revolutionary vagina monologue (lines 148–68):

Я думаю, а что, может, и правда вагина погубит это государство,
прогонит незаконного президента,
отправит в отставку правительство,
отменит армию, налоги для бедных,
фсб как структуру самой гнусной власти и подавления,
разберётся с полицией,
консерватизмом и реваншизмом,
расформирует несправедливые суды, освободит
политических заключенных,
сделает невозможным тухлый русский национализм,

унижение угнетённых, сфабрикованные дела,
разъебёт олигархат и патриархат,
парализует войска,
движущиеся в чужих государствах—
всё дальше и дальше:
в пизду милитаризм!

Моя вагина—это любовь, история и политика.
Моя политика—это тело, быт, аффект.
Мой мир—вагина. И я несу мир,
но для некоторых я—опасная вагина,
боевая вагина. Это мой монолог

I think, well, maybe the vagina will bring down this state for real,
drive out the illegitimate president,
disband the government,
abolish the army, taxes on the poor,
the FSB as a structure of utterly vile power and oppression,
will deal with the police,
with conservatism and revanchism,
will dismantle unjust trials, free
the political prisoners,
make impossible putrid Russian nationalism,
the humiliation of the oppressed, fabricated cases,
will shatter oligarchy and patriarchy,
paralyze the troops deployed in other states—
farther and farther
into militarism's pussy!

My vagina is love, history and politics.
My politics is the body, the everyday, affect.
My world is the vagina. And I bear peace.
Yet for some I am a dangerous vagina,
a fighting vagina. That is my monologue.

The famous phrase "The personal is political"—the title of an essay by the American feminist Carol Hanisch (1970)—takes on new meaning in Rymbu's poem. It is not just that so-called domestic or sexual "women's problems" reflect gender inequality and implicit or explicit forms of repression. Anything but. "My Vagina" actually argues for turning the most personal and intimate into an instrument of political struggle. Here, one cannot help but think of the play *Lysistrata*—which, as it happens, gave its name to a large and still unfinished cycle of antiwar poems by Elena Fanailova (see chapter 30). Rymbu's method consists of reclaiming agency—not rationalistic, but corporeal, affective, and sexual agency. How can the various forms of violence listed in this long stanza be resisted? "My Vagina" has an answer: through transgressions, symbolic and otherwise. After all, these forms of violence, like those of contemporary Russian authoritarianism, are based on centuries-old patriarchal models. And this means that their rejection—first by one, then by several generations of women—is indeed fraught with revolution.

33

Polina Barskova, "Children's Literature" (2019)

THE GARDEN OF EARTHLY DELIGHTS

Книжки с картинками

Они пытали их обоих.
Какого цвета на обоях
Они оставили следы?
Конечно только золотые,
Конечно только голубые,
Горения слюны слюды.
Смотри ж на дивные оттенки:
Они остались на застенке,
Сюда идём мы как в музей.
Что видим мы в музее этом?
Вот видим: стрекозиным летом
Блуждает череда друзей,
Хармс сторонится
Шварц хохочет,
Олейников его не хочет,
Знать, он лежать у речки хочет
И жабу палочкой крушить.
Их путь ещё не кончен,—начат,
И все они уже да значат
Поэзию и крутят нить.
Сквозь стрекозу, сквозь паутину,
Смотрю на жаркую картину
И вижу их живыми не.
Один во льду, другой на дыбе,

Введенский плавает на рыбе,

Мерцает Вагинов на дне.[1]

Children's Literature

Both were tortured.
What color traces
did they leave on the wallpaper?
I bet you golden
I bet you blue
Burns of crystal, drool.
Observe droll colors
preserved in the confines.
We come here to a museum.
What do we see in this museum?
We see: a trail of fellows
who dragonfly on summer days.
Kharms shies away Shvartz ha-has
to Shvartz Oleinikov prefers
to slug by a stream
poking a toad to death.
Their journey has just begun,
not ended, they stand
for poetry and weave their thread.
Through the web, through a dragonfly's wing,
I watch a blistering scene
and see them living not:
one in the ice, another on the rack,
poet Vvedensky floats atop a pike,
poet Vaginov twinkles on the river's bed.

(TRANSLATED BY VALZHYNA MORT)

Polina Barskova started her literary career in Perestroika-era Leningrad. Her first book of poems was published in 1991, when she was barely fifteen years old. Critics have observed that her verses continue the tradition of neomodernism, grown and nurtured in the Leningrad underground and represented by such poets as Mikhail Kuzmin,

Joseph Brodsky, Elena Shvarts, and Viktor Krivulin. Barskova remains faithful to this tradition, but she is always on the lookout for ways to open it toward a new understanding of history and culture, experimenting with form and not shying away from themes and subjects that are, in this tradition, surrounded by a halo of sacredness.

Though Barskova has been living in the United States since 1998 and is pursuing a successful career as a university academic (currently at Berkeley), she continues to relate herself and her work to the so-called Petersburg text. According to Vladimir Toporov, who pioneered this concept and field of studies, the Petersburg text is characterized by the antithesis between eschatological motifs (natural cataclysms, historical catastrophes, everyday chaos) and strict forms of harmony (architecture, art):

> on the one hand, there is a dark and ghostly chaos, in which nothing can be seen with any certainty but a haze and blur, a treacherous duality, where being and nonbeing interplay, merge, one pretending to be the other, teasing the observer (mirages, dreams, ghosts, shadows, doppelgängers, reflections [. . .]) On the other hand, there is a lucid cosmos, an ideal unity of nature and culture, characterized by logic, harmony, and maximum visibility (clarity)—up to clairvoyance and providential revelations.[2]

In her poems of the 2010s and 2020s, Barskova significantly redefines this tradition. As an ominous Surrealist continuation of the Petersburg text, her poems,[3] prose,[4] and scholarship[5] address the Siege of Leningrad. To her, the giant death camp that the city became under the siege is inseparable from the tragedy of the Great Terror, which she also inscribes into the Petersburg text. Her very own Petersburg/Leningrad text, then, not only incorporates the tragic experience of twentieth-century history, but also, in a sense, embeds its roots in the cultural past. In this version of the Petersburg text, the horrors of the Stalinist terror and the siege are anticipated within the literary tradition in the nightmares of Gogol's and Dostoevsky's characters.

In conjunction, St. Petersburg, with its keen cultural memory, processes this unbearable experience in its own way, turning it into a cultural fact. In her poetry and prose, Barskova invariably centers on artists who found new and different means to transform their tragic historical experience into a courageous and harmonious art. Sometimes, she focuses on neoclassicists, sometimes on avant-gardists, or underground artists, or even socialist realists. All of them let the chaos of the Petersburg text pass through their lives and bodies: this is the price of turning it into art. In this process of rethinking the Petersburg text, Barskova turns her attention to OBERIU and affiliated authors: Daniil Kharms, Alexander Vvedensky, Nikolai Oleinikov, Nikolai Zabolotsky, Konstantin Vaginov, and Evgeny Shvarts.

It is the OBERIU writers to whom she dedicated "Picture Books" ("Children's Literature" in Valzhyna Mort's translation). The poem makes very little reference to a real historical drama. Instead, it foregrounds a vision, a poetic fantasy. But this fantasy turns out to be saturated with historical and cultural meaning, arguably providing deeper insights than mere facts ever could.

The present volume discusses the aesthetics of OBERIU in chapters on Kharms, Oleinikov, Vvedensky, and Zabolotsky. As for Barskova, what interested her most was their fate. It will suffice here to recapitulate a few facts, touched on in the respective chapters, that are significant for the context of Barskova's poem. Kharms and Vvedensky were arrested in 1931. It was only thanks to the efforts of Kharms's father, a veteran of the revolutionary movement, that they were sent into exile, to Kursk (where they went on to spend a year instead of the appointed three), rather than to a concentration camp. However, soon after the German attack on the Soviet Union, both were arrested again. In December 1941, Kharms was declared mentally ill and sent to a psychiatric prison, where he died (probably from starvation) during the siege winter of 1942. In September 1941, Vvedensky was arrested in Kharkov, where he was living at the time, for "anti-Soviet agitation" (which could refer to anything, even the most innocent conversation). He died during the prisoner transport a few months later, in the course of the same winter as Kharms. Oleinikov, the only OBERIU member to join the Communist Party, was arrested at the height of the Great Terror in 1937, accused of belonging to a Trotskyist organization, and shot a few months later after a brutal "investigation." Zabolotsky was also arrested during this period, in 1938. He, too, had been beaten, abused, and tortured during the investigation, but he still never pleaded guilty, which is perhaps the reason why he escaped with his life. He went on to survive the Gulag, was released in 1944, and continued to write until his death in 1958. Vaginov and Shvarts were never arrested—in the case of Vaginov, because he died of tuberculosis before the Great Terror, in 1934, at the age of thirty-four. It is not clear what saved Shvarts. Threatened with arrest more than once, he survived Stalin, the siege, and the war, and became a celebrated author of plays, including *The Shadow* (1939) and *The Dragon* (1943), which combined fairy-tale motifs with deep and dangerous political overtones. Shvarts died in 1958, leaving behind detailed diary entries about the OBERIU circle, which we believe to be a crucial source for Barskova's poem—after all, she has been exploring Shvarts's prose for many years.

The poem begins with a phrase that, as the poet confirmed in a conversation, was taken from a newspaper article about the fate of OBERIU: "Both were tortured." It refers to Zabolotsky, who was driven to madness by torture, and the painter Vera Ermolaeva, a student of Malevich and book designer, who was arrested and shot in a concentration camp in 1937. The motif of torture reappears in line 24 of the poem: "One in the ice, another on the rack" (line 23 in the translation), and the context suggests that the first description refers to Kharms, whose death in a prison hospital dates to February 1942, the most terrible time of the siege, its coldest and hungriest moment. The rack is a reference to Oleinikov: the documents relating to his arrest and interrogation (the "interrogation protocol") show that, at first, he flatly denied the accusations of the investigator, but eventually he was forced to concede all the charges. As a researcher writes, "This interrogation was final. Most likely, the physical condition of the person under investigation ruled out the possibility of obtaining evidence from him in the near future."[6]

However, Barskova defiantly refuses to look into the horrific details of her characters' fates. What does she put in their place? Surprisingly, the answer is beauty: "Observe droll colors / preserved in the confines. / We come here to a museum" (lines 7–9). What does "here" refer to? The most likely answer is the prison *replaced* by a museum. The imperative "look at the marvelous hues" ("observe droll colors" in the present translation) in line 7 is echoed in line 21: "I watch a blistering scene" (the original noun here, *kartina,* literally means "painting"). These lines frame the description of the friends "who dragonfly on summer days" (line 12), and they are Kharms, Shvarts, and Oleinikov. In the final lines, they are joined by Vvedensky and Vaginov. Each poet is described as succinctly as possible (Oleinikov in the greatest detail), but a train of literary associations encompasses many a characteristic. Almost all of these associations can be traced back to Shvarts's autobiographical writing, that is, his diary entries and the notes published posthumously under the title *The Phone Book.*[7]

The scene of summer *dolce far niente,* which forms the center of the poem, mimics children's literature of the 1930s. Fun in and near a river was a frequent subject of the children's poetry of those years, including texts by OBERIU poets as in Vvedensky's "On the fisherman and the pike" ("O rybake i sudake"):

По реке плывет челнок,
На корме сидит рыбак,
На носу сидит щенок,
В речке плавает судак.
Речка медленно течет,
С неба солнышко печет.[8]

On the river, there's a boat:
someone fishing by a dike,
and a puppy, all afloat.

In the river, there's a pike.
On the river, there's a boat,
and the sun is very hot.[9]

Such happy *idleness* in many OBERIU children's poems, as well as in Barskova's work, is described through a series of multidirectional, not goal-oriented, *activities*. For instance:

Шел я лесом по тропинке,
Недалеко от реки.
Мне показывали спинки
Убегавшие жуки.

[. . .]

Рыбы в речке тихо плыли,
Тучи по небу ползли,
Птицы всюду говорили:
Ля-ля-ля и ли-ли-ли!

Ветры в поле пробегали,
Травы тихо шевеля.
Всюду птицы щебетали:
Ле и ли и лю и ля![10]

I was walking in the woods,
leaving wet and shiny tracks
and I saw the beetles scurry,
showing me their polished backs.
[. . .]

Fish were swimming in the river,
clouds were crawling in the sky,
everywhere, the birds were saying:
tra-la-la and try-ly-ly!

Winds were blowing in the meadows,
and the grasses went swoosh-swish.
Everywhere, the birds were saying:
tra-la-la and troosh-trysh-trish![11]
(Vvedensky, "Birdies")

Barskova adds to an impression of children's verse by using deliberately simple, sometimes tautological, rhymes: *oboikh/oboiakh, zolotye/golubye, khokhochet/khochet/khochet, nachat/znachat, na dybe/na rybe, pautinu/kartinu*.

It is the context of children's literature that explains the phrase "Kharms shies away" (line 13): though he was the most popular children's writer in the OBERIU set, Kharms declared that he hated children. Yevgeny Shvarts wrote, "Kharms couldn't stand children and was proud of it. Actually, it suited him. It defined a facet of his being. He was, of course, the last offspring of his family. Had he had kids, they would have been absolutely horrible. That's why even other people's children frightened him."[12] Meanwhile, Kharms's last wife, Marina Malich (Durnovo), points out that, despite his alleged hatred of children, Kharms enjoyed enormous success with this audience: "As soon as Daniil came onstage, something unimaginable began. The children shouted, squealed, clapped. They stomped their feet in excitement. He was adored."[13] Apart from this alienation from the "children's world," Kharms is surrounded by an aura of tragedy that isolates him from the happy world of childhood invented by OBERIU. The essence of this tragedy and its significance are impossible to miss: the cheerful utopia of childhood is created by poets, above all by Kharms himself, in the midst of a historical catastrophe. Terror has touched them all, and a sense of danger never disappears.

The next phrase of the poem, "Shvarts ha-has" (line 13), is ambiguous. On the one hand, it is a detail of the happy "dragonfly summer." On the other, it can be read as a reference to Shvarts's *The Phone Book*, in which he speaks eloquently of the relationship between daily life, creativity, laughter—and the terror that affects and threatens everyone:

> How do you flee if you don't believe yourself guilty? How do you hold up under interrogation? People perished, confessing to terrorism, to sabotage, as if delirious. And they disappeared without a trace, and their wives and children, whole families, were sent after them. There was nobody who was not afraid for their life, nobody who did not go to sleep or wake up feeling the unprecedented tragedy that had befallen the country, that was unlike anything. But nothing is more stagnant than everyday life. Outwardly, we lived as before. We had parties at the Writers House. We ate and drank. And we laughed. In our slavishness, we laughed even about our shared tragedy—what else could we do? Love remained love, life remained life, but every moment was saturated with terror. And the threat of infamy.[14]

In this context, laughter temporarily replaces terror, or rather shields one from terror. The issue here is not just everyday life, but rather first and foremost creative work. After all, the magnificently funny and frivolous OBERIU poems and stories were written in the 1930s, as though designed to stand in total relief to the historical background of unnamed horrors. In that regard, they remind us that sources of joy and humor survive even the most tragic moments of history: "Love remained love, life remained life . . ."

The phrase "Shvarts ha-has" also refers to another fragment from Shvarts's diaries, which immediately follows the passage quoted above. Shvarts recalls his last meeting with Oleinikov in early July 1937, shortly before the latter was arrested. The lines "to Shvarts Oleinikov prefers / to slug by a stream / poking a toad to death" (lines 14–16) reverberate with details from this entry. Let us consider a somewhat abbreviated version:

> Summer, a clear day, hot in a non-Leningrad way—all this conspired to take us back to the first days of our acquaintance, the time in Donbas, that brief time when we were really friends. But, conspire as it may, it couldn't quite take us back. Too much had occurred between us since then, both of us had changed too much. Especially Nikolai [Oleinikov]. [. . .] We were walking to our dacha, and, on the way, we saw a boy on the balcony. He was reading a book, as one reads at that age, utterly absorbed. He was reading and laughing, and Oleinikov pointed at him with tenderness and envy. Nikolai and I were very different people. Sometimes he'd vent his feelings and mock me behind my back with great pleasure, which always became known to me in one way or another in our small and closed circle [. . .] We often felt repelled by each other, but there were some occasions of perfect understanding—however, they grew ever rarer toward the end. Such perfect understanding flashed up for a moment when he pointed to that boy reading a funny book. Paradise lost—and hell, whose stench was about to get us.[15]

It might well have been this entry that gave rise to the crucial motifs of Barskova's poem. First, there is the motif of the *funny children's book,* in which the boy is so happily absorbed on his balcony. This motif establishes the dominant trope of the poem, namely, that of a happy "picture book," "children's literature." Second, the motif of laughter ("Shvarts ha-has"), albeit reversed: in the fragment cited, it is Oleinikov who mocks Shvarts, which is strangely echoed by the image of the poet torturing a river creature ("poking a toad to death"). Most importantly, both in Shvarts's diary and in Barskova's poem, the motif of a hot summer forms a borderline between paradise and hell. This single moment of liminality in itself condenses a key structure in the Petersburg text: "Paradise lost—and hell, whose stench was about to get us."

And what occurs in Barskova's poem is precisely a transition from paradise to hell. It is achieved by a strange agrammatism (*zhivymi ne*), correctly rendered by Valzhyna

Mort as: "I watch a blistering scene / and *see them living not* . . ." (lines 21–22 in the translation). This sharp shift in grammar (an example of the modernist use of *sdvig*) conceptually ratchets up the tension a notch. As images succeed one another, a hellish torment supplants paradise ("one in the ice, another on the rack," line 23). While the motif of ice, as mentioned above, refers to the icy winter in which Kharms died in the prison hospital, in this context it also evokes an association with Dante's hell:

Now was I, and with fear in verse I put it,
There where the shades were wholly covered up,
And glimmered through like unto straws in glass.

Some prone are lying, others stand erect,
This with the head, and that one with the soles;
Another, bow-like, face to feet inverts.[16]

However, unlike Dante, who placed Lucifer and the worst sinners—traitors—at the icy bottom of hell, for Barskova, it is poets who enter the hell of history. The question is why and also what for. The answer seems to lie in the following lines of the poem (18–23 in the Russian, 17–22 in the translation):

Их путь ещё не кончен,—начат,
И все они уже да значат
Поэзию и крутят нить.
Сквозь стрекозу, сквозь паутину,
Смотрю на жаркую картину
И вижу их живыми не.

Their journey has just begun,
not ended, they stand
for poetry and weave their thread.
Through the web, through a dragonfly's wing,
I watch a blistering scene
and see them living not

What Mort renders as "they stand / for poetry" is even stranger in the original: the most literal translation would read "they mean / signify poetry" (lines 19–20). For Barskova, then, it is less the texts than the poets themselves who *are* poetry. Her work can thus be read as a meta-fantasy of what poetry can do. Its main product is a thread which—almost literally, from line to rhyming line—connects the author with the dead poets, one era with another, happiness with horror, the paradise of childhood with the hell of torture, the visible with the invisible. The image of a thread embodies an understanding of poetry as the joining of the disjointed, the crossing of boundaries, the breaking of limits. In one word: transgressions. And they, by their very definition, must violate religious (and other) prohibitions. Hence the connection with Dante's hell. From a religious, hierarchical point of view, poets with their all-connecting and all-defying threads of verse are sinners who belong in icy hell next to the border-crosser Lucifer.

In this sense, the last two lines are of particular interest (lines 25–26 in the Russian, lines 24–25 in the translation):

Введенский плавает на рыбе,
Мерцает Вагинов на дне.

poet Vvedensky floats atop a pike,
poet Vaginov twinkles on the river's bed.

Why is Vvedensky swimming on a fish? Why is Vaginov twinkling on the bottom? The vision of Vvedensky once again refers to his children's poems, among which fishermen and fish occupy an exceptional place. Apart from "On the Fisherman and the Pike"[17] (cited above), he also wrote at least two poems titled "The Fisherman" (1929 and 1940), and one with the title in the plural, "The Fishermen" (1929). Vvedensky was not the only member of OBERIU fascinated by fish and fishing. In Kharms's 1941 "Unexpected Catch" we witness something very much like what Vvedensky describes in "Guest on a Horse" (see the analysis in the present volume) in adult terms: the appearance of the Messiah.

—Замолчишь ты наконец!
Крикнул с яростью отец.
Он вскочил, взглянул на небо . . .
Сердце так и ухнуло!
И мгновенно что-то с неба
В воду с криком бухнуло.

Сын, при помощи отца,
Тащит на берег пловца,
А за ним на берег рыбы
Так и лезут без конца!
Сын доволен. Рад отец.
Вот и повести конец.[18]

"Will you ever shut your trap!"
finally the father snapped.

He jumped up, looked at the skies—
in his heart, he felt an ache:
suddenly, right from the skies
something splashed into the lake.

Son and father pull together
and the fallen man they gather.

Fish now start to climb ashore—
more, and more, and more, and more!
Fishermen now have their quarry—
that's the end of this strange story.[19]

The identity of the swimmer who falls from the sky and is followed by fish climbing ashore remains open. All these ichthyological OBERIU poems resonate with Barskova's work, and arguably the strongest connection of all is with one of Vvedensky's final works, the complex philosophical text "Inviting Myself to Think" (1941). It contains the following lines:

в морей соленом водоеме
нам как-то побывать пришлось,
где волны издавали скрип,
мы наблюдали гордых рыб:
рыбы плавали как масло
по поверхности воды,
мы поняли, жизнь всюду гасла
от рыб до Бога и звезды.[20]

The salty water of the sea
had once been our abode.
The waves kept making creaking sounds,
we watched proud fish make stately rounds,
like oil, the fish swam on the water,
we saw them close, we saw them far,
we saw how life was fizzling out
from fish to God and every star.

Here, fish appear beside God, foreshadowing the apocalypse. In "Where. When," also written by Vvedensky in 1941, we read:

Прощай тетрадь.
Неприятно и нелегко умирать.

FIGURE 33.1. Details from Hieronymus Bosch's *The Garden of Earthly Delights* (1490–1500), Madrid, Museo del Prado. Wikipedia: https://commons.wikimedia.org/wiki/The_Garden_of_Earthly_Delights.

Прощай мир. Прощай рай.
Ты очень далек человеческий край.[21]

My notebook, goodbye.
It isn't pleasant or easy to die.
Goodbye, Earth. Goodbye, Paradise.
So far away the human world lies.

In this context, the image of Vvedensky floating on a fish embodies in Barskova's poem a farewell to the world and to creation, foreshadowing the apocalypse. In his famous book *The Sense of an Ending*, Frank Kermode argues that references to apocalypses suggest a vision of time that corresponds not to the historical *chronos* but to *kairos*, "a point in time filled with significance charged with a meaning derived from its relation to the end."[22] This observation also applies to Barskova's poem: in the perspective of impending torture and execution, the paradisial picture of the OBERIU poets happily at rest becomes a vision of *kairos*, a time when history moves from one disaster to the next. It is *the hell of history* in which poets are sent to its most torturous circle because they, unlike others, try to break the unity of *kairos*, piercing it with a needle of poetry whose thread connects and transcends (hi)stories. Poets are doomed to this hell even as they rest in the paradise of their own invention.

However, the final couplet can also be read differently, in a way that is diametrically opposed to a sense of doom. The entire composition of Barskova's poem recalls Bosch's triptych *The Garden of Earthly Delights*, in which scenes in paradise and hellish torments are linked by a shared horizon. Moreover, in Bosch's heaven, the idyll does not exclude cruelty. In the foreground of the paradisial panel, right at the feet of Adam and Eve, we see the circle of life at its most brutal: one beast devours another, and, far from lying down with the lion, the lamb is trying, in vain, to escape. This resonates with Barskova's poem, where the paradisial state of the "dragonfly summer" does not prevent Oleinikov from poking a toad with a stick and enjoying its misery.

Much of Bosch's central panel, the one actually depicting the Garden of Earthly Delights, is dedicated (sometimes allegorically, sometimes more directly) to various forms of sexuality. Among sexual symbols, fish play a not insignificant role: "fish, which crop up several times here, referenced the phallus in Old Netherlandish proverbs," points out a researcher of Bosch.[23] Readers of Barskova's poem do not have to be familiar with the Bosch research to glean a sexual reference: this aspect of the last two lines is actualized by the "genital" association in the pseudonym of the poet and novelist Konstantin Vaginov (Vagenheim), author of the novel *The Goat Song*, dedicated to the daily apocalypse of the 1920s. Thus, the image of the phallus and the vagina keep "flickering" (as Barskova/Mort puts it in the final line), acquiring here a new significance as the reference to earthly delights and the creation of new life. In translation, this reference is strengthened by happy coincidence: the most obvious equivalent for *dno* is "river *bed*," with "bed" becoming the final word.

New life does not contradict the idea of the apocalypse, which, after all, promises a new heaven and a new earth. By concluding with a playful erotic motif, the poem introduces the carnivalesque semantics of eternal renewal. Carnivalesque eroticism appears as the reverse of a body suffering and being tortured. In his book on Rabelais, Bakhtin writes that the grotesque body is "a body in the act of becoming. It is never finished, never completed; it is continually built, created, and builds and creates another body. Moreover, the body swallows the world and is itself swallowed by the world."[24] More than that: "If we consider the grotesque image in its extreme aspect, it never presents an individual body; the image consists of orifices and convexities that present another, newly conceived body. It is a point of transition in a life eternally renewed, the inexhaustible vessel of death and conception."[25] Bakhtin endows the grotesque body with optimistic meaning—but it can also be read as belonging to a victim of violence and terror, as researchers have repeatedly suggested.

Barskova inverts Bakhtin's logic. Describing the OBERIU poets as victims of violence, she transforms the suffering body into a carnivalesque one. By overcoming doom in this manner, she turns the scene of the apocalypse into a (Boschian) carnival in which "the beginning and end of life are closely linked and interwoven."[26] An erotic motif is the final link completing the chain of metamorphoses that begins with the history of terror ("both were tortured"), continues with a paradisial idyll of children's literature, and concludes with a mythologized hell of history bordering on the apocalyptic. This is how the thread of poetry unwinds, linking distant or even incompatible states and realities, historical eras and metaphysical realms. Its ability to permeate time is fraught with danger for poets. It also fills the very act of poetic creation with indestructible optimism.

34

Maria Stepanova, "A little like this: instead of coming out of the closet" (2021)

A QUIET APOCALYPSE

Как-нибудь так: вместо того, чтобы выйти из шкафа,
Люди ходят в шкафу—и оказываются в другом месте.
Или они только заглянули в шкаф
И слышат, как за спиной проворачивается ключ,
И вот они уже в другом месте,
Под носами тапок утренний снег.

Или так: они никогда не знали, что это шкаф, пока
Дверца не захлопнулась, медленно рассвело
И стало ясно, что вот, мы в другом месте
И над нами сыплется нафталин.
На городских площадях, на улицах города
Пусто так, словно война, словно революция,
Словно эпидемия, словно финал чемпионата мира—
И над ними идет утренний снег.

Нынче видно все, и что все одновременно:
В каждой квартире горит свет, одновременно
Каждый в своем шкафу садится за стол, поливает плющ,
Встает, садится, ложится, не гасит свет,
Сияет в окне ослепительно сонной лампой,
Как девушки в витринах красных кварталов,
Перед которыми нет никого, улицы пустые,
И над ними сыплется нафталин.

Одинаковые, обрюзгшие, тяжкие как животы,
В воздухе стояли воздушные шары:
Воздушные шкафы на невидимых нитках,
В каждом никого не веселящий газ.
В темной воде, состоящей из льда и воды,
Возвышались этажи фосфоресцирующих рыб.
В зимнем небе, состоящем из неба и снега,
Светились окна многоквартирных домов,
Пустые, товарами полные магазины,
Рестораны со стульями, прислоненными к столам,
Учрежденья с прошлогодними календарями,
Забытыми на странице с мартовской девушкой.
И над ними шел утренний свет.

Иногда на лед выходили фавны
Опушенные смуглой шерсткой,
На тонких копытцах,
Стесняющиеся
Лишний раз
отпечаток раздвоенный ставить на белое.[1]

A little like this: instead of coming out of the closet
They crowd inside it, and find themselves in another place.
Or they only went briefly into this wardrobe
But heard the key turn behind them—
And now they're in another place,
The morning snow under the tips of their slippers.

Or perhaps they didn't know it was a wardrobe, until
The door slammed shut, the light slowly grew
And it was suddenly clear—we're in another place,
Naphthalene sprinkling down from above.
Emptiness, like war, like revolution
On the city squares and in the streets
Like an epidemic, or the world cup final—
And the morning snow falling from above.

Now everything can be seen, how it all happens at once:
A light glowing in every apartment, at the same time

Each man in his closet sits at his table, waters his houseplant
Stands, sits, lies, leaves the light burning
Shines blinding bright like a lamp in the small hours
Like girls in the windows of red light districts
With no one to see them, the streets are empty,
And the naphthalene falls softly.

Lonely, bloated, drooping like paunches
These balloons hanging in the air:
Aerial wardrobes on invisible strings
Filled with un-laughing gas.
In dark water, made of ice and water
Rose the many stories of phosphorescent fish.
In the winter sky, made of snow and sky,
Gleamed the windows of many-storied buildings
Empty shops, piled high with goods
Restaurants with the chairs leaned against the tables
Offices with last year's calendar
Fixed on the page with March's girl
And from above fell the morning light.

Sometimes fauns came out onto the ice
Downy dark wool
On thin little hooves
Fearing
To leave too many
Cloven prints on the white.

(TRANSLATED BY SASHA DUGDALE)

Maria Stepanova (b. 1972) left Russia almost immediately after the full-scale invasion of Ukraine in February 2022 to become one of the most outspoken critics of Putin's regime and one of the most respected Russophone public intellectuals across the world. In the West, Maria Stepanova is better known as a prose writer than as a poet. Translated into English by Sasha Dugdale, Stepanova's nonfictional "romance" *In Memory of Memory* (*Pamiati pamiati*, 2017) has garnered significant literary accolades, including the short list of the International Booker Prize and the long list of the US National Book Award (for the best book in translation). Two books of poems have also been published in English, *War of the Beasts and the Animals* (*Voina zverei i zhivotnykh*)[2] and *The Voice Over*, which also includes selected essays.[3] Among fans of Russian poetry, since the early 2000s Stepanova has been regarded as the most innovative of the poets working within a paradigm of Russian modernist poetry (a lineage defined by Mandelstam, Akhmatova, Tsvetaeva, Khodasevich), her work further enriched by a serious interaction with Anglophone poetry (see, for example, Stepanova's collection of free translations *For Stevie Smith* [*Za Stivi Smit*]).

Praised by the British newspaper the *Guardian* as "Russia's next great writer" and "a writer who will likely be spoken about in the same breath as Poland's Olga Tokarczuk and Belarus's Svetlana Alexievich in years to come,"[4] Stepanova in fact persistently eludes any attempt to pin her down to a trend or typology. She is at once classical and experimental, modernist and postmodernist. She is equally intuitive and rational, both intellectually and emotionally sensitive. While being a sophisticated stylist, she is at the same time receptive to the voices of popular culture and street speech. Stepanova's original voice constantly oscillates between two opposite strategies. One strategy is defined by the quest for freedom through an escape from narrow and debilitating identity into a multitude of performed selves. The second is to ventriloquize the voices (or even "truths") of others who would otherwise remain muted. Her freedom turns out to be a form of dependence, almost an addiction to diverting selves. This is one of her many aporias.

The critic Mikhail Iampolski made the following observation about the fluidity of Stepanova's poetic subject: "Stepanova's 'personalities' are unstable, they reflect each other and flow into each other [. . .] This indeterminacy transcends similarities based upon kinship, and mutates into an almost Ovidian stream of metamorphoses."[5] Curiously enough, his words precede by a number of years the appearance of Stepanova's poetic cycle *Holy Winter*, in which Ovid emerges as one of the central voices. It is a work overwhelmingly dominated by the logic of metamorphoses. One may reasonably assume that Stepanova's Ovid emerged from Covid. As a collection, *Holy Winter 20/21*, written during a time of pandemic and published in the shadow of Russia's war with Ukraine, is full of images of snow and emptiness, its subjects taking refuge from a blizzard of events or exiled by hostile forces. Characters and works inhabiting this wondrous book include Kai from Hans Christian Andersen's *The Snow Queen*, the Empress Catherine the Great and her general and lover Potemkin, Tchaikovsky's *Sleeping Beauty*, C. S. Lewis's *The Chronicles of Narnia* (the wardrobe in this poem originates with the first book), and frozen sounds from the tales of Baron Munchausen. But at its center we see and hear the exiled Ovid complaining about eternal cold and night in passionate poems that defy death and despair. With Ovid's help, Stepanova unleashes a stream of metamorphoses blurring the borderlines not only between the self and others, but also between life and death, defeat and triumph. While all are seemingly controlled by a winter representing forces beyond everyone's control, poets and translators prove able to thaw voices lost to repression and accidents of history.

Stepanova has a knack for aporias, and it may even be her preferred method of exploration. Stepanova's aporias dwell on the impossibility of what is deemed necessary and the vital necessity of the impossible. She cannot avert her gaze from the yawning gap between what we see in reality and how we interpret what we see. There, in this baffling gray area, she detects a glimpse or rather a hope for the light.

Holy Winter explores the continuing condition of living-within-death—whether it is provisional or final, no one can say. This condition results from both the Covid pandemic and the Russian political winter, both of which may very well last longer than an individual's own life. Stepanova's vision in this book is simultaneously pessimistic and optimistic, and her wise conclusion is that one has to abandon hope in the knowledge that there will be no release and no escape from our historical condition. When one pandemic ends, another will begin. When this dictator dies, another will replace him. But this condition is not incompatible with creativity and metamorphoses—in other words, with life. We simply have to learn to live *within* this condition, whatever that seems to be.

To one degree or another, all the poems in the collection *Holy Winter* investigate the simultaneous flowing of life and death into another: of death on one level of existence and of life (which also means art) on another. These conditions are mutually contradictory, and yet they coexist. Stepanova wrote concerning this collection:

> This winter [2020–21] I was struck by the inseparability of time-space-political winter in our general situation, and the fact that the pandemic was experienced as a 'removal' (including in the spatial sense) began to seem like a natural continuation of the dead end in which we had found ourselves. And the fact that, in this fatal dead end, it is still possible to write books and make jam doesn't cancel out anything, but simply divides life into first and second stories, as in a wooden folk puppet booth. We live on one story (where miracles and texts, and the happiness of understanding are all possible), on the other—we know what is on the other.[6]

The simultaneous presence of normal life and the condition of symbolic death, and also the parallelism of pandemic isolation and the political winter, which also leads to isolation, acquired new significance in February 2022, when Russia launched its war against Ukraine. Stepanova was one of the first Russian writers to declare her opposition to the war and the entirety of Russia's national policy.[7] The destruction of "all our notions of the contemporary world and a social contract," and the realization of "the unthinkable," had already been intimated by Stepanova in *Holy Winter*. Retrospectively, one cannot help reading poems like the one treated in this chapter as a foreshadowing of the global catastrophe marked first by the Covid pandemic disrupting the everyday social fabric, and second by Russia's invasion of Ukraine, signifying the brutal destruction of the thirty-year attempt to build a new, post–Cold War, world.

Stepanova's poem is composed of five stanzas of unequal length (6, 8, 8, 13, and 6 lines). Numerous repetitions unite them. These repetitions pull the free verse together, endowing it with a firm rhythm. In the first stanza, there are repetitions of phrases with variations on the words *shkaf* ("closet," "wardrobe" in the translation) and *drugoe mesto* ("another place"): *vyiti iz shkafa* ("coming out of the closet"); *khodiat v shkafu* ("they crowd inside it"); *zaglianuli v shkaf* ("went briefly into the wardrobe"); *okazyvaiutsia v drugom meste* ("find themselves in another place"); *uzhe v drugom meste* ("now they're in another place"), together with the use of anaphora in lines 3–5.

These same phrases recur in the second stanza: *nikogda ne znali, chto eto shkaf* ("they didn't know it was a wardrobe"), *vot my v drugom meste* ("we're in another place"). But now other repetitions also occur: *Na gorodskikh ploshchiadakh, na ulitsakh goroda* ("On the city squares and in the streets," line 12); *slovno voina, slovno revoliutsiia / Slovno epidemiia, slovno final chempionata mira* ("like war, like revolution," "Like an epidemic, or the world cup final," lines 12–13 in the Russian, lines 11 and 13 in Sasha Dugdale's translation). In the third stanza, the words *vse* ("everything"), *odnovremenno* ("at the same time"), and *kazhdyi* ("each") are repeated. Here also the almost importunate motif of light moves into the foreground: "A light glows in each apartment" (line 16), "Shines blinding bright like a lamp in the small hours" (line 19).

In the fourth stanza the eye is caught by a striking rhythmical anaphora (lines 24–29): *V vozdukhe* ("hanging in the air"); *V kazhdom* ("in each"); *V temnoi vode* ("In dark water"); *Vozvyshalis'* ("Rise"); *V zimnem nebe* ("In the winter sky"). But here also we find an almost tautological repetition of the motif of "elements" constituting a void: "These balloons hanging in the air, / Aerial wardrobes on invisible strings" (lines 24–25); "In dark water, made of ice and water" (line 27); "In the winter sky, made of snow and sky" (line 29). Note also the syntactical parallelism that unites these lines.

Finally, running throughout the poem is the motif of snow transforming into naphthalene, and, moreover, sometimes the lines literally repeat or syntactically imitate each other—Sasha Dugdale's translation inventively preserves these parallelisms: "Naphthalene sprinkling down from above" (line 10); "and the morning snow falling from above" (line 14); "And the naphthalene falls softly" (line 22); "And from above fell the morning light" (line 35). This motif reaches its culmination in the final verse, where the snow/naphthalene is transformed into ice and fauns come out onto it. The rhythm of the repetitions is so insistent that it almost sounds monotonous. The same phrases, appearing in new contexts, sound like a stuck gramophone record. They erase themselves, leaving a void. The snow or naphthalene also becomes an equivalent for this inexorably advancing emptiness.

The first stanza creates a microplot about disappearance from the closet reminiscent of Daniil Kharms's text *The Trunk* (*Sunduk*, 1937) from the cycle *Incidences* (*Sluchai*). Written at the height of the state terror, this novella describes the escape of an unnamed individual—"a man with a long, skinny neck"—who "crawled into a trunk, closed the cover behind him and began to suffocate." His death throes are intensified by the fact that there is "an appalling smell of naphthalene in the trunk," a motif that also occurs in Stepanova's poem. However, the process of dying is unexpectedly interrupted, and the man finds himself outside the trunk: "The man with the long, skinny neck got up off the floor and looked around. The trunk was not around. Strung up on the chairs and on the bed the things that had been taken out of the trunk were lying on the chairs and the bed, but the trunk was nowhere to be seen." The novella concludes with the phrase: "That means that life defeated death by a method unknown to me."[8]

Stepanova also borrows from Kharms the motif of isolation—which verges on death—as the portal to a different life, a different reality. But in her poem, just as in Kharms's text, the "other place" in which people find themselves is indistinguishable from the quasi-existence of an afterlife. The victory of life over death by an "unknown method" can equally well be understood as the victory of death over life. However, by contrast with Kharms, in Stepanova's case the transition to an indefinite state between life and death is experienced not by a single individual, but rather by a society as a whole.

The second stanza consists of a variation on the initial microplot. It is not by accident that it starts with the words "Or perhaps" (*Ili tak*, line 7). The main difference between the two scenarios is that, in the first stanza, "instead of coming out of the closet / They crowd into the cupboard" (lines 1–2), whereas in the second stanza "they didn't know it was a wardrobe, until / The door slammed shut" (lines 7–8). The view from the outside ("they") is replaced at this point by the view from the inside ("we"). The isolation may or may not be consciously realized, but the outcome remains the same: "we're in another place, / Naphthalene sprinkling down from above" (lines 9–10). The "other place" seems to acquire a concrete character. It is a city stilled by a catastrophe of some kind: "like war, like revolution, / [. . .] Like an epidemic, or the world cup final" (lines 11, 13). Even though the poem was written about a year before Russia's invasion of Ukraine, we can see the specter of war already hovering above the surrealistic picture of a society stupefied by an epidemic of a deadly virus. War, revolution, epidemic, and, what's more, the final of a world championship—one presumes that Stepanova has in mind the soccer World Cup that took place in Russia in 2018—shifted the whole of society into a state of symbolic death. Sometimes this is provisional, as when a major championship eclipses everything that constitutes the normal course of life, and sometimes it is more tragic and protracted, as in war or revolution.

The visual technique of the third stanza is reminiscent of a camera zooming out. The viewpoint from within ("we") once again yields to an exterior view ("they"), but this time in a more generalized form. In the foreground, we have "everything at the same time," "each apartment," and "Each man in his closet" (lines 15–17). Why is it, however, that the motif of light sounds so insistent here, and what is the reason for the comparison with "girls in the windows of red light districts" (line 20)? The answer probably lies in the possibility that life has seemingly returned to normal: "sits at his table, waters his houseplant, / Stands, sits, lies, leaves the light burning" (lines 17–18). Nonetheless, the life that flows "in the closet," that is, in isolation, proves to be a mere imitation of life, akin to the way girls in a red-light district act out a certain kind of everyday routine while on display behind a window. The light emanating from isolated segments of life is replaced by the light of red lanterns, and in Stepanova's poem this is reduced to simply "red districts."

In the fourth stanza, the camera "zooms out" even further, so that the people disappear from view. All that remains is the new architecture of the world. Stepanova constructs this world out of parallelisms that expand both upward and downward. On the one hand, the "aerial wardrobes" are compared with "balloons" (lines 24–25):

> В воздухе стояли воздушные шары:
> Воздушные шкафы на невидимых нитках,

> These balloons hanging in the air:
> Aerial wardrobes on invisible strings.

On the other hand, the windows of apartment blocks are syntactically and visually compared to "many stories of phosphorescent fish" suspended "in dark water" (l.28). Moreover, both sky and water literally break down into "elements" (lines 27–30):

> В темной воде, состоящей из льда и воды,
> Возвышались этажи фосфоресцирующих рыб.

В зимнем небе, состоящем из неба и снега,
Светились окна многоквартирных домов

In dark water, made of ice and water
Rose the many stories of phosphorescent fish.
In the winter sky, made of snow and sky,
Gleamed the windows of many-storied buildings

The parallel drawn between bright sky and dark water brings a new concreteness to the motif of an isolated existence hovering between life and death: "up" and "down" turn out to resemble and reflect each other. The indistinguishability of life and death is emphasized by the disappearance of people from the peaceful interiors of shops, restaurants, and institutions. Why is it, however, that in this stanza the line that occurred earlier—"And the morning snow falling from above" (line 14)—is replaced by "And from above fell the morning light" (line 35)? What is the explanation for this shift?

This may be Stepanova's way of emphasizing the dialogue between her own poem and Joseph Brodsky's "Eclogue 4th (Winter)" (1980). In the first line of this rather long poem, Brodsky calls snow "a dry, condensed form of light." The following lines by Brodsky resonate especially clearly with Stepanova's poem:

—мир, не слыхавший о лондонах и парижах,
мир, где рассеянный свет—генератор будней,
где в итоге вздрагиваешь, обнаружив,
что и тут кто-то прошел на лыжах.[9]

a world that has never heard of any London or Paris,
where diffuse light is a generator of humdrum routine,
where at the last you shudder on discovering
that someone passed by even here on skis.[10]

The "Eclogue" also includes the motif of isolation, and an association between light and daily routine, and tracks in the snow are the only thing that disrupts the freezing over. In Brodsky's poem, however, the winter landscape stimulates thoughts of time: "Time is coldness," "time that has fallen far below zero," "time looks at itself in the mirror, like a singer," "the more time there is, the colder it is." And finally, even the all-conquering void is understood by Brodsky as an excess of time:

Вас убивает на внеземной орбите
отнюдь не отсутствие кислорода,

но избыток Времени в чистом, то есть
без примеси вашей жизни, виде.[11]

What kills you in your extraterrestrial orbit
is by no means the lack of oxygen,
but an excess of Time in a pure form—
that is, with no admixture of your life.

In Stepanova's poem, however, time—even in the form of simple marker—is completely absent, being supplanted by space. This effect was also foreshadowed by Brodsky:

В разговорах о смерти место
играет все большую роль, чем время.[12]

In conversations about death
place plays a far more important role than time.

The disappearance of time in Stepanova's poem is comparable to the way an isolated world drops out of history, to what is in effect its historical death. It is precisely this loss of a connection with history that Stepanova understands as the transition of society into a state in which life and death are indistinguishable. Put more simply, this is a *quiet apocalypse.*

The contrast between Stepanova's poem and Brodsky's "Eclogue 4th" is nowhere sharper than in the final stanza. Ice also appears in Brodsky's finale, but his lyrical hero dons his skates and inscribes the ice with his tracks:

. . . И голос Музы
Звучит как сдержанный, частный голос.
Так родится эклога. Взамен светила
загорается лампа: кириллица, грешным делом,
разбредаясь по прописи вкривь ли, вкось ли,
знает больше, чем та сивилла,
о грядущем. О том, как чернеть на белом,
покуда белое есть, и после.[13]

. . . And the voice of the Muse
Sounds like a reserved, private voice.
Thus an eclogue is born. In place of the sun
a lamp lights up: the Cyrillic, straggling haphazardly,
I regret to say, across the copy-book,

knows more than that sybil
about the future. About marking black on white,
while there still is white, and after.

The finale of Stepanova's poem describes a similar situation. Fauns, the companions of Dionysus, come out onto the ice that has shackled the world in its isolation. It would seem that, as in Brodsky's "Eclogue," the purging of the world by cold and solitude will lead to the rebirth of life and inspiration; the snow-bound universe will be transformed into a sheet of paper, ready to receive the new word. Yet no, for in Stepanova's poem no hope remains of a renaissance of the word. The fauns are daunted, "Fearing / To leave too many / Cloven prints on the white" (lines 39–41). The apocalypse that has occurred is irreversible.

Stepanova's poem is an allegory that has moved beyond its own limits. Conceived as a micromodel of a world struck down by a pandemic, it has turned into an image of a world that has doomed itself to isolation from time, from history and also, therefore, from life and logos. To a certain extent, this poem throws into relief the semantics of the allegory as a method of cognizing modern times. Stepanova's use of allegory bears resemblance to Walter Benjamin's concept of this trope as expressed in *The Origin of German Tragic Drama*: "In allegory there lies before the eyes of the observer the *facies hippocratica* [lit. 'Hippocratic face'—the sunken, hollow, and pinched features exhibited by the dying] of history as petrified, primal landscape. History, in everything untimely, sorrowful and miscarried that belongs to it from the beginning, inscribed in a face—no, in a death's head [*Totenkopfe*]."[14] A similar image also occurs in Stepanova's poem—the death of history, imprinted on a "primal landscape"—only one that is not petrified, but icebound.

ACKNOWLEDGMENTS

We would like to thank a number of colleagues at Princeton University Press: first and foremost Ben Tate for his interest and guidance in the development of this book, and Josh Drake, Kathleen Cioffi, and Leah Caldwell for their contributions to its production. Many thanks to Leah Morin for help preparing the typescript and to Dr. Panayiotis Xenophontos for his assistance in negotiating and securing permissions to reproduce the poems. We express our warm gratitude to all the translators whose work plays such an important part in this critical anthology, and we are particularly grateful to those who contributed new versions of poems, including Alexandra Berlina, Andrew Bromfield, Sasha Dugdale, Boris Dralyuk, Peter France, Helena Kernan, Ainsley Morse, Valzhyna Mort, Eugene Ostashevsky, Kevin M. F. Platt, G. S. Smith, Joanne Turnbull, and Matvei Yankelevich. For advice on various matters we are grateful to Daniel Altshuler, the late John Burnside, Nicholas Cronk, Sasha Dugdale, Ilja Kukuj, Patrick McGuinness, Mikhail Pavlovets, and Lucy Silbaugh. We owe a considerable debt to the anonymous readers of the book manuscript for their careful scrutiny and helpful reports. We thank the following institutions for funding: the Harriman Institute at Columbia University; the John Fell Fund and the Humanities Research Support Fund at the University of Oxford; the Fellows' Research Fund at St. Edmund Hall; the Lockert Fund and Princeton University Press. We would also like to express appreciation to the Warner Fund at the University Seminars, Columbia University for their help in this publication. Material from this book was presented to the University Seminar on Slavic Studies.

We acknowledge the following publishers and individual rights holders for giving us permission to reprint their translations and poems:

Bella Akhmadulina, "Year after painful year." The English translation is published with the permission of Alexandra Berlina.

Anna Akhmatova, "Secrets of Craft." The English translation is published by permission of Sasha Dugdale.

Polina Barskova, “Knizhki s kartinskami” and “Both were tortured” in the English translation of Valzhyna Mort reprinted from Polina Barskova, *Air Raid*, trans. Valzhyna Mort (New York: Ugly Duckling Presse, 2021), with the permission of Polina Barskova, Valzhyna Mort and Ugly Duckling Presse.

Alexander Blok, “Free Thoughts. About death.” The English translation is published by permission of Peter France.

Joseph Brodsky, “Posviashchaetsia Chekhovu”. Copyright © 1993 by Joseph Brodsky, used by permission of The Wylie Agency (UK) Limited. “Homage to Chekhov” from Joseph Brodsky, *Collected Poems in English*. Copyright © 2000 by the Estate of Joseph Brodsky. Reprinted by permission of Farrar, Straus and Giroux; Joseph Brodsky, Ed: Ann Kjellberg, Translated by Anthony Hecht; *Collected Poems in English* (Paperback). Carcanet Press Ltd.

Elena Fanailova, “Again they’re off for their Afghanistan.” Reproduced from Elena Fanailova, *The Russian Version*, ed. Aleksandr Skidan, trans. Genya Turovskaya and Stephanie Sandler (New York: Ugly Duckling Presse, 2009). “Again they’re off for their Afghanistan” © Elena Fanaiolva, Translation © Genia Turovskaya, from Elena Fanailova, *The Russian Version* (Ugly Duckling Presse, Brooklyn, New York, 2009). Russian and English reprinted with permission of Elena Fanailova and Ugly Duckling Presse.

Alexander Galich, “The Night Watch” from Alexander Galich, *Songs and Poems*, trans. and edited by Gerald Smith (Michigan: Ardis, 1983). Reprinted with permission of Gerald Smith.

Gennadii Gor, “I lie together with my wife”. Permission for the Russian from Kira Gor: © 2007 by estate of Gennadij Gor. For the English “I lie together with my wife, the two of us in an apartment” by Gennady Gor, Translation © Ben Felker-Quinn, Eugene Ostashevsky, and Matvei Yankelevich, from *Written in the Dark: Five Poets in the Siege of Leningrad*, ed. Polina Barskova (Ugly Duckling Presse, Brooklyn, New York, 2016).

Linor Goralik, “Kak v nore lezhali” is reprinted with the permission of Linor Goralik. The English “Little Star” is published with the permission of Helena Kernan.

Nikolai Gumilev, “Sixth Sense.” The English translation is printed by permission of Peter France.

Elena Guro, “Gone to Sleep.” The English translation is published by permission of Matvei Yankelevich.

Daniil Kharms, “Werld.” Reproduced by permission of Matvei Yankelevich and Overlook Press from *Today I wrote Nothing: The Selected Writings of Danill Kharms*, translated by Matvei Yankelevich, Overlook Press, New York. 2009.

Velimir Khlebnikov, "Esli ia obrashchu chelovechestvo . . ." For permission to publish the Russian text from V. Khlebnikov, *Sobranie sochinenii v shesti tomakh*, ed. R. V. Duganov (Moscow: IMLI, RAN, 2001), we are grateful to the Institut mirovoi literatury im. A.M. Gor'kogo RAN. Translated reprinted by permission of Harvard University Press from *The Collected Works of Velimir Khlebnikov*, vol. 3: *Selected Poems*, translated by Paul Schmidt (Cambridge, MA: Harvard University Press, 1997).

Vladislav Khodasevich, "Ballad" reproduced by permission of Peter Daniels and Angel Classics from Vladislav Khodasevich, *Selected Poems*, translated by Peter Daniels with an introduction by Michael Wachtel (Angel Classics, London 2013).

Igor Kholin, "Zabory. Pomoiki. Afishi. Reklamy." Reprinted from Igor' Kholin, *Zhiteli Baraka. Stikhi* (Moscow: Prometei, 1989). All best efforts were made to secure permission to reprint these poems by Igor Kholin. The English translation is published by permission of Ainsley Morse.

Mikhail Kuzmin, "Not a governor's lady with an officer." The English translation is published by permission of Peter France.

Lev Losev, "Odin den' L'va Vladimirovicha." Reprinted from Lev Losev, *Stikhi* (St Petersburg: Ivan Limbakh, 2012) with permission of the estate of Lev Losev. The English translation "One Day in the Life of Lev Vladimirovich" is printed with permission of G. S. Smith.

Osip Mandelstam, "The Horseshoe-Finder." The English translation is published by permission of Sasha Dugdale.

Vladimir Mayakovsky, "Listen!" The English translation is published by permission of Alexandra Berlin.

Vladimir Nabokov, "Lilith." The Russian and English poems are reproduced from *Collected Poems* by Vladimir Nabokov published by Penguin Classics. Copyright © Vladimir Nabokov, 1991 Translation Copyright © Dmitri Nabokov, 2012 . Reprinted by permission of Penguin Books Limited. For the original Russian poem "Lilith" from SELECTED POEMS OF VLADIMIR NABOKOV by Vladimir Nabokov, copyright ©2012 by The Estate of Vladimir Nabokov. Used by permission of Alfred A. Knopf, an imprint of the Knopf Doubleday Publishing Group, a division of Penguin Random House LLC.

Ry Nikonova, "Beshenestvo beshenstvo vzbeshenstvo" from *Transfuristy. Izbrannye teksty Ry Nikonovoi, Sergeia Sigeia, A. Nika, B. Konstriktora*, ed. Petr Kazarnovsky with Boris Konstriktor (Moscow: Gilea, 2016). Reprinted by permission of the publisher and estate of Ry Nikonova. The English translation "furious furious rabious" is published with the permission of Sasha Dugdale.

Nikolai Oleinikov, "The Cockroach." The English translation is published by permission of Alexandra Berlina.

Boris Pasternak, "Poetry". The English translation is published by permission of Peter France.

Dmitry Prigov, "Ia vsiu zhizn' provel v myt'e posudy," "Ia s domashnei borius' entropiei," and "Banal'noe russuzhdenie na temu svobody" reproduced from Dmitry Prigov, *Monady: kak-by-iskrennost'*, ed. Mark Lipovetsky (Moscow: Novoe Literaturnoe Obozrenie, 2012). Reprinted by permission of the publisher and estate of Dmitry Prigov. For the English "I've spent all my life washing dishes," "I wrestle with domestic entropy," and "Banal rumination on the topic of freedom" by Dmitrii Prigov, Copyright © Novoe Literaturnoe Obozrenie, Moscow; Translation Copyright © Simon Schuchat and Ainsley Morse, from Dmitry Prigov, *Soviet Texts* (Ugly Duckling Presse, Brooklyn, New York, 2020), reprinted with the permission of Ugly Duckling Presse.

Lev Rubinshtein, "Eto ia." Reproduced from Lev Rubinshtein, *Bol'shaia kartoteka* (Moscow: Novoe izdatel'stvo, 2015). Reprinted with permission from Lev Rubinshtein and the publisher. "It is I" Reprinted from *Here I am: Performance poems* by Lev Rubinshtein (Glas, 2001), with permission from Joanna Turnbull.

Galina Rymbu, "Moia vagina" is reprinted in Russian with permission of Galina Rymbu. The translation is from Galina Rymbu, Eugene Ostashevsky, and Ainsley Morse, eds. *F-Letter: New Russian Feminist Poetry*. New York: Isolarii, 2020. Used with permission of the translator Kevin Platt.

Ian Satunovsky, "Yesterday, late on my way to work". The English translation is published by permission of Andrew Bromfield and Andrew Kahn

Olga Sedakova, "Kuznechik i sverchok" is reprinted with the permission of Olga Sedakova. The English translation "The Grasshopper and the Cricket" printed by permission of Helena Kernan.

Elena Shvarts, "Svalka." Reproduced from Elena Shvarts, *Stikhotvoreniia i poemy* (St. Petersburg: Inapress, 1999) with permission from the estate of Elena Shvarts to republish (in Russian) and in translation. The English translation "Rubbish Heap" is published with the permission of Sasha Dugdale.

Maria Stepanova. "Kak-nibud' tak . . ." The Russian is reproduced from Maria Stepanova, *Sviashchennaia zima 20/21* (Moscow: Novoe izdatel'stvo, 2022), with the permission of the author and publisher. The English translation is published with the permission of Maria Stepanova and Sasha Dugdale.

Marina Tsvetaeva, "I embrace you like the horizon." The English translation is published by permission of Sasha Dugdale.

Alexander Vvedensky, "Guest on a Horse." Reproduced form Alexander Vvedensky, An Invitation from Me To Think. Selected and Translated by Eugene Ostavesky (New York: New York Review of Books, 2013). First published in English by *New York Review of Books*. Translation Copyright © 2013 by Eugene Ostashevsky.

Vladimir Vysotsky, "My Gypsy Song." The English translation is published with agreement of Alexandra Berlina.

Nikolai Zabolotsky "Somewhere in a field near Magadan." The English translation is published with the permission of Boris Dralyuk.

NOTES AND REFERENCES

Introduction: Enduring Modernism

1. See Evgeny Dobrenko's works developing the concept of socialist realism as a cultural institution in his *Late Stalinism: The Aesthetics of Politics* (New Haven, CT: Yale University Press, 2021). On the particularities of the "Soviet poet" see Mark Lipovetsky, "Soviet Poet," in *The Oxford Handbook of Russian Poetry* (Oxford: Oxford University Press, forthcoming).

2. G. S. Smith, "Russian Poetry: The Lives or the Lines?" *Modern Language Review* 95, no. 4 (2000): xxix–xli (xl); on the view of poetry as the supreme artistic form, see Joseph Brodsky, "The Condition We Call Exile," in *On Grief and Reason: Essays* (New York: Farrar, Straus & Giroux, 1995), 22–35 (33). That perspective persists in the typical view that "the place of poetry in [American] culture is much smaller than it is for Russians" offered in Reginald Gibbons, "On Russian Meta-Realist Poetry: A Conversation with Ilya Kutik," *American Poetry Review* 36, no. 2 (2007): 19–25 (24–25) ("The Situation of Poetry in America and in Russia").

3. Smith, "Russian Poetry," xxxv.

4. See Svetlana Boym, *Death in Quotation Marks: Cultural Myths of the Modern Poet* (Cambridge, MA: Harvard University Press, 2013). For a succinct backward-looking account, see Igor' Shaitanov, "Poet v Rossii," *Arion* 2 (1998): 16–25; on continuity into the present see Dmitrii Kuz'min, "Russkaia poeziia v nachale XXI veka," *Rets* 48 (2008), http://www.litkarta.ru/dossier/kuzmin-review/ (accessed June 17, 2023).

5. For an overview, see Sidney Monas, "Modern Russian Poetry and the Prophetic Tradition," *World Literature Today* 59, no. 2 (1985): 190–93; and for an earlier chapter in this cultural myth, Pamela Davidson, "Simeon Polotskii and the Origins of the Russian Tradition of the Writer as Prophet," *Modern Language Review* 112, no. 4 (2017): 917–52.

6. Nadezhda Mandel'shtam, *Hope against Hope: A Memoir*, trans. Max Hayward (New York: Atheneum, 1970), 159.

7. S. S. Vilenskii, ed., *Poeziia uznikov GULAGa. Antologiia* (Moscow: Mezhdunarodnyi fond "Demokratiia" / Izdatel'stvo "Materik," 2005).

8. Irina Shevelenko, "Introduction," in Maria Stepanova, *The Voice Over: Poems and Essays*, ed. Irina Shevelenko (New York: Columbia University Press, 2021), viii–xxii (xi).

9. On the literary dynamics and regroupings typical of the early Soviet period, see the overview in Lazar Fleishman, *Boris Pasternak: The Poet and His Politics* (Cambridge, MA: Harvard University Press, 1990), 59–83 ("In the Futurist Camp"). For an overview of Russian poetry in the entire twentieth and early twenty-first centuries, see Andrew Kahn et al., *A History of Russian Literature* (Oxford: Oxford University Press, 2018), 565–643.

10. The phrase "Silver Age" gained traction in the 1960s and 1970s with the publication of pioneering studies about Alexander Blok and until recently has been widely and popularly used. Revisionist scholarship has heavily qualified our understanding of the origins and applicability of the term. The new consensus is that it is a retrospective cultural construct coined to position the prerevolutionary period

from around 1900 to 1921 as a pendant to the Pushkinian Golden Age. See Omry Ronen, *The Fallacy of the Silver Age in Twentieth-Century Literature* (Amsterdam: Harwood Academic Publishers, 1997); and Boris Gasparov, introduction to *Cultural Mythologies of Russian Modernism*, eds. Boris Gasparov, Robert P. Hughes, and Irina Paperno (Berkeley: University of California Press, 1992), 1–10.

11. For a comprehensive historiography of Russian modernism, see now Leonid Livak, *In Search of Russian Modernism* (Baltimore, MD: Johns Hopkins University Press, 2018), esp. 1–77.

12. For example, see Nikolai Gumilev, "Nasledie simvolizma i akzmeizm," *Apollon* 1 (1913): 42–45.

13. For a comparative perspective and succinct overview, see Christopher Butler, *Early Modernism: Literature, Music and Painting in Europe 1900–1916* (Oxford: Clarendon Press, 1994).

14. Linda Hutcheon, *A Poetics of Postmodernism: History, Theory, Fiction* (New York: Routledge, 1988), xiii.

15. On the process, see the still relevant Hugh Kenner, "The Making of the Modernist Canon," *Chicago Review* 34, no. 2 (1964): 53–57.

16. Evidence of contemporary awareness of the point can be found widely in the émigré press of the period. For example, see Evgenii Anichkov, *Novaia russkaia poeziia* (Berlin: I. Ladyzhnikov, 1923).

17. Russian intergenerational tension was no outlier, as can be seen in Ann Ardis, *Modernism and Cultural Conflict, 1880–1922* (Cambridge: Cambridge University Press, 2002).

18. Andrei Belyi,"Simvolizm kak miroponimanie," in *Simvolizm kak miroponimanie* (Moscow: Respublika, 1994), https://traumlibrary.ru/book/beliy-simvolizm-kak-miroponimanie/beliy-simvolizm-kak-miroponimanie.html#s002002010 (accessed May 10, 2023).

19. Osip Mandel'shtam, "The Morning of Acmeism," trans. Jane Gary Harris, in *Russian Silver Age Poetry: Texts and Contexts*, eds. Sibelan Forrester and Martha M. F. Kelly (Boston, MA: Academic Studies Press, 2015), 329–33 (330).

20. Iurii Levin et al., "Russkaia semanticheskaia poetika kak potentsial'naia kul'turnaia paradigma," *Russian Literature* (Hague) 7–8 (1974): 47–82 (49, 50).

21. Maxim Shapir, "Esteticheksii opyt XX veka: Avangard i postmodernism," *Philologica* 2 (1995): 135–38. For a well-informed discussion of the avant-garde that sees its "logological conceptions" of language as the distinctive creative principle, see Vladimir Feshchenko, *Russian and American Poetry of Experiment: The Linguistic Avant-Garde* (Leiden: Brill, 2023), 1–16.

22. Louis Menand, *Discovering Modernism: T. S. Eliot and His Context* (Oxford: Oxford University Press, 2007), 5.

23. Daniel Beer, *Renovating Russia: The Human Sciences and the Fate of Liberal Modernity, 1880–1930* (Ithaca, NY: Cornell University Press, 2008), 7.

24. Livak, *In Search*, 9.

25. For a multidisciplinary overview, see Jean-Michel Rabaté, *1913: The Cradle of Modernism* (Oxford: Blackwell, 2007).

26. Marina Tsvetaeva, "Iskusstvo pri svete sovesti," in *Sobranie sochinenii*, vol. 5, *Avtobiograficheskaia proza. Stat'i. Esse, Perevody*, eds. Anna Saakiants and Lev Mnukhin (Moscow: Ellis Lak, 1994), 346–75 (354).

27. See Barret Watten, "Post-Soviet Subjectivity in Arkadii Dragomoschenko and Ilya Kabakov," *Postmodern Culture* 3, no. 2 (1993), https://muse.jhu.edu/pub/1/article/27402 (accessed June 18, 2023); and on poetry's contribution to the "cultural originality and specificity" of Russian postmodernism, see Mark Lipovetsky, *Russian Postmodernist Fiction: Dialogue with Chaos* (Armonk, NY: M. E. Sharpe, 1999).

28. Roman Jakobson, "On the Generation That Squandered Its Poets," in *Language in Literature*, eds. Krystyna Pomorska and Stephen Rudy (Cambridge, MA: Harvard University Press, 1987), 273–301 (296).

29. Randall Jarrell, "The Poet's Essay," *American Scholar* 28, no. 3 (1959): 277–92 (290).

30. For a very different, Marxist-informed take on the nature of the post-Soviet avant-garde that sees its development as distinct from dominant narratives about formal and aesthetic continuities, see Marijeta Bozovic, *Avant-Garde Post–:Radical Poetics after the Soviet Union* (Cambridge MA: Harvard University Press, 2023), esp. 1–17.

31. Elena Shvarts, *Khomo Musaget*, http://www.newkamera.de/shwarz/escwarz_05.html.

32. Joseph M. Conte, *Unending Design. The Forms of Postmodern Poetry* (Ithaca, NY: Cornell University Press, 1991), 3.

33. Claude Lévi-Strauss and Roman Jakobson, "Charles Baudelaire's 'Les Chats,'" in Roman Jakobson, *Language and Literature*, eds. Krystyna Pomorska and Stephen Rudy (Cambridge, MA: Harvard University Press, 1987), 180–97.

1. Alexander Blok, "Free Thoughts. On Death" (1908): In Baudelaire's Shadow

1. A. A. Blok, *Polnoe sobranie sochinenii v dvadtsati tomakh*, vol. 2 (Moscow: Nauka, 1997), 205–9.

2. Avril Pyman, *A History of Russian Symbolism* (Cambridge: Cambridge University Press, 1994), 305–22.

3. Avril Pyman, *The Life of Aleksandr Blok: The Distant Thunder, 1880–1908*, vol. 1 (Oxford: Oxford University Press, 1979), 280.

4. John E. Bowlt, "Through the Glass Darkly: Images of Decadence in Early Twentieth-Century Russian Art," *Journal of Contemporary History* 17, no. 1 (1982): 93–110 (101).

5. On Baudelaire's flâneur as a "man of the world" rather than Paris-centric, see Mary Gluck, "The Flâneur and the Aesthetic Appropriation of Urban Culture in Mid-19th-Century Paris," *Theory, Culture and Society* 20, no. 5 (2003): 53–80 (53); Keith Tester, *The Flâneur* (Abingdon, UK: Routledge, 2015).

6. Irina Paperno, "The Meaning of Art: Symbolist Theories," in *Creating Life: The Aesthetic Utopia of Russian Modernism*, eds. Irina Paperno and Joan Delaney Grossman (Stanford, CA: Stanford University Press, 1994), 13–23 (22–23); and, more extensively, Auge Hansen-Löwe, "Kontseptsii *Zhiznetvorchestva* v russkom simvolizme nachala veka," *Blokovskii sbornik* 14 (1970): 57–85.

7. For an extensive treatment of the subject, see Dina Magometova, *Avtobiograficheskii mif v tvorchestve Bloka* (Moscow: Martin, 1997), esp. 1–59.

8. See the famous essay by Roman Jakobson, "O pokolenii, rastrativshem svoikh poetov. Smert' Vladimira Maiakovskogo" (The Hague: Mouton, 1975), available as "On the Generation That Squandered Its Poets"; and Svetlana Boym, *Death in Quotation Marks: Cultural Myths of the Modern Poet* (Cambridge, MA: Harvard University Press, 2013), 119–91.

9. Andrei Belyi, "Sharl' Bodler," *Vesy* 6 (1909): 71, cited in Adrian Wanner, "Populism and Romantic Agony: A Russian Terrorist's Discovery of Baudelaire," *Slavic Review* 52, no. 2 (1993): 298–317 (298).

10. Anne Marie Brumm, "Death, Poetry, and the City," *Zeitschrift für Religions- und Geistesgeschichte* 36, no. 4 (1984): 346–60 (348).

11. On the autobiographical nature of Blok's lyric persona, see Boris Eikhenbaum, "Sud'ba Bloka," in *Skvoz' literaturu: Sbornik statei* (The Hague: Mouton, 1962), 215–52.

12. On the notion of the journey in Blok, see Dmitrii Maksimov, "Ideia puti v poeticheskom soznanii Al. Bloka," in *Poeziia i proza Al. Bloka* (Leningrad: Sov. pisatel', Leningr. otd-nie, 1975), 6–143; and Lidiia Ginzburg, "Nasledie i otkrytiia," in *O lirike* (Moscow: Intrada, 1997), 229–91.

13. For a discussion of the city and flâneur figure in other poems by Blok, see Milica Ban'ianin, "The Mutual Reflection of Scene and Spectator in the Works of Alexander Blok," *New Zealand Slavonic Journal* (2000): 59–77; the same author's more delimited discussion of Baudelaire's influence in earlier collections before "Vol'nye mysli" can be found in M. Ban'ianin, "Bodlerovskoe ekho v gorodskoi poezii Bloka," in *Aleksandr Blok. Issledovaniia i materialy* (St. Petersburg: Pushkinskii dom, 2011), 142–62.

14. See Adrian Wanner, *Baudelaire in Russia* (Gainesville: University of Florida Press, 1996).

15. On the influence of mass culture and the urban newspaper on nineteenth-century fiction, see Stephen Rachman, "Reading Cities: Devotional Seeing in the Nineteenth Century," *American Literary History* 9, no. 4 (1997): 653–75 (660).

16. Cheryl Krueger, "Telling Stories in Baudelaire's 'Spleen of Paris,'" *Nineteenth-Century French Studies* 30, no. 2 (2002): 281–99 (281–82).

17. On the Baudelairean street as a site of alienation, see Ross Chambers, "Baudelaire's Street Poetry," *Nineteenth-Century French Studies* 13, no. 4 (1985): 244–59; and on Russian symbolist repurposing, see B. Tench Coxe, "Valery Briusov and the Construction of Urban Forms," *Ulbandus Review* 8 (2004): 27–46. On the earlier history of Baudelaire in Russia leading up to Blok, see Joan Delaney Grossman, *Valery Bryusov and the Riddle of Russian Decadence* (Berkeley: University of California Press, 1985).

18. This characteristic of the flâneur as a man of the crowd is discussed in Walter Benjamin's classic essay "Charles Baudelaire: A Lyric Poet in the Era of High Capitalism" in his collection *Illuminations*, trans. Harry Zohn (London: Fontana, 1973), 35–66.

19. In a letter to his wife in May 1907, Blok wrote that he had a few days earlier been in the town of Lesnoy and, as he walked past a hippodrome, witnessed the death of a "yellow jockey" in a fall (Blok, *Polnoe*, 870).

20. Z. G. Mints, "Lirika Bloka perioda pervoi russkoi revoliutsii," in her *Blok i russkii simvolizm* (St. Petersburg: Iskusstvo, 1999), 46–98 (97).

21. For a comprehensive view of the structuring of space and creation of depth in Blok's lyric collections, see Z. G. Mints, "Struktura 'khudozhestvennogo prostranstva' v lirike A. A. Bloka," in *Blok*, 444–539. She notes (511) that the creation of a "real space" accompanies an erosion of temporal markers, which is the case in this poem and *Free Thoughts* as a collection.

22. Charles Baudelaire, *Les Fleurs du mal*, in *Œuvres complètes*, vol. 1, ed. Claude Pichois (Paris: Gallimard, 1975), 31.

23. Jeffrey Brooks, "The Russian Nation Imagined: The Peoples of Russia as Seen in Popular Imagery, 1860s–1890s," *Journal of Social History* 43, no. 3 (2010): 535–57 (538).

24. Aleksandr Pushkin, *Sobranie sochinenii v desiati tomakh*, vol. 2, ed. D. D. Blagoi, (Moscow: Khudozhestvennaia literatura, 1959), 264.

25. A. A. Blok, *Zapisnye knizhki, 1901–1920*, eds. V. N. Orlov, A. A. Surkov, and K. I. Chukovskii (Moscow: Khudozhestvennaya literatura, 1965), 198.

26. Martha M. F. Kelly, "Alexander Blok's Other Body," *Russian Review* 70, no. 1 (2011): 118–36 (119).

27. Charles Baudelaire, "The Artist, Man of the World, Man of the Crowd, and Child," in *The Painter of Modern Life and Other Essays*, trans. Jonathan Mayne (London: Phaeton Press, 1964), 5–12 (7).

28. Pushkin, *Sobranie sochinenii*, 299 ("Elegiia").

29. An account of Ibsen's influence on Blok, especially in these years, can be found in Nils Åke Nilsson, *Ibsen in Russland* (Stockholm: Almquist and Wiksell, 1958), 207–19.

30. Bjørn Hemmer, "Ibsen and the Realistic Problem Drama," in *The Cambridge Companion to Ibsen*, ed. James McFarlane (Cambridge: Cambridge University Press, 1994), 68–88 (71).

2. Elena Guro, "Gone to sleep, gone quiet now, so kind" (1912): Performing Sincerity

1. Elena Guro, *Nebesnye verbliuzhata: Izbrannoe*, ed. Alsen Mizaev (St. Petersburg: Limbus Press, 2001), 31–32.

2. Zara Mints, "Futurizm i 'neoromantizm': K probleme genezisa i struktury 'Istorii bednogo rytsaria' El. Guro," in *Blok i russkii simvolizm: Izbrannye Trudy*, vol. 3: *Poetika russkogo simvolizma* (St. Petersburg: Iskusstvo–SPb, 2004), 317–26.

3. The title could also be translated as *Autumn Sleep* but will be referred to as *Autumn Dream* in the present chapter.

4. Andrew Kahn et al., *A History of Russian Literature* (Oxford: Oxford University Press, 2018), 619.

5. Translated by Alexandra Berlina.

6. Elena Guro, *Nebesnye verbliuzhata. Bednyi rytsar'. Stikhi i proza*, ed. L. Usenko (Rostov-on-Don: Izdatel'stvo Rostovskogo universiteta, 1993), 164.

7. Guro, *Nebesnye verbliuzhata*, 161.

8. Vladimir Toporov, *Mif. Ritual. Simvol. Obraz. Issledovaniia v oblasti mifopoėticheskogo* (Moscow: Progress-Kul'tura, 1992), 402.

9. Toporov, *Mif. Ritual*, 402.

10. Toporov, *Mif. Ritual*, 406.

11. See Sarah Julie Dadswell, "The Spectacle of Russian Futurism: The Emergence and Development of Russian Futurist Performance, 1910–1914" (PhD diss., University of Sheffield, 2005).

12. Kornei Chukovskii, "Obraztsy futurliteratury," in *Sobranie sochinenii* (Moscow: Khudozhestvennaia literatura, 1969), 249.

13. Schamma Schahadat, *Iskusstvo zhizni* (Moscow: Novoe literaturnoe obozrenie, 2014), 12.

14. Schahadat, *Iskusstvo*, 15.

15. Understandably, as the adjective, *khoroshii* has many facets and can also be used as a term of endearment, the translation only partially recreates this repetition, rendering it twice as "kind" and once as "good-natured."

16. D. A. Prigov, *Mesta*, eds. Mark Lipovetsky and Zhanna Galeeva (Moscow: Novoe literaturnoe obozrenie, 2018), 278.

3. Vladimir Mayakovsky, "Listen!" (1914): Love and the Egotistical Sublime

1. V. V. Mayakovskii, *Polnoe sobranie sochinenii v 13 tomakh*, vol. 1 (Moscow: Khudozhestvennaia literatura, 1955), 60–61.

2. See Stefanie Hajak, *V.V. Majakovskijs "Jas am": Untersuchugen zur Struktur einer futuristischen Autobiographie* (Wiesbaden: Otto Harrassowitz, 1989), esp. 31–68.

3. Paul A. Klanderud, "Maikovskii's Myth of Man, Things, and the City," *Russian Review* 55, no. 1 (1996): 45.

4. For an accessible account of the relationship between Mayakovsky and the Briks, see Ann and Samuel Charters, *I Love: the Story of Vladimir Mayakovsky and Lili Brik* (London: André Deutsch, 1979); indispensable is the edition of their correspondence, *Eto serdtse sego. V. V. Maiakovskii i L.Iu. Brik, 1915–1930*, ed. Bengt Jangfeldt (Moscow: Kniga, 1991).

5. V. V. Maiakovskii, "Neskol'ko slov o moei zhene," in *Polnoe sobranie*, vol. 1, 46.

6. P. Shchegolev, "Mooing" ("Mychanie"), in *Vladimir Maiakovskii. Pro et Contra* (St. Petersburg: Izd-vo Russkoi Khristianskoi gumanitarnoi akademii, 2006), 335–38 (335).

7. D. Burliuk et al., *Poshchechina obshchestvennomu vkusu* (Moscow: Izdanie G. L. Kuz'mina, 1912), 1.

8. On his key images, see Lawrence Stahlberger, *The Symbolic System of Mayakovskii* (The Hague: Mouton, 1964).

9. V. V. Maiakovskii, *L. Iu. Brik, Perepiska, 1915–1930*, ed. Bengt Jangfel'dt (Moscow: Kniga, 1991), 39. In a 1921 letter, Mayakovsky, signing off as a puppy, compares Lilya to a fox (in fact, a "little fox" or "foxy" [*lisik*]) and adds a list of attributes starting with "dear" (*milyi*) and ending with "little star" (*zvezdochka*).

10. See Bengt Jangfel'dt, *"Stavka-zhizn'." Vladimir Maiakovskii i ego krug* (Moscow: Kolibri, 2009), 68–70.

11. On this topic, see Maria Gough, "*Faktura*: The Making of the Russian Avant-Garde," *Res* 36 (1999): 32–59.

12. Robert Langbaum, *The Poetry of Experience* (London: Chatto and Windus, 1957), 53.

13. Mayakovsky's recording of the poem can be found on YouTube. See "Владимир Маяковский - Послушайте!" posted June 30, 2014, https://www.youtube.com/watch?v=V4tCY7SV5BI (accessed May 12, 2023).

14. Benjamin Hrushovski, "Poetic Metaphor and Frames of References," *Poetics Today* 5, no. 1 (1984): 5–43 (7).

15. Victor Erlich, "The Dead Hand of the Future: The Predicament of Vladimir Mayakovsky," *Slavic Review* 21, no. 3 (1962): 433–40.

16. V. V. Maiakovskii, *Polnoe sobranie sochinenii v 13 tomakh*, vol. 10 (Moscow: Khudozhestvennaia literatura, 1941), 281.

17. See Iurii Tynianov, "Promezhutok," *Russkii sovremennik* 4 (1924): 209–23, reprinted in Iurii Tynianov, *Arkhaisty i Novatory* (Moscow: Priboi, 1929), esp. 553–57.

18. Thomas Weiskel, *The Romantic Sublime: Studies in the Structure and Psychology of Transcendence* (Baltimore: Johns Hopkins University Press, 2019), 4.

19. Weiskel, *Romantic Sublime*, 141.

20. Frederick Garber, "Point of View and the Egotistical Sublime," *English Studies* 49, nos. 1–6 (1968): 409–18 (409).

21. Andrei Sinyavskii, "Osnovnye printsipy estetiki V.V. Maiakovskogo," *Znamia* 2 (1950): 151–57 (153).

22. Mayakovsky himself set out the principles in his 1926 essay *How to Make Verse* (*Kak delat' stikhi*). A pithy analysis of his change in artistic orientation can be found in Halina Stephan, "Mayakovskij's Post-Revolutionary Poetics and the 'LEF' Concept of Art," *Russian Language Journal* 33, no. 116 (1979): 123–33.

23. See Natalia Karakulina, "Vladimir Maiakovskii and the National School Curriculum," in *Twentieth-Century Russian Poetry: Reinventing the Canon*, eds. Katharine Hodgson, Joanne Shelton, and Alexandra Smith (Cambridge: OpenBook Publishers, 2017), 95–122. For an important appreciation by a contemporary written just after Mayakovsky's suicide, see Boris Pasternak, "On Mayakovsky," an extract from his memoir *Safe Conduct in Russian Silver Age Poetry: Texts and Contexts*, eds. Sibelan Forrester and Martha M. F. Kelly (Boston, MA: Academic Studies Press, 2015), 508–20.

24. See the review by Boris Pasternak, "Vladimir Maiakovskii: *Prostoe kak mychanie*," in *Vladimir Maiakovskii. Pro et Contra*, 356–59 (first published in 1965, as the journal for which Pasternak wrote this piece in 1917 never appeared).

4. Nikolai Gumilev, "The Sixth Sense" (1920): Poetic Darwinism

1. Nikolai Gumilev, *Stikhotvoreniia i poemy*, eds. M. D. Elzon with Aleksei Pavlovskii (St. Petersburg: Akademicheskii proekt [Novaia Biblioteka Poeta], 2000), 333–34.

2. For an overview, see the commentary to Gumilev's ten-volume collection *Polnoe sobranie sochinenii v desiati tomakh*, vol. 4 (Moscow: Voskresenie, 2001), 312–15.

3. See Irina Vinokurova, "Zhestokaia, milaia zhizn'," *Novyi mir* 5 (1990): 253–54; Aleksandr Etkind, *Sodom i Psikheia: Ocherki intellektual'noi istorii Serebrianogo veka* (Moscow: Gnozis, Progress-Kompleks, 1996), 220; Irene Delich, "Nikolai Gumilev," in *Istoriia russkoi literatury. XX vek. Serebrianyi vek*, eds. George Nivat and Il'ia Serman (Moscow: Progress, Litera, 1995), 488–501 (495).

4. Nikolai Bogomolov, "Gumilev i okkul'tizm," in *Russkaia literatura nachala XX veka i okkul'tizm* (Moscow: Novoe literaturnoe obozrenie, 1999), 113–44 (136–37).

5. M. Jovanovich, "Nikolai Gumilev i masonskoe uchenie," https://gumilev.ru/about/21/ (accessed May 15, 2023).

6. Alexander Zholkovsky in his analysis of the poem focuses on the relation between subject and syntax. He rightly observes that "The Sixth Sense" is saturated with inversions and decelerations, and he argues that its style replicates the sexual act with a delayed culmination. Alexander Zholkovsky, "Grammatika liubvi," https://dornsife.usc.edu/alexander-zholkovsky/erot83 (accessed June 17, 2023).

7. In his 1913 manifesto "The Legacy of Symbolism and Acmeism," Gumilev wrote: "Every movement is in love with some other creator and epoch. Beloved tombs connect people best. In circles close to Acmeism, the names uttered most often are those of Shakespeare, Rabelais, Villon, and Théophile Gautier. This selection is not arbitrary. Each of these names is a cornerstone for the building of Acmeism, the apotheosis of one or another of its elements. Shakespeare showed us the inner world of the human being, the wisely physiological Rabelais demonstrated the body and its joys, Villon told us

about life that does not doubt itself, although it knows everything—God, vice, death, and immortality. For this life, Théophile Gautier found in art worthy garments of impeccable form. To combine these four aspects within oneself is the dream that now unites people who so boldly decided to call themselves Acmeists." *Nikolai Gumilev on Russian Poetry*, trans. David Lapeza (Ann Arbor, MI: Ardis, 1977), 21–24 (21).

8. Osip Mandel'shtam, *Sobranie sochinenii v 4 tt.*, vol. 1 (Moscow: Art-Biznes-Tsentr, 1993), 218.

9. Mandel'shtam, *Sobranie*, 218–19.

10. Mandel'shtam, *Sobranie*, 220.

11. Mandel'shtam, *Sobranie*, 221.

12. Blok's speech relied in many ways on Viktor Zhirmunsky's influential book *German Romanticism and Modern Mysticism* (1914).

13. Grigorii Fridlender, "Shestoe chuvsto," in *Pushkin. Dostoevskii. "Serebrianyi vek"* (St. Petersburg: Nauka, 1995), 452 (435–55).

14. Aleksandr Blok, *Sobranie sochinenii v vos'mi tomakh*, vol. 6 (Moscow: Gosizdat Khudozhestvennoi literatury, 1962), 359–72, "On Romanticism" (364).

15. The word *uslovnyi*, which is used here, is difficult to translate: deriving from *uslovie* ("convention," "condition"), it means neither "conventional" nor "conditional" in the usual sense. Rather, it suggests that a work of art is transparently and tacitly based on certain internal rules and on contracts established by the author and accepted by the reader, rather than on absolute verisimilitude.

16. Blok, *Sobranie*, 365–66.

17. N. Volkovysskii, "N. S. Gumilev," in N. S. Gumilev: *Pro et Contra. Lichnost' i tvorchestvo Nikolaia Gumileva v otsenke russkikh mysliteleii issledovatelei* (St. Petersburg: Izd-vo RGKhA, 2000), 337.

5. Vladislav Khodasevich, "Ballad" (1922): The Return of Orpheus

1. Vladislav Khodasevich, *Stikhotvoreniia* (Leningrad: Biblioteka Poeta, 1989), 152–53.

2. Vladislav Khodasevich, *Selected Poems*, trans. Peter Daniels (London: Angel Classics, 2013), 122–23.

3. On the collection as the summation of the poet's Petersburg period, see David Bethea, "Following in Orpheus's Footsteps: A Reading of Khodasevich's 'Ballada,'" *SEEJ* 25, no. 3 (1981): 55–58. For a critical biography, see David Bethea, *Khodasevich: His Life and Art* (Princeton, NJ: Princeton University Press, 1983).

4. For Khodasevich's record of their rootless existence, see Vladislav Khodasevich, "Vladislav Khodasevich to Mikhail Karpovich: Six Letters (1923–1932)," eds. Robert Hughes and John Malmstad, *Oxford Slavonic Papers* 19 (1986): 71–88.

5. Henry Gifford, "Khodasevich and Tradition," *Grand Street* 7, no. 2 (1988): 136–54 (136).

6. Nina Berberova, "Vladislav Khodasevich: A Russian Poet," *Russian Review* 11, no. 2 (1952): 78–85 (79).

7. See the obituary Nabokov wrote under his pen name: V. Sirin, "O Khodaseviche," *Sovremennye zapiski* 69 (1939): 262; and the brief appreciation "On Hodasevich" in his *Strong Opinions* (New York: McGraw-Hill, 1973), 223–37; on debates in the diaspora about cultural conservatism and Khodasevich's view that émigré literature written abroad was part of a national literature, see Greta Slobin, *Russians Abroad: Literary and Cultural Politics of the Diaspora (1919–1939)* (Boston: Academic Studies Press, 2019), 170–76.

8. On their friendship, see David Bethea, "Nabokov and Khodasevich," in *The Garland Companion to Vladimir Nabokov*, ed. Vladimir Alexandrov (New York: Garland, 1995), 452–63.

9. See Irina Surat, *Pushkinist Vladislav Khodasevich* (Moscow: Labirint, 1994)

10. V. F. Khodasevich, *Sobranie sochinenii v chetyrekh tomakh*, eds. I. P. Andreeva et al. (Moscow: Soglasie, 1996), vol. 2, 118.

11. Vladislav Khodasevich, *Stat'i o russkoi poezii* (Petersburg: Epokha, 1922), 114.

12. George Nivat, "Angoisse et classicisme dans la poésie de Hodasevic," *Cahiers du monde russe et soviétique* 30, no. 3/4 (1989): 309–20 (311).

13. Khodasevich, *Stikhotvoreniia*, 103.

14. See Margarita Nafpaktitis, "Multiple Exposures of the Photographic Motif in Vladislav Khodasevich's *Sorrentinskie fotografii*," *SEEJ* 52, no. 2 (2008): 389–413.

15. Khodasevich, *Stikhotvoreniia*, 174.

16. An analysis of Khodasevich's use of the pronoun, arguing for a distinction between the empirical and transcendental "I," can be found in Kiril Postoutenko, "'Ia, ia, ia. Chto za dikoe slovo . . .' Vladislav Khodasevich's Deconstruction of the First-Person Personal Pronoun," *New Zealand Slavonic Journal* (2022): 225–35.

17. On the visual motif, see Alexandra Kirilcuk, "The Estranging Mirror: The Poetics of Reflection in the Late Poetry of Vladislav Khodasevich," *Russian Review* 61, no. 3 (2002): 377–90.

18. Khodasevich, *Stikhotvoreniia*, 112.

19. Khodasevich, *Stikhotvoreniia*, 113.

20. V. Vejdle, "Poeziia Khodasevicha," *Sovremennye zapiski* 34 (1928): 452–69.

21. Aleksandr Pushkin, *Sobranie sochinenii v desiati tomakh*, ed. D. D. Blagoi, vol. 2 (Moscow: Khudozhestvennaia literatura, 1959), 149.

22. Pushkin, *Sobranie sochinenii*, 149.

23. For a discussion of inspiration as a theme in Khodasevich's essays, see Kristen Welsh, "Rapture, Sweat and Tears: Nabokov and Khodasevich on Inspiration," *SEEJ* 54, no. 2 (2010): 334–53. It does not take into account the Pushkinian model.

24. Pushkin, *Sobranie sochinenii*, 149.

25. Readings oriented toward a biographical interpretation identify the location as Khodasevich's room in the House of Arts, as described by him in the essay "Dom iskusstv." But, as Bethea admits ("Nabokov and Khodasevich"), Khodasevich's room was semicircular rather than circular.

26. Pushkin, *Sobranie sochinenii*, 295.

27. See David Bethea, *Khodasevich: His Life and Art* (Princeton, NJ: Princeton University Press, 1983), 237–48, for an excellent discussion of the versification and a different interpretative emphasis.

28. On the dream of wordless music in symbolist practice, see Ada Steinberg, *Word and Music in the Novels of Andrey Bely* (Cambridge: Cambridge University Press, 1982), chap. 1; and D. J. Mossop, *Pure Poetry: Studies in French Poetic Theory and Practice 1746–1945* (Oxford: Clarendon Press, 1971), chap. 4 (esp. 65–91).

29. Eduard Waysband, "'Translatio studii,' Orpheus, and the Poetry of Revolution," in *Evropa v Rossii*, eds. Pekka Pesonen, Gennadii Obatnin, and Tomi Huttunen (Moscow: Novoe literaturnoe obozrenie, 2010), 312–40.

6. Velimir Khlebnikov, "Suppose I make a timepiece of humanity" (1922): The King of Time

1. Velimir Khlebnikov, *Sobranie sochinenii*, ed. R. V. Duganov, vol. 2 (Moscow: IMLI RAN "NASLEDIE," 2000), 363.

2. Velimir Khlebnikov, *Collected Works of Velimir Khlebnikov*, trans. Paul Schmidt, vol. 3 (Cambridge, MA: Harvard University Press, 1997), 118–19.

3. For an accessible summary, see Willem G. Weststeijn, "Another Language, Another World: The Linguistic Experiments of Velimir Khlebnikov," *L'Esprit créateur* 38, no. 4 (1998): 27–37; and for a discussion that integrates Khlebnikov's experimentalism in avant-garde practice, see Vladimir Feshchenko, *Russian and American Poetry of Experiment: The Linguistic Avant-Garde* (Leiden: Brill, 2023), 57–70.

4. See, for example, Dmitrii Petrovskii, *Povest' o Khlebnikove* (Moscow: Biblioteka Ogonek, 1926).

5. Vladimir Markov, "The Literary Importance of Khlebnikov's Longer Poems," *Russian Review* 19, no. 4 (1960): 338–70 (339).

6. Noteworthy among the meticulous analyses of Khlebnikov's linguistic experimentation are Ronald Vroon, *Velimir Xlebnikov's Shorter Poems: A Key to the Coinages* (Ann Arbor, MI: Department of Slavic Languages, 1983), and Natalia Pertsova and R. Vroon, *Slovotvorchestvo Velimir Khlebnikova* (Moscow: Izd-vo Moskovskogo universiteta, 2003).

7. Osip Mandel'shtam, *Critical Prose and Letters*, ed. Jane Gary Harris (Ann Arbor, MI: Ardis, 1979), 122.

8. Mandel'shtam, *Critical Prose* ("Some Notes on Poetry"), 165.

9. See Ronald Vroon and Andrea Hacker, "Velimir Khlebnikov's 'Perevorot v Vladivostoke': History and Historiography," *Russian Review* 60, no. 1 (2001): 36–55 (36); and on the theme of prophesy, see L. Jurgenson, "Khlebnikov—ochevidets: sozdanie mifo-dokumenta, in *1913: Slovo kak takovoe*, eds. Jean-Philippe Jacard and Annik Morar (St. Petersburg: European University, 2015), 144–59.

10. See Raymond Cooke, *Velimir Khlebnikov* (Cambridge: Cambridge University Press, 1987), chap. 5 ("The Single Book").

11. Aage A. Hansen-Löve, "Platonov's *Chevengur* between Defamiliarization and Compassion," *Ulbandus Review* 14 (2011/2012): 3–36 (3); on Khlebnikov's application of mathematics to find numerological patterns in historical events and to divine the future in *Doski sud'by* (*Slates of Fate*), see Andrea Hacker, "Introduction to Velimir Chlebnikov's *Doski Sud'by*," *Russian Literature* 63, no. 1 (2008): 5–55.

12. Khlebnikov, *Sobranie sochinenii*, 77 ("Slava tebe, koster chelovechestva").

13. Khlebnikov, *Sobranie*, 28.

14. Henry Pickford, "Review of *The Collected Works of Velimir Khlebnikov*," *Harvard Book Review* 15/16 (1990): 3–4 (4).

15. Khlebnikov, *Sobranie sochinenii*, 28 ("Vnov' trudu doveril ruki / I doveril razum svoi").

16. Quoted in Weststeijn, "Another Language, Another World," 31.

17. For a description, see Nancy Perloff, "*Mirskontsa* (*Worldbackwards*) and Russian Futurism," *Art in Print* 8, no. 4 (2018): 14–15.

18. Velemir Khlebnikov, *Collected Works of Velemir Khlebnikov*, vol. 1 (Cambridge, MA: Harvard University Press, 1987), 417 ("Tables of Destiny").

19. For an overview, see Robert C. Williams, "The Russian Revolution and the End of Time: 1900–1940," *Jahrbücher für Geschichte Osteuropas* 43, no. 3 (1995): 364–401 (387).

20. Quoted in Williams, "The Russian Revolution," 386.

21. Williams, "The Russian Revolution," 387.

22. The poem was originally published in the author's own pamphlet, *Vestnik Velimira Khlebnikova*, no. 1 (1922), and then in the collection *Doski sud'by* (1922).

23. Osip Mandel'shtam, *Polnoe sobranie sochinenii i pisem v trek tomakh*, vol. 1 (Moscow: Progress-Pleiada, 2009), 97. During the civil war, the Mandel'shtams, who held Khlebnikov in high regard as a poet, shared their own scant board with him.

24. On salvation and gender identity, see, for example, Alexander Etkind, *Khlyst. Sekty, literatura i revoliutsiia* (Moscow: Novoe literaturnoe obozrenie, 1998), and Laura Engelstein, *Castration and the Heavenly Kingdom: A Russian Folk Tale* (Ithaca, NY: Cornell University Press, 1999), 17–19, 89–91.

25. Olga Matich, *Erotic Utopia: The Decadent Imagination in Russia's Fin de Siècle* (Madison: University of Wisconsin Press, 2005).

7. Boris Pasternak, "Poetry" (1922): Experiencing Lyric

1. Boris Pasternak, *Stikhotvoreniia i poemy* (Moscow: Sovetskii pisatel' [Biblioteka Poeta], 1965), 193.

2. Lazar' Fleishman, *Boris Pasternak i literaturnoe dvizhenie 1930-kh godov* (St. Petersburg: Akademicheskii proekt, 2005), 253–312.

3. Victor Erlich, "The Concept of the Poet in Pasternak," *SEER* 37, no. 89 (1959): 325–35 (325).

4. See Guy de Mallac, *Boris Pasternak: His Life and Art* (Norman: University of Oklahoma Press, 1981), chap. 5, and Guy de Mallac, "Pasternak's Critical-Esthetic Views," *Russian Literature Triquarterly* 6 (spring 1973): 503–33.

5. See her essay "Svetovoi liven'," in *Sobranie sochinenii v 7-i tomakh*, vol. 5 (Moscow: Ellis Lak, 1994), 231–45.

6. On Pasternak's involvement in literary theoretical groups, most especially OPOIAZ (Obschestvo izucheniia poeticheskogo iazyka, the Society for the Study of Poetic Language) and MLK (the Moscow Linguistic Circle), and their influence on his poetics and, above all, sound structure, see V. V. Ivanov, "Pasternak i Opoiaz," *Tret'i Tynianovskie chteniia* (Riga: Zinatne, 1988), 70–82, and Catherine Depretto, "Boris Pasternak et la philologie des années 1910–1920," *Revue des études slaves* 76, no. 4 (2005): 429–36. On the effect of techniques of painting on Pasternak's poetic skill, see Zbigniew Folejewski, "Some Problems of Semantics in Painting and in Poetry: Maiakovskii, Pasternak, and the Italian Manifesto of Futurist Painting," *Canadian Slavonic Papers* 25, no. 1 (1983): 108–16.

7. Krystyna Pomorska, *Themes and Variations in Pasternak's Poetics* (Lisse: Peter de Ridder Press, 1975), 10–14.

8. The classic discussion of the relation between the poetic mind and Nature in English poetry, as grounded in German poetry and philosophy, remains M. H. Abrams, *The Mirror and the Lamp: Romantic Theory and the Critical Tradition* (Oxford: Oxford University Press, 1953).

9. It has been observed that the "music of poetry" has a particular significance for Pasternak, whose use of sound orchestration, while clearly influenced by futurist techniques, was also a way of carrying over into his verbal art the youthful passion he felt for musical composition. See Christopher Barnes, "Pasternak as Composer and Scriabin-Disciple," *Tempo* 121 (1977): 13–19.

10. Bodo Zelinsky, "Selbstdefinitionen der Poesie bei Pasternak," *Zeitschrift für Slavische Philologie* 38, no. 2 (1975): 268–78 (271).

11. Alexander Zholkovsky, "Iz zapisok po poezii grammatiki: On Pasternak's Figurative Voices," *Russian Linguistics* 9 (1985): 375–86 (378).

12. In his late "Notes to Translations of Shakespeare's Tragedies" ("Zamechaniia k perevodam iz Shekspira," 1956), Pasternak noted aphoristically, "Metaphoricity is the transcript of a great personality, the shorthand of its spirit." See "Zamechaniia k perevodam iz Shekspira," in *Vozdushnye puti* (Moscow: Sovetskii pisatel', 1983), 394.

13. Peter France records (private communication) that the poet's son Evgenii Pasternak, a keen commentator on his father's work, pointed him to one of Prosper Merimée's most famous stories, "The Taking of the Redoubt" ("L'Enlèvement de la redoute"), as a source of the line. The story and poem share a vivid evocation of the moon shining on the battlefield.

14. It. Pomorska, *Themes*, 10.

15. On the prominence of word play and sound play, see Kiril Taranovsky, "On the Poetics of Pasternak," *Russian Literature* 10 (1981): 339–57 (343–45).

16. On Pasternak's scientific interest in motion, see Darlene Reddaway, "Pasternak, Spengler, and Quantum Mechanisms: Constants, Variables, and Chains of Equations," *Russian Literature* 26 (1992): 37–70.

17. I. P. Smirnov, "B. Pasternak. Metel'," in *Poeticheskii stroi russkoi liriki*, ed. G. M. Fridlender (Moscow: Nauka, 1973), 236–54 (252)

18. Paul M. Waszink, "The Recurring Grip of the Poem on the Reader: Observations on Metonymy in Pasternak's *Poverkh bar'erov*," *Canadian Slavonic Papers* 38, nos. 1–2 (1996): 109–33 (111). On Pasternak's own writings about metonymy, the reader will find a set of sources given in n. 16 of Waszink's article.

8. Osip Mandelstam, "The Horseshoe Finder (A Pindaric Fragment)" (1923): Time Future, Time Past

1. The text is slightly adapted from Osip Mandel'shtam, *Polnoe sobranie stikhotvorenii*, ed. A. G. Mets (St. Petersburg: Novaia biblioteka poeta, 1995), 170–73. The extraordinary length of some of the lines has proved to be a challenge to typesetters. Modern editions cope variously by shunting

final words into phrases that spill over into a short line printed flush right. The length of the phrase on the next line is mostly an editorial choice. The appearance of the poem is strikingly different in its original printing on the pages of the journal *Red Virgin Soil* (*Krasnaia nov'*) no. 2, 1924: 135–37, since the margins were spacious and most of the lines up to about twenty syllables did not spill over into adjunct phrases. For this reason the more fragmentary, short layout of the final two sections looks expressively designed. In an effect not reproduced here, line 83 (describing how the liquid in a vase splashes when carried home) is divided into three lines, with each line dropping forward on the page mimetically.

2. See Aleksandr Blok's essay "Krushenie gumanizma," in *Sochineniia v dvukh tomakh*, vol. 2 (Moscow: Khudozhestvennaia literatura, 1955), 338–52.

3. For a comparative treatment setting Mandelstam in the European and American context, see Clare Cavanagh, *Osip Mandelstam and the Modernist Creation of Tradition* (Princeton, NJ: Princeton University Press, 1995).

4. Dmitrii Segal, *Osip Mandel'shtam: istoriia i poetika* (Berkeley, CA: Berkeley Slavic Specialties, 1998).

5. See Clarence Brown, *Mandelstam* (Cambridge: Cambridge University Press, 1973), 53–69.

6. Drawing on the work of Marcel Detienne, Leon Burnett sees a connection between Mandelstam's use of myth and the adoption in the 1920s of the symbolic language of the mythologeme as a code for the nocturnal word. See Leon Burnett, "The Guests of Reality: Mandelstam and Anamnesis," in *Mandelstam Centenary Conference*, eds. Robin Aizlewood and Diana Myers (Tenafly, NJ: Ermitazh, 1984), 155–72 (168).

7. Translated by J. Smithers. See Perseus Digital Library, "C. Valerius Catullus, Carmina, Leonard C. Smithers, Ed.," accessed June 17, 2023, http://www.perseus.tufts.edu/hopper/text?doc=Perseus%3Atext%3A1999.02.0006%3Apoem%3D64.

8. For other examples of time as a negative force, see Kirill Taranovsky, *Essays on Mandel'stam* (Cambridge, MA: Harvard University Press, 1976), 68–83 (82).

9. M. L. Gasparov, "Orpheus Faber. Trud i postoianstvo v poezii O. Mandel'shtama," in *Izbrannye stat'i. O stikhe. O stikhakh. O poetakh* (Moscow: Novoe literaturnoe obozrenie, 1995), 221–30.

10. A. S. Pushkin, *Polnoe sobranie sochinenii v desiati tomakh*, vol. 2 (Moscow: Khudozhestvennaia literatura, 1959), 382–83.

11. The classic discussion remains Iurii Tynianov, "Oda kak oratorskii zhanr," in *Arkhaisty i novatory* (Leningrad: Priboi, 1929), 48–87.

12. D. S. Carne-Ross, *Pindar* (New Haven, CT: Yale University Press, 1985), 40–79; Mandelstam's Greek sources remain unknown. See Tatiana Smoliarova, "Pindar and Mandelstam," *Toronto Slavic Quarterly*, Vol. 13 (2005), online.

13. Gasparov, *Izbrannye stat'i*, 351.

14. Steven Broyde, *Osip Mandel'štam and His Age: A Commentary on the Themes of War and Revolution in the Poetry 1913–1923* (Cambridge, MA: Harvard University Press, 1975).

15. J. Hillis Miller, *Poets of Reality: Six Twentieth-Century Writers* (Cambridge: Belknap, 1966), 11.

16. A. L. Crone, "Echoes of Nietzsche and Mallarmé in Mandlestam's Metapoetic 'Petersburg,'" *Russian Literature* 30 (1991): 405–30.

17. See Jay Bergman, *The French Revolutionary Tradition in Russian and Soviet Politics, Political Thought, and Culture* (Oxford: Oxford University Press, 2019).

18. Kahn, *Mandelstam's Worlds: Poetry, Politics, and Identity in a Revolutionary Age* (Oxford: Oxford University Press, 2020), 159–89.

19. Omry Ronen, *An Approach to Mandel'stam* (Jerusalem: Magnes Press, 1983).

20. Osip Mandel'shtam, *Polnoe sobranie sochinenii i pisem v trekh tomakh*, vol. 2 (Moscow: Progress-Pleiada, 2009), 287. For a more pessimistic reading of the poem, and specifically on the destiny of the devalued coin, what she calls a "surrogate of the self" rather than an emblem of culture or language, see Clare Cavanagh, *Osip Mandelstam and the Modernist Creation of Tradition* (Princeton, NJ: Princeton University Press, 1995), 186–90.

9. Mikhail Kuzmin, "Not a governor's lady with an officer" (1924): Exit God

1. Mikhail Kuzmin, *Stikhotvoreniia*, ed. N. A. Bogomolov (St. Petersburg: Akademicheskii proekt [Novaia Biblioteka Poeta], 1996), 666.

2. For an authoritative overview of his poetry that also disposed of much untruth about Kuzmin, see the essay by Vladimir Markov in Mikhail Kuzmin, *Sobranie stikhov*, eds. John E. Malmstad and Vladimir Markov, vol. 3 (Munich: Wilhelm Fink Verlag, 1977–78), 321–426.

3. Laura Engelstein, review of *Mikhail Kuzmin: A Life in Art* by John E. Malmstad and Nikolay Bogomolov, *Journal of the History of Sexuality* 9, no. 3 (2000): 373–76 (373).

4. See Simon Karlinksy, "The Death and Resurrection of Mikhail Kuzmin," in *Freedom from Violence and Lies: Essays on Russian Poetry and Music*, eds. Robert Hughes, Thomas A. Koster, and Richard Taruskin (Boston, MA: Academic Studies Press, 2013), 125–31.

5. Irina Paperno, "Dvoinichestvo i liubovnyi treugol'nik: poeticheskii mif Kuzmina i ego pushkinskaia proektsiia," *Wiener Slawistischer Almanach* 24 (1989): 57–82.

6. Quoted from his poem "Why does the moon, arisen, turn pink" ("Zachem luna, podniavshiis. Rozoveet"), no. 6 in the cycle *Liubov' etogo leta* (1906).

7. For an introductory overview, see Andrew Kahn, "Poetry of the Revolution," in *The Cambridge Companion to Twentieth-Century Russian Literature*, eds. Evgeny Dobrenko and Marina Balina (Cambridge: Cambridge University Press, 2011), chap. 3.

8. See Simon Karlinsky, *The Woman, Her World, and Her Poetry* (Cambridge: Cambridge University Press, 1985), 191.

9. There is a good introduction to the question of Pasternak's historical engagement in Christopher Barnes, "Pasternak's Revolutionary Year," *Forum for Modern Language Studies* 11 (1975): 46–60. More detailed treatments can be found in Il'ia Serman, "*Vysokaia bolezn'* i problema eposa v 1920-e gody," in *Boris Pasternak, 1890–1990*, ed. Lev Loseff (Northfield, VT: Russian School at Norwich University, 1991), 81–100; and Catherine Ciepiela, *The Same Solitude: Boris Pasternak and Marina Tsvetaeva* (Ithaca, NY: Cornell University Press, 2006), chap. 4 ("Lyricism and History").

10. See Konstantin Polivanov, "K intimizatsii istorii," in *Themes and Variations: In Honor of Lazar Fleishman* (Stanford, CA: Department of Slavic Languages and Literatures, 1994), 71–80.

11. N. Bogomolov, "'Liubov'—vsegdashniaia moia vera'," in M. Kuzmin, *Stikhotvoreniia*, ed. N. Bogomolov (St. Petersburg: Akademicheskii proekt, 1996), 37.

12. Kuzmin, *Stikhotvoreniia*, 323.

13. John Malmstad and Nikolay Bogomolov, *Mikhail Kuzmin: A Life in Art* (Cambridge, MA: Harvard University Press, 1999), 264; on the volatile cultural situation of the time, see Mark von Hagen, "Toward a Cultural and Intellectual History of Soviet Russia in the 1920s," *Révue des études slaves* 68 (1996): 283–302.

14. Georg Lukács, *The Theory of the Novel: A Historico-Philosophical Essay on the Forms of Great Epic Literature*, trans. Anna Bostock (Cambridge, MA: MIT Press, 1996), 88; and see Galin Tihanov, *The Master and the Slave: Lukács, Bakhtin, and the Ideas of Their Time* (Oxford: Oxford University Press, 2000), 83–111.

15. The date, accepted in the Biblioteka Poeta edition used as a source here, comes from Kuzmin's working notebooks. See Kuzmin, *Stikhotvoreniia*, 687.

16. Kuzmin, *Stikhotvoreniia*.

17. David E. Powell, *Antireligious Propaganda in the Soviet Union: A Study of Mass Persuasion* (Cambridge, MA: MIT Press, 1975), 34.

18. Barry P. Scherr, *Russian Poetry: Meter, Rhythm, and Rhyme* (Berkeley: University of California Press, 1986), 220–24. See chapters 1 and 8 for other poems written in this meter that further illustrate these characteristics.

10. Vladimir Nabokov, "Lilith" (1928): Decadent Reverie

1. V. V. Nabokov, *Stikhotvoreniia*, ed. L. A. Nikolaeva (St. Petersburg: Gumanitarnoe agentstvo Akademicheskii proekt, 2002), 221 (no. 247).

2. Vladimir Nabokov, *Collected Poems*, ed. Thomas Karshan (London: Penguin Books, 2013), 83–84.

3. On the numbers and collections, see Barry Scherr, "Poetry," in *The Garland Companion to Vladimir Nabokov*, ed. Vladimir Alexandrov (New York: Garland Publishing, 1995), 608–23.

4. For an overview and critical appreciation, see Paul Morris, *Vladimir Nabokov: Poetry and the Lyric Voice* (Toronto: University of Toronto Press, 2010).

5. See G. S. Smith, "Notes on Prosody," in *The Garland Companion*, 561–66; on the contemporary reception of the poetry in the Berlin and Paris years, see Paul D. Morris, "Vladimir Nabokov's Poetry in Russian Émigré Criticism: A Partial Survey," *Canadian Slavonic Papers* 40, nos. 3–4 (1998): 297–310.

6. Vladimir Nabokov, *Strong Opinions* (New York: McGraw-Hill, 1973), 160–61.

7. Nabokov, *Stikhotvoreniia*, 302.

8. Nabokov, *Stikhotvoreniia*, 575.

9. See Julian W. Connolly, "The Precursors to Nabokov's Lolita," in *A Reader's Guide to Nabokov's Lolita* (Boston, MA: Academic Studies Press, 2017), chap. 2.

10. See Olga Matich, *Erotic Utopia: The Decadent Imagination in Russia's Fin de Siècle* (Madison: University of Wisconsin Press, 2005), 10–27.

11. A helpful discussion of the context if not of this poem can be found in John Burt Foster, Jr., *Nabokov's Art of Memory and European Modernism* (Princeton, NJ: Princeton University Press, 1993), esp. 73–91 ("Encountering French Modernism").

12. "Ces nymphes, je veux les perpétuer"; Stéphane Mallarmé, "L'après midi-d'un faune," in *Collected Poems and Other Verse*, trans. E. H. and A. M. Blackmore (Oxford: Oxford World's Classics, 2006), 38.

13. Thomas Karshan, "Nabokov's 'Homework in Paris': Stéphane Mallarmé, *Bend Sinister*, and the Death of the Author," *Nabokov Studies* 12 (2009): 1–3 (3). The first signs of Nabokov's engagement with Mallarmé's poem date from decades earlier.

14. Mallarmé, *Collected Poems*, 41.

15. On Lilith's identity, see Nancy Mandeville Caciola, "Serpents and Lies," *Speculum* 93, no. 1 (2018): 101–11 (102). On Pan and Lilith, see Kostas Boyiopoulos, "'Esoteric Elements': The Judeo-Christian Scheme in Arthur Machen's *The Great God Pan*," *Neophilologus* 94 (2010): 363–74. There is no evidence as to whether Nabokov knew Remy de Gourmont's monodrama *Lilith* (1892) or the works by Arthur Machen, a popular writer of horror. Depictions of Pan and Lilith were typical of the period, attracting the interest of Swinburne, Rossetti, and Yeats, among others. (Stephen Blackwell, an expert on Nabokov's sources, believes Nabokov read Fraser. Private communication, 2021.)

16. On the importance of the poem and the connection, see D. Barton Johnson, "'L'inconnue de la Seine' and Nabokov's Naiads," *Comparative Literature* 44, no. 3 (summer 1992), 225–48 (232).

17. On the position of the poet as a commentator on the fauns and the ambiguities in voice, see Lloyd James Austin, *Essais sur Mallarmé*, ed. Malcolm Bowie (Manchester: Manchester University Press, 1995), 183–97.

18. On Nabokov's recursive textual strategies and the "sinuosity" of construction, see Duncan White, *Between Late Modernism and the Literary Marketplace* (Oxford: Oxford University Press, 2017), 95–114.

19. For a discussion of parallel, contemporary lyric about masturbation, see Edward Waysband, "The Poetics of Shock: 'The Pitiful Vice' in Khodasevich's 'Under the Ground,'" *Slavic Review* 80, no. 4 (2021): 769–91.

20. Nabokov's eroticism here bears a striking resemblance to Pavel Vasiliev's even more graphic "Love at the Kuntsevkaia dacha" ("Liubov' na Kuntsevskoi dache," 1931), a poem in which the lovers

are "damned, doomed": https://45parallel.net/pavel_vasilev/lyubov_na_kuntsevskoy_dache.html (accessed May 17, 2023).

21. Clive Scott, "The Poetry of Symbolism and Decadence," in *Symbolism, Decadence, and the Fin de Siècle: French and European Perspectives*, ed. Patrick McGuinness (Exeter: University of Exeter Press, 2000), 57–72 (65).

22. On the pervasive image of the truncated or aborted paradise in Nabokov's writing of the 1920s, see Alexander Dolinin, "Caning of Modernist Profaners: Parody in *Despair*," https://epi-revel.univ-cotedazur.fr/publication/item/426 (accessed June 5, 2023).

23. For a discussion of the "codes of decadence" and such phrases, see Vincent Sherry, *Modernism and the Reinvention of Decadence* (Cambridge: Cambridge University Press, 2014), 1–36.

24. For an overview, see the discussion especially of Remy de Gourmont's monodrama *Lilith* (1892) in Boyiopoulos, "Esoteric Elements," 363–74.

25. For a full survey of Nabokov's reputation as a poet, including Struve's judgment, see Morris, "Vladimir Nabokov's Poetry," 309.

26. See Yuri Leving, *Keys to The Gift: A Guide to Nabokov's Novel* (Boston, MA: Academic Studies Press, 2011), 17–19 and passim.

27. Vladislav Khodasevich, *Sobranie sochinenii*, vol. 1 (Moscow: Russkii put', 2009), 145.

28. For a study of Nabokov's otherworldly beliefs, see Vladimir Alexandrov, *Nabokov's Otherworld* (Princeton, NJ: Princeton University Press, 1990).

29. As quoted in Nabokov, *Collected Poems*, 4.

30. On the contemporary and later debate about whether Nabokov's künstlerroman have a plot, see Paul D. Morris, "Nabokov and the Surprise of Poetry," *Connotations* 15, nos. 1–3 (2005–6): 30–57.

31. Jonathan Culler, *Theory of the Lyric* (Cambridge, MA: Harvard University Press, 2015), 229.

11. Daniil Kharms, "Myr" / "The Werld" (1930): I Think Therefore . . .

1. Daniil Kharms, *Polnoe sobranie sochinenii*, vol. 2 (St. Petersburg: Akademicheskii proekt, 1997), 301 (as part of the cycle *Izmerenie veshchei* [*The Measure of Things*], made up of eight works, including sets of equations).

2. Daniil Kharms, *Today I Wrote Nothing: The Selected Writings of Daniil Kharms*, ed. and trans. Matvei Yankelevich (New York: Ardis, 2009), 144–45.

3. For an excellent overview with comments on the importance of Kharms to the theater of the absurd, see the introduction to Daniil Kharms, *"I Am a Phenomenon Quite Out of the Ordinary": The Notebooks, Diaries and Letters of Daniil Kharms*, ed. and trans. Anthony Anemone and Peter Scotto (Boston, MA: Academic Studies Press, 2013), 9–42.

4. Numerous other pen names included Charms, Daniil Dandan, Garmonius. See Neil Cornwell, "The Rudiments of Daniil Kharms," *Modern Language Review* 93, no. 1 (1998): 133–45 (133).

5. Cornwell, "Rudiments," 136 (with n. 14).

6. On this period in his life, see Aleksandr Kobrinskii, *Daniil Kharms* (Moscow: Molodaia gvardiia, 2008), chap. 6; and I. S. Marshak, "Moi mal'chik, tebe etu pesniu dariu . . . ," in *Ia dumal, chuvstvoval, ia zhil . . . Vospominaniia o Marshake* (Moscow: Sovetskii pisatel, 1988), 74–108.

7. On the publication history, see Adrian Wanner, "Russian Minimalist Prose: Generic Antecedents to Daniil Kharms's 'Sluchai,'" *SEEJ* 45, no. 3 (2001): 451–72.

8. See Ellen Bunker, "The Overuse of Proper Nouns and the Creation of the Absurd in the Works of Daniil Kharms," *Russian Literature* 116 (2020): 1–16.

9. José Vergara, "Cognitive Play in Daniil Kharms's 'Blue Notebook No. 10,'" in *The Linguistic Worldview*, eds. Adam Glaz, David Danaher, and Przemyslaw Lozowski (Warsaw: De Gruyter, 2013), 115–34 (115).

10. Craig Brandist, "Deconstructing the Rationality of Terror: William Blake and Daniil Kharms," *Comparative Literature* 49, no. 1 (1997): 59–75 (59); on the impact of these formalist methods on

OBERIU writers in the 1920s, see Geoffrey Cebula, "Aleksandr Tufanov's *Ushkuiniki*, Historicist *Zaum'*, and the Creation of OBERIU," *SEEJ* 58, no. 1 (2014): 93–112 (99).

11. See I. D. Levin, "The Collision of Meanings: The Poetic Language of Daniil Kharms and Aleksandr Vvedesnkii" (PhD diss., University of Texas at Austin, 1986).

12. See Jean-Philippe Jaccard, *Daniil Harms et la fin de l'avant-garde russe* (Bern: Peter Lang, 1991), 48–69.

13. Eugene Ostashevsky, "'Numbers Are Not Bound by Order': The Mathematical Play of Daniil Kharms and His Associates," *SEEJ* 51, no. 1 (2013): 28–48 (35) ("A universe where we can forget the number sequence is one without the automatism of success; any concatenation of numbers there is wholly arbitrary . . ."). On the notebooks, an excellent description can be found in the introduction to Kharms, *"I Am a Phenomenon Quite Out of the Ordinary,"* 15–18.

14. Daniil Kharms, "Byl odin ryzhii zhelovek," in *Polnoe sobranie sochinenii*, vol. 2, 118.

15. Matvei Yankelevich, "Introduction," in *Today I Wrote Nothing*, 11–41 (32).

16. See, for example, of another formal hybrid, a work like "Sonnet": http://www.sevaj.dk/kharms/stories/sonnet.htm (accessed My 17, 2023).

17. Paul Hetherington and Cassandra Atherton, *Prose Poetry: An Introduction* (Princeton, NJ: Princeton University Press, 2020), 9.

18. Hetherington and Atherton, *Prose Poetry*, 15.

19. Hetherington and Atherton, *Prose Poetry*, 6; on the prose poem in Russian literature, see Adrian Wanner, *Russian Minimalism: From the Prose Poem to the Anti-Story* (Evanston, IL: Northwestern University Press, 2003).

20. Jeremy Noel Tod, *Penguin Book of the Prose Poem: From Baudelaire to Anne Carson*; quoted in Hetherington and Atherton, *Prose Poetry*, 12.

21. Hilary Fink traces the absurd in Kharms to the general "modernist spirit of anti-Kantianism." Hilary Fink, "The Kharmsian Absurd and the Bergsonian Comic: Against Kant and Causality," *Russian Review* 57, no. 4 (1998): 526–38 (527).

22. See Jaccard, *Daniil Harms*, 88–90; Bunker, "The Overuse of Proper Nouns," 3.

23. For a suggestive argument (without reference to "Myr") about the connection between Kharms's verbal techniques and the Five Year Plan, see Maya Vinokour, "Daniil Kharms and the Liquid Language of Stalinism," *SEEJ* 60, no. 4 (2016): 676–99 (677).

24. Daniil Kharms, *Polnoe sobranie sochinenii*, vol. 4 (St. Petersburg: Akademicheskii proekt, 1997), 30.

12. Alexander Vvedensky, "Guest on a Horse" (1931–34): Time–Space Conundrum

1. Aleksandr Vvedenskii, *Vse*, ed. Anna Gerasimova (Moscow: OGI, 2011), 181–83.

2. Aleksandr Vvedenskii, *An Invitation for Me to Think*, trans. Eugene Ostashevsky with Matvei Yankelevich (New York: New York Review Books, 2013), 82–84.

3. Iuliia Valieva, *Igra v bessmylitsu. Poeticheskii mir Aleksandra Vvedenskogo* (Moscow: Dmitrii Bulanin, 2007), 86.

4. See V. V. Feshchenko, "Chinari i muzyka," http://www.d-harms.ru/library/chinary-i-muzika.html (accessed June 5, 2023). On their early association in a different circle (Levyi flang, or Left Flank) and the influence of Aleksandr Tufanov's theory of *zaum'* on their youthful work, see I. D. Levin, "The Collision of Meanings: The Poetic Language of Daniil Kharms and Aleksandr Vvedesnkii" (PhD diss., University of Texas at Austin, 1986), 22–24.

5. Anthony Anemone, "The Anti-World of Daniil Kharms: On the Significance of the Absurd," in *Daniil Kharms and the Poetics of the Absurd*, ed. Neil Cornwell (Basingstoke: Macmillan, 1991), 71–79.

6. Cited in Evgeny Pavlov, "Aleksandr Vvedensky's Rhetoric of Temporality," *New Zealand Slavonic Journal* 43 (2009): 115–30 (118).

7. Levin, "The Collision of Meanings," 3.

8. Anna Gerasimova, "Predislovie," in Vvedenskii, *Vse*, 7–24 (17).

9. Vvedenskii, *Vse*, 15.

10. Alice Stone Nakhimovsky, *Laughter in the Void: An Introduction to the Writings of Daniil Kharms and Alexander Vvedenskii*, special issue, *Wiener Slawistischer Almanach* 5 (1982): 2.

11. Levin, "Collision," 29.

12. Aleksandr Vvedenskii, *Polnoe sobranie proizvedenii v dvukh tomakh*, vol. 2 (Moscow: Gileia, 1993), 158.

13. See Aleksandr Vvedenskii, *Polnoe sobranie sochinenii v dvukh tomakh* (Moscow: Gilei, 1993), 20, 43, 200, passim.

14. Aleksandr Pushkin, *Sobranie sochinenii v desiati tomakh*, ed. D. D. Blagoi, vol. 2 (Moscow: Khudozhestvennaia literatura, 1959), 149.

15. Pushkin, *Sobranie sochinenii*, 149.

16. David Bethea, *The Shape of Apocalypse in Modern Russian Fiction* (Princeton, NJ: Princeton University Press, 1989).

13. Nikolai Oleinikov, "Cockroach" (1934): A Farcical Tragedy

1. Nikolai Oleinikov, *Puchina strastei*, eds. Aleksandr Oleinikov with Lidiia Ginzburg (Moscow: Sovetskii pisatel', 1990), 156–59.

2. Lidiia Ginzburg, *Zapisnye knizhki. Vospominaniia. Ėsse* (St. Petersburg: Iskusstvo-SPb, 2002), 487.

3. Ginzburg, *Zapisnye*, 493.

4. Ginzburg, *Zapisnye*, 494.

5. Oleinikov, *Puchina strastei*, 155.

6. Oleinikov, *Puchina strastei*, 121.

7. Ginzburg, *Zapisnye*, 502.

8. Joseph Brodsky, "Nobel Lecture," December 8, 1987, www.nobelprize.org/prizes/literature/1987/brodsky/lecture (accessed May 18, 2023).

9. Fedor Dostoevskii, *Sobranie sochinenii: v 30 tt.*, vol. 10 (Leningrad: Nauka, 1974), 141.

10. Translated by Alexandra Berlina. As Lidiia Ginzburg points out, Captain Lebyadkin's "fable," in its turn, harks back to a poem by Ivan Miatlev (1796–1844) titled "Fantastic Tale": "A cockroach / In a glass / Will fall / Will disappear, / Onto the glass /—For it is hard—/ He will not crawl out. Like me / My life / Faded away / Departed; / I am captive, / I am in love, / But with whom?"

11. Ginzburg, *Zapisnye*, 486.

12. Ginzburg, *Zapisnye*, 486.

13. Ginzburg, *Zapisnye*, 502.

14. Nikolai Oleinikov, "Chislo neizrechennogo," in *Zhizn' i stikhi Nikolaia Oleinikova*, eds. Oleg Lekmanov and Mikhail Sverdlov (Moscow: OGI, 2015), 11–215 (160).

15. Kornei Chukovskii, *Tarakanishche* (Moscow: Malysh, 1990), 12.

16. Kornei Chukovskii, "Cock-the-Roach," trans. Tom Botting, http://freebooksforkids.net/chukovsky-cock-the-roach.html#:~:text=Like%20other%20fish.&text=Cock%2Dthe%2DRoach%20was%20named,Lord%20of%20All%20the%20Land (accessed May 29, 2023).

17. Lev Loseff, *On the Beneficence of Censorship: Aesopian Language in Modern Russian Literature* (Munich: Verlag Otto Sagner, 1984), 199, 202.

18. Iosif Stalin, *Sobranie sochinenii*, vol. 13 (Moscow: Gospolitizdat, 1951), 14. For more on the Stalin-related interpretation of Chukovsky's tale, see M. Lipovetskii, "Skazkovlast': 'Tarakanishche' Stalina," *Novoe literaturnoe obozrenie* 5 (2000), https://magazines.gorky.media/nlo/2000/5/skazkovlast-tarakanishhe-stalina.html (accessed May 18, 2023).

19. Osip Mandel'shtam, *Sobranie sochinenii v 4-kh tomakh*, eds. Pavel Nerler and A. Mikitaev, vol. 3 (Moscow: Art-Biznes-Tsentr, 1994), 61.

20. *The Poems of Osip Mandelstam*, trans. Ilya Bernstein (New York: EPC Digital Edition, 2014), 23–24.

21. "Oleinikov couldn't stand Mandelstam. About people he despised, he'd say through his teeth: 'He must like Mandelstam.'" Cited from Nikolai Khardzhiev, "Iz poslednikh zapisei," in *Studi escritti in memoria di Marzio Marzaduri a cure di Giovanni Pagani-Cesa e Ol'ga Obuchova*, ed. Mikhail Meilach (Padova: CEUP, 2002), "O Kharmse," 49–62.

22. "Aesopian language" refers to a system of substitutions, lacunae, allusions, allegories, and similar techniques enabling authors to tackle forbidden topics under the conditions of censorship. The most detailed study of (anti-)Soviet Aesopian language remains Loseff's *On the Beneficence of Censorship*.

23. Kornei Chukovskii, *Moidodyr* (Petrograd: Raduga, 1923), 16.

24. Kornei Chukovskii, *Wash 'Em Clean* (Moscow: Raduga, 1988), 15. Translated by E. Felgenhauer.

25. Verb-based rhymes are discouraged in serious Russian poetry as too facile because of identical suffixes.

26. *King Lear*, act 4, scene 1.

27. Leonid Pinskii, *Shekspir: Osnovnye nachala dramaturgii* (Moscow: Khudozhestvennaia literatura, 1971), www.w-shakespeare.ru/library/leonid-pinskiy-shekspir18.html (accessed May 18, 2023), chap. 6 (italics in the original).

14. Marina Tsvetaeva, "I Embrace You Like the Horizon" (1936): Transcendent Love

1. Marina Tsvetaeva, *Stikhotvoreniia i poemy*, ed. E. B. Korkina (Leningrad: Biblioteka Poeta, 1990), 451.

2. See Irma Kudrova, *Posle Rossii*, vol. 1 (Moscow: Rost, 1997).

3. A textual milestone was the five-volume edition of all her poetry published by Russian publishers in New York between 1980 and 1990, edited by Alexander Sumerkin and Viktoria Shveitser, paving the way for new post-Soviet editions, including an expanded and revised single-volume Biblioteka Poeta edition of 1990, edited by Elena Korkina.

4. Noteworthy early lives were by Viktoria Shveitser, *Byt i bytie Mariny Tsvetaevoi* (Fontenay-aux-Roses: Sintaksis, 1988), published in English as *Tsvetaeva*, ed. Angela Livingstone, trans. Robert Chandler (London: Harvill, 1992), and Anna Saakiants, *Marina Tsvetaeva, Zhizn' i tvorchestvo* (Moscow: Ellis Lak, 1997). The most significant correspondences, providing essential information about chapters of her life abroad, include the letters to her Czech friend Anna Tesková (there are several editions, the fullest being a 2008 Moscow version), and letters to the young poet Anatoly Shteiger and to Konstantin Rodzevich, the subject of the two great love epics of the Prague period.

5. Diana Burgin, "Mother Nature versus the Amazons: Marina Tsvetaeva and Female Sexuality," *Journal of the History of Sexuality* 6, no. 1 (1995): 62–88 (63).

6. For a helpful overview of earlier work and new insights that advanced the next critical wave, see Burgin, "Mother Nature versus the Amazons." In recasting his pathbreaking first book of 1966, Simon Karlinsky's second book gave new weight to these aspects. See his *Marina Tsvetaeva: The Woman, Her World, and Her Poetry* (Cambridge: Cambridge University Press, 1985); and Catriona Kelly, *A History of Russian Women's Writing, 1820–1992* (Oxford: Oxford University Press, 1992), 301–18.

7. Her romantic capacity to establish a stunningly metaphysical relationship with figures she admired even at a distance can be followed in a celebrated three-way correspondence available in English as Boris Pasternak, Rainer Maria Rilke, and Marina Tsvetaeva, *Letters, summer 1926*, eds. Konstantin Azadovskii et al., trans. Jamey Gambrell (Oxford: Oxford University Press, 1985).

8. See M. L. Gasparov, "'Poema vozdukha' Mariny Tsvetaevoi. Opyt interpretatsii," in *Izbrannye stat'i* (Moscow: Novoe literaturnoe obozrenie, 1995), 259–75.

9. A comparison noted by Catherine Ciepiela, "The Demanding Woman Poet: On Resisting Marina Tsvetaeva," *PMLA* 111, no. 3 (1996): 421–34 (421), and explored in depth in Michael Naydan, "Marina Tsvetaeva and Sylvia Plath," *Ulbandus Review* 18 (2016): 13–22.

10. See Olga Peters Hasty, "*Poema* vs. Cycle in Cvetaeva's Definition of Lyric Verse," *SEEJ* 323 (1988): 390–98.

11. And not only Rilke: see Alyssa W. Dinega, "Sexual Transcendence in Tsvetaeva's Poems to Pasternak," *Slavic Review* 59, no. 3 (2000): 547–71.

12. For a convenient description of the affair and literary record, see Alexandra Kirilcuk, "Moving Mountains: The Spiritual Topography of Prague in Marina Tsvetaeva's 'Poema kontsa,'" *Russian Review* 65, no. 2 (2006): 194–207; in greater depth, see Catherine Ciepiela, *The Same Solitude: Boris Pasternak and Marina Tsvetaeva* (Ithaca, NY: Cornell University Press, 2006), 82–130.

13. On her sexual intensity, see Catherine Ciepiela, "The Demanding Woman Poet: On Resisting Marina Tsvetaeva," *PMLA* 111, no. 3 (1996): 421–34.

14. On her inventive use of relatively unusual accentual meters, see G. S. Smith, "Logaoedic Metres in the Lyric Poetry of Marina Tsvetayeva," *SEER* 53, no. 132 (1975): 330–54; for an interpretation of their contribution to theatrical speech, see Andrew Kahn, "Chorus and Monologue in Marina Tsvetaeva's *Ariadna*," in *Marina Tsvetaeva: One Hundred Years*, eds. V. Schweitzer and Jane Taubman (Berkeley, CA: Slavic Special Studies, 1994), 162–93.

15. Marina Tsvetaeva, *Sobranie sochinenii v semi tomakh*, vol. 3: *Poemy. Dramaticheskie proizvedeniia* (Moscow: Ellis Lak, 1994), 667.

16. Marina Tsvetaeva, *Sobranie sochinenii v semi tomakh*, vol. 2: *Stikhotvoreniia. Perevody* (Moscow: Ellis Lak, 1994), 70. See also Liza Knapp, "Marina Tsvetaeva's Poetics of Ironic Delight: The 'Podruga Cycle' as Evist Manifesto," *SEEJ* 41, no. 1 (1997): 94–113.

17. Marina Tsvetaeva, *Sobranie sochinenii v semi tomakh*, vol. 7: *Pis'ma* (Moscow: Ellis Lake, 1995), 2 (italics in the original).

18. For a reading and biographical context, linking the cycle to her feelings for Pasternak, see Jane Taubman, *A Life Through Poetry: Marina Tsvetaeva's Lyric Diary* (Columbus, OH: Slavica, 1989), 230–37; and Viktoria Schweitzer, *Tsvetaeva* (New York: Farrar, Straus and Giroux, 1992), 273–85.

19. On separation in the cycle *Provoda* with relevant general comments, see Karlinsky, *Marina Tsvetaeva*, 134.

20. On the episode, see Irma Kudrova, *Put' komet. Zhizn' Mariny Tsvetaevoi* (Moscow: Vita Nova, 2002), 230–50.

21. Peters Hasty, "Poèma vs. Cycle," 390.

22. Gasparov, "'Poema vozdukha,'" 259–74.

23. Cited in Ciepiela, "The Demanding Woman Poet," 425.

24. For similar imagery, see the poem Tsvetaeva wrote after she and her husband Sergei Efron separated in 1920: "Kto sozdan iz kamnia, kto iz gliny" ("This one is made from stone, this one from clay") in Tsvetaeva, *Sobranie*, vol. 2, 524.

25. The line contains a quotation from a 1912 poem by Akhmatova: "Kak vplelas' v moi temnye kosy / Serebristaia nezhnaia priad'" ("How woven into my dark braid / There was a silver strand").

15. Anna Akhmatova, "Secrets of Craft" (1936–60): The Forms of Inspiration

1. Anna Akhmatova, *Stikhovoreniia i poemy*, ed. V. M. Zhirmunskii (Moscow: Biblioteka Poeta, 1976), 201–10.

2. Akhmatova, *Stikhovoreniia i poemy*, 480.

3. Vera Dunham, "Poems about Poems: Notes on Recent Soviet Poetry," *Slavic Review* 24, no. 1 (1965): 57–76 (62).

4. Il'ia Kukulin, *Proryv k nevozmozhnoi sviazi. Stat'i o russkoi poezii* (Ekaterinburg—Moscow: Kabinetnyi uchenyi, 2019), 92.

5. "Doklad tov. A. A. Zhdanova o zhurnalakh *Zvezda* i *Leningrad*," https://www.domarchive.ru/history/part-2-construction-of-socialism/8848 (accessed June 12, 2023).

6. See Sonia I. Ketchian, "Akhmatova's Civic Poem 'Stansy' and Its Pushkinian Antecedents," *SEEJ* 37, no. 2 (1993): 194–210.

7. Image, biography, and text have to an unusual degree been conflated in the creation of the Akhmatova myth. The famous notebooks of Lidia Chukovskaia, *Zapiski ob Anne Akhmatovoi*, remain an indispensable source in public perception of the poet. For a deconstruction of the myth and demonstration of how skillfully Akhmatova herself scripted her image, see Alexander Zholkovsky, "The Obverse of Stalinism: Akhmatova's Self-Serving Charisma of Selflessness," in *Self and Story in Russian History*, eds. Laura Engelstein and Stephanie Sandler (Ithaca, NY: Cornell University Press, 2000), 46–68. Much anecdotal material is to be found in Anatolii Naiman, *Rasskazy o Anne Akhmatovoi* (Moscow: Khudozhestvennaia literatura, 1989), also available as Anatolii Naiman, *Remembering Anna Akhmatova* (London: Halban, 1991), much criticized for inaccuracies; on Akhmatova's influence, see Maxim D. Shrayer, "Two Poems on the Death of Akhmatova: Dialogues, Private Codes, and the Myth of Akhmatova's Orphans," *Canadian Slavonic Papers* 35, no. 2 (1993): 45–68 (59–60). Also indispensable if highly idiosyncratic are the memories of Nadezhda Mandel'shtam, gathered in *Ob Akhmatovoi* (Moscow: Novoe izdatel'stvo, 2007).

8. Joseph Brodsky, "On Richard Wilbur," trans. Carl Proffer, *American Poetry Review* 2, no. 1 (1973): 52.

9. C. K. Williams, "Solitary Caverns: On Globalization and Poetry," *Poetry* 193 (2009): 549–54 (550); and his "Keening Muse," in *Less Than One: Selected Essays* (London: Viking, 1986), 34–53.

10. Mary Gordon, "Journal," *American Scholar* 69, no. 2 (2000): 133–36 (134).

11. See Seamus Heaney, "Crediting Poetry: The 1995 Nobel Lecture," *World Literature Today* 70, no. 2 (1996): 253–59 (255); and Philip McDonagh, "Poetic Truth and Public Justice: Reflections on the Purposes of Poetry from Pushkin to Heaney," *Poetry Ireland Review* 106 (2012): 65–85 (82).

12. Carolyn Forché, "Twentieth-Century Poetry of Witness," *American Poetry Review* 22, no. 2 (1993): 9–16.

13. Eavan Boland, *Object Lessons: The Life of the Woman and the Poet in Our Time* (London: Vintage, 1996), 174; Tess Gallagher, "The Poem as a Reservoir for Grief," *American Poetry Review* 13, no. 4 (1984): 7–11 (7). Medbh McGuckian, a prominent Irish poet of a younger generation, called Akhmatova the "poet who defined Tess" ("Essay: Crucial Collection," *Poetry Ireland Review* 87 [2006], 17–19 [17]).

14. Kukulin, *Proryv*, 94.

15. Andrew Kahn, *Mandelstam's Worlds: Poetry, Politics, and Identity in a Revolutionary Age* (Oxford: Oxford University Press, 2020), 244–99.

16. On the metrical shape of her cycles, see T. S. Gvozdikovskaia, "Metrika Anny Akhmatovoi i tsiklizatsiia liricheskikh stikhotvorenii," in *Poetika realizma i sotsialisticheskogo realizma* (Frunze: Kirgizskii gosudarstvennyi universitet, 1984), 31–39.

17. The term *tvorchestvo* itself has a rich history, traced in Kåre Johan Mjør, "Metaphysics, Aesthetics, or Epistemology? A Conceptual History of *Tvorchestvo* in Nineteenth-Century Russian Thought," *SEEJ* 62, no. 1 (2018): 4–25.

18. Boris Gasparov, "'He said that for a woman to be a poet is nonsense': Anna Akhmatova in a Quest for a Lyrical Voice," *Ulbandus Review* 8 (2004): 119–34 (121).

19. See A. S. Pushkin, *Polnoe sobranie sochinenii v 16-i tt*, eds. M. Gorkii et al., vol. 12 (Moscow: AN USSR, 1949), "Zametki na poliakh stat'i P.A. Viazemskogo 'O zhizni i sochineniiakh V.A. Ozerova,'" 213–42 (229).

20. A. S. Pushkin, *Sobranie sochinenii v desiati tomakh*, ed. D. D. Blagoi, vol. 3 (Moscow: Khudozhestvennaia literatura, 1959), 179.

21. Instances of other repeated uses of the word "secrets" (*tainy*) in Akhmatova's poetry dating to these years can be found in R. D. Timenchik, *Poslednii poet. Anna Akhmatova v 1960-e gody*, vol. 1 (Moscow: Mosty kul'tury, 2014), chap. 3 (147–207).

22. Pushkin, *Sobranie sochinenii v desiati tomakh*, 179.

23. Osip Mandel'shtam, *Polnoe sobranie sochineii i pisem*, vol. 1 (Moscow: Progress-Pleiada, 2009), 176.

24. For a bravura demonstration of the range of citational and critical practices modernist Russian poets invite, see Alexander Zholkovsky, "Quote the Poets Ever More: Micro-Analyzing Intertextual Gems by Anna Akhmatova, Vladislav Khodasevich, and Osip Mandel'shtam," *SEEJ* 61, no. 1 (2017): 111–28.

25. "Vnov' podaren mne dremotoi" (1916).

26. "Govoriat deti" (1950).

27. Akhmatova, *Stikhovoreniia i poemy*, 193.

28. "Zashchitnikam Stalina" (1962).

29. "O net, ia tebia liubila" (1925).

30. Akhmatova, *Stikhovoreniia i poemy*, 208.

31. On Akhmatova's lifelong and intricate relationship with all aspects of Pushkin, see David Wells, *Akhmatova and Pushkin: The Contexts of Akhmatova's Poetry* (Birmingham: Department of Russian Language and Literature, 1994).

32. A. S. Pushkin, *Sobranie sochinenii v desiati tomakh*, ed. D. D. Blagoi, vol. 2 (Moscow: Khudozhestvennaia literatura, 1959), 16.

33. Boris Eikhenbaum, *Anna Akhmatova. Opyt analiza* (Petersburg: Academia, 1923), 48.

34. On Akhmatova's renewed vitality at this time, see Susan Amert, *In a Shattered Mirror: The Later Poetry of Anna Akhmatova* (Stanford, CA: Stanford University Press, 1992), esp. chap. 1.

16. Ian Satunovsky, "Yesterday, late on my way to work" (1939): Poetics of the Ethical

1. Ian Satunovskii, *Stikhi i proza k stikham*, ed. Ivan Akhmet'ev (Moscow: Virtual'naia galereia, 2012), 9.

2. Satunovskii, *Stikhi i proza k stikham*, 207.

3. For a detailed account of Satunovsky's life, see Oleg Burkov, "Ian Satunovskii: Popytka biografii" (2012), https://imwerden.de/pdf/burkov_yan_satunovsky_biografiya_2012.pdf (accessed May 22, 2023). See also Galina Zykova and Elena Penskaia, "Ian Satunovskii. Materialy k izucheniiu tvorchestva i literaturnogo konteksta," in *"Lianozovskaia shkola": Mezhdu barachnoi poeziiei i russkim konkretizmom*, ed. Galina Zykova, Vladislav Kulakov, and Mikhail Pavlovets (Moscow: Novoe literaturnoe obozrenie, 2022), 593–624.

4. Satunovskii, *Stikhi i proza k stikham*, 399.

5. Vladislav Kulakov, "Ian Satunovskii: 'Ia—ne poet,'" https://www.ruthenia.ru/60s/satunovskij/kulakov.htm (accessed May 29, 2023). On Satunovsky's poetics, see also Kirill Korchagin, "'Konstrikom, no s novolefovskim uklonom' Ian Satunovskii i evoliutsiia konstruktivistskoi poetiki," in *"Lianozovskaia shkola,"* 547–71; Georg Vitte, "'Vmesto priblizitel'noi tochnosti—tochnaia priblizitel'nost'.' 'Bednaia poeziia' Iana Satunovskogo," in *"Lianozovskaia shkola,"* 572–92; Ilya Kukulin, "Vid na bereg s ruinami progressa: O stikhotvorenii Iana Satunovskogo 'Prishel rybak . . .' (1966)," in *"Lianozovskaia shkola,"* 625–37.

6. Mikhail Aizenberg, "Tochka soprotivleniia," in *Vzgliad na svobodnogo khudozhnika* (Moscow: Gendalf, 1997), http://www.vavilon.ru/texts/aizenberg/aizenberg6-4.html (accessed May 22, 2023).

7. On Satunovsky's poems about the Holocaust and Soviet antisemitism, see, Lev Oborin and Linor Goralik analysis of Satunovsky's poem "Ia Moisha z Berdycheva" ("I am Moysha from Berdichev") in the podcast *Mezhdu strok* (Between the lines), https://polka.academy/podcasts/807. On Satunovsky's

war poetry, see Luba Golburt, "Ian Satunovskii: Identity and Biography, from the War to the Lyric," *Slavic Review* 82, issue 3 (Fall 2023): 640–647.

8. "Concerning measures for regularizing labor discipline, improving the practice of state social insurance, and measures to counter abuse in this area" (December 27, 1939), http://docs.historyrussia.org/ru/nodes/242666-o-meropriyatiyah-po-uporyadocheniyu-trudovoy-distsipliny-uluchsheniyu-praktiki-gosudarstvennogo-sotsialnogo-strahovaniya-i-borbe-s-zloupotrebleniyami-v-etom-dele-postanovlenie-snk-sssr-tsk-vkp-b-i-vtssps-ot-28-dekabrya-1938-g (accessed May 29, 2023). See also Peter H. Solomon, Jr., *Soviet Justice under Stalin* (Cambridge: Cambridge University Press, 1996), 299–336.

9. *Pravda* (January 21, 1939): 3 (italics in the original).

10. "Comrade I. V. Stalin's speech to a preelection meeting of the electorate of the Stalin Electoral District of the City of Moscow. December 11, 1937, at the Bolshoi Theater," *Pravda* (December 11, 1937): 2 (italics added).

11. *Pravda* (December 11, 1938): 1.

12. Mikhail Bakhtin, *The Dialogic Imagination: Four Essays*, ed. Michael Holquist, trans. Caryl Emerson and Michael Holquist (Austin: University of Texas Press, 1981), 159, 160.

17. Gennady Gor, "I lie together with my wife, the two of us in the apartment" (1942–44): Is There Life after Death?

1. The poem (in both Russian and English) is published in *Written in the Dark: Five Poets in the Siege of Leningrad*, ed. Polina Barskova, with an afterword by Ilya Kukulin (Brooklyn, NY: Ugly Duckling Presse, 2016), 45–47.

2. Polina Barskova and Andrei Muzhdaba, "Gor ne tol'ko mozhet pokazat'sia nerovnym, no i byl nerovnym pisatelem" (January 27, 2021), www.colta.ru/articles/literature/26472-polina-barskova-andrey-muzhdaba-literaturnyy-put-gennadiy-gor (accessed May 22, 2023).

3. See the case study in Andrew Kahn et al., *A History of Russian Literature* (Oxford: Oxford University Press, 2018), 545–49.

4. Aleksandr Laskin, "Gor i mir," *Zvezda* 5 (2002), https://7iskusstv.com/2011/Nomer3/Laskin1.php (accessed May 22, 2023).

5. Oleg Iuriev, "Zapolnennoe ziianie-2," *Novoe literaturnoe obozrenie* 1 (2008), https://magazines.gorky.media/nlo/2008/1/zapolnennoe-ziyanie-2.html (accessed May 22, 2023). Review of Gennadii Gor, *Blockade: Gedichte, aus dem Russischen übersetzt und herausgegeben von Peter Urban* (Vienna: Edition Korrespondenzen, 2007).

6. Gennadii Gor, *Krasnaia kaplia v snegu. Stikhotvoreniia 1942–1944 godov*, ed. Andrei Muzhdaba (Moscow: Gileia, 2012).

7. Barskova and Muzhdaba, "Gor ne tol'ko."

8. Gor, *Krasnaia*, 25, 27, 30–31. Translated by Ben Felker-Quinn and Eugene Ostashevsky.

9. *Written in the Dark*, 46. Translated by Alexandra Berlina.

10. Translated by Ben Felker-Quinn and Eugene Ostashevsky. See *Written in the Dark*, 38–39.

11. Iuriev, "Zapolnennoe."

12. Though the name Ludmila is repeated several times in the poem, A. Muzhdaba notes that "names usually have no real referents in Gor's poetry" (Gor, *Krasnaia*, 145).

13. Muzhdaba, in Gor, *Krasnaia*, 147.

14. Andrei Muzhdaba, "Poeziia Gennadiia Gora," in Gor, *Krasnaia*, 11–22 (15).

15. Varlam Shalamov, "On prose," trans. Brian Johnson, in *Late and Post-Soviet Russian Literature: A Reader*, vol. 2: *The Thaw and Stagnation*, eds. Mark Lipovetsky and Lisa Ryoko Wakamiya (Boston, MA: Academic Studies Press, 2015), 116.

16. Theodor W. Adorno, "Cultural Criticism and Society," in *Prisms* (Cambridge, MA: MIT Press, 1983), 17–34 (34).

18. Igor Kholin, "Fences. Trash-heaps. Flyers. Ads" (mid-1950s): The Slums of Communism

1. Igor' Kholin, *Izbrannoe: Stikhi i poemy*, ed. Tatiana Mikhailovskaia with Genrikh Sapgir (Moscow: Novoe literaturnoe obozrenie, 1999), 4.

2. R. Karpel', "Zhretsy 'pomoiki no. 8,'" *Moskovskii komsomolets* (September 29, 1960).

3. Iu. Ivashchenko, "Bezdel'niki karabkaiutsia na Parnas," *Izvestiia* (September 2, 1960).

4. Alexei Konakov, "Pesnia o Kholine," https://www.colta.ru/articles/literature/3576-pesnya-o-holine (accessed May 22, 2023).

5. Galina Rymbu, "Vspomnit' Kholina," https://www.colta.ru/articles/literature/3753-vspomnit-holina (accessed May 22, 2023).

6. Vladislav Kulakov, *Poeziia kak fakt* (Moscow: Novoe literaturnoe obozrenie, 1999), 18.

7. Evgenii Kropivnitskii, *Izbrannoe: 736 stikhotvorenii i drugie materialy*, ed. Ivan Akhmet'ev with Iurii Orlitskii (Moscow: Kul'turnyi sloj, 2004), 107.

8. Kholin, *Izbrannoe*, 35.

9. Kholin, *Izbrannoe*, 30.

10. Kholin, *Izbrannoe*, 31.

11. "Mikhail Epstein: Seriality is an attempt to characterize a language, in which each picture is a separate utterance, i.e., every utterance immediately trails in along with it the entire language in which it is produced; extending from each picture is an entire series, like a presentation of the grammar and the rules for combining images.

"Ilya Kabakov: [. . .] This is a very good explanation. The fabrication of a multiplicity [. . .] In Moscow they used to say: 'It's already clear! Why twenty pictures?' But the paradox is that it's clear, precisely because there are twenty pictures. You have to establish a language, then one picture can remain in 'this' language." (M. Epstein and I. Kabakov, *Katalog* (Vologda: B-ka moskovskogo kontseptualizma, 2010), 307.)

12. Olga Sedakova, "Chetyrekhstopnyi amfibrakhii ili 'Chudo' Pasternaka v poeticheskoi traditsii," http://www.olgasedakova.com/Poetica/228 (accessed May 22, 2023).

13. Nikolai Zabolotskii, *Sobranie sochinenii v trekh tomakh*, vol. 1 (Moscow: Khudozhestvennaia literatura, 1983), 192.

14. Zabolotskii, *Sobranie sochinenii*, 192.

15. Zabolotskii, *Sobranie sochinenii*, 192.

16. Sedakova, "Chetyrekhstopnyi."

17. A. Volodin, "'Skuchno zhiteliam baraka': o poezii Igoria Kholina," https://gorky.media/context/laquo-skuchno-zhitelyam-baraka-raquo-o-poezii-igorya-holina (accessed May 22, 2023).

18. Kholin, *Izbrannoe*, 53.

19. Valerii Podoroga, *Vremya posle Osventsima. GULAG: myslit' absoliutnoie Zlo* (Moscow: Logos, 2015), 82, 86.

20. Rymbu, "Vspomnit' Kholina."

21. Giorgio Agamben, *Homo Sacer: Sovereign Power and Bare Life*, trans. Daniel Heller-Roazen (Stanford, CA: Stanford University Press, 1998), 170–71.

22. Agamben, *Homo*, 188.

23. Agamben, *Homo*, 115.

24. Thanks go to Mikhail Pavlovets for his important comments and advice.

19. Nikolai Zabolotsky, "Somewhere not far from Magadan" (1956): A Gulag Elegy

1. Nikolai Zabolotskii, *Stikhotvoreniia i poemy* (Moscow: Sovetskii pisatel' [Biblioteka poeta], 1965), 144.

2. See Sarah Pratt, *Nikolai Zabolotsky: Enigma and Cultural Paradigm* (Evanston, IL: Northwestern University Press, 2000).

3. For a summary and new arguments, see Irene Masing-Delic, "Zabolotsky's *The Triumph of Agriculture*: Satire or Utopia?" *Russian Review* 42, no. 4 (1983): 360–76.

4. For the poems and an analysis of their tenor, see Kevin F. M. Platt, "N. A. Zabolotskii na stranitsakh *Izvestii.* K biografii poeta 1934–1936 godov," *Novoe literaturnoe obozrenie* 44 (2000): 91–107.

5. The first Russian publications of this memoir appeared in the late 1980s, following a translation by Robin Milner-Gulland published in the *Times Literary Supplement* on 9 October 1981. For a succinct account of Zabolotsky's detention, penal colony years, and release, see Darra Goldstein, *Nikolai Zabolotsky: Play for Mortal Stakes* (Cambridge: Cambridge University Press, 1993), 86–107.

6. Goldstein, *Nikolai Zabolotsky,* 83–85.

7. Zabolotskii, *Stikhotvoreniia,* 85.

8. Zabolotskii, *Stikhotvoreniia,* 153.

9. Barry Scherr, *Russian Poetry: Meter, Rhythm, and Rhyme* (Berkeley: University of California Press, 1986), 75–84 (81).

10. Andrea Gullotta, "Gulag Poetry: An Almost Unexplored Field of Research," in *(Hi-)Stories of the Gulag: Fiction and Reality,* eds. Felicitas Fischer von Weikersthal and Karoline Thaidigsmann (Universitätsverlag Winter: Heidelberg, 2016), 175–92.

11. See the results of the two searches for "merzlyi tuman" and "merzlyi vozdukh" in the *Natsional'nyi korpus russkogo iazyka*: https://ruscorpora.ru/results?search=CqcBEo0BCooBEhkKFwoDbGV4EhAKDtC80LXRgNC30LvRi9C5Em0KFQoDbGV4Eg4KDNCy0L7Qt9C00YPRhQoKCgRmb3JtEgIKAAoLCgVncmFtbRICCgAKCQoDc2VtEgIKAAoVCgdzZW0tbW9kEgoKCHNlbXxzZW14CgsKBWZsYWdzEgIKAAoMCgRkaXN0IgQIARABKg4KCAgAEAoYMiAKIABABTICCAE6AQEwAQ==// (accessed May 23, 2023).

12. Charlie Louth, "The Romantic Lyric," in *The Cambridge Companion to German Romanticism,* ed. Nicholas Saul (Cambridge: Cambridge University Press, 2009), 67–84 (68).

13. Aleksandr Pushkin, *Polnoe sobranie sochinenii,* vol. 3.1 (Moscow: AN USSR, 1948), 330.

20. Bella Akhmadulina, "Along My Street" (1959): An Elegy on Betrayal

1. Bella Akhmadulina, *Sochineniia v trekh tomakh,* vol. 1 (Moscow: PAI, Korona-Print, 1997), 33–34.

2. Akhmadulina, *Sochineniia,* 50.

3. "I am attracted to the ancient style" (1959). All excerpts from poems by Akhmadulina in this chapter are translated by Alexandra Berlina.

4. What Alexandra Berlina translates as "penchant" here literally reads *tainstvennaia strast',* "mysterious passion." Vasily Aksenov used this phrase as the title of his last novel, an autobiographical text about the poets and writers of the 1960s (not translated into English as of February 2023). He is talking about the self-betrayal of his—and Akhmadulina's—generation.

5. See Evgenii Pasternak, *Boris Pasternak: Materialy dlia biografii* (Moscow: Sovetskii pisatel', 1989), 642–52.

6. Boris Messerer, "Promel'k Belly: Romanticheskaia khronika," *Oktiabr'* 1 (2013), https://magazines.gorky.media/znamia/2011/9/promelk-belly.html (accessed May 23, 2023).

7. This suggests that the meeting took place probably in late October 1959. The meeting could not have taken place in October 1960 because Pasternak died on May 30, 1960.

8. Akhmadulina, *Sochineniia,* 100.

9. Arnold Van Gennep, *The Rites of Passage* (Chicago, IL: University of Chicago Press, [1914] 1969), and Victor Turner, *The Ritual Process: Structure and Anti-Structure* (Chicago, IL: Aldine Publishers, 1969).

10. Turner, *From Ritual to Theatre* (New York: Performing Arts Journal Publications, 1982), 25.

11. Turner, *From Ritual,* 44.

12. Akhmadulina, *Sochineniia,* 100.

13. Akhmadulina, "Plokhaia vesna," in *Sochineniia,* 131–35 (134).

14. Akhmadulina, *Sochineniia*, 165.

15. Akhmadulina, *Sochineniia*, 152.

16. Akhmadulina, *Sochineniia*, 153.

17. *The Princeton Encyclopaedia of Poetry and Poetics*, ed. Alex Preminger (Princeton, NJ: Princeton University Press, 1965), 215.

21. Alexander Galich, "The Night Watch" (1963): History as the Uncanny

1. Aleksandr Galich, *Stikhotvoreniia i poemy*, ed. V. Betaki (Moscow: Novaia Biblioteka Poeta, 2006), 64.

2. Aleksandr Galich, *Songs and Poems*, ed. and trans. G. S. Smith (Ann Arbor, MI: Ardis, 1983), 99–100.

3. On the mass consumption of songs through radio transmission or performance, see David MacFadyen, *Red Stars: Personality and the Soviet Popular Song, 1955–1991* (Montreal: McGill-Queen's University Press, 2001), 79.

4. Mikhail Aronov, *Aleksandr Galich. Polnaia biografiia* (Moscow: Novoe literaturnoe obozrenie, 2012), 390.

5. Aronov, *Aleksandr Galich*, 387.

6. "Neskol'ko voprosov Bulatu Okudzhave." Radio interview given in Munich on October 23, 1987 (cited in G. S. Smith, "Okudzhava Marches On," *SEER* 66, no. 4 [1988]: 553–63 [560]).

7. Galich, *Stikhotvoreniia i poemy*, 6.

8. See David C. Gillespie, "The Sounds of Music: Soundtrack and Song in Soviet Film," *Slavic Review* 62, no. 3 (2003): 473–90; G. S. Smith gives figures for the availability of open-reel tape recorders in the 1960s, which numbered more than a million by the end of the decade; G. S. Smith, *Songs to Seven Strings: Russian Guitar Poetry and Soviet "Mass Song"* (Bloomington: Indiana University Press, 1984), 79.

9. Galich, *Songs and Poems*, 28.

10. For a detailed account of the event and its consequences, see Aronov, *Aleksandr Galich*, 244–81.

11. Aronov, *Aleksandr Galich*, 851.

12. Smith, "Okudzhava Marches On," 559.

13. Rachel Platonov, "Bad Singing: *Avtorskaia pesnia* and the Aesthetics of Communication," *Ulbandus Review* 9 (2005): 87–113 (88).

14. The definitive history of the form is Smith, *Songs to Seven Strings*; on Galich in this context, see chap. 8 (218–28).

15. The pioneering and highly influential discussion remains Freud's essay "The Uncanny," reflected on and taken further in Hélène Cixous, "Fiction and Its Phantoms: A Reading of Freud's *Das Unheimliche* (The 'Uncanny')," *New Literary History* 7, no. 3 (1976): 525–48.

16. For insights on Galich's use of polymetrical structures, see, with bibliography, O. A. Fomina, "Polimetriia Galicha i Vysotskogo. Opyt tipologicheskogo analiza," in A. Galich, *Novye stat'i i materialy*, ed. A. E. Krylov (Moscow: Bulat, 2009), 128–43.

17. Boris Groys, *The Total Art of Stalinism: Avant-Garde, Aesthetic Dictatorship, and Beyond* (London: Verso, 2011), 51.

18. Sigmund Freud, "The 'Uncanny'" (1919), in *The Complete Psychological Works*, vol. 17 (London: Hogarth Press, 1955), 217–56 (218).

19. For a more detailed comparison, see Iu. S. Karpukhina, "Romanticheskaia traditsiia V. A. Zhukovskogo v tvorchestve Galicha," in *A. Galich. Novye stat'i i materialy*, ed. A. E. Krylov (Moscow: Iupaps, 2003), 69–75.

20. On the legend and Pushkin's appropriation, the classic study remains Roman Jakobson, *Pushkin and His Sculptural Myth* (The Hague: Mouton, 1975), 41.

21. Paul Zanker, *The Power of Images in the Age of Augustus* (Ann Arbor: University of Michigan Press, 1988).

22. See David Brandenberger, *Propaganda State in Crisis: Soviet Ideology, Indoctrination, and Terror under Stalin, 1927–1941* (New Haven, CT: Yale University Press, 2011), 1–8.

23. Jan Plamper, *The Stalin Cult: A Study in the Alchemy of Power* (New Haven, CT: Yale University Press, 2012).

24. A thorough overview of Pushkin's symbolic statuary can be found in Jakobson, *Pushkin and His Sculptural Myth*.

25. Sergei Gandlevskii, "O Galiche," https://znamlit.ru/publication.php?id=8388&fbclid=IwAR1No0fqeKwsLUCAIxhaIjt2QdfHQeSiwgHZ6_vWJTPtn9ujWP6eHiyWAAM (accessed May 24, 2023).

26. A. E. Krylov, "O dvukh 'Okudzhavskikh' pesniakh Galicha," in Galich, *Novye stat'i i materialy*, 291.

27. Boris Slutskii, *Sobranie sochinenii v 3-kh tomakh*, vol. 1 (Moscow: Khudozhestvennaia literatura, 1991), 184; another example by Slutsky, possibly dated later than Galich, is "Nazvaniia i pereimenovaniia" ("Names and Renamings").

28. Robert C. Tucker, ed., *The Marx-Engels Reader* (New York: Norton, 1978), 340.

22. Vladimir Vysotsky, "My Gypsy Song" (1967–68): Choreography of Despair

1. Vladimir Vysotskii, *Sobranie sochinenii*, eds. Vladimir Novikov and Olga Novikova, 4 vols. (Moscow: Vremia, 2008), vol. 1, 157–58.

2. See Nataliia Krymova, *Imena. Kniga chetvertaia. Vysotskii. Nenapisannaia kniga* (Moscow: GKTsM V. S. Vysotskogo, 2008).

3. See Natalia Krymova, "O poezii Vladimira Vysotskogo," in Vladimir Vysotskii, *Izbrannoe* (Moscow: Sovetskii pisatel', 1988), 481–502.

4. Nikolai Bogomolov, "Chuzhoi mir i svoe slovo," in *Mir Vysotskogo*, vol. 1 (Moscow: GKTsM V. S. Vysotskogo, 1997), http://vysotskiy-lit.ru/vysotskiy/kritika/bogomolov-chuzhoj-mir-i-svoe-slovo.htm (accessed 24 May, 2023).

5. "Okhota na volkov" (1968), in Vysotskii, *Sobranie*, vol. 1, 171.

6. Translation by "Trotta.Gnam," https://wysotsky.com/1033.htm?1742 (accessed 24 May, 2023).

7. *The Visible and the Incredible* was a Soviet popular-science TV show from the 1970s and 1980s; the Psychiatric Hospital no.1 in Kanatchikovo on the outskirts of Moscow was popularly known as "Kanatchikova Dacha."

8. See the chapter "'Ia tol'ko malost' ob'iasniu v stikhe.' Kontseptsiia cheloveka i mira," in Andrei Skobelev and Sergei Shaulov, *Vladimir Vysotskii—Mir i Slovo* (Voronezh: Logos, 2001), http://vysotskiy-lit.ru/vysotskiy/kritika/skobelev-shaulov-mir-i-slovo/index.htm (accessed May 24, 2023).

9. Vysotskii, *Sobranie*, vol. 3, 165.

10. Skobelev and Shaulov, *Vladimir Vysotskii*.

11. "Monument" (1973), in Vysotskii, *Sochineniia*, vol. 2, 87.

12. "Ariadne's Thread" (1973), in Vysotskii, *Sochineniia*, vol. 3, 103–4.

13. On the motif of the extreme in Russian romantic songs, see Miron Petrovskii, "Ezda v Ostrov liubvi, ili Chto est' russkii romans," *Voprosy Literatury* 5 (1984): 55–90.

14. "Koni priveredlivye" (1972), in Vysotskii, *Sochineniia*, vol. 2, 43.

15. "Solodov's Song" (1973), in Vysotskii, *Sochineniia*, vol. 2, 254.

16. "Grateful to Be Alive" (1979), in Vysotskii, *Sochineniia*, vol. 3, 170.

17. "The Song of the Singer at the Microphone" (1971), in Vysotskii, *Sochineniia*, vol. 2, 16–17.

18. See, for example, M. N. Kaprusova, "Stikhotvorenie V. Vysotskogo 'Moia tsyganskaia': Tekst i podtekst," http://vysotskiy-lit.ru/vysotskiy/kritika/kaprusova-moya-cyganskaya-tekst-i-podtekst

.htmь (accessed May 24, 2023); I. Sokolova,"'Tsyganskie' motivy v tvorchestve trekh bardov," http://vysotskiy-lit.ru/vysotskiy/kritika/sokolova-cyganskie-motivy.htm (accessed May 24, 2023); N. V. Krylova, "'Kabatskie' motivy u Vostskogo: genealogiia i mifologiia," *Mir Vysotskogo* 3 (2000): 398–416; Aleksei Krasnoperov, "'Net, rebiata, vse ne tak . . .': 'Tsyganskaia pesnia i russkii romans v tvorchestve Vladimira Vysotskogo," https://v-vysotsky.com/articles/Net_rebiata/text03.html (accessed May 24, 2023); V. Andrei Skobelev, "Moia tsyganskaia (zima 1967/1968)," in *"Mnogo neiasnogo v strannoi strane . . ." Materialy k kommentirovaniiu izbrannykh proizvedenii V. S. Vysotskogo*, vol. 3 (Voronezh: Ekho, 2012), 72–75; N. Rudnik,"Ob odnom stikhotvorenii. Ego tsyganskaia," *Vagant* 3 (1990): 11–12.

19. Sokolova, "Tsyganskie."

20. Apollon Grigor'ev, *Stikhotvorenia. Poemy. Dramy*, ed. Boris F. Egorov (St. Petersburg: Akademicheskii proekt, 2001), 135.

21. Translated by Alexandra Berlina.

22. Grigor'ev, *Stikhotvorenia*, 135.

23. Aleksandra Nabiullina, "Spetsifika realizatsii zvukovoi metafory v pesniakh V. S. Vysotskogo (na materiale russkogo i frantsuzskogo iazykov)," *Iazyk i kul'tura* 31, no. 3 (2015): 44–54 (46).

24. Skobelev and Shaulov, "Kontseptsiia."

25. Vysotskii, *Sobranie*, vol. 2, 135.

26. M. Kaprusova reads this line as a reference to Korovyev's fatal pun in Bulgakov's novel *The Master and Margarita*: "This knight once made an unfortunate joke [. . .] his pun, which he made while talking about light and darkness, was not very good" (Kaprusova, "Stikhotvorenie"). Andrei Skobelev notes that, unfortunately, this version does not stand up to criticism, since the versions of Bulgakov's novel published by the winter of 1967–68—both in the USSR and abroad—did not contain this fragment.

27. Vasilii Shukshin, "I Believe!," in *50 Writers: An Anthology of 20th-Century Russian Short Story*, trans. Valentina Brougher and Frank Miller with Mark Lipovetsky (Boston, MA: Academic Studies Press, 2011), 456–64 (457).

28. Shukshin, "I Believe!," 461.

29. Shukshin, "I Believe!," 464.

30. Victor Turner, *The Ritual Process: Structure and Anti-Structure* (Chicago, IL: Aldine Publishers, 1969), 73, 95.

31. Turner, *The Ritual Process*, 75, 60.

23. Dmitri Prigov, Three Poems about Dishwashing (1980s): The Banality of the Romantic

1. Dmitrii Prigov, *Monady: kak-by-iskrennost'*, ed. Mark Lipovetskii (Moscow: Novoe literaturnoe obozrenie, 2012), 65, 139, 69.

2. Dmitrii Prigov, *Soviet Texts*, trans. Simon Schuchat and Ainsley Morse (New York: Ugly Duckling Presse, 2020), 63, 64, 71.

3. D. A. Prigov, *Mysli*, eds. Mark Lipovetskii and Ilya Kukulin (Moscow: Novoe literaturnoe obozrenie, 2019), 644.

4. Andrei Zorin, "Slushaia Prigova (Zapisannoie za chetvert' veka)," in *Nekanonicheskii klassik: D. A. Prigov (1940–2007)*, ed. Evgenii Dobrenko et al. (Moscow: Novoe literaturnoe obozrenie, 2010), 407–29 (426).

5. Aleksandr Barash, "'Da ia ved' chto, da ia s liubov'iu . . .' Prigov kak deiatel' tsivilizatsii," in *Nekanonichieskii klassik*, 263–78 (268, 273).

6. D. A. Prigov, *Mesta*, eds. Zhanna Galeeva and Mark Lipovetskii (Moscow: Novoe literaturnoe obozrenie, 2018), 246.

7. Prigov, *Mesta*, 246.

8. Merab Mamardashvili, "Soznanie i tsivilizatsiia," in *Kak ia ponimaiu filosofiiu* (Moscow: Progress-Kul'tura, 1992), http://psylib.org.ua/books/_mamar02.htm (accessed May 25, 2023).

9. A search in the Russia State Library for 1979–84 gives titles for books of prose and poetry including *The Law of Eternity, The Eternal Call* (in numerous reeditions), *The Eternal Wind, The Eternal Aviator, Personal Eternity, The Eternal City, The Eternal Campfire, A Moment Is an Eternity, A Ticket for All Eternity, A Taste of Eternity, Touching Eternity, Hours for Eternity, A Conversation with Eternity, A Minute of Eternity, The Song of Eternity, The Circle of Eternity, From the Viewpoint of Eternity,* and dozens of books with the titles *The Eternal Battle* and *The Eternal Fire.*

10. "It is not the case that Pushkin was killed by D'Anthès's bullet. What killed him was the lack of air. His culture died with him." Aleksandr Blok, "O naznachenii poeta. Rech', proiznesennaia v Dome literatorov na torzhestvennom sobranii v 84-iu godovshchinu smerti Pushkina," in *Sobranie sochinenii v vos'mi tomakh,* vol. 6 (Moscow: Gosizdat, 1962), 167.

24. Elena Shvarts, "A Rubbish Heap" (1983): An Ode to Rot

1. Elena Shvarts, *Stikhotvoreniia i poemy* (St. Petersburg: Inapress, 1999), 142.

2. Elena Shvarts, "Dnevniki," *Novoe literaturnoe obozrenie* 115 (2012), https://nlobooks.ru/magazines/novoe_literaturnoe_obozrenie/115_nlo_3_2012/article/18770/ (accessed May 25, 2023).

3. Elena Shvarts, *Opredelenie v durnuiu pogodu* (St. Petersburg: Pushkinskii fond, 1997), 72.

4. "The Labors and Days of Lavinia" is a series of poems written on behalf of a nun of the fictional Order of the Circumcision of the Heart and published by her sister after Lavinia had lost her mind.

5. Volchek is referring to the discussion of Shvarts's and Viktor Krivulin's poetry at the Leningrad Writers Union in 1985.

6. Dmitrii Volchek, "Poet zolotogo veka. Vospominaniia o Elene Shvarts" (March 18, 2010), https://www.svoboda.org/a/1987645.html (accessed May 25, 2023).

7. Elena Shvarts, *Opredelenie,* 48.

8. Aleksandr Skidan, "Summa poetiki," *Novoe literaturnoe obozrenie* 60, no. 2 (2003), https://magazines.gorky.media/nlo/2003/2/summa-poetiki.html (accessed May 25, 2023)

9. Oleg Dark, "Volna i pamiat': O poezii Eleny Shvarts," *Znamia* 8 (2004), http://www.litkarta.ru/dossier/dark-o-shwartz-volna/dossier_4681 (accessed May 25, 2023).

10. "Elegy to the South" (1990), in Shvarts, *Stikhotvoreniia i poemy,* 94.

11. In the original, the rhyme *Sulla/iiulia* (July) also brings to mind the Roman origin of the month's name.

12. Shvarts, *Opredelenie,* 82–83.

13. Shvarts, *Opredelenie,* 84.

14. Shvarts, *Opredelenie,* 85.

15. Shvarts, *Opredelenie,* 86.

16. Oleg Iuriev, "Svidetel'stvo: O stikhakh Eleny Shvarts," http://www.litkarta.ru/dossier/yuriev-o-shwartz/dossier_4681 (accessed May 25, 2023).

17. Valerii Shubinskii, "Sadovnik i sad (O poezii Eleny Shvarts)," http://www.newkamera.de/shubinskij/vsh_o3.html (accessed May 25, 2023).

18. Dark, "Volna i pamiat'."

19. See chapter 15 on Akhmatova, where this poem is analyzed along with others.

20. Mikhail Bakhtin, *Sobranie sochinenii,* vol. 4.2 (Moscow: Iazyki slavianskikh kul'tur, 2010), 18.

21. Bakhtin, *Sobranie,* 19–20.

22. Bakhtin, *Sobranie,* 20.

23. Yurii Tynianov, *Permanent Evolution: Selected Essays on Literature, Theory and Film,* trans. Ainsley Morse and Philip Redko (Boston, MA: Academic Studies Press, 2019), 81.

24. Lev Pumpianskii, "Ob ode A. Pushkina 'Pamiatnik,'" http://pushkin-lit.ru/pushkin/articles/pumpyanskij-ob-ode-pushkina-pamyatnik.htm (accessed May 25, 2023).

25. Ry Nikonova, "furious furious rabious" (1985): Threading the Avant-Garde

1. *Transfuristy. Izbrannye teksty Ry Nikonovoi, Sergeia Sigeia, A. Nika, B. Konstriktora*, ed. Petr Kazarnovsky with Boris Konstriktor (Moscow: Gilea, 2016), 18.

2. Boris Konstriktor, "Zaum zum Ende (Trans-Mission)," in *Transfuristy*, 273–80 (276).

3. On the Uktusskaya School, see Anna Nikonova-Tarshis, "Uktusskaia shkola," in *Avangardnye napravleniia v sovetskom izobrazitel'nom iskusstve* (Ekaterinburg: Ural'skii gosudarstvennyi universitet, 1993), 58–65; T. Zhumati, "The Uktus+ School: Coding Changes," in *Bookwork, Rea Nikonova & Serge Segay* (Eindhoven: LS Collection Van Abbemuseum, 2016), 29–34.

4. A collection of highly informative articles is devoted to the group's activities: *Transpoetika: Avtory zhurnala 'Transponans' v issledovaniiakh i materialakh*, eds. Pyotr Kazarnovsky and A. Mudzhaba (St. Petersburg: Art-Tsentr "Pushkinskaia 10," 2021).

5. "Vmesto manifesta," in *Transfurizm. Katalog k vystavke v Art-tsentre "Pushkinskaia, 10" (23 dekabria 2017–21 ianvaria 2018)*, ed. Ilja Kukuj (St. Petersburg: DEAN, 2017), 18–22 (19).

6. Il'ia Kukui, "Laboratoriia avangarda: Zhurnal 'Transponans,'" *Russian Literature* 59, nos. 2–4 (2006): 225–59 (230).

7. Kukui, "Laboratoriia avangarda," 229.

8. On the publications of the historical avant-garde in *Transponans*, see Andrei Ustinov, "Mesto pechati 'Transponans': K istorii mashinopisnykh izdanii 1980-kh godov," in *Transpoetika*, 31–90.

9. See, for example, I. Kolosova, "Name—Text—Ritual: The Role of Plant Characteristics in Slavic Folk Medicine," *Folklorica* 10, no. 2 (January 2005), 44–61.

10. V. I. (Viacheslav Ivanov) and V. T. (Vladimir Toporov), "Leshii," in *Mify narodov mira. Entsiklopediia*, vol. 2 (Moscow: Sov.ėntsiklopediia, 1982), 52.

11. Sigey refers to its 1982 edition in his article about Vasilisk Gnedov, and we can assume that Nikonova was also familiar with it.

12. A. Afanasiev, *Drevo zhizni*, eds. Y. Medvedev with V. Kirdan (Moscow: Sovremennik, 1982), http://litena.ru/books/item/f00/s00/z0000011/st017.shtml (accessed May 25, 2023). See also *vzimanie dyn'* (lit. "levy of melons") in Nikonova. We shall return to the mysterious original phrase *vzimanie dyn'* later. Suffice it to say here that, after *vzimanie* (levying), one expects *dan'* (tribute exacted by a conqueror). Instead, with the change of one letter, we are facing melons: *dyn'*.

13. Vladimir Maiakovskii, *Polnoe sobranie sochinenii v 13 tomakh*, vol. 1 (Moscow: GIKhL, 1955), 195–96 (173–96).

14. Translated by Andrey Kneller, https://www.unlikelystories.org/old/archives/cloudintrousers4.html (accessed June 6, 2023).

15. See https://traumlibrary.ru/book/gnedov-egufuturnalia/gnedov-egufuturnalia.html#s002013 (accessed June 11, 2023).

16. Translated by Alexandra Berlina.

17. See Mikhail Pavlovets, "'Pars pro toto': Mesto 'Poemy Kontsa' v strukture knigi Vasiliska Gnedova 'Smert' iskusstvu' (1913)," *Toronto Slavic Quarterly* 70 (2019), http://sites.utoronto.ca/tsq/27/pavlovec27.shtml (accessed May 25, 2023).

18. V. Gnedov, *Egofuturnaliia bez smertnogo kolpaka. Stikhotvoreniia i risunki*, ed. S. Sigei (Eisk: Meotida, 1991), 3.

19. Vasilisk Gnedov, *Sama poeziia*, ed. Il'ia Kukui (Moscow: Tsiolkovskii, 2018), 308.

20. Velimir Khlebnikov, *Sobranie sochinenii v 6 tomakh*, ed. R. V. Duganov, vol. 6.2 (Moscow: IMLI RAN, 2006), 99.

21. Khlebnikov, *Sobranie sochinenii*, 332 (italics added). Our sincere thanks to Igor Loshchilov for pointing out these Khlebnikov references.

22. Translated by Alexandra Berlina.

23. See, for example, https://www.vysokovskiy.ru/anekdot/podlezhastcee/ (accessed May 25, 2023).

24. See *Etimologicheskii onlain slovar' N. M. Shanskogo* (etymological online dictionary), https://lexicography.online/etymology/к/карапуз (accessed May 25, 2023).

25. *Transponans* 1 (1979): 24, https://samizdatcollections.library.utoronto.ca/islandora/object/samizdat%3A5791 (accessed May 25, 2023).

26. *Transponans* 7 (1980): 10, https://samizdatcollections.library.utoronto.ca/islandora/object/samizdat%3A7717 (accessed May 25, 2023).

26. Olga Sedakova, "The Grasshopper and the Cricket" (1979–85): The Music of the Earth

1. Olga Sedakova, *Vrata, okna, arki* (Paris: YMCA Press, 1968), 64–65.

2. On the theme of eternity in Sedakova's work, see D. Bavil'skii, "Malen'kaia vechnost'," *Postskriptum. Literaturny zhurnal* 3 (1996): 109–32.

3. See, for instance, her autobiographical letter-cum-essay "Pokhvala poezii," https://www.olgasedakova.com/prose/98/search (accessed May 26, 2023).

4. See Stephanie Sandler, "Introduction," in Olga Sedakova, *In Praise of Poetry*, ed. and trans. C. Clark, K. Golubovich, and S. Sandler (Rochester, NY: Open Letter, 2014), 5–16.

5. W. Jackson Bate, *John Keats* (Cambridge, MA: Belknap, 1978), 120.

6. On birds as redolent of "nineteenth-century musicality," see Angela Leighton, "Heaney and the Music," *Irish Review* 49–50 (2014–2015): 19–21, and Pearl Faulkner Eddy, "Insects in English Poetry," *Scientific Monthly* 33, no. 1 (1931): 53–73.

7. Suresh Raval, "Intention and Contemporary Literary Theory," *Journal of Aesthetics and Art Criticism* 38, no. 3 (1980): 261–77 (265); and Tilottama Rajan, "Keats, Poetry, and 'The Absence of the Work,'" *Modern Philology* 95, no. 3 (1998): 334–51.

8. Seamus Heaney, "Crediting Poetry," in *Opened Ground: Poems 1966–1996* (London: Faber, 1998), 445–69 (466).

9. Paula Feldman and Daniel Robinson, *A Century of Sonnets: The Romantic-Era Revival 1750–1850* (Oxford: Oxford University Press, 1999), 12.

10. John Keats, *The Complete Poems*, ed. John Barnard (Middlesex: Penguin, 1978), 94.

11. That ear for weighted silence is one of the properties Sedakova values in the poetry of Gennadiy Aygi, as she notes in her essay "Aigi: Ot'ezd," *Novoe literaturnoe obozrenie* 79 (2006), 200–4.

12. M. V. Lomonosov, *Izbrannye proizvedeniia* (Moscow: Sovetskii pisatel' [Biblioteka poeta], 1986), 276.

13. See "Ершов Петр Павлович," http://az.lib.ru/e/ershow_p_p/text_0020.shtml (accessed June 12, 2023).

14. M. V. Lomonosov, *Polnoe sobranie sochinenii*, vol. 8 (Moscow: Akademiia nauk, 1959), 736. The original title is "Verses composed during a journey to Peterhof when I in 1761 traveled to request the confirmation of a patent for the Academy, having already done the same many times" ("Stikhi, sochinennye na doroge v Petergof, kogda ia v 1761 godu ekhal prosit'o podpisanii privilegii dlia Akadamii, byv mnogo raz prezhde za tem zhe").

15. A. S. Pushkin, *Sobranie sochinenii v desiati tomakh*, eds. D. D. Blagoi et al., vol.2 (Moscow: Khudozhestvennaia literatura, 1959), 297.

16. On Sedakova's representation of void and abyss overcome by transcendence, see Andrew Kahn, "Sedakova's Book of Hours and the Devotional Lyric: Reading 'Fifth Stanzas,'" in *The Poetry and Poetics of Olga Sedakova: Origins, Philosophies, Points of Contention*, eds. Stephanie Sandler et al. (Madison: University of Wisconsin Press, 2019), 141–65.

17. See Ketevan Megrelishvili, "The Topography of the Other World in Olga Sedakova's Poetics," in *The Poetry and Poetics*, 214–41.

18. Osip Mandel'shtam, *Polnoe sobranie sochinenii i pisem v trekh tomakh*, ed. A. G. Mets, vol. 1 (Moscow: Progress-Pleiada, 2009).

19. Translated by Andrew Kahn.

20. Osip Mandel'shtam, *Polnoe sobranie*, 115.

21. On Sedakova's cycle of poems about Tristan, see Kseniia Golubovich, "Tristan i Izol'da v ispolnenii Ol'gi Sedakovoi," https://magazines.gorky.media/volga/2011/9/tristan-i-izolda-v-ispolnenii-olgi-sedakovoj.html (accessed June 12, 2023).

22. Olga Sedakova, "O chem Tristan i Izol'da," https://www.olgasedakova.com/Poetica/2018/search (accessed May 26, 2023).

23. Sedakova, "O chem Tristan i Izol'da."

24. Sedakova, "O chem Tristan i Izol'da."

27. Lev Losev, "One Day in the Life of Lev Vladimirovich" (1985): Self-Portrait in a Cloudy Mirror

1. Lev Losev, *Stikhi* (St. Petersburg: Izdatel'stvo Ivana Limbakha, 2012), 165–67.

2. The two writers resident in Vermont are Aleksandr Solzhenitsyn and Sasha Sokolov.

3. Standard translations of Losev's "untranslatable" words: *istina*, "truth"; *volia*, both "will" and "freedom"; *uiut*, "comfyness"; *khamstvo*, "crude behavior"; *padlo*, any kind of unpleasant person, "piece of shit."

4. "D. P." was normal post–World War II official parlance: "Displaced Person."

5. G. S. Smith, "Flight of the Angels: The Poetry of Lev Loseff," *Slavic Review* 47, no. 1 (1988): 76–88 (82).

6. Losev, *Stikhi*, 79.

7. Yasha Klots, "The Ultimate City: New York in Russian Immigrant Narrative," *SEEJ* 55, no. 1 (2011): 38–57 (39).

8. Iambic pentameter remained a popular meter in Russian émigré poetry from the mid-century. See G. S. Smith, "The Metrical Repertoire of Shorter Poems by Russian Emigres, 1971–1980," *Canadian Slavonic Papers* 27, no. 4 (1985): 385–99 (389).

9. The terms and approach come from Ilya Kukulin, "Documentalist Strategies in Contemporary Russian Poetry," *Russian Review* 69, no. 4 (2010): 585–614 (586).

10. Smith, "Flight of the Angels," 77.

11. Losev's ingenious rhymes are all the more marked against a metrical conservatism that characterized his generation of émigré poets. On the metrical repertoire, see Smith, "The Metrical Repertoire of Shorter Poems."

12. See the *Bol'shoi akademicheskii slovar' russkogo iazyka*, vol. 4 (Moscow: RAN, 2006), 601.

13. Arnold McMillin, "Bilingualism and Word Play in the Work of Russian Writers of the Third Wave of Emigration," *Modern Language Review* 89, no. 2 (1994): 417–26 (418 on Losev/Loseff).

14. Petr Vail', *Stikhi pro sebia* (Moscow: Kolibri, 2011), 578–90.

15. Smith, "Flight," 78.

16. Svetlana Boym, "Estrangement as a Lifestyle: Shklovsky and Brodsky," *Poetics Today* 17, no. 4 (1996): 511–30 (511).

17. The translator confirmed his decision as perhaps more of a subjective choice than a matter of actual ambiguity in the expression. (G. S. Smith, private communication, June 2022.)

28. Joseph Brodsky, "Homage to Chekhov" (1993): Pastiching the Prosaic

1. Iosif Brodskii, *Peizazh s navodneniem* (Dana Point, CA: Ardis, 1995), 126–27.

2. Joseph Brodsky, *Collected Poems in English*, ed. Ann Kjellberg (New York: Farrar, Straus and Giroux, 2000), 428–29.

3. Alexander Zholkovsky, "Writing in the Wilderness: On Brodskij and a Sonnet," *SEEJ* 30, no. 3 (1986): 404–19 (405).

4. Aaron Beaver, "Lyricism and Philosophy in Brodsky's Elegiac Verse," *Slavic Review* 67, no. 3 (2008): 591–609 (591).

5. The subject, in need of further study, is treated in Jane Elizabeth Knox, "Iosif Brodskij's Affinity with Osip Mandel'shtam: Cultural Links with the Past" (PhD diss., University of Texas, 1978); on the role of abstract categories in his poetic thinking, see Aaron Beaver, "Brodsky, Kierkegaard, Language and Time," *Russian Review* 67, no. 3 (2008): 415–37.

6. See Lev Losev, "Chekhovskii lirizm u Brodskogo," in *Solzhenitsyn i Brodskii kak sosedi* (St. Petersburg: Izdatel'stvo Ivana Limbakha, 2010), 185–98.

7. J. Brodsky and D. Weissbort, "The Rustle of Acacias," *Iowa Review* 9, no. 4 (1978): 1.

8. G. S. Smith, "The Versification of Joseph Brodsky, 1988–89," *SEER* 80, no. 3 (2002): 417–38 (423), has argued convincingly for Brodsky's later verse that there is no evidence for a coupling between metrical form and content, also observing that the anapest is the only ternary meter that forms a core of his metrical repertoire. The use of an amphibrachic foot looks unpoetic or prosaic in the context of his usual metrical practice.

9. Lines 12–13 ("v predchustvii aviatsii, / plyvut v napravlen'ii Germanii" ("foreshadowing aviation / drift toward Germany") may be inspired by the finale of Shaw's *Heartbreak House*, an openly Chekhovian play that ends with the bombing of England.

10. Michael Finke, *Seeing Chekhov: Life and Art* (Ithaca, NY: Cornell University Press, 2005).

11. Andrew Kahn, "Joseph Brodsky's 'The Bust of Tiberius,'" *Stanford Slavic Studies* 35 (2008): 243–61.

12. For a rich study of his use of visual media, see Panayiotis Xenophontos, "Joseph Brodsky and the Visual Arts: Consumer, Practitioner, Interpreter" (PhD diss., University of Oxford, 2022).

13. See Losev, "Chekhovskii lirizm u Brodskogo," 194, and Andrew Kahn, "Brodsky's Darwinian Aesthetic," *Stanford Slavic Papers* 2 (2014): 301–20.

14. "Interview with Joseph Brodsky" by Eva Burch and David Chin, *Columbia: A Journal of Literature and Art* 4 (1980): 50–68 (53).

29. Lev Rubinshtein, "That's me" (1995): The Self as Card Index

1. Lev Rubinshtein, *Here I Am: Performance Poems*, trans. Joanne Turnbull (Moscow: GLAS New Russian Writing, 2001), 145–72.

2. Lev Rubinshtein, *Bol'shaia kartoteka* (Moscow: Novoe izdatel'stvo, 2015), 568–84.

3. See Ilya Kukulin's posting from January 14, 2024: https://www.facebook.com/ilya.kukulin, and Mikhail Pavlovets's posting from January 15, 2024: https://www.facebook.com/pavlovez

4. See: Anastasiia Belousova, Vera Polilova. "Nenapisannaia stat'ia M.I. Shapira o 'stikhakh na kartochkakh' L.Rubinshteina," *M. I. Shapir. Universum versus: Iazyk—stikh—smysl v russkoi poezii XVIII—XX vekov.* Moscow: Iazyki slavianskoi kul'tury, 2015, vol. 2, 483–95.

5. Printed on the back cover of an English-language edition of poetry and prose by Rubinshtein: Rubinstein, *Here I Am.*

6. Published on the cover of Lev Rubinshtein, *Reguliarnoe pis'mo* (St. Petersburg: Izd-vo Ivana Limbakha, 1996). For more detailed comment on the correspondence between Rubinshtein's aesthetic and Chekhov's, see Aleksandr Ulanov, "L. S. Rubinshtein: golos slukha," *Tsirk-Olimp* 15 (1996): 13.

7. In the sense in which Mikhail Bakhtin suggested using the term "metalinguistics": "the dialogical relationships between utterances, also permeating speech and individual utterances from within, belong to metalinguistics"; Mikhail Bakhtin, "Problema teksta v lingvistikie, filologii i drugikh gumanitarnykh naukakh. Opyt filosofskogo analiza," in *Polnoe sobranie sochinenii*, vol. 5 (Moscow: Iazyki russkoi kul'tury, 1996), 306–26 (321).

8. Mikhail Epshtein, *Postmodern v Rossii* (Moscow: Izd-vo R. Elinina, 2000), 151.

9. See Vladimir Lettsev, "Kontseptualizm—chtenie i ponimanie," *Daugava* 8 (1989): 107–13.

10. Boris Groys, *History Becomes Form: Moscow Conceptualism* (Cambridge, MA: MIT Press, 2010), 42.

11. Andrei Zorin, "Katalog," in *Gde sidit fazan: Ocherki poslednikh let* (Moscow: Novoe literaturnoe obozrenie, 2003), 70–76. Zorin also elaborates a similar point of view in other articles about Rubinshtein and Moscow conceptualism. See Andrei Zorin, "Stikhi na kartochkakh. Poeticheskii iazyk L'va Rubinshteina," *Daugava* 8 (1989): 100–102, and Andrei Zorin, "Muza iazyka i sem' poetov," *Druzhba narodov* 4 (1990): 240–49.

12. Mikhail N. Aizenberg, "Vokrug kontseptualizma," in *Vzgliad na svobodnogo khudozhnika* (Moscow: Gendal'f, 1997), 128–54 (149).

13. Aizenberg, "Vokrug," 149, 150.

14. Rubinshtein, *Reguliarnoe pis'mo*, 7.

15. Rubinshtein, *Reguliarnoe pis'mo*, 7.

16. See Zorin, "Muza iazyka," 247–48.

17. Gerald Janecek, "Lev Rubinshtein's Early Conceptualism: The Program of Works," in *EndQuote: Sots-Art Literature and Soviet Grand Style*, eds. Marina Balina, Nancy Condee, and Evgeny Dobrenko (Evanston, IL: Northwestern University Press, 2001), 107–22.

18. Something similar occurs with the recognizable metrical schemes employed by Rubinshtein. As Mikhail L. Gasparov has noted: "In his compositions consisting of verse and prose fragments, Rubinshtein is most interesting where he [. . .] proffers a selection of ordinary, everyday utterances that fit impeccably into an iambic tetrameter [. . .] With Rubinshtein, one has to make an effort to recall that this is the same meter in which *Onegin* was written [. . .] Rubinshtein has gone further than [Kibirov]; his iambic tetrameter is no longer parodic." Mikhail Gasparov, "Ruskii stikh kak zerkalo postsovetskoi kul'tury," *Novoe literaturnoe obozrenie* 32 (1998): 77–83 (82, 83).

30. Elena Fanailova, ". . . Again they're off for their Afghanistan" (2003): Scars of Imperial Eros

1. Elena Fanailova, *The Russian Version*, ed. Aleksandr Skidan, trans. Genya Turovskaya and Stephanie Sandler (New York: Ugly Duckling Presse, 2009), 52, 54 (in Russian), 53, 55 (in English).

2. See Mikhail Efremov, Dmitrii Bykov, and Andrei Vasil'ev, *Grazhdanin poet: na smert' proekta* (Moscow: Azbuka-Attikus, 2012).

3. See the discussion between Valerii Shubinsky and Linor Goralik, "Bor'ba za *Znamia*," http://www.openspace.ru/literature/projects/130/details/1986/ (accessed June 1, 2023).

4. Fanailova, "Russkaia versiia," *Znamia* 11 (2004), https://znamlit.ru/publication.php?id=2487 (accessed June 12, 2023).

5. See Stephanie Sandler, "New Lyrics," in *Russian Literature since 1991*, eds. Evgeny Dobrenko and Mark Lipovetsky (Cambridge: Cambridge University Press, 2015), 234–37.

6. Mikhail Aizenberg, "Shag v storonu" (July 7, 2008), OpenSpace.ru (accessed June 1, 2023) (italics in the original).

7. Linor Goralik, "Interview [with Elena Fanailova]," *Vozdukh* 1–2 (2009): 32–35 (32).

8. Goralik, "Interview," 33.

9. Fanailova, *The Russian Version*, 57.

10. V. Dubin, "Kniga neuspokoennosti," *Kriticheskaia massa* 1 (2006), https://polit.ru/article/2006/03/18/fanailovadubin/ (accessed June 12, 2023).

11. Yurii Leving, "V dome durakov: pesni nevinnosti, oni zhe—opyta," *Novoe literaturnoe obozrenie* 4 (2003), https://magazines.gorky.media/nlo/2003/4/v-dome-durakov-pesni-nevinnosti-oni-zhe-8212-opyta.html (accessed June 1, 2023).

12. Fanailova, *The Russian Version*, 59.

13. Fanailova, *The Russian Version*, 57.

14. Iosif Brodskii, *Uraniia* (Ann Arbor, MI: Ardis, 1987), 97–99 (97–98) (italics added).

15. Joseph Brodsky, *Collected Poetry in English* (New York: Farrar, Straus and Giroux, 1987), 254–55 (256), translated by Joseph Brodsky.

16. Brodskii, *Uraniia*, 99.

17. Glossing *uzdechka* as the penis's frenulum, Yuri Leving in his perceptive commentary to Fanailova's poem reads the line "Unbraiding bridles with their tongues" as a reference to oral sex (Leving, "V dome durakov").

18. "I saw their scars: the man had a laparotomy (most likely for a perforated ulcer). The woman, surgery related to a cyst. Probably several abortions too, taking into account their social status, and you can determine that by the swimming trunks alone (the speech, the faces of former defense industry workers who went into small business at the right moment)" (Fanailova, *The Russian Version*, 59).

19. Fanailova, *The Russian Version*, 59.

20. Goralik, "Interview," 33.

31. Linor Goralik, "Little Star" (2010): The Tale of the Hare and the Wolf

1. Linor Goralik, *Podsekai, Petrusha* (Moscow: ARGO-RISK; Knizhnoe obozrenie, 2007), 43–44.

2. To convey the fairy-tale aura, Helena Kernan in her translation of the poem uses "hare"—a frequent protagonist of fairy tales—rather than "bunny," despite the suggestion of childishness and cuteness inherent in "bunny."

3. In Russian, verb-based rhymes are frowned upon, verb endings being identical by virtue of morphology.

4. Joseph Brodsky, *Collected Poems in English*, ed. Ann Kjellberg (New York: Farrar, Straus and Giroux, 2000), 53 (1972, translated by Alan Myers and Joseph Brodsky).

5. Brodsky, *Collected Poems in English*, 351 (1987, translated by Joseph Brodsky).

6. Brodsky, *Collected Poems in English*, 389 (1989, translated by Seamus Heaney).

7. Brodsky, *Collected Poems in English*, 427 (1992, translated by Joseph Brodsky).

8. *New Yorker* (December 18, 2000), 72 (1995, translated by Seamus Heaney).

9. In one of her interviews, Goralik says: "I'm quite afraid of all these global things, and constantly afraid of local disasters, too—afraid for my loved ones, afraid for the stability of my tiny world, and so on . . . In any disaster, as far as I know from what I read and see, the first thing people try to do is to build for themselves some tiny island of everyday normality. In Teffi's memoirs, there is a passage about how emigrants—people who have lost everything, on their way to exile on a ship in third class, almost in the ship's bowels—immediately try to construct for themselves a semblance of home comfort using shawls, rags, some tiny surviving household objects . . . This is what one does in the first place—building a sort of everyday normality out of whatever one can find. Then again, when it is the mundanity of everyday life that cuts off everything else, it turns out to be very hard, too" (https://yeltsin.ru/news/linor-goralik-chelovek-vystraivaet-povsednevnost-v-pervuyu-ochered [accessed June 2, 2023]).

10. Helena Kernan has opted for a more erotic tuning of this line, thus emphasizing the queer aspect of the duo (in Russian, both the hare and the wolf are male): "when I'm swaddled up warm in your fur" (line 29).

11. Compare "Brodsky's recurring depiction of Christ not as one who eternizes, but as one who makes finite"; Michael Lavers, "A Sense of Our Uniqueness: Gender and Time in Joseph Brodsky's 'Lullaby,'" *College Literature* 40, no. 1 (winter 2013): 32–44 (36).

12. Yuri Lotman, *Culture and Explosion*, trans. Benjamin Paloff (Boston, MA: Academic Studies Press, 2020), 66–67.

13. Georg Wilhelm Friedrich Hegel, *Lectures on the Philosophy of World History: Introduction, Reason in History*, ed. H. B. Nisbet (New York: Cambridge University Press, 1975), 79.

14. *The Hegel Dictionary*, ed. Glenn Alexander Magee (London: Continuum, 2010), 218.

15. As Eleazar M. Meletinskii wrote, "In a fairy tale, etiological endings vanish even more quickly, giving way (at the last stage) to endings of a completely different type, which hint at the fictitiousness, unreliability of the narrative. Mythic times and aetiology merge to an inseparable whole with the cosmic scale of the myth and its attention to the collective destiny of the tribe, subjectively identified with humanity as a whole ('real people'). [. . .] As one moves from myth to the [fairy] tale, the scale changes, the interest shifts to the personal fate of the protagonist. [. . .] Even the 'altruistic' noble hero

of a magic tale—one who quests for 'water of life' and other miraculous objects, saves his sick father or a princess kidnapped by a dragon—acts in the interests of a rather narrow circle (his community, his king, or his family—father, father-in-law, etc.). In his own way, he thus also opposes the 'cosmism,' the 'collectivism,' the 'aetiology' of myth"; Eleazar Meletinskii, "Mif i skazka," in *Izbrannye stat'i. Vospominaniia* (Moscow: RGGU, 1998), 290; see also https://www.ruthenia.ru/folklore/meletinsky11.htm (accessed June 2, 2023).

32. Galina Rymbu, "My Vagina" (2018): The Personal Is the Political

1. Galina Rymbu, *Ty—budushchee* (Moscow: Tsentr Voznesenskogo, Tsentrifuga, 2020), 154–61.

2. In *F-Letter: New Russian Feminist Poetry*, eds. Galina Rymbu, Eugene Ostashevsky, and Ainsley Morse (New York: Isolarii, 2020), 220–43 (in Russian and English).

3. See Helena Goscilo, *Dehexing Sex: Russian Womanhood during and after Glasnost* (Ann Arbor: University of Michigan Press, 1996).

4. Maria Bobyleva and Iulia Podlubnova, *Poetika feminizma* (Moscow: AST, 2021), 12.

5. On the significance of obscene vocabulary for Russian F-poetry, see Bobyleva and Podlubnova, *Poėtika*, 231–35.

6. See, for example, *Setka Tsetkin: Antologiia feministskoi kritiki* (Ekaterinburg-Moscow: Kabinetnyi uchenyi, 2021); Aleksandr Skidan, "Stronger Than Uranus: On 'Women's Poetry,'" *Russian Studies in Literature* 54, nos. 1–3 (2018): 32–57; Ilya Kukulin, "Dvadtsat' piat' let peniia bez akkompanimenta: Vzlet i prevrashcheniia zhenskoi innovativnoi poezii v postsovetskoi Rossii," in *Imidzh, dialog, eksperiment: polia sovremennoi russkoi poezii*, eds. Henrieke Stahl and Marion Rutz (Munich: Verlag Otto Sagner, 2013), 119–54.

7. Rymbu, Ostashevsky, and Morse, *F-Letter*.

8. See Sophie Pinkham, "No More Mother-Saviors," *New York Review of Books* (April 29, 2021), https://www.nybooks.com/articles/2021/04/29/russian-poetry-no-more-mother-saviors/ (accessed June 5, 2023), and Suyin Haynes, "How Russia's Feminist Poets Are Changing What It Means to Protest," *Time* (December 21, 2020), https://time.com/5908168/russia-feminist-poets-protest (accessed June 5, 2023).

9. Galina Rymbu, *White Bread*, trans. Joan Brooks (New York: After Hours LTD, 2016).

10. Cited from Bobyleva and Podlubnova, *Poėtika*, 130.

11. Joan Brooks, "A Conversation with Galina Rymbu," *Music and Literature* (February 4, 2016), https://www.musicandliterature.org/features/2016/1/31/a-conversation-with-galina-rymbu (accessed June 5, 2023).

12. For a detailed analysis of public reactions to Rymbu's poem, see Josephine von Zitzewitz, "Case Study: Galina Rymbu, 'Moia vagina,' June 2020," *Poetics and Politics by Women in the Post-Soviet Space*, special issue, *Internationale Zeitschrift für Kulturkomparatistik* 6 (2022): 187–210.

13. See Галина Рымбу, "ВЕЛИКАЯ РУССКАЯ ЛИТЕРАТУРА," Facebook, July 3, 2020, https://www.facebook.com/GalinaRymbu/posts/1632746380224687 (accessed June 12, 2023).

14. Translated by Alexandra Berlina.

15. Jacques Rancière, *Dissensus: On Politics and Aesthetics*, ed. and trans. Steven Corcoran (London: Continuum, 2010), 38.

16. See Toril Moi, *What Is a Woman? and Other Essays* (Oxford: Oxford University Press, 1999), 16–83.

17. Kathleen Lennon, "Feminist Perspectives on the Body," *Stanford Encyclopedia of Philosophy* (June 28, 2010; rev. August 2, 2019), https://plato.stanford.edu/entries/feminist-body (accessed June 5, 2023).

18. For a discussion of the revolutionary element in the poem, see Dmitrii Gerchikov, "'Delat' revoliutsiiu vaginoi: Vremia i telo v knige *Ty—budushchee* Galiny Rymbu," *Colta* (September 21, 2021), https://www.colta.ru/articles/literature/28325-dmitriy-gerchikov-kniga-ty-buduschee-galina-rymbu-vremya-i-telo (accessed June 5, 2023).

33. Polina Barskova, "Children's Literature" (2019): The Garden of Earthly Delights

1. Polina Barskova, *Air Raid,* trans. Valzhyna Mort (New York: Ugly Duckling Presse, 2021), 16 (in Russian), 17 (in English).

2. Vladimir Toporov, "Peterburg i 'Peterburgskii tekst russkoi literatury' (Vvedenie v temu)," in *Mif. Ritual. Simvol. Obraz: Issledovaniia v oblasti mifopoèticheskogo: Izbrannoe* (Moscow: Izdatel'skaia gruppa Progress—Kul'tura, 1995), 259–367.

3. Most of her poems dedicated to the Siege of Leningrad are included in the following bilingual collection: Polina Barskova, *Air Raid,* trans. Valzhyna Mort (Brooklyn, NY: Ugly Duckling Presse, 2021).

4. See Polina Barskova, *Living Pictures,* trans. Catherine Ciepiela, ed. Eugene Ostashevsky (New York: New York Review Books, 2022), and Polina Barskova, *Sed'maia shcheloch': Teksty i sud'by blokadnykh poetov* (St. Petersburg: Izd. Ivana Limbakha, 2020).

5. Polina Barskova, *Besieged Leningrad: Aesthetic Responses to Urban Disaster* (DeKalb: Northern Illinois University Press, 2017).

6. *"Sborishche druzei, ostavlennykh sud'boi . . ." "Chinari" v tekstakh, dokumentakh i issledovaniiakh,* ed. V. Sazhin, vol. 2 (Moscow: Ladomir, 2000), 602. Oleinikov was arrested on July 20, 1937, a terrible time: "In July 1937 in Moscow, at the briefing of regional NKVD heads during the preparation of mass arrests, Commissar [head of NKVD] Yezhov and his deputy Frinovsky told the Chekists in no uncertain words that they 'could use physical methods of influence'"; https://bessmertnybarak.ru/article/pytki_ot_stalina (accessed June 6, 2023).

7. Evgenii Shvarts, *Telefonnaia knizhka* (Moscow: Iskusstvo, 1997).

8. Vladimir Glotser, ed., *Chasy v korobochke: Stikhi, rasskazy, skazki. Vvedenskii, Oleinikov, Kharms* (St. Petersburg: Amfora, 2005), 29.

9. Aleksandr Vvedenskii, "The Fisherman and the Pike." All poetry excerpts in this chapter are translated by Alexandra Berlina unless otherwise stated.

10. *Chasy v korobochke,* 18–19.

11. Aleksandr Vvedenskii, "Birdies."

12. Shvarts, *Telefonnaia knizhka,* 226.

13. Vladimir Glotzer, *Marina Durnovo: Moi muzh Daniil Kharms* (Moscow: IMA-Press, 2001), 71.

14. Evgenii Shvarts, *Zhivu bespokoino . . . : Iz dnevnikov,* 630.

15. Shvarts, *Zhivu,* 631–32.

16. Dante Alighieri, *The Divine Comedy: Hell,* trans. Henry Wadsworth Longfellow, Canto 34, https://www.gutenberg.org/files/1001/1001-h/1001-h.htm (accessed June 6, 2023).

17. The particular pike parallel only arises in translation: in Vvedenskii's original, the fish is a zander, and, in Barskova's original, just an unnamed fish. Both translators, Berlina and Mort, respectively, turn to pikes in their translations, presumably partly due to their rhyming properties. In Mort's case, the pike yields an additional bonus: a pike can refer to both a fish and a sharp prong, so that, in translation, this line oscillates between a summer scene and a scene of torture.

18. Daniil Kharms, *Polnoe sobranie sochinenii,* ed. Vladimir Sazhin, vol. 3 (St. Petersburg: Akademicheskii proekt, 1997), 84.

19. Daniil Kharms, "Unexpected Catch" (1941).

20. Aleksandr Vvedenskii, *Vse,* ed. Anna Gerasimova (Moscow: OGI, 2011), 194.

21. Vvedenskii, *Vse,* 264.

22. Frank Kermode, *The Sense of an Ending: Studies in the Theory of Fiction* (New York: Oxford University Press, 1967), 47. Moreover, as Kermode observes, *kairos* becomes formalized in literature, especially in the novel: "In the midst of voluminous detail intended to ensure realism, everything became *kairos* by virtue of the way in which letters coincide with critical moments" (50). This, too, resonates with Barskova's poem and most especially with its title, which turns the whole scene into an allegory of literature.

23. Alexxa Gotthardt, "Decoding Bosch's Wild, Whimsical 'Garden of Earthly Delights,'" https://www.artsy.net/article/artsy-editorial-decoding-boschs-wild-whimsical-garden-earthly-delights (accessed June 6, 2023).

24. Mikhail Bakhtin, *Rabelais and His World*, trans. Helene Iswolsky (Bloomington: Indiana University Press, 1984), 317.

25. Bakhtin, *Rabelais*, 318.

26. Bakhtin, *Rabelais*, 317.

34. Maria Stepanova, "A little like this: instead of coming out of the closet" (2021): A Quiet Apocalypse

1. Maria Stepanova, *Sviashchennaia zima 20/21* (Moscow: Novoe izdatel'stvo, 2022), 21.

2. Maria Stepanova, *War of the Beasts and the Animals*, trans. Sasha Dugdale (Hexham: Bloodaxe Books, 2021).

3. Maria Stepanova, *The Voice Over: Poems and Essays*, ed. Irina Shevelenko (New York: Columbia University Press, 2021).

4. Matthew Janney, "'Love's Labours Should Be Lost': Maria Stepanova, Russia's Next Great Writer," *Guardian* (February 11, 2021), https://www.theguardian.com/books/2021/feb/11/maria-stepanova-russia-in-memory-of-memory (accessed June 6, 2023).

5. Mikhail Iampol'skii, "Podzemnyi patefon (Ob odnom motive v poezii Marii Stepanovoi)," *Novoe literaturnoe obozrenie* 6 (2014), https://magazines.gorky.media/nlo/2014/6/podzemnyj-patefon.html (accessed June 6, 2023).

6. Personal communication with Mark Lipovetsky. The puppet booth to which Stepanova refers is called *vertep*, and it traditionally depicts nativity scenes.

7. In an article published in the *Financial Times*, she wrote about this war: "What we are living through might be termed the death of the conceivable. Over many decades, the western imagination (across many genres and forms, from high literature to Hollywood and television series) has used the industry of the imagination as a sort of training ground for experience. Fearful dystopian scenarios are played out, tested for accuracy, and thereby become normalised and safe, like films about zombies and aliens. After all, they're just inventions! [. . .] Having to accept that the unthinkable, what we have rejected from the collective imagination as both impossible and impermissible, could actually come to pass on an unremarkable winter's morning would be a catastrophe. It destroys all our notions of the contemporary world and a social contract that recognizes the need for mutual understanding, empathy, common sense (and a certain scepticism towards alarmist pronouncements). But today all this has come to pass and we are standing among the ruins"; Maria Stepanova, "The War of Putin's Imagination," trans. Sasha Dugdale, *Financial Times* (March 18, 2022), https://www.ft.com/content/c2797437-5d3f-466a-bc63-2a1725aa57a5 (accessed June 6, 2023).

8. Daniil Kharms, *Today I Wrote Nothing: The Selected Writings of Daniil Kharms*, ed. and trans. Matvei Yankelevich (New York: Ardis, 2009), 55.

9. Iosif Brodskii, *Uraniia* (Ann Arbor, MI: Ardis, 1987), 119.

10. Here Brodskii's poem is translated by Andrew Bromfield.

11. Brodskii, *Uraniia*, 122.

12. Brodskii, *Uraniia*, 122.

13. Brodskii, *Uraniia*, 123.

14. Walter Benjamin, *The Origin of German Tragic Drama*, trans. John Osborne (New York: New Left Books, 2003), 174.

SUGGESTIONS FOR FURTHER READING

Anthologies in English Translation

An Anthology of Contemporary Russian Women Poets. Edited by Valentina Polukhina and Daniel Weissbort. Manchester: Carcanet, 2005.

The Ardis Anthology of Russian Futurism. Edited by Ellendea Proffer and Carl R. Proffer. Ann Arbor, MI: Ardis, 1980.

Crossing Centuries: The New Generation in Russian Poetry. Edited by John High et al. Jersey City, NJ: Talisman House, 2000.

In the Grip of Strange Thoughts: Russian Poetry in a New Era. Edited by J. Kates. Newcastle upon Tyne: Bloodaxe Books, 1999.

The Penguin Book of Russian Poetry. Edited by Robert Chandler, Boris Dralyuk, and Irina Mashinski with Robert Chandler. London: Penguin Books, 2015.

Russian Silver Age Poetry: Texts and Contexts. Edited by Sibelan Forrester and Martha M. F. Kelly. Boston, MA: Academic Studies Press, 2015.

Critical Works (Historical, General, and Individual Studies)

Agamben, Giorgio. *The End of the Poem*. Translated by Daniel Heller-Roazen. Stanford, CA: Stanford University Press, 1999.

Azarova, Natalia. *Iazyk filosofii i iazyk poezii: Dvizhenie navstrechu*. Moscow: Logos, 2010.

Bowie, Malcolm. *Selected Essays: Dreams of Knowledge*. Edited by Alison Finch. Leeds: MHRA, 2013.

Boym, Svetlana. *Death in Quotation Marks: Cultural Myths of the Modern Poet*. Cambridge, MA: Harvard University Press, 2013.

Bozovic, Marijeta. *Avant-Garde Post–: Radical Poetics after the Soviet Union*. Cambridge MA: Harvard University Press, 2023.

Burnside, John. *The Music of Time: Poetry in the Twentieth Century*. Princeton, NJ: Princeton University Press, 2020.

Burt, Stephanie. *The Poem Is You: 60 Contemporary American Poems and How to Read Them*. Cambridge, MA: Harvard University Press, 2016.

Carson, Anne. *Economy of the Unlost*. Princeton, NJ: Princeton University Press, 1999.

Culler, Jonathan. *Theory of the Lyric*. Cambridge, MA: Harvard University Press, 2015.

Doherty, Justin. *The Acmeist Movement in Russian Poetry: Culture and the Word*. Oxford: Clarendon Press; New York: Oxford University Press, 1995.

Etkind, Efim. *Materiia stikha*. Paris: Institut d'études slaves; St. Petersburg: Izd-vo "Gumanitarnyi soiuz," 1998.

———. *Tam vnutri: O russkoi poezii XX veka*. St. Petersburg: Maksima, 1996.

Gasparov, Mikhail. *Metr i smysl: ob odnom iz mekhanizmov kul'turnoĭ pamiati*. Moscow: Fortuna El, 2012.

———. *Poet i poeziia*. Moscow: Ripol-Klassik, 2018.

Gin, Ia. I. *Problemy poetiki grammaticheskikh kategorii*. St. Petersburg: Akademicheskii proekt, 1996.

Ginzburg, Lydia. *O lirike*. Leningrad: Sov. pisatel', 1974.

Hansen-Löve, Aage Ansgar. *Russkii simvolizm: sistema poeticheskikh motivov: mifopoeticheskii simvolizm nachala veka: kosmicheskaia simvolika*. St. Peterburg: Akademicheskii proekt, 2003.

Heaney, Seamus. *The Redress of Poetry*. London: Faber and Faber, 1995.

Hodgson Katharine, Joanne Shelton, and Alexandra Smith, eds. *Twentieth-Century Russian Poetry: Reinventing the Canon*. Cambridge: OpenBook Publishers, 2017.

Jakobson, Roman. *Selected Writings*. Vol. 5, *On Verse, Its Masters and Explorers*. Edited by Stephen Rudy. The Hague: Mouton, 1978.

Janecek, Gerald. *Sight and Sound Entwined: Studies of the New Russian Poetry*. New York: Berghahn Books, 2000.

Jauss, Hans Robert. *Aesthetic Experience and Literary Hermeneutics*. Translated by Michael Shaw. Minneapolis: University of Minnesota Press, 1982.

Kahn, Andrew, Mark Lipovetsky, Irina Reyfman, and Stephanie Sandler. *A History of Russian Literature*. Oxford: Oxford University Press, 2018.

Kukulin, Il'ia. *Proryv k nevozmozhnoi sviazi. Stat'i o russkoi poezii*. Ekaterinburg: Kabinetnyi uchenyi, 2019.

Lacoue-Labarthe, Philippe. *Poetry As Experience*. Translated by Andrea Tarnowski. Stanford, CA: Stanford University Press, 1999.

Leighton, Angela. *On Form: Poetry, Aestheticism, and the Legacy of a Word*. Oxford: Oxford University Press, 2007.

Levin, Yurii, Dmitrii Segal, Roman Timenchik, Vladimir Toporov, Yuri Tsiv'ian. "Russkaia semanticheskaia poetika kak potentsial'naia kul'turnaia paradigma." *Russian Literature* (Hague) 7–8 (1974): 47–82.

Lotman, Yurii. *O poetakh i poezii*. Edited by Mikhail Gasparov. St. Petersburg: Iskusstvo-SPB, 1996.

Markov, Vladimir. *O svobode v poezii*. St. Petersburg: Izda. Chernyshev, 1994.

———. *Russian Futurism: A History*. Berkeley: University of California Press, 1968.

Miller, J. Hillis. *Poets of Reality: Six Twentieth-Century Writers*. Cambridge, MA: Harvard University Press, 1966.

Perloff, Marjorie. *Unoriginal Genius: Poetry by Other Means in the New Century*. Chicago, IL: University of Chicago Press, 2009.

Perloff, Marjorie, and Craig Dworkin, eds. *The Sound of Poetry / The Poetry of Sound*. Chicago, IL: University of Chicago Press, 2009.

Rabaté, Dominique. *Le Sujet lyrique en question*. Bordeaux: Presses universitaires de Bordeaux, 1996.

Riffaterre, Michael. *Semiotics of Poetry*. Bloomington: Indiana University Press, 1978.

Ronen, Omry. *The Fallacy of the Silver Age in Twentieth-Century Russian Literature*. Amsterdam: Harwood Academic, 1997.

Sandler, Stephanie. *Commemorating Pushkin: Russia's Myth of a National Poet*. Stanford, CA: Stanford University Press, 2004.

———. *The Freest Speech in Russia: Poetry 1989–2022*. Princeton, NJ: Princeton University Press, 2024.

———, ed. *Rereading Russian Poetry*. New Haven, CT: Yale University Press, 1999.

Scherr, Barry P. *Russian Poetry: Meter, Rhythm, and Rhyme*. Berkeley: University of California Press, 1986.

Skidan, Aleksandr. *Summa poezii*. Moscow: Novoe literaturnoe obozrenie, 2013.

Smith, G. S. *Vzgliad izvne: stat'i o russkoi poezii i poetike*. Moscow: Iazyki slavianskoi kul'tury, 2001.

Stewart, Susan. *Poetry and the Fate of the Senses*. Chicago, IL: University of Chicago, 2002.

Vendler, Helen. *The Breaking of Style: Hopkins, Heaney, Graham*. Cambridge, MA: Harvard University Press, 1995.

Wachtel, Michael. *The Development of Russian Verse: Meter and Its Meanings*. Cambridge: Cambridge University Press, 1998.
Zholkovsky, Alexander. *Novaia i noveishaia russkaia poeziia*. Moscow: Rossiiskii gos. gumanitarnyi universitet, 2009.
Zubova, Liudmila. *Iazyki sovremennoi poezii*. Moscow: NLO, 2018.

INDEX